FEMINISM
AND
COMPOSITION

FEMINISM AND COMPOSITION

A Critical Sourcebook

EDITED BY

Gesa E. Kirsch
Bentley College, Waltham, MA

Faye Spencer Maor
Lincoln University of Missouri

Lance Massey
University of Illinois, Urbana-Champaign

Lee Nickoson-Massey
University of Illinois, Urbana-Champaign

Mary P. Sheridan-Rabideau
Rutgers, The State University of New Jersey

Published in cooperation with the
National Council of Teachers of English

BEDFORD / ST. MARTIN'S Boston • New York

For Bedford / St. Martin's

Executive Editor: Leasa Burton
Executive Assistant: Brita Mess
Associate Editor, Publishing Services: Maria Teresa Burwell
Senior Production Supervisor: Joe Ford
Production Associate: Christie Gross
Marketing Manager: Brian Wheel
Art Director: Donna Dennison
Text Design: Anna George
Cover Design: Donna Dennison
Composition: Stratford Publishing Services, Inc.
Printing and Binding: Haddon Craftsmen, an RR Donnelley & Sons Company

President: Joan E. Feinberg
Editorial Director: Denise B. Wydra
Editor in Chief: Karen S. Henry
Director of Marketing: Karen R. Melton
Director of Editing, Design, and Production: Marcia Cohen
Manager, Publishing Services: Emily Berleth

NCTE Stock No. 16760
Published in cooperation with the
National Council of Teachers of English
1111 W. Kenyon Road
Urbana, Illinois 61801-1096
www.ncte.org

Library of Congress Control Number: 2002114118

Manufactured in the United States of America.

8 7 6 5 4 3
f e d c b a

For information, write: Bedford / St. Martin's, 75 Arlington Street, Boston, MA 02116   (617-399-4000)

ISBN: 0-312-40764-5

ACKNOWLEDGMENTS

Acknowledgments and copyrights appear at the back of the book on pages 608–610, which constitute an extension of the copyright page. It is a violation of the law to reproduce these selections by any means whatsoever without the written permission of the copyright holder.

We dedicate this book to all those in rhetoric and composition studies—students, teachers, scholars, and administrators—who have made it possible for us to "take our women students seriously" (to borrow Adrienne Rich's much cited phrase); to experiment with new forms of writing; to develop interactive pedagogies; to conduct reflective, feminist research and scholarship; and to begin improving working conditions for women (where much more remains to be done). We also dedicate this book to each other, in mutual friendship and admiration. Because the whole has become so much greater than the sum of our individual contributions, we ask that all future citations of this book acknowledge all five editors—Gesa E. Kirsch, Faye Spencer Maor, Lance Massey, Lee Nickoson-Massey, and Mary P. Sheridan-Rabideau.

ACKNOWLEDGMENTS

We would like to thank Gail Hawisher for her support and valuable insights through all stages of this book's development; Teresa Bertram for the use of her office and help with locating articles, and for her cheerful disposition all along; Kristen V. Edwards for her patience and good humor with all of our meetings; the reviewers of this book for their valuable suggestions regarding the selection of articles — Patricia Bizzell, Lisa Ede, Susan Jarratt; colleagues in the field who made important recommendations — Andrea Lunsford, Joy Ritchie, Eileen Schell; Leasa Burton for her enthusiasm for the project and her recognition of the importance of feminist work; Brita Mess for her careful reading and editing of the manuscript and her helpful suggestions for revisions; Emily Berleth and Maria Burwell for their fine attention to detail and guidance in the production process; Susan Petrie and Joy Matkowski at Publisher's Studio for their expertise, project management, and superb copyediting work; Joan Feinberg for her strong and ongoing commitment to the field of composition studies and her fine leadership of Bedford/St. Martin's; and last, but not least, our families and friends for all their support, patience, and love along the way.

CONTENTS

Dedication   *v*

Acknowledgments   *vii*

FOREWORD

Forwarding a Feminist Agenda in Writing Studies   *xv*
GAIL E. HAWISHER

INTRODUCTION

Charting Our Ways in Feminism and Composition   *1*
GESA E. KIRSCH, FAYE SPENCER MAOR, LANCE MASSEY,
LEE NICKOSON-MASSEY, AND MARY P. SHERIDAN-RABIDEAU

SITUATING THE FIELD

Feminism in Composition: Inclusion, Metonymy,
and Disruption   *7*
JOY S. RITCHIE AND KATHLEEN BOARDMAN

Part One   **EARLY FEMINIST VOICES AND VISIONS**   *27*

Introduction   *29*
FAYE SPENCER MAOR

1   Identity and Expression: A Writing Course
for Women   *33*
FLORENCE HOWE

2 The Feminine Style: Theory and Fact *43*
MARY P. HIATT

3 Teaching Griselda to Write *49*
JOAN BOLKER

4 The Womanization of Rhetoric *53*
SALLY MILLER GEARHART

5 Style as Politics: A Feminist Approach to the Teaching of Writing *61*
PAMELA J. ANNAS

Part Two   **FEMINIST THEORIES AND RESEARCH** *73*

Introduction *75*
MARY P. SHERIDAN-RABIDEAU

6 Confronting the "Essential" Problem: Reconnecting Feminist Theory and Pedagogy *79*
JOY S. RITCHIE

7 Writing Against Writing: The Predicament of *Écriture Féminine* in Composition Studies *103*
LYNN WORSHAM

8 Feminism and Methodology in Composition Studies *124*
PATRICIA A. SULLIVAN

9 Beyond the Personal: Theorizing a Politics of Location in Composition Research *140*
GESA E. KIRSCH AND JOY S. RITCHIE

10 Beside Ourselves: Rhetoric and Representation in Postcolonial Feminist Writing *160*
SUSAN C. JARRATT

11 Rhetoric, Feminism, and the Politics of Textual Ownership *180*
ANDREA ABERNETHY LUNSFORD

12   Feminist Methods of Research in the History of Rhetoric:
      What Difference Do They Make?   *194*
      PATRICIA BIZZELL

13   A View from a Bridge: Afrafeminist Ideologies
      and Rhetorical Studies   *206*
      JACQUELINE JONES ROYSTER

      REFLECTIVE ESSAY
      Revisiting "Confronting the 'Essential' Problem"   *234*
      JOY S. RITCHIE AND BARBARA DIBERNARD

Part Three   **GENDER AND FORMS OF WRITING**   *237*

              Introduction   *239*
              LANCE MASSEY

14   Composing as a Woman   *243*
      ELIZABETH A. FLYNN

15   Rhetoric in a New Key: Women and Collaboration   *256*
      ANDREA ABERNETHY LUNSFORD AND LISA EDE

16   Feminism and Composition: The Case for Conflict   *263*
      SUSAN C. JARRATT

17   Beyond Argument in Feminist Composition   *281*
      CATHERINE E. LAMB

18   Discourse and Diversity: Experimental Writing Within
      the Academy   *294*
      LILLIAN BRIDWELL-BOWLES

19   Recomposing as a Woman—An Essay in Different
      Voices   *314*
      TERRY MYERS ZAWACKI

20   Writing Multiplicity: Hypertext and Feminist Textual
      Politics   *321*
      DONNA LECOURT AND LUANN BARNES

REFLECTIVE ESSAY

Contextualizing "Composing as a Woman"   *339*
ELIZABETH A. FLYNN

REFLECTIVE ESSAY

Reflections on "Feminism and Composition: The Case
for Conflict"   *342*
SUSAN C. JARRATT

Part Four   **GENDER, TEACHING, AND IDENTITY**   *345*

Introduction   *347*
FAYE SPENCER MAOR

21   The Other "F" Word: The Feminist in the Classroom   *351*
DALE M. BAUER

22   A Symposium on Feminist Experiences in the
Composition Classroom   *363*
JILL EICHHORN, SARA FARRIS, KAREN HAYES,
ADRIANA HERNÁNDEZ, SUSAN C. JARRATT,
KAREN POWERS-STUBBS, AND MARIAN M. SCIACHITANO

23   Participatory Rhetoric and the Teacher as Racial/
Gendered Subject   *388*
CHERYL L. JOHNSON

24   Rend(er)ing Women's Authority in the Writing
Classroom   *398*
MICHELLE PAYNE

25   Coming Out in the Classroom: A Return to the
Hard Place   *411*
MARY ELLIOTT

26   "When and Where I Enter": Race, Gender, and
Composition Studies   *425*
SHIRLEY WILSON LOGAN

27   Reading and Writing Differences: The Problematic
of Experience   *436*
MIN-ZHAN LU

28   On Becoming a Woman: Pedagogies of the Self   *447*
SUSAN ROMANO

29   Bi, Butch, and Bar Dyke: Pedagogical Performances
of Class, Gender, and Sexuality   *466*
MICHELLE GIBSON, MARTHA MARINARA,
AND DEBORAH MEEM

REFLECTIVE ESSAY

Masks and Other Drapings: A Reconsideration (or
Reconciliation?) of "Participatory Rhetoric and the
Teacher as Racial/Gendered Subject"   *488*
CHERYL L. JOHNSON

Part Five   **FEMINISM AND THE POLITICS
OF THE PROFESSION**   *491*

Introduction   *493*
LEE NICKOSON-MASSEY

30   Learning Our Own Ways to Situate Composition and
Feminist Studies in the English Department   *496*
WENDY BISHOP

31   Composing "Composing as a Woman": A Perspective
on Research   *512*
ELIZABETH A. FLYNN

32   The Feminization of Composition   *520*
SUSAN MILLER

33   Teaching College English as a Woman   *534*
LYNN Z. BLOOM

34   The Feminization of Rhetoric and Composition
Studies?   *542*
JANICE M. LAUER

35   The Feminization of Composition: Questioning the
Metaphors That Bind Women Teachers   *552*
EILEEN E. SCHELL

36   Gender and Publishing Scholarship in Rhetoric and
      Composition   *558*
      THERESA ENOS

      REFLECTIVE ESSAY
      On "Learning Our Own Ways"   *573*
      WENDY BISHOP

      A Selected Annotated Bibliography in Feminism
      and Composition   *575*

      Further Readings in Feminism and Composition   *591*

      Notes on the Authors   *597*

      Notes on the Editors   *606*

      Index   *611*

FOREWORD

Forwarding a Feminist Agenda in Writing Studies

GAIL E. HAWISHER

There is no book that I have enjoyed watching emerge more than *Feminism and Composition*, a much needed historical rendering of the many faces of feminism in writing studies. I watched each Wednesday evening for over a year as Gesa Kirsch, without fail, climbed the English Building's flights of stairs with an energy that belied the long day she had already put in as associate executive director at the National Council of Teachers of English. I watched as promptly at five o'clock a group of graduate students—Faye, Lance, Lee, and Mary, who had all been part of Gesa's University of Illinois summer course on feminist research and theory—waited to meet in the mostly comfortable space of the Center for Writing Studies office. And, if I ever accidentally forgot about the Wednesday evening gatherings as I noisily moved through the office and halls, Kristen, Faye's then nine-year-old daughter, would gently and sometimes not so gently remind me that an important meeting was going on. From these meetings and from the more than a hundred articles that the group reviewed for the project there emerges a fascinating chronicle of the several paths feminism has followed these past thirty years through composition studies.

Thirty years ago I was in Georgia, and I remember with a jolt that I was living through my first year of teaching, as well as my first year after a divorce that would have been impossible without my new degree and teaching job. Those years were made up of telling feminist moments when I found myself without any sort of financial credit with which to buy a car or refrigerator or any of those other things a single working mother with two children needs to support her family. And, not unlike some other women during the seventies,[1] I found that my most serious nemesis seemed to be represented by the Sears Company, whose nameless service managers insisted on my earning $12,000 a year before I might qualify for a Sears credit card. Although the salary of my (male) colleagues *with* Sears credit cards was substantially below that amount—in the 1970s few, if any, teachers in Georgia earned such a sum—it didn't seem to matter. As a *divorcée* (fortunately a word not much used today) with no previous single credit history, I was not entitled to credit, or so I assume the reasoning went.

Thus when I read Florence Howe's 1971 article on written expression and identity, I am thrown back to those times and realize yet again that my own life in the profession closely parallels the women's movement and the tremendous initiatives women have undertaken during the years since Howe's essay. I am gratified that this book will ensure that stories will not go untold of the turmoil and exasperation many of us in composition experienced during the last decades of the century. These were the years before second-wave feminists had fully theorized the seriousness of women's predicament. They represent years of struggle over the Equal Rights Amendment; they represent the times when many of us battled to come to identity—to have some authorship over our own lived experiences and teaching lives.

But little of this struggle is news to the many feminist readers of *Feminism and Composition*. What may be surprising, however, and what these collected pieces surely reveal is that feminist activism has had a long and enduring presence within composition studies. Even as the field of rhetoric and composition fought to establish itself in the seventies, it did not, as is commonly believed, neglect important feminist issues that were making themselves felt in other parts of the academy. Although there was a dearth of feminist publications in composition during the first half of the eighties,[2] time and again, the thirty-six essays presented here and published from 1971 through 2000 underscore the ongoing importance of feminist thinking to the field. The collected essays are framed by Joy Ritchie and Kathleen Boardman's opening essay in which the two authors map out and analyze converging feminist paths through the field. The volume then moves on to present feminist writing in composition chronologically in each section. Beginning with the strikingly varied 1970 early essays of Howe, Mary P. Hiatt, Joan Bolker, and Sally Miller Gearhart, this volume asks readers to pay attention to women as writers, to women as students in writing classes, to women as researchers, and to women as faculty writing their way through the hierarchies of the academy. Taken together, these essays highlight at least two sites for activism that I'd like to consider in greater depth. Each points to ways in which feminists in composition work to change not only the writing and sometimes the lives of our students but also the very fabric of the academy in which each of us labors.

CLASSROOM PRACTICE HAS ALWAYS BEEN A SITE FOR ACTIVISM FOR FEMINISTS IN COMPOSITION STUDIES

> The kind of writing I finally want these students to be able to do brings together the personal and the political, the private and the public, into writing which is committed and powerful because it takes risks, because it speaks up clearly in their own voices and from their experience, experiments with techniques of argumentation and skillful organization, and engages, where appropriate, with the insights of other writers.
> —PAMELA ANNAS, 1985, THIS VOLUME

> [Reform in the English curriculum] requires a methodology consistent with what theory has taught us about how human beings learn, a

methodology that takes into account the diverse political and social realities of our lives as well as our students' lives, a methodology that encourages a critical practice that continually turns back on itself, continually
monitors, challenges, and changes itself.

—Joy Ritchie, 1990, this volume

The essays in this collection repeatedly demonstrate a commitment to
classroom practice as a site of activism for feminists in composition. Time and
again, they call for not only a thoughtful practice but also a theory of teaching
that is grounded in the conditions of students' lives. Yet despite many having
worked for a number of years to create a feminist pedagogy, there remain
strong disagreements over what constitutes a feminist approach to teaching. Sometimes that pedagogy has taken the form of displacing authoritarian
teaching while creating supportive, nurturing classroom contexts (e.g., Howe).
At other times that pedagogy seeks ways of establishing authority as a feminist writing teacher (e.g., Eichhorn et al.). And at still other times, feminist
pedagogy takes an oppositional turn, in the best sense of that phrase, with the
aim of providing opportunities for dissent or, in Susan Jarratt's words, for the
engagement of "productive conflict."

Yet even as we disagree as to the forms a feminist pedagogy might take,
the goals of that pedagogy remain remarkably similar. They seek to elicit in
students a critical awareness of that which was once invisible—to provoke in
students through reading, thinking, writing, and talk a sense of agency, a
sense of possibility. They aim to forward, through teaching, a feminist agenda
that probes the dominant discourses of sexism, gender preference, and, increasingly in the 1980s and 1990s, racism and classism. Feminism perhaps
found a home in composition because of the shared interest in pedagogy. In
1989, Janice Lauer and Andrea Lunsford reminded us that pedagogy has
always occupied a special place within the field of rhetoric and composition
and that, unlike other disciplines, it is a relationship we prize rather than dis-
dain. The authors of these collected essays would agree.

"Diverse Discourses" Are Appropriate—Even Necessary— Kinds of Writing for Students and the Feminists Who Teach Them

If we are to invent a truly pluralistic society, we must envision a socially
and politically situated view of language and the creation of texts—one
that takes into account gender, race, class, sexual preference, and a host of
issues that are implied by these and other cultural differences. Our language and our written texts represent our visions of our culture and we
need new processes and forms if we are to express ways of thinking that
have been outside the dominant culture.

—Lillian Bridwell-Bowles, 1992, this volume

Lillian Bridwell-Bowles argues persuasively for the adoption of feminist
writing for our teaching and ourselves—for our trying on what she has come
to call "diverse discourse." Essays such as hers and Catherine Lamb's earlier

piece on mediation and negotiation show us differently how to fold into our classes these "new processes and forms." Sometimes using the form of narrative, at other times experimenting with the textual space of paper or screen, students often show a capability with these different forms that eludes them, and us, in the traditional academic essay. As I have worked to incorporate feminist writing in my classes, I have been enormously impressed with the students' experimental writing and attempts to go beyond, in Lamb's words, "the monologic argument." Although *écriture féminine,* as Lynn Worsham points out, is likely to alter either our writing classes or *écriture féminine* beyond recognition, there are many other kinds of diverse discourses that can contribute to students' learning. Students in my classes, for example, commonly create an online portfolio of their semester's work. While online writing does not in itself constitute a feminist project, there are ways that the new technologies, used critically, can further a feminist agenda. Electronic writing can encourage students to try out a different way of being in the world—their Web sites are read by their classmates as well as by students and colleagues from as far away as Australia and Zimbabwe—and to become proficient Web authors in the process. These small examples underscore the many ways that feminists in composition have contributed to changing the kinds of texts that our students, and ourselves, write.

Several feminists represented here also collaboratively author texts with students. These co-authored texts demonstrate departures from traditional academic writing and foreground the value that we place on connections between the writing that students do and the writing that we do. Within the pages of this book, for example, Susan Jarratt and her students and colleagues give us the polyphonic "A Symposium on Feminist Experiences in the Composition Classroom." Other examples of multivoiced texts orchestrated by composition feminists are Susan Miller and her University of Utah undergraduates' survey of "Cross-curricular Underlife," Andrea Lunsford and the Ohio State graduate students' introduction to *Ethics and Representation,* and Nedra Reynolds and her students' review of *Fragments of Rationality.*

Certainly another kind of writing with which composition feminists and their students experiment is the personal essay.[3] Whether the powerful teaching narrative of Cheryl Johnson struggling as an African American feminist to teach her students even as they display a remarkable blindness to issues of difference, the moving tale of Michelle Payne teaching as a graduate student, or the horror story of Lynn Bloom's early life in the profession, all take the kinds of risks often asked of students but that we ourselves resist. In the case of these essays, however, all three authors convey a certain vulnerability in their willingness to share stories that enrich our understanding, another hallmark of feminists working in composition.

Finally, as you read the essays presented here, you will see that they speak with and back to one another. Oftentimes edited collections are criticized as a series of single essays that fail to talk to one another. Clearly that is not the case with those collected here. Lunsford and Lisa Ede cite Anne Gere's study of women's writing groups and Jackie Jones Royster's work with African American women writers; Bridwell-Bowles, Lamb, and Jarratt engage with Sally Miller Gearhart's controversial essay on the violence of persuasion; and Wendy Bishop engages with Elizabeth Flynn's telling essay on composing "Composing as a Woman." And these are just a few of the many references and citations that feminists in composition continually make to one another's work.

I should also note that the conversations are not limited to the printed page. They also occur at the many conferences to which compositionists contribute and which they attend. Papers at the Conference on College Composition and Communication, the convention of the Modern Language Association, the Computers and Writing Conference (founded by Bridwell-Bowles), and, more recently, the biannual Feminist Rhetorics Conference attest to ongoing, vital conversations. More often than not, feminists in composition not only know the scholarly work of their feminist colleagues but also know them face-to-face, with most being only an e-mail message away. But lest I sound too sanguine about the state of feminism in composition, the essays here also remind us that much work remains to be done. As Wendy Bishop, Susan Miller, Eileen Schell, Ritchie and Boardman, and numerous others reveal in this volume, far too many women are still working as handmaidens to those who count as real members of departments of English, the elite literary workforce that grows more elite as it grows smaller. But as the essays in this volume also suggest, there have been far worse times for feminists in composition.

This volume, then, is the first comprehensive effort to map those times and give feminism in composition a history—to foreground the critical position that feminism has occupied in our field and to demonstrate that feminism has always in composition studies been a powerful force in shaping women's identity. Yet there will be its detractors. It won't surprise you, for example, that I would have liked to have seen more essays by compositionists working at the intersections of feminism and technology.[4] Electronic writing can contribute to many of the goals of feminism, but it cannot contribute in any way if feminists eschew the online world. If we omit considerations of the new technologies from our field of vision, we contribute to reproducing the same hierarchies in the online world that already exist in our everyday lives in and out of academe. But, regardless of what I or others might have added to the table of contents, this volume makes an enormous contribution to the profession. The job of the editors for *Feminism and Composition* was to collect, review, arrange, and determine the selections. I can only applaud the superb choices they have made. My only real regret is that those Wednesday evenings with Gesa, Faye, Lance, Lee, and Mary have, like many good things in our lives, necessarily come to an end. But then, I need to remind myself, they live on in the pages of their remarkable collection.

NOTES

I am grateful, as always, for Janet Carey Eldred's careful reading of my writing.

1. See Joan Wallach Scott's "Deconstructing Equality-Versus-Difference: Or, the Uses of Post-structuralist Theory for Feminism" for her analysis of the Sears case, a sex discrimination suit launched against Sears in 1979 by the Equal Employment Opportunity Commission.

2. See Ritchie and Boardman, this volume, for further discussion regarding the relationship between published articles and feminist activism in composition.

3. Expressivist writing pedagogy also asks students to engage with their experiences, but I would argue that the feminist impulse and subsequent writing are different. Although both encourage students to become more involved in their writing, feminist assignments also prompt students to examine critically, sometimes but not always through narrative, their own lived lives and their own positioning within society. Some of these assignments may be classified as critical pedagogy but, in the hands of feminists, reflect a feminist agenda.

4. See, for example, essays by Emily Jessup (Decker), Cynthia Selfe, and myself and Purdue's Patricia Sullivan, and the many excellent essays in *Feminist Cyberscapes* by Kris Blair and Pamela Takayoshi. See also a 1999 special issue on gender of *Computers and Composition*, edited by Lisa Gerrard, to which readers might also want to refer.

WORKS CITED

Anderson, Worth, Cynthia Best, Alycia Black, John Hurst, Brandt Miller, and Susan Miller. "Cross-curricular Underlife: A Collaborative Report on Ways with Academic Words." *College Composition and Communication* 41.1 (February 1990): 11–36.

Blair, Kristine, and Pamela Takayoshi. *Feminist Cyberscapes: Mapping Gendered Academic Spaces.* Stamford: Ablex, 1999.

Gere, Anne. *Writing Groups: History, Theory, and Implications.* Carbondale: Southern Illinois UP, 1987.

Gerrard, Lisa, guest editor. *Computers and Composition.* Special issue: *Computers, Composition, and Gender* 16.1 (April 1999).

Hawisher, Gail E., and Patricia Sullivan. "Fleeting Images: Women Visually Writing the Web." *Passions, Pedagogies, and 21st Century Technologies.* Ed. Gail E. Hawisher and Cynthia L. Selfe. Logan: Utah State UP, 1999. 268–91.

Hawisher, Gail E., and Patricia Sullivan. "Women on the Networks: Searching for E-Spaces of Their Own." *Feminism and Composition Studies: In Other Words.* Ed. Susan C. Jarratt and Lynn Worsham. New York: MLA, 1998. 172–97.

Jessup, Emily. "Feminism and Computers in Composition Instruction." *Evolving Perspectives on Computers and Composition Studies: Questions for the 1990s.* Ed. Gail E. Hawisher and Cynthia L. Selfe. Urbana: NCTE, 1991. 336–55.

Lauer, Janice, M., and Andrea Lunsford. "The Place of Rhetoric and Composition in Doctoral Studies." *The Future of Doctoral Studies in English.* Ed. Andrea Lunsford, Helene Moglen, and James Slevin. New York: MLA, 1989. 106–10.

Lunsford, Andrea A., Melissa A. Goldthwaite, Gianna M. Marsella, Sandee K. McGlaun, Jennifer Phegley, Rob Stacy, Linda Stingily, and Rebecca Greenberg Taylor. "Foreword: Considering Research Methods in Composition and Rhetoric." *Ethics and Representation in Qualitative Studies of Literacy.* Ed. Peter Mortensen and Gesa E. Kirsch. Urbana, IL: National Council of Teachers of english, 1996. vii–xv.

Reynolds, Nedra, et al. "Fragments in Response: An Electronic Discussion of Lester Faigley's *Fragments of Rationality.*" *College Composition and Communication* 45 (1994): 264–73.

Royster, Jacqueline Jones. "Contending Forces: The Struggle of Black Women for Intellectual Affirmation." Columbus, Ohio. March 1, 1989.

Scott, Joan Wallach. "Deconstructing Equality-Versus-Difference: Or, the Uses of Poststructuralist Theory for Feminism," *Conflicts in Feminism.* Ed. Marianne Hirsch and Evelyn Fox Keller. New York: Routledge, 1990. 134–48.

Selfe, Cynthia L. "Technology in the English Classroom: Computers Through the Lens of Feminist Theory." *Computers and Community: Teaching Composition in the Twenty-First Century.* Ed. Carolyn Handa. Portsmouth, NH: Boynton/Cook, 1990. 118–39.

FEMINISM
AND
COMPOSITION

INTRODUCTION

Charting Our Ways in Feminism and Composition

GESA E. KIRSCH, FAYE SPENCER MAOR, LANCE MASSEY, LEE NICKOSON-MASSEY, AND MARY P. SHERIDAN-RABIDEAU

Feminist composition studies is a well-established sub-field within composition studies. Journals in the field regularly publish feminist scholarship in composition, several edited collections present feminist rereadings of the field, and a growing number of single-author books address feminist concerns in the teaching of writing, in composition theory and research, and in professional matters. Yet, until now no single book has compiled the most frequently cited articles published in feminism and composition. When this group of editors gathered for a seminar in Feminism and Composition at the University of Illinois Urbana-Champaign, we lamented the absence of such a collection. By editing *Feminism and Composition,* we set out to change that. This book collects what we consider to be the most influential and important articles published in feminism and composition in the last thirty years.

For the purposes of our collection, we define feminism broadly. Thus, different articles have different theoretical orientations, and many reflect the cultural and social concerns of the times when they were written. Our collection chronicles how various feminisms, as political, social, and historical movements, informed how composition scholars attended to issues of gender in the classroom. The early essays (1970s) reflect the fledgling status of both second-wave feminism and composition within the university. While composition and feminism grew in prominence, it was not until Elizabeth Flynn's 1988 piece that composition journals published feminist work with any regularity. From that time forward, feminist compositionists drew from various feminisms, debating issues surrounding essentialism, social constructionism, and identity politics; exploring personal writing, adversarial arguments, and community considerations; and advocating activism, experimentation, and institutional reform—in order to advance as well as question the idea that gender is a difference that makes a difference. What unites this diversity is that each of the authors invokes feminist frames to understand and advocate what is or what should be happening in the classroom.

The diverse voices included in this collection also reflect the group of five people who came together to bring this project to fruition, people with markedly diverse histories and intellectual interests who all share a keen interest in exploring feminism and composition. Gesa E. Kirsch approached the collection as an accomplished scholar in the field whose knowledge of and experience with feminism and composition served to guide much of the work represented here. Faye Spencer Maor brought her experiences in journalism and communication to the project, as well as the perspective of an African American woman, graduate student, and experienced writing teacher. Lance Massey, the sole male voice of the group, brought interests in antifoundational theory and its relationship to composition and feminism to the project, while Lee Nickoson-Massey's interest and involvement in writing program administration and composition pedagogy suited her well for working with issues of the profession. Finally, Mary P. Sheridan-Rabideau's experience with feminist theory, computers and composition, and empirical research in women's studies provided the group with fresh insight into feminist composition.

As we worked on the collection, each of us discovered new directions for research and teaching in feminism and composition. For example, when one of us (Mary P. Sheridan-Rabideau) taught a graduate seminar in feminism and composition in the fall of 2001, she found that students did not see the dynamic and varied nature of feminism within composition studies. In a climate where "feminism" may be simultaneously seen as a dirty word and absorbed into other projects, she wondered how we could best represent feminist work, work by writers, teachers, and students of composition who may not come with (or want) a "feminist" label. By putting this collection together, then, we asked each other and ourselves about the overly determined definitions of both feminism and composition. We noted, for example, that in recent years feminism has become "mainstreamed" in composition studies. For instance, whereas a few years ago there were special sessions at the Conference on College Composition and Communication devoted to feminist theory, feminist teaching, feminist ways of writing, and feminist ways of refiguring the field, we now find that feminism has been absorbed into an array of conference sessions but rarely stands out in its own right, in its challenge to the status quo, and in its radical potential to question what and how we know.[1] In our opinion, this trend—the mainstreaming of feminism—represents a bittersweet development. It indicates both the strength and weakness of feminism at this time: It is here to stay and has taken its rightful place in our conversations, publications, and conferences, but it seems to have lost, in part, its radical, transformative edge.

Other persistent questions continued to trouble us. How, we wondered, could we best represent the varied and multicolored voices of composition scholars? As we imagined the motivations for academics of color refusing or reframing the conversations in which we were engaging, we wondered if feminism and composition had and could explain why so many women of color foreground race over gender or why lesbian and gay teachers and researchers foreground sexual orientation. What effect does that foregrounding have on theory and pedagogy? Are there ways in which ideas of difference can be utilized to empower students of composition racially, ethnically, and in terms of gender or sexual orientation? Complicating these questions are the impacts of technology, professional politics, and numerous other factors on feminism and composition. As articles in this collection make clear, these questions are constantly evolving, and much remains to be done. This collection, we hope, will help readers navigate the ongoing discussions, recognize gaps and absences, and enrich their understanding of what it means to be a feminist in the field of composition.

By offering readers key essays in one place, we intend *Feminism and Composition* to serve as a resource for scholars who want to familiarize themselves with the history of feminist thought in the field. We imagine that this sourcebook will be read alongside other collections of feminist work that have distinctly different foci than this book, such as Susan Jarratt and Lynn Worsham's collection of postmodern essays, *Feminism and Composition Studies: In Other Words;* Louise Phelps and Janet Emig's experientially based essays, *Feminine Principles and Women's Experience in American Composition and Rhetoric;* Cynthia Caywood and Gillian Overing's early pedagogical volume, *Teaching Writing: Pedagogy, Gender, and Equity;* Jan Zlotnik Schmidt's edition of personal, reflective essays, *Women/Writing/Teaching;* Joanne Addison and Sharon McGee's collection of feminist research studies, *Feminist Empirical Research;* and Joy Ritchie and Kate Ronald's *Available Means: An Anthology of Women's Rhetoric(s).* In this way, *Feminism and Composition* provides a framework for some of the newer, more specialized collections of feminist work.

Several features distinguish this sourcebook. First, we invited five authors of frequently cited essays to reflect on their work's reception, interpretation, and influence, thereby offering readers of this collection a unique and timely perspective on these touchstone essays. Second, we offer readers an annotated bibliography of articles in feminism and composition that we reviewed for this collection but could not include here. This annotated bibliography highlights the important body of feminist work these articles constitute and allows readers to pursue specific interests in greater depth. Third, we provide a list of further readings that includes works by frequently cited feminist theorists from across the disciplines: women's studies, cultural studies, critical theory, queer theory, philosophy, political science, psychology, education, anthropology, and other fields. This list of further readings underscores our position that feminism and composition is situated at the nexus of many disciplines. *Feminism and Composition* presents one reading of the history of feminist thought in composition studies, but the special features, we hope, will alert readers to the many other possible renderings of that same history.

Included in this book are articles from composition and rhetoric journals, as well as from edited book collections published in the last thirty years. All essays have been previously published, with the exception of five reflective essays that were solicited especially for this collection from influential feminist scholars. We did not include excerpts from full-length books, except the last chapter from Jacqueline Jones Royster's *Traces of a Stream: Literacy and Social Change among African American Women,* because of its important contribution to feminist theory and research methodology. In selecting key articles to include in this book, we focused on major areas of composition studies—teaching, theory, research, and the profession—before choosing other, equally important areas, such as technical and scientific writing, basic writing, and writing program administration. In narrowing our selection, we chose essays that have shaped ongoing conversations, that are cited in current scholarship time and again, that have moved the conversation in a particular way, and that have become "touchstone" pieces.

Other criteria for the selection of essays included our desire to balance authors' diverse voices and theoretical perspectives. We included no more than two essays by any single author—except when multi-authored—even though some leading figures in feminist composition studies have published numerous essays that merit republication. We also aimed for diversity in authorship— diversity in terms of authors' backgrounds, ethnicity, sexual orientation, and race. Thus, we included several essays by scholars who add an important new perspective to the field, but whose essays may not be cited as frequently as other essays in this volume. We also valued readability as a criterion, since we intend this book to be a resource for both graduate students and scholars who want to familiarize themselves with the history of feminist thought in the field.

We did not include work in the history of rhetoric, such as feminist re-readings of the rhetorical tradition, work on women's rhetorical education, and feminist historiography. This new and burgeoning area is too large to represent comprehensively here. We refer interested readers to such works as *With Pen and Voice: A Critical Anthology of Nineteenth-Century African-American Women* (Shirley Wilson Logan), *Reclaiming Rhetorica: Regendering the Rhetorical Tradition* (ed. Andrea Lunsford), and *Rhetoric Retold: Regendering the Tradition from Antiquity Through the Renaissance* (Cheryl Glenn), as well as to journals that focus on the history of rhetoric, such as *Rhetoric Review, Rhetorica: A Journal of the History of Rhetoric* and *Rhetoric Society Quarterly.*

Finally, we decided to limit our choices to the field of *composition and rhetoric.* Subsequently, we did not draw on feminist work in education, women's studies, psychology, critical theory, cultural studies, and other related fields. Our list of suggested readings at the end of the book points readers to critical works in these areas, such as bell hooks's *Talking Back: Thinking Feminist, Thinking Black;* Lisa Delpit's *Other People's Children: Cultural Conflict in the Classroom;* Kathleen Weiler's *Women Teaching for Change;* Patti Lather's *Getting Smart: Feminist Research and Pedagogy With/In the Postmodern;* and Magda Gere Lewis's *Without a Word: Teaching Beyond Women's Silence.*

We open our collection with two framing pieces, both offering a different way into the history of feminism and composition. By way of the foreword, Gail Hawisher poetically highlights how the essays in this collection reflect individually and collectively embodied struggles and triumphs. She narrates her own early experiences as a woman, a scholar, and an emerging feminist in composition studies, followed by her current perspective as an eminent scholar whose research focuses on gender and technology. Following our introduction, we present Kathleen Boardman and Joy Ritchie's essay, which provides a critical overview of feminism in composition studies and situates many of the essays we include in this collection.

The essays that follow these pieces are organized thematically, with each of the five parts addressing a major topic in feminism and composition.

Within each part, we offer a brief introduction to situate the selected articles and then present them in chronological order. Part One presents the early voices and visions of feminist scholars who led the way and identified major issues in the field. Extensive conversations rarely appeared in composition journals until the late 1980s, though feminism and composition interacted in productive and multiple ways much earlier. The apparently sporadic representation of feminist composition parallels the obstacles feminist work has faced historically: resistance, silencing, or marginalization. As detailed in later parts, not all journals were receptive to scholarship in feminist composition (e.g., Elizabeth Flynn's "Composing 'Composing as a Woman'"), and some feminists experimented with new forms of writing, such as blurred genres, thereby not easily fitting into traditional publication venues (e.g., Terry Zawacki). Nonetheless, this part offers some of the earliest essays that take gender as a point of departure for scholarship in composition. These essays are also noteworthy because they vary greatly in length, depth, and topic covered and because many of them lack a list of works cited, indicating both the novelty of feminist work in composition and the essays' status as editorials or "staffroom interchange" pieces rather than full-fledged articles.

Part Two includes articles that address the changing nature of theory and research as examined through feminist lenses. One early and much debated topic in this part is essentialism—whether we can generalize about women's ways of writing, knowing, learning, and arguing, or whether we unfairly stereotype and limit women's potential as soon as we speak about women as a group. This debate is far from resolved, although scholars now take into consideration other factors of identity when they discuss essentialism. They ask, for instance, how do race, gender, class, educational background, religion, age, nationality, and other factors shape our ways of knowing, seeing the world, and constructing identity? How does that identity change over time? Feminist composition scholars have also been influenced by a number of different theoretical perspectives—postmodern, French feminist, Marxist, and postcolonial perspectives among them. These and other theoretical approaches have shaped what it means to conduct research or write from a feminist perspective. This part, then, provides a cross-section of the many ways in which feminist scholars have both been influenced by and questioned different theories and methodologies.

Part Three focuses on gender and writing, another topic that received much attention from feminist scholars in the late 1980s and throughout the 1990s. Based on the influential work by Mary Belenky et al. and Carol Gilligan, many scholars began to ask questions about gender, such as "Are there differences in the way men and women write and read? If so, what are these differences, and what might account for them? Are some kinds of writing more suited to women than to men and vice versa? What kinds of writing should we teach and why? Should we prepare students for academic forms of writing or introduce them to many different genres, purposes, and audiences? What is the role of personal and multivoiced writing in the academy?" Authors in this section explore—as well as illustrate—the many possible answers to these questions.

Part Four addresses the heart of writing studies—how we teach writing and how questions of identity play out in the social context of the classroom. These essays explore questions of power, gender, equity, and identity in the classroom. Writing teachers have long noted that their status in the academy directly influences students' perception of the importance of writing classes. To this day, the relative low status and low pay of composition instructors, many of whom are employed in part-time or full-time temporary positions, affect how students respond to and evaluate writing teachers, a topic addressed by Dale Bauer. When considering how other factors of both students' and teachers' identity shape interactions in the classroom, we can recognize a social microcosm that reflects the assumptions—and prejudices—of our larger society. Authors in this part take up many different ways of responding to students (and student resistance) and of teaching writing while challenging students' assumptions about gender, power, and identity.

In the final section, Part Five, authors examine the context of institutional life and professional development and raise critical questions about the politics of the profession, including issues such as working conditions, opportunities for publication, the gendered nature of teaching, the status of composition studies in the academy, and women's roles in the field. They ask, for instance, what the "feminization" of composition studies means. Is it cause for alarm or for celebration? How can we improve the working conditions of all composition instructors, not only a few? How do we best train doctoral students and prepare them for all aspects of faculty work, including writing program administration? How can women (and men) in the profession balance family and work? While exploring these questions, the authors examine the material conditions and consequences for those who work in composition studies.

In assembling this collection, we tried to highlight not only the importance and continuity of feminist work in composition but also the often overlooked ways it interacts with and influences other perspectives in composition studies. As feminism continues to develop as an influential perspective within composition studies, we hope this book's historical perspective will offer feminist composition one possible corpus of work. As with any corpus, this body of work can be reread in alternative ways. We have suggested one way that the essays speak to (or against) one another, thereby forming conversational strands. We invite you, the reader, to find connections between and among these essays, to trace lines of conversations by rearranging essays according to different principles, and to challenge the linear, chronological narrative inevitably inscribed in a book like this one. Such re-visions mark the richness, diversity, and complexity of the many possible histories of feminist composition. The writers whose work is included here each contributed to and challenged the field in some way. So, too, must we challenge ourselves as students, teachers, researchers, and professionals if we are to continue the conversations so critical to the future of feminism and composition.

NOTE

1. There are a few notable exceptions, such as the annual feminist preconvention workshop, devoted solely to feminist issues, and the annual Wednesday night session sponsored by the Coalition of Women Scholars in the History of Rhetoric and Composition.

Feminism in Composition: Inclusion, Metonymy, and Disruption

JOY S. RITCHIE AND KATHLEEN BOARDMAN

At a time when composition is engaged in clarifying its theoretical, political, and pedagogical histories, it is appropriate to construct a story of feminism's involvement in the disciplinary conversations. Despite the recent burgeoning of feminist perspectives in our discipline, it is not easy to delineate how feminism has functioned over the past three decades to shape and critique our understandings of the gendered nature of writing, teaching, and institutions. Although some accounts suggest that feminism, until recently, has been absent or at least late-blooming in the field, we find a more complex relationship in our rereading of essays and books in composition written from a feminist perspective—in particular, the many accounts of personal experience in the field written by feminists and by women since the 1970s. In this essay we look, and look again, at the few articles and notes that appeared in *CCC, College English,* and *English Journal* in the early 1970s. We also focus on feminist retrospective accounts—re-visions of composition written since the mid-1980s.

In writing this brief critical historical survey, we have found ourselves working from various impulses. First, we want to document and celebrate the vitality of feminism in composition, from its early manifestations in the small scattering of essays published in the 1970s (some of them frequently cited, others forgotten) to the explosion of feminist theory and well-documented feminist practice of the last decade. We wish to point out that much early feminist work in composition is not documented in our official publications, having occurred in informal conversations, in classrooms, and in committee meetings. At the same time we want to suggest ways to examine and theorize experiential accounts—both published and unpublished—of feminism in composition. We must also consider seriously the causes and consequences of the delay in feminism's emergence in the published forums of our discipline and the extent to which feminism, despite its recent vitality, has remained contained or marginalized in composition. Finally, we hope to speculate on the positive and negative potential of inclusive, metonymic, and disruptive strategies for feminism's contribution to composition's narratives.

From *College Composition and Communication* 50 (1999): 585–606.

In the past decade, feminists have been visibly active in our discipline. They have examined the subjectivity of the gendered student and the position of women writers in the profession. Questioning assumptions about genre, form, and style, they have provided an impetus to seek alternative writing practices. Feminist perspectives have produced analyses of the gendered nature of the classroom, the feminization of English teaching, the working conditions for female teachers, and the implications of feminist theory for scholarship. Feminist scholars like Andrea Lunsford and Cheryl Glenn have begun rewriting the rhetorical tradition by reclaiming, refiguring, and regendering "Rhetorica." They are also critiquing earlier constructions of history and scholarship in composition. And from a different direction, scholars are drawing upon feminist, African American, lesbian, Native American, and class-based examinations of difference in order to complicate definitions of diversity within composition. Two recent essay collections, Susan Jarratt and Lynn Worsham's *Feminism and Composition Studies: In Other Words* and Louise Phelps and Janet Emig's *Feminine Principles and Women's Experience in American Composition and Rhetoric,* especially highlight the strength of feminism(s) in composition and show how important feminism has been in shaping women's definitions of themselves, their work, and their commitment to pursuing questions of equity in the field.

Yet in the 1970s, while the work of composition as an emerging discipline was occurring right next door to, down the hall from, or in the basement under the work of feminist linguists and literary scholars, composition's official published discussions were largely silent on issues of gender. There is little explicit evidence of systematic theorizing about gender from the 1950s to the late 1980s. As late as 1988, Elizabeth Flynn could write, "For the most part . . . the fields of feminist studies and composition studies have not engaged each other in a serious or systematic way" (425). Indeed, when we began this study, we framed it as a paradox: prior to the mid-1980s, feminism seemed absent from composition but present among compositionists. From those early investigations we pulled one useful reminder: that the connections of composition and feminism have not been an inevitable result of the presence of so many women in the field. But subsequent conversations with a number of longtime teachers and scholars, who spoke to us about their own feminist beliefs and activities in composition dating back to the 1960s, reminded us that the near-absence of feminism from our publications does not constitute absence from the field.

The absence-presence binary also did not help us explain our own history as feminists in composition. As secondary English teachers, teaching women's literature and applying our feminist perspectives to high school courses in the 1970s, we moved into graduate courses and tenure track jobs in composition in the late 1980s and 1990s. Reflecting on our own experience, we recognized that much of the creative feminist energy in composition's history is not visible in the publications we searched: it appeared in informal conversations, in basement classrooms, and in committees on which women served. This energy might be viewed as ephemeral, yet we can testify, along with others, that it created solidarity among women, influenced students and colleagues, and helped form an epistemology on which later feminist work could grow. Sharon Crowley reminds us further that composition allowed and acknowledged women's participation in teaching and scholarship before many other disciplines began to do so—as we see from the important work of Josephine Miles, Winifred Horner, Ann Berthoff, Janet Emig, and others. Still, Theresa Enos' collection of anecdotes from women in the field over the last several decades cautions us that the job conditions and security for many of these practitioners were terrible.

Crowley's and Enos' different perspectives point again to a history of women and feminism in composition that cannot be constructed in a tidy narrative. In the documents and accounts we have read and heard, we find three overlapping tropes that shed light on the roles feminism has played in composition and in the strategies women have used to gain a place in its conversations: (1) Following the pattern of developing feminist thought in the 1970s and 1980s, many early feminist accounts in composition sought *inclusion* and equality for women. (2) More recent accounts like those of Louise Phelps and Janet Emig posit feminism as a "subterranean" unspoken presence (xv), and Susan Jarratt and Laura Brady suggest the *metonymy* or contiguity of feminism and composition. (3) Also developing during this time has been what feminist postmodernists define as *disruption* and critique of hegemonic narratives—resistance, interruption, and finally redirection of composition's business as usual.

While it's tempting to posit this as a linear, evolutionary set of tropes—that women have grown out of and into as we've matured theoretically—we find it too restrictive to do so. These narratives coexist and have multiple functions, often depending on the historical or theoretical context in which they are read. For example, some early attempts at inclusion, based on experiential accounts, function also as disruptive narratives, and a number of very recent accounts might be characterized as primarily metonymic narratives. Furthermore, each of these tropes has both advantages and disadvantages for feminism in composition: for example, a narrative aimed at *including* women may also function to *contain* feminism within narrow boundaries. We also emphasize that we are not interested in categorizing narratives (and narrators) as "inclusionist," "disruptionist," and so on. Rather we hope to tease out the tropes, show how these narratives can be reread in multiple ways, and suggest how each one enacts one or more epistemological positions with respect to women's experience, identity, and difference.

As we reread for these rhetorical strategies, we find that the conceptions of experience in each of these sets of narratives also require examination. Most of the feminist writing in composition is grounded in accounts of personal experience. For example, many women have told powerful stories of their first recognition of their marginality in a field they had previously thought of as theirs. We must beware of reading these moving accounts too transparently and untheoretically. In her essay "Experience," Joan W. Scott offers a useful caution:

> When experience is taken as the origin of knowledge, the vision of the individual subject (the person who had the experience or the historian who recounts it) becomes the bedrock of evidence upon which explanation is built. Questions about the constructed nature of experience, about how subjects are constituted as different in the first place, about how one's vision is structured—about language (or discourse) and history— are left aside. (25)

Scott reminds us that narratives of experience should be encountered not as uncontested truth but as catalysts for further analysis of the conditions that shape experience.

We want to be clear about our view of experience: we are not dismissing such accounts but only suggesting ways to read and listen to them. The problem is not that these narratives are personal or that they are experiential, but that they are often untheorized. In understanding both the value and the limitations of feminist uses of experience in our field, we have found the work of Scott and of Rosemary Hennessy particularly useful. Both address "experience" as a construct and show ways to continue to value women's experiences as sources of knowledge; but they also suggest ways to theorize experience to make it a more critical rhetorical tool. Scott advises us to keep in mind that "experience is at once always already an interpretation and is in need of interpretation. What counts as experience is neither self-evident nor straightforward; it is always contested, always therefore political" (37). Hennessy views experience as a critical tool for examining the values and ideologies used to construct women's experiences, but she adds an important qualification for ensuring that women's experience is not narrowly read. Any critical theorizing of women's experience must be undertaken in the context of a continual "re-contextualization of the relationship between personal and group history and political priorities" (Minnie Bruce Pratt, qtd. in Hennessy 99) and in relation to the "counterhegemonic discourses" of others (99). We have found that by attending to certain feminist tropes in our discipline, we can not only begin to tease out the relationships between composition and feminism, but also gain a better sense of the important dialectical relationships between experience and theory.

ADDING WOMEN: NARRATIVES AIMED AT INCLUSION

Correcting the long absence of women from intellectual and political landscapes, inserting women's perspectives into contexts dominated by patriarchy, and giving women equal status with men have constituted one of the central feminist projects—that of *inclusion*. This effort to add women has been criticized retrospectively as ineffective because it arises from Enlightenment conceptions of individual autonomy and the unquestioned "truth" of individual experience. Discussions of inclusion of women *as* women may reinforce essentialist or biological definitions of gender, and they often neglect to theorize the discourses that keep women and minorities marginalized. Most critically, many attempts to include women in the conversations of the field have in fact added only white, middle-class, heterosexual women. Despite these criticisms, we need to reread these attempts from their cultural context and for their first steps toward gender awareness. As Suzanne Clark reminds us, "feminists challenging a certain kind of feminism in composition represent a luxury: women now have a sufficient number to play out [their] anxieties of influence" (94). Our analyses need to take into account cultural and historical contexts out of which women were working that made these assumptions viable at the time.

Some of the first published evidence of the initiative to add women to the conversation came in NCTE publications aimed primarily at secondary teachers. The March 1972 *English Journal* printed "The Undiscovered," Robert A. Bennett's NCTE presidential address of the previous November. In highlighting "the undiscovered human resources of our professional organization" (352), Bennett includes girls and women among "those peoples of American society who have not yet been allowed to make their fullest contribution":

> The talents of the great number of women teachers who are today still nonmembers of the Council or who are inactive in Council affairs provide another undiscovered resource. As a professional organization, we must reach out to these women and encourage them . . . to become full partners in our common effort. (353)

After urging the organization to examine wage and promotion policies, document discriminatory practices, and work for recognition of women in curriculum and pedagogy, Bennett declares, "NCTE must take a stand for recognition of the contribution of women to society and to our profession. We have not done it. Let's get at it" (353).

Two months later, *English Journal* carried a short "Open Letter from Janet Emig, Chairwoman, NCTE Committee on the Role and Image of Women," asking the membership to nominate committee members and to send information about any "instances of discrimination against women in the profession, either in the form of a brief narrative or, if you are the woman involved, as a signed or as an anonymous case history" (710). A direct result of NCTE's new commitment to include women, Emig's committee was soliciting stories that would potentially disrupt business-as-usual in the profession (a practice that Theresa Enos repeated more than 20 years later for *Gender Roles and Faculty Lives in Rhetoric and Composition*). The CCCC Committee on the Status of Women also continues to solicit narratives, in various forums, in order to ascertain more clearly the status of women in the field.

While a review of *CCC* from the late 1960s through the late 1980s uncovers few essays or other documents that would indicate a gendered feminist consciousness in composition, two landmark special issues of *College English*, in 1971 and 1972, report on the newly formed MLA Commission on the Status of Women in the Profession and document courses designed by feminists in

English to reshape the curriculum from the standpoint of women students. The narratives in these special issues set the pattern for the impulse a decade or more later in composition to add women to its perspectives. Arising from the writers' own consciousness-raising experiences, the narratives articulate the potential for student and teacher subjectivities that are not neutral or universal but uniquely influenced by the textual, social, and political context of gender. Florence Howe's impassioned 1971 essay, in which she inserts her own personal account of discrimination, reports the inequities in women's status she uncovered as chair of the MLA commission. In addition to these first attempts to address women's low status in the profession, Howe and Elaine Showalter both illustrate their efforts to rectify the lack of women's texts and perspectives in English courses. Showalter describes her newly organized course, "The Educated Woman in Literature," in practical terms, and Howe presents a writing course she designed to help women alter their self-image "from centuries of *belief* in their inferiority, as well as from male-dominated and controlled institutions" (863). A second special issue of *College English* (October 1972) contains important essays concerning women's inclusion in the discipline of English, among them Tillie Olsen's "Women Who Are Writers in Our Century: One Out of Twelve" and Adrienne Rich's "When We Dead Awaken: Writing as Re-Vision." Each of these essays seeks to insert women—their perspectives, their writing, their lived experiences—into a discipline from which they had been excluded.

In "Taking Women Students Seriously," her important 1978 essay emphasizing the necessity of including women's perspectives in education, Adrienne Rich described how the experience of changing from one teaching context to another allowed her to translate the critical questions she asked as a writing instructor of minority students into parallel questions she needed to ask about women students:

> How does a woman gain a sense of her *self* in a system . . . which devalues work done by women, denies the importance of female experience, and is physically violent toward women? . . . How do we, as women, teach women students a canon of literature which has consistently excluded or depreciated female experience? (239)

These early essays set a pattern for subsequent inclusive questions that women in composition began asking. Beginning by describing their own consciousness-raising experiences in their essays, the writers moved on to document the concrete changes in teaching and critical perspectives they advocated. What are women's experiences in classrooms, in institutions? How do women use language? How are women writers different from male writers? Questions like these included women in ways that had not been possible in a "gender-blind" field of composition; they set the stage for writers in the 1980s like Pamela Annas and Elizabeth Flynn to engage them further in work that again sought women's inclusion in the field and sparked feminist discussions for a newer generation of women.[1]

In the late 70s, the trope of inclusion appeared in essays applying feminist language research to composition by investigating claims made by Robin Lakoff in her 1975 *Language and Woman's Place*—that women, by using a lady-like middle-class language, contributed to their own oppression. Lakoff's argument reflected the "dominance" approach to women's language use that was prominent among feminists of the 70s: attributing gender differences in language mainly to social oppression of women. Joan Bolker's 1979 *College English* article, "Teaching Griselda to Write," is a practitioner's account of her experience struggling with the absence of voice and authority in the work of "good-girl" student writers. The many citations of this short article in the past 19 years suggest that it has resonated with feminists in composition. In 1978, two articles examining women's "different" style appeared in *CCC*. In "The Feminine Style: Theory and Fact," Mary P. Hiatt discusses her study of the stylistic features of women's and men's writing. She reports "clear evidence of a feminine style . . . [that] is in fact rather different from the common assumptions about it" (226). Contrary to Lakoff's generalizations about women's oral language, women's written style, according to Hiatt, has "no excesses of length or complexity or emotion" (226). In "Women in a Double-Bind: Hazards of the Argumentative Edge," Sheila Ortiz Taylor draws composition instructors' attention to the "invisible, though real, disadvantage" that women students face in writing courses because "both the methods and the goals of such classes are alien to them" (385). She argues that the competitive, impersonal style of traditional argument alienates women; she urges instructors to validate "conversational tone, dramatic technique, and intimate reader involvement" (389).

Among the first composition articles to train the spotlight on women's language experiences, these essays highlight deficiency. (Ironically, as in Lakoff's book, an essentialized "woman" is both *included* and *found lacking*.) Bolker, Taylor, and Hiatt respond differently to the idea that women students must have special problems because a feminine style represents deficiency. Taylor uses the language of victimization to describe the woman student: "She must feel that something is wrong with her, a self-destructive disapproval common enough in women . . . of course, much of the damage has been done by the time our students reach us. They have been taught a special language" (385). But Taylor adds that a feminine style of argument is only "deficient" because society has refused to validate it. Bolker believes that with more self-esteem and voice, the good girl can be a contender in the arena of the dominant discourse. Hiatt implies that readers need to be more discerning about the gender differences they *think* they see. None of these articles is heavily theorized; with the possible exception of Hiatt's, they arise from and return directly to classroom experience. Because they do not attend closely to larger systemic issues of power and discourse, these studies also make it possible for feminist concerns to be contained, encapsulated, or dismissed as "women's issues." Yet essays like these deserve credit for challenging the field's gender-blindness by insisting that women be included in narratives of classroom writing practices. They have contributed to a sense of intuitive connection between composition and those who ask, at least implicitly, "What difference might it make if the student (or teacher) is female?"

MAKING INTUITIVE CONNECTIONS: NARRATIVES OF METONYMIC RELATIONSHIP

In their introduction to *Teaching Writing: Pedagogy, Gender, and Equity,* one of the first books to connect writing and feminism in composition, Cynthia Caywood and Gillian Overing say that despite the absence of explicit discussion, they had experienced as practitioners an "intuitive understanding" of a "fundamental connection" between feminism and revisionist writing theory. While highlighting an absence of attention to gender, they also posit a more complicated reading of this absence by pointing to the nearly parallel lives of composition and feminist theory. According to this story, the two have run for years in the same direction, along close trajectories; to bring the fields together it is necessary only to notice the shared goals and common directions, and to make connections more visible and explicit. Caywood and Overing ask, "At what point did our parallel interests in feminism and revisionist writing theory converge?" (xi). More recently Susan Jarratt, Laura Brady, Janet Emig, and Louise Phelps have suggested that the boundaries have been permeable between feminist work in literary studies, the social sciences, and composition. This resonates with our own sense, as practitioners in the 70s, that boundaries between feminism and composition were often marked by unarticulated overlaps and crossovers. This permeability may have been partly the result of the interdisciplinary nature of composition, which drew for its theoretical substance from linguistics, cognitive and developmental psychology, and literary criticism. But while this intuitive connection may have created alliances among women in composition and feminists in other fields, it may also have delayed the emergence of feminist theory and continued its marginalization in the field.

Various factors account for the intuitive sense of connection that many of us have experienced and narrated. First, emerging pedagogical theories spoke a language that resonated with feminism's concerns of the time: coming to voice and consciousness, illuminating experience and its relationship to individual identity, playing the believing game rather than the doubting game, collaborating rather than competing, subverting hierarchy in the classroom. These watchwords characterized composition's link to liberal political and social agendas shared by feminist scholars in other disciplines and aimed at challenging established traditions, epistemologies, and practices of the academy.[2] Sharon Crowley explicitly connects Dewey's progressivism with Janet Emig's development of "process pedagogies," arguing that this link between progressivism and process pedagogies was vitally important in reconceptualizing composition "as an art rather than a course," and "because its theorists discovered a way to talk about student writing that authorized teachers to think of themselves as researchers" (17). This reconceptualization resonated for feminists theoretically and politically.

Secondly, at that time many women in the profession were doing double-duty as composition and literature teachers. Among the *College English* authors represented in the special issues we have pointed out, Florence Howe taught composition and wrote about how her course focused on women, and Adrienne Rich taught writing with Mina Shaughnessy in the SEEK program at CCNY. Many feminist composition instructors, coming from literary critical backgrounds, continued reading in their fields and appropriating whatever feminist approaches seemed useful—much as compositionists of the 80s and 90s have appropriated the work of Belenky, Clinchy, Goldberger, and Tarule and poststructuralists feminists.

The material conditions surrounding women in composition have also contributed to a felt sense of the feminist connections to our work. Composition was and still is constructed as women's work, and the majority of workers were women; many of us teaching writing or working on composition degrees during the 70s and 80s were newly arrived from secondary teaching. Surrounded by colleagues with similar career patterns, we entered conversations that enacted an interplay between our lives and our professional work. The drawbacks of the "feminization" of the field were not theorized until several years later.

Finally, as the field developed in the 1970s, although journal editors and the professional hierarchy were primarily male, the names of women were also moving into prominent places: Mina Shaughnessy, Janet Emig, Ann Berthoff, Sondra Perl, Anne Gere, Lillian Bridwell-Bowles, and others were writing many of the important articles and books we studied. Many feminists refer with appreciation to the "foremothers," first for their presence as models, and secondly for their ideas which, though not articulated in terms of gender, are often read, in retrospect, as consistent with feminist practice. In many cases, these ideas have to do with nurturing, collaboration, revisioning, and decentering.

Some retrospective accounts use theory to make the composition-feminism connections less intuitive, more explicit. Turning from foremothers to "midwives," Carolyn Ericksen Hill uses feminist theory to read composition history through the gendering of practices, of theories, and of the field itself.[3] She reads the label "midwives" back onto male composition theorists active in the 60s and early 70s: Peter Elbow, Ken Macrorie, John Schultz, and William Coles, Jr. Without necessarily claiming them as feminists, she can, with the aid of postmodern theory, gender their approach as feminine and place their work in a certain feminist context: they helped "birth" the experiential self. The expressivist/nurturing feminist connection has often been made in passing, but Hill's label "midwives" claims these key composition figures for feminist theorizing—and also marginalizes them. In the 1990s, Hill argues, these four "expressivist" figures have been pushed to the edge of a newly theorized and professionalized field; their gender-blindness and humanistic model of the autonomous self have had to make way for gender difference and shifting subject positions, powerful constructs for feminist analysis. Hill sees in the compartmentalization—rather than dynamic rereading—of the four men's so-called expressivism a parallel with the "othering" of "woman," and of feminism, that continues to occur.

The rereading of "foremothers"—or even "midwives"—as feminist precursors may also be problematic if it ignores context and complexity, as we see from a few examples of foremothers who resist labeling. In the late 1970s, Ann Berthoff roundly rejected the gendering of logic and the either/or-ism of all discussions of women's ways of knowing; she reaffirmed this rejection at the 1998 CCCC convention. Still, the foremother figures can both exemplify and disrupt the notion of the feminization of the field. As fore*mothers* they are both marginalized and typically characterized as nurturers. But insofar as they are envisioned as *fore*mothers, as founders, they are not feminized but rather constructed in a traditionally masculine position.

Evidence that stories of connection continue to resonate with us may be found in Jan Zlotnik Schmidt's introduction to *Women/Writing/Teaching,* a 1998 collection of essays by women writers and teachers. Schmidt emphasizes the importance of women's experience in making writing-teaching connections and expresses her hope that readers will also "explore their own life stories, their development of selfhood, their multiple identities as writers, teachers, and writing teachers" (xii). Retrospective narratives that create foremothers, midwives, connections, and nurturing community in composition's history foreground the double potential of the metonymic relationship between feminism and composition. This intuitive connection helps to create a sense of solidarity and vitality. But it may also reinforce the very structures that keep feminist perspectives contained in a separate, benign category rather than giving feminist analysis a central place, or at least keeping it insistently, vocally disruptive of the discipline's metanarratives. For example, some feminist practitioners have told powerful stories about replacing hierarchical, agonistic classroom environments with decentered, nurturing classrooms based on an ethic of care. But, as Eileen Schell argues, "femin*in*ist pedagogy, although compelling, may reinforce rather than critique or transform patriarchal structures by reinscribing what Magda Lewis calls the 'woman as caretaker ideology'" ("The Cost" 74, our italics).

Granting feminism's intuitive connections with a discipline that challenged current-traditional conceptions of language and introduced new decentered writing pedagogies, it is also important to recognize that some feminist agendas were more likely to disrupt than to aid composition's early progress toward full disciplinary status. Composition needed to build institutional legitimacy in the traditional academy; a fundamental feminist goal was to disrupt rather than extend patriarchal discourses and their assumptions about knowledge. Composition sought a single theory of the writing process and the writing subject; feminist theorists challenged notions of a singular universal concept of truth. The trope of metonymy may have difficulty expanding to cover some of these adversarial relationships.

FEMINIST DISRUPTIONS

Composition has many narratives of feminist disruption which emphasize neither inclusion nor intuitive connection but rather represent some form of feminism (newly experienced or theorized) reaching back to reread and even reconfigure past experience and practice. We see increasing numbers of current feminists drawing on postmodern theories to analyze and critique the basic "process" narratives of composition's first 20 years, to raise questions about difference(s), and to critique disciplinary practices and structures that have shaped composition. Disruption is often linked to postmodern theories of power, discourse, and ideology rather than to consciousness-raising sessions, discussions of pedagogy, or attempts to create equitable and inclusive conditions for women. In order to intervene significantly in power structures that keep women subordinate, feminists investigate and uncover the contradictions in those dominant structures. The feminist narratives we have reread remind us, however, that efforts at inclusion, connection, and disruption often work synthetically rather than as adversaries or as unequal partners. As Theresa Enos says, her book's "most powerful use of 'data' is the narrative, in the stories that help us define our places in academia so that we can better trace our future" (1).

The explicit recognition of composition's lack of attention to women's material lives has led women in anger, frustration, and recognition to tell the stories of their coming to awareness. A classic feminist narrative of the early 70s is the story of a "good girl," silenced by her compulsion to please, whose recognition of her oppression releases an anger strong enough to overcome politeness and fear; thus she finds both her voice and an agenda for change. The consciousness-raising sessions of the late 60s and early 70s provided a model for this narrative, as did the two special women's issues of *College English*, 1971–72, that we have mentioned. In "When We Dead Awaken," Rich told her own story of frustration at the demands that she be good at all the roles women were supposed to play, while Howe, after narrating how she had acquiesced in years of inequitable treatment, wrote, "Eighteen months as commission Chairwoman [of the MLA Commission on the Status of Women] has eroded that wry smile. I feel now a growing anger as I come to realize that . . . I am not alone in my state" (849).

Many of today's feminist accounts of the 60s and 70s follow a similar pattern. Lynn Z. Bloom's essay, "Teaching College English as a Woman" (1992), is a scathing look at the bad old days in college English, when a woman in the field—whether student or teacher—would be exploited if she did not get angry and speak up. Bloom recalls a conversion experience when, as a part-time composition instructor, she finally was able to obtain office space: in a basement room full of desks, on the floor under the stairs, next to the kitty litter. Surveying these wretched conditions, she told herself, "If I ever agree to do this again, I deserve what I get" (821). Separated by more than 20 years, Bloom's and Howe's angry accounts illustrate what we might call individual, liberal disruption: the idea that once a women sees clearly, her life is changed, and she is thus empowered to become effectively active for change and reform. These accounts show the "re-visioning" that feminist thinking has enabled individual women to do. We read these accounts as disruptive because in addition to realizing that the liberal Enlightenment agenda hasn't included *her,* each of these women also recognizes that she must take action to disrupt and change the structures that have kept her subordinate.

Other women who are currently doing feminist work in composition studies have provided similar testimonies of naive compliance, oppressed silence, eventual recognition, and new outspokeness.[4] That we now have so many such narratives may mean that women in composition today are finally in a position to claim the authority of the autobiographical; it may also mean that, largely due to feminist efforts, the conventions of scholarly discourse have expanded to include the personal narrative as a way of situating oneself in one's scholarship. But perhaps the personal testimony remains an effective—and still necessary—tool of disruption. Many of these stories are disruptive because they expose "the pattern of well-rewarded, male supervision of under-rewarded, female workers" that has existed in composition and "is entrenched in our whole culture" (Enos vii). The disruption that is so central to the consciousness-raising narrative itself also highlights gaps in our reading of our past and of business as usual. Rereading the consciousness-raising essays that have recurred in composition over the past 25 years can show us more sites where women have been silent but where feminists want to rupture that silence.

Many narratives deal with experiences in teaching and department politics, but a 1993 retrospective account by Nancy McCracken, Lois Green, and Claudia Greenwood tells how they acquiesced as researchers to a field characterized by "a persistent silence on the subject of gender" in its "landmark research studies on writing development and writing processes" (352). Now writing collaboratively, they return to studies of teacher responses to student writing that they had published earlier (and separately), reinterpreting those studies in terms of gender differences. These authors emphasize that until the late 80s the climate in composition studies had made it difficult to notice or report gender differences in empirical studies: "None of us went looking for gender differences. When the data began to speak of gender, we dared not listen" (356). They recount their worries about being accused of biological determinism, about seeming to exclude men, about appearing unprofessional, and about calling attention to themselves as women. Now, they say, they feel empowered not only to note gender difference but to insist on it. Theirs is not a story of breaking silence by themselves. Instead, the current "research environment in which it is both important and safe to study the interplay between students' gender and their development as writers" (354) has made it possible to revise their findings. Their story is not about singular heroism but about collaboration, in a network of mutual support, in a research/scholarly environment that has made discursive structures more visible. Their story is not about going solo against a hostile discipline but about rereading the field and their own complicity. Their reading disrupts, among other things, their *own* research, by requiring that they return to it and revise it.

Some of the early disruptive narratives we have mentioned are reformist, and they may even be read as attempts at inclusion as well as disruption. Another form of disruptive narrative is less grounded in the impulse for individual disruption and change, but seeks wider consideration of difference. Such critiques often create conflict and may evoke more resistance because they demand changes in institutional and epistemological structures that conflict with composition's continuing need to establish legitimacy. They support the emergence of different perspectives rather than suppressing them. In these accounts difference is expanded from the single male/female binary to differences, taking into account multiple inflections of social class, sexual orientation, and race. For example, Harriet Malinowitz's study of lesbian and gay students in writing classes and Shirley Wilson Logan's writing on the confluence of race and gender in composition both attempt to expand our understanding of what differences can mean in composition classrooms. They articulate the connections among differences as well as show the privileging or erasure of some categories by others. Writing out of her own experience as a Chinese student speaking several languages, Min-Zhan Lu has drawn upon third-world and minority feminisms as well as other cultural theorists to disrupt composition teachers' view of the conflicts students face in negotiating the political, linguistic, and rhetorical "borderlands" between home and school. She reopens a debate about the processes of acculturation and accommodation at work in writing classrooms, particularly those that serve minority and immigrant students. In doing so, she rereads the work of Mina Shaughnessy, Thomas Farrell, Kenneth Bruffee, and others in light of current contexts in order to critique the wider public debates about literacy and to highlight the cultural conflicts and necessary resistances of today's students on the margins.

At times these disruptions can create tension and anger even among feminists, highlighting the way feminism itself is shaped by and embedded in existing hierarchical discourses. This conflict may seem to undermine any sense of solidarity that existed when feminism appeared in a more intuitive rather than carefully articulated and scrutinized form. But in fact, such conflict may produce one of feminism's most important benefits—the proliferation of differences. Nedra Reynolds argues: "Feminists daring to criticize other feminists have opened up spaces for analyzing difference; they interrupted the discourses of feminism in the singular to make possible feminism in the plural" (66). Other disruptive narratives of difference are only now emerging and await further exploration. Constructs like Gloria Anzaldua's *mestiza*, Trinh T. Minh-ha's subject-in-the-making, Donna Haraway's cyborg, and Judith Butler's performer of gender extend postmodern notions of difference in disruptive directions with their advocacy of multiplicity, fluidity, hybridity, and indeterminacy.

Feminists in composition in the past decade have used postmodern theories to reread the feminization and the femin*in*ization of composition as problematic and to seek to revise institutional frameworks. The preponderance of women in composition has not led inevitably to the triumph of feminist interests and values in the field. For example, Susan Miller tells the story of the "sad women in the basement" and describes feminization as the "female coding" of the "ideologically constructed identity for the teacher of composition" (123); it involves constructing composition as "women's work." Feminization refers to the gendering of the entire field of composition and of various activities that have taken place within it (nonhierarchical pedagogy, the writing process movement, "romantic" philosophies, nurturing of writers). For Miller, feminization points to the devaluation of the composition instructor, and the subordination of composition to literature, throughout the history of the field. For Rhonda Grego and Nancy Thompson, compositionists "still reside within our gendered roles," but we are not limited to a traditional "wifely" role because the field has lately been "developing terms and methods through which to name our work at least to ourselves, if not yet fully to the ruling apparatus of the academic system" (68). In *Gypsy Academics and Mother-Teachers,* Eileen Schell combines materialist feminist and postmodern perspectives, labor and institutional history, and the personal narratives of women non-tenure-track teachers to analyze the gendered division of labor in composition and to critique femin*in*ization—the coopting of the "ethic of care." She also provides strategies for coalition-building and tangible plans of action for reconceptualizing women's positions and reshaping institutional structures. Feminization narratives like these work disruptively in two directions: their analysis foregrounds the political position of composition within institutional structures, but it also highlights tensions within women's roles and interests in composition.

Finally, disruptive narratives in composition have begun to analyze the established narratives of the discipline and the agency of students and teachers constructed by those narratives. They explore the ideologies underlying the discourses where composition has been situated, including those espoused by feminists, to underscore the contradictions and dangers that those create for women as well as for the field in general. An early example is Susan Jarratt's rereading of Peter Elbow's work and of the tendency in feminism and expressivism to suppress conflict and promote consensus.[5] She argues that such a stance fails to arm women students and teachers with the tools to confront the power relations inherent in their positions. An important recent example of disruption is Nedra Reynolds' rereading of several major narratives in the field. Reynolds emphasizes that interruption—talking back, forcibly breaking into the prevailing discourse of a field—is a way to create agency: "Agency is not simply about finding one's own voice but also about intervening in discourses of the everyday [this would include personal experience narratives] and cultivating rhetorical tactics that make interruption and resistance an important part of any conversation" (59). She points out the tendency of "some of the most important voices in composition today . . . to ignore work in feminism that might complement or complicate their ideas" (66). She not only "interrupts" some of the major cultural studies theorists but also analyzes the conceptions of subjectivity and agency in the work of James Berlin, John Trimbur, and Lester Faigley. She criticizes the dominant narrative's tendency to compartmentalize interrupters and disrupters as "rude women," thereby denying them agency. As part of the evidence for her argument, she tells stories about a cultural studies conference where bell hooks and other women participants analyzed the "terror" of the typical "white supremacist hierarchy" (65). Reynolds urges women to develop strategies for interrupting dominant discourses in composition and challenges them to offer their students the means to resist rigid forms of discourse.

CONCLUSION: IN EXCESS

These three different but also converging narratives of feminism suggest a rich tradition of feminist thought and activity in composition: pushing for admission, working intuitively alongside, and interrupting the conversation. We believe these three tropes may help us read and revise feminism's evolving place in the narratives of composition; they provide useful insight for feminists about existing tensions in the relationship of theory to experience and practice, and they point to strategies feminists may seek to promote or avoid in the future.

In composition's last three decades, the impulse has been toward legitimation, theory-building, and consolidation. The disruption and the assertion of difference that feminists and others represent have come slowly and with struggle; they have been delayed and even suppressed by the need to build a more unified disciplinary discourse. In several recent metanarratives that assess where composition has come from and where it is going, we find traces of these three lines of feminist thought that may help us see where feminism might most usefully lead composition and where they might go together. These recent commentaries demonstrate that tropes of inclusion and metonymic connection still define feminism's relationship to the field.

In *Fragments of Rationality,* Lester Faigley practices inclusion as he credits feminism for its efforts to theorize a postmodern subject with agency; he also cites the contributions of feminists in foregrounding important pedagogical and political questions. James Berlin's *Rhetorics, Poetics, and Cultures* does not mention feminism, but this book, like Faigley's, does cite several postmodern feminists' efforts to theorize subjectivity and difference. In Joseph Harris' *A Teaching Subject: Composition Since 1966,* the connections between women practitioners, feminism, and "the teaching subject" are neither articulated nor connected; they remain an unspoken presence. Like Berlin, Sharon Crowley argues in *Composition in the University* that despite its progress over the past 30 years, composition has remained a conservative discipline, still trapped in current-traditionalism, still shackled to the service role of Freshman English, and still bound to the limitations of humanism in English departments. Unlike Berlin, she looks to feminist thought for its disruptive power, as one of several theoretical perspectives that might help dislodge composition from narrow disciplinary confines.

The representation of feminist perspectives in these recent commentaries suggests that in the future these relationships will persist—with unspoken alliances between feminist thought and composition, and inclusive reliance on postmodern feminism(s) where they advance the general argument. But it is to the disruptive strategy, framed in dialogue with inclusivity and metonymy, that we return. It is tempting to see disruption as the newest and best hope for feminism and to privilege theorizing as the most worthwhile activity for feminism and composition. But it's also clear that different emphases may be more effective as rhetorical contexts shift and historical moments change. While efforts at inclusion suffer from the limitations we've outlined, and untheorized or unarticulated practices also create risks of marginalization and erasure, disruptive strategies, by themselves, also have limitations. The history of feminism suggests that it is necessary to do more than interrupt a disciplinary conversation. Disruption may be only temporary, and as Reynolds and others point out, it's easy to push disrupters to the sidelines, to stop listening to them and to marginalize them once again. In addition, the task of disruption requires rhetorical skill. Those who interrupt may gain momentary attention, but those who can't sustain the conversation, hold up the argument, or tell an absorbing story will soon drop—or be dropped— from the discussion.

Certainly feminists in composition have provided the field with models for persuasive and beautiful writing that tells and disrupts stories of experience. (Lynn Worsham's "After Words: A Choice of Words Remains" is a recent example.) If theorizing and disruption are detached from lived experience and material history, they may remain irrelevant. And if disruption only fractures and doesn't again create connection, a sense of an even tentatively inclusive agenda, it will lack the vital energy and supportive alliances to sustain its own taxing work. Over the last 30 years, feminists have demonstrated that critique and disruption are never finished and that coalition-building and collaboration are vital for change.

Our rereading of 30 years of feminist writing suggests that in both early and more recent work, feminism has been most challenging and disruptive and also provided a sense of alliance and inclusion when it has maintained a dialogical relationship between theory and experience. Despite its short history, feminist work in composition can certainly provide many revitalizing demonstrations of this dialogical relationship as one of its contributions to academic feminism. Virtually all the feminist work we've reviewed and see emerging has, at least in part, claimed, interpreted, and revised accounts of experience and history: the personal history of one's life as a woman, the practice of the teacher, or the experience of the scholar. As Suzanne Clark points out, narratives of experience theorized become possible sites of agency: "At the same time that stories of personal experience invoke and re-cite determinant categories of identity . . . such stories also produce an excess not easily retrofitted as the norm" (98). Rather than dismissing stories of experience, Clark suggests that we look at them for what is "excessive," that is, for parts of the narrative that do not fit our current explanations: "What refuses, despite the sometimes daunting applications of straitjacket pseudo-sciences, to be contained?" (98). One of feminism's most potentially powerful tools is the deployment of what is excessive, what is other. Difference, "otherness," disrupts, as Rosemary Hennessy argues, because the "gaps, contradictions, *aporias*" that otherness creates force dominant perspectives into crisis management to "seal over or manage the contradictions. . . . But they also serve as the inaugural space for critique" (92).

Many gaps remain for feminists to explore in composition and in its relationship to English and the broader culture. Although researchers have now examined from a feminist perspective the status of women in composition and the feminized status of composition within English studies, many women still teach composition in the "basement," and the wider institutional, economic, and cultural conditions continue to create barriers against improving their status. Although women and men in our field have considered how class, gender, and race may shape their pedagogy, we have not thoroughly come to terms with students' or teachers' gendered, classed, or raced position in the academy—or the continuing failure to provide a viable education for many minority students or encouragement for minority colleagues in our field. Although various critics have highlighted the gender blindness of liberatory and critical pedagogies, we have not thoroughly considered how such theories and pedagogies stop short of realizing their goals where women students, minorities, and gay and lesbian students are concerned. Although we have a body of metacommentary on research methodologies and ethical representation of research subjects, we have only begun to explore effective ways to connect our research to wider public concerns and debates about literacy.

Our own interest in diversity and multiplicity makes us curious about the possible uses of "excess" as a trope for feminists in composition of the present and future. Already we are exploring feminist or "diverse discourses," which are in excess of what a singular linear argument requires. We are pushing for notions and accounts of agency that exceed limited ideas of the determined subject. Might the re-visionary stories of the next generation refer to greedy visions of *more* as well as angry recognitions of *lack*? Can we envision narratives of a disruptive practice that overflows as well as challenges? Excess might be proposed as inclusion with a difference: uncontained and without limits.

At this time when composition is reviewing its past and seeking to chart new directions, a glance beyond the academy suggests that political and economic conditions will create continuing intellectual and practical "straitjackets" in composition's next 50 years. The energy of feminists will be vital to the disruption of restrictive theory and practice. This energy will be important for sustaining coalitions for change; it is our best hope for inclusion and proliferation of difference, multiplicity, and uncontainable excess.

NOTES

1. In two recent collections of essays on composition, Villaneuva's *Cross-Talk in Comp Theory*, and Bloom, Daiker, and White's *Composition in the Twenty-First Century*, the only essay specifically from a feminist perspective is Flynn's 1988 "Composing as a Woman." The frequent inclusion of

this essay suggests the impact it has had; the fact that it is the only one included suggests that, in some venues at least, it has been used to contain feminism at the same time.

2. For example, the February 1970 issue of *CCC* contains articles by Donald Murray and by William Coles articulating many of the crucial progressive assumptions emerging in composition: the value of individual students' writing as an articulation of agency and selfhood rather than merely as an object of diagnosis and correction. The *CCC* journals of that year also contain several proposals for alternative freshman English courses for minority students, and the October 1972 issue contains the CCCC Executive Committee's Resolution, "The Student's Right to His Own Language." Although they remain steadfastly gender-blind, essays like these attest to the profession's increasing attempts in the late 60s and 70s to redefine writing and writing instruction. These disciplinary calls for cultural diversity in the curriculum and for the students' rights to their own language caused a great deal of ferment in the profession and foregrounded issues of difference, yet they still did not open a discursive space for women to speak as women writers and teachers or to consider the gendered implications of Coles' goal for writing: "to allow the student to put himself together" (28).

3. Belenky, Clinchy, Goldberger, and Tarule are noted for their use of "midwife" in their discussion of educators who promote constructed knowledge. But the term was applied to writing instructors much earlier. In 1970, Stephen Judy wrote in *English Journal* (which he was later to edit): "We need to discard the structure of the composition teacher as one who passes on knowledge about writing, makes assignments, and corrects errors on themes. A more appropriate role can be described as that of coach or catalyst, or one that I prefer, that of midwife: one who assists in the process of bringing something forth but does not participate in the process himself" (217). This passage suggests possibilities for metonymy; the masculine pronoun may simply illustrate composition's gender-blindness, but it may also be a trace of the gender-shifting that Hill does 20 years later. Judy adds, "It would be difficult for a midwife to do *her* job adequately if the expectant mother knew she were going to be graded on the results" (217, italics ours).

4. Wendy Bishop, Lillian Bridwell-Bowles, Louise Phelps, and Nancy Sommers are just a few of the women who have written personal narratives that practice and reflect on disruption of a status quo. Jacqueline Jones Royster writes, "I have been compelled on too many occasions to count to sit as a well-mannered Other" (30). Theresa Enos' *Gender Roles and Faculty Lives in Rhetoric and Composition* contains a number of anonymous stories from women in composition, along with her narrative of her own experience as an "academically battered woman" (ix). Gesa Kirsch's interviews with women in various academic disciplines explore their interpretations of their experiences as writers and raise "questions of gender and language, women's participation in public discourse, and women's 'ways of writing'" (xvii). A new collection, *Women/Writing/Teaching*, edited by Jan Zlotnik Schmidt, presents ten previously published and ten new essays by women that examine their personal experiences as writers and teachers.

5. We could cite numerous other examples: Patricia Sullivan's rereading of Stephen North's *The Making of Knowledge in Composition*; Nancy Welch's use of feminist theory and her own experience to reread Lacan and other theorists and to disrupt composition's conceptualization of revision; and the important work of increasing numbers of feminists rereading and regendering the rhetorical tradition from Aspasia to Ida B. Wells, from Gertrude Buck to Toni Morrison.

WORKS CITED

Annas, Pamela J. "Style as Politics: A Feminist Approach to the Teaching of Writing." *College English* 47 (1985): 360–71.

Belenky, Mary Field, Blythe McVicker Clinchy, Nancy Rule Goldberger, and Jill Mattuck Tarule. *Women's Ways of Knowing: The Development of Self, Voice, and Mind.* New York: Basic, 1986.

Bennett, Robert A. "NCTE Presidential Address: The Undiscovered." *English Journal* 61 (1972): 351–57.

Berlin, James. *Rhetorics, Poetics, and Cultures: Refiguring College English Studies.* Urbana: NCTE, 1996.

Berthoff, Ann E. "Rhetoric as Hermeneutic." *CCC* 42 (1991): 279–87.

Bishop, Wendy. "Learning Our Own Ways to Situate Composition and Feminist Studies in the English Department." *Journal of Advanced Composition* 10 (1990): 339–55.

Bloom, Lynn Z. "Teaching College English as a Woman." *College English* 54 (1992): 818–25.

Bloom, Lynn Z., Donald A. Daiker, and Edward M. White, eds. *Composition in the Twenty-First Century: Crisis and Change.* Carbondale: Southern Illinois UP, 1996.

Bolker, Joan. "Teaching Griselda to Write." *College English* 40 (1979): 906–8.

Brady, Laura. "The Reproduction of Othering." Jarratt and Worsham, 21–44.

Bridwell-Bowles, Lillian. "Freedom, Form, Function: Varieties of Academic Discourse." *CCC* 46 (1995): 46–61.

Caywood, Cynthia, and Gillian Overing, eds. *Teaching Writing: Pedagogy, Gender, and Equity.* Albany: State U of New York P, 1987.

Clark, Suzanne. "Argument and Composition." Jarratt and Worsham 94–99.

Coles, William, Jr. "The Sense of Nonsense as a Design for Sequential Writing Assignments." *CCC* 21 (1970): 27–34.

Crowley, Sharon. *Composition in the University: Historical and Polemical Essays.* Pittsburgh Series in Composition, Literacy, and Culture. Pittsburgh: U of Pittsburgh P, 1998.

Enos, Theresa. *Gender Roles and Faculty Lives in Rhetoric and Composition.* Carbondale: Southern Illinois UP, 1996.

Faigley, Lester. *Fragments of Rationality: Postmodernity and the Subject of Composition.* Pittsburgh Series in Composition, Literacy, and Culture. Pittsburgh: U of Pittsburgh P, 1992.

Flynn, Elizabeth A. "Composing as a Woman." *CCC* 39 (1988): 423–35.

Fontaine, Sheryl I., and Susan Hunter, eds. *Writing Ourselves into the Story: Unheard Voices from Composition Studies.* Carbondale: Southern Illinois UP, 1993. 1–17.

Grego, Rhonda, and Nancy Thompson. "Repositioning Remediation: Renegotiating Composition's Work in the Academy." *CCC* 47 (1996): 62–84.

Harris, Joseph. *A Teaching Subject: Composition Since 1966.* Upper Saddle River: Prentice, 1997.

Hennessy, Rosemary. *Materialist Feminism and the Politics of Discourse.* Thinking Gender Series. New York: Routledge, 1992.

Hiatt, Mary P. "The Feminine Style: Theory and Fact." *CCC* 29 (1978): 222–26.

Hill, Carolyn Ericksen. *Writing from the Margins: Power and Pedagogy for Teachers of Composition.* New York: Oxford UP, 1990.

Howe, Florence. "A Report on Women and the Profession." *College English* 32 (1971): 847–54.

———. "Identity and Expression: A Writing Course for Women." *College English* 32 (1971): 863–71.

Jarratt, Susan C. "Feminism and Composition: The Case for Conflict." *Contending with Words: Composition and Rhetoric in a Postmodern Age.* Ed. Patricia Harkin and John Schilb. New York: MLA, 1991. 105–23.

Jarratt, Susan C., and Lynn Worsham, eds. *Feminism and Composition Studies: In Other Words.* New York: MLA, 1998.

Judy, Stephen. "The Search for Structures in the Teaching of Composition." *College English* 59 (1970): 213–18.

Kirsch, Gesa E. *Women Writing the Academy: Audience, Authority, and Transformation.* Studies in Writing and Rhetoric. Carbondale: Southern Illinois UP, 1993.

Kirsch, Gesa E., and Patricia A. Sullivan, eds. *Methods and Methodology in Composition Research.* Carbondale: Southern Illinois UP, 1992.

Lakoff, Robin. *Language and Woman's Place.* New York: Harper, 1975.

Logan, Shirley W., ed. *With Pen and Voice: The Rhetoric of Nineteenth Century African-American Women.* Carbondale: Southern Illinois UP, 1995.

Lu, Min-Zhan. "Conflict and Struggle: The Enemies or Preconditions of Basic Writing?" *College English* 54 (1992): 887–913.

———. "From Silence to Words: Writing as Struggle." Perl, 165–76.

Malinowitz, Harriet. *Textual Orientations: Lesbian and Gay Students and the Making of Discourse Communities.* Portsmouth: Boynton, Heinemann, 1995.

McCracken, Nancy, Lois Green, and Claudia Greenwood. "Gender in Composition Research: A Strange Silence." Fontaine and Hunter 352–73.

Miller, Susan. *Textual Carnivals: The Politics of Composition.* Carbondale: Southern Illinois UP, 1991.

Murray, Donald M. "The Interior View: One Writer's Philosophy of Composition." *CCC* 21 (1970): 21–26.

Olsen, Tillie. "Women Who Are Writers in Our Century: One Out of Twelve." *College English* 34 (1972): 6–17.

"Open Letter from Janet Emig, Chairwoman, NCTE Committee on the Role and Image of Women." *College English* 61 (1972): 710.

Perl, Sondra, ed. *Landmark Essays on Writing Process.* Landmark Essays Series 7. Davis: Hermagoras, 1994.

Phelps, Louise W. "Becoming a Warrior: Lessons of the Feminist Workplace." Phelps and Emig 289–339.

Phelps, Louise W., and Janet Emig, eds. *Feminine Principles and Women's Experience in American Composition and Rhetoric.* Pittsburgh Series in Composition, Literacy, and Culture. Pittsburgh: U of Pittsburgh P, 1995.

Reynolds, Nedra. "Interrupting Our Way to Agency: Feminist Cultural Studies and Composition." Jarratt and Worsham, 58–73.

Rich, Adrienne. "When We Dead Awaken: Writing as Re-Vision." *College English* 34 (1972): 18–25.

———. "Taking Women Students Seriously." *On Lies, Secrets, and Silence: Selected Prose 1966–1978.* New York: Norton, 1979. 237–45.

Royster, Jacqueline Jones. "When the First Voice You Hear Is Not Your Own." *CCC* 47 (1996): 29–40.

Schell, Eileen. *Gypsy Academics and Mother-Teachers: Gender, Contingent Labor, and Writing Instruction.* Portsmouth: Boynton, 1998.

———. "The Costs of Caring: 'Femininism' and Contingent Women Workers in Composition Studies." Jarratt and Worsham, 79–93.

Schmidt, Jan Zlotnik, ed. *Women/Writing/Teaching.* Albany: State U of New York P, 1998.

Scott, Joan. "Experience." *Feminists Theorize the Political.* Ed. Judith Butler and Joan W. Scott. New York: Routledge, 1992. 22–40.

The Secretary's Report of Executive Committee. "The Student's Right to His Own Language." *CCC* 21 (1970): 319–28.

Showalter, Elaine. "Women and the Literary Curriculum." *College English* 32 (1971): 855–62.

Sommers, Nancy. "Between the Drafts." Perl, 217–24.

"The Students' Right to Their Own Language." *CCC* 25 Special Issue (1974): 1–32.

Sullivan, Patricia A. "Feminism and Methodology." Kirsch and Sullivan, 37–61.

Taylor, Sheila Ortiz. "Women in a Double-Bind: Hazards of the Argumentative Edge." *CCC* 29 (1978): 385–89.

Villanueva Jr., Victor, ed. *Cross-Talk in Comp Theory.* Urbana: NCTE, 1997.

Welch, Nancy. *Getting Restless: Rethinking Revision in Writing Instruction.* Portsmouth: Boynton, 1997.

Worsham, Lynn. "After Words: A Choice of Words Remains." Jarratt and Worsham, 329–56.

PART ONE

Early Feminist Voices and Visions

Part One: Introduction

FAYE SPENCER MAOR

As the second wave of the feminist movement took hold in the mid-1960s and an atmosphere of free love, psychedelic music, and black power pervaded the land, women focused on raising the consciousness of society regarding the struggles of women. Colleges and universities were in the center of the fray. These second-wave feminists began their work in college classrooms, and writing classrooms were no exception. In writing courses, the problem for some women students, it seemed, was that they did not see themselves as intellectuals. As an early participant in the feminist movement on college campuses, Florence Howe saw that women students had needs that were different from male students. Howe reports her experiences with teaching a writing course for women in her essay "Identity and Expression: A Writing Course for Women." Although this piece was published in 1971, it actually represents her reflections on five years of teaching women in college writing classes.

As a result of her experiences, Howe proposes a theory of teaching women to write. The first aspect of her theory suggests that the writing classroom can challenge women's "learned sense of inferiority" and the "passive dependent" patterns they often adopt as a result of this learned inferiority. Second, Howe theorizes that the composition classroom can, and should, raise women's consciousness. Writing, she suggests, can help women to resist their socialization into inferior and supporting roles. Howe's classroom experiences also reveal that her approach to teaching composition was not the approach she had been taught. Ultimately, she seeks to answer the question of whether "identity"—specifically the identity of being female—affects written expression, a question the field of feminism and composition continues to address today.

Mary Hiatt, some seven years after Howe, investigates further what it means to be a woman writing. Her approach, however, is a traditional statistical analysis of writing by men and women. In "The Feminine Style: Theory and Fact," Hiatt analyzes, by computer, four hundred samples of writing by male and female writers in hopes of discovering and delineating stylistic differences between the two. She begins her analysis with the hypothesis that the way men are taught to write is, in fact, the way society encourages, and often demands, everyone to write. Hiatt concludes that there is indeed a feminine style of writing, but the style she finds is not the style most often attributed to women, one characterized as emotional and verbose. Her analysis characterizes women's style as "conservative, structurally sound and balanced." Hiatt's essay represents one of the early attempts by the field to gain legitimacy in the academy. The use of traditional research methodology proves that women's needs in the writing classroom are different and valid and that it is possible to investigate these issues in traditional, discipline-based ways.

In a 1985 essay, Pamela Annas echoes Florence Howe's point that women's writing should be grounded in the self, in personal experience, and in women's lives. However, Annas complicates that point by observing that writing grounded in the self can be, and almost always is, political. In addition, she argues that there can be both rigor and subjectivity in this type of writing. Since political expression most often emerges from the lives and experiences of marginalized groups of students (e.g., urban, African American, Hispanic, working class), Annas asks whether it is fair to require these students to ignore their lived experiences in order to achieve the distance that traditional academic writing demands. For many of these marginalized students, it is impossible to create that distance, Annas concludes. These students' writing must be based on their lives; through their experiences, students can validate "who they are." And as instructors, we can assist students while also providing them with the skills needed to survive in the world of academia.

The notion of politics emerging from writing that is centered in students' sense of self brings with it the concept of "bilingualism"—that is, the idea that students, based on their gender, ethnicity, race, and class, enter the academy with a language of communication that is not always recognized and accepted in the traditional college classroom. Once in college, instructors often ask these students to reject one method of expression, their "home" language, and accept another. In "The Womanization of Rhetoric," Sally Miller Gearhart asks whether it is an act of violence, a continuation of the imperialist ideal of "conquest and conversion," to demand that students, through the instruction and practice of persuasive discourse, give up their "home" ways of expression.

Rhetoric's traditional focus on persuasive discourse does force students to give up individuality, ethnic mores, and a home culture, Gearhart argues. Feminism, she contends, rejects the "conquest and conversion" model in favor of notions of learning and dialogue subsumed under the broader term "communication." For Gearhart, this term implies the creation of a classroom space where students are *invited* to change. The term, she says, "feminizes" rhetoric. This idea, along with Pamela Annas's call for a politicized approach to writing, takes feminism and composition to a place where all aspects of the self (race, ethnicity, culture, etc.) come together to stimulate and create change. Gearhart asserts that people must be invited to change themselves. They cannot be forced. Consequently, feminism moves composition from a model of conquest and conversion and of persuasion and argumentation to one of "listening and receiving" for change.

Many of the early voices and visions in feminism and composition centered on students who were perceived to have some type of deficiency (skills, confidence, depth, vocabulary, etc.). However, not all women in the academy were having difficulty succeeding in the traditional and patriarchal practices considered the norm. But what was happening with these women, the "good girls" or "Griseldas," as Joan Bolker calls them? They made good grades, and, Bolker argues, they knew how to write good papers. What she discovered was that they really did not know *how* to write in their own voices or present their own ideas; what they did well was to imitate traditional academic discourse. These women often complained of not "owning" their writing.

In her essay "Teaching Griselda to Write," Bolker explores the difficulties "good girls" have in balancing notions of audience with their own goals, ideas, and voice as writers. She argues that these women have been socialized to consider audience so much that they have lost themselves, and as a result they write stiff and sterile pieces. Therefore, for Griseldas, composition teachers must concentrate not so much on deficiencies as on assisting them in expressing their true and authentic voices, ideas, and feelings.

The essays in this section, spanning the years of 1970 to 1985, started the "flow" of discussion and debate on seminal issues in feminism and composition. Many of the theories, issues, and pedagogies these authors grappled with, sometimes as the sole voice, continue to be complicated and grappled with today. These writers and teachers led the way.

How should we continue these scholars' discussions more than thirty years later? How would an African American woman today, for instance, in a classroom like Florence Howe's writing course, value or see herself as a result of her socialization? Or what sense of self, or perhaps sense of inferiority, exists today for Latino students? How do such students wrestle with the various stereotypes that confront them in their everyday lives as well as in the college classroom? Can the idea of "communication," of learning and dialogue, really create a space where people listen to one another and initiate self-change? Can the writing classroom help students find their true voices while also equipping them to succeed in an oppressive world? What should we do when the internal desire for change is not there?

To answer these questions, we must examine what has changed as a result of these authors' work. Has the work of these women affected changes in the academy that have resulted in more feminist classrooms and use of critical pedagogy? Do classrooms today better address the needs of women? Or are we still producing students whose writing conforms to traditional notions of academic, impersonal, and distanced discourse? There is much to discover as we forge ahead, riding the third wave of feminism.

1   *Identity and Expression:*
A Writing Course for Women

FLORENCE HOWE

My women students consistently consider women writers (and hence themselves, though that is not said outright) inferior to men. If women believe themselves inferior writers, so it will be. Why should naturally inferior writers attempt anything ambitious? How to convince young women that their self-images grow not from their biology but from centuries of *belief* in their inferiority, as well as from male-dominated and controlled institutions? How to convince them of this when even the brightest of them reviews the past in a lengthy essay and concludes that since there have been few great intellectual women, women must be inferior as a biological group?

A device I began to use two or three years ago was helpful in that it allowed me to bring the problem directly to my students, as well as to assess some of its depth and complexity. On the first day of class, after I had talked about the course a bit, enough to establish the beginnings of a non-threatening atmosphere, I asked students to write for ten minutes on their assessment of themselves as writers: do they like to write? what are their "hangups" about writing? I read the papers and returned them the next day marked only with + or – signs, or occasionally with a +– or a –+. I was attempting to gauge, crudely of course, their self-images as writers. If there was a sign of pleasure or achievement, I rated them +; if there was none—only a legend of pain or failure—I rated them –. Some of the pain ranged from "I never enjoy writing" to "When I have to write anything, I get a headache for the whole day before." More serious still were the self-indictments: "My English teacher last year said I can't think logically"; or "I don't have any ideas"; or "I don't have any imagination"; or "I can't write anything really interesting." I have never had more than six "positives" from a group of 15 or 20; in my last group of 15, there were 14 "negatives." I have used this device to initiate discussion about why students feel as they do: do such feelings reflect the alleged inferiority of women? do they indict the teaching of composition? etc. Such discussions have led to

From *College English* 32 (1971): 863–71.

admissions from many students that they secretly want to write, that they should like to have "ideas" and "imagination," but that they feel it's too late for them. They are asking to be told, of course, that it is not too late, and I certainly oblige.

There was some correlation between those students who liked to write and those who could; also between those who liked to write and those who kept some sort of journal or wrote lengthy and elaborate letters daily. For several terms I asked students to bring a journal-notebook to class each day and to spend the time from arrival to ten minutes past the bell writing in that book. I used the time in the same way. In another term, I asked that students write for ten or fifteen minutes each day in a journal outside of class. In still another variation, I asked that students keep a journal that recorded what went on in each hour of class, though they were to write it in the evenings. In all cases, students were not obliged to show me their journals, though some wished to do so; in conference, we usually discussed the effect of journal-writing. And in all cases, students reported at least a notable rise in fluency: those students able to write only twenty words in the first ten-minute session, for example, were writing several pages long before the end of the term.

The group experience for women is a particularly crucial one for several reasons. If they have come from co-ed classes, they have experienced the domination by men of intellectual discussion; if they have come from a women's high school, they may still never have had serious discussion with their peers, and with an adult present, about the nature of women's lives. In either case, they have been taught to dislike each other, to regard other women as competitors for men's favors. Intense group discussion about their lives is meant to build students' respect for one another even as it should allow them to trust themselves to sustain intellectual discussion—and hence to attempt it in writing.

There are several associated problems in this regard. The passivity and dependency of women students—these characteristics are of course not innate but socially conditioned in schools and the culture at large—need special attention, as does their avoidance of conflict. The role of the teacher in the open-ended group discussions is, therefore, important. Obviously, it is helpful for students to have before them a model of a strong woman teacher-intellectual. At the same time, given the social conditioning of freshmen women, a strong woman may arouse negative reactions. Assuming a relatively unobtrusive role in the classroom, on the other hand, may also arouse some negative reactions, especially from those who want what they have been accustomed to: directions that tell them clearly "what the teacher wants" so that they may continue their passive-dependent patterns. Since it is important to break those patterns, I have risked the anger or bewilderment of students, calculating that it may be of benefit to the group as well as to individuals. On the whole I have been correct, though I was not always wise enough (especially in the beginning) to rescue those students for whom independence was terrifyingly traumatic.

Once women students feel confidence in the possibility of their functioning as intellectuals, they can choose whether they wish to commit themselves to the work involved. Writing is hard work; thinking is hard work. Women are trained in school and out to follow directions well—which means passivity. It is not that passive-dependent people don't work conscientiously at a given job, but such people find it easier to be told what to do than to figure it out for themselves, or even to decide what they really *want* to do.

If the first aspect of the theory of teaching women to write involves the breaking of passive-dependent patterns and assumptions of inferiority, the second has to do with informing them about the processes of social conditioning, helping them to analyze sexual stereotyping and to grow conscious of themselves as women. Hence the theme of the course is explicitly "the identity of *women*." In the sections that follow, I shall describe course materials as well as procedures. Here I will add only one more note about theory. Consciousness or knowing fosters power and control: all of these terms are essential for the writer, even as they are also political terms. None of a teacher's theory, therefore—at least if she is intent upon helping her students to free themselves—should be a secret from them. I did not know this to begin with, nor did I know all the "theory" that I have presented here—it has grown into theory from the five years and fifteen courses of experiences. But from relatively early on, I have tried to be open about why I asked students to do particular things, or why I was interested in experimenting with the journal-writing, for example. While I do not tend to spend time lecturing about anything in this course, I have taken some of the first hour to explain at least my theory about the ways in which reading and discussion are related to writing. I also state such facts as I do not put grades on themes; no themes are ever classified as "late"; the class is to agree on a schedule, though individuals can establish their own deviations from it or even their own patterns; I do not take attendance; no reading is required; there are no exams; etc. At the same time, I try to explain that a writer learns to write by writing, that the class and individuals in it are responsible for arranging a schedule that will spread themes through the term and so allow for rewriting and improvement.

II

How the Course Works: Just as the material above summarized what was in fact a cumulative development, what follows is a summary of fifteen different classroom patterns. The individual pattern is always a result both of what I have learned from previous experiences and of the particular nature of any single class. Thus, when I have had two sections in one term, their patterns have been different. In each case, however, my purpose has been identical, and in each case I have told the class as much of it as I then understood: to improve their ability to write through helping them to understand their own social identities as women and their potential as feeling and thinking people. I shall describe the three aspects of the course—reading, discussion, and writing—separately, but of course in practice they are always going on at the same time.

About the Readings (Section III contains an annotated bibliography): In the beginning, I relied on readings to begin discussions and as early subjects of themes. Of late, I have been freer to begin with the lives of students. In the beginning, I could count on a negative reaction from women students to the reading list: "too many lady writers" was a typical comment, often stated sneeringly. Of late, particularly this past year, I have felt a decided shift in attitude, less hostility and more interest in the subject. This past year, for the first time, I used underground literature from women's liberation; this past year also, students brought in those issues of national magazines that had devoted special attention to the subject of women. Some of this provoked, I might add, some analytical papers on women's magazines.

To students bored with the readings, I suggested looking at children's books or school texts, and from them I had papers and reports on such subjects as sexual stereotyping in third-grade arithmetics.

No readings have been "required" in the sense that students were to be tested on content. It was clear enough, however, that discussions died or had to be diverted when an insufficient number of people had read what the group had decided to read. If that was the case, we usually talked about the reasons: if the text agreed upon was declared "boring," we talked about why and decided whether to try it again or to go on to something else. When students decided to read Kate Chopin's *The Awakening,* not one turned out not to have read it to the end; when students decided to read James's *Washington Square,* on the other hand, only a few had read far into the novel on the day it was to be discussed. We spent perhaps half a dozen hours on the Chopin book, and only one on the James. Almost all students wrote essays on the Chopin book; one or two on the James. I have ordered as many as ten paperbacks for a ten-week course—a procedure that allows students some choice.

About Writing: The English Department has, in the past, set flexible guidelines for the number and length of themes. Students in my courses have generally written up to twice the amount set by guidelines. Those with special problems of dependency know that they have at least to meet the guidelines. When there were ten weeks to the term and five papers suggested, the class usually agreed on a schedule of a paper every two weeks. Dates were mandatory, not for my convenience, but for the convenience of those writing on the same subject and for those whose job it was to select papers for class discussion. Students were also quick to learn that some writing each day or each week brought rewards they could feel: greater ease and fluency and, especially in rewriting, a sense of control about the development of paragraphs, for example, that they had not had before. I should add also that many students discovered that, under non-threatening conditions, they enjoyed writing; they were willing to experiment, even to "fail," since the worst they might expect was a note from me saying they ought to revise this or that. Thus some students who had never dared to try writing a story or a poem were eager to do so. Others who had never dared to try a difficult intellectual subject—their thoughts about religion, for example—did that. Most were eager to write what some of them began to call an "ideas" or "argument" paper: most had never tried to take a "position" on a subject and literally debate it. This was terribly difficult for many since, typically, women students try to see "both sides," possibly to avoid being part of some "conflict." It is safer to be neutral or "open-minded" if you are a woman. But of course it is difficult, if not impossible, to be a neutral writer.

Since students write at will or at class-arranged will, and with no punitive deadlines established by the teacher, one obvious sign of trauma is the absence of any writing at all from particular students. They need individual attention in conferences, special support, and encouragement. Even so, such students may not begin writing until mid-term. Their pattern has been to write prolifically in the last half or even the last third of the term and to end the term wishing it were the beginning. By the term's end, the writing of these students will not have improved as much as others', but generally the students and I have felt that their gain in self-direction was at least as important an achievement.

If, on the other hand, the course offers freedom and independence to experiment with both form and subject, it also asks women to write several serious essays on themselves and the social conditions of being women. Early essays have been focused either on their own lives or on the lives of characters in novels or on some combination of the two. Usually, students have written "identity" papers during the concluding weeks of the term. But once I asked students to write identity papers early, and the results sparked another set from that group. Several of the students had written very intimately; others had avoided dealing with their lives by theorizing about the idea of identity; and still others had disguised their views in a story or a poem. After discussion, students were interested in trying modes they had not tried before. Discussion served particularly to evoke from those students who had avoided the personal both admiration for those who had not and confessions that they tended not to trust people, especially not a group of women.

On Open-ended Discussion and Open Questions: The purpose of reading is different from what it might be in a literature course. I am not teaching students an interpretation (mine or anyone else's) of literature. I am not leading them—through skillfully arranged questions—to conclusions that I have reached about a novel. I am not conducting Socratic dialogues. Instead, I am establishing a classroom tone and organization in which students may learn to react to literature as well as to analyze those reactions. "React" means to respond to such questions as "Do you like this story?" or "How did the ending make you feel?" or "Did you identify with a particular character?" These are questions designed to evoke affective responses rather than solely cognitive ones—a process that is more difficult than it may seem, since students are school-conditioned not to respond at all but to guess the cognitive response that the teacher is searching for. Even when there is a response, when students learn what this teacher "wants," they are typically puzzled that I expect them to "explain," develop, or defend that response. I want to know "why" they feel as they do, a question that leads both back to the piece of literature and into their own experiences, assumptions, etc. More importantly, the process connects feelings and thoughts and is essential to analysis.

There are problems galore in this kind of discussion: How to keep it from becoming a dialogue between a student (who then feels "picked on") and the teacher? How to keep it from wandering into trivia? How to keep it from petering out altogether? How to decide where to begin on each day? Should the teacher begin each day? How to know which leads from students to follow? How to know when or whether to interrupt a discussion? And so forth. Briefly, the secret for the teacher is to experiment and to be as conscious as possible during the period, even to keep a journal immediately afterward of what happened. For example, silence is extraordinarily difficult, embarrassing for a group of students, sometimes shocking as well. Try silence for a minute or two. Try it and eye contact at the same time. The purpose of such efforts is not "sensitivity-training" in the ordinary sense, but rather to establish that the teacher is not totally responsible for thought and movement in the circle of discussants. As the term continues, students ought to begin to initiate discussion, either because of something that interested them in the reading—e.g., "I found Edna less appealing as the book went on, and I just couldn't believe that she'd kill herself. What did you think about the ending?"—or because of writing problems—"I found that the topic we'd decided on is impossible, and I have started something else. Is that all right?"—or personal/social problems of possible interest to the class either for discussion or as a possible subject for writing or both—"I invited my brother to come to this class, and the first question he asked me was, 'Have you a man or a woman teacher?'"

An open question is one that facilitates discussion. "How did you feel about . . . ?" is perhaps the most open question of all; "Do the rest of you agree?" is another. It is different from a "closed question" in that the answer is not known in advance. Thus, I ask no questions about factual events in a novel. If in the course of discussion someone offers an inaccurate piece of information, another student will usually challenge the error; the issue is settled by referring to the text. The text is authority. If I am asked a question, I answer it, attempting to be precise about whether I am stating "fact" or "opinion." Generally, I conclude by asking what others in the group think. If possible and polite, and if the question is clearly one of opinion, I try to turn it back to the students in the group. I still find myself asking "closed" or "leading" questions occasionally; when I do, I stop, explain what I've been doing, and offer the piece of information or opinion instead, as though I were simply a member of the group. As teacher, my problem is to find a role for myself somewhere between the traditional person of authority and a "member of the group." My position depends usually on the relative strength or dependency of the particular group of students.

A Final Note on Attendance and Class Tone: Students don't take notes in this class, nor do I keep attendance records, nor are they ever "tested" on anything that goes on. Why, then, do they attend with special regularity? The question itself has come up with regularity, generally mid-way through or late in the term. Sometimes the student who poses the question does so with some hostility, sometimes with curiosity, sometimes as a joke. The replies have not essentially varied. They amount to the outburst of one student a couple of years ago: "It's just *interesting*—I'm afraid I'm going to miss something if I stay away." My guess is that students are really commenting also on the experience of controlling a classroom. Many of them understand the relationship between that classroom experience and the papers they are writing. Others, struggling with the writing, find the classroom experience rewarding—they can talk even if they can't write! When classes have begun to function as "groups" they have not wished to part. Thus, there are typically scheduled "extra classes" in the last week or weeks of term, as well as lunch sessions or a "party." For some students, the class has become a "reference group," in which they feel free either to try out pieces of writing or to talk of a particular problem or decision. Obviously, this latter has happened relatively rarely, and only of late, when I have known better how to conduct the class.

III

Annotated Bibliography: D. H. Lawrence's *Sons and Lovers* has been very useful for starting the course, since students enjoy reading the book and are therefore interested in initiating discussions on such topics as the relative guilt of mother or father in their bad relations with each other and with the children; or for identification with either of the two young women in the novel.

Doris Lessing's *The Golden Notebook* proved too complex for the kind of student-initiated discussion that I wanted. Lessing's stories in *A Man and Two Women* were much better for this purpose, even though students by and large considered several of them "horrid" or "unpleasant." I plan to use *Martha Quest,* since it has recently become available again.

Ralph Ellison's *Invisible Man:* For several years in a row, no matter what other books I had ordered or what discussions or readings students initiated, I left a week or two at the end for reading and discussion of this book, accompanied by a request for an "identity paper." I used the depth of the papers as a personal gauge of my "success" in raising the consciousness of students. Often, as one might expect, they contained the best writing of the term, since students generally combined in them their own term's experience as well as their ability to analyze what had occurred. Interestingly, students read *Invisible Man* as though it were written about them, not about a black male. They found the concept of invisibility particularly apt.

I experimented with many other texts, chiefly *The Group* by Mary McCarthy and some essays and novels of Virginia Woolf. *The Group* aroused more negative feelings than I could deal with except through coercion, possibly because the identification of Goucher students with students in the novel is a potent one. I gave up the struggle with that one after two attempts, but I may return to it. The Woolf materials seemed remote to their lives, and I finally gave them up too.

In the last two years, I have begun to use, as openers in the course, Ibsen's *A Doll's House* followed immediately by Kate Chopin's *The Awakening,* and then later, as students asked for it, *Sons and Lovers.* In the fall of 1970 I began with Hardy's *Tess of the D'Urbervilles.* Obviously, I don't believe that a particular group or order of books needs to be fixed. In fact I believe rather that some books need to be changed to suit changing students, but also to relieve the teacher from potential boredom.

Poetry: I tried several volumes of Denise Levertov last year, especially because she was to be on campus for several days. Students were very interested in reading and discussing poems, and in writing them. I found much of this valuable and will repeat the attempt—using other poets coming to campus—though it becomes difficult, if not impossible, to keep students to essay-writing! (For the sake of future text-users, perhaps I should add that Ellen Bass and I are preparing for the University of Massachusetts Press an anthology of poetry by twentieth-century women poets on their conceptions of women.)

Non-fictional Materials: Though I have ordered Simone de Beauvoir's *The Second Sex* for class after class, until last year it was largely unread by students. Students never chose to discuss this book in class and rarely brought references from it into their writing or discussion; and yet no class voted to abandon it when I asked at the end of term for suggestions about reading lists for the next term.

For the past three years I have ordered *Women in America* (ed. R. J. Lifton, Beacon Press, 1965, repr. 1970), and occasionally I have asked students to read particular essays for discussion when particular factual questions have come up, especially about sociological or psychological questions. But again there was little independent use of this text before this past year, though students would not vote to abandon it.

This past year I used *Born Female* (Carolyn Bird, Pocket Books, 1970) for the first time and found that students read it rather disbelievingly. It provoked lively discussions and, in a few cases, papers. More surprisingly, students in another section read and demanded detailed discussion of *The Second Sex.* Both groups shared each others' books and were eager for more material. Anne Moody's *Coming of Age in Mississippi* (Dell, 1968) has recently proved valuable. (From the reactions of my class in the fall of 1970, I suspect that autobiographical materials will be more useful than fiction.)

I put on library reserve—since there wasn't time to order and no available resources here—copies of all the underground women's liberation literature I had. Sources for some of this material are:

New England Free Press, 791 Tremont Street, Boston, 02118

Radical Education Project, Box 561A, Detroit, 48232

Women: A Journal of Liberation, 3028 Greenmount Avenue, Baltimore, Md. 21218

Off Our Backs: A Woman's News-Journal, P.O. Box 4589, Cleveland Park Station, Washington, D.C. 20008

It Ain't Me Babe, Berkeley Women's Liberation, P.O. Box 6323, Albany, Calif. 94706

Voice of the Women's Liberation Movement, Joreen Freeman, 5336 South Greenwood, Chicago, 60615

New York Radical Women, 799 Broadway, Room 412, New York 10003

Aphra, Box 332, Springtown, Pa. 19081.

Up from Under, 339 Lafayette St., New York, N.Y. 10012

Two helpful collections are:

Sisterhood Is Powerful: An Anthology of Writings from the Women's Liberation Movement (ed. Robin Morgan, Vintage, 1971)

Notes from the Second Year: Women's Liberation (Major writings of the Radical Feminists, a collection of some 35 essays for $1.50.) Write to: Notes (From the Second Year): Radical Feminism, P.O. Box AA, Old Chelsea Station, New York, 10011

There are other kinds of materials available from the following sources:

Know, Inc., P.O. Box 10197, Pittsburgh, Pa. 15232

National Organization for Women (NOW), Executive Director, Dolores Alexander, 33 West 93 St., New York, 10025

United Nations at UN Place, New York. Studies of women around the world.

Woman's Bureau, U.S. Dept. of Labor, Washington, D.C. Leaflet #10 lists numerous publications on women, especially as workers. Also available are the original reports of the President's Commission on the Status of Women.

Feminist Press, 5504 Greenspring Ave., Baltimore, Md. 21209

IV

Conclusion: The story of this course has no conclusion, but I should like to indicate one of its possible directions. The growth of my own feminist consciousness has led me back to the theory of teaching composition. As a student and teacher, I learned and then taught conventional methods of organizing papers. I grew skillful at analyzing a student's research and especially the paper she had written, and directing her into a revised outline. I taught many students how to proceed from note-cards to outline to paper-writing. But as I began to write (and the period of my own writing coincides with the period of experimentation I have been describing), I noticed that I did not follow my own precepts. In fact, I could not follow them. Why not? When I began to collaborate on a book with my husband, it was clear that we had two different modes of working. He spent from days to weeks staring into space with a pad before him, working out a detailed outline—all before writing a line. I wrote sometimes as much as 40 or 50 pages—most of which I threw away—before I "knew what I was doing"—which sometimes amounted to an outline. Sometimes the form grew very naturally from the associative process I allowed to develop at the typewriter. At any rate, I began last year to describe both processes to my classes and to ask that students grow conscious of which was theirs or whether theirs was still different. If an understanding of "identity" contributes to "expression," might not a conscious sense of the writing process lead back into the self and forward again to the written page?

2   *The Feminine Style: Theory and Fact*

MARY P. HIATT

Critics often have trouble dealing with style, probably for two reasons. In the first place, stylistic theory itself ranges widely. Some stylisticians hold that style is totally a matter of one individual's writing—that, in effect, there is no such thing as a group or mass style. Others take an opposing view and maintain that it is possible to describe the characteristics of a group of writers or of writers of a certain era. Stylisticians further differ on whether style is the sum total of the characteristics of the writing or whether it describes in what way the writing departs from a norm, roughly defined as a standard or commonplace manner of writing. Some theorists also hold that any style can only be adequately described in the context of another style, whether individual or group. The state of the theory itself is therefore conflicting and confusing.

In the second place, the metalanguage of style often relies on inadequate descriptors. Thus, in considering an individual's writing style, impressionistic adjectives abound: "muscular," "manly," "clear," "hothouse," "lush," "lean," etc. And in considering group style—or types of style—we are confronted with the traditional adjectives such as "plain," "high," and "grand," as well as "Baroque," "Ciceronian," "Attic," "Augustan," and so on. Few of these descriptors, whether of individual or group styles, have been objectively assayed, for upon close evaluation, they might vanish, leaving the critic at an unendurable loss for words.

Castigation of the manifold efforts at stylistic description serves little purpose. Nonetheless, an awareness of some of the pitfalls and complexities involved in the task of such description is essential to any adequate consideration of written style. To some degree, the critic of style is faced with choosing or developing a theory.

As mentioned above, a theory has persisted over the years that common characteristics in the writing of certain groups, perhaps during certain eras, do exist, despite the abjurations of those theorists who claim that style can only

---

From *College Composition and Communication* 27 (1978): 222–26.

be an individual matter. This group-style theory is reflected in the descriptors "masculine" style and "feminine" style. Men and women, it is commonly believed, write differently. The conviction has run strong. Notably absent are any data to support the conviction.

But whereas data are missing, we generally find, once again, a plethora of adjectives being flung about. The "masculine" style is held to be terse, strong, rational, convincing, formidable, and logical. The "feminine" style is thought to be emotional, illogical, hysterical, shrill, sentimental, silly, and vapid. The "masculine" style seems to be described in terms of a male view of *men* — not necessarily of men's style. And the "feminine" style is described in terms, often pejorative, of a male view of *women* — not of women's style. Whether or not the difference exists at all is important to establish, but most certainly the stereotyped descriptors are impressionistic, biased, and consequently less than useful.

Opting for the theory, however, that style need not always be an individual matter and that there do exist types of style consisting of linguistic features shared by groups of writers at particular times, I have studied a large sample of contemporary American prose to see, first, whether there are discernible differences between the way men write and the way women write, and, second, if there are differences, what these differences are.[1] One hundred books, 50 by women and 50 by men, were objectively selected for the study. Objectivity was maintained by *not* choosing books on the basis of literary "merit," for merit is a subjective matter. To have selected books because anyone in particular — I, my friends, critics in general — liked them would have seriously prejudiced the study. In the study, therefore, the books include non-fiction by Albert Ellis, Telford Taylor, Marjorie Holmes, and Frances Fitzgerald, and fiction by Charles Simmons, Bernard Malamud, Andrea Newman, and Joyce Carol Oates.

The two categories (women's books and men's books) were subdivided equally into fiction and non-fiction. From each of the 100 books, four 500-word selections of running text were randomly chosen. Each book, therefore, contributes a 2,000-word sample to the study, which finally consists of 200,000 words of contemporary prose.

If one is attempting to discern stylistic differences between two sets of 100,000 words each, one can, of course, try to read all these words and note the occurrence of such stylistic matters as sentence-length and complexity, inserts, types of modification, and so on. One can try to do this, but no one should. The human mind is often an inaccurate perceiver, and errors inevitably occur. A mechanical mind is not inaccurate. Hence, the only objective and accurate way to deal with such a vast amount of text is to use a computer.

The 200,000 words of prose were therefore keypunched onto IBM cards. Each of the 100 samples was scanned by computer for such major aspects of style as sentence-length and complexity, logical sequence of ideas, similes, *-ly* adverbs, parenthetical expressions, structural parallelism, and rhetorical devices.

The findings indicate that contemporary male and female authors do write differently. I can report, with a fair degree of confidence, that there is a feminine style that is not the same as a masculine style. I definitely do not postulate, however, that either style is a "norm," from which the other style varies, although the way men are thought to write tends to be considered the way *to* write, probably because there are so many more male authors and critics than female authors and critics. The emergence of specific differences between the two groups of writers does, however, lend valid support to the theory that types of styles or styles characteristic of groups of writers do exist.

Of greater interest, perhaps, is the discovery that the masculine style and the feminine style do not always differ in the commonly perceived or described ways. A consideration of some specific results bears out this conclusion.

For example, close study of sentence-lengths[2] and average sentence-lengths of all the authors reveals that the men are not terse and that the women are not verbose. Of the non-fiction authors, the men's average sentence-length is 23 words; the women's, 21 words. The gross averages are not significantly different. All that can be said is that the women do not go on and on—if anything, their thoughts are phrased in shorter units. But if the sentences of all the non-fiction authors are divided into two groups, those of twenty words or fewer ("short" sentences) and those of more than twenty words ("long" sentences), a statistical analysis indicates that the women use significantly more short sentences—58 percent, versus 48 percent of the men's sentences.

Generally speaking, the longer the sentence, the more likely it is to be structurally complex. And, in the non-fiction studied, both the men's and the women's long sentences are certainly complex. But they are complex in different ways. The structure of the long sentences of *each author* in the men's non-fiction exhibits specific, often repeated aspects of style. Norman Mailer's long sentences, for example, are highly complicated, involving lengthy seriation, many parenthetical phrases and clauses, and many self-interrupters; Frank Mankiewicz uses many introductory and inserted adverbial phrases and clauses and many appositives; Frederick Cartwright often uses right-branching sentences; Rudolf Bing employs many complicated series, all in perfectly parallel constructions. In other words, the long sentences of each male non-fiction author usually offer readily identifiable types of complexity that are characteristic of that author.

With the exception of two women non-fiction authors, the long sentences of the women do not generally display individual patterns of complexity. The exceptions are Eda LeShan and Joyce Maynard, both of whom use dashes and parentheses in their long sentences. The constructions delineated by dashes and parentheses, however, could just as well have been delineated by periods. In other words, their long sentences do not display the subordinate constructions that are the hallmark of complexity. Their long sentences thus are not so complex as those of the men. Among the other women writers, the long sentences are carefully organized syntactically but cover a range of types of complexity. It is difficult to discern any one constructional characteristic for any one of these writers. The complexity of their sentences therefore is not so individually delineated as the complexity of the men's sentences.

As for the fiction writers, the average sentence-length for men is 17 words; for women, 16 words per sentence—again not really a significant difference. But the men tend to write longer sentences than the women and *more* longer sentences than the women. Nine men produce fourteen sentences of over 80 words, whereas only five women write even one sentence of more than 80 words, none of them longer than 90 words.

The *range* of sentence-lengths in fiction is also quite different between the two groups. Using as examples the two writers of the longest sentences in each group, we find that John O'Hara's longest sentence is 116 words, his shortest is two, and his range is 114 words; Tom Wicker's longest sentence is 104 words, his shortest is two, presenting a range of 102 words. On the other hand, Ruth Macdowell's longest sentence is 90 words, her shortest is two, and her range is 88; Daphne DuMaurier's longest sentence is 86 words, her shortest is three, and her range is 83 words. The foregoing are only examples, but the relatively narrow range of sentence-lengths is a repetitive feature of the women writers of fiction.

In fiction, sentence complexity is not a particularly cogent parameter of style, because fiction is so studded with dialogue. But in sentence-length, it does not seem that the women writers vary as widely as do the men. In this respect, their writing is perhaps less daring, more conservative.

Another aspect of style is the logical development of ideas. Examination of this feature was confined to non-fiction writers and carried out by studying the occurrence of certain words or phrases that often indicate a particular kind of logical sequence. There are, of course, many ways of indicating a particular logical process without the use of specific words. Instead of the word "because," for example, indicating that a reason is being offered, a writer may simply choose to say, "Another reason is that. . . ." The existence of a logical sequence without the use of specific "signaling" words cannot be gainsaid. However, a search for what may be called "signals of logic," occurring at the beginning or within the sentence, reveals a difference in the writing of the men and the women.

Logical-sequence indicators (or the particular group of words or phrases signaling a particular process of logic) may be divided into five types:[3] (1) Illustratives ("for example," "that is," "for instance"); (2) Illatives ("therefore," "(and) so," "thus," "hence"); (3) Adversatives ("however," "but," "yet," "nevertheless," "on the other hand"); (4) Causatives ("because," "for," "since"); and (5) Additives ("and," "so . . . did").

The women use 190 of these logical-sequence indicators, whereas the men use 160. On the basis of the indicators, therefore, the women cannot be said to write illogically. But there is a difference in the type of logic used by the women writers. The men and the women use approximately the same number of Adversatives, but the women employ 50 percent fewer Illustratives and Illatives and 50 percent more Causatives and Additives. The logic of the feminine style would thus seem to depend on reasons and extra information rather than on exemplifications and conclusions. In terms of the low ratio of Illatives—those words indicating conclusions—the logic of the women is less definitive than that of the men. In terms of the high ratio of Causatives, their logic is more self-justifying. Neither the men's nor the women's style is, however, "illogical." Both are logical in different ways.

The occurrence of *-ly* adverbs offers another measure of style. Women's speech has been reported to contain many more adverbs ending in *-ly* than that of men, with high use of such words as "simply," "utterly," and "awfully" as modifiers of adjectives. The unadorned adjective is presumably the province of men.

Such may indeed be the case in women's speech, but in this study, it does not carry over into their writing. There is no significant difference between the men's and the women's writing in either the total number of *-ly* adverbs used or in the number of different adverbs, and the type-token ratio for both groups is almost exactly the same in fiction and in non-fiction. But the adverb "simply" is used more often by the men than by the women; the adverb "utterly" is rarely used by either group; and the adverb "awfully" is used only by the men.

In the interest of discovering whether women writers are, as frequently claimed, "hyperemotional," adverbs of emotion (such as "amiably," "abjectly," "coldly," "angrily," etc.) were studied. That emotion is often expressed verbally or nominally is true; the expression of emotion via adverbs is only one means. Nonetheless, the two groups' use of adverbs of emotion is startlingly different in fiction and scarcely different at all in non-fiction. In fiction, the women use twice as many adverbs of emotion as do the men, a finding that probably is the basis for calling women writers "hyperemotional."

But if another type of adverb is examined, the adverb of pace (such as "gradually," "hastily," "slowly," etc.), a reverse trend is seen. The men's fiction contains twice as many of these adverbs as the women's, and again there is no difference in the non-fiction of the two groups. The men's fiction style thus seems to be "hyperactive" as compared to the women's.

If both types of adverbs are considered together, however, a more accurate evaluation of the two fiction styles is possible. In all, the women fiction writers use approximately the same number of adverbs of emotion and adverbs of pace, whereas the men fiction writers use four times as many adverbs of pace as adverbs of emotion. Thus, in fiction, where the major differences occur, there is evidence that the feminine style balances pace of action and expression of emotionality. The women writers are not hyperemotional, except in terms of the men writers. There seems to be far less basis for labeling the feminine styles as hyperemotional than for labeling the masculine style as *hypo*-emotional.

The adverb *really* deserves special mention. The women writers use the word two and a half times more often than the men writers in non-fiction, and one and a half times as often in fiction. One male novelist (Anthony Burgess) accounts for the lessening of the difference in fiction by using that particular adverb more often than any woman writer. If his sample is disregarded, the same high proportion of *really*'s exists in the women's fiction as in their non-fiction. The relatively high occurrence as characteristic of the feminine style is probably at least unconsciously and generally recognized. It actually is very consciously recognized in the words of one male character in a woman writer's novel when he says to a woman character, "'Really,' 'really,' 'really'! That's all you can say!" Its use probably reflects women's feelings that they will not be believed, that they are not being taken seriously or "really." These feelings would quite naturally lead women to claim sincerity and validity more frequently than do men.

To recapitulate, in those areas of style discussed here, the way women write emerges as distinct from the way the men write. This distinction is borne out in the study of other areas of style, such as the use of similes, certain adjectives and verbs, parallel structures, and various aspects of rhetoric. There is, in other words, clear evidence of a feminine style and sound justification for the theory of group style.

But the feminine style is in fact rather different from the common assumptions about it. Solely on the basis of just those aspects discussed in this paper, it can be claimed that the feminine style is conservative, structurally sound, logical in its own way, balanced in terms of emotionality and pace. There are no excesses of length or complexity or emotion. Its only excess lies perhaps in the protesting use of *really*—an understandable protest against being disbelieved.

NOTES

1. See Mary P. Hiatt, *The Way Women Write: Sex and Style in Contemporary Prose* (New York: Teachers College Press, Columbia University, 1977) for the complete report, including the list of the 100 authors forming the basis of the study.

2. A sentence is defined as any word or words beginning with a capital letter and ending with end punctuation. This is not a grammatical definition but one that accommodates the vagaries of dialogue and speech patterns.

3. The logical-sequence indicators were suggested by a system of eight logical relationships posited by Louis T. Milic, *Stylists on Style* (New York: Scribners, 1969), p. 21.

3   *Teaching Griselda to Write*

JOAN BOLKER

When I was a medievalist studying Chaucer's *Canterbury Tales* I was tantalized by the Clerk's Tale of Patient Griselda. What captivated me was that an interesting character, one of the most intelligent on the pilgrimage, could speak about the quality of goodness raised to its apotheosis, and turn out to be so thoroughly dull.

Griselda comes to mind now because I have tried recently to teach her natural descendants, two marvelous young women, to write. Both are very good students, at Harvard and Yale respectively, the sort of well-organized, well-read, conscientious, and bright persons whom their less fortunate or less hardworking classmates want to murder. Their papers are always handed in on time (in fact, are often finished early, but they have learned not to tell anyone), are well proofread, and properly bibliographied. Both students have pursued a writing process which includes thorough reading, careful note-taking, and assiduous thinking, writing, and revision; they have constructed the sort of outlines that are supposed to make English teachers smile with pleasure. And those papers usually come back with grades of high Bs or As on them. Why, then, have I chosen to write about these two young women as a "problem," and to compare them to Griselda?

Because each of them has come to speak to me about her writing, uncomfortable with it, yet not knowing quite why, or what to do about it. As we have talked, some interesting things have emerged: Meg, the Yalie, tells me that her friends complain about the letters she writes to them, that her professors write comments on her papers that let her know she has not quite met their standards. Nancy, the Harvard student, also senses that her readers are dissatisfied with her papers (neither she nor Meg is someone who worries about grades, just about what they indicate), and she herself feels that they are somehow not quite right. Each of these women describes a lack of personality in her papers, and her sense of non-ownership, and of disappointment at not being able to make herself heard.

From *College English* 40 (1979): 906–8.

Fine, you may say, but these are not real writing problems—any student who can hand in a technically perfect paper and get it back with a B+ or an A− on it isn't really in any trouble; perhaps they are both just expressing the dissatisfaction that any writer feels after she's finished a piece of work. Perhaps, but I don't think so.

I take their complaints as seriously as I do those of the student who writes totally unacceptable papers. While Meg and Nancy have both learned how to write papers, they have not yet learned to write—that is, to be able to communicate by expressing their own ideas, feelings, and voices on paper, whether they are writing a letter to a friend, a personal journal, or a letter to the editor. They want to be able to do more than write papers, and for them the B+ or A− is not a sign of academic failure, but a sign that something is wrong with their writing itself. The student who writes unacceptable papers and knows that she or he is at the beginning of a process of growth may find that discouraging, but I think it is even more so to feel as if you are nearly at the end, nearly "fully baked," but still haven't gotten it quite right. And, perversely, it can be even harder to undo learning than to start from the beginning. So I take Meg's and Nancy's complaints even more seriously than those of the students who have trouble writing papers, because the problem of not being able to write threatens to stay with Meg and Nancy longer.

But why have I compared them to Griselda? Because one of the outstanding traits which these two women share is blatant goodness: they are the sorts of people whom other parents hold up to their own offspring as shining examples, the sort who are almost always kind, considerate, well-mannered; they don't throw tantrums; they are warm and smiling without being insincere or mushy; they are, in short, what one understands by the phrase, "good girls." When I was growing up, if someone described a young woman as a "good girl," it was the kiss of death. That phrase translated as "dull and insipid." Neither Meg nor Nancy is dull or insipid in person, yet their writing has some of that quality about it. What is more, I suspect, and would like to argue here, that the problems they have with their writing have something to do with Meg's and Nancy's being "good girls." Let me try to explain that.

When we teach writing, one of the things we try to explain to students is that they have to pay attention to the reader, to their audience. Many beginning writers have great trouble doing so. It is hard enough to think about what is in their own heads without having to worry about what is in someone else's. Besides, they often cannot imagine anyone else other than the grader ever reading this stuff they have been writing. The furthest many students get toward "considering the reader" is to try to "psyche out the teacher"—a much more limited (and limiting) enterprise.

The Griseldas of this world have another problem: part of learning to be "a good girl" means learning what pleases those around you, and acting that way. Griselda has no difficulty thinking about the reader of her writing—she *always* thinks about the reader, because she is used to thinking about others. She has a different problem: she thinks too little about the writer. When Meg tells me she is saddened because her papers cease to be hers after she has written them, I believe she means that the reader is all-important, and that it is too easy to forget that she herself did the writing, because she thought so little about herself while she was doing it.

What are the results of ignoring the writer and paying undue attention to the reader? A style that aims to please all and offend none, one which "smiles" all the time, shows very little of a thought process, but strives instead to produce a neat package tied with a ribbon. Ambivalence is out, changes of mind are out, the important nagging questions are out, because they are not neat, and they might offend—and because they involve paying some attention to one's own state of mind while one is writing. Such papers are highly polished, so much so that it is hard to catch a human voice in them. And, like Griselda, they are dull; competence is all.

Several people have asked me, and I have wondered myself, if the Griselda syndrome is confined to women students. I cannot say for sure, but I suspect this is a far more common problem among them than it is among young men; it is part of being "a good girl," or of what Lucille Clifton calls "the lady cage." Meg herself suggested I subtitle this essay "The Masochistic Writer." At first I couldn't see why. Now I begin to understand that Griselda's approach to writing stifles herself for the sake of the reader, puts aside the excitement of chasing a good idea, ignores her doubts, and works very, very hard to be sure that the finished product is very good. This all leaves very little room for fun. It also, not incidentally, protects her from having to flex her muscles, or shout, or try out her full powers, while assuring her that she has "done the right thing." So there is a payoff, but the personal costs are high.

If my understanding of Griselda's problem is accurate, what does it imply we might suggest to her? I have tried out some approaches which seem promising. One is to let her know that most readers are more pleased by the sloppy sound of the human voice in a piece of writing than they are by neatness and goodness. Another is to encourage her to work on developing personal voice in a variety of ways: I assign journal writing, for herself, with no corrections allowed, and no attention paid to technical matters if she can manage it. I encourage some outrageous behavior in writing: fictional letters to enemies, telling them, in full color, how she would like to do them in; complaining letters; free writing, involving poetry, or playing with words, or even, God help us, with obscenities. I sometimes assign reading, choosing it because it includes strong and even outrageous voice (but not too outrageous, because that feels too far from the possible to "good" students; Virginia Woolf's *A Room of One's Own*, Mary McCarthy's writing, and Dorothy Sayers' books have all worked well). I encourage her to try out other kinds of writing than the writing of papers—fiction, poetry, journals, occasional essays—and emphasize that the development of a personal style takes time. (Meg has already felt some good results: a friend has written her to comment on the change in her letters, on how lively and interesting they have suddenly become, and Meg has fired off an angry letter in a situation where, she observes, she would earlier have said nothing, or phoned—"but suddenly I wanted to write it." And just this week I had a postcard from her: "P.S. I feel really good about . . . writing assignments. . . . They're fun!") And I push, very strongly, writing that begins with the personal, with issues of great personal importance, that begins with the self—even with the selfish. Griseldas are superb at sensing and bending to the demands of the outer world. For their writing to develop—as they want it to, and as their readers want it to—they need to begin to listen to the demands of the inner world as well.

4   *The Womanization of Rhetoric*

SALLY MILLER GEARHART

My indictment of our discipline of rhetoric springs from my belief that any intent to persuade is an act of violence. In this first section I'd like briefly to review our culpability as teachers of persuasion, explore the distinction between change and intent-to-change, and finally describe a culture-wide phenomenon, the conquest/conversion mentality, in which I find public discourse to be but one of many participants.

The patriarchs of rhetoric have never called into question their unspoken assumption that mankind (read "mankind") is here on earth to alter his (read "his") environment and to influence the social affairs of other men (read "men"). Without batting an eye the ancient rhetors, the men of the church, and scholars of argumentation from Bacon, Blair, and Whately to Toulmin, Perelman, and McLuhan, have taken as given that it is a proper and even necessary human function to attempt to change others. As modern critics and practitioners of public discourse we have been committed to the improvement in our students of the fine art of persuasion. In fact, our teaching, even if it were not the teaching of persuasion, is in itself an insidious form of violence. The "chicken soup" attitude or the "let me help you, let me enlighten you, let me show you the way" approach which is at the heart of most pedagogy is condescending and acutely expressive of the holier-than-thou mindset. Void of respect and openness, it makes even the informative lecture into an oppressive act.

Until the last few decades speech or rhetoric has been a discipline concerned almost exclusively with persuasion in both private and public discourse; it has spent whole eras examining and analyzing its eloquence, learning how to incite the passions, move the will. Over the centuries rhetoric has wearied itself in the ancient and honorable act of finding the available means of persuasion, the better to adapt a discourse to its end. Of all the human disciplines, it has gone about its task of educating others to violence

From *Women's Studies International Quarterly* 2 (1979): 195–201.

with the most audacity. The fact that it has done so with language and meta-language, with refined functions of the mind, instead of with whips or rifles does not excuse it from the mindset of the violent.

The indictment of the profession is not an attack on the tools of rhetoric; nor does it suggest that we, its practitioners, serve the world best by forsaking education or committing suicide. With our expertise in persuasion, rhetoricians and rhetorical theorists are in the best position to change our own use of our tools. The indictment is of our *intent* to change people and things, of our attempt to educate others in that skill. The indictment is of our participation in the conquest/conversion mindset that sends us now as a species pell-mell down the path to annihilation.

It is important to know that we can and do change each other daily. Our physical bodies respond to energy; even without our will they react in measurable ways to objects or people generating high energy. We are constantly being changed by each other. Further, we come closer each day to a recognition in our lives of the meaning of Einstein's reduction of matter to energy. It is only in density that the energy fields surrounding each of us differ from the solid energy that is our physical bodies; it is only in density that the energy we generate in our minds or our psyches differs from our auras. As Kurlian photography tracks down revolutionaries by the energy exuded from their very bodies and as Western medicine adopts techniques of visualization and fantasy in the curing of cancer, we realize that to thrust a sword into another person does not differ significantly from wishing them ill or from fantasizing a sword thrust into their heart. Our physical being, our movement, our thoughts, our metaphors: all are forms of energy in constant and infinitely varied exchange.

It is important that we recognize the communication that takes place between entities as well as between humans and entities that we do not count as human. Just as the lunacy of "talking to yourself" has now become a highly recommended technique of intrapersonal communication, even so has the lunacy of "talking to your plants" become recognized as an exchange of energy that revitalizes both communicators. (Here in the Bay Area of California you are thought taciturn if you do not talk to your plants, and plants have been known to resent such neglect.) We have been human chauvinists too long, calling consciousness our own, cornering the market upon it, setting ourselves above everything nonhuman because of our "higher awareness." Chimpanzees and porpoises more and more frequently make mockery of the Crown of Creation we have thought ourselves to be.

To change other people or other entities is not in itself a violation. It is a fact of existence that we do so. The act of violence is in the *intention* to change another. The cultural manifestation of that intention makes up the pages of our history books. It is the *conquest* model of human interaction. More significantly, it is the *conversion* model of human interaction, a model more insidious because it gives the illusion of integrity. In the conquest model we invade or violate. In the conversion model we work very hard not simply to conquer but to get every assurance that our conquest of the victim is really giving her what she wants. In fact, a lot of excitement and adventure would go out of our lives if conquest were the only model. It is conversion that gives us our real kicks; it is the stuff of all our pornography, the stuff of Hollywood, the stuff of romance.

Our history is a combination of conquest and conversion. We conquered trees and converted them into a house, taking pride in having accomplished a difficult task. We conquered rivers and streams and converted them into lakes, marveling in ourselves at the improvement we made on nature. We tramped with our conquering spaceboots on the fine ancient dust of the Moon and we sent our well-rehearsed statements of triumph back for a waiting world to hear. We'd like to think that much as the Moon resisted us, she really, down deep, wanted us—her masters—to tame her and to own her.

We did not ask permission of trees, river, Moon. We did not in any way recognize the part of the victim in the process. They were the conquered. We were the conqueror. The more "fight" they gave us and the more difficult the task, the more exhilarating was the contest and the more arrogant we became at winning over them. Many of us have heard it too often: "I like a woman who gives me a little fight." While there is satisfaction in conquering, the real rush comes if she resists and then gives in, if you make her want you, if you convert her, if the trees are big, if you fail the first few times to harness the river, if the Moon is hard to get to.

Since the Middle Ages scholars have been fond of classifying rhetoric into three brands: that which flows from the pulpit, that which is found at the bar of justice, and that which rings out on the senate floor. All three efforts demonstrate precisely a violence not just of conquest but also of conversion, whether it be conversion of the sinner, the jury, or the worthy opposition. Preachers, lawyers, and politicians may congratulate themselves that they are men of reason who have chosen civilized discourse above fighting. Yet where the intent is to change another, the difference between a persuasive metaphor and a violent artillery attack is obscure and certainly one of degree rather than of kind. Our rational discourse, presumably such an improvement over war and barbarism, turns out to be in itself a subtle form of Might Makes Right. Speech and rhetoric teachers have been training a competent breed of weapons specialists who are skilled in emotional maneuvers, expert in intellectual logistics, and, in their attack upon attitude and belief systems, blissfully ignorant of their violation of nature or her processes.

Somewhere in a dark corner of human history we made a serious evolutionary blunder. We altered ourselves from a species in tune with the Earth, with our home, into a species that began ruthlessly to control and convert its environment. At that point, when we began to seek to change any other entity, we violated the integrity of that person or thing and our own integrity as well.

Political speculations about the origin of alienation, theological agitations about the beginning of evil, psychological ruminations about the birth of "the other," and philosophical explorations of the mind-body split—all have shown us the futility of trying to determine the cause of our violence as a species. Was it our coming to consciousness? Or some leap from our subjective ego to the recognition of another subjective ego? The drive to civilization or the drive to death through civilization? Perhaps the creative urge or the birth of language itself or the first time someone claimed private property? Did it occur when men discovered that they had some role in conception and got so carried away that they organized the patriarchy? Is the violence inherent in the nature of the human being, a product of the natural urge to compete or of the hierarchical mindset? Did it occur from something so practical as the planning ahead for survival through the storing of surplus goods? Or from something so ontological as the realization of death and the planning ahead against its occurrence?

The evidence is plain that somehow our energy has gone haywire, that we are riding roughshod over the biosphere, that we have no species consciousness, that we produce, reproduce, and consume in a constantly expanding pattern that is rapidly depleting our natural resources and driving us to the destruction of each other and of the planet which sustains us. "Rape of the Earth" is not simply a metaphor, or if it is a metaphor it is one so strong that it brings into sharp relief both the reality of the female/male relationship in Western culture and the separation of ourselves as a species from the original source of our being. The earth seems now to be giving us clear and unmistakeable signals that she will not endure our rule over her much longer, that we are a renegade civilization, a dying civilization which may have passed up its opportunity for survival. We need to come to a halt and reawaken ourselves, to refresh and resource ourselves at the lost wells of our own origin. Already it may be too late.

––––––––––

To pose the value question, "Can it be an act of integrity to seek to change another person or another entity?" is to open the door to alternatives to persuasion. I will explore here a nonpersuasive notion of communication and show how I believe our discipline has been moving toward that notion in the recent past. Finally I will draw connections between recent understandings of communication and the womanization of culture that I believe is necessary for the survival of the planet.

If we are not to attempt to change our world, then is the alternative to sit forever in a quiet and desperate passivity? Must we choose between being an invader, a violent persuader, and a patient Griselda twiddling our thumbs and curbing our energy in the hope that some miraculous process will do it all for us? Surely it is of value to seek to alter injustices, to change oppressive societal institutions. Is there a way to relate to each other, to other entities, in acts that participate in the changing of our world but which do not themselves recapitulate our heritage of violence? Is there a difference between wanting circumstances to change and wanting to change circumstances?

Mao Tse Tung in his essay "On Contradiction" gave us the metaphor of the egg and the stone. No one can change an egg into a chicken. If, however, there is the potential in the egg to be a chicken—what Mao called the "internal basis for change"—then there is the likelihood that in the right environment (moisture, temperature, the "external conditions for change") the egg will hatch. A stone, on the other hand, has no internal basis for hatching into a chicken and an eternity of sitting in the proper conditions of moisture and temperature will not make possible its transformation into a chicken.

If we think of communicative acts not as attempts to change others or even as attempts to inform or to help them, then perhaps we can understand Mao's metaphor. Communication can be a deliberate creation or co-creation of an atmosphere in which people or things, if and only if they have the internal basis for change, may change themselves; it can be a milieu in which those who are ready to be persuaded may persuade themselves, may choose to hear or choose to learn. With this understanding we can begin to operate differently in all communicative circumstances, particularly those wherein *learning* and *conflict encounter* take place.

What might take place in the learning circumstance could be best understood as a mutual generation of energy for purposes of growth; what would take place in the conflict encounter is best described for lack of a better word as dialogue. In either case, persons entering the interaction would be certain:

1. that no intent to enlighten or to persuade would be made but rather that each party would seek to contribute to an atmosphere in which change for both/all parties can take place;

2. that there are differences among those who participate—in the case of learning, differences of degree and quality of knowing specific subject matter, and in the case of conflict genuine disagreements between/among people;

3. that though there are differences, the persons involved feel equal in power to each other;

4. that communication is a difficult achievement, something to be worked at, since the odds are great that moments of miscommunication will outnumber moments of communication;

5. that each participant is willing on the deepest level to yield her/his position entirely to the other(s).

If the circumstance is one of learning, then instructors must genuinely prepare to learn, prepare to be changed with students in the mutually created setting. As we observe from changes already taking place in classrooms across the country, the number of words spoken by any one individual—teacher or student—in such an atmosphere is far less important than the manner and the intentionality with which they speak the words.

If the circumstance is one of conflict, then all that we are already learning about dialogue comes into play. Somehow the mind-body split experienced by rhetoric or speech communication as well as by other disciplines will have to be bridged in the process of dialogue. Some unity will have to occur there of personality differences with the principled advocacy of positions; some techniques of interpersonal clarification and openness will have to blend with the use of good reason in the controversy. We functioned from Socrates to the 1950s with reason as our standard; then, with the advent of sensitivity training and small group communication, we seemed almost to exchange the tyranny of the mind for the tyranny of the emotions. What we now know is that, in any conflict circumstance, there are positions and arguments, but there are as well the multi-leveled dynamics of human personalities at work.

It is at this point, when we address emerging notions of learning and dialogue, that we appreciate the recent changes of the rhetoric and public address that have occurred within the discipline of rhetoric and public address. It is fair to say that until the 1950s speech-making has been practiced and taught on the conquest/conversion model, on a very male chauvinist model, one that not only implied but explicitly assumed that all the power was in the speaker, just as we believed at one point in history that all power was in the sperm. He stood before the crowd, one hero, one persuader. He believed that he did it all, and, unfortunately, his audience believed the same thing. His was the message, his the act of converting his hearers; his was the enlightened truth which sought a womb/audience in which to deposit itself and grow. Little attention was paid to the listener, and even less to the circumstances or the environment of the persuasive process.

In the last decades, however, the listener has come into her own. By drawing our attention away from the masses transfixed by one orator and toward the interactions that transpire in our daily lives, by sitting more often in groups or in dyads and less often in lectures, we have come to realize that in its more common and more natural setting communication does not have to be an invasion of enemy territory but can at least be a two-way street. We have begun to admit the listener's presence, perhaps even her participation in the speech-making process. And the field of *rhetoric*—persuasion—has broadened into the field of *communication,* a change which in itself is a symptom of the change in our concerns.

In recent semantic and communication theory we move closer to the concern for environment, for climate; particularly this is true in a general systems approach and transactional models. Though the term is only beginning to be used, it is important that the whole communication environment be understood as a *matrix,* a womb. A matrix is that within which or from which something takes form or begins. A matrix "produces" a seed (like the sperm), only we call it an egg. Yet the matrix is not simply a generating substance. It is also a nurturing substance, the atmosphere in which growth and change take place. In terms of communication it is an atmosphere in which meanings are generated and nurtured. We could even say, "The meaning is the matrix."

It is a new thing that we do in this century: to turn again toward the wholeness of the communication process instead of separating ourselves out from it, to think in terms of an organic atmosphere that is the source of meanings instead of waiting for an outsider who will, like a god, give us the meanings. We are perhaps on the brink of understanding that we do not have to be persuaders, that we no longer need to intend to change others. We are not the speaker, the-one-with-the-truth, the-one-who-with-his-power-will-change-lives. We are the matrix, we are she-who-is-the-home-of-this-particular-human-interaction, we are a co-creator and co-sustainer of the atmosphere in whose infinity of possible transformations we will all change.

Modern communication theory has not yet articulated its own process of change. With all of its extensive research into human behavior, with all its imagination and creative models, modern communication theory still is concerned almost exclusively with the *how* and the *what* of communication, how it works and what its definition is. At best it asks questions about the role of values in attitude change and fails as yet to ask essential value questions about its own intent.

The conquest/conversion rhetoricians of the first 2,400 years of our discipline constantly asked questions of value: Can virtue be taught? Can we allow a dangerous enemy to speak to the masses? What does a lie do to the speaker's credibility? Should teachers of rhetoric take fees for teaching? They too failed to ask the crucial value question, "Can we with integrity intend to change another?" But at least they reflected on their actions in the light of ethics. We recall, though, that rhetoric has always found its home in the humanities where value questions are the norm. Modern communication theory participates more readily in the social sciences where questions of value hide under the search for objective reality. Until such theory begins to entertain those ethical questions or until communicators in the humanities challenge modern theory on just such questions, we will be little better off than with our commitment to the old conquest/conversion assumptions.

In what is called the second wave of feminism, the rise of the women's movement in the sixties and seventies of this century, there are threads that may connect a society presently violent to a nonviolent past and to a nonviolent future. One of the threads is an understanding of communication as essentially the womanlike process we have been describing.

Feminism is at the very least the rejection of the conquest/conversion model of interaction and the development of new forms of relationship which allow for wholeness in the individual and differences among people and entities. At the same time it means some sense of how that infinite variety thrives within a unity. Feminism is an ideology of change which rises out of the experiences of women, out of the experiences of our bodies, our experiences of our conditioning both in our individual lives and over the centuries.

It is important to the field of communication that biologically and historically we women have been thought of and think of ourselves as receptacles, as listeners, as hearers, as holders, nurturers, as matrices, as environments and creators of environments. It is important to the field of communication that, though we women now begin to discover what the suppression of our violence has meant to us, violence has been associated almost exclusively with men in our culture. The change in the discipline of speech from the concentration on speaker/conqueror to an interest in atmosphere, in listening, in receiving, in a collective rather than in a competitive mode—that change suggests the womanization of that discipline.

Many of us in the speech field, women and men alike, will be uncomfortable with that idea: that communication, like the rest of the culture, must be womanized, that in order to be authentic, in order to be nonviolent communicators, we must all become more like women. We have all learned that though women are okay they are somehow lesser human beings. It is a blow to the ego to suggest that we may be like a woman. It will be hard for men to think of changing because never having been environments they need lots of practice in becoming so. It will be hard for women in the field to think of changing because though we have been environments, we've spent most of our professional careers trying not to be so, trying not to be women, trying instead to scale ourselves to the conquest/conversion model of the speechmaker, the speech teacher.

We have all diligently studied our Aristotle and learned how to persuade others, how to enlighten them. We have all enjoyed the rush of power that has come with that. How can we forsake all this and think of ourselves not as bearers of great messages but as vessels out of whose variety messages will emerge? We have been practicing conquer-and-convert for centuries; struggling for survival in a self-perpetuating system of violence and power conflicts. There is reason, good reason, for us to be uncomfortable with such a "weak" and "yielding" model of communication. There is reason enough to be insecure about giving up our desire to change others since our entire identity has been bound up in our power to change others. When all we've done for centuries is to penetrate the environment with the truth we've been taught to believe is ours alone, then it is difficult to enjoy being just a listener, just a co-creator of an atmosphere. Yet that is precisely the task.

Feminism is a source, a wellspring, a matrix, an environment for the womanization of communication, for the womanization of Western civilization. It calls for an ancient and deep understanding and ultimately for a fundamental change of attitude and perspective. In its challenge to history and to the present social order feminism in this, its second wave, feminism this time around, in this century, is playing for keeps for all of us—for women, for men, for children, animals, and plants, and for the earth herself. The stakes are that high.

5

Style as Politics: A Feminist Approach to the Teaching of Writing

PAMELA J. ANNAS

My interest in the politics of style begins in two immediate personal concerns: my own efforts to write as a woman who is both a feminist and an academic and who therefore wants to reach more than one audience, and my work in writing classes with women students who are trying to find an authentic and effective writing voice in classroom situations, for an audience, and in the context of approved models of writing that often seem puzzling and alien to them. I think that particularly those of us who have worked with students' writing in the context of women's studies classes are aware of being caught in a dilemma. We have been trained to teach expository writing in a particular way—one which values writing that is defended, linear, and "objective." Indeed, many writing classes seem designed to teach the use of abstract, logical, and impersonal rather than sensual, contextual, and committed language. How many of us teach writing in a way that moves during the semester from image to argument, from the particular to the abstract, and that attempts gradually to "wean" students from subjectivity into objectivity? Yet our observation of students lets us know how necessary it is for them to discover their own voices in an expression, assertion, and grounding of their own identity in their own experience.

So we may sometimes feel that on one hand there is experiential writing—journals, sketches, response papers—which we perhaps won't grade or will read with our usual critical faculties suspended. We may value women's creative writing while at the same time feeling that it is very different from expository writing, the actual essay or research paper, which on the other hand we have been trained to think should be based on what the authorities say rather than on personal experience, and on "hard" data rather than "soft." It should be objective rather than subjective; it should be linear and logical in a particular way, with a beginning, a middle, an end, and a clear thesis statement. The word that comes to mind here is *rigor,* and we might remember what Adrienne Rich says in "Taking Women Students Seriously" (in *On Lies, Secrets, and Silence*

From *College English* 47 (1985): 360–71.

[New York: Norton, 1979]): That we need to be finding ways to train women students to write rigorously as women, rather than either not insisting that they write rigorously or accepting established (and, for Rich, patriarchal) notions and standards of what constitutes rigor (p. 244). I want to suggest a third alternative in teaching writing, one which is rigorous without sacrificing subjectivity.

People write well—with passion and color—when they write out of their experience and when that experience is seen as valuable so that they have the confidence to write it. A successful approach to the teaching of writing, at least for the urban, older, often working-class students in my classes at the University of Massachusetts–Boston, cannot focus on the writing product to the exclusion of the person writing. Students' lives will "intrude" into their classroom performance, their attendance, their attention, and their writing. They need to ground their writing in their lives rather than to surmount their lives before they write. Though this is not the only writing problem students encounter, much awkwardness in sentences and paragraphs simply disappears when students are no longer alienated from language, their subject, and themselves, when they are writing with the confidence that what they have to say is worth saying and that someone wants to hear it.

Can we teach writing to our students in a way that validates who they are, that allows them to handle their materials confidently and comfortably, with discipline and integrity, and that also gives them the survival skills to write in a way that will be acceptable to the world that we are training them to enter? This pedagogical dilemma may be grounded in part in our conflicts about our own writing as women who are trying to be heard in a profession that values hierarchy, competitiveness, detachment, and objectivity and who may, on the other hand, also wish to be heard by a range of women and men, not all of whom are academics. We have a real problem here. As Marilyn Frye says in "On Second Thought":

> our need for respectability generates tiresome articles in which some glimmer of insight has been drowned in jargon, charts, and footnotes and strangled by professional defensiveness. We are caught in a position where we keep trying to contribute to building a world in which the vocation of women no longer is the pleasing of men, by producing scholarship about women that will be pleasing to men. . . .
>
> The path we open is the path we will train our students to follow, and if it deviates little from the path we took ourselves, then we will not go far beyond just putting them through the same paces we went through. (*Radical Teacher*, No. 17 [1980], p. 37)

Much of what I will be saying here is adaptable to the teaching of writing to members of other groups disadvantaged in their relationship to language. I am going to focus specifically, however, on the relation between gender and language and the particular situation of women students as writers, though even that reality is complex since many of us are marginalized in more ways than one. For example, one of my students is a southern black woman in her mid-forties who was dealing with issues of race, class, and regional alienation in relation to language as well as with the issue of gender.

Robin Lakoff remarked in 1975 that writers who are women are in effect bilingual, required to be competent in two dialects:

> though her command of both is adequate for most purposes, she may never feel really comfortable using either, and never be certain that she is using the right one in the right place to the right person. Shifting from one language to another requires special awareness to the nuances of social situations, special alertness to possible disapproval. It may be that the extra energy that must be (subconsciously or otherwise) expended in this game is energy sapped from more creative work, and hinders women from expressing themselves as well, as fully, or as freely as they might otherwise. (*Language and Women's Place* [New York: Harper and Row, 1975], p. 7)

The white woman who is from a working-class background is to some extent bilingual, as is the white woman who is a lesbian, for both must make a choice whether or not to "pass" in their use of language, as well as in other areas of their life. The question of bilingualism becomes even more pressing for women who are black or who, as third world women, are literally caught between two languages as well as two cultures. June Jordan writes in "White English/Black English: The Politics of Translation" that "*white power uses white English as a calculated, political display of power to control and eliminate the power-less* . . . the white child is rewarded for mastery of his standard, white English: the language he learned at his mother's white and standard knee. But the Black child is punished for mastery of his non-standard Black English; for the ruling elite of America have decided that *non*-standard is *sub*-standard, and even dangerous, and must be eradicated."[1] One consequence of being either literally or metaphorically bilingual is that we may spend a lot of time acting as interpreters for ourselves and others, as we stand, writes Audre Lorde in her poem "A Litany for Survival," "upon the constant edges of decision/ crucial and alone." Or, as Kate Rushin puts it in "The Bridge Poem," "I do more translating/than the Gawdamn U.N."[2] The internal struggle with one's relation to one's audience can often distort and deflect the relation a writer has to her subject and to her own creativity.

In Writing as Women, a sophomore-level expository writing course I teach at the University of Massachusetts–Boston, we study the stylistic strategies that various women essayists have used to deal with the problem of writing as women in an authentic female voice in a context that often does not value what women have to say and often insists that we neutralize what we say in the way we say it.[3] Given this situation a writer's choices (whether conscious or not) are political, engaging, and frequently difficult. Whenever a woman sits down to write, she is engaged in a complex political act in which the self and the world struggle in and through the medium of language. No wonder writing is so exhausting and so many of us suffer from writing blocks. No wonder it feels like such a triumph to get something even conditionally true and readable onto the page.

What is style? Virginia Woolf asks obliquely in *A Room of One's Own* whether there is such a thing as a female sentence ([New York: Harper and Row, 1929], pp. 79–80). Mary Hiatt, in "The Feminine Style: Theory and Fact" (*College Composition and Communication* 29 [1978], 222–6), did a computer analysis of one hundred samples of prose fiction writing by men and women, studying sentence length and complexity, logical sequence of ideas, similes, -*ly* adverbs, parenthetical expressions, rhetorical devices. I break style down even further and say it includes many elements as specific as the few I name here: choice of words; amount, type, and pattern of imagery; length, rhythm, and complexity of sentences; use of humor, satire, and irony; choice of genre elements; variety and length of paragraphs; choice of subject; the way an argument is constructed; and the complex interrelationships between the writer's attitude toward her subject, toward her audience, and toward the self writing and the self in the writing.

Here are passages taken from the prefaces of two explicitly political books published in the mid-1970s, books which stand on the border between being for an academic audience and for a wider audience. Harry Braverman comes from a working-class background, and in *Labor and Monopoly Capital: The Degradation of Work in the Twentieth Century* (New York: Monthly Review Press, 1974) he has produced what is probably the most important and readable book in Marxist economics in the last couple of decades. Robin Lakoff is a feminist from a middle-class background whose *Language and Women's Place* helped found the field of feminist linguistics. Both are white. Both of these writers, doing germinal work in their respective fields, attempt to explain in these passages what their methodology is—that is, what the relation is between themselves and their subjects. Their concern here revolves around the question of objectivity. Each is aware of the standard of objectivity that is part of the criteria by which the truth and value of their work will be judged by a segment of their audience they consider important. Braverman writes:

> As the reader will see in the appropriate chapters, I have tried to put this experience [his work years as a laborer and artisan] to some use in this book. I have also had the benefit of many conversations—with friends, acquaintances, strangers met at social gatherings or while traveling— about their work (and it may be that some of them, if they chance to read this, will now understand why I was curious to the point of rudeness). But while this occupational and conversational background has been useful, I must emphasize that nothing in this book relies upon personal experience or reminiscences, and that I have in the formal sense included almost no factual materials for which I could not give a reference which can be checked independently by the reader, as is proper in any scientific work. (pp. 8–9)

Robin Lakoff, starting from what appears to be the same situation—the construction of an argument grounded in personal experience and observation—

comes to a very different conclusion about the use and validity of her methods. She writes:

> The data on which I am basing my claims have been gathered mainly by
> introspection: I have examined my own speech and that of my acquain-
> tances, and have used my own intuitions in analyzing it. I have also made
> use of the media: in some ways, the speech heard, for example, in com-
> mercials or situation comedies on television mirrors the speech of the
> television-watching community. . . . The sociologist, anthropologist, or
> ethnomethodologist familiar with what seem to him more errorproof
> data-gathering techniques, such as the recording of random conversa-
> tion, may object that these introspective methods may produce dubious
> results. But first, it should be noted that *any* procedure is at some point
> introspective: the gatherer must analyze his data, after all. Then, one nec-
> essarily selects a subgroup of the population to work with . . . and finally,
> there is the purely pragmatic issue: random conversation must go on for
> quite some time, and the recorder must be exceedingly lucky anyway, in
> order to produce evidence of any particular hypothesis, that there is sex-
> ism in language, that there is not sexism in language. If we are to have a
> good sample of data to analyze, this will have to be elicited artificially
> from someone; I submit that I am as good an artificial source of data as
> anyone. (pp. 4–5)

Both writers have internalized a sense of audience—the academic establishment with its criteria of scientific objectivity—and the audience nudges
them toward a particular relation between themselves and their subject. Both
struggle with this problem, sensing that their truth, because it is new, because
it challenges old beliefs, can't be contained inside the bounds of traditionally
defined objectivity. Braverman is disturbed but finally capitulates and gives
up personal experience as part of the evidence for his conclusions. Lakoff in
her passage is mildly apologetic but finally pugnacious. She knows she's
going to get in trouble with her academic audience when she makes the choice
to use intuition, introspection, and her own experience as data. She chooses to
speak to a general feminist audience rather than exclusively to the (at that
time) largely male community of academic linguists. Both in this preface and
throughout *Language and Women's Place* the painful cost of that decision is
apparent. That Lakoff still has one foot in the academic world has caused her
to be criticized by some feminists who point out, for example, that she still
uses the generic *he* in a monograph on sexism in language.

An example of powerful writing that can be produced out of the very tension between writer and audience is, of course, *A Room of One's Own*. Woolf's
long opening paragraph (which I have condensed somewhat here) explains
and embodies her own methodology, her relation to her subject, her audi-
ence(s), and herself in the writing.

> But, you may say, we asked you to speak about women and fiction—
> what has that got to do with a room of one's own? I will try to explain.
> When you asked me to speak about women and fiction I sat down on the
> banks of a river and began to wonder what the words meant. . . . The title

women and fiction might mean, and you may have meant it to mean, women and what they are like; or it might mean women and the fiction that they write; or it might mean women and the fiction that is written about them; or it might mean that somehow all three are inextricably mixed together and you want me to consider them in that light. . . . I soon saw . . . I should never be able to come to a conclusion. I should never be able to fulfill what is, I understand, the first duty of a lecturer—to hand you after an hour's discourse a nugget of pure truth to wrap up between the pages of your notebooks and keep on the mantelpiece forever. All I could do was offer you an opinion upon one minor point—a woman must have money and a room of her own if she is to write fiction. . . . I am going to develop in your presence as fully and freely as I can the train of thought which led me to think this. . . . One can only give one's audience the chance of drawing their own conclusions as they observe the limitations, the prejudices, the idiosyncrasies of the speaker. . . . I propose . . . to tell you the story of the two days that preceded my coming here—how, bowed down by the weight of the subject which you have laid upon my shoulders, I pondered it, and made it work in and out of my daily life. . . . Lies will flow from my lips, but there may perhaps be some truth mixed up with them; it is for you to seek out this truth and to decide whether any part of it is worth keeping. If not, you will of course throw the whole of it into the waste-paper basket and forget all about it. (pp. 3–4)

First, like Robin Lakoff and unlike Harry Braverman, Woolf is validating not only the importance but the primacy of grounding one's conclusions in personal experience. Second, she is asserting that the process of reasoning is as crucial as the product or conclusions that emerge from it, that indeed process is the other nine-tenths of the iceberg against which unwary readers may bump and sink their boat. Third, she proposes that thought and creativity are not separate from the material conditions in which they take place. This claim is, of course, the thesis of the whole book, and she demonstrates it in miniature in this opening paragraph. Fourth, her method is inclusive; it connects rather than separates, assumes complexity, is circular rather than linear. Then she demonstrates how one does not necessarily have to accept the given topic (or the assumptions underlying a topic) but can reframe it to suit oneself. And she mixes genres, using narration, characterization, and image to construct an argument. Finally, here as in other essays, Woolf eschews an authoritative stance. She puts the responsibility for reaching conclusions on her audience. If there is such a thing as truth, she says, she hasn't got it; what she has are opinions and fictions, and it is up to us to sift through them.

Woolf's relation to her audience is complex and subversive. Built into the very structure of Woolf's sentences is a combative stance in regard to the shadowy but real male audience which stands behind her real but shadowy audience of women. "But," she begins her essay, acknowledging at the outset that she will be speaking in part to people who are not predisposed to agree with her or even understand her. By addressing her remarks directly to her audience, to "you," she pulls the reader into the essay itself, where that reader can be controlled, characterized, manipulated, picked up, turned inside out, shaken out the back door, patted back into shape, and set on the sofa again. She employs flank rather than direct attacks. She lulls her readers into thinking we have control over where we're going when in fact she is firmly at the wheel. She breaks all the rules about thesis statements by burying hers in the middle of a two-page paragraph and undercutting it by calling it "an opinion upon one minor point." Throughout *A Room of One's Own* she uses the method of contrast which acknowledges division, setting male and female realities against each other and letting readers draw their own conclusions— Oxbridge and Fernham, the young male researcher in the library and herself, Shakespeare and his sister, and so on. The prose is powerful in part because it is so centered on this problematic relationship between writer, subject, and audience, and because it finds a delicate resolution between hostile elements.[4] It is a traditionally "feminine" style, yet it is so sure, so effective, and so in the command of the writer that it becomes almost a tongue-in-cheek criticism of the linguistic etiquette of powerlessness at the moment she employs it.

––––––––––

Our discussion of the politics of style comes about two-thirds of the way through the course Writing as Women. In addition to *A Room of One's Own* we study examples of a variety of essay styles, including Meridel LeSueur's 1932 article about unemployment among women during the Depression, "Women on the Breadlines," Adrienne Rich's essay on feminist ethics, "Women and Honor: Some Notes on Lying," Gloria Anzaldúa's discussion of cultural exclusion in "Speaking in Tongues: A Letter to 3rd World Women Writers," and Judy Syfer's satiric definition of woman's role in "Why I Want a Wife."[5] This turning outward to study the stylistic choices other women writers have made is preceded by a number of writing assignments which help students become conscious of their own writing styles, writing processes, and the contexts in which they write.

One of our first acts as a group is to compile a list of our own writing blocks and what underlies them. Some of these are perfectionism, fear of criticism or judgment, depression, numbness or blankness, fear of taking risks, fear of success, coping with an alien subject matter, fear of one's own power or anger, worry that one has nothing to say, writing for an audience indifferent or hostile to what one wants to say, fear of knowing oneself, getting stuck between objectivity and subjectivity, fear of being trivialized or conforming to what's expected, private vs. public writing, talking vs. writing, having the right to one's opinions, discomfort with the mechanics of writing and organizing a paper, fear of being boring, dumb, insignificant, or ridiculous.[6]

The forms that these writing blocks take are various, and I mention only a few of the more common ones here. First, students may block to the extent that they don't write at all. Or they may procrastinate in a dazzling and creative variety of ways, leaving themselves so little time that they can't possibly write something that satisfies them, thus self-fulfilling their expectation of failure. As one student in the course remarked, there is active procrastination, where you decide that now is the time to sort out your winter socks even though it's April, passive procrastination, which may involve making endless notes on the subject instead of writing the paper, and then there's being so overwhelmed, guilty, and numbed out by your overdue work that you can't even get started.[7] They may write but not revise, which always makes me think of Adrienne Rich's comment in "Taking Women Students Seriously" that "a romantic sloppiness, an inspired lack of rigor, a self-indulgent incoherence, are symptoms of female self-depreciation" (*On Lies, Secrets and Silence,* p. 244). They may block at the point when they're supposed to go public with their writing and share it with other people in the class. They may write the paper but present it in scrawled illegible handwriting or as a blurred photocopy or in a typescript almost too faint to read. They may know what they want to say but edit it, giving the audience (often a teacher) what they think that teacher wants to hear. They may do this out of discomfort at self-revelation or out of fear they will be punished, rejected, or annihilated if they say or write what they actually think. And frequently they censor themselves so well that they don't know what they think.

Different students block at different points in the semester. Some block because of outside pressures in their lives, or because of internal pressure about the writing as the semester goes on and on and they have to keep producing paper after paper. Sometimes a writing block has to do with resistance to the assignment. One semester two women in the course blocked when I asked them to write about their backgrounds in relation to writing and language. One said in class, "Thinking about my background. Well, you can't do anything about it, but . . . my attitude was, I'm mad, I'm angry, I'm bitter, so I'm not finishing this paper." She was upset at the anger she had found in herself, but she also thought that what she really had to say wouldn't be acceptable. So she turned in something that was bland, numb, and lifeless. During this discussion I suggested that she rewrite the paper, beginning with "I'm mad, I'm angry, I'm bitter," and go on from there. When she did that, her writing unblocked, and though much of what she wrote in the rest of the semester had a bitter edge, her writing was prolific and vivid. Another woman stuck for two weeks on the same assignment, then turned in a powerfully written account of how her father had molested her from age eleven to fourteen and had beaten her up when she tried to speak about it to her mother. She had never written about that experience before and she dated the development of her particular form of silence—a polished, distant, ironic style—from that period.

Other women have a tough time making their writing a priority because the very act of writing seems to them selfish and self-indulgent, like going back to school and getting an education; it is something they are doing for themselves and therefore suspect: "My baby started crying. He was just lying there looking at me, and all of a sudden I felt so guilty because I was indulging myself in my work and I wasn't paying attention to him. And I found myself going over to him, playing with him" instead of writing. Another woman, who wants to be a professional writer, gives an account of "freezing" during an exam.

Oh, how I loathe myself. My husband will say if I tell him, but I will not, "I told you so. You are wasting your time in a Liberal Arts program." Maybe he is right. After all, he usually is. The idea of making a career by the power of my pen is a high flight into fancy. If I had any sense I would go to Northeast Regional and become a plumber or a carpenter, as he has so often suggested.[8]

I ask students to become self-conscious about their writing process so that they can make it less mysterious and have more control over it. The writing process paper asks them to describe in step-by-step detail *how* they go about writing a paper, from the moment they get the assignment to the time they turn it in—with particular emphasis on the material conditions of their writing and what their lives are like when they're writing. *Where* do they write (in the library, in bed, at the kitchen table); *when* do they write (the night before the paper's due, as soon as they get the assignment, one page a day for a week); *on what* do they write (note cards, long ruled yellow pads, a typewriter, a word processor); *what techniques* do they feel most comfortable with: do they use an outline, do they need to get the first paragraph right before they can go on, do they write pages of notes or rough draft before they can really get started? Is there consistently a place in their writing process where they block and stop? Sometimes simply knowing that their writing block is there, lurking around that particular corner of the process, makes it slightly less terrifying. At least the element of surprise is gone. Are there methods they can develop to maneuver themselves past that particular sticking place? Not only identifying their most usual writing process, but also learning that they can vary it is useful to the students. Are there different kinds of writing processes for different kinds of writing—for poems, stories, research papers, position papers, or argumentative essays? Do they have a different writing process depending on their relation to the subject or assignment—depending on whether, for example, they are reluctant or eager to do it? Under what conditions do they work best? How can they replicate these conditions? Sometimes I suggest that they find an extended metaphor for their writing process and structure the paper around that. One student imagined her "anti-muse" as a plump little old lady, Aunt Emma, who, every time she sat down to write, urged her to look under the furniture for dust balls instead. Another student imaged her writing process as putting a jigsaw puzzle together. A third saw it as similar to finding an old chair in a garbage pile and slowly and lovingly refinishing it; that same student wrote, "Each time I am assigned a paper I suck in my breath as if I had to move a hundred pound stone from the entrance to my apartment in order to go on living."[9]

I have found two overall types of writing problems among women students: there are those students who early learned how to turn out polished, correct, and fluent essays which generally engage only the surface of their selves, which are detached, objective, passionless, and take few risks. Another type of woman student writes regularly or occasionally in a journal, or poetry, or fiction but does so in a diffuse and scattered way. She writes for herself, not for an audience, and though she writes about what really matters to her, she protects herself by writing almost in a private code. She dislikes criticism intensely and she does not want to revise. What I am describing here, of course, are two extremes. As women writers we have walked a fine line between objectivity and subjectivity, between self-censorship and self-indulgence, silence and noise, rigid control and little or no control. This is a tension with which I am more comfortable (or at least more accustomed) than are most of my students, one of whom wrote:

> This paper needs a purpose.
> It needs a thesis. The thesis needs a question.
> The question needs an answer. Sooner or later we
>   all must settle
> down to the business of communicating clearly and
>   concisely.
> Look at Sylvia Plath. She wrote poetry thesaurus
>   in hand.
> She killed herself.
>   What do we learn about "real" writers,
>   women
>   They are very
>   unhappy.
>   They go crazy.
>   They kill
>   themselves.
>   They are deadly
>   serious.[10]

In Writing As Women we try to mediate between these modes through exercises that ask the students who are primarily public writers to commit themselves in language by writing about what matters to them, and that ask students who are essentially private writers to consider an audience and to use a more conventional, slightly less free associative style in order that communication can take place. The overall goal is to have a personal investment in the subject, the medium, one's self in the writing, and the audience the writer has chosen. Because historically women have been channeled toward private forms and denied access to more public forms, it has seemed to me particularly important to teach women how to write political essays—by which I mean any essay that places the self in the world, is addressed to an audience, and takes a position.[11]

The last assignment of the semester is a six- to eight-page position paper, in which students choose a topic of intense interest to them and base their arguments at least as much on lived personal experience as on more conventional sources of information. One woman wrote out of her seventeen years of working at the telephone company a biting description and analysis of female managerial types. Another wrote about her experience with mental institutions and the ways in which people who have been institutionalized are treated by their friends, neighbors, relatives, and co-workers once they are out. A third argued for a re-engineering of buildings and cities for the physically challenged, based on her recent experience of breaking both her wrists and being unable to use her hands for four months.[12] A fourth woman wrote about the chronic physical pain in her knees and the reasons people in pain want to keep their pain private. Another woman wrote a scathing critique of the proficiency exam at our school after having taken it herself and passed it; she talked with others who had both passed and failed the exam and with the tutors who coached them and concluded that the exam was part of the University's attempt to "eliten" itself by systematically dropping out working-class, black, Third-World, and many women students. A top U.S. competitor in karate who happened to be in the class argued that women should learn karate to build their confidence so that they can deal with the violence against women that they will inevitably encounter. Finally, a student did a critical analysis of the bourgeois liberalism of *Ms.* magazine's September back-to-school issue and its colossal irrelevance for working-class women students like herself.[13]

The kind of writing I finally want these students to be able to do brings together the personal and the political, the private and the public, into writing which is committed and powerful because it takes risks, because it speaks up clearly in their own voices and from their experience, experiments with techniques of argumentation and skillful organization, and engages, where appropriate, with the insights of other writers.

Women students need to move from a kind of writing bounded at one end by what Robin Lakoff in *Language and Women's Place* calls "women's language," a hesitant ladylike language characterized (in speech) by tag questions, rising inflections, and vague intensifiers and by a focus on the particular which is crippling and limited. They need to travel *through* what the French feminist linguists have been calling the transforming power of silence in which one discovers (somewhat mystically, I admit) one's own meanings in the holes in patriarchal discourse,[14] to discover or rediscover a new women's language, a kind of writing which is confident in asserting the particulars of women's experience—both in content and in form. The writing product as the end of this process may or may not be outside the range of what we are accustomed to recognize as strong expository writing.[15] However, as teachers of writing we need to be aware that the route to a good essay is sometimes very different for women than for men. And I believe that the essay form itself is being strengthened and revived as women begin to write from our own center. For what sometimes has been perceived as the weaknesses in women's writing—an emphasis on the particular, the contextual, the narrative, the imagistic, what Meridel LeSueur has called circular rather than linear writing; and the different content and conclusions that emerge as women write from a specific reality as women (including, for example, what goes on around kitchen tables)—these are in fact some of the strengths of women's writing. Those of us who are, as composition teachers, in the powerful position of judging our students' writing need to extend our definition of what good and effective writing is and to transfer that sense of possibility to students alienated from the connections between language and experience. Women students need to stop learning primarily how to translate their own experience into a foreign language and instead to spend some time learning their mother tongue.

Editors' note to this edition: In her computer analysis, Mary Hiatt included both fiction *and* non-fiction prose. For more details, see Hiatt, this volume.

NOTES

1. In *Civil Wars* (Boston: Beacon Press, 1981), p. 65. Later in the essay Jordan writes that "the subject of 'Black English' cannot be intelligently separate from the subject of a language as translation and translation as a political process distinguishing between the powerless and the powerful" (p. 70).

2. "A Litany for Survival," in *The Black Unicorn* (New York: Norton, 1978), p. 31; "The Bridge Poem," in *This Bridge Called My Back: Writings by Radical Women of Color,* ed. Cherrie Moraga and Gloria Anzaldúa (Watertown, Mass.: Persephone Press, 1981), p. xxi.

3. Writing as Women requires seven or eight papers of varying lengths and a portfolio of three revisions. No incompletes are allowed in the course. It is crosslisted in the English department and in Women's Studies. The prerequisite for the course is the university's required two semesters of introductory composition. This means that students generally are in control of the rudiments of writing and allows us to take on the question of style. However, I have begun to adapt some of the writing assignments in Writing as Women, including the writing process paper, for my introductory composition courses.

4. Adrienne Rich says, in "When We Dead Awaken: Writing as Re-Vision," that the tone of *A Room of One's Own* "is the tone of a woman almost in touch with her anger," "who is determined not to appear angry, who is *willing* herself to be calm, detached, and even charming in a roomful of men. . . . Virginia Woolf is addressing an audience of women, but she is acutely conscious—as she always was—of being overheard by men" (*On Lies, Secrets and Silence,* p. 37).

5. "Women on the Breadlines," in *Ripening: Selected Work, 1927–1980,* ed. Elaine Hedges (Old Westbury, N.Y.: The Feminist Press, 1982); "Women and Honor: Some Notes on Lying," in *On Lies, Secrets and Silence;* "Speaking in Tongues: A Letter to 3rd World Women Writers," in *This Bridge Called My Back;* "Why I Want a Wife," in *Radical Feminism,* ed. Anne Koedt, Ellen Levine, and Anita Rapone (New York: Quadrangle Books, 1973).

6. For a longer list of writing blocks, see *Women's Studies Quarterly* 12, No. 1 (1984), 39.

7. Judy Bosquin, "Unfinished Business," in *Writing as Women,* supplement to *Wavelength* (Spring 1982), p. 16.

8. Catherine Walsh. "The Block," in *Writing as Women,* p. 8.

9. Karen McDonald, "My Writing Process," *WSQ* 12, No. 1 (1984), 40.

10. Marilyn Stern, "Words," in *Writing as Women,* p. 25.

11. See Dale Spender's discussion of public and private writing in Chapter 7, "Women and Writing," of *Man Made Language* (London: Routledge & Kegan Paul, 1980), pp. 191–233.

12. Kayla Kirsch, "Disarmed," in *Writing as Women,* pp. 21–23.

13. Deb Whippen, "Writing Proficiency," pp. 6–7; Pam Glaser, "Anger into Action," pp. 12–13; "On Taking Women Students Seriously: The September Issue of *Ms.* 'save these pages,'" p. 18; in *Writing as Women.*

14. See especially the selections from Helene Cixous, Marguerite Duras, Chantal Chawaf, Madeleine Gagnon, Xaviere Gauthier, and Julia Kristeva in *New French Feminisms,* ed. Elaine Marks and Isabelle de Courtivron (New York: Schocken Books, 1981).

15. For an excellent discussion of the new feminist essay, see Julia Penelope (Stanley) and Susan J. Wolfe, "Consciousness as Style: Style as Aesthetic," in *Language, Gender, and Society,* ed. Barrie Thorne, Cheris Kramarae, and Nancy Henley (Rowley, Mass.: Newbury House Publishers, 1983), pp. 125–39.

PART TWO

Feminist Theories and Research

Part Two: Introduction

MARY P. SHERIDAN-RABIDEAU

Just as there is no one feminism, there is no one feminist theory or research methodology. In fact, definitions of feminist theory and methodology are hotly contested as feminist composition scholars draw upon theories from French feminism, postmodernism, and postcolonialism, as well as methodologies from the humanities, the social sciences, and the natural sciences. To compound this complexity, for feminist composition scholars, theory and research inform and are informed by classroom practices. What, for example, are the implications of adopting certain theories or methodologies for our students and ourselves? What obligations do we have in speaking for and with others? What forces shape the rhetorical ability to name "others" in the classroom? To locate ourselves in our research? To define intellectual property within and beyond the academy? What role does ethics play in our practice, and who determines what is ethical? Whose "truths" do we ask our students to seek? How can different feminisms help students and ourselves methodologically and theoretically challenge dominant systems of representation? What forms of writing could this foster? As the following essays illustrate, responses differ. Nonetheless, by critiquing prevalent composition practices, often by noting the absence or apparent misrepresentation of gender-informed analyses, feminist composition scholars share a goal of articulating theoretical and methodological practices that better address feminists' concerns. This re-articulation is evident in the following essays.

Joy Ritchie opens this section by calling for a stronger connection between feminist theory and practice. Foregrounding pedagogical practice, Ritchie argues that for our teaching to be meaningful to students, we cannot maintain the either-or thinking of binaries such as intellect-reason-theory versus emotion-experience-practice. Instead, Ritchie calls for both-and thinking that cannot separate theory from practice. Susan Jarratt similarly wrestles with and challenges "essential" ways of labeling and representing. Rather than advocate a pedagogy that engages the essentialism–social constructivism debate as Ritchie does, Jarratt draws on postcolonial theory. By examining the dilemma of representing and speaking for others—in large part by attending to how "others" are made to speak—Jarratt argues that teachers should reflect on their own practice, as well as help students understand the many rhetorical constructions of themselves and others.

Andrea Lunsford also focuses on feminist rhetorical constructions, in this case on changing constructions of authorship and intellectual property. Although Lunsford has long challenged originary notions of a solitary author, she is decidedly uneasy about recent legal and corporate efforts to reimagine authorship as intellectual property. As Lunsford makes clear, these constructions of authorship and the decisions about who owns the resulting "property" should concern composition scholars. Urging us to pay attention to the commercialization of intellectual property, Lunsford turns to feminist theory to develop alternative models of textual ownership that would safeguard free access to and exchange of information.

While Ritchie, Jarratt, and Lunsford all draw on theory to rethink practices in and beyond the classroom, Lynn Worsham explicitly cautions against too easily absorbing prevailing theories without first examining the implications. Specifically addressing the limits of French feminist theory for composition pedagogy, Worsham argues that compositionists' attempts to harness *écriture féminine* have been misguided: Either *écriture féminine*'s call for radical change will challenge or dismantle the university or, more likely, the institutional positioning of composition itself will domesticate and therefore radically alter *écriture féminine*. Without reaching a consensus, these articles examine feminists' responses to the promise and perils of adapting current theories to the classroom.

A second group of articles in this part focuses on research methodology. While the methods vary, each of these articles explores the politics of knowledge making by examining the implications of conducting and interpreting research. In the earliest article, Patricia A. Sullivan argues that composition research has been too slow in examining how gender informs writing. Analyzing research and teaching practices, classroom and mentoring experiences, and student and published writing, Sullivan details the pervasive androcentrism within composition studies. To remedy this bias, Sullivan foregrounds the importance of asking how gender may shape the meaning of a writing situation.

Gesa Kirsch and Joy Ritchie also offer alternative ways of making meaning within composition studies by probing a different research practice, the practice of locating the "personal" within public discourse. Examining the politics of locating ourselves—and others—in our work, Kirsch and Ritchie challenge research practices that merely claim the personal as a site from which to speak. To avoid essentializing others or forwarding master narratives, Kirsch and Ritchie argue for methods that problematize and expand our assessments of these locations within cultural and ideological frameworks. Invoking feminist research from several disciplines, Kirsch and Ritchie challenge composition researchers to scrutinize their research practices, to think about who has the privilege to conduct and interpret research and what responsibilities go along with that privilege. This, they contend, may encourage researchers to address different ethical questions, such as the implications of the personal in research.

Jacqueline Jones Royster similarly focuses on ethics as she puts forward a methodology based on what she calls an afrafeminist ideology. Enacting this ideology requires researchers to balance ethical behavior with sound scholarly practice. Researchers do this, in part, by positioning themselves as members of both their academic and research communities. In negotiating a role between these communities, researchers inhabit an "in-between" space where they may be better able to make new meanings, to question who should be the audiences and the agents of scholarly work, and to advance research methodologies that both privilege and question researchers' analytical frameworks, passionate attachments, ethical actions, and social responsibilities.

In positing a new methodology and implicitly challenging more traditional research methodologies, Royster articulates a growing trend in recent feminist research in the history of rhetoric, as Patricia Bizzell makes clear. Acknowledging the role emotion may play in research practices, Bizzell argues that instead of traditionally defined universal "truth," many feminist researchers seek relative truths as defined by both the academy and the participants affected by the research. To acknowledge their situatedness within and allegiance to both of these communities, Bizzell details a "hybrid" methodology that allows these researchers to use traditional academic methods for nontraditional ends. Highlighting the complexity of research and offering strategies for feminist compositionists to ethically engage in meaning making, each of these articles challenges and expands the ways composition researchers make meaning.

In the final selection, Joy Ritchie and Barbara DiBernard reflect on how theory and research shape and are shaped by the personal lives of their authors. This sentiment—echoed in Ritchie's engagement with a women's literature class, Kirsch and Ritchie's locating themselves as researchers, Lunsford's personal desire for collaboration, and Royster's call to acknowledge our passionate attachments to our research—reinforces the falseness of prevalent binaries such as the personal versus the academic. By challenging false representations and producing alternatives, the essays in this section encourage us to examine the complexity of feminist work and illustrate how theory and research enrich and animate that work.

6

Confronting the "Essential" Problem: Reconnecting Feminist Theory and Pedagogy

JOY S. RITCHIE

In the current flowering of feminist writing, there is considerable debate about essentialism and constructivism. One consequence of this debate has been to divide feminist theorists and feminist teachers. On one side, feminist theorists assume that feminist pedagogy is "essentialist" because it often seems to be founded on an ahistorical, uncritical celebration of a fixed female position, a stance many theorists find reductive and dangerous. On the other side, feminist teachers often assume that to "do" theory, to explore the linguistic, social, and political construction of women as gendered subjects, is to participate in an esoteric activity (at best) and an activity tainted by reliance on male methodology and philosophy (at worst). Therefore, despite the fundamental feminist assertion that knowledge cannot be separated from the knower, many feminist academicians continue to operate within a binary perspective, placing intellect against emotion, separating reason from experience, and, ultimately, setting theory against practice. As a result, important connections between feminist theory and practice are masked, and we lose sight of our common purposes.

Furthermore, we lose sight of our students. Adrienne Rich observes that "it is easier, especially for academically trained white women, to get an intellectual/political 'fix' on the *idea* of racism than to identify with black female experience: to explore it emotionally as part of our own" ("Disloyal" 281). I believe this split among feminists occurs, in part, because it has also been easier for academically trained feminists to get a "fix" on abstract theories of gender construction than to explore the immediate implications of these theories for the lives of women students. While we have a profusion of feminist theoretical writing and a profusion of writing about feminist teaching and learning, we have little writing that seeks to connect the two or that demonstrates what might be the impact of feminist teaching and feminist theory on the lives of students in our composition and literature classes.

From *Journal of Advanced Composition* 10 (1990): 249–73.

To begin exploring what these connections might be and how feminist teaching and theory might influence students' lives, I became a participant-observer in an undergraduate women's literature class taught by my colleague, Barbara DiBernard, a feminist teacher.[1] I was attempting to understand how students' experience in such a class might differ from their experience in other reading and writing classes, and, also, attempting to reconcile for myself some of the profound and troubling divisions I saw between the positions of feminist teachers and feminist theorists in academia.

Literary education has traditionally been justified by the claim that literature provides a mirror in which readers may examine the human experience and come to understand better their place within it. But women have been absent or invisible in that mirror. Thus, the attempt of women's literature classes has been to provide a new mirror filled with images of women and to help women arrive at a new definition of their human identity, one of presence rather than absence, of power rather than lack. In Barbara's class, I observed women taking part in literary study, in a process of reclaiming women's literature and history. But they were also examining social, political, and personal definitions of themselves as women. In short, they were exploring a central issue of current feminist theory—their own interpretation of gender construction in our culture.

The reality of the feminist classroom, as I observed and participated in it, demonstrates that the split between feminist theory and practice is artificial. In the women's literature class, the explicit agenda of feminist literary theory—to examine the symbolic and social-political structures that construct women as gendered subjects—also became the students' agenda. Although most students would shun the label "feminist" for themselves, the questions they explored in the women's literature class arose from the same basic question that academic feminists—theorists, critics, and teachers—have been exploring for two or three decades. And for these students, pursuing this problem was fraught with as much conflict as it is for feminist teachers and theorists. Carol voiced the feelings of a number of students: "I'm not sure how to absorb this way of thinking about women. I've never faced it before. I don't like all the anger and bitterness in this class. If this is what feminism is about, I'm not sure I want any part of it. It's really bothering me."

As I participated in the course, I was struck by the number of students who experienced conflicts as they read, wrote about, and discussed literature. The women in the course, aged nineteen to fifty, were frustrated and angry for a variety of reasons: at having their old myths challenged, at the contradictions that they began to see in their lives, at other women's denial and passivity, and at their own failures. But the tension that resulted in many class sessions was a version of the feminist community's longstanding debates.

The contradictions and questions that the students explored are inextricably connected to the central questions discussed by feminist theorists today. For both students and their feminist teachers, these questions arise from the problem Simone de Beauvoir articulated over forty years ago:

> If we . . . admit, provisionally, that women do exist, then we must face the question: what is a woman?
>
> . . . If I wish to define myself, I must first of all say: "I am a woman"; on this truth must be based all further discussion. A man never begins by presenting himself as an individual of a certain sex; it goes without saying that he is a man. (xvii)

The problem seems deceptively simple. But as the course progressed, the students became aware that asserting one's identity as a woman necessitates more than a joyous celebration of womanhood. Embedded within de Beauvoir's question are social, economic, political, linguistic, aesthetic, epistemological, and ethical questions. Students confronted the traditions that have positioned them as women and that they had consequently accepted as universal givens not to be questioned. The literature they read led them to acknowledge the immediate contradictions in their own political and social positions as women and to examine the historical consequences of these contradictions for their mothers and foremothers.

Initially, many students articulated a narrow, fixed "essentialist" female identity, but the dialogic nature of the class continually challenged this view by highlighting contradictory images of women. The perspectives of white, black, and Native American women, from the fifteenth century to the present, lesbian women, old and young, divorced and married women, childless women and women with children, poor women and privileged women—all these were articulated in the literature and, equally powerfully, in the voices of students themselves. Thus, the class became a rich source of multiple definitions of women that were continually posited, affirmed, examined, challenged, discarded, and rearticulated. The image of women that emerged in the class was not the singular, fixed, and universal image of the humanist mirror; instead, the course projected varied images in a multidimensional mirror; images that were not infinite duplications but each a variation, contradiction, or transformation of women's identity. As Amy's words suggest, the result was a changed vision of herself and the world, a vision so powerful that the old images were permanently transformed:

> I really had no idea of what to expect from this class. I just needed another class. I thought it would just be another English class, but when I first glanced at the required texts, I about gagged. Before this course I never really thought much about women, their history, their art, or even how my mother or grandma or I lived our lives. It was just not there. The class helped me take on a whole different way of looking at my family, my education, even my relationship with my boyfriend—the different points of view of a lot of people. These stories and poems and books have opened up a whole new way of seeing myself and the world. I won't be able to see it in the old way again.

The process that students experienced as they recognized and reexamined multiple perspectives on women's subjectivity suggests a crucial connection between theory and practice.

I would like to examine this process through the students' experience and view it in relation to the essentialism-constructivism debate in feminism. Using excerpts from students' journals and their comments in class discussions and interviews, I will trace their exploration of the contradictory and conflicting social-sexual identities that the class presented. I will examine their answers to the question "What is a woman?" and point to connections between questions that they wrestled with and fundamental issues that feminist theory examines. Finally, I'll argue that the power of this experience to change *what* students think and *how* they think presents us with insight for revisioning our discipline. The critical activity of examining and articulating women's positions as gendered subjects can serve as a model for education in composition and literature, an alternative to the one-dimensional critical processes that academia often promotes.

THE TEACHER-MIDWIFE: TEACHING FROM A FEMINIST PERSPECTIVE

The first assigned reading was an article on feminist teaching that Barbara had written. Barbara believed that sharing her philosophy of teaching from the outset of the class was consistent with her desire to help them see "teaching as a political act." During the first class session, she talked about why the class was important to her:

> As professors, we may like to think we're off in some ivory tower, but someone is making a decision about what to teach and what to leave out, about how we get information. That is a political decision. I realize that my college education was characterized by silences. Women's voices were not a part of the literature I read, and many women, including myself, were silent because we were not comfortable with the combative, hierarchical nature of those classes.

Barbara wanted to create a different kind of atmosphere, allowing students access to women's writing, offering them the historical and social perspective that women's literature allows, and breaking down "the hierarchical views that denigrate the ways in which many women have expressed their experience" (DiBernard 3). She also wanted students to see beyond the view of human experience that mainstream Western European tradition depicts, to understand that our experience in that tradition is not universal. Women's literature, she said, gives us access to different experiences that encompass women from other social classes, age groups, races and ethnic backgrounds, sexual orientations, and ablebodiedness. She wanted students to reexamine their definitions of art by looking at poetry and novels, but also by thinking about women's letters, journals, and quilts as art forms. Furthermore, she wanted students to develop modes of reading and analyzing literature that would allow them to rely on their own experience and to consider multiple perspectives and methods of response. She believed that students who are not encouraged to take themselves seriously as intellectuals, to recognize their own capacity to solve problems, cannot be expected to take responsibility for bringing about change. She summarized her own role as that of teacher-midwife: "one who helps students give birth to their own ideas, to integrate the personal and the academic, and to empower themselves as readers and critics."

The class structure reflected this philosophy. Students wrote a reading-response journal for each week's assigned reading. Barbara explained that daily work is the kind of work women are most in touch with, and that doing daily work also "keeps us in touch with our own perceptions, reactions, and responses and allows us to journey back through the course to see ourselves, our former selves, because we will be different by the end of the semester." During almost every class, students did some sort of writing connected to the reading, and they worked in small groups to share ideas and questions and to bring them to the whole class. They also participated in activities in the university and the wider community and wrote papers on these activities. Barbara asked them to learn one another's names, to listen to one another, to support and encourage one another in their work, and to be patient and tolerant of others' ideas, something that was not always easy given the questions that students began struggling with. At the beginning of the semester, Barbara told me:

> I don't expect everyone to be comfortable. Some students will be upset by some of the texts. Some will be very angry, especially during the first few weeks. But I hope they'll hang on with enough trust to keep coming and reading and listening. I want them to learn information, but I want them to arrive at their own conclusions about literature and, more important, to become confident in themselves as learners and to think about their lives.

THE PROBLEM OF ESSENCE: WHAT IS A WOMAN?

This question has set the agenda for feminist theory for twenty years, but it and a constellation of surrounding questions also lie at the heart of the students' experience in the class. Their responses to the question ranged from affirmation, recognition, and celebration to anger, contestation, and revision of their understanding of themselves as women. For feminist teachers and theorists, the pursuit of de Beauvoir's question has raised serious epistemological, philosophical, and political conflicts that parallel those of the women students. Before considering students' responses, I want to outline some of these theoretical questions in order to illuminate better the complexity of the conflicts that they faced.

De Beauvoir's question has pointed feminists toward an examination of the social, economic, and linguistic structures that give meaning to the biological sex differences that have traditionally defined women. As they attempt to analyze these questions, feminist theorists take philosophical perspectives that result in complicated and often indistinctly defined political and theoretical divisions. These divisions often fall under such labels as liberal, radical, cultural, socialist, Anglo-American, French, and poststructuralist feminism.[2]

Each of these theoretical strands falls somewhere along a continuum on which gender is defined according to essentialist or constructivist paradigms. In an attempt to define essentialism, Linda Alcoff points out that women have always been seen as "essential"—easily defined, captured, always apprehendable as the object of male definition (258). Thus, as Alcoff notes, from the beginning of the women's movement, women have felt compelled to redefine their history, biology, psychology, literature, and epistemology as separate from the circumscribed definition that the masculine patriarchal tradition imposes. American feminists, in particular, have attempted to end the erasure and powerlessness that characterize women's place in the social order and to affirm women, selfhood, and community. In American academic institutions, women's studies courses have grown out of this tradition and, to the extent that such courses are perceived as subscribing to an essentialist position, they have become theoretically suspect. For as women articulate and celebrate what is intrinsically "female," they risk coming full circle to the very psychobiological determinism—the "essentialism"—that has circumscribed women for so long. When women make a claim for a unique and powerful female identity, they are left once again in a traditional binary, oppositional position: male versus female, power versus lack.

Central to the problem of gender definition and the essentialist-constructivist issue is the problem of language itself. Working out of a psychoanalytic tradition, French feminists connect women's oppression to the symbolic forms in which they have been represented. Language, arising from the phallic-patriarchal order, has controlled the way that women's biological and social position is defined. Thus, in a sense, women have not had a language for articulating their identities apart from the language of patriarchy, a language that binds them into definitions of self that they cannot escape. Julia Kristeva points out that "as soon as the insurgent . . . speaks, it gets caught up in the discourses allowed by and submitted to the Law" ("From Ithaca" 511). Thus, the methodology and language that women use in the process of defining themselves are grounded in and tainted by the very structures that they are attempting to subvert ("Il n'y a pas" 134–35).

One theoretical solution to this dilemma, posited by radical feminists such as Mary Daly, is to create a new language, a new symbolic order separate from that offered by the male tradition. This new language, they suggest, is necessary to help women rediscover their true feminine essence—beneath the misdefinitions and perversions that male culture has perpetrated—and to develop a truly female culture. French feminists Hélène Cixous and Luce Irigaray are also linked to this essentialist position, proposing that the symbolic formations in which women have been fixed as "other" be fractured and destructured. Cixous proposes that female energy and imagination be celebrated, and Irigaray proposes that phallocentric categories be displaced through a continual reconnection of the female to the female body. While these positions are essentialist, they also arise from an awareness of the role that language and culture play in constructing women's identity; thus, they force an acknowledgment of "woman" as a political position. In this respect, Cixous and Irigaray are less aligned with essentialist theorists and more aligned with feminist theorists working from Marxist, psychoanalytic, and poststructuralist theories, theorists who hold that the "authentic self" — conceived by Western humanist tradition as existing below a veneer of ideology and cultural socialization — is merely a construct, part of the "apparatus" that the culture uses to maintain the individual in a "subjected" position, inscribed by ideology.

They argue that because human beings are constructed by the social discourse surrounding them, the concept of a special female essence is also a fiction, part of a binary system of discourse — male/female, culture/nature — to be dismantled and deconstructed. Thus, as Kristeva argues, if woman's position is a shifting social construction, then the only effective feminist position is one of negativity: "A woman cannot 'be'; it is something which does not even belong in the order of *being*. It follows that a feminist practice can only be negative, at odds with what already exists, so that we may say, 'That's not it' and 'that's still not it'" ("Woman" 137). Kristeva rejects discussions of woman's identity and calls for discussions of "woman" as a position within language. She offers women the possibility of what Alcoff describes as "the 'free-play' of gender, of plurality and difference unhampered by predetermined gender identity" (270). But as many feminists argue, these positions do not offer women a clear direction for changing the political and social realities of their lives. The essentialist position leaves women trapped in a separate, idealistic, but ultimately powerless position as "other"; the constructivist position leaves women in an eternally fluid position of indeterminacy or in a position of negativity, constantly rejecting and deconstructing but also risking invisibility and the possibility for action and change.

This theoretical thicket might leave feminists paralyzed, but the very diversity of positions within feminism, what Paul Smith describes as the "internal heterogeneity of the feminist discourse" (138), points toward an understanding of women's identity that does not rely on binary positions of essentialism or constructivism. The strength of feminism is its ability to hold in tension an array of theoretical and practical perspectives and, thus, to arrive at a clearer understanding of the varied nature of women's positions.

While I do not intend to suggest that their positions are the same, Gayatri Spivak, Jane Gallop, and Teresa de Lauretis posit a "both/and" perspective that recognizes the complexity of women's identity. Such a perspective has allowed me to interpret more clearly the contradictory and conflict-filled experience of the students as they attempted to understand their position as women in our culture. For example, while Spivak opposes an "essential feminism," she argues that if we allow for the multiplicity of women's identities, we must acknowledge the role that women's experience of their bodies — and especially the subjugation of women's bodies by men — plays in shaping women's identities. Thus, she argues that women must "take the risk of essence" in order to increase the possibility of substantive resistance (150). In short, the claim of "essence" is a beginning point of contestation, but Spivak demands a continual process of historicization, even for those who posit an identity defined by the female body; any claim of women's identity must be analyzed in light of the multiple historical and social circumstances in which women live their lives.

In a similar vein, Gallop argues for multiple definitions, continually redefined:

> Both psychoanalysis and feminism can be seen as efforts to call into question a rigid identity that cramps and binds. But both also tend to want to produce a 'new identity,' one that will now be adequate and authentic. . . . I do not believe in some 'new identity' which would be adequate and authentic. But I do not seek some sort of liberation from identity. That would lead only to another form of paralysis . . . of undifferentiation. Identity must be continually assumed and immediately called into question. (xii)

De Lauretis argues that women's subjectivity can best be defined through a continual analysis of the contextual conditions and contradictions inherent in social life. An understanding of subjectivity lies

> not in femininity as a privileged nearness to nature, the body, or the unconscious . . . not in female tradition simply understood as private, marginal, and yet intact . . . not finally in the chinks and cracks of masculinity, the fissures of male identity . . . but rather in that political, theoretical, self-analyzing practice by which the relations of the subject in social reality can be rearticulated from the historical experience of women. (*Alice* 186)

De Lauretis further describes a concept of women's identity that is neither fixed, powerless essence nor endlessly dissolving and invisible, but multiple and changing within a social, linguistic, and political context and that has agency because of its reflective, self-analyzing power (*Feminist* 8–9). I believe this process can be seen clearly at work in the experience of students in the women's literature class.

Theoretical debates among academic feminists are complex and subtle (more complex and subtle, certainly, than I've presented them here). And because many feminists see them as peripheral to the goals of women's literature courses, they keep these political and theoretical conflicts in the professional closet, separate from their students and classrooms. Barbara's students were undergraduates, not feminist theorists or critics, yet the questions that emerged as they read and wrote about women's literature have a clear resonance with the problems that feminist theorists debate in professional meetings and publications.

Pursuing these questions, students engaged in a critical examination of the nature of language and its role in constituting women and their subjectivity; they considered aesthetic questions about the nature of art and literature; and they explored problems of racism and class, political power, and ethical responsibility. But they did not simply explore these questions on an abstract level; rather, they found themselves inevitably drawn into an examination of their own experience, the historical conditions surrounding their lives, and the dissonance inherent in them. These women began to recognize themselves as the outsider, as "other." Confronting contradictory views of themselves was painful and difficult for many, impossible for a few, and reaffirming for others. I want to avoid suggesting that all the women had the same response to the class or that every student went through a series of stages or transformations during the semester. Although they experienced the class in a variety of ways, it allowed them, some for the first time, to see the conflict between images of themselves as women that they confront daily (that some had accepted uncritically throughout their lives) and their actual experience as students, members of families, and people who participate in a network of social relationships. For some students, the class affirmed or clarified conflicts they had already recognized as women in our culture. The analysis of those contradictions, framed in a classroom taught according to feminist pedagogy, was the central feature in the students' experience. It demanded that they practice a new form of critical thinking and that they develop a new stance toward their own experience, toward other women, and, ultimately, toward knowledge and truth.

DENIAL AND RESISTANCE: DETHRONING THE MYTH OF FEMININITY

Adrienne Rich writes:

> A radical critique of literature, feminist in its impulse, would take the work first of all as a clue to how we live, how we have been living, how we have been led to imagine ourselves, how our language has trapped as well as liberated us, how the very act of naming has been till now a male prerogative, and how we can begin to see and name—and therefore live—afresh. ("When We Dead" 35)

From the first week, the class focused on the way women have been trapped by the myths and "names" that culture circumscribes them in, determining even the way women think about themselves. Students read the stories of Eve and Pandora and several contemporary women poets' revisions of these myths. Many students reacted with confusion and anger, demonstrating immediately the contradictions they experienced between the poets' views of women and the notion of femininity they had always accepted. Here are two students' comments:

> BEV: What's the big deal? So I'm a woman. This isn't sexism; it's just tradition or biology. Why are we making a big deal about women's differences from men? We're all human beings.
>
> CAROL: Why do we have to look at the negative aspects of womanhood? I've always been treated fairly, gotten what I deserved. I can't say I've been discriminated against. Of course there were times when school officials would seem more interested in the football players or would select more guys than girls for academic teams, but it was just something to live with. That's just the way things are and have always been.

Like other women in the class, Bev and Carol held the view that "male" and "female" are fixed biological and social-psychological categories that resist examination. Paradoxically, they also believed that differences between male and female held few social or political consequences for people's lives. They resisted Barbara's attempts to point out that these distinctions promote a circumscribed and negative identity for women.

In general, the readings ignited intense discussion and evoked anger, resistance, and denial. For example, several students thought Stevie Smith's "How Cruel Is the Story of Eve," and other poems about Eve and Pandora, were "trashing men" and "putting down" traditional religious beliefs. Jennifer argued in class discussion, "That's not fair to the Bible. It's the authority of my life and I choose to believe what I believe and no one can change that." And Carol wrote in her journal about the danger and discomfort of talking about such ideas:

> I want to figure out why these women are so angry. Does it have any validity? Isn't there some possibility that women have been happy in some part of their lives, their history? If the object is to open our eyes to the oppression of women, then I'm not sure I want to be a part of it. Isn't it possible that men aren't always happy with their lives? They can't experience bearing a child—is that discrimination? I worry that I'll end up hating men.

Carol was not simply denying the identity that language and cultural myths had inscribed for her. She assumed a deterministic, essentialist position for women, believing that male and female roles are biological and should not be questioned. In this "common-sense" stance, Carol and others participated in the erasure of their own experience as they discounted the power of social structures to position them as females in society. They believed that their situations in academia and society were "inevitable," and they were uncomfortable with any contradiction of these beliefs.

Anger and Recognition: When We Dead Awaken

While some students denied that being a woman had consequences for them, others responded with recognition and anger. Amy wrote the following journal entry in response to these lines from Stevie Smith's poem about Eve: "He must make woman lower then / So he can be higher then."

> When I read those lines, my mind began to race. Time and time again, I come across events that seem to make women lower than men. When I first came to college I was enrolled in architecture, but now I am in civil engineering. Nonetheless, people (usually male, although some narrow-minded females tend to do the same) respond with much surprise. They cannot believe that a female, the sex which is less intelligent, is an engineering major. I am supposed to be submissive, a follower, basically a shadow of all males.

Recognizing her experience in these poems, Amy acknowledged that rigidly prescribed definitions of female subjectivity had affected her life. In contrast to Carol, Amy and other women recounted with anger the circumstances of their lives. Bonnie, a business major, spoke most vehemently: "Yes, this anger has validity. I'm thirty-eight years old, and I've seen sexism and discrimination in my own life, in my mother's life. I've seen it in the way I was raised, in my first marriage, and even still in my sons. We still send the boys out to play football and the girls to the kitchen."

To encourage the students to analyze their roles as women and to ground their reading in an examination of their own history and experience, Barbara asked them to do a response writing: "A number of you have pointed out that what we're talking about here is the powerful role language has in shaping our view of ourselves. Think about your own experience. Does language matter?" Students wrote their responses to Barbara's question and then shared them with other members of the class. For an hour and a half they poured out stories—of classes in which professors told them, "Don't worry about your grade; just stay home and have babies"; of art and history classes that ignored women's contributions to their culture; of myths that led them to feel embarrassed about their bodies and religious groups that would not allow women to participate fully. They spoke of the effects of language in families with grandparents who felt that women should be in the kitchen, about construction workers and fraternity men who yelled demeaning comments at them as they walked across campus, of films that left them embarrassed to be women.

Many feminist theorists have written about the powerful, even poisonous effects that the language of patriarchy has on women. Mary summarized its effect on her life in words that echo theirs: "I feel like all my life I have been brainwashed, like something was poisoning me without my knowing it, and it makes me angry." Bonnie also acknowledged her anger: "To change, you have to have it brought before your brain or you will stay with the status quo. The anger and bitterness are necessary." As Bonnie pointed out, anger allows women to begin to be truthful about their lives and provides momentum for change.

Carolyn Heilbrun says that women have often been dishonest in examining their lives, even in their autobiographies. She continues, "And, above all other prohibitions, what has been forbidden to women is anger, together with the open admission of the desire for power and control over one's life. . . . Nostalgia . . . is likely to be a mask for unrecognized anger" (13–15). Thus, the contradictions that some students resisted and glossed over with nostalgia or denial became a point of anger and recognition.

While some women found a beginning point for registering resistance against culturally prescribed identity, Carol and others refused to accept what they saw as a negative, critical view of gender relations. But at the same time, Carol was beginning to acknowledge the possibility of other perspectives. During the third week of class, she wrote in her journal:

> I'm getting extremely frustrated with this class because I'm realizing there is no right or wrong answer here. It's all opinions. That's why I like journalism, because you just deal with facts. But I suppose if I can organize my beliefs and formulate my own opinion about this whole "woman" issue, then I will have gained a great deal from this course. Right now, I'm not sure what I think, what my religion would think.

Although Carol was uncertain about the definition of women's experience she would accept, the class was providing her with a new way of thinking about women's identity. She also recognized an epistemology radically different from the dualistic one she experienced elsewhere in her academic life. In the first few class sessions, this course suggested to her that there were multiple perspectives to take into account in answering the question "What does it mean to be a woman?" Something in this process also suggested that she possessed the capacity to formulate answers, and she seemed almost willing to claim agency for herself.

Part of Carol's struggle is an echo, albeit a naive and paradoxical one, of the debate among feminists about defining women's subjectivity. She believed woman's position is "just the way things are," a natural part of the universal order. At the same time, she also resisted the view that women's history consists entirely of tragic oppression. She was moving toward a recognition of the contradiction in her position that female experience is "naturally" determined. In the literature and voices of women in class, she saw mounting evidence that women have been frustrated and angry in the roles prescribed for them by "the natural order." Paradoxically, Carol wanted to believe that women do possess agency and the responsibility to act in the world, that they are not simply the product of biology or of the "ideological apparatus" of culture, constructed as man's other.

Taking the Risk of Essence: Celebrating Women

Simone de Beauvoir writes,

> One is not born a woman; one becomes one. . . . The peculiarities that identify her as specifically a woman get their importance from the significance placed upon them. They can be surmounted . . . when they are regarded in new perspectives. (809)

It was toward these new perspectives that the readings pushed students in the next few weeks, particularly as we read *Daughters of Copper Woman,* Judy Grahn's *Common Woman* poems, and Alice Walker's "In Search of Our Mother's Gardens."

While Carol, Amy, and other students were articulating resistance, anger, and recognition in the face of contradictions between the image of woman they had come to accept and those the course was revealing, they needed to place women's identity in a new perspective in order to move beyond denial and anger to productive action. In *Daughters of Copper Woman,* Ann Cameron's version of stories told to her by northwest Native American women (a female mythology-history of a matrilineal culture), students experienced the affirmation that women are creative and powerful and can produce a culture that is strong and viable. Jennifer said, "For me it was like reading the Bible, in a woman's form." Amy wrote, "I was envious of those women. They knew where they came from, who they were. Their roles as women were prepared for and celebrated. I wish I were part of a society of women who thought of their bodies and bodily functions as sacred and powerful." And Mary said:

> Suzi in *Copper Woman* reminded me of my years of drug and alcohol dependency, the insanity of my divorce, the splitting up of my children. In all of that I thought I was crazy. But I could relate to her courage. Women all over and through time have been walked on, subservient; they have learned to be strong, to endure, to survive. We are no less.

In her journal, Carol summarized the shift of the class mood: "The discussion was so much more positive. Up until now there has been a lot of bitterness and disagreement in class. This book made us all feel better about ourselves as women."

Discussion of *Copper Woman* allowed students to continue examining women's place in our culture, but it did so by holding up the mirror of an alternative woman's culture, of strong, proud, clever, wise, and enduring women. As Patrocinio Schweickart says, "As women have come to examine women's literature, not just the traditional male canon, a different reading task emerges for us and for our students. We no longer must occupy ourselves with . . . the negative hermeneutic of ideological unmasking" (51). That is, we can also engage in the task of recovering, exploring, and articulating literature that elaborates women's point of view and celebrates their strength, endurance, and wisdom. This more affirming task, Schweickart says, allows a woman "to read without condemning herself to the position of 'other'" (51).

The celebration of women continued as students read Walker's and Grahn's affirmations of artistry and richness in women's everyday lives. Amy wrote her own "Common Woman" poem, in which she celebrated herself and her capabilities. Many students wrote about the art that they had never fully appreciated—their mothers', aunts', and grandmothers' artistry. Carol wrote: "My grandmother makes quilts, and she has a love for flowers and always keeps a roomful. I think my grandma's most creative outlet is through cooking. She makes the most wonderful Czech pastries and bread. I believe cooking can be an art form, and my grandma is the Renoir of cooking!"

In the academic community, women's literature and women's studies courses have gained a negative reputation for this sort of celebratory affirmation of women, although the purpose of such celebrations is to reverse the effects of centuries of erasure by restoring to women their history and literature and by allowing them to become participants rather than bystanders in history and culture. For some academicians, this celebration represents an uncritical, emotional, and anti-intellectual approach to literature and art. But, in some circumstances, it is equally criticized by feminist theorists because it asserts a coherent, biologically defined identity and because it fails to acknowledge the social and political contradictions in which women live.

Yet those who criticize this process have only seen it in isolation from the total intellectual and social dynamic of the course, a context that allowed for celebration and affirmation but also always demanded the reconsideration and decentering of women's identity. Having recognized themselves in the position of "other," defined and circumscribed by their culture, students needed to move away from the negative critique, to stand back from the "unmasking" of myths and language that they had first engaged in. Part of the process is to "take the risk of essence," as Spivak argues women must. The search for identity demands that woman's position as "other" be recognized. That recognition in itself takes women into an "essentialist" position. But that should be only a temporary point. The process of defining oneself as female doesn't stop with the assertion of essence. As Annette Kolodny says, the process is "female consciousness turning in upon itself attempting to grasp the deepest condition of its own unique and multiplicitous realities, in the hope, eventually, of altering the very forms through which the culture perceives, expresses, and knows itself" (159). The women's class provided an environment in which students could first take the risk of asserting an identity, a process necessary to self-definition, but it also provided that this assertion was never separated from an examination of the immediate social, historical, and political conditions in which one lays claim to a particular identity. Furthermore, it allowed the continual challenge and reexamination of those definitions and consideration of other perspectives.

RECOGNIZING CONTRADICTIONS: ANGER IS FOLLOWING US AROUND

It was not possible to sustain affirmation and celebration for long. As students went on to read Margery Kempe's "On Female Celibacy," Anne Bradstreet's poems, and essays by Virginia Woolf and Adrienne Rich, they recognized that the contradictions inherent in these women's writing and in their own lives are always lurking in the corner at every celebration.

Reading Bradstreet, Woolf, and Kempe on the heels of *Daughters of Copper Woman* was difficult for some students because even though they tried to consider the conditions under which each author lived and wrote, some were angry and disappointed with the contradictions they saw. Kempe's mystical religious enthusiasm seemed to contradict any image of women resisting authoritarian and patriarchal institutions, despite her repudiation of the sexual responsibilities of marriage and her exhortations against Church fathers. In Bradstreet's writing, contradictory swings between self-effacement and self-assertion also confused them. The tensions in Woolf's writing and life—her patrician, intellectual background, her radical perspective on women and society, and her eventual suicide—didn't match some students' expectations that women writers should be unambiguous exemplars of stability and strength. In one contentious class discussion, several students said they felt that Bradstreet, Woolf, and even Kempe were weak and "waffling," caving in to the established religious authority and abdicating to their husbands and social norms. "They were playing it 'safe,'" Betty said. "I think Kempe really was something of a freak," Karin said. "Why didn't they just rise up and do what they wanted to do?" Betty argued.

While Barbara attempted to help them recognize the contradictions they were experiencing, it was other students who spoke about the clear representation of the reality of women's lives that they found in Bradstreet and others. They recognized that women sometimes are able to resist and subvert social structures, but also sometimes negotiate or acquiesce in order to survive. Reading these writers, they began to view women's identity as a constant movement between shifting identities as the social context makes varying demands. But they also saw how women who become critically aware of conflicts refuse to live totally within the myth of a unified femininity. Woolf, Bradstreet, and Kempe located points at which they could resist and subvert the identities in which they had been circumscribed. Bonnie and Amy spoke about the double-bind women are often placed in and the multiple identities they often assume. Both women recognized that even in their own "liberated" circumstances with access to jobs and education, they often seemed ambivalent, made compromises, and felt alienated. Amy wrote in her journal:

> I feel I can tell you what's going on because it relates to what Woolf is saying about women writers and what Rich is saying about Woolf. Women are still only allowed to be a certain way. Like Woolf says, women cannot sound angry or write about their feelings. It made them bitter and angry and depressed, and I know what that's like. Last night my boyfriend said he was scared about our relationship because I had gotten an "A" on the calculus test and he hadn't. Chauvinistic! I could not believe that he could think that as a male he should automatically do better than me. I have had to deal with this all my life. What does this say about our society? It really makes me mad.

Bonnie spoke about "warping herself" to fit into male and female expectations: "Pretty soon you don't even know who you really are, because you've spent so much time sort of pulling yourself in here and then pushing yourself that way, tailoring yourself this way and that into something that's prim and proper." During class discussion, she said: "I can sympathize with Bradstreet. It isn't that easy. I feel uncomfortable when I'm the only woman out of fifty in accounting or management class. I wonder if I really ought to be there, if I'm capable of doing the work. I find myself keeping quiet a lot. I find it's not hard to be invisible." Mary added, "I have to fight this doubt all the time, wondering if I'm smart enough. I feel sometimes in classes like my ideas are way out on a limb. Sometimes I do risk saying something, but a lot of times I realize I'm playing the academic game, and for me that means playing it by men's rules."

These women understand the untenable position they are in. On one hand, they can submit to accepted ways of thinking and speaking, give themselves over to the symbol systems of the patriarchy. The alternative, to refuse to participate, forces them back once again to the margins of language and power. Bonnie and Amy pointed out the necessity of articulating women's experience in order to establish a point of resistance. Carol wrote in her journal that week: "I remember a line from *Copper Woman:* 'Who sees the other half of Self sees truth.' That applies to what we've been discussing in this class. We need to be able to see all sides of ourselves. Is it so bad to recognize who and what we are?"

ACKNOWLEDGING DIVERSITY: SPEAKING THE UNSPOKEN

In one of her most famous speeches, Sojourner Truth says:

> That man over there says that women need to be helped into carriages, and lifted over ditches, and to have the best place everywhere. Nobody ever helps me into carriages, or over mud-puddles, or gives me any best place! And ain't I a woman? (253)

If reading Bradstreet and Woolf evoked the contradictions in women's experience, the writing of black, lesbian, and Native American writers and the presence of these women in class intensified the increasingly complex view of women's subjectivity. These women were loud reminders that to speak of a universal woman's experience is to erase the effects of racism, economic and social deprivation, and discrimination arising from differences in women's sexual orientation.

These students' voices, coupled with reading Toni Morrison, Leslie Silko, Gertrude Stein, Adrienne Rich, Audre Lorde, and Judy Grahn, brought the diversity of women's experience to the fore. Although I noted an increasing rapport and openness in speaking of their lives, I also noted continuing tensions as a few students enunciated diverse perspectives and values. I was also aware that some perspectives were not being articulated at all, though they were simmering in the background. Roberta told me in an interview:

> I was so disgusted the first few classes. I almost felt like dropping out. I had counted so much on finding a comfortable group here. But I couldn't say anything, because I realized my experience, my orientation, is so much different. I know it sounds arrogant, but I felt this class, with all these blind women in it, held nothing for me. I'm learning to deal with other people's realities even though they're in conflict with mine, without compromising myself or hiding the lesbian side of me. I struggle not to hide that side.

Although lesbian women, like Roberta, were a quiet presence in the class, their situations were tacitly evoked by the writing of lesbian writers. Students reacted less with disapproval or disgust than with a sense of strangeness and unfamiliarity. Amy wrote in her journal:

> Oh yuck! I'm sorry, but for the first time this semester, I didn't like what was assigned. Stein was so hard to read and understand. On the other hand, Richardson was very good. I was confused for a bit, but finally understood at the end. It really helped me to think about what it would be like to go through that.

Carol was more ambivalent:

To be honest, I don't really know how to react to these pieces. I'm not sure I understand what's going on in Richardson's "Two Hanged Women." I am uncomfortable with this topic because I don't understand how lesbians feel. It is not for me to decide how people should run their lives or who should sleep in what bed. Although I try to be open-minded about homosexuality, I can't help but stand in disbelief. I am ignorant and I'm not completely sure I want to know. I have talked to a girl on my floor about it. Perhaps this is part of God's plan after all. I want to talk to my priest to find out more. This topic has really given me a chance to think, and this class is giving me a chance to evaluate my previous beliefs and is forcing me to see new perspectives. I like to be challenged to sort a moral question out.

Although students like Roberta may have felt that their experience had to be suppressed, from the beginning the class allowed women to challenge homogenizing pronouncements about women. In other circumstances the "blind women" that Roberta spoke about could have avoided challenges to their perspective, but this class, with its variety of social-sexual orientations, brought students face to face with alternate perspectives. By demonstrating that cherished myths about women do not hold, it challenged students like Amy and Carol to reexamine their values and assumptions about women's lives. As both of these students' journals show, the feminist classroom's focus on the lived experience of women fostered the exploration of differences in a tolerant and safe environment and, in doing so, added another set of images to the mirror in which women see themselves represented.

The most powerful challenge to the homogenizing impulse came from three black women in the class. Jennifer, Anna, and Karin reminded us over and over again that living as black women in a racist society had given them different experiences. Their responses to the writing of black women forced all of us to confront, in more than an intellectual way, what it means to be black in our culture. At the beginning of class discussion of Morrison's *The Bluest Eye,* several students posed the question "What is this Dick and Jane business doing in the story?" This discussion followed:

> **KARIN:** "I grew up with that in school and on television. People of color are faced with those Brady Bunch, blond and blue-eyed images every day of our lives. Black people are just not there. But people think of that as the standard."

> **JENNIFER:** "Yeah, if you're not light and bright, you're not right. That's what the blue eyes mean to Piccola."

> **KARIN:** "Yes, but even if you're light, people want you to behave in a certain way. In high school when I didn't hang out with a lot of the black kids, white people said, 'What's wrong with you? You aren't like a black.' I can't win."

Several white students countered that at least black people had the Jeffersons and Bill Cosby on television, that racism was mostly a thing of the past since black people's lives had improved drastically in the past few years. Jennifer argued, "It's just a pacifier. It's a cover-up, a big white lie. No one wants to watch Bill Cosby because he's black." Another white student asked, "What *do* you want then?" Anna answered:

> I just want people to see me as a person. You can all say anything you want about how things have improved, but the fact still remains that none of you in this class would want to wake up tomorrow morning and be black, Bill Cosby or not. You would probably kill yourself. People right across there in the library will not take money from my hand because it is black.

Anna's words were more persuasive than any intellectual analysis of racism could have been. Carol wrote in her journal: "This was the first time in my life I experienced a black person's anger face to face. What Anna said stunned me. I guess, honestly, I found *The Bluest Eye* pretty horrifying, eye-opening. I never thought about the Dick and Jane mentality until now. A lot of people's lives don't fit that mold."

Confronting racism in this way allowed students to see the wider effects of oppression, to understand the anger they found baffling in some of the writers and the "negative" attitudes they saw in class. The experience was important for students like Amy and Carol, but it was also important for lesbian, black, and older women in the class as an affirmation of their experience and an opportunity to find some reconciliation with women from whom they felt separated.

The rejection of a universal "woman's" essence was vital because it contradicted the strong tendency to erase the experience of women of different race, class, and sexual orientation. But it was also important because it allowed women to speak about parts of their lives that had often been unrecognized and unspoken. In *The Cancer Journals,* Lorde says:

> I have come to believe over and over again that what is most important to me must be spoken, made verbal and shared, even at the risk of having it bruised or misunderstood. . . . In the cause of silence, each one of us draws the face of her own fear. . . . But . . . we fear the very visibility without which we also cannot truly live. (19–21)

The class allowed women to name the unspeakable and the unspoken: racism, lesbianism, sexism, physical and mental abuse, failures in their pasts, struggles with social-sexual relationships, having one's children taken away, or having lived with breast cancer. It also allowed them to hear the words of other women whose experiences were not their own, women they had often feared or rejected. But Lorde argues further that finding words to name and interpret one's experience is not enough. Transforming silence into language must lead to action.

ACTION AND RESPONSIBILITY: ETHICS IN FEMINIST TEACHING

Though not the overt organizing themes of the course, personal responsibility and agency emerged as a crucial dimension of women's identity. The course began by reexamining the language, myths, and images that shape women's lives, but it did something many courses fail to do. As Judith Newton and Deborah Rosenfelt point out, most educational experience divorces the study of ideas, language, and literature from the study of personal, social, political, and economic conditions in which people live. Academic life often fosters the view that intellectual activity is a solitary undertaking without social origins and political implications.

Barbara, on the other hand, presented students with a model of intellectual life that integrated her own life as a reader-scholar with life in the university, surrounding community, and wider culture. She demonstrated how women can continually examine their own experience, monitor conditions in the world, make decisions about the implications of these conditions, and act in relation to them. On the first day of class, she remarked to the students that feminist theory enabled her to bring together all the parts of her life and work. At one point she said: "I would rather think that everything I do matters rather than that nothing matters. So I have to act accordingly, even if it is in seemingly small ways." Ethical considerations and the importance of individual decisions were also a prominent theme in the readings. For example, in her poem, "A Woman Is Talking to Death," Grahn writes of women's responsibility to one another, a theme also addressed in Susan Glaspell's play *Trifles*. Morrison, in *The Bluest Eye*, speaks about the responsibility members of a community have for the lives of its people. Lorde challenges, "Because I am a woman, because I am black, because I am lesbian, because I am myself, a black woman warrior poet doing my work, come to ask you, are you doing yours?" (21).

Barbara tried to create opportunities for students to connect their lives to the readings and to connect both to action, to sensitize themselves to react to what goes on around them. She began every class with announcements of events on and off campus, and she required them to attend at least two outside activities and to write reports connecting them to the reading selections. Students' growing sensitivity to these events was apparent. They began writing about outside events in their journals or referring in class discussion to something they had seen or experienced. They increasingly applied ideas from class and the readings to their own situations.

The concept of responsibility and action that students took from this course was far from the aggressive militancy that Lorde urges women toward, and far from the vocal activism that many feminists would like to see in this "postfeminist" generation. Instead, it was a redefinition of responsibility, along the lines that Flynn and Schweickart point to. Traditionally, responsibility is linked to legal terms—accepting responsibility means not impinging on the rights of others and accepting the risk of liability that comes with authority. Flynn and Schweickart note that in female discourse "responsibility is more closely associated with responsiveness to the needs of others" (xx).

In class, students spoke and wrote most about their responsibility to support and encourage other women, to acknowledge their mothers' and grandmothers' accomplishments, and even to write about or speak out on issues that concerned them. One student said: "It bothers me a little, because now

I've become so observant, so critical in a way. I can't let things go the way I used to—like even how waiters treat me differently from my boyfriend in a restaurant or how my dad talks about blacks, or when a professor uses text-books that are sexist." The readings and the manner in which the course was taught clearly asserted that women are capable of critically interpreting the circumstances of their lives and that their actions do make a difference.

CRITIQUE AND TRANSFORMATION: PUSHING AT THE BOUNDARIES

In attempts to define human subjectivity, the problem of human agency is important, particularly in some versions of poststructuralist and Marxist theory. The question stated very simply is this: if human beings are constructed by cultural and linguistic relationships, what, if anything, allows them to resist, to transform the conditions of their existence? Paul Smith says that many versions of the human subject leave us either with a deterministic definition of the individual as one who has neither agency nor autonomy or, at the other extreme, with a concept of the self that is constantly shifting, fading, and dissolving and, thus, that also has no possibility of claiming agency.

From its earliest tradition, feminist theory has assumed that although women are positioned and defined by a set of sexual and political ideologies, they nevertheless are not condemned to be pawns of these forces. Though poststructuralist feminists seem to imply a genderless "subject" in opposition to the biological "essential" subject of other feminists, theorists like de Lauretis point to a conception of the female subject that allows us to reconceive women's identity via the constant "engagement of a self or subject in social reality" and "political, theoretical, self-analyzing practice" (*Alice* 182, 186). She stresses the idea, reinterpreted from Lacan, that human beings are structured through language, through discursive practices, but not in a totalizing way, because language is not the only source of meaning and, also, because language itself allows the potential for resistance to discursive constructions. Language makes possible a continual reflective, critical analysis of unique histories and experiences. As in the class, this process gives people access to evidence of the nonunity, the discontinuous, in individual lives. Confronting what is contradictory and alienating in human experience allows women and men to resist definitions that society would impose. Seeing the cracks and fissures in such homogenizing definitions allows for the possibility of resisting, of reconsidering and reexamining our positions, and of claiming responsibility and action in the world.

Heilbrun urges women to return to such a critical process when she says that women must return to telling their own and other women's stories, not simply through the texts we read but also "in oral exchanges among women in groups hearing and talking to one another" (46). With de Lauretis, she concludes that women need to reclaim their life stories for these stories' potential to critique and revise women's lives (45). I believe Heilbrun is suggesting more than a return to naive consciousness-raising groups; she is asserting the importance of women's stories as an enactment of "womenness," a dramatic portrayal through women's own life stories of the diversity and contradictions in which they live. This enactment holds within it the potential for historical, critical analysis and, thus, for action. It allows women to understand that the multiplicitous realities of their existence exceed all descriptions of essence.

Women's stories had such a dramatic power in the class, a power seen most tangibly in the students' writing. Amy's final essay described how themes in women's literature allowed her to "reestablish" her views in important areas of her life: her family, death, sexuality, physical appearance, and her conception of herself as a complicated person: "Of course I have a better understanding of women authors, but I also see growth in myself and more understanding of other people." Carol's final paper focused on a theme that she defined as "the power of women and the strength women give to other women." Her essay drew on the writing of Zora Neale Hurston, Audre Lorde, Susan Glaspell, Sarah Orne Jewett, and Ann Cameron to trace transformations in women's lives as they rejected traditional definitions and attempted to reinterpret their identities, gaining power not only for themselves but also for other women. As she traced this theme, she also reexamined her own intellectual process:

> Strength and power were in the characters and the writers, but they are also in the women in our class. I began to gain self-confidence because of the opportunity to listen to the views of women in class. The process was a slow one. At the beginning of the course I was frustrated and felt like I was being forced to think about things I didn't want to think about. It wasn't until later that I realized I could think any way I wanted so long as I wasn't hypocritical, blind, or unthinking. This new opinion came about as my previous beliefs were challenged and I was forced to reevaluate. For me, this may well be the greatest growing I did this semester. This ability to see reason in someone else's opinion is something I can and will carry with me for a long time to come.

REDEFINING LITERARY EDUCATION

This class provided all of us—students, teacher, and participant-observer—with multiple images of women's identity, a clear alternative to the false unity of the universal female essence and, also, to an endlessly dissolving, yet deterministic, identity. It gave us images of ourselves as women committed to complexity, to responsibility, and to change. As a participant-observer, I came away with a sense of the inseparability of feminist theory and practice and of the importance of what, together, they offer as a model for education in both composition and literature.

Rich, Heilbrun, and others assert that feminist theory has potential for revolutionizing literary education, but this revisionary activity is highly suspect in the current debate about the nature of education in English. Some would consider Amy and Carol's experience and the "feminist teaching" that produced it as contributors to the "demise" of literary education today. Barbara Herrnstein Smith notes that Lynne Cheney's report, *Humanities in America*, not only decries the political and ideological turn that literature instruction has taken, but also argues for a return to an emphasis on the transmission of knowledge, information, and fact in place of the current emphasis on self-reflective processes. As Teresa Sullivan notes, women's studies and women's literature classes are especially suspect, both pedagogically and philosophically. Women's literature stands outside the boundaries of canonic texts, lacks the signs of methodological rigor, and appears to indulge in unrestrained ideological indoctrination and emotional, solipsistic examination of self. Still others, as Charles Paine acknowledges, assert that the relativism inherent in "radical pedagogies" leads students to a disabling nihilism. The experience of students in the class provides a much different view of the results of "radical" feminist pedagogy.

Feminist classrooms are not simply revisionary because they break with canonical content; they are also revisionary because they demand critical rather than solipsistic modes of thought and because they assert an ethical rather than a nihilistic stance. The women's literature course demonstrates that the diverse and multidimensional perspectives such a course makes available do not emerge simply from the literature students read or from the theoretical "correctness" of the class or its teacher; rather, they emerge from the dynamic of the entire course, from students' reading and interaction and the critical dialogue with lived experience that interaction makes possible.

This course engaged students in intellectual processes that offer much to the ongoing debate about the nature of education in English. According to de Lauretis, the process of "collective articulation of one's experience of sexuality and gender has produced, and continues to elaborate, a radically new mode of understanding the subject's relations to social-historical reality." Furthermore, de Lauretis points out, this process constitutes an "original critical instrument that women have developed . . . toward the analysis of social reality, and its critical revision" (*Alice* 186). Thus, the critical process that the students engaged in enabled them to develop and practice intellectual processes, to use "critical instruments" that can serve as models of processes that would benefit all students, if they are to live in a pluralistic society.

Revising the *content* of the English curriculum is not enough, then, and the reform needed in the English curriculum runs much deeper than a correct theoretical stance. It requires a methodology consistent with what theory has taught us about how human beings learn, a methodology that takes into account the diverse political and social realities of our lives as well as our students' lives, a methodology that encourages a critical practice that continually turns back on itself, continually monitors, challenges, and changes itself. In a recent essay, Arthur Schlesinger writes about the perils he sees in the rise of "absolutist" thinking in the United States, of the inability of our society to identify and value contradicting and multiple perspectives, and of our tendency to settle for reductive, monolithic representations of issues and ideas.

Feminism's "internally heterogeneous" perspectives offer a remedy to this habit of mind. But feminism will be handicapped if feminists maintain a division between theory and pedagogy. Contrary to the view of feminists like Nina Baym, who suggests that feminists must operate outside the theoretical questions, and contrary to the argument that feminist theory has only to do with the critical project of reading and analyzing texts and that pedagogy is peripheral, we cannot separate theory from practice. To do so endangers the effectiveness of feminism itself by stripping away the interrelationship between the personal, political, and theoretical and by perpetuating a hierarchical dichotomy. Such a separation subverts one of the most important contributions of feminism: the model of a discipline that constantly connects intellectual activity—the study of literature, language, and ideas—to the history and experience of people's lives. This interrelationship provides intellectual practice that allows students to see that we make our own knowledge rather than simply acquire "the facts," and that we do so in a reciprocal process of rethinking and reinterpreting the "word and the world," in Paulo Freire's phrase (35). A model of education that understands the reciprocal nature of theory and practice and constantly places students' experience at its center provides a check against narrowly ideologic forms of teaching that feminists and nonfeminists alike cannot indulge in. Many of our students make little connection between themselves and feminism of any sort, and they believe, further, that reading and writing are alien to their lives. The critical processes made available in the women's literature class—a class that allowed ideas to be held up to reexamination, to contradiction, and to the multiple stories of women's lives—hold at least some promise to counter the absolutist forms of thinking that prevail in our society and to allow more students to remake their view of the world.

NOTES

1. This course, Introduction to Women's Literature, was taught during the fall semester, 1988. My study was one of several participant-observation studies that my colleagues and I have conducted in the Department of English at the University of Nebraska in an effort to understand the contexts for student learning in academic cultures. I used standard participant-observation methodology in collecting data during the course: I participated in and took field-notes at every class session, read the assigned literature and did other assignments, and read students' weekly journals and their midterm and final essays. I also interviewed eight students and the teacher three times during the semester to gain their perceptions of the course.

2. These distinctions are more thoroughly outlined in Weedon.

WORKS CITED

Alcoff, Linda. "Cultural Feminism versus Post-Structuralism: The Identity Crisis in Feminist Theory." *Reconstructing the Academy*. Ed. E. Minnich et al. Chicago: U of Chicago P, 1988. 257–88.

Baym, Nina. "The Madwoman and Her Languages: Why I Don't Do Feminist Literary Theory." *Feminist Issues in Literary Scholarship*. Bloomington: Indiana UP, 1987. 45–61.

Bradstreet, Anne. "The Prologue." *The Norton Anthology of Literature by Women*. Ed. Sandra M. Gilbert and Susan Gubar. New York: Norton, 1985. 61–63.

Cameron, Ann. *Daughters of Copper Woman*. N.p.: Press Gang, 1981.

Cixous, Hélène. "The Laugh of the Medusa." Marks and de Courtivron, 245–64.

Daly, Mary. *Gyn/Ecology*. London: Women's P, 1979.

De Beauvoir, Simone. *The Second Sex*. New York: Random, 1952.

De Lauretis, Teresa. *Alice Doesn't: Feminism, Semiotics, Cinema*. Bloomington: Indiana UP, 1984.

———. *Feminist Studies/Critical Studies*. Bloomington: Indiana UP, 1986.

DiBernard, Barbara. "Feminist Teaching." *Women's Journal-Advocate* 6 (1987): 1–3.

Flynn, Elizabeth, and Patrocinio Schweickart. *Gender and Reading: Essays on Readers, Texts, and Contexts*. Baltimore: Johns Hopkins UP, 1986.

Freire, Paulo, and Donaldo Macedo. *Literacy: Reading the Word and the World*. South Hadley, MA: Bergin, 1987.

Gallop, Jane. *The Daughter's Seduction: Feminism and Psychoanalysis*. London: Macmillan, 1982.

Gilbert, Sandra M., and Susan Gubar. *The Norton Anthology of Literature by Women*. New York: Norton, 1985.

Glaspell, Susan. *Trifles*. Gilbert and Gubar, 1389–99.

Grahn, Judy, "The Common Woman." *The Work of a Common Woman*. Trumansburg, NY: Crossing, 1978. 59–73.

———. "A Woman Is Talking to Death." *The Work of a Common Woman*. Trumansburg, NY: Crossing, 1978. 112–31.

Heilbrun, Carolyn. *Writing a Woman's Life*. New York: Norton, 1989.

Irigaray, Luce. "This Sex Which Is Not One." Marks and de Courtivron, 99–106.

Kempe, Margery. "On Female Celibacy." Gilbert and Gubar, 22–27.

Kolodny, Annette. "Dancing Through the Minefield: Some Observations on Theory, Practice, and Politics of Feminist Literary Criticism." *The New Feminist Criticism*. Ed. Elaine Showalter. New York: Pantheon, 1985. 144–67.

Kristeva, Julia. "From Ithaca to New York." *Polylogue*. Paris: Seuil, 1977.

———. "Il n'y a pas de maître à langage." *Nouvelle Revue de Psychanalyse* 20 (1979): 119–40.

———. "Woman Can Never Be Defined." Marks and de Courtivron. 137–41.

Lorde, Audre. *The Cancer Journals*. San Francisco: Spinsters/ Aunt Lute, 1980.

Marks, Elaine, and Isabelle de Courtivron. *New French Feminisms*. New York: Schocken, 1981.

Morrison, Toni. *The Bluest Eye*. Gilbert and Gubar, 2068–184.

Newton, Judith, and Deborah Rosenfelt. *Feminist Criticism and Social Change*. New York: Methuen, 1985.

Paine, Charles. "Relativism, Radical Pedagogy, and the Ideology of Paralysis." *College English* 51 (1989): 557–70.

Rich, Adrienne. "Disloyal to Civilization: Feminism, Racism, Gynephobia." *On Lies, Secrets, and Silence, Selected Prose 1966–78*. New York: Norton, 1979. 275–310.

———. "When We Dead Awaken: Writing as Re-Vision." *On Lies, Secrets, and Silence, Selected Prose 1966–78*. New York: Norton, 1979. 33–49.

Richardson, H. H. "Two Hanged Women." Gilbert and Gubar, 1210–14.

Schweickart, Patrocinio. "Reading Ourselves: Toward a Feminist Theory of Reading." Flynn and Schweickart, 31–62.

Silko, Leslie Marmon. "Lullaby." *The Norton Anthology of Literature by Women*. Ed. Sandra M. Gilbert and Susan Gubar. New York: Norton, 1985. 2383–90.

Smith, Barbara Herrnstein. "Limelight: Reflections on a Public Year." *PMLA* 104 (1989): 285–93.

Smith, Paul. *Discerning the Subject*. Minneapolis: U of Minnesota P, 1988.

Smith, Stevie. "How Cruel Is the Story of Eve." Gilbert and Gubar, 1684–86.

Spivak, Gayatri C. "French Feminism in an International Frame." *In Other Worlds: Essays in Cultural Politics*. New York: Routledge, 1987. 134–53.

Stein, Gertrude. "Ada." Gilbert and Gubar, 1334–36.

Sullivan, Teresa, et al. "Valuing and Devaluing Women's Studies." *Academe* 75 (1989): 35–42.

Truth, Sojourner. "Ain't I a Woman?" Gilbert and Gubar, 253–55.

Walker, Alice. "In Search of Our Mother's Gardens." Gilbert and Gubar, 2374–82.

Weedon, Chris. *Feminist Practice and Poststructuralist Theory*. London: Basil Blackwell, 1987.

Woolf, Virginia. "From *A Room of One's Own*." Gilbert and Gubar, 1376–83.

7

Writing Against Writing: The Predicament of Écriture Féminine in Composition Studies

LYNN WORSHAM

T o get to the point of writing a paper, I had to combat the writing in me.

—Hélène Cixous

Academic discourse, and perhaps American university discourse in particular, possesses an extraordinary ability to absorb, digest, and neutralize all of the key, radical, or dramatic moments of thought, particularly, a fortiori, of contemporary thought.

—Julia Kristeva

Politics makes strange bedfellows indeed—and composition studies and *écriture féminine* provide an excellent example.[1] On the one hand, we have a discipline that defines itself largely as a discourse community whose positive task it is to teach academic discourse(s); on the other, we have a language "event" that, in its more accessible moments, unleashes a damning critique and denunciation of academic discourse as the instrument par excellence of phallocentrism. What the French might say about an entire discipline that would reinvent the university in every student requires little speculation. Still open for consideration, however, is an effort by composition theorists to bring together two discourses that will surely lock in mortal combat—a battle royal—over the issue of academic language. Curiously, this antagonism does not seem to pose any serious obstacle for the handful of essays importing *écriture féminine* into the institutional discussion of writing (see Caywood and Overing for a limited treatment of French feminism). Perhaps the hostility does not run as deeply as it first appears, making détente conceivable through a profitable exchange of terms and methods. Or perhaps composition simply seeks to display its cultural capital by contending with the newest of the new intellectual fashions, and French feminism is certainly haute couture. This explanation is simultaneously too cynical and too reductive; *écriture féminine* is one of the most dramatic developments in recent writing theory and

From *Contending with Words: Composition and Rhetoric in a Postmodern Age.* Ed. Patricia Harkin and John Schilb. New York: MLA, 1991. 82–104.

pedagogy, not only because it may reformulate our notion of literacy and its consequences but also because it could produce a crisis in composition's self-understanding. The hostility, in other words, is deep and abiding, as the epigraphs opening this essay are meant to suggest. What difference, then, do their differences make?

Before considering that question, I want to address another one, which concerns the way we read *écriture féminine*. Especially useful in the task of discriminating our hermeneutical options is a distinction, developed by Julia Kristeva, between two styles of reading: the political and the postmodern.[2] These two styles of reading articulate and open up two rather different fates for *écriture féminine* in American university discourse. While it can be read either way, the dominant tendency, both in composition studies and elsewhere in the academy, has been to read it politically, as political discourse.

In the notion of political interpretation, Kristeva links everyday language and the so-called specialized discourses of the university. Political interpretation, which is truly "political" in the ancient Greek sense of "popular" (of the people), is "only the ultimate consequence of the epistemological attitude which consists, simply, of the desire *to give meaning*"; hence, it seems so natural, so fundamental that it is beyond partisan interests (Kristeva, "Psychoanalysis" 303–4). The desire to give meaning, to explain, to interpret certainly plays a fundamental role in human experience and characterizes our ordinary relation to the world, but it is never innocent. It is rooted in our need for meaning when confronted by meaninglessness, our need for mastery when confronted by what we fear most: the enigmatic other that exceeds and threatens every system of meaning, including individual identity. Although the desire for meaning appears to be the least personal (both transpersonal and objective), it is based on subjective needs and desires. When the epistemological attitude encounters the unknowable, it becomes resourceful. It takes a stance vis-à-vis the other as an object of knowledge and thereby draws the other into its circle of desire, reducing otherness to sameness, trading a relation of difference for a regime of domination. Political interpretation begins as a quest for a meaning and ends as phallocentric obsession with one meaning. Its most paranoid form occurs in the totalitarian demand of the Enlightenment for one truth, one mind.[3] Even when political interpretation openly acknowledges its status as fiction, a gesture typifying poststructuralist philosophy and literary criticism, it does so without abandoning its goal of stating the true meaning of the discourse it interprets ("Psychoanalysis" 314). If meaning is the obsession of political interpretation, then total consensus is its deepest fantasy.

When French feminists say that *écriture féminine* is a new language, epistemologists in several disciplines quite predictably set to work trying to identify and isolate its distinctive features and the source of its coherence as a system of discourse. They expect to find, if not a theory, then a loosely related group of theories or propositions about language, "woman," "the feminine," or "female experience," including the nature of "feminine" textual practice. They assume an interpretive stance toward *écriture féminine* as an object of knowledge and a repository of truth. Submitted to the discursive obligations of political interpretation, however, *écriture féminine* is typically found lacking, fraught with contradictions, riddled with (theoretical) inconsistencies, and short on concrete strategies for changing the material conditions of everyday women's lives (see, e.g., Jones; Rabine; Spivak; Plaza). Since the feminine has been defined as lack within patriarchy, the fact that *écriture féminine* is found lacking may not come as a surprise, though we should be profoundly suspicious of an approach reaching specifically this conclusion. The challenge now is to read *écriture féminine* politically but as a form of postmodern discourse, which arises not from the desire to give meaning but from the desire to go beyond meaning to a topos of pure invention where discourse becomes more radically political to the extent that it approaches the heterogeneous in meaning.

This approach conserves the differences between composition and *écriture féminine* and hence makes possible an examination of the specific way in which French feminism has been read into composition as a form of political discourse. In the second part of this essay, I show how previous attempts to give meaning to French feminism within composition (1) neutralize its radical potential and (2) tell us something about the ideological investments of writing theory and pedagogy. The second part of my discussion, then, rests on an explanation, undertaken in the first part, of the specific way in which *écriture féminine* should be considered "radical," a term that perhaps has too much commerce in this most postmodern age. Thus, before turning to the way that *écriture féminine* has been read by composition theorists, I want to explore the way it might be read, assuming that the decision can be, as it should be, made again. The appropriate term for such a revision is Lillian Hellman's *pentimento*, which she describes as a form of repentance that occurs when a painter changes his or her mind and redraws the lines expressing an artistic conception. When the paint ages and becomes transparent, it is sometimes possible to see the original lines and the initial conception still etched in the memory of paint and canvas. Pentimento is "a way of seeing," Hellman writes, "and then seeing again" (1). It is still possible to repent, to redraw the lines determining our approach to *écriture féminine* and, in this context, see something of its truly radical potential.

What's Radical About Radical French Feminism?

Dick Hebdige's *Subculture: The Meaning of Style* is an indispensable read for anyone who has been fascinated, repelled, or amused by any of the spectacular youth subcultures emerging onto the cultural scene since World War II. Beatniks, rockers, punks, skinheads—all receive a semiotic analysis, inspired primarily by Roland Barthes, in which Hebdige argues that these music-centered subcultures begin as a movement away from consensus and take shape as symbolic challenges to the inevitability and the unquestioned status of the meanings and values governing a society. They are a form of resistance to hegemony but a resistance that is indirect. The deepest objections to the prevailing ideology are obliquely represented at the level of appearance and the cultivation of a style (17). Clothes, dance, music, and a special idiom work together to produce a subcultural style that communicates a "refusal" of a way of life, a refusal that also affirms identity for a subordinate group. What participants in a subculture seek, to echo Sartre, is a way to "make something of what has been made of [them]" (qtd. in Hebdige 139).

I want to explore *écriture féminine* more fully in terms of Hebdige's analysis of subcultures, as a new language and a form of postmodern expression. Specifically, I suggest a functional analogy between dominant culture and spectacular subcultures, on the one hand, and, on the other, political discourse and *écriture féminine* as a spectacular discourse subculture.[4] Functioning within and against political interpretation in a manner analogous to other spectacular subcultures, *écriture féminine* also arises in response to particular historical conditions and constitutes a style and an identity for a subordinate group, the members of which seek ways to make something of what has been made of them, directly and indirectly, by phallocentrism.[5] "Woman must write her self," Hélène Cixous says, and thereby put herself "into the world and into history" ("Laugh" 279). *Écriture féminine* becomes "*the very possibility of change, . . .* a springboard for subversive thought," refusing every reduction of difference to sameness; thus it is destined to become an exile within (and a hostage to) a political economy of meaning ("Laugh" 283).

Écriture féminine may be considered radical precisely in the same sense that punk subculture, for example, is radical. Both are essentially phenomena of style, disrupting the dominant order of meanings by expressing forbidden content—specifically, consciousness of difference—in forbidden terms (Hebdige 91). Spectacular subcultures, in general, serve as vehicles of semantic disorder by inscribing within the dominant order what it cannot immediately account for, what it cannot easily interpret and explain: safety pins through the cheek or lip, hair dyed bright yellow or lime green with pink polka dots or bleached-in question marks, and, of course, the swastika—to name only a few of the ways in which punk style fractures the syntax of everyday life. Violations of the accepted codes through which the social world is organized and experienced have the power to disorient and disturb. In their most extreme forms, they may even signify what mainstream culture fears most—nihilism and anarchy. Yet a subculture relies on what it resists for the elements of its style, taking the objects, values, and attitudes of dominant culture and using them in a way that perverts their "straight" meaning (e.g., a safety pin becomes a form of facial ornamentation; jewelry, a form of self-mutilation) (Hebdige 102–6). Through parody and pastiche, subcultural styles block the system of representation—that is, the apparatus of political interpretation that tames every enigma by assimilating it to an existing framework of meanings—and expose arbitrary social codes to open up the world to new oppositional readings.

The "object" French feminists do their subversive work on is language—in particular, the discursive operation of phallocentrism in academic language. This focus explains, in part, why French feminism elicits from its American audience responses that are not entirely unlike responses to the outrages of subcultural styles. Phallocrats and feminists alike have been fascinated, repelled, and perplexed by the very idea of "writing the body," which, in the guise of philosophy or criticism, parades before its readers every feature of female anatomy and physiology, every sexual and textual taboo. Cixous's insistent refrain, "I want vulva!" is emblematic of the kind of profane articulation that violates the authorized codes across which we typically construct and disseminate knowledge, and it raises the specter of epistemological, if not cultural, anarchy. Spectacular in its rhetoric, *écriture féminine* is shocking and outrageous, alienating, and, for others, exhilarating. It is the latest scandal wrought by a postmodern temperament. *Style* becomes the critical term—not a style of writing but writing as style, style as a form of cultural critique.[6] If *écriture féminine* is a social and political struggle waged at the level of style, then how does it dress itself, so to speak, to resist the desire to give meaning?

Luce Irigaray writes that the issue is one not "of elaborating a new theory of which woman would be the subject or the object, but of jamming the theoretical machinery itself, of suspending its pretension to the production of a truth and of a meaning that are excessively univocal" (*This Sex* 78). In her books *Speculum of the Other Woman* and *This Sex Which Is Not One*, Irigaray stages a rereading of Western philosophical discourse "inasmuch as this discourse sets forth the law for all others, inasmuch as it constitutes the discourse on discourse" (*This Sex* 74). She calls for "an examination of the operation of the 'grammar' of each figure of discourse, its syntactic laws or requirements, its imaginary configurations, its metaphoric networks, what it does not articulate at the level of utterance: its silences" (75). Only this work—a work on the figurations of the fathers—will jam the theoretical machinery and block the system of representation that defines the feminine as lack and deficiency and that ultimately controls the material conditions of women's lives.

Irigaray thus sets to work on dominant university discourses (such as philosophy and pyschoanalysis) through a stylistic strategy she calls "mimicry." It is the only path, she says, in the initial phase of *écriture féminine,* which must articulate itself in terms of the historical conditions it resists so that feminism does not simply set itself up as another exclusionary practice. Mimicry works indirectly to hollow out the structures of a discourse from within those structures and therefore is a form of infidelity that, like marital infidelity, operates within an institution to ruin it (see Gallop, *Daughter's Seduction* 48). Mimicry requires that women assume the feminine role deliberately and thereby convert a form of subordination into an affirmation and then into a process of subversion. For a woman to play with mimesis

> means to resubmit herself—inasmuch as she is on the side of the "perceptible," of "matter,"—to "ideas," in particular to ideas about herself, that are elaborated in/by a masculine logic, but so as to make "visible," by an effect of playful repetition, what was supposed to remain invisible: the cover-up of a possible operation of the feminine in language. (*This Sex* 76)

Irigaray rejects "a direct feminine challenge" to phallocentrism because it demands that women speak as masculine subjects and hence maintain the sexual indifference of political discourse. A practice of self-exile, mimicry repeats and parodies phallocentric modes of argument to exaggerate their effects and expose their arbitrary privilege.

Working as a mime artist, then, Irigaray resubmits woman to the idea that she is "body." Her critics understand this literally to mean that the female body is the source for *écriture féminine*. They ask: In going back to female sexuality to describe or foresee a feminine textual practice, isn't Irigaray, like Freud, "falling back upon anatomy as an irrefutable criterion of truth" (*This Sex* 70)? Irigaray responds that she goes back "to the question not of the anatomy but of the morphology of female sex" ("Women's Exile" 64). The structure of political discourse possesses an isomorphism with the masculine sex; that is, working through an unstated correspondence—a "morphologic"—of sexuality and textuality, it privileges unity, form, coherence, oneness, the visible. Yet this morphologic has nothing to do with the female sex; it does not correspond to the feminine, because there is not *a* female sex. Irigaray uses the morphology of female sexuality—the logic of the female form, its multiplicity of erogenous places—to show that "it is possible to exceed and disturb this [masculine] logic" ("Women's Exile" 64).

In Irigaray's construction of *écriture féminine*, which may appear to be a positive effort to theorize a feminine style, the mime artist is still at work, disturbing masculine logic by refusing to theorize *écriture féminine*. She reminds us again and again that no objective or objectifying account of this syntax, this other mode of writing, exists or can exist. "It is spoken," Irigaray says, "but not in metalanguage" (*This Sex* 144). It cannot be theorized because *écriture féminine* is not, precisely speaking, an inscription of a specific content (e.g., the essence of woman) but an inscription of heterogeneity. Thus, her comments do not represent or refer to *écriture féminine* but only obliquely indicate a direction in which to think its operation. The mime artist reverses phallocentrism and puts *écriture féminine* into discourse as its opposite to resist and disrupt the dominant semantic order. Inasmuch as phallocentric discourse privileges the logic of noncontradiction, Irigaray therefore says: "Hers are contradictory words, somewhat mad from the standpoint of reason, inaudible for whoever listens to them with ready-made grids, with a fully elaborated code in hand" (*This Sex* 29). Since phallocentrism involves an obsession with property, propriety, proper names, proper terms, Irigaray says that *écriture féminine* "tends to put the torch to fetish words, proper terms, well-constructed forms" (*This Sex* 79). Since phallocentric discourse relies on the logic of the clear and the distinct through which identities are established and proprieties maintained, the mime artist says that a feminine "syntax" involves "nearness, proximity, but in such an extreme form that it would preclude any distinction of identities, any establishment of ownership, thus any form of appropriation" (*This Sex* 134). If *écriture féminine* can be said to have a "propriety," Irigaray suggests we locate it in a dynamics of "proximity" and "simultaneity" to refuse the linearity of phallocentric discourse and its tendency toward stasis and systematization through opposition and hierarchy.

Spinning possibilities from an analogy with fluid mechanics, Irigaray suggests that *écriture féminine* is "continuous, compressible, dilatable, viscous, conductive, diffusible" and therefore never remains within "the same type of utterance as the one that guarantees discursive coherence" (*This Sex* 78, 109). It breaks up the orderly arrangement of discourse and the dominant framework of meanings: "There would no longer be either a right or a wrong side of discourse, or even of texts, but each passing from the one to the other would make audible and comprehensible even what resists the recto-versal structure that shores up common sense" (*This Sex* 80). Because phallocentric discourse, through the strategies of representation, posits the full presence of meaning and a relation of reference between signifier and signified, Irigaray says that *écriture féminine* sets the signifier free from the signified, and the imagination free from words:

> One would have to listen with another ear, as if hearing an "other meaning" always in the process of weaving itself, of embracing itself with words, but also of getting rid of words in order not to become fixed, congealed in them. For if "she" says something, it is not, it is already no longer, identical with what she means. What she says is never identical with anything, moreover; rather it is contiguous. It touches (upon). (*This Sex* 29)

Irigaray may stand phallocentric logic on its head, but her style becomes more flagrantly subversive with her refusal to take seriously her construction of *écriture féminine*.[7] "To escape from a pure and simple reversal of the masculine logic," she says, "means in any case not to forget to laugh." She laughs at the "seriousness" of any discourse (including her own) that, in claiming to state its meaning, forgets that what moves discourse, what moves through meaning is untranslatable, unrepresentable, irrecuperable within discourse (*This Sex* 163). She warns her readers, therefore, that even the motif of proximity, "isolated as such or reduced to utterances, could effectively pass for an attempt to appropriate the feminine to discourse" — that is, to the status of an object of epistemological speculation (*This Sex* 79). In all our efforts to construct from Irigaray's musings a metalanguage whose object is *écriture féminine*, we should hear her laughing, as if to say: "That is not it at all. That is not what I meant, at all."

Laughter is also a key figure and practice of resistance for Cixous. "The Laugh of the Medusa," for example, reclaims the myth of the Medusa as a positive figure of the feminine, and this time she is not deadly: "She's beautiful and she's laughing" (289). *Écriture féminine* laughs at the philosopher's obsession with meaning, taking pleasure in breaking up "the truth" with laughter, "in jumbling the order of space, in disorienting it, in changing around the furniture, dislocating things and values, breaking them all up, emptying structures, and turning propriety upside down" ("Laugh" 291). Such violations of the semantic order are the discursive equivalent of laughter, the principal form of which is a refusal to theorize *écriture féminine*. What could be more subversive to the epistemologist than to assert the existence of something that is not defined, that always exceeds every instrument of theorization? *Écriture féminine* is an outlaw, a fugitive from epistemological justification, taking place in "areas other than those subordinated to philosophic-theoretical domination." Cixous knows that by daring to create *écriture féminine* outside the theoretical, she will be "called in by the cops of the signifier, fingerprinted, remonstrated, and brought into the line of order [she is] supposed to know" ("Laugh" 287, 296). She will, in effect, be required to be systematic, theoretically consistent, and politically transparent.

Cixous refuses the epistemological stance, and, like Irigaray, she also rejects the economy of proper meaning, proper nouns, and common nouns because they "disparage . . . singularity by classifying it into species" ("Laugh" 296). She takes on the very concept of concept and the mode of thought that constantly produces concepts in order to take possession of the world.[8] In the etymology of *concept,* Cixous identifies the basic unit of thought in philosophical discourse or in what I call, following Kristeva, "political interpretation": "concept: etymologically, means something that seizes. Violent grip, rape, abduction. A concept has something of the seducer about it" ("Rethinking" 73). Academic language is also, in a sense, specialized: It is a way of speaking and thinking that captures and appropriates an external reality through models and concepts. "What organize, imprison, censure, are models," she charges; "the fact that there are modes of thought, models, ready-made structures into which one pours all that is still fermenting in order to congeal it" ("Rethinking" 71). Models immobilize; that is their purpose, and that is the pleasure they provide (cf. Lyotard, "Pseudo-Theory").

If what immobilizes us is the medusa of academic language, then Cixous projects *écriture féminine* as a force that steals into language to make it fly ("Laugh" 291; cf. Lyotard, "Pseudo-Theory"). Whatever is coded as profane or "other" by the phallocentric order therefore offers the terms for thinking *écriture féminine* as a practice of resistance and an inscription of heterogeneity that "doesn't annul differences but stirs them up, pursues them, increases their number" ("Laugh" 288). Since academic language immobilizes thought through the limits imposed by concepts, models, and methods, *écriture féminine* is a "spreading-overflowing. It spills out, it is limitless, it has nothing to do with limits" ("Rethinking" 74). Because academic language seizes, captures, and appropriates, thinking *écriture féminine* through the metaphor of gift giving provides terms for thinking another practice and another relation to the world: *Écriture féminine* gives. It allows departures, breaks, partings, separations in meaning, the effect of which is to make meaning infinite and, like desire, nontotalizable. While the epistemologist maintains the propriety of thesis and position, origin and closure, *écriture féminine* works on the beginning but not on the origin, "for the origin is a masculine myth and it does not haunt the feminine unconscious." A feminine text starts on all sides at once, refusing to move logically, linearly, from beginning to end: "a feminine text can't be predicted, isn't predictable, isn't knowable and is therefore very disturbing" (Cixous, "Castration" 53). In particular, *écriture féminine* disturbs the logic of academic language, which depends on a scission between oral speech and written text, by working with the oral otherness of discourse, the nondiscursive possibilities of voice and rhythm that, in discussions of orality, Walter

Ong rather abstractly calls "the somatic component" (*Orality* 67). Cixous calls these possibilities "the flesh of language," which is not a meaning—*écriture féminine* does not rush into meaning—"but [is] straightway at the threshold of feeling. There's tactility in the feminine text, there's touch, and this touch passes through the ear" ("Castration" 53).

Cixous places *écriture féminine* close to the voice—"writing and voice . . . are woven together"—but she does not do what Toril Moi claims she does, namely, produce "a full-blown metaphysical account of writing as voice, presence, and origin" (*Sexual/Textual Politics* 119). Her account of a writing close to the voice does not posit a relation between meaning and sound; it does not make meaning(s) its obsession. It is concerned instead with writing and touch. The rhythms of the voice do not have the effect of socialization but simply move us to move with rhythm and sound (cf. Sloterdijk xviii). This intimacy between language and the body once again puts into discourse the sense that our deepest relation to language is concrete, material, existential—and rhetorical—not epistemic.

Kristeva, more than Irigaray or Cixous, directly theorizes our material relation to language in terms that generally coincide with the notion that *écriture féminine* functions as a spectacular discourse subculture.[9] She argues that *écriture féminine* is not a new and distinct language as such (see "Women's Time" 202–11). Rather, the feminine is a subversive operation within language and the distinctive trait of postmodern discourse, which Kristeva also describes as a transgressive practice of laughter (see "Postmodernism"). Postmodern discourse is produced by a specific *positioning* within language, offered by the "semiotic disposition." Heterogeneous to meaning and its ideology, the semiotic is "pre-meaning" and "pre-sign" or "trans-meaning" and "trans-sign." It is the otherness within language identified with the body and with what traditionally has been coded as the feminine. The semiotic manifests itself in transgressions from the grammatical rules of language that ensure meaning and communication and achieves its effects through contradiction, rhythm, disruption of syntax, and absences or gaps of meaning that are nonetheless significant—in short, through the effects we have traditionally associated with style. Yet postmodern style is interpretation, Kristeva writes; its unobjectifiable, unnameable "nonobject" is emotion, drive, instinct, desire—in particular, the emotion experienced when a writer confronts the meaninglessness existing in spite of, in the midst of, all systems of meaning that are created precisely to hide this existential fact ("Psychoanalysis" 310–17). Face to face with the void—the irreducible otherness—across which all our meanings are stretched like iridescent skin, postmodern "interpreters" do not pretend to communicate a meaning directly. They "musicate" to keep from being frightened to death and in so doing "individuate" themselves and their experiences, not as subjects or objects of knowledge, but in the creation of a style ("Postmodernism"; *Powers of Horror* 1–32).

Kristeva names that which is heterogeneous to meaning "desire" or "emotion" and thus suggests that our deepest relation to language and to the world is not epistemic but emotional and material. She also acknowledges that the semiotic always exceeds every effort to name it and therefore to place it within any system of meanings. Although we can observe important differences among Kristeva, Cixous, and Irigaray, they share some common concerns, not the least of which is their refusal of the epistemological attitude. In their effort to put into discourse what dominant discourse has relegated to meaningless-ness—the feminine, the body, desire, emotion, sound, voice, rhythm, contra-diction—they are not simply theorizing *écriture féminine* as the opposite of phallocentrism, simply reversing its hierarchical structure and creating a new language. Such objectives would confirm the charge that they are epistemo-logically inept essentialists who attack philosophical essentialism while cre-ating a new language of "woman" (see Moi, *Sexual/Textual Politics;* Plaza). Instead, they reverse phallocentric logic to draw attention to its arbitrary priv-ilege, its historical contingency. Furthermore, they put *écriture féminine* into discourse as the opposite of phallocentric discourse to resist the notion that it is a separate language cut off from the language and the historical conditions it arises to oppose. *Écriture féminine* is a practice of self-exile within the domi-nant order of meaning. This is its "meaning." Yet *écriture féminine* is a moving phenomenon, a language event with a sense of its own historical specificity, and as such its contours will change as the material conditions of women's lives change.

Écriture féminine (more precisely, for Kristeva, postmodern discourse) functions now as an inscription of heterogeneity that, in refusing to become an object of knowledge, seeks always to subvert our ordinary relation to the world. A spectacular discourse subculture, *écriture féminine* is spectacular in its effects, but it is not "specularizable"—in other words, it resists every effort to make it an object of knowledge and a spectacle for the gaze of the epistemolo-gist. It insists on passage *out* of the system, any system, every system, toward what is "'other,' which if it is truly 'other,' there is nothing to say, it cannot be theorized" (Cixous and Clément 71). If it refuses to be objectified, if it exceeds any system's power of recuperation, then it cannot be brought within the uni-versity as we know it. It cannot become the object of research and scholarship; it cannot become the basis for a pedagogy. Indeed, *écriture féminine* does not want to be brought, from its position on the margin of official culture, into the university. It is more likely to decimate, not invent or reinvent, the univer-sity and its discourses, because it is in places like the university that people are crushed "by highly repressive operations of metalanguage, the opera-tions, that is, of the commentary on commentary, the code" (Cixous, "Castra-tion" 51). "Let's get out of here," Cixous says. "Not another minute to lose" ("Laugh" 289). In spite of our efforts to "know" it, *écriture féminine* is "some-where else entirely," "conceived of [and performed] only by subjects who are breakers of automatisms, by peripheral figures that no authority can ever sub-jugate" (Cixous and Clément 137; Cixous, "Laugh" 287).

Because of these predispositions, *écriture féminine* cannot be freely imported into the writing classroom to work alongside academic discourse toward the goal of literacy—that is, to the extent that literacy and the literate mind are governed by the epistemological attitude and its positioning of the speaker or writer in a phallic position of mastery over discourse. To the extent that literacy is aligned with the ideology of the clear and distinct, the transparency of communication, the overriding need for consensus and communication, *écriture féminine* laughs in defiance of this narrowly political project for improving the human condition. This laughter is not that of an anarchist or nihilist. It should suggest instead that literacy itself is a regime of meaning to be interrogated regarding its power to recuperate the power of those already in a position to order and give meaning to the social world. While E. D. Hirsch's "cultural literacy" project seems to be the ultimate consequence of political interpretation, we must consider the possibility that multicultural literacy also arises from the need to bring the other within the circle of epistemological desire. As Alice Jardine observes, "There is, after all, a difference between really attempting to think differently and thinking the Same through the manipulation of difference" (*Gynesis* 17). *Écriture féminine,* in contrast to both these literacy projects, inscribes an effort to think differently, to repent and repossess writing as an experience of the limits of meaning. It indirectly inscribes, within and against the dominant discourse, an experience in which writing does not contain, possess, or appropriate but steals into language to make it fly, to make it move, to make *us* move without our ever knowing what worked or works on us and toward what end. *Écriture féminine* is a raid on the articulate.

This discussion, however, has moved inexorably toward the following articulation of the predicament: If composition studies were to make any sustained contact with *écriture féminine,* one of two things would happen. Either composition would neutralize the radical potential of *écriture féminine* in an effort to appropriate it to serve the current aims of the profession and, beyond this, the university, or *écriture féminine* would cast such suspicion on the whole enterprise of composition studies as an accomplice of phallocentrism that composition would be transformed beyond recognition. It would not be entirely inaccurate to say that composition would cease to exist as we know it, and by implication the university, along with its constituent discourses, would come tumbling down.

How to Take Out a Radical

The dilemma posed above becomes moot because every spectacular subculture is destined to be brought back in line, incorporated, and located within the dominant framework of meanings. Social order can only be maintained through the appropriation and definition—hence, the neutralization—of subcultures of resistance (cf. Hebdige 85). Dominant culture develops and depends on elaborate strategies of containment and incorporation to bring all competing definitions and interests within its range of influence, so that subcultures are, if not controlled, then at least contained within an ideological space that does not seem ideological, that appears instead to be neutral, nonaligned, and beyond particular interests (see Hebdige 16). Thus, subcultural styles, which begin as symbolic challenges to the dominant ideology, inevitably end by creating new conventions of meaning, new commodities, new industries, or by renewing old ones (Hebdige 96). What begins as a practice of resistance gets incorporated and ultimately trivialized as "fashion."

Two essays—Robert de Beaugrande's "In Search of Feminist Discourse: The 'Difficult' Case of Luce Irigaray" and Clara Juncker's "Writing (with) Cixous"—offer an opportunity to observe the machinery of hegemony working to neutralize the radical potential of *écriture féminine*. Neither essay, it should be noted, expressly intends to defuse what Juncker calls the "political dynamite" of French feminism (432). Both are meticulous, even masterful readings that offer much insight, including the sense that French feminism could produce "a genuine renewal of language and all that rides upon it" (de Beaugrande 272). Yet apart from any conscious intention or expressed hope, we must also be concerned with what happens above and beyond our willing and doing. And these essays, in their desire to give French feminism meaning within composition, unwittingly contain and neutralize it within an ideological space that it resists and refuses.

Neither essay reaches the impasse that requires either the neutralization of *écriture féminine* or the evacuation of composition theory and teaching. Neither essay addresses, through French feminism, the ideological investments of the profession. These remain unthought and unspoken. Neither asks questions, in short, that would focus attention at a metatheoretical level of analysis. Both writers are concerned instead with showing how *écriture féminine* works so that they can make it work in the interest of current writing theory and pedagogy. This strategy—"know how it works" in order "to make it work"—is part of the habitual gesture of scholarship in composition and is symptomatic of a dominant mode of political interpretation within the university.[10] Cixous indicates that this strategy is fundamental to the logic of mastery characterizing phallocentrism ("Laugh" 291). Pursued in these terms, French feminism cannot make a serious critique of composition but finds its potential indentured to serve the present system's equilibrium. The following discussion not only considers two specific cases in which *écriture féminine* is incorporated and neutralized but also exposes some of the values, rituals of appeal, and habits of mind characterizing the ethos of composition studies.

The first form of incorporation is already familiar to us as political interpretation, for which the fundamental move is a denial of difference. Juncker's title—"Writing (with) Cixous"—indicates her awareness of the process by which otherness is reduced to sameness, that is, assimilated to an existing regime of meaning. It suggests that she knows her essay both rewrites—and therefore distorts—Cixous and attempts to (re)model theory and practice in terms of Cixous's brand of *écriture féminine*. The object of interpretation, in other words, exists and it does not exist as such; it is both opaque and transparent (see Jardine, "Opaque Texts"). In the body of her essay, Juncker calls attention to the strangeness, the foreignness of French feminist thought and then enters into the circle of epistemological desire, assuming the task of making *écriture féminine* less strange, less threatening, and more palatable to a specific audience composed of those who are least likely to see anything useful in the often wildly obscure statements of French feminists. It is no accident, then, that Juncker explains *écriture féminine* by suggesting ways in which it "parallels" empirical studies of gender and writing. Certainly, the unknown becomes known through a hermeneutical operation in which existing structures of thought translate the unknown into the domain of the known. Yet it is impossible to understand how French feminism, which regards empiricism and humanism as part of the logic of masculine privilege, could have much to say that *parallels* any empiricist and humanist investments in composition studies.[11]

Juncker further naturalizes and domesticates *écriture féminine* by seeing it as a source for new textual and pedagogical models and strategies. If *écriture féminine* operates against models, concepts, ready-made modes of thought, then it is just as likely to operate against strategies, routines, plans, procedures—against techniques of any kind that, because they can be applied generally across different writing situations and by different writers, deny differences and annul singularities. Yet Juncker wants to inscribe a place for *écriture féminine* in the writing classroom because, as she says, "by opening ourselves to French (feminist) theories of writing, we teachers of composition, male and female, might actually engender new textual and pedagogical strategies within our field and beyond" (424). This single statement reveals a determining force in Juncker's essay, which I call a "pedagogical imperative" or the "will to pedagogy." This imperative is at the heart of a discipline requiring every theory of writing to translate into a pedagogical practice or at least some specific advice for teachers. (To be sure, the burden of my own discussion is to articulate if and how French feminism makes a difference ultimately in the way I teach writing.) The pedagogical imperative receives its most recent justification from the critical-pedagogy movement, which reinvigorates the study of pedagogy as concrete political practice, but a more visceral commitment to the notion that theories and techniques serve as instruments for the control and prediction of "writing behavior" still operates within the field of composition. And even when writing "specialists" refrain from demanding that theory operate in such mechanistic terms, they nonetheless demand that theoretical questions receive explicit answers that are theoretical or practical or both. Such specialization excludes the possibility that questions in some provinces of thought refuse to be answered and instead lead to further questions in the spirit of radical invention. French feminists, in short, do not offer a theory or even a set of theories of writing—that is, if *theory* is understood as a systematic explanation of some phenomenon. They are not interested in formalizing *écriture féminine* to offer us what we think we need—a nugget of pure truth about writing.

Under pressure from the profession's pedagogical imperative, however, Juncker seems to have little choice but to outline new strategies suggested by *écriture féminine* and to recontextualize old ones already familiar to writing teachers. These strategies are what we might expect: Students should be allowed, even assigned, to write "experimental texts"; students should be allowed to take possession of their own voices; writing assignments should focus on invention, emphasizing beginnings rather than closure; students should read noncanonical, even outrageous, literature in a nonaggressive, nonmastering mode; teachers should assume a nonmastering pedagogical stance. While Juncker's appropriation of *écriture féminine* simply confirms much of what is already considered standard practice in the field, thus neutralizing the very real differences between French feminist and American discourses on writing, it does not successfully alter the deeply entrenched power relations between student and teacher in the university system. Despite any pedagogical posturing to the contrary, students know that power and knowledge flow from the top down: teachers still determine assignments and still have the power to give or deny students the right to their own voices.

What Juncker offers as the most radical innovation inspired by *écriture féminine* turns out to be our oldest pedagogical model. She suggests that if teachers assume the role of Kristeva's "phallic mother," they can "bring about a quick revolution [in the classroom]—and not just in language" (434). Here Juncker eliminates a specific difference between Kristeva and Cixous and writes against Cixous, who argues that teachers who position themselves as phallic mothers actually have been "assigned by force of trickery to a precise place in the chain that's always formed for the benefit of a privileged signifier." The phallic mother, in other words, is only a new twist in the chain of significations that leads back to the "Name-of-the-Father" and to the logic of mastery ("Laugh" 296). The issue is not that Juncker's appropriation fails or that she fails to understand Cixous. Rather, any attempt to appropriate *écriture féminine* as a theory of writing or as a course for pedagogical strategies swallows up its specific force in the epistemological desires of a discipline that would rather not be questioned, for example, about the ways in which culture is reproduced through its theories and pedagogies, through its reliance on the ideas of theory and pedagogy.

The very process of political interpretation occurring in Juncker's essay cannot be meaningfully separated from a second form of incorporation—namely, commodification, which relies on the conversion of a subcultural style into mass-produced style. Once a subcultural style becomes generally available, it becomes frozen; it is emptied of its radical potential (see Hebdige 94–96). The process of political interpretation, which turns *écriture féminine* into an object of knowledge, is in effect a process of commodification. In other words, once objectified, it can be systematized, theorized, codified, and ultimately taught. By such means, it passes into fashion, a commodity generally available for consumption. The introduction and incorporation of this new intellectual commodity serves to rejuvenate or renew the industry of composition studies. That *écriture féminine* could (be made to) rejuvenate writing theory and pedagogy, without cracking its foundations, is a persuasive advertisement, but the power to rejuvenate belongs not to the specificity of *écriture féminine* but to the industriousness of composition. One can foresee a day, in the not too distant future, when a cottage industry of research and scholarship supplies textbooks on the production of so-called experimental texts; a day when summer seminars, conducted perhaps in the streets of Chicago rather than on Martha's Vineyard, are available for composition teachers who wish to "retool" themselves in the image of the phallic mother. We have seen this happen before with deconstruction and the decentered classroom.

I am not suggesting, however, that we ignore French feminism or regard it (or that it asks to be regarded) as a pure object, as irreducibly other, which would place it beyond analysis, beyond interpretation, and, most important, outside history. As I have said, I consider the conjunction of French feminism and composition studies a critical moment in the life of the profession. To regard *écriture féminine* as a pure object is simply another strategy of containment—one that works to defuse resistance by rendering heterogeneity meaningless as pure spectacle, pure exotica (see Barthes 152). *Écriture féminine*, in effect, receives a tweak on the cheek for being cute (but useless) and gets sent back whence it came. If the process leading from resistance to incorporation and neutralization is inevitable, then perhaps we can exercise prudence about the level at which *écriture féminine* is introduced into and incorporated by composition studies. We may conserve some of its energy by realizing that it has less to contribute to the industry of composition—to the development of a new theory of writing or to the design of textual and pedagogical strategies—than it does to an examination of how composition conducts itself as a theoretical enterprise. It is relevant, in short, not as a critical model but as a force of resistance that indirectly calls into question the needs and desires governing the field. The epistemological attitude is one such need; the pedagogical imperative, another. Working at this level of analysis, I turn finally to "the difficult case" of Irigaray and the specific way de Beaugrande's essay works to neutralize *écriture féminine* by aligning it with the values of modernism, which are synonymous with those of the Enlightenment project. If de Beaugrande's essay represents the values and interests of the field, and I think it does, then composition is, at this point in its historical development, more nearly a modernist discipline than a postmodern intervention in the discourse on knowledge.[12]

On the level of conscious intention, de Beaugrande makes a determined effort to refuse the operation of metalanguage by weaving into his essay a tremendous number of quotations from Irigaray's two principal books. He gets beyond his reactions to her discourse, he claims, "by not filtering it through . . . paraphrase" (258). His concern is to create the proper relation to her discourse, to get on the "right" side of it—her side. Yet he arranges and quotes her words without acknowledging that his selection and arrangement are already the culmination of a process of (in)filtration and political interpretation. Then, too, there is the matter of the essay's title. What are we to understand by the choice of the word *difficult*, the importance of which is further emphasized by quotation marks? Certainly, it calls to mind a negative (male) stereotype of women. More generously, perhaps the word *difficult*, thus emphasized, is meant to indicate the interpreter's sense of humor, if not of irony, about his relation to his object. While his title may problematize the hermeneutical relation, it nevertheless calls attention to the fact that the interpreter chooses to play the part of the analyst explaining (curing?) the case of the difficult, the enigmatic female (discourse).

Taking up the position of the subject who knows, the subject with power over discourse (both his and his patient's), which is the subject position typifying modernism, de Beaugrande claims that although feminism is beginning to have an effect throughout the English profession, as yet "we find no widespread consensus about the detailed consequences that we should expect [from feminism]." He goes on to say that feminism seeks "experimental forms of discourse that attempt to propose and practice a radically different mode of communication" (253). These two statements reveal two of the three standards that work to neutralize *écriture féminine*—namely, communication and consensus. The third occurs in what I believe is de Beaugrande's estimation of the value and promise of (French) feminist discourse. He asks, "Can we deconstruct our entrenched conceptions, and the discourses that presuppose them, to the point where a genuinely nonaligned system of discourse might enable a free and commensurate communication among all humans, be they women or men?" (257). Consensus, commensurability, communication, "nonaligned" discourse—these are the old dreams of the Enlightenment as well as of the philosopher and phallocrat. They are motivated by one desire: the desire for the same mind, the same meaning, the same standard, and the same language. They promise enlightenment, emancipation, and empowerment. Yet in a postmodern culture, *écriture féminine* joins with other forms of postmodern discourse in regarding "consensus [as] an outmoded and suspect value," as an instrument of totalization and totalitarianism (Lyotard, *Postmodern* 66). It breaks with the ideology of communication and seeks instead to explore the limits of language as a communicative system (Kristeva, "Postmodernism"). Although de Beaugrande does not detail what he means by a "genuinely nonaligned system of discourse," my best guess is that "nonaligned" means "neutral"—neutral with respect to position, bias, prejudice, ideology. He might have said "rational" discourse, for this definition precisely reflects the Enlightenment dream of rationality. A "free and commensurate communication among all humans"—male and female—is a communication that transcends or brackets difference. It is communication unmarked by (gender) difference. De Beaugrande quite shrewdly navigates the issue of difference, appropriating *écriture féminine* in a way that makes difference a nonissue when for French feminists it is the only issue. This maneuver strikes me as a rather poignant example of the difference between really thinking differently and thinking the same through the manipulation of difference.

This kind of appropriation, I suspect, will be the fate of *écriture féminine* in composition studies, especially if the two articles discussed here do in some sense speak the desires of the field. Composition theorists will effectively manipulate *écriture féminine* to shore up the foundations of their field as a modernist discipline committed to the old dreams of the Enlightenment. I say this despite the many overt ways in which the profession has abandoned the rhetoric of totality and opted instead for a rhetoric of multiplicity, suggesting that it wants to locate itself on the side of diversity and heterogeneity and perhaps identify itself with a postmodern sensibility.[13] The notion of distinct discourse communities, for example, which fractures the dominant discourse into many discourses, each with its own conventions for producing and evaluating knowledge, seems to move us toward a sensitivity to difference. In this regard, students' discourse, though few of us would call it particularly spectacular, operates as a subculture openly resisting conventions of academic discourse. Students, by virtue of their marginality to those conventions, seem to occupy a feminine position, regardless of the gender of individual speakers or writers. This, in fact, is Juncker's claim (434).

Yet despite these appearances, the idea of discourse community and the definition of literacy supporting it represent a redeployment, and not a refusal, of the values associated with modernism. The profession is deeply committed to the Enlightenment dreams of communication and consensus, emancipation and empowerment, and the idea of discourse community has appeal because it promises to empower students to (re)produce the "proper" kind of discourse by learning, as David Bartholomae says:

> to extend themselves . . . into the commonplaces, set phrases, rituals, and gestures, habits of mind, tricks of persuasion, obligatory conclusions, and necessary connections that determine the "what might be said" and constitute knowledge within the various branches of our academic community. (146)

Not only does this approach reproduce the ideology of proper meaning criticized by Cixous and Irigaray, it also reproduces the relation of mastery characterizing modernist knowledge. Students must, as Bartholomae says, "appropriate (or be appropriated by) a specialized discourse" (135). It's a big fish–little fish system. Though they may be marginalized with regard to the conventions of academic discourse, students nevertheless are probably conspicuous consumers of the dominant meanings and values of their culture, and these are in no way alien to academic discourse. Students may not move with finesse in the game of academic discourse, but they are well versed, though perhaps unconsciously, in the forms of incorporation and neutralization by which the social order wins their consent and enlists their conformity to a carefully controlled range of values and meanings. If students occupy a feminine position—and I am not at all convinced that they do—it is not because of their marginality in the academy but because they are so thoroughly constructed by the culture in which they live that they are, in effect, exiled from anything remotely resembling "individual expression." The idea of discourse community simply reinforces this relation. It does not individuate; it assimilates. As Bartholomae says, students "have . . . to know what I know and how I know what I know . . . they have to learn to write what I would write, or to offer up some approximation of that discourse" (140). They have to learn to think and write, in other words, like a big fish. This imperative produces a discipleship model of knowledge and education, which, according to Gregory Ulmer, is the least thoughtful relation to knowledge because it only reproduces authorities and the authority of tradition (*Applied Grammatology* 164–69). It is also the antithesis of what French feminists attempt to approach through *écriture féminine*. Our students know only too well the way of life that, despite all the rhetoric of individual choice, demands they take their place in line. The question is whether composition teachers can position themselves so that they do not further prevent individual expression.

In a big fish–little fish system, writing can ultimately evidence possession of or by a dominant framework of meaning or work as a form of resistance. Though the fate of every practice of resistance may be incorporation and neutralization, it is still possible to set resistance in motion again as such. This is the work of *écriture féminine*. If all of us have the responsibility to invent our own styles of resistance, as teachers we are faced with an impossible desire: to teach an unteachable relation to language. While we worry over this problem, and since we have much work yet to do, we can take whatever we glean from the excesses of *écriture féminine* and expand our notions of literacy to their widest possible circumference, to a point where literacy must involve us, and our students, in more than an epistemic relation to the world and to the earth. We can also recognize that *écriture féminine* arises from an ability to read culture, to read the ways hegemony works to win and shape consent so that the power of dominant meanings and dominant groups appears natural and beyond question. This ability can be taught. It involves students in the ongoing criticism of everyday life, of prominent forms of political discourse that shape their lives—such as advertising, film, photography, television, fashion, music, the news media, religious ritual, common sense, and academic discourse. We have numerous "models" to guide us and, within these broad divisions of discourse, numerous cultural texts on which to work, for the desire to give meaning is endless and endlessly fascinating. I find Hebdige's analysis of subcultures particularly suggestive as a reading of attempts by postwar youths to think and live differently. More generally, Hebdige offers an insightful application of Barthes's semiological and rhetorical approach to cultural analysis, which examines not only the literature and images of high art but also the texts of everyday life (eating, drinking, cleaning, vacationing).

The purpose of refashioning composition as cultural criticism, however, is not to stay within an epistemological justification but to liberate a different way of feeling, another sensibility.[14] Our emphasis should shift from the notion of writing as a mode of learning to that of writing as a strategy, without tactics or techniques, whose progress yields "unlearning." This result does not mean that writing produces ignorance; rather, it produces a sense of defamiliarization vis-à-vis unquestioned forms of knowledge. Writing would no longer function primarily as an agency in the articulation of knowledge and redistribution of power; instead, it would become an indispensable agency for making the world strange and infinitely various. Barthes calls this experience *sapientia*: "no power, a little knowledge, a little wisdom, and as much flavor as possible" (478). Students may discover ways to make something of what has been made of them; they may begin to discover and to invent the "flavor" of life in a society whose general tendency is toward conformity. Scholarship in composition, in the meantime, should examine ways in which culture is reproduced in its theory and in its practice—with a view toward becoming a site for the production of difference.

NOTES

1. In this essay I leave *écriture féminine* untranslated whenever possible, to emphasize its difference from any of our appropriations of it, including my own. Among the translations of this term: "feminine writing," "writing said to be feminine," "writing the body."

2. Kristeva develops this distinction across several essays; see especially "Psychoanalysis and the Polis," "The System and the Speaking Subject," "Women's Time," "Freud and Love." Her distinction between political and postmodern interpretation closely parallels Jean-François Lyotard's distinction between "metanarratives" of explanation, typical of modernism, and "petite narratives," typical of postmodern knowledge (*Postmodern* 3–23). Also, her definition of political interpretation seems synonymous with Barthes's sense of *myth*, which itself is synonymous with *ideology* (see *Mythologies* 109–59).

3. For more on the discussion about modernism, the Enlightenment, and postmodernism, see Lyotard's *Postmodern Condition* and Habermas's *Philosophical Discourse of Modernity*. For a discussion of postmodernism and feminism, see Flax; Moi, "Feminism, Postmodernism, and Style."

4. The analogy proposed here does not attempt to make a perfect match. Significant differences may be observed between *écriture féminine* and spectacular youth subcultures, which Hebdige argues arise out of a working-class ethic and the influence of race and race relations. French feminism, in contrast, has been criticized (e.g., by Spivak) as a phenomenon of and for elite, "First World" women. Most critics, however, see *écriture féminine* as being part of and contributing to a growing consciousness of racial difference (not tension), leading to a politics of diversity (not oppression). In spite of differences between *écriture féminine* and youth subcultures, the similarities seem numerous enough to make speculation productive. This approach, in particular, helps us resist the tendency to see *écriture féminine* simply as an alternative discourse or counterdiscourse constituting a counterculture. Counterculture has been distinguished from subculture by its overtly political and ideological forms of opposition to the dominant culture (e.g., through coherent philosophies giving rise to organized political action) and by its development of alternative institutions (e.g., alternative newspapers and presses, communes as alternative models of family organization) (Hebdige 148n6). The distinction between counterculture and subculture seems to turn on the degree of organization, formalization, and commitment to the elaboration of a system of meanings. To read French feminism as counterdiscourse therefore would be to freeze it within the demands of political interpretation. *Écriture féminine* ultimately hopes to create a different culture, a different articulation of meaning and heterogeneity, but it will do so indirectly by first opening a space in dominant culture in which we can begin to think differently. It does not, in or of itself, lead directly to a counterculture.

5. *Écriture féminine* is conceived by and for women, who form a subordinate group, in the context of this discussion, in the sense that "they have been driven away [from writing] as violently as from their bodies" (Cixous, "Laugh" 279). Men are not excluded from *écriture féminine*, though women come to it more readily by virtue of their position within phallocentrism. For more on men and *écriture féminine*, see Cixous, "The Laugh of the Medusa"; Kristeva, "Women's Time"; Conley.

6. Several critics investigate the style of *écriture féminine*. See Duren; Gallop, *Daughter's Seduction*; Jardine, *Gynesis*; Rabine; Richman; Stanton; Suleiman.

7. Irigaray uses analogy extensively but with no guarantee that her reader will catch the mimic at work. Indeed, her critics often entirely overlook the importance of mimicry and argue that she commits the same errors of thought that brand the philosopher a phallocrat. In defense of her use of analogy, she says:

> And didn't Aristotle, a "giant thinker" according to Marx, determine the relationship between form and matter through an analogy with the relationship between male and female? To return to the question of sexual difference is therefore rather a new passage through analogism. (*This Sex* 170)

Irigaray, the subcultural bricoleur, steals into the dominant language and uses it against itself. This new passage makes visible what has been rendered invisible by the phallocentric use of analogy—not sameness but difference or, more precisely, differences.

8. See Eric A. Havelock, who argues that pre-Socratic philosophers began to develop conceptual language once they discovered the power of abstraction and the ideas of system and totality.

His discussion, in general, coincides with and supports many of the statements French feminists make about conceptual language, though he is not attempting to expose a sexual ideology at work in the process leading from a narrative logic to a logic of the written text.

      9. Hebdige actually employs Kristeva's notion of language as a signifying practice to discuss the construction of subcultures. He does not, however, extend this discussion to the feminine or to *écriture féminine*.

      10. Heidegger also examines the instrumentalist logic at work in this strategy. He associates it with "the technical interpretation of thought" typical of "research" in the university. See Worsham, "The Question Concerning Invention."

      11. For more on humanism, modernism, and postmodernism, see Jardine, *Gynesis*; Moi, *Sexual/Textual Politics*.

      12. I have developed the argument that composition is part of the Enlightenment project at greater length in "The Question of Writing Otherwise."

      13. See Louise Wetherbee Phelps, for example, who situates composition in terms of a postmodern "consciousness."

      14. Gilles Deleuze writes, "The point of critique is not justification but a different way of feeling, another sensibility" (*Foucault* vii).

WORKS CITED

Barthes, Roland. *Mythologies.* Trans. Annette Lavers. New York: Hill, 1972.

Bartholomae, David. "Inventing the University." *When a Writer Can't Write: Studies in Writer's Block and Other Composing Problems.* Ed. Mike Rose. New York: Guilford, 1985. 134–65.

Caywood, Cynthia L., and Gillian R. Overing, eds. *Teaching Writing: Pedagogy, Gender, and Equity.* New York: State U of New York P, 1986.

Cixous, Hélène. "Castration or Decapitation?" Trans. Annette Kuhn. *Signs* 7 (1981): 41–55.

———. "The Laugh of the Medusa." Trans. Keith Cohen and Paula Cohen. *The Signs Reader: Women, Gender, and Scholarship.* Ed. Elizabeth Abel and Emily K. Abel. Chicago: U of Chicago P, 1983. 279–99.

———. "Rethinking Differences." Trans. Isabella de Courtivron. *Homosexualities and French Literature.* Ed. George Stambolian and Elaine Marks. Ithaca: Cornell UP, 1979. 70–86.

Cixous, Hélène, and Catherine Clément. *The Newly Born Woman.* Trans. Betsy Wing. Minneapolis: U of Minnesota P, 1986.

Conley, Verena Andermatt. *Hélène Cixous: Writing the Feminine.* Lincoln: U of Nebraska P, 1984.

de Beaugrande, Robert. "In Search of Feminist Discourse: The 'Difficult' Case of Luce Irigaray." *College English* 50 (1988): 253–72.

Duren, Brian. "Cixous' Exorbitant Texts." *SubStance* 32 (1981): 39–51.

Flax, Jane. "Postmodernism and Gender Relations in Feminist Theory." *Feminism/Postmodernism.* Ed. Linda J. Nicholson. New York: Routledge, 1990. 39–62.

Gallop, Jane. *The Daughter's Seduction: Feminism and Psychoanalysis.* Ithaca: Cornell UP, 1982.

Habermas, Jürgen. *Communication and the Evolution of Society.* Trans. Thomas McCarthy. Boston: Beacon, 1979.

———. *The Philosophical Discourse of Modernity: Twelve Lectures.* Trans. Frederick Lawrence. Cambridge: MIT P, 1987.

Havelock, Eric A. "The Linguistic Task of the Pre-Socratics." *Language and Thought in Early Greek Philosophy.* Ed. Kevin Robb. La Salle: Monist Library of Philosophy, 1983. 7–82.

Hebdige, Dick. *Subculture: The Meaning of Style.* London: Methuen, 1979.

Hellman, Lillian. *Pentimento: A Book of Portraits.* New York: NAL, 1973.

Hirsch, E. D., Jr. *Cultural Literacy: What Every American Needs to Know.* Boston: Houghton, 1987.

Irigaray, Luce. *Speculum of the Other Woman.* Trans. Gillian G. Gill. Ithaca: Cornell UP, 1985.

———. *This Sex Which Is Not One.* Trans. Catherine Porter with Carolyn Burke. Ithaca: Cornell UP, 1985.

———. "Women's Exile." *Ideology and Consciousness* 1 (1977): 57–76.

Jardine, Alice. *Gynesis: Configurations of Woman and Modernity.* Ithaca: Cornell UP, 1985.

———. "Opaque Texts and Transparent Contexts: The Political Difference of Julia Kristeva." Miller 96–116.

Juncker, Clara. "Writing (with) Cixous." *College English* 50 (1988): 424–35.

Kristeva, Julia. "Freud and Love: Treatment and Its Discontents." Trans. Leon S. Roudiez. Moi, *Kristeva* 238–71.

———. "Postmodernism?" *Romanticism, Modernism, Postmodernism.* Ed. Harry R. Garvin. Lewisburg: Bucknell UP, 1980. 136–41.

————. *Powers of Horror: An Essay on Abjection.* Trans. Leon S. Roudiez. New York: Columbia UP, 1982.

————. "Psychoanalysis and the Polis." Trans. Margaret Waller. Moi, *Kristeva,* 301–20.

————. "The System and the Speaking Subject." Moi, *Kristeva,* 25–33.

————. "Women's Time." Trans. Alice Jardine and Harry Blake. Moi, *Kristeva,* 188–213.

Lyotard, Jean-François. "For a Pseudo-Theory." *Yale French Studies* 52 (1975): 115–27.

————. *The Postmodern Condition: A Report on Knowledge.* Trans. Geoff Bennington and Brian Massumi. Minneapolis: U of Minnesota P, 1984.

Miller, Nancy K., ed. *The Poetics of Gender.* New York: Columbia UP, 1986.

Moi, Toril. "Feminism, Postmodernism, and Style: Recent Feminist Criticism in the United States." *Cultural Critique* 9 (1988): 3–22.

————, ed. *The Kristeva Reader.* New York: Columbia UP, 1986.

————. *Sexual/Textual Politics: Feminist Literary Theory.* London: Methuen, 1985.

Ong, Walter J. *Fighting for Life: Contest, Sexuality, and Consciousness.* Amherst: U of Massachusetts P, 1989.

————. *Orality and Literacy: The Technologizing of the Word.* London: Methuen, 1982.

Plaza, Monique. "'Phallomorphic Power' and the Psychology of 'Woman.'" *Ideology and Consciousness* 4 (1978): 4–36.

Rabine, Leslie W. "*Écriture Féminine* as Metaphor." *Cultural Critique* 8 (1988): 19–44.

Richman, Michele. "Sex and Signs: The Language of French Feminist Criticism." *Language and Style* 13 (1980): 62–81.

Sloterdijk, Peter. *Critique of Cynical Reason.* Trans. Michael Eldred. Minneapolis: U of Minnesota P, 1987.

Spivak, Gayatri Chakravorty. *In Other Words: Essays in Cultural Politics.* New York: Methuen, 1987.

Stanton, Domna C. "Difference on Trial: A Critique of Material Metaphor in Cixous, Irigaray, and Kristeva." Miller 157–82.

Suleiman, Susan Rubin. "(Re)Writing the Body: The Politics and Poetics of Female Eroticism." *The Female Body in Western Culture: Contemporary Perspectives.* Ed. Suleiman. Cambridge: Harvard UP, 1986. 7–29.

Ulmer, Gregory L. *Applied Grammatology: Post(e)-Pedagogy from Jacques Derrida to Joseph Beuys.* Baltimore: Johns Hopkins UP, 1985.

Worsham, Lynn. "The Question Concerning Invention: Hermeneutics and the Genesis of Writing." *Pre/Text* 8 (1987): 197–244.

————. "The Question of Writing Otherwise: A Critique of Composition Theory." Diss. Univ. of Texas, Arlington, 1988.

8

Feminism and Methodology in Composition Studies

PATRICIA A. SULLIVAN

T he contemporary feminist movement and the field of composition studies have, in a sense, grown up together. Both emerged in the sixties, the former as an organized movement to counter large-scale sex discrimination and social inequality in American culture, the latter as an institutional response to a widely perceived literacy crisis. Both came into their own on university campuses in the 1970s, when women's studies programs were developed to research women's issues and concerns long neglected by the traditionally masculinist agendas of the academy, and composition established itself as a research specialization within doctoral programs in education and English. By the late eighties, feminism had made inroads into nearly all academic disciplines and had made a profound impact on literary criticism and the social sciences. Composition studies, too, had expanded its initial focus on freshman composition to include writing across the disciplines and the writing of professionals in both academic and nonacademic settings. While the contemporary feminist movement and the field of composition emerged in the same historical period, however, they developed independently of each other. Feminist research has not made the same inroads in composition studies as it has in other disciplines. Indeed, research on writing has remained silent on issues of gender until quite recently.[1]

Why has composition studies remained virtually unaffected by feminist inquiry and critique until recent years? Feminist critiques of male bias and androcentrism in the academy are usually leveled against established disciplines whose canons, theories, and discourses inscribe patriarchal values and perpetuate sexist and exclusionary practices. When feminist literary scholars in English departments were critiquing sexism in male-authored texts and recovering the work of women writers, composition scholars were engaged in a different kind of political struggle, a struggle for recognition and status in those same departments. Composition itself was marginalized, and composition scholars had to constitute the discipline as a viable field of inquiry and peda-

From *Methods and Methodology in Composition Research.* Ed. Gesa E. Kirsch and Patricia A. Sullivan. Carbondale: Southern Illinois UP, 1992. 37–61.

gogy. They had to argue the need for scholarship in literacy against the more narrowly defined field of literary studies and clear a space for student writing in a house that was built for canonized authors. Some scholars made the case for composition explicitly, like Maxine Hairston in her address to the 1985 Conference on College Composition and Communication, while others demonstrated the value of composition studies implicitly through their own research, like Mina Shaughnessy in her landmark study of basic writing (*Errors and Expectations*). The fact that women have been at the forefront of composition's struggle for autonomy also has bearing on why composition has thus far been relatively exempt from the kinds of feminist critique leveled at other disciplines: women have been present and influential in the field from the start.

Unlike other, more established disciplines, composition counts a significant number of women among its first and second generations of scholars. Women such as Hairston and Shaughnessy, Janet Emig, Ann Berthoff, Andrea Lunsford, Nancy Sommers, and Linda Flower have played an influential role in defining the field—articulating questions and issues for research, crafting new pedagogies, and overseeing program design and administration. While the ground-breaking work of many of these scholars was not explicitly or self-consciously feminist, the very fact that women helped to chart composition's course over two decades has enabled composition studies to avoid some of the more overtly androcentric practices that inform the research methodologies of other disciplines. Unlike the fields of psychology and medicine, for example, where conclusions about human intellectual development and aging have often been drawn exclusively from studies of male populations, empirical studies of the composing process have always included both male and female subjects, reflecting a more egalitarian ethic. A liberal ethic of equal rights and equal opportunity, in fact, has resided in "the political unconscious" of our discipline from its inception. The emergence of composition was coincident not only with a nationally perceived literacy crisis but with open admission policies that drew a broad and diverse cross section of American culture into college classrooms. Many composition scholars and teachers served as advocates for all students' rights to literacy regardless of a student's age, race, gender, socioeconomic background, or national origin. It is composition's humane disregard for difference under an egalitarian ethic, however, that now renders it pervious to feminist inquiry and critique. For the assumption of equality tends to mask difference, the critical difference it makes, from a feminist perspective, whether a writer, or a researcher for that matter, is a man or a woman.[2]

Some of the earliest and most influential studies of our discipline have forged general propositions about "the way writers write" without considering the influence of gender on the composing process and on the texts and contexts of written communication. We have been slow to take into account either the patriarchal structures and values embedded in our culture that students bring to the classroom or the ways that men's and women's differential relationships to various cultural institutions, including the academy, influence their discursive practices. Women students enter an academic community in which men have largely determined what is important to know, how knowledge is organized, how knowledge is made, and, most importantly for composition scholars and teachers, how knowledge is expressed. The academic discourses that men and women students must "master" in order to succeed in the academy are largely inscriptions of male subjectivities; women have inherited modes of discourse that they have had little voice in shaping.[3]

At issue for feminist composition researchers and teachers is not whether women can accommodate themselves to the knowledge or discourses of academe, for women have proven that they can "cross-dress," that they can master the male idiom, that they can engage in either adversarial or disinterested modes of discourse and succeed by whatever standards we choose to measure success. Rather, feminist scholars take issue with the assumption that discourse is gender neutral, that the literate practices of male and female writers and readers bear no traces of their differential relationships to culture. Feminist scholars emphasize that gender is "basic to all aspects of human experience; it functions as a lens through which all other perceptions pass" (Foss and Foss 67). In composition studies, feminists are concerned with identifying the androcentrism of the academy at large and of our own discipline as it affects research and teaching practices; with uncovering the gendered nature of the written discourses and the writing processes we teach; and with learning what women deem important to know, how women organize and express knowledge, and how women make meaning in a world in which they are differentially situated as subjects. As both an ideology and a praxis, feminism not only reinterprets but seeks to change the dominant, patriarchal structures and categories of experience that have rendered women's activities and social relations analytically invisible. Feminist scholarship in composition thus has both reactive and proactive components: it focuses on received knowledge—on the existing studies, canons, discourses, theories, assumptions, and practices of our discipline—and reexamines them in the light of feminist theory to uncover male bias and androcentrism; and it recuperates and constitutes distinctively feminine modes of thinking and expression by taking gender, and in particular women's experiences, perceptions, and meanings, as the starting point of inquiry or as the key datum for analysis. These two components of feminist scholarship offer the researcher two general strategies or approaches, one derived from the historical, critical, and interpretive practices of humanistic inquiry, the other from experimental and field-research models of the social sciences. While these strategies are not mutually exclusive (both involve theory construction and both draw upon the findings and insights of the other during the research process), I will focus on each of them in turn to foreground some of the procedural and ideological issues germane to each.

FEMINIST RE-VISIONS: ANALYSIS AND CRITIQUE

Like feminist literary analysis, feminist critique in composition involves a reinterpretation of the extant literature of our discipline. But since our literature includes empirical studies and textbooks in addition to theoretical and historical scholarship, reinterpretation often involves a metatheoretical critique of methodological assumptions as well as a critical reexamination of a particular study or text. The scholar's purpose may be to expose and deconstruct the latent androcentrism or overt sexism in a text; to pluralize a given perspective by locating an alternate feminist perspective alongside it; to refine or lend an interpretive richness to an existing study by incorporating issues of gender; or to supplant a previous reading or interpretation with a reading grounded in feminist research. In each case, the scholar challenges or problematizes traditional assumptions and theories to help us gain a fuller understanding of the cultural contexts of written communication.

Within this general framework, of course, it would be possible to critique any study that failed to take into account the influence of gender on the rhetorical practices of the writers and readers under study or on the research process. Nearly all of the research that has been conducted in composition studies in the last two decades would fall into this category, rendering feminist critique a formidable if not impossible project. Thus it would be more fruitful at this stage to focus on those cases where a feminist reading or interpretation is clearly at odds with the analysis or interpretation provided by the researcher and/or where considerations of gender might have led the researcher to different results or different conclusions. By implication, I am suggesting that there is a core of knowledge and theory in composition that, if reexamined in light of feminist assumptions, would still elicit our assent, a body of research that does not explicitly take gender into account but that offers no grounds for feminist critique because the conclusions drawn are deemed to be valid across gender categories. I am also implying, however, that the mere inclusion of both men and women subjects at the stage of data collection, either through random sampling or deliberate selection procedures, does not necessarily ensure that a study will be free of androcentric bias. Such inclusiveness, as I suggested earlier, may be a liability in that it may induce a researcher, in some instances, to overlook the potential significance of gender in interpreting her results.

One of my own earlier studies is just such an instance. Several years ago I conducted a study of graduate-student writing that involved case studies of two master's and two doctoral students, each enrolled in a different literature seminar ("From Student to Scholar"). I was careful to include both men and women in my study and, as often as possible, to describe in their own words their writing experiences in their respective courses. But when it came time to analyze the experience of one of the master's students, a woman who found it difficult to meet her professor's expectations about what constituted successful writing in a seminar on Shakespeare, I overlooked connections between gender and composing. In the six position papers the student was required to write, she tended to explore thematic issues she discovered in the plays she was reading rather than argue with critics' assessments of those plays, and she chose to proceed inductively and recursively rather than adopt the "thesis-proof model" her professor specifically asked for. Her term paper similarly reflected exploratory rather than critical modes of discourse. Though she perceived herself as a good writer and had been an *A* student as an undergraduate, in this course she received a grade of only satisfactory on the best of her position papers and a *B* on her term paper. In my analysis of this student's writing, I concurred with her (male) professor and indeed with her own judgment that she had not mastered the standard conventions of literary argumentation, and while I noted that she often expressed a lack of confidence in her own critical authority, I traced both her lack of confidence and her inability to engage in conventional modes of argument to her inexperience in graduate school. In other words, instead of regarding her resistance to these modes as significant in itself and analyzing the modes of thinking and expression with which she did choose to do her intellectual work, I concentrated solely on the disjuncture between her writing performance and her teacher's expectations. Hence, I "saw" deficiency where I might only have seen difference, and I attributed this deficiency to her inexperience as a graduate student rather than to her own sense as a woman "that the terms of academic discourse [were] not her language" (Rich 244). Had I interpreted her experience through the lens of gender, I might not have concluded that I had observed a substandard writing performance born of inexperience, but only a nonstandard performance in a course where male conventions of discourse were allowed to define the standard.

I offer this critique of my own study to illustrate how an analysis of data based on an assumption of gender difference rather than universality can radically alter the conclusions we draw, indeed even the events we observe. To provide a more extensive example of feminist critique in composition and to illustrate the ways that androcentrism can blind an author to the influences of gender not only on composing but on his or her own methodology, I turn to Stephen North's *The Making of Knowledge in Composition: Portrait of an Emerging Field,* where we can find a narrative that has many parallels to my own case study of a graduate-student writer. I could begin by pointing out that nowhere in North's portrait of our field is there any mention of feminism as an ideology or praxis, an omission that says a great deal, depending on a reader's perpective, about composition studies in general or about North's own ideological orientation to the field. But rather than review North's book, I wish to focus on several passages that occur in an early chapter, when North is discussing practitioners as knowledge makers (37–42).

Practice-as-inquiry, North tells us, requires six steps, the first two of which are identifying a problem and searching for causes. When practitioners identify a problem for inquiry, they do so because "routine somehow fails them." "In my own experience," he writes, "this discomfiture has taken the form of a graduate student who, despite serious preparation, had been unable to pass her M.A. comprehensive exam in English in three tries." He then tells the following story to offer his readers a "typical account" of the practitioner's search for causes:

> The graduate student I described above as preparing for her M.A. comprehensive exam worked with me for nearly 1½ years. To prepare her, we

studied her failing exams, compared them to passing exams written by other people, had her write (and rewrite) literally hundreds of practice exam questions, reviewed the material—in short, we tried every approach I could think of. I did identify what seemed to be a few significant textual patterns: answers developed in a form that reflected her progress through the text(s) in question rather than some conceptual or analytical organization; odd uses of critical terms; a tendency to not address questions. But these were symptoms, not causes. The real question was why: Why did she write answers in these ways? Exam pressure? Lack of understanding of the material? The genre of comprehensive exam writing? Or was she merely the victim of an unreliable grading system?

The instructional breakthrough seemed to come after about a year when, angry with me, and probably sick of the whole business, the student wrote a rather hostile analysis of Jonson's "To Penshurst." For the first time, her persona seemed to have the kind of authority that had been missing from all her other answers. And just a few months afterward, she retook the comprehensives, and passed—pretty handily, I gather. Why? What had changed? That shift in persona marked a significant turning point for both of us, but what exactly did it signify? That is, what cause or causes of her unsuccessful exam writing had our interaction, and her work, affected? (41–42)

In his analysis of this student's writing problems and subsequent breakthrough, North relinquishes his search for causes because "clear though they may be in retrospect, causes are seldom much more than cloudy, changeable hypotheses." Indeed, North's purpose in telling this story is to make this very point. But the story that North tells is likely to strike a dissonant chord in many feminist readers, and the point he makes, while not in itself antithetical to feminist theories of knowledge, is premised on a model of inquiry that is inhospitable to feminist issues and methods of inquiry.

Practitioners, according to North, are interested in finding solutions to the problems they have identified, and thus, they do not search for reasons, explanations, or underlying cirmcumstances that might account for a student's literate behavior but for *causes;* they want to find the antidote that will eradicate the problem at its source and not merely treat the symptoms. Practitioner inquiry for North is thus grounded in a deterministic model of human behavior, in a behavioristic psychology that is the clinical offspring of positivist science. Writing problems are symptoms of an underlying illness; if the teacher-doctor can locate the problem at its source, he can prescribe the proper antidote or exercise that will cure the writer of her ills. The behavioristic dimensions of North's model explain his tendency to locate the problem in the writer, or more specifically, in the psychology of the writer rather than in the cultural and political circumstances of her situation: she succumbs to exam pressure, or she lacks understanding of the material, or she's unfamiliar with the genre of comprehensive exam writing. When he turns to the writer's environment to search for a probable cause of her problems, he posits an improbable cause—"an unreliable grading system." (She's failed three times, after all.) The positivist elements in North's model also explain why he relinquishes his search for the causes responsible for the student's instructional break-through: by the terms of his own epistemology, he must discover what is actually the case; he must separate reality from a range of appearances, symptoms, and speculations. But since practitioner inquiry, for North, always proceeds through guesswork, he has no methodological means of distinguishing reality from his own "half-formed guesses and cloudy intuitions." Thus, the "true" cause forever, and necessarily, remains elusive.

Most problematic from a feminist perspective, however, is that North's model functions, in effect, to suppress the underlying issues of gender his story inscribes. North does not consider gender as a possible source of the graduate student's difficulty, nor, in the positivist terms in which he casts his notion of causality, can he, for he would have to posit her sex as the *cause* of her difficulty and hence, as something that could be cured or that would be amenable to treatment. He could, of course, introduce gender at the point where he speculates about why the student writes answers as she does. Since he allows that the genre of comprehensive exam taking might be responsible for the student's difficulties, he could also allow that the gender of comprehensive exam writing has something to do with her difficulties. Indeed, by replacing the word *genre* with the word *gender,* he might have placed himself in a more advantageous position to begin to account for the significant textual patterns he has just identified. But (again) for North, the practitioner's desire for an immediate solution to a problem that resides solely in the writer leaves the cultural, political, and historical circumstances of the writer's situation beyond the pale of practitioner inquiry.

If North's model suppresses issues of gender, it also leaves no room for feminist approaches to practitioner research. North most clearly reveals the androcentrism of the framework in which he is working when he bypasses the student herself, her subjectivity, as a place to search for "causes." Nowhere in North's account is the woman herself allowed to speak. We simply do not know what she would say if she could tell the story for herself, how she would interpret her three failures or her eventual success. Hers is an untold story, a story we're not permitted to hear, an "other" perspective we're not allowed to share. In North's model of practitioner inquiry, the roles of teacher and student are clearly demarcated. It is the teacher-researcher who diagnoses the patient and searches for a solution ("we tried every approach I could think of"); the student is the object of inquiry, her mind, but not her subjectivity, a place to search for answers. Her subjective experiences and her writing itself never count for more than symptoms.

Interestingly, however, even as North abandons the search for causes, he leaves a door open to his readers to continue their own speculations by asking a question that his own methodological apparatus leaves him unable to answer: What does the student's turning point signify? From a feminist perspective, North's account of this student's hard-won success in taking her exams and her subsequent change in status is rich indeed in its significations. We notice first in North's narrative that it is when the student becomes angry, writing a "rather hostile" analysis of "To Penshurst," that her persona assumes a kind of authority that seemed to be missing in her earlier answers, and she goes on to pass her exams pretty handily. In other words, when she assumes an agonistic relation to a text, when she criticizes a text, she writes with what North and her exam committee recognize as authority and passes her exams. To a feminist reader the implication is obvious: the student masters the genre/gender of comprehensive exam writing. But we also notice in North's account that it is not the woman's voice that assumes a kind of authority, but a persona. Her anger, in other words, affords her a mask through which to speak. Would North have chosen to describe the student as writing behind a persona rather than speaking with authority if the student were male? Why must her hostility to a poem like "To Penshurst" (which celebrates male ownership of an estate that includes not only bountiful woods and gardens but a "fruitful" wife, "chaste withal," such that the lord of the manor may call his children "his own") be interpreted as a guise that permits her to critique and resist the text? Quite possibly, the anger with which this woman responds to a male teacher and critiques what she perceives as a sexist poem is born of her own experiences as a woman in a male-dominated culture. But if so, then this very culture ensnares her in a paradox. She must become angry to speak with the kind of critical authority required by English professors on exam committees. Her subjectivity must speak itself in traditionally defined ways, in the disputational discourse or father tongue of the academy. But when she does become angry, she is not, as a woman, allowed to own her anger, nor the authority it generates. Her authority must be perceived as speaking through a mask in order to be deemed acceptable to a male reader. We can understand the full implications of this paradox if we ask how this woman's subjectivity speaks itself (or writes itself) when it isn't speaking with (a masculinist conception of) authority. North may have provided a partial answer when he identified those "significant textual patterns" that he dismissed as symptoms. Quite possibly, she develops answers in a form that reflects "her progress through the text(s) in question rather than some conceptual or analytical organization"; she makes "odd uses of critical terms"; she has "a tendency to not address questions." Quite possibly, her writing speaks in the voice of a woman "taught early," as Adrienne Rich says, "that tones of confidence, challenge, anger, or assertiveness are strident and unfeminine" (243). Seen in this light, the shift in persona that marks a significant turning point for North and his student may indeed be a shift from voice to persona. But if so, then North may have been the unwitting agent (even as I was in my own case study) of the very process by which women's voices are rendered inaudible in the academy.

As my rereading of North and the critical reassessment of my own case study are meant to show, the aim of feminist criticism is never simply criticism for its own sake; rather, it hopes to contribute to our understanding of the gendered nature of composing, including those texts we compose under the name of "research." Feminist rereadings of the stories we have told may reveal to us the stories we have yet to tell; they may raise questions we have not thought to ask, issues (such as how women are socialized into academic discourse communities) that have remained invisible under the assumption that gender has no impact on experience. Feminist critiques may also challenge the ways in which we have traditionally constructed our stories, the processes by which we ascertain truth and impart knowledge to the larger research community. I have objected to North's search for causes and to his omission of his student's perceptions of her experiences, for example, on epistemological and procedural grounds. In doing so, I have implicitly suggested that there are fundamental differences between traditional approaches to inquiry and feminist methodology. In the next section, I hope to make these philosophical and methodological differences more explicit.

FEMINIST CONSTRUCTIONS OF KNOWLEDGE

If feminist critique is essentially reactive, focusing on the extant studies, theories, and text(book)s that comprise the literature of our discipline, feminist empirical research is essentially proactive: it seeks to generate new knowledge about the relationships between gender and composing that can help us counteract the androcentrism that leaves women's modes of thinking and expression suppressed and undervalued. While there are no uniquely feminist methods for gathering evidence, feminist inquiry is distinct from other types of inquiry in at least one respect: it takes gender as its starting point. Whether the researcher is specifically interested in invention, forms of expression, ways of making meaning, or the role that audience plays in text production, he or she seeks to learn more about the ways that men's and women's different relationships to culture affect their writing processes or the specific rhetorical and linguistic features of their written texts. Examples of studies in composition that take gender issues as their starting point include Geoffrey Sirc's "Gender and 'Writing Formations' in First-Year Narratives," Donnalee Rubin's "Gender Influence: Reading Student Texts," and Cinthia Gannett's *Gender and the Journal: Diaries and Academic Discourse*. Each relies on a different set of techniques for data collection and analysis, but in each case the specific features of written discourse that form the ostensive topic of inquiry are actually subsumed under a problematic of gender.

Obviously, not all studies that locate their problematics in issues of gender can be characterized as feminist. Throughout the history of modern science, male researchers have undertaken studies of gender difference—from comparisons of male and female skull and brain size to men's and women's different methods for resolving conflict—to establish male superiority and legitimate women's exclusion from education and from positions of leadership (Fee, "Nineteenth-Century Craniology"; Gilligan).[4] Taking gender as the starting point of inquiry, then, is a necessary but not a sufficient condition of feminist methodology, for feminism has as its ideological goal the overturning of patriarchal assumptions and practices that render women's experiences invisible and undervalued. In composition studies, research on gender difference may be characterized as feminist, at least at this moment in our institutional history, if it explores relationships between gender and writing to illuminate women's distinctive modes of thinking and expression. This does not mean, as Sandra Harding points out, that feminist researchers "try to substitute one set of gender loyalties for the other—'woman-centered' for 'man-centered' hypotheses. They try instead, to arrive at hypotheses that are free of gender loyalties" (*The Science Question* 138). But since women's experiences and ways of knowing have been suppressed in the history of Western culture, we first "often have to formulate a 'woman-centered' hypothesis in order even to comprehend a gender-free one" (138). In other words, we may need to focus on discourse from the perspective of women's experiences even to understand men's communicative practices as gendered rather than as representing the human.

Harding identifies three characteristics of feminist research in the social sciences that are relevant to feminist research in composition. First, it "generates its problematics from the perspective of women's experiences" and "uses these experiences as a significant indicator of the reality against which hypotheses are tested." Second, it "is designed for women." That is, "the goal of this inquiry is to provide women explanations of social phenomena that they want and need." And third, it "insists that the inquirer her/himself be placed in the same critical plane as the overt subject matter. . . . That is, the race, class, culture, and gender assumptions of the researcher her/himself must be placed within the frame of the picture that she/he paints" ("Is There a Feminist Method?" 8–9). Each of these characteristics represents a more or less radical departure from traditional assumptions and paradigms of knowledge making in the field in composition: we tend to generate our problematics from gender-neutral perspectives; we assume that we already are providing women with explanations of composing they want and need by including both men and women subjects in our various investigations and by publishing our theories and findings for a gender-inclusive audience; and those of us who conduct empirical research generally assume that we must control for our personal biases and cultural situatedness in order to be objective, to paint an accurate and reliable picture of the reality we observe. Harding's characteristics, then, problematize "business as usual" in composition studies by challenging assumptions of gender neutrality, gender inclusiveness, and researcher disinterestedness. In the remainder of this chapter, I will elaborate on each of these issues in turn, though all, I believe, merit a fuller discussion than I am able to lend to them here.

In composition studies, we tend to generate our problematics from gender-neutral perspectives. We have asked what it means to compose as basic writers, nontraditional students, college freshmen, technical writers, graduate students, biologists, chemical engineers, corporate executives, and so on, and we have generally assumed that the gender of the writer was irrelevant to the problematics of composing that formed the basis of our inquiry. Thus, we have not systematically explored, as Elizabeth Flynn points out, what it means for the women writers within any of these discourse communities to compose as women ("Composing as a Woman"). In some instances, of course, the influence of gender on the writing practices of the group we are studying will be negligible. But in other cases, the assumption of gender neutrality could conceal an androcentric bias or allow men's experiences to define characteristic ways of thinking and writing for both men and women. Consider, for example, a study in which we are interested in the discourse processes by which students in an engineering class learn to become effective problem solvers. We observe the class, collect the students' writing over the course of the term, and code and analyze the data for instances of problem solving. If we do not differentiate between the male and female students in the class and do not take into account the fact that engineering is a male-dominated discipline, the mere fact that men outnumber women in the class will allow men's problem-solving and discourse practices to define the standard, the reality against which individual performances are measured. Women's cognitive styles and discourse strategies will be suppressed or marginalized, their underrepresentation in the discipline reified by our methods. Or consider, on the other hand, studies of writing and the teaching of writing where women comprise the majority of the group we are investigating. The persons we designate under the label nontraditional students, for example, are most often women, women who have raised families or who have delayed their own education to further their partners' careers. Most part-time composition faculty, too, are women—a fact we have yet to acknowledge in our professional guidelines and recommendations for the postsecondary teaching of writing.[5] Studies that concentrate on the distinctive curricular requirements of adult learners or on the inequitable labor conditions and earnings of instructors but that overlook the explicit correlation between gender and status—the fact that it is because these students and teachers are women that they have been defined as nontraditional students or have taken part-time positions—once again leave women's experiences suppressed. In the first example, generating our problematics from the perspective and experiences of the women in the engineering course could help us to learn more about the ways in which the genres and contexts of engineering discourse are gendered; instead of universal descriptions of how engineers compose in response to various writing tasks, we might uncover gender-related strategies for solving problems and hence, perhaps, empower voices we were previously unaccustomed to hearing. In the second example, enlisting the perceptions of the women and men whose experiences we are studying can tell us more about the specific educational needs of returning students and the working conditions of part-time faculty than if we assume from the outset that gender roles are irrelevant to the situation and status of these groups. Instead of the stereotypical and hierarchical modes of thinking that so often accompany outsider perspectives, our curricula and policies will be shaped and guided by those in the best position to reveal what they should be.

While generating problematics from the perspective of women's experience may, in itself, provide women with theories of composing they want and need—Harding's second characteristic—there is no guarantee that composition research designed specifically for women will reach its intended audience. Dale Spender has documented the difficulty that feminist scholars in various disciplines have had in placing research about and for women in the principal journals of their fields (*The Writing or the Sex?*), and there is evidence to suggest that similar gatekeeping practices occur in composition. In her essay, "Composing 'Composing as a Woman,'" for example, Elizabeth Flynn recounts how reviewers of her earlier essay, "Composing as a Woman," were reluctant to publish her article because her explicitly feminist and metatheoretical approach did not conform to their conceptions of research. Flynn's second piece—itself a reflective and metatheoretical essay—was published in the section of the journal normally reserved for curricular issues and pedagogical strategies, the Staffroom Interchange. Apparently, studies of writing must take everyman as their audience, to borrow the apt and ideologically revealing term that recently adorned the cover of *College English* ("Everyman's Guide to Critical Theory," March 1990) in order for those studies to be regarded as research and as worthy of professional publication. Women, of course, are tacitly assumed to be included in this generic representation of readership (everyman presumably means every man and woman) and are also, therefore, automatically assumed to be interested and concerned with issues relevant to men. But reversing this semantic configuration reveals the problem with "inclusiveness." Men cannot be subsumed under the category everywoman. And so men are not automatically assumed, at least by journal editors, to be interested in research about and for women. Indeed, the publication of Flynn's work in a regular issue of *College Composition and Communication* is something of an anomaly, for research for women is nearly always assigned to special journal issues and to essay collections devoted exclusively to feminist scholarship and pedagogy.[6] Such research is published in regular issues of our principal journals only when editors narrow their perceptions of audience exclusively to women or to feminist women and men. Research by and for men requires no such narrowing because the universal audience of composition scholarship, figured in the generic everyman, is already male. The androcentrism that pervades our conceptions of audience and the potential for sexism that attends the fact that most of our journal editors are men are feminist issues in their own right, issues, I would add, in pressing need of study.

What Harding has identified as the third characteristic of feminist research—its insistence that the inquirer her/himself be placed in the same critical plane as the overt subject matter—is likely to be especially problematic for many composition researchers because it runs counter to long-held notions about what constitutes good empirical research, perhaps even research itself. The dominant paradigm, reflected throughout works such as Lauer and Asher's *Empirical Designs* and in parts of North's *The Making of Knowledge in Composition*, dictates that the researcher must detach herself from the object of inquiry and keep personal bias and values from influencing her observations and analysis if she is to paint an objective and undistorted picture of reality. Introducing into analysis the subjective elements of the researcher's own assumptions of race, class, culture, and gender would undermine the reliability and validity of the results; in effect, the researcher would have to relinquish whatever claims to knowledge she would like to have made for her study and assign her study to the domain of opinion or speculation.

As feminist philosophers and historians of science have pointed out, however, the concept of dispassionate, disinterested inquiry has itself arisen from patriarchal ideology. Methods of analysis that presumably guarantee the objectivity of a researcher's results are actually by-products of an androcentric epistemology that has historically equated subjectivity with the feminine mind. Empirical science, in its quest for socially transcendent truths and value-neutral facts about the world, detached the knower (or the scientist) from the object of study and insulated its objects of inquiry from the contingencies of lived experience. Women's lived experiences were rendered inaccessible to inquiry, and women themselves were excluded from knowlege making. "The Enlightenment vision," Harding writes:

> explicitly denied that women possessed the reason and powers of dispassionate, objective observation required by scientific thinking. Women could be objects of (masculine) reason and observation but never the subjects, never the reflecting and universalizing human minds. Only men were in fact envisioned as ideal knowers, for only men (of the appropriate class, race, and culture) possessed the innate capacities for socially transcendent observation and reason. ("The Instability" 292)

Elizabeth Fee similarly notes that the objective-subjective and rational-emotional dichotomies central to the scientific enterprise are distinctively masculine, rising from man's self-definition as a being of pure rationality and man's definition of woman as the repository of emotional life and of all the nonrational elements of human experience ("Women's Nature" 11–12). The methodological underpinnings of modern science, then, have developed according to male prescriptions and proscriptions of knowledge. But since they purport to hold a nondistorting mirror up to reality, to register objectively and dispassionately reality as it is, they appear to be value-neutral and hence gender-neutral as well. Feminist scholars point to the gender bias inscribed in the history and methodology of positivist science to show that the scientific enterprise itself is ideologically interested—and to argue, therefore, that no individual project that is based on a scientific methodology can claim to be disinterested. The realities recorded and reported via so-called objectivist methodologies are always versions of a reality that is subject to revision; reality "as it is" is always someone's perception, even if a collective perception or representation. The perspective from which this reality is glimpsed, moreover, is always a situated perspective. There is no "view from nowhere," as Susan Bordo writes, no "God's eye-view" from which "one can see nature as it really is, undistorted by human perspective" (143). The researcher's own race, class, culture, and gender assumptions are not neutral positions from which he or she observes the world but lenses that determine how and what the researcher sees. In choosing to make these assumptions explicit, the feminist researcher does not decrease the reliability of her observations nor the validity of her conclusions but only the objectivism, as Harding notes, that serves to hide this kind of evidence from the public ("Is There a Feminist Method?" 9). Put another way, feminist inquiry wears its heart on its sleeve: it originates in an ideological agenda that, instead of masking, it declares up front. But all empirical research, the feminist argues, is similarly interested or ideologically motivated; the difference between feminist inquiry and the dominant, hypothetico-deductive model of inquiry is that the latter has produced no self-generated practice of reflection on its racial, class, and gender biases.

While the three characteristics of feminist research that Harding delineates reveal fundamental differences between a feminist approach and traditional approaches to empirical research in composition, they do not represent a wholesale rejection of empiricism by feminists but only of the positivist elements that still linger in the dominant paradigm of scientific inquiry. Feminist researchers often seek out or devise alternative empirical methodologies whose principles and procedures are consonant with feminist ideology and praxis. Many are drawn, for example, to the cluster of methods that fall under the rubrics of qualitative and naturalistic inquiry. Techniques such as open-ended interviews and case studies enable researchers to generate descriptions of composing from the point of view and in the language of the writers they are studying. Participant observation, a defining feature of ethnomethodology, allows researchers to reflect critically on their own subject position, both as researchers and as authors, in the twin sites of study—in the field and on the page. And emergent forms of teacher research are helping researchers learn more about women's and men's different experiences within the classroom contexts in which they compose, about the cultural differences among individual writers in these contexts, and about the fluid and ever-shifting nature of these contexts themselves. But whether individual researchers are appropriating or revising conventions of empirical scholarship, their work is informed by the same purpose: they are consciously seeking to create the conditions and circumstances whereby voices, stories, and discourses too long silent in the academy can be heard.

In this chapter I have sought to claim for feminist research and scholarship a central role in composition studies. I have argued that we will have to resist the desire to subsume problematics of gender under universal descriptions of how writers write and ask, instead, what difference it makes to the writing situation whether a writer is a man or a woman. To do otherwise, I have suggested, is to give our tacit assent to an ideology that has allowed men's discursive practices to define the standard against which women's writing is judged. One of the places this ideology has found expression is in the traditional methodologies—the research practices and assumptions—of our discipline. Thus, we need to inquire not only into relationships between gender and composing but into the gendered nature of our research practices, including the cultural and historical traditions that have produced them.

What is finally at stake, I believe, if feminism is to become a fully realized voice within composition studies, is considerably more than the special interests of a subgroup of scholars in our field. If we do not as a research community undertake to understand issues of gender difference and sexual politics, we can never hope to achieve the full understanding of composing that has been the goal of composition studies from its inception.

NOTES

1. Elizabeth Flynn in her essay "Composing as a Woman" similarly notes that "the fields of feminist studies and composition studies have not engaged each other in a serious or systematic way." My debt to Flynn's essay will be apparent throughout this chapter. I also wish to acknowledge a number of colleagues whose insights and comments on various drafts of this chapter have proven invaluable: Gesa Kirsch, Cinthia Gannett, Donna Qualley, Elizabeth Chiseri-Strater, Bonnie Sunstein, and Sherrie Gradin.

2. While I view gender as a social construction rather than a biologically determined characteristic, my references to gendered dualisms such as "male and female modes of thinking" and "men's and women's differential relationships to culture" throughout this chapter would seem to commit me to a view of homogenized difference and thus to a form of essentialism. I certainly recognize that women and men come in different races, classes, and cultures, and I believe it would be mistaken to speak collectively of "woman's experience" or "man's experience." But race, class, and culture are also always categories within gender, and our culture, as Susan Bordo writes, is in fact constructed by gender duality: "Our language, intellectual history, and social forms are 'gendered'; there is no escape from this fact and from its consequences on our lives. . . . [L]ike it or not, in our present culture, our activities *are* coded as 'male' or 'female' and will function as such within the prevailing system of gender-power relations" (152).

3. A number of works in recent years have discussed the androcentrism of academic discourse stemming from women's historical exclusion from formal education, including Aisenberg and Harrington; Bleich; Presnell; and Spender (*Man Made Language*).

4. For additional examples and analyses of gender-based distortions in the history and practices of science, see Schiebinger; Harding (*The Science Question*); and Keller.

5. See the *Statement of Principles and Standards for the Postsecondary Teaching of Writing* published by the Conference on College Composition and Communication, October 1989.

6. Composition journals that have devoted special issues to feminist theory and to studies of gender and writing include *Journal of Advanced Composition* 10.2 (1990) and *College English* 51, 52 (1990). For edited collections on feminist theory, research, and pedagogy in composition, see Caywood and Overing and Phelps and Emig.

WORKS CITED

Aisenberg, Nadya, and Mona Harrington. *Women of Academe: Outsiders in the Sacred Grove.* Amherst: U of Massachusetts P, 1988.

Bleich, David. "Sexism in Academic Styles of Learning." *Journal of Advanced Composition* 10 (1990): 231–47.

Bordo, Susan. "Feminism, Postmodernism, and Gender-Scepticism." *Feminism/Postmodernism.* Ed. Linda J. Nicholson. New York: Routledge, 1990. 133–56.

Caywood, Cynthia L., and Gillian R. Overing, eds. *Teaching Writing: Pedagogy, Gender, and Equity.* Albany: State U of New York P, 1987.

Fee, Elizabeth. "Nineteenth-Century Craniology: The Study of the Female Skull." *Bulletin of the History of Medicine* 53 (1980): 414–33.

———. "Women's Nature and Scientific Objectivity." *Woman's Nature: Rationalizations of Inequality.* Ed. Marian Lowe and Ruth Hubbard. New York: Pergamon, 1982. 9–27.

Flynn, Elizabeth. "Composing as a Woman." *College Composition and Communication* 39 (1988): 423–35.

———. "Composing 'Composing as a Woman': A Perspective on Research." *College Composition and Communication* 41 (1990): 83–89.

Foss, Karen A., and Sonia K. Foss. "Incorporating the Feminist Perspective in Communication Scholarship: A Research Commentary." *Doing Research on Women's Communication.* Ed. Kathryn Carter and Carole Spitzack. Norwood, NJ: Ablex, 1989. 65–91.

Gannett, Cinthia. *Gender and the Journal: Diaries and Academic Discourse.* Albany: State U of New York P, 1992.

Gilligan, Carol. *In a Different Voice: Psychological Theory and Women's Development.* Cambridge, MA: Harvard UP, 1982.

Hairston, Maxine. "Breaking Our Bonds and Reaffirming Our Connections." *College Composition and Communication* 36 (1985): 272–82.

Harding, Sandra. "The Instability of the Analytical Categories of Feminist Theory." *Sex and Scientific Inquiry.* Ed. Sandra Harding and Jean F. O'Barr. Chicago: U of Chicago P, 1987. 283–302.

————. "Is There a Feminist Method?" *Feminism and Methodology.* Ed. Sandra Harding. Bloomington: Indiana UP, 1987. 1–14.

————. *The Science Question in Feminism.* Ithaca: Cornell UP, 1986.

Keller, Evelyn Fox. *Reflections on Gender and Science.* New Haven: Yale UP, 1984.

Lauer, Janice, and William Asher. *Composition Research: Empirical Designs.* New York: Oxford UP, 1988.

North, Stephen M. *The Making of Knowledge in Composition: Portrait of an Emerging Field.* Upper Montclair, NJ: Boynton/Cook, 1987.

Phelps, Louise Wetherbee, and Janet Emig, eds. *Feminine Principles and Women's Experience in American Composition and Rhetoric.* Pittsburgh: U of Pittsburgh P, 1995.

Presnell, Michael. "Narrative Gender Differences." *Doing Research on Women's Communication.* Ed. Kathryn Carter and Carole Spitzack. Norwood, NJ: Ablex, 1989. 118–36.

Rich, Adrienne. "Taking Women Students Seriously." *On Lies, Secrets, and Silence.* New York: Norton, 1979. 237–45.

Rubin, Donnalee. "Gender Influence: Reading Student Texts." Diss. U of New Hampshire, 1989.

Schiebinger, Londa. "The History and Philosophy of Women in Science: A Review Essay." *Sex and Scientific Inquiry.* Ed. Sandra Harding and Jean F. O'Barr. Chicago: U of Chicago P, 1987. 7–34.

Shaughnessy, Mina. *Errors and Expectations.* New York: Oxford UP, 1979.

Sirc, Geoffrey. "Gender and 'Writing Formations' in First-Year Narratives." *Freshman English News* 18 (1989): 4–11.

Spender, Dale. *Man Made Language.* London: Routledge, 1980.

————. *The Writing or the Sex?* New York: Pergamon, 1989.

Statement of Principles and Standards for the Postsecondary Teaching of Writing. Conference on College Composition and Communication. October 1989.

Sullivan, Patricia A. "From Student to Scholar: A Contextual Study of Graduate-Student Writing in English." Diss. Ohio State U, 1988.

9

Beyond the Personal: Theorizing a Politics of Location in Composition Research

GESA E. KIRSCH AND JOY S. RITCHIE

In recent years, feminist scholarship has begun to inform much research in composition studies. One particular emphasis has been on admitting the "personal" into our public discourse, on locating ourselves and research participants in our research studies. In what Adrienne Rich calls "a politics of location," theorizing begins with the material, not transcending the personal, but claiming it. The goal is, Rich says in an echo of Hélène Cixous, "to reconnect our thinking and speaking with the body of this particular living human individual, a woman" (213).[1] This new emphasis on the personal, on validating experience as a source of knowledge, raises a number of recurring questions: How does a politics of location inform—and change—research practices? How do we both affirm the importance of "location," and yet understand the limitations of our ability to locate ourselves and others? How do issues of power, gender, race, and class shape a politics of location? What ethical principles are consistent with feminist scholarship and can guide researchers? Although these questions are clearly important in feminist scholarship, they are not merely feminist issues. They mark an important point where feminist theories can inform composition studies. And although we believe women's experiences are an important starting point for research because they have been ignored and omitted in studies of many kinds, we also believe that what can be learned from women's experiences and from feminist theory has wider implications for composition research; it can become a location for reconsidering what counts as knowledge and for revitalizing research in composition.

In this article, we begin by examining what it means to bring a politics of location to composition research and by foregrounding some of the difficulties of assuming that perspective. We argue that it is not enough to claim the personal and locate ourselves in our scholarship and research. In doing so, we risk creating another set of "master narratives," risk speaking for and essentializing others, and risk being blinded by our own culturally determined

From *College Composition and Communication* 46 (1995): 7–29.

world views. Instead, we propose that composition researchers theorize their locations by examining their experiences as reflections of ideology and culture, by reinterpreting their own experiences through the eyes of others, and by recognizing their own split selves, their multiple and often unknowable identities. Further, we propose changes in research practices, such as collaborating with participants in the development of research questions, the interpretation of data at both the descriptive and interpretive levels, and the writing of research reports. Finally, we raise ethical questions that arise from these new research practices. We illustrate our argument with examples drawn from composition, including our own research, but also from scholarship in anthropology, oral history, and sociology. Scholars in those fields have a long history of using ethnomethodological research, have reflected on the role of the personal in research, and have encountered a range of ethical dilemmas.

A POLITICS OF LOCATION IN FEMINIST RESEARCH

We begin this essay by locating ourselves in this writing, although we recognize that any location is fluid, multiple, and illusive. The impulse to write this article came from a day-long conversation among several women during a workshop on feminism and composition at the 1992 CCCC.[2] These women, though mostly tenured and tenure-tracked and with successful teaching and publication records, were nevertheless frustrated because of the conflicts they experience as feminists in composition living in English departments. The issues we talked about that day suggested that we have been taught to devalue our own experiences as researchers and writers, our relationships with students and other teachers, and our own histories as sources for research and scholarship. As a result, we have often stripped the personal from our writing and research.

As we continued to think about the conflicts women expressed in that group, we began to realize that, in part, these conflicts arise from our varied and shifting locations in our discipline, particularly from attempts to hold feminist values and to focus on issues of gender in research, while we still accept the existing epistemologies and methodologies in the field—methodologies that often presuppose objectivity and gender-neutrality. We recognize this tension in our own research. Instead of working to question, resist, and transform traditional research practices, we often find ourselves attempting to live within the contradictions between our feminist beliefs and those traditionally valued in our discipline, even as we write this essay. As we explored these contradictions, we found that many feminists in other disciplines have already begun this work.

We believe researchers in composition must engage in the same kinds of discussions that feminist researchers are having in other disciplines concerning the "politics of location" in research. We hope to advance that discussion by presenting some of the feminist critiques of philosophical, methodological, and ethical assumptions underlying traditional research. In doing so we assert the importance of interrogating the motives for our research and the unspoken power relationships with the "subjects" of our research, considerations we hope will assist us in developing a more ethical approach to research.[3]

If we are to move beyond what Sandra Harding calls an "add women and stir" approach to research (*Feminism* 3), we need to examine just what a politics of location means for research, what are its implications and its limitations. How might we achieve a more problematized politics of location? Rich says that we can no longer utter phrases like "women always. . . ." Instead, she argues: "If we have learned anything in these years of late twentieth-century feminism, it's that that 'always' blots out what we really need to know: When, where, and under what conditions has the statement been true?" (214). But Rich does not suggest that research simply needs to provide the ethnographer's "thick descriptions" of context or to engage in superficial reflexivity. It is not enough to make the facile statements that often occur at the beginning of research articles, to say, "I am a white, middle-class woman from a midwestern university doing research." She urges women to investigate what has shaped their own perspectives and acknowledge what is contradictory, and perhaps unknowable, in that experience.

In addition to acknowledging our multiple positions, a politics of location must engage us in a rigorous ongoing exploration of *how* we do our research: What assumptions underlie our approaches to research and methodologies? And a politics of location must challenge our conception of *who* we are in our work: How are our conflicting positions, histories, and desires for power implicated in our research questions, methodologies, and conclusions? A politics of location allows us to claim the legitimacy of our experience, but it must be accompanied by a rigorously reflexive examination of ourselves as researchers that is as careful as our observation of the object of our inquiry (Harding, *Whose Science?* 149–50, 161–63). Thus, for example, researchers need to acknowledge the way race (and for most composition scholars this means examining their whiteness), social class, and other circumstances have structured their own thinking and how that, in turn, has shaped their own questions and interpretations. Rich observes: "Marginalized though we have been as women, as white and Western makers of theory, we also marginalize others because our lived experience is thoughtlessly white, because even our 'women's cultures' are rooted in some Western tradition" (219).

Finally, a postmodern feminist perspective leads us to continually question our ability to locate ourselves as researchers and to locate the participants in our research. We need to take into account what psychoanalytic, hermeneutic, and postmodern critics have already shown us about the limitations of our ability to fully understand our own motivations and perspectives. These scholars remind us that we can never fully step outside our culture in order to examine our assumptions, values, and goals. Pretending to do so amounts to what Stanley Fish calls the "theory hope of antifoundationalism" (qtd. in Bizzell 40), the belief that although we reject foundational truth as the basis of knowledge, we can nevertheless use critical analysis to interrogate the historical, political, and social contexts of our knowledge. But, as Fish reminds us, no attempt at analyzing our assumptions is neutral or value-free; it is always a culturally and politically charged activity.

This problematized "politics of location" may seem to make our task impossible; it may make us wonder if we can claim anything for our research. But instead of falling into inaction and despair, we move forward with the awareness that we can only approximate an understanding, noticing the multiple and contradictory positions researchers and participants occupy, complicating and politicizing our investigation, valuing the individual and the local, although we can never hope to understand them fully. We move forward with a willingness to pursue the difficulties inherent in a politics of location accompanied by an equal willingness to be unrelentingly self-reflective.

THE RISK OF ESSENTIALISM

While locating research questions in ourselves and our own experience is vital, it also creates unsettling problems and possibilities for the way we think about knowledge, authority, and power. Feminists have rightly challenged the claims to objectivity in traditional research, arguing that inattention to the researcher's location and subjectivity has led to what Donna Haraway calls the "god trick," researchers' false claims to an ahistorical and universal perspective that has caused gross omissions and erasures in claims of knowledge (qtd. in Harding, *Whose Science?* 153). But feminist theorists have also argued against the uncritical celebration of female experience situated in a fixed or "natural" female identity (Ritchie 255). In fact, it would be dangerous for women, as Teresa Ebert argues, to invest so much in the "local," the individual, the unique, that we forget the global power structures that oppress women (902).

It is not enough, then, to begin locating ourselves and our experiences. In doing so naively, we risk ignoring hierarchies and creating the same unifying and totalizing master narratives that feminist scholars have sought to revise and oppose. More specifically, we risk defining gender biologically rather than recognizing it as a varied set of social relationships. We risk limiting our definitions to a binary of male and female as opposite, inherently different human beings, without seeing the multiple permutations of gendered experience. Jane Flax argues that this will prevent us from adequately asking and answering the questions we need to articulate in order to understand how both men and women are affected by cultural contexts (*Thinking Fragments* 182).

In composition studies we risk making essentializing distinctions about writers: If they are male they must write or think *this* way; if they are female, they must write or think another. New research on gender and writing has made important contributions to composition studies and moved the field from being "gender-blind to gender-sensitive" (Peaden 260), but there remains the tendency to polarize—to essentialize—accounts of gender differences.[4] Don Kraemer suggests that in considering gender and language we look at the "range of social relations they imply" rather than read gender as "one monolithic language" (328). We argue that composition researchers need to resist the drive to generalize about men and women, that we can learn much from studying the multiple ways in which both men and women can express themselves, and that composition teachers need to develop pedagogical practices that encourage students to write in a wide variety of discourse forms, a task that Lillian Bridwell-Bowles has begun to map out successfully in "Discourse and Diversity."

Claiming our experience, then, may be as inadequate for making claims to knowledge as traditional claims from objectivity are. Harding points out that "our experience may lie to us" just as it has lied to male researchers who believed their positions were value-free or universal (*Whose Science?* 286). A number of African-American, lesbian, and Third World feminists, including bell hooks, have argued that simply privileging our experience may lead us to posit rigid and exclusionary definitions of experience that erase the interlocking structures of race, social class, and heterosexist oppression for men and women ("Feminist Politicization" 107–8). The result is that we create definitions of experience that produce dominant group "common-sense" norms so exclusive that the experience of non-white, non-dominant people is eliminated, while dominant gender, class, race, and sexuality produce more airtight, fastened down, comprehensive theories. Sidome Smith observes that feminist researchers "from the dominant culture" can easily appropriate the experiences of others if they are "unselfconscious about the possibility of such cultural appropriation" (401). Consider, for example, the experience that taught one of us (Ritchie) about the problems of cultural appropriation and representation.

Joy Ritchie: As I observed the writing of two women students in an advanced composition class—Manjit Kaur, a Punjabi from Malaysia, and BeeTin Choo, a Chinese woman from Singapore—I was struck by the rich and contradictory construction of selfhood in their writing. When I decided to report on their writing, I quickly recognized the political and ethical problems involved in writing *about* them, speaking *for* them, or attempting to represent their experiences. Instead, I invited them to co-author an article, thinking that allowing them to speak for themselves would help me avoid appropriating their writing for my purposes. But I discovered that we still faced many difficult decisions because of the complexity and multiplicity of each of our identities and motivations, most obviously because of our cultural differences, because of the complex power relations between students and professor, and because of the constraints of academic writing. For example, during the time we were writing our essay, after our proposal had been accepted by the editors, BeeTin became increasingly committed to a Christian perspective and was, therefore, uncomfortable with the feminist theoretical framework the other two of us favored. Both women were concerned particularly that their representations of their cultures, written in the relative safety of a classroom, would be misinterpreted by readers and used to solidify existing negative stereotypes of their culture. Whose theory, whose language, whose interpretation, and whose narrative voice would prevail? We had to negotiate these and other questions. I drafted the introduction and conclusion for the essay because I felt some responsibility for ensuring coherence among our three distinct voices, but I struggled, without complete success, to minimize the dominance of my narrative voice.

In a continuing dialogue as we wrote together, I learned more about the way my own cultural context constrained my perspective and often caused me to objectify "others." First, I had to recognize that my assumptions about international students and "Asian women students" led to limited and essentialized understanding of their lives as students, as women, and as writers. BeeTin's silence was not Asian acquiescence to authority; it was a form of resistance. Manjit's exploration of the roles of women in Malaysia and in the United States did not necessarily fit within my Western feminist assumptions about women's oppression. I realized that I set apart Manjit and BeeTin as essentialized "others" as I sought to define their voices and to analyze the style, form, and rhetorical features of their writing according to my own training in rhetoric. Although we finished the article, we considered abandoning it at several points because each of us felt at least slightly compromised in the essay that resulted (Ritchie, Kaur, Choo-Meyer).

If researchers are to preserve the value of experience as a source of knowledge, they need to locate the experience of others, especially those previously excluded or devalued. But they also need to recognize the impossibility of ever fully understanding another's experiences and to question their motives in gathering, selecting, and presenting those stories. It is important to step back from our own experience, to understand it as a reflection of ideology and culture. But this may not be enough. As Ritchie's work with her students suggests, the tendency to essentialize is only one symptom of what Michelle Fine calls the "knotty entanglement" of self and other (72). As researchers examine more carefully the relationship between themselves and participants, they will need to consider the provocative advice of Trinh Minh-ha: "In writing close to the other of the other, I can only choose to maintain a self-reflexively critical relationship toward the material, a relationship that defines both the subject written and the writing subject undoing the *I* while asking 'what do I want, wanting to *know* you—or me?'" (76).

Since researchers cannot assume that they understand what is relevant in the lives of others or even what are the important questions to ask, research participants must be invited to articulate research questions, to speak for themselves, to choose the occasions for and forms of representing their experiences. Inevitably, as in Ritchie's work with her students, participants' perspectives will reshape the assumptions and methodologies on which research is based, leading to more collaborative, complex, and "knottily entangled" research practices.

RELATIONSHIP OF THE KNOWER TO THE KNOWN

We have been focusing on the "knower" and her perspective on research. But feminist researchers have another significant and related concern—the "known" and its relationship to the "knower." One of the methodological changes proposed by feminist scholars is to establish more interactive, collaborative, and reciprocal relations between researchers and participants. These changes have come to us from pioneering work of scientists like Barbara McClintock and Evelyn Fox Keller, whose ideas about "objectivity" and the relationship between subject and object of study have complicated feminist research. McClintock's discoveries (documented by Keller) about genetic transposition in maize arose from her unconventional view of the role of the scientist and the relationship of observer and the observed. She no longer thought of the scientist as combative, manipulative, or dominant but rather in a relationship of intimacy and empathy with nature (Keller 117).

As scholars in composition we are uniquely positioned to interact closely with participants since much of our work involves us directly in the lives of students, teachers, and writers as we study their written and oral language. Our research strategies often bring us into lived daily relationships with research participants in ways not possible for biologists or even sociologists. Shirley Brice Heath's *Ways with Words* provides examples of daily lived interactions among research participants and researcher, although she mentions them only occasionally in her narrative: Heath's children played with the children in her study; she transported them in her car; she socialized with them in homes and churches. In the context of her work, Heath's participants became partners in research. Black and white teachers, mill workers, businessmen, and parents whose communities Heath was studying began themselves to observe and analyze the patterns of language use around them and could therefore begin to formulate questions and initiate change.

One of the assumptions underlying collaboration between researchers and participants is that it will benefit all parties involved in the interaction: Researchers can gather additional insights by getting to know participants in the context of their daily lives, and participants can gain new knowledge about themselves and their lives through the research project. Collaborative research practices often bring about methodological changes as well. One frequently quoted example of methodological innovation resulting from collaborative research is Ann Oakley's interview study of working-class pregnant women. When Oakley encountered women who asked her about prenatal care or other medical information, for example, she found that she could not follow traditional interview procedures: to deflect questions, withhold information, and maintain the role of distanced interviewer. Instead, Oakley decided that she had a moral obligation to assist these women in their quest for information. Consequently, she changed her research methodology in response to research participants: she engaged in dialogue with the women, provided them with information available to her, and helped them get access to prenatal care. Thus, she launched one of the early feminist critiques of social science research methodology. In composition studies, we need to be similarly sensitive to research procedures. Whether we study basic or professional writers, we need to ask participants to collaborate with us, to help us design our research questions, to ask for their feedback, to answer their questions, and to share our knowledge with them.

This formulation of collaborative research still does not go far enough. A feminist politics of location would require the learning about self to be as *reciprocal* as possible—with the researcher also gaining knowledge about her own life or at least reexamining her cultural and gender biases. Sherry Gorelick suggests that "the researcher is transformed in the process of research—influenced and taught by her respondent-participants as she influences them. Theory and practice emerge from their interaction" (469). In composition there are few published accounts in which researchers reflect on the knowledge they gained about themselves and their relations with others due to the research they conducted, and in the few places where such accounts appear, they are often relegated to a preface or epilogue. We suspect this has to do with the format of traditional research reports which do not invite researchers' self-reflections and introspections. But we have anecdotal evidence from colleagues and friends who have discovered that interactive, collaborative research leaves them with a changed understanding of themselves. We have already mentioned one such example: the collaborative writing project Ritchie undertook with two students and the profound questions it raised for her and her position as a white female university professor. Another example emerged in an interview study Kirsch conducted with academic women (*Women Writing the Academy*).

Gesa Kirsch: In my effort to learn more about the concerns of academic women in different disciplines and at different stages of their careers, I invited participants to collaborate with me during various stages of the research: I developed interview questions with the help of women who participated in the study, adding and revising questions in response to initial conversations. I also collaborated with women in the interpretation of interviews. As I began to record and transcribe interviews, I consulted with women about the themes I identified as important in their lives. Thus, I entered into a cycle of conversation whereby both researcher and participants shaped, to some extent, the interpretation of interviews. In many cases, the collaboration between myself and participants was mutually beneficial: the stories women told me transformed my sense of self as writer, as scholar, and as participant in the academic community; women themselves also reported gaining insights into their writing and research processes through the interviews. In some cases, the interviews led to friendships that extended well beyond the duration of my research.

But the cycle of collaboration also had limitations. For example, it was cut short by time constraints I faced as researcher and by participants' interest, availability, and willingness to collaborate with me. I also have to assume that some participants may have felt disappointed, misunderstood, or even manipulated. Although no woman directly expressed this sentiment to me, lack of interest in follow-up conversations and resistance to collaboration suggest that possibility.

Relations between researcher and participants will always retain the potential for misunderstandings, even exploitation—much like other human relationships do. This potential risk, however, should not lead to inaction; rather, researchers can learn to explore sites of conflict for the shifting, multiple, and contradictory positions researchers and participants inevitably occupy and for the ethical questions raised by collaborative research.

ETHICAL QUESTIONS: ISSUES OF POWER AND COLONIZATION

So far we have argued that a politics of location must begin with researchers who recognize their own subjectivity, who draw on their experiences to formulate research questions even as they recognize the limitations of their perspective, experiences, and understanding. Researchers' reflective and critical stance, however, is only the beginning. They must also investigate the relation between the knower and the known and explore the possibilities of collaboration with participants as they develop research questions, collect data, interpret findings, and write research reports. Finally, they must be open to change themselves, reexamining their own perspective continually as they collaborate with participants and come to recognize how their cultural, ethnic, gendered, and personal histories influence the shape of their research. Ideally, a politics of location enables reciprocal, dialogic, collaborative, and mutually beneficial relations between researchers and participants. However, this "ideal" research scenario often remains just that—an ideal. More often, researchers encounter epistemological, methodological, and—perhaps most troubling—ethical dilemmas. We now turn to ethical issues, such as questions of power and colonization, that scholars are likely to face in the research process.

The work of Michel Foucault and others has allowed us to see how observation, classification, and codification in the discourse of the academy are always exercises of power, sometimes more coercive than others. Issues of power and colonization can become particularly prominent in studies of oppressed or disenfranchised groups, as the example of Daphne Patai's work illustrates. She reflects on her experience of interviewing working-class women in Brazil, many of whom lived in poverty and lacked access to adequate health care and education:

> The dilemma of feminist researchers working on groups less privileged than themselves can be succinctly stated as follows: is it possible—not in theory, but in the actual conditions of the real world today—to write about the oppressed without becoming one of the oppressors? (139)

Patai ultimately answers this question in the negative, arguing that the material, economic, and political conditions that separate privileged feminist researchers from disenfranchised or oppressed women cannot easily be overcome, no matter how emancipatory the research methods are or how much good will the researcher brings to the project. She does not, however, suggest that scholars abandon all research that involves oppressed or disenfranchised people; instead, she suggests that scholars abandon their naiveté and learn to make professional judgments about the context, consequences, and potential benefits and drawbacks of their work.

Other ethical dilemmas can emerge when researchers solicit highly personal information from participants. Judith Stacey, a sociologist, faced an ethical dilemma when she interviewed a fundamentalist Christian woman. This woman revealed that she had been involved in a lesbian relationship before her marriage, but asked Stacey not to disclose that information. Thus, the researcher faced a dilemma:

> What feminist ethical principles could I invoke to guide me here? Principles of respect for research subjects and for a collaborative, egalitarian research relationship demand compliance, but this forced me to collude with the homophobic silencing of lesbian experience, as well as consciously to distort what I considered to be a crucial component of the ethnographic "truth" in my study. Whatever we [the interviewer and interviewee] decided, my ethnography was forced to betray a feminist principle. (114)

At times researchers will find that feminist principles are at odds with ethnographic ones. Feminist principles urge researchers to listen to women's voices, to cooperate with women in the telling of their stories, and to honor their trust. Ethnographic principles, on the other hand, urge researchers to be as accurate, exhaustive, and frank as possible in the process of gathering and presenting information about other people and cultures.

The kinds of ethical dilemmas Patai and Stacey describe also concern composition researchers. While composition research does not necessarily involve "disenfranchised groups," it often concerns groups who have less power and fewer resources than the researchers, such as students, basic writers, K–12 teachers, minorities, and women. Furthermore, composition scholars frequently solicit highly personal information from research participants, much in the same way that writing teachers who assign autobiographical essays can find themselves confronted with details about their students' lives that they never anticipated.[5] Researchers need to consider, for example, the dynamics of the interview situation. Although it may be dishonest to assume the stance of objective, detached interviewer, Sheila Riddell points out that it is equally problematic to position oneself as "just another woman" whose concerns in life are similar to those of the research participant (83–84). Because it creates a false atmosphere of equality and mutuality in which women are often eager to talk, this stance may seem to break down barriers between the researcher and participants, but it may also be manipulative or even coercive, while giving participants a false sense of control. Riddell's interviews with teenaged girls led her to speculate that women may talk more openly in some situations because of their social powerlessness and are thus easily exploited. In a long-term study of English teachers Ritchie faced similar issues.

Joy Ritchie: As my colleague David Wilson and I conducted a study of teachers' developing knowledge of their discipline and its pedagogy, I interviewed Carol Gulyas, one of our participants, several times over a period of four years while she completed her course work and began teaching. Because of the many hours I spent in interviews with her and because her position as a student in some of our classes and as a research and teaching assistant in our project, we developed a closer relationship with Carol than with other participants, a relationship she described as one of "love and caring." My position of authority, but also our frequent and extended contacts, as well as my position as a woman with similar concerns about children and parents, for example, no doubt caused Carol to be less reserved in revealing connections between her personal life and the development of her voice as a writer, as a teacher, and as a woman. According to Carol, our frequent prompts to reflect on and articulate her learning over several semesters encouraged and deepened her learning. Because Carol was so articulate, self-reflective, and astute in her analyses of herself and her peers, the data she provided, and especially the connection between her personal history and her theoretical learning, were crucial in shaping our conclusions. David and I recognized that our representation of her personal experience in our writing might be a distortion or an appropriation. But because we had been so intrusive in Carol's life, we could not withdraw—nor would we have wanted to—from Carol after the study was over. We felt more than the usual obligation to become an advocate for Carol in her emerging career, to encourage her to write her own account of her learning, even in counterpoint to our representation of it, and to continue to learn from her as a colleague (Gulyas; Wilson and Ritchie).

A final ethical dilemma we want to discuss concerns anthropologists, oral historians, and composition scholars alike: How can or should researchers respond to participants who do not share the researcher's values, who oppose feminist research goals, or who do not identify with feminist causes? We draw on another example from oral history to illustrate this ethical issue. Sondra Hale, an anthropologist who studies African and Middle Eastern women, reports on the dissonance she experienced in interviews with women who either did not identify themselves as feminists or did not share the researcher's notion of what it means to be a feminist. Hale describes her disappointment with an interview of a Sudanese women's movement leader who ignored Hale's invitation to reflect on her role and position in the movement. Instead, the woman chose to use the interview as an occasion to promote the "party line," to enhance the image of the Sudanese women's movement, even when it meant providing inaccurate information or exaggerating accomplishments. In composition studies, we can face similar dissonances in our interactions with research participants. In the interview study of academic women mentioned above, Kirsch also faced questions of how to interpret women's lives.

Gesa Kirsch: I interviewed a history professor who chose to distance herself from the feminist movement and repeatedly disavowed any interest in, sympathy with, or connections to feminist ideas. Yet she had been a "pioneer" in a field dominated by men and made many comments that were feminist in nature, such as pointing to the discrepancy between her values and those of her male colleagues, describing herself as a woman living in a "foreign" male culture, and expressing an interest in experimenting with forms of writing that went "against the academic grain." How was I to represent her views and comments? Should I use her comments that emphasized dissonance from feminist ideas, or should I offer my feminist reading of her interview? Taking my cues from feminist scholars, I addressed these questions by doing both; I juxtaposed her comments (in extended interview quotes) with my analysis and commentary, thereby giving readers evidence that allowed both perspectives to emerge. Of course, as the writer of the research report, I still retain authority by selecting interview quotes, arranging the text, and drawing on supporting theories.

To some degree, researchers cannot escape a position of power and the potential for appropriating or manipulating information. The point here, however, is not to suggest that scholars ignore or omit data that seem to contradict their views. Rather, the point is to encourage researchers to view dissonances as opportunities to examine deeply held assumptions and to allow multiple voices to emerge in their research studies, an act that will require innovation in writing research reports. (We discuss possibilities for new forms of writing below.) Only in that manner will researchers be able to allow readers to see the conflicting pieces of information they often gather in their work and the potential contradictions inherent in their interpretations.

We are not advocating a relativist approach to research here, however. Instead, we argue that feminist research goals should guide researchers' decisions. Feminist research can be distinguished from other research traditions by its emancipatory goals.[6] Feminist researchers not only set out to study and describe women's lives and experiences, but actively seek to understand and change the conditions of women's social and political realities. Thus, feminist researchers advocate using guiding questions like these for responding to ethical dilemmas: Who benefits from the research/theories? What are the possible outcomes of the research and the possible consequences for research participants? Whose interests are at stake? How and to what extent will the research change social realities for research participants? There are no easy solutions to the range of ethical dilemmas researchers can face. Like Patai, we do not think:

> that generic solutions can be found to the dilemmas feminists [and other researchers] face in conducting research, nor do [we] for an instant hold out the hope of devising exact "rules" that will resolve these issues for us. In [our] view, this is impossible because ethical problems do not arise as absolutes requiring "blind justice." (145)

Researchers will face difficult decisions in the research process, but a politics of location requires that researchers interrogate their relations with the people they study and the power they hold over them. Linda Alcoff suggests that "in order to evaluate attempts to speak for others in particular instances, we need to analyze the probable or actual effects of the words on the discursive and material context" (26). At times, researchers will have to refocus their research questions, find additional or different participants, assume roles other than that of participant-observer, leave some data unpublished, or even abandon a research project.

Toward an Ethics of Research

In the previous section we have raised some of the ethical questions inherent in a feminist politics of location. Although we do not claim to have all the answers, we want to suggest how composition researchers can begin to address these questions. As we have shown, these questions are intertwined with—and highlight the necessity for articulating—ethical concerns. However, as we have attempted earlier in this essay to problematize our understanding of a politics of location, we also need to problematize ethics, informing our view with the vigorous discussion of ethics in which feminists from various disciplines have recently engaged.[7] First we will consider how we might revise our definition of ethics based on caring, collaborative relationships with participants. Next, we suggest changes in research methods and forms of writing to meet these ethical demands, changes that allow multivocal, dialogic representations in our research narratives. Finally, we propose a reexamination of the goals and implications of research in a further attempt to examine an ethical stance in our work.

Feminist discussions of ethics call for a fundamental change in the way ethics is conceived. Traditional ethics are based on a fixed set of principles determined through rational means to guide one's approach to all problems. That approach assumes a universal applicability and fails to question beliefs in objectivity and neutrality. It also homogenizes differences in contexts and perspectives and fails to take into account the connection between political and moral questions. In general, feminist philosophers disavow traditional rule-governed ethics based on "universal" principles and on unbending rules, because acting from principle entails acting without experience and context, without a politics of location (e.g., Noddings, Schweickart, Young). An ethic of care often comes to different conclusions than an ethic of principle. Ethical behavior must be guided by natural sentiment or what Noddings calls "caring" within the context of human relationships. Unlike rule-bound ethics, "caring" requires one to place herself in an empathetic relationship in order to understand the other's point of view. For this reason an ethic of care is dependent on the engagement of "the personal"—a particular person of ethical character engaged in the examination of context, motivations, relationships, and responsibility (Tronto, "Beyond Gender" 657–58).

But empathy is not an unproblematic concept. Gregory Clark, paraphrasing Wyschogrod, notes that "an act of empathy is inherently an interpretation that eclipses, at least partially, the full reality of another's difference: it directs me to 'understand' another in my own terms" (66). Feminist critics, while acknowledging the importance of an ethic of care, point out the inherent hierarchies, paternalism, and inequalities even in this "caring" ethical model. Patrocinio Schweickart observes that "an ethic of care is no guarantee against self-deception—a discourse of care can be used to mask exploitative and uncaring conditions" (187). Further, Sarah Hoagland suggests that Noddings's ethic still posits a one-way relationship rather than a truly reciprocal relationship between the caring and cared-for. Such unidirectional relationships of care, she argues, reinforce oppressive institutions (250–53).

Hoagland's concern seems especially relevant for composition researchers because of the problems inherent in seemingly benevolent but unequal relationships. It suggests that researchers continually interrogate their relations with participants, working toward dialogic, mutually educative, caring relations while at the same time recognizing that the complex power dynamics between researcher and participants can undermine, threaten, or manipulate those relations. Engaging in more collaborative approaches to research can help reduce the distance between researchers and participants. Participants can be brought in as co-researchers; those who have been marginalized can be encouraged to join in posing research questions that matter to them. Not only should participants co-author the questions, they can also work with researchers to negotiate the interpretations of data at both the descriptive and interpretive level. bell hooks is most insistent that white, privileged researchers and writers stop asking disempowered women to tell their stories so that these women can rewrite them in their own language, making their stories their own ("Choosing the Margin" 152). Madeleine Grumet provides further suggestions for reciprocal relationships between researchers and participants:

> So if telling a story requires giving oneself away, then we are obligated to devise a method of receiving stories that mediates the space between the self that tells, the self that told, and the self that listens: a method that returns a story to the teller that is both hers and not hers, that contains her self in good company. (70)

Inevitably caring, reciprocal, collaborative research will lead to complications, but it may also lead to richer, more rigorously examined results. Despite the potential problems of an ethic of care, we prefer, along with Toronto, "a moral theory that can recognize and identify these issues [problems of otherness, privilege, and paternalism] . . . to a moral theory that, because it presumes that all people are equal, is unable even to recognize them" (*Moral Boundaries* 147).

Reciprocal relations also imply that researchers attempt to open themselves to change and learning, to reinterpreting their own lives, and to reinventing their own "otherness" (Harding, *Whose Science?* 217). This means doing more than listening to and becoming more sensitive to the experiences of those who are disenfranchised. It requires researchers to attempt to identify what may be repressed and unconscious in their own experiences and to claim their own contradictory social and gendered identities. Women can explore their marginality, for example, by considering that a woman scholar is at some level a contradiction in terms, that women in the academy still continue to occupy marginal positions because of their gender (Harding, "Who Knows?" 103). Marginality is not merely determined by sex or skin color; we sometimes make choices that place us in such positions. Men in composition studies, for example, can explore how their work as teachers and scholars often positions them as "other" in English departments that tend to privilege the study of literature and critical theory.[8] African-American scholars have theorized the importance of using this perspective to generate new understandings of our discipline (Collins 40–41; hooks, "Choosing the Margin" 149). Collins argues that our own devalued identities can be powerful resources for knowing because the tension that arises from assuming the perspective of "outsiders within" allows us to see what privileged insiders can not (59). Patricia J. Williams in *The Alchemy of Race and Rights* combines her privileged perspective as a legal scholar and her marginalized personal history as an African-American woman to analyze the social and political contexts of such seemingly arcane matters as contract law.[9]

Working from a marginal position also offers the potential for research that moves beyond analyzing gender or race as though they are someone else's problem—not ours. It can lead the more privileged to consider themselves as potential "subjects" of study, and, therefore, reveal more clearly their privileged positions as well as their unacknowledged marginality. In her analysis of self-other relations, Michelle Fine describes the study of one of her students, Nancy Porter. Porter interviewed white "Main Line" women in Philadelphia and revealed how white people's lives are protected from surveillance and how scholars have "sanitized" evidence of the dysfunctional in such privileged lives (73).[10] Historian Minnie Bruce Pratt provides another example of this process. She uses her identity as a white Southerner at the center, but also her identity as a lesbian on the margin, to analyze her understanding of Southern history, to see how her white perspective is challenged by the perspective of African-American lives, and by her own "outsider" position as a lesbian. We are not suggesting that scholars engage in self-indulgent privileging of their own stories or that they superimpose their stories on those of others; instead, we suggest that they can place their stories and those of their research participants in dialogue with each other to gain new insights into their own and others' lives. As the women in our discussion group at CCCC acknowledged, because our gender and our position in composition still locates us in a marginal position in many English departments, it gives us one important site from which to see with the perspective of outsiders.

We have already asserted the importance of rigorous self-reflection on the part of the researcher in order to avoid essentializing others and to clarify her own motives, desires, and interests. We also understand that to some extent these will always remain unconscious and unknowable. However, neutrality and objectivity are also myths that mask the power-relations always present in research endeavors. That does not mean that relativism is the only alternative, however. Harding's notion of "strong objectivity" may help us understand how to negotiate this apparent dichotomy between a humanist belief in our ability to represent experience and a paralyzed postmodernist stance that denies the possibility of making any claims or taking action. "Strong objectivity" recognizes the historical, social, culturally situated nature of our motives and values, continually theorizes the impact of those values on our work, and searches for what is being eliminated, distorted, or masked in the process (*Whose Science?* 145–47).[11] As part of this activity we can look at the relationship between our theories and our conclusions. The questions that guide our data collection, the stories we decide to tell or eliminate from our research narratives, the range of conclusions we suppress or include—all are guided by our own positionality and must be acknowledged. This process is difficult because "working from a perspective in which we are trained to want to give a reasoned and connected account, we face live material [such as interviews and ethnographic observations] that is constantly in the process of transformation, that is not organized in the way of academic theories" (Acker, Barry, and Esseveld 149).

In addition to acting from an ethic of care and from the perspective offered by rigorous ongoing scrutiny of our motivations and methods, an ethical stance also suggests that we encode in our research narratives the provisional nature of knowledge that our work generates and the moral dilemmas inherent in research. We need to reconsider our privileging of certain, coherent, and univocal writing and include multiple voices and diverse interpretations in our research narratives, highlighting the ideologies that govern our thinking as well as those that may contradict our own. These "rupturing narratives," as Michelle Fine describes them, "allow us to hear the uppity voices of informants and researchers" (78). Finally, of course, we must be prepared to make the case for new forms of research and writing in our discipline as McCarthy and Fishman and others have begun to do. Traditional research reports, for example, urge writers to come to conclusions and announce their findings. That process demands that researchers make coherent what might be fragmented, and thus that they might sometimes reduce complex phenomena or erase differences for the sake of developing coherent theories.[12]

To avoid such erasing of differences, we need to continue experimenting with new ways of reporting research. In composition, a number of scholars have begun to invent writing that highlights multiple narratives and diverse perspectives. Several examples come to mind: Beverly Clark and Sonia Wiedenhaupt published an article on writers' block that took the form of a dialogue between the researcher and the writer, thereby allowing two distinct voices to tell the story from two different vantage points; Jill Eichhorn, Sara Farris, Karen Hayes, Adriana Hernández, Susan Jarratt, Karen Powers-Stubbs, and Marian Sciachitano used a symposium to reflect on and theorize their experiences as feminist teachers, writing "both as a collective and in [their] seven different voices" (297); and Susan Miller collaborated and coauthored a study of "academic underlife" with several of her undergraduate students, Worth Anderson, Cynthia Best, Alycia Black, John Hurst, and Brandt Miller.[13] Such innovative writing challenges scholars to find new ways of presenting research, challenges journal editors to develop a greater tolerance for ambiguity and unconventional forms of discourse, and challenges readers to learn new ways of reading and interpreting texts. Fine observes, "When we construct texts collaboratively, self-consciously examining our relations with/for/despite those who have been contained as Others, we move against, we enable resistance to, "Othering" (74). Multivocal reports also disrupt the smooth research narratives we have come to know and expect, highlight rather than suppress the problems of representation in our writing, and expose the multiple, shifting, and contradictory subject positions of researchers and participants.[14]

Finally, a problematized politics of location leads us to research centered in the local and the individual while at the same time acknowledging that research has social consequences in the world. If we work from an ethic of care, we cannot ignore the political and cultural conditions that place us in unequal power relationships with the participants of our research (Hoagland 260). We have seen in the studies of Patai and Oakley and in our own research how deeply implicated issues of power are in our work. Patti Lather is one of many feminist thinkers who argues strongly that we cannot be satisfied with more research and better data concerning women (or other groups we choose to study). If our research is centered on a politics of location it demands an extra measure of responsibility and accountability on our part. It requires using research as "praxis" to help those who participate with us in research to understand and change their situation, to help those who have been marginalized to speak for themselves. Under these circumstances, it will not be possible to walk away from the research site or those who live in it. Our research instead will need to extend to theory-generating in a self-reflexive and mutually dialogic context to help researchers and participants challenge and change the conditions that keep oppressive structures in place. Only in this extra measure of "care" can our research truly be ethical.

Pursuing the difficulties inherent in a politics of location may lead us beyond some of the frustrations we experience in our work in English departments, because these discussions will inevitably lead us to question our accommodation with the status quo in our discipline, to more seriously question the discipline's traditional ways of asking and answering research questions, to examine the internalized structures, the standard conventions for generating and communicating knowledge in the discipline, and to reshape our agendas for research and action in the field. It will engage us in a rigorous process of analyzing the meaning of the "personal" in our work.

NOTES

Acknowledgments: We wish to thank colleagues, friends, and CCC reviewers for their comments and encouragement as we developed this essay: Lil Brannon, Robert Brooke, Gregory Clark, Lisa Ede, Elizabeth Flynn, Min-Zhan Lu, and Kate Ronald.

1. We frame our article with Adrienne Rich's words realizing that she has been criticized for some of her earlier writing in which she seems to advocate an essentialist position that reinscribes bourgeois individualism and an unproblematic universal feminism. We think her position is an important starting point for discussions of a politics of location, however, because Rich was one of the early theorists attempting to reintroduce the personal in order to challenge the impersonal authority and false universality of interpretive practices that exclude women's writing and women's lives altogether from the academy and other public sites. In the essay we quote she does acknowledge the social and psychological construction of women's lives defines "location" as a space in which we move, not as a fixed site. She also foregrounds the tension we want to explore between the degendered, depoliticized subject of post-modernist aesthetics and the universalizing, unified, humanist subject—both positions which can erase the specificity and lived experience of particular women.

2. We realize that our attempt to locate the origins of this article in a single event misrepresents the many origins our work inevitably has. In the first place we had to be motivated to attend the workshop, a motivation we could trace to our reading of feminist literature, to conversations with colleagues and friends, and to our lived everyday experiences as women in the academy and in the culture at large. If we continue this search for origins, we quickly come to realize that questions of location are complex and call for an analysis of the many conflicting layers of reality we experience in our multiple and shifting subject positions.

3. People participating in research studies are traditionally called "subjects." This term, however, is problematic, implying a division if not hierarchy between researchers and subjects, thereby positioning participants as objects of study, not as the complex and contradictory human beings they are. Since we are questioning precisely this division between researchers and subjects, we have chosen to use the terms "research participants" or simply "participants" throughout this article when we are referring to human beings involved in research studies.

4. Heather Brodie Graves, for example, argues that traditional "feminine" and "masculine" traits can be found in writers of both genders; she analyzes the writing of Kenneth Burke for "feminine" traits and that of Julia Kristeva for "masculine" traits to illustrate her point.

5. For discussions of writing teachers faced with highly personal and at times disturbing information in their students' writing, see Carole Deletiner; Cheryl Johnson; Richard E. Miller.

6. For discussions of feminist research goals and methods, see *Beyond Methodology* (Fonow and Cook), *Feminism and Methodology* (Harding), *Feminist Research Methods* (Nielsen), *Feminist Methods in Social Research* (Reinharz).

7. Space does not permit a full discussion of feminist approaches to ethics, particularly an ethic of care. We refer interested readers to discussions in political science (Tronto, Young), in feminist theory and philosophy (Card, Friedman, Hoagland, Houston, Lather, Schweickart), in education and psychology (Fine, Gilligan, Grumet, Noddings, Punch), and in composition studies (Clark, Mortensen, and Kirsch).

8. We do not mean to suggest that only scholars who are marginalized can engage in feminist or care-based approaches to research. Rather, we argue for a sense of location that one can actively learn to choose. But we believe that attending to the experiences of marginalized people as well as examining aspects of one's identity that are suppressed are important points of departure for a critical perspective on research.

9. We do not wish to minimize differences among women of different backgrounds, generations, race, class, ethnicity, or other identity-shaping factors. In fact, the position of African-American women in the academy is distinctly different from those of white, middle-class women and has caused much debate and tension among feminist theorists. We use this example only to suggest that a marginal position can be a source of strength and insight, allowing researchers to formulate new research questions and gain knowledge not readily available to those who occupy more privileged positions.

10. For another revealing study of "whiteness," see *White Women, Race Matters: The Social Construction of Whiteness* by Ruth Frankenberg.

11. Harding's concept of "strong objectivity" is not unproblematic. Flax, for example, argues that it is still based on a notion of "transcendental truth" because it suggests that once we eliminate or reduce gender biases we will have come closer to "the truth" (*Disputed Subjects* 141–47). We concur with Flax's critique but find Harding's notion useful as a working concept for researchers trying to assess the ethical dimensions of their work.

12. We recognize the irony of the text we have produced: a relatively univocal, coherent text that argues for experimental, multivocal writing. We have attempted to present multivocality by writing in our individual voices when describing our own research projects and in our collective voice in other sections of this text, but we can imagine more experimental and innovative ways of writing.

13. We list names of all collaborators/authors here to give full credit to the nature of collaborative work; all too often multiple authors disappear in the "et al." convention, a practice that reinforces the dominant single-author model of scholarship.

14. The multivocal texts we advocate are not without risk; besides making new demands on readers, writers, and editors, these texts pose special risks for untenured faculty and graduate students who still have to "prove"—or feel that they still have to prove—their disciplinary membership by using conventional research methods and forms.

WORKS CITED

Acker, Joan Kate Barry, and Johanna Esseveld. "Objectivity and Truth: Problems in Doing Feminist Research." *Beyond Methodology: Feminist Scholarship as Lived Research.* Ed. Mary Fonow and Judith Cook. Bloomington: Indiana UP, 1991, 133–53.

Alcoff, Linda. "The Problem of Speaking for Others." *Cultural Critique* 20 (1991–92): 5–32.

Anderson, Worth, Cynthia Best, Alycia Black, John Hurst, Brandt Miller, and Susan Miller. "Cross-Curricular Ablex: A Collaborative Report on Ways with Academic Words." *CCC* 41 (1990): 11–36.

Bizzell, Patricia. "Foundationalism and Anti-Foundationalism in Composition Studies." *Pre/Text* 7 (1986): 37–56.

Bridwell-Bowles, Lillian. "Discourse and Diversity: Experimental Writing Within the Academy." *CCC* 43 (1992): 349–68.

Card, Claudia, ed. *Feminist Ethics*. Lawrence: UP of Kansas. 1991.

Clark, Beverly Lyon, and Sonja Wiedenhaupt. "On Blocking and Unblocking Sonja: A Case Study in Two Voices." *CCC* 43 (1992): 55–74.

Clark, Gregory. "Rescuing the Discourse of Community." *CCC* 45 (1994): 61–74.

Collins, Patricia Hill. "Learning from the Outsider Within: The Sociological Significance of Black Feminist Thought." *(En)Gendering Knowledge: Feminists in Academe*. Ed. Joan Hartman and Ellen Messer-Davidow. Knoxville: U of Tennessee P, 1991. 40–65.

Deletiner, Carole. "Crossing Lines." *College English* 54 (1992): 809–17.

Ebert, Teresa. "The 'Difference' of Postmodern Feminism." *College English* 53 (1991): 886–904.

Eichhorn, Jill, Sara Farris, Karen Hayes, Adriana Hernández, Susan Jarratt, Karen Powers-Stubbs, and Marian Sciachitano. "A Symposium on Feminist Experiences in the Composition Classroom." *CCC* 43 (1992): 297–322.

Fine, Michelle. "Working the Hyphens: Reinventing Self and Other in Qualitative Research." *Handbook of Qualitative Research*. Ed. Norman Denzin and Yvonna Lincoln. Thousand Oaks, CA: Sage, 1994. 70–82.

Flax, Jane. *Disputed Subjects: Essays on Psychoanalysis, Politics, and Philosophy*. New York: Routledge, 1993.

———. *Thinking Fragments: Psychoanalysis, Feminism, and Postmodernism in the Contemporary West*. Berkeley: U of California P, 1990.

Fonow, Mary M., and Judith Cook, eds. *Beyond Methodology: Feminist Scholarship as Lived Research*. Bloomington: Indiana UP, 1991.

Foucault, Michel. *Discipline and Punish: The Birth of the Prison*. Trans. Alan Sheridan. New York: Vintage Books, reprint ed. 1995.

———. *Madness and Civilization: A History of Insanity in the Age of Reason*. New York: Vintage, 1965.

Frankenberg, Ruth. *White Women, Race Matters: The Social Construction of Whiteness*. Minneapolis: U of Minnesota P, 1993.

Friedman, Marilyn. "Beyond Caring: The De-Moralization of Gender." *Science, Morality, and Feminist Theory*. Ed. Marsha Hanen and Kai Nielsen. Calgary: U of Calgary P, 1987. 87–110.

Gilligan, Carol. *In a Different Voice: Psychological Theory and Women's Development*. Cambridge, MA: Harvard UP, 1982.

Gorelick, Sherry. "Contradictions of Feminist Methodology." *Gender and Society* 4 (1991): 459–77.

Graves, Heather Brodie. "Regrinding the Lens of Gender: Problematizing 'Writing as a Woman.'" *Written Communication* 10 (1993): 139–63.

Grumet, Madeleine R. "The Politics of Personal Knowledge." *Stories Lives Tell: Narrative and Dialogue in Education*. Ed. Carol Witherell and Nel Noddings. New York: Teachers College P, 1991. 67–77.

Gulyas, Carol. "Reflections on Telling Stories." *English Education* 18 (1994): 189–94.

Hale, Sondra. "Feminist Methods, Process, and Self-Criticism: Interviewing Sudanese Women." *Women's Words: The Feminist Practice of Oral History*. Ed. Sherna Gluck and Daphne Patai. New York: Routledge, 1991. 121–36.

Haraway, Donna. "Situated Knowledges: The Science Question in Feminism and the Privilege of Partial Perspective." *Feminist Studies* 14 (1988): 575–99.

Harding, Sandra, ed. *Feminism and Methodology: Social Science Issues*. Bloomington: Indiana UP, 1987.

———"Who Knows? Identities and Feminist Epistemology." *(En)Gendering Knowledge: Feminists in Academe*. Ed. Joan Hartman and Ellen Messer-Davidow. Knoxville, TN: U of Tennessee P, 1991. 100–15.

———. *Whose Science? Whose Knowledge? Thinking from Women's Lives*. Ithaca: Cornell UP, 1991.

Heath, Shirley Brice. *Ways with Words: Language, Life, and Work in Communities and Classrooms*. New York: Cambridge UP, 1983.

Hoagland, Sarah Lucia. "Some Thoughts about 'Caring.'" *Feminist Ethics*. Ed. Claudia Card. Lawrence: UP of Kansas, 1991. 246–63.

hooks, bell. "Choosing the Margin as a Space of Radical Openness." *Yearning: Race, Gender, and Cultural Politics*. Boston: South End P, 1990. 145–54.

———. "Feminist Politicization: A Comment." *Talking Back: Thinking Feminist, Thinking Black*. Boston: South End P, 1989. 105–11.

Houston, Barbara. "Rescuing Womanly Virtues: Some Dangers of Moral Reclamation." *Science, Morality, and Feminist Theory*. Ed. Marsha Hanen and Kai Nielsen. Calgary: U of Calgary P, 1987. 237–62.

Johnson, Cheryl L. "Participatory Rhetoric and the Teacher as Racial/Gendered Subject." *College English* 56 (1994): 409–19.

Keller, Evelyn Fox. "Dynamic Objectivity: Love, Power, and Knowledge." *Reflections on Gender and Science.* New Haven: Yale UP, 1985. 115–26.

Kirsch, Gesa E. *Women Writing the Academy: Audience, Authority, and Transformation.* Carbondale: Southern Illinois UP, 1993.

Kraemer, Don J. "Gender and the Autobiographical Essay: A Critical Extension of the Research." *CCC* 43 (1992): 323–39.

Lather, Patti. *Getting Smart: Feminist Research and Pedagogy With/In the Postmodern.* New York: Routledge, 1991.

McCarthy, Lucille, and Stephen Fishman. "A Text for Many Voices: Representing Diversity in Reports of Naturalistic Research." *Ethics and Representation in Qualitative Studies of Literacy.* Ed. Peter Mortensen and Gesa E. Kirsch. Urbana, IL: National Council of Teachers of English, 1996. 155–76.

Miller, Richard E. "Fault Lines in the Contact Zone." *College English* 56 (1994): 389–408.

Minh-ha, Trinh T. *Women, Native, Other: Writing Postcoloniality and Feminism.* Bloomington: Indiana UP, 1989.

Mortensen, Peter, and Gesa E. Kirsch. "On Authority in the Study of Writing." *CCC* 44 (1993): 556–72.

Nielsen, Joyce McCarl, ed. *Feminist Research Methods: Exemplary Readings in the Social Sciences.* San Francisco: Westview, 1990.

Noddings, Nel. *Caring: A Feminine Approach to Ethics and Moral Education.* Berkeley: U of California P, 1984.

Oakley, Ann. "Interviewing Women: A Contradiction in Terms?" *Doing Feminist Research.* Ed. Helen Roberts. New York: Routledge. 1981. 30–61.

Patai, Daphne. "U.S. Academics and Third World Women: Is Ethical Research Possible?" *Women's Words: The Feminist Practice of Oral History.* Ed. Sherna Gluck and Daphne Patai. New York: Routledge, 1991. 137–53.

Peaden, Catherine Hobbs. Rev. of *Gender Issues in the Teaching of English.* Ed. Nancy McCracken and Bruce Appleby. *Journal of Advanced Composition* 13 (1993): 260–63.

Pratt, Bruce Minnie. "Identity: Skin Blood Heart." *Yours in Struggle: Three Feminist Perspectives on Anti-Semitism and Racism.* Ed. Elly Bulkin, Minnie Bruce Pratt, and Barbara Smith. Ithaca, NY: Long Haul P, 1984. 11–63.

Punch, Maurice. "Politics and Ethics in Qualitative Research." *Handbook of Qualitative Research.* Ed. Norman Denzin and Yvonna Lincoln. Thousand Oaks, CA: Sage, 1994. 83–97.

Reinharz, Shulamit. *Feminist Methods in Social Research.* New York: Oxford UP, 1992.

Rich, Adrienne. "Notes on a Politics of Location." *Blood, Bread, and Poetry.* New York: Norton, 1989. 210–31.

Riddell, Sheila. "Exploiting the Exploited? The Ethics of Feminist Educational Research." *The Ethics of Educational Research.* Ed. Robert Burgess. New York: Falmer, 1989. 77–99.

Ritchie, Joy S. "Confronting the Essential Problem: Reconnecting Feminist Theory and Pedagogy." *Journal of Advanced Composition* 10 (1990): 249–71.

Ritchie, Joy S., Manjit Kaur, and BeeTin Choo Meyer. "Women Students' Autobiographical Writing: The Rhetoric of Discovery and Defiance." *Situated Stories: Valuing Diversity in Composition Research.* Ed. Emily Decker and Kathleen Mary Geissler. Portsmouth, NH: Boynton/Cook Heinemann, 1998. 173–89.

Schweickart, Patrocinio. "In Defense of Femininity: Commentary on Sandra Bartky's *Femininity and Domination.*" *Hypatia* 8 (1993): 178–91.

Smith, Sidonie. "Who's Talking/Who's Talking Back? The Subject of Personal Narrative." *Signs: Journal of Women in Culture and Society* 18 (1993): 392–407.

Stacey, Judith. "Can There Be a Feminist Ethnography?" *Women's Words: The Feminist Practice of Oral History.* Ed. Sherna Gluck and Daphne Patai. New York: Routledge, 1991. 111–19.

Tronto, Joan. "Beyond Gender Difference to a Theory of Care." *Signs: Journal of Women in Culture and Society* 12 (1987): 644–63.

———. *Moral Boundaries: A Political Argument for an Ethic of Care.* New York: Routledge, 1993.

Williams, Patricia J. *The Alchemy of Race and Rights.* Boston: Harvard UP, 1991.

Wilson, David E., and Joy S. Ritchie. "Resistance, Revision, and Representation: Narrative in Teacher Education." *English Education* 18 (1994): 177–88.

Young, Iris Marion. *Justice and the Politics of Difference.* Princeton: Princeton UP, 1990.

10 Beside Ourselves: Rhetoric and Representation in Postcolonial Feminist Writing

SUSAN C. JARRATT

The value of postcolonial theory for teachers of writing arises in part from its focus on the rhetorical situation of intellectual work applied to the question of difference. By pointing out that academic traditions of Western universities are built on several centuries of economic and cultural imperialism, this theory demands that scholars and teachers of literature and literacies ask rhetorical questions the answers to which had been for many years assumed: who speaks? on behalf of whom? who is listening? and how? It interrogates the assumption of any group identification and more specifically the relationship of the single "I" to a collective "we" (see Anderson, Mohanty, Roof, and Wiegman[1]).

My aim in this essay is to address the problem of speaking for others by looking at how "others" speak. Employing the figures of metaphor and metonymy, I analyze the ways three postcolonial feminists open up the workings of representation—of the self, groups, and audiences—such that participants are no longer disposed in the classical rhetorical position, a single subject facing an audience, but rather, "beside themselves." This colloquial expression calls to mind situations of deep emotional turmoil—worry, anger, or maybe grief. Perhaps it means that, in times of intense emotional distress, one loses bodily or mental integrity and manufactures another version of oneself to express or absorb the pain. My appropriation of the expression bears some relation to its everyday use, in the sense that oppressed groups experience the pain of self-distancing or alienation (Fanon). As a rhetorician, though, I am interested in the way an experience of suffering is turned into a tool of language: an artful, rhetorical practice of self-multiplication used by speakers in response to their historical, rhetorical, and institutional circumstances. I am also interested in the way a painful image of self-division could be transformed into a hopeful vision of alliance. Tracing representational strategies of postcolonial feminist rhetoric might offer ways for composition teachers and students to imagine that scene—a difficult task in a culture that values indi-

---

From *Journal of Advanced Composition* 18 (1998): 57–75.

vidualism so highly. I hope this essay will contribute to that project in three ways: by analyzing changes in concepts of ethos and audience under the historical conditions of postcoloniality; by describing complex processes of writing the self; and by attending to the ways teachers and students in U.S. universities "read" (about) formerly colonized people.

FIGURING STRUCTURES OF RELATION

How can differences be imagined? In what forms of relation? Rhetoric is useful for addressing these questions because it gives names to figures which structure relations in language and in the material world. Any choice of a figure is a discursive act that also simultaneously configures a material relationship of power and difference. One of the ways postcolonial theory has heightened attention to the politics of representation is to point out that exercises of domination occur not only in the sphere of politics proper but also through cultural practices. They insist on the dual functions of rhetoric as both political and figurative representation.[2] Gayatri Chakravorty Spivak, in her now-canonical essay "Can the Subaltern Speak?" warns first-world intellectuals about the danger of obscuring their own acts of discursive imperialism in the process of facilely "representing" the interests of apparently silent subjects of oppression. She makes her point historically and philologically, using Marx's essay on the mid-nineteenth-century coup d'etat of Louis Bonaparte, who came to "represent" a peasant class politically through an exercise of executive power without their having any consciousness of themselves as a class, i.e., without participating in an imaginative or political construction of themselves as a class (Marx 602, 608). The typical translation of two different German words (*Vertretung and Darstellung*) into a single English word, "representation," emblemizes for Spivak the danger of collapsing these two distinct processes: the first, a political or legal process of standing for members of a constituency group; the second a symbolic process of creating images of such groups ("Subaltern" 276; see also Landry and MacLean 198). She associates these two forms of representation with two kinds of rhetoric, persuasion and trope, graphically captured in the analogies of "proxy" and "portrait" —arguing that in her historical example of Louis Bonaparte the former assumes or enacts the latter: "The event of representation as [a political process] . . . behaves like an [imaging], taking its place in the gap between the formation of a (descriptive) class and the nonformation of a (transformative) class" ("Subaltern" 277). In other words, when someone uses power over others to represent them politically—to act for them—there is an unavoidable, concomitant symbolic process underway: the represented group is sketched, painted, described in a particular way through that process. And this description may or may not "represent" them in ways they themselves would endorse.

The reason Spivak writes "nonformation" is to emphasize that "identity" as a class does not take place naturally (at what she calls "ground level consciousness"), but rather must be constructed through acts of political agency and self-description ("Subaltern" 277–8). One cannot assume a class identity for the French peasants Louis Bonaparte forcibly represented in the absence of their own representations of themselves or of acts on their own behalf as a class. The backlash against feminism in the U.S. (and other countries as well) offers a contemporary example of processes of "nonformation" and transformation. Many women on university campuses reject feminism—i.e., reject being identified as a politicized class, "women"—because they believe they haven't had a hand in constructing the symbolic representations of the class. In Women's Studies classes, female students actually read and discuss the works of feminists (as opposed to absorbing uncritically the grotesque caricatures offered on talk radio and other popular media). As they talk and write about the ways their self-identification fits with or differs from the representations they read, a process of class-formation/transformation takes place, creating a locally grounded understanding of the class "women" from which some will actually go forward to act out of that class consciousness (in campus activism, volunteer work, or career choices). Inevitably, their subsequent actions as "women" on behalf of other "women" will recreate the gap between political agency and self-description.[3]

Discovering the workings of these two forms of representation at any site, the interwoven operations of imaging—textual descriptions of otherness—and political representation—entailing identification of or with a group—is the work of teachers and students of language practices. Rhetoric mobilizes an interaction between representation (political) and re-presentation (cultural), possibly enabling the transformative practices Marx found missing in the nineteenth-century French peasants: i.e., driving the movement from descriptive to transformative class, or at least calling attention to where and by whom groups are described. It is my argument that some postcolonial feminists have been particularly useful in activating rhetoric in these two senses, and that an analysis of their work in these terms might advance the argument over identity politics, helping to delineate with more care and refinement the bases on which identities are constructed, claimed, and linked with others. This framework might serve the ethical aim of "recognizing the responsibility for linking" (Faigley 237).

My method in the body of the essay is to use rhetorical figures—metaphor and metonymy—to analyze the ways postcolonial feminist writing calls attention to these dual processes of representation: political and pictorial. In this analysis, I take metaphor as a figure of substitution: one thing or person standing in for another, and in the process, obscuring some particularities of what it represents.[4] A metaphoric style of representation occurs any time a speaker or writer functions as a spokesperson for a particular category of people—workers, women, voters in a particular constituency—the partiality of the single member standing in for the whole. Here is an example of a critic using this definition of metaphor to distinguish autobiography from *testimonio:*

> In rhetorical terms, whose political consequences may be evident, there is a fundamental difference here between the *metaphor* of autobiogra-

phy and heroic narrative in general, which assumes an identity-by-substituting one (superior) signifier for another (I for we, leader for follower, Christ for the faithful), and metonymy, a lateral move of identification-through-relationship, which acknowledges the possible differences among "us" as components of a centerless whole. (Sommer 61)

Metonymy, on the other hand, as the passage above suggests, creates a chain of associations. It configures a relationship based on contiguity and context (Jakobson 79, 83, 90–91; Irigaray; Brady). The example of metonymy provided by Jakobson has an eerie resonance for postcolonial history. A hut may metonymically be associated with "thatched roof," "family of twelve," or "burnt by the army," each association creating a narrative or contextualized understanding of the word without displacing or blocking out the word itself. Applying metonymy to identity politics suggests that differences can be spoken of not in terms of exclusive categories but rather as places, descriptions, or narratives of relation. The writings of Gayatri Spivak and Trinh T. Minh-ha offer eloquent illustrations of what I see as a metonymic process of subject construction; each simultaneously makes visible the intellectual work of theorizing and gives voice to varieties of otherness, placing themselves not at the head of some silent group of followers but rather beside themselves. But in so doing, they unavoidably participate in a metaphoric process of representing "others," thus enacting a tension between these two modes. After analyzing rhetorics of linkage and spatial location in texts of the Spivak and Trinh, I will turn to a very different text. The 1983 *testimonio* of Rigoberta Menchú Tum,[5] a Quiché Indian peasant and peace activist, arose from the midst of the Guatemalan civil war, a situation calling forth different strategies of representation from those used by postcolonial feminist academics writing within the context of the U.S. academy.[6]

IMMIGRANT ACADEMICS AS METONYMIC SUBJECTS

My first two subjects are both professional "representers," engaged in literary criticism and cultural critique (Spivak); in documentary filmmaking, ethnography, and cultural theory (Trinh). These feminist theorists are hypersensitive to the constructed nature of the discourse of personal experience yet, nonetheless, acknowledge the need for the representation of others—to give others a vocal and visible presence. They both meet this need through the production of what Spivak terms "counter-sentences" by subjects of imperialism: alternatives to re-presentations—images of the "other"—produced from within dominant cultures. Such counter-sentences come into being through the strategic placement and voicing of narrative, but both Trinh and Spivak seek to avoid speaking for the other through displacement and indirection. Unlike the "Third World intellectuals" in metropolitan universities described by Ahmad, who "materially represent the undifferentiated colonized Other . . . without much examining of their own presence in that institution" (92), Trinh and Spivak figure themselves with an awareness of their placement within systems of privilege and draw attention to the modes of production and consumption of their academic work.

I turn first to cultural critic Gayatri Spivak, an upper-caste Indian, an economic immigrant from Calcutta, who has studied and taught in English departments in U.S. universities since the early sixties. This biographical sentence introduces Spivak to those who don't know of her work but, by consolidating her into a unified, coherent subject, works against the grain of her own rhetoric. In the second half of the "Subaltern" essay, Spivak calls into question the desire of first world intellectuals for an authentic native voice when that desire is directed toward people like her.[7] Spivak is at pains to point out her difference from that Other. She complicates the illusion of a single "native voice" by delineating various positions among Indians under British occupation. Setting off a silent underclass from those in closer contact with their colonizers, Spivak uses as her prime example a colonial subject whose agency and voice had the least possibility of being heard—Indian widows who became victims of sati, sacrificial burning—to demonstrate how many of the historically colonized had in fact no legitimate platform from which to speak ("Subaltern" 297–308; see also Mani). Spivak argues that this situation is a problem not only for first-world intellectuals but for diasporic postcolonial academics as well in their own production of knowledge about their homelands. Her conclusion is that a postcolonial intellectual cannot speak for these unrepresented groups but only to them in an imagined conversation across class lines and historical distances ("Subaltern" 295). The emphasis here is on "imagined," for of course Spivak assumes no possibility of reaching the present-day remnants of this group through the rarified discourses of Western academies.[8] Rather, she uses this formulation to displace the representative potential of her own voice, opening a space for others. "Speaking to" might be construed as a movement from the metaphoric to the metonymic. Instead of substituting one voice for another, the speaker adds another voice to the parallel strands of discourse, a voice without its own clear origin. Her writings stand alongside other accounts and the person herself who continues to re-generate a speaking subject.

The ethical implications of Spivak's performance lie in its difference from, on the one hand, a rhetoric of substitution, and on the other, from what Mohanty calls a "Western, postmodernist notion of agency and consciousness which often announces the splintering of the subject, and privileges multiplicity in the abstract" (37). Spivak's performance should be understood as an ethical practice of seeking to displace any fixed sense of knowledge of the "other" a Western listener might be tempted to grasp through an encounter with an elite, immigrant academic. When "card-carrying hegemonic" listeners listen for someone speaking as an Indian, a Third World woman speaking as a Third World woman, Spivak asserts, ignorance of a complex history is covered over with a fabricated homogeneity ("Alterity" 270). Within her chosen area of literary and cultural studies,[9] Spivak puts before a Western audience a multitude of postcolonial subjects—the Indian widow of 1829, the sixteen-year-old member of an Indian independence group who committed suicide in Calcutta in 1926, the women workers in today's Export Processing Zones—along with her own "selves."

Indeed, it seems that part of Spivak's strategy for multiplying others is achieved through the manufacture of more and more versions of herself. She has experienced an amazing degree of public scrutiny, and I'm interested in examining how she has negotiated her self-constitution through that process. *The Post-Colonial Critic,* a series of interviews, collects and multiplies the many versions of this "highly commodified academic," as she ironically calls herself ("Word" 130). In an interview with Ellen Rooney, she acknowledges complaints that "Spivak talks too much about herself" ("Word" 130). Though this focus on the self might suggest the seduction of "representativeness," it might also be read as a continuing attempt to disperse the representative Indian in the U.S. academy.

Spivak is meticulous about her own processes of self-identification. Refusing several of the available options for self-representation—unmediated accounts of experience, the philosophical voice from nowhere, and the hollow echoes of the now-dead "author"—Spivak instead practices "deidentification . . . a claiming of an identity from a text that comes from somewhere else."[10] Resisting the Western academy's attempt to hear from her the voice of the native, she differentiates "talking about oneself" from a process of "graphing one's bio" such that it becomes representative of certain histories ("Word" 130). In this formulation, the text represents, not the self. This process of contexture and displacement begins when Spivak identifies herself with contingent and polemical labels—"woman," "literary critic," "Asian intellectual," "Non-Resident Indian." She then reveals the persistence of imperialist and sexist attitudes by recounting situations when one or another of those labels provoked conflict or effected marginalization in public forums. But instead of grounding these claims in authenticity, Spivak practices what she calls a reactive strategy, adopting different identities at different times to create a consciousness of the hazards of fixity and substitution. She seems to be saying, If you take me to be a feminist, I'll show how I'm not the same as Western feminists. If you take me for an Indian, I'll explain elite immigrant privilege. If you define me as anti-institutional, I show you the disciplinarian. Spivak consistently cannot be found where she is sought. She signals the relatively minimal significance of color and former colonial status (those markers of difference through which she appears as the representative Indian) through references to her high caste status, the historical moment within which her immigration took place (the early '60s brain drain of Indians to the UK and U.S.), and the benefits accruing to her as the product of a British education from American academics' Anglophilia. In specifying the geographical, economic, and class locations of her background and academic formation, she engages in the project Ahmad calls "periodizing": connecting academic practices with modes of production and larger historical movements, rather than assuming their distance from the material world (Ahmad 36).

In introductory passages contextualizing the essays in her latest book, *Outside in the Teaching Machine,* Spivak reflects on her positions in relation to other women (see especially 121–29, 141–46). Returning to early writing enables her to place positions side by side in a narrative sequence:

> When I wrote "French Feminism in an International Frame" my assigned subject-position was actually determined by my moment in the United States and dominated my apparent choice of a postcolonial position. . . . Now it seems to me that the radical element of the postcolonial bourgeoisie must most specifically learn to negotiate with the structure of enabling violence that produced her. (145)

Spivak now seeks to negotiate " 'white feminism' " rather than simply resisting it; she seeks not "to neglect the postcolonial's particular generalization in the vaster common space of woman" (145). Throughout these passages she rearticulates the problematic of representation: "It is obvious that these positions [feminism, European Enlightenment, nationhood, etc.], logically defined, swirl in the inaccessible intimacy of the everyday, giving hue to being. To fix it in paint is to efface as much as to disclose" (144–5).

It is through a carefully crafted rhetoric that Spivak revises her early position.[11] Sometimes tortured, almost always tortuous, her prose seems at times almost to parody classical philosophical argument. Deeply engaged with the most traditional philosophical issues, Spivak's prose is full of "lurches": unconventional word use (e.g., "to operate" as a conceptual process), abrupt transitions, unexpected juxtaposition of subjects. Where most academic readers are accustomed to the Aristotelian format—state your case and prove it—Spivak seems to work laterally, moving from case to case, point to point, rarely offering examples.[12] Despite all her efforts, we see an operation of substitution emerging when Toril Moi suggests that Spivak's texts might be representative of "an enactment of the violent clash of discourses experienced by the subject in exile" (20). Though her writing at first seems radically different from the *écriture féminine* of French feminists, I find common elements: along with deep engagements with the canonical male texts of Western culture, there is "a courageous effort to explode linear sequentiality, a deliberate desire to enact the decentering of the subject and its discourses" (Moi 21). Simultaneous with the pretense of what Catherine Clément calls "democratic transmission" (Cixous and Clément)—i.e., the implicit agreement with a reader that she seeks to communicate—we find at times "a text where the connections are so elusive as to become private" (Moi 20). I've seen some of the same patterns in the writing of female students: a struggle under the burden of a masculine literary heritage, a movement from public communication into the realm of private codes, a break-down in the conventional structures of argument. I'm suggesting not that these textual features be celebrated as expressions of a gendered essence, nor praised as the curious idiosyncrasies of a brilliant thinker, but rather be read as symptoms—textual traces of a strained encounter with multiple forms of dominance. Within, then, Spivak's meticulous and principled renunciation of a representation of substitution, her highly artful theory and practice of metonymic association with others, I find an informing if painful case of writing difference.

Trinh T. Minh-ha claims writing without equivocation as the defining act for "Third World women," a phrase she chooses despite its anachronistic assumption of a tri-partite division of world powers and the risk of homogenization. From the jacket of her first book, *Women, Native, Other: Writing Postcoloniality and Feminism,* we learn that she is a writer, filmmaker, composer, and academic. But, despite the fact that her text is full of first person pronouns both singular and plural, her one moment of specific self-definition is delayed until late in the book and displaced into third person: "From jagged transitions between the headless and bottomless storytelling, what is exposed in this text is the inscription and de-scription of a nonunitary female subject of color through her engagement, therefore also disengagement, with master discourses" (43). The self she creates in her text is figured by the broken mirror. It destroys a pure relation of "I to I" (23), but does not cease reflecting: "here reality is not reconstituted, it is put into pieces so as to allow another world to rebuild (keep on unbuilding and rebuilding) itself with its debris" (23). The subject is dispersed throughout her text, yet Trinh speaks at times with complete presence, easily adopting the role of "writing woman" (as opposed to "written woman") and using conventions of the "priest-god scheme" (her version of the critique of the author). Her discussion of commitment, responsibility, and guilt capture Trinh as a most consolidated subject: "In a sense, committed writers are the ones who write both to awaken to the consciousness of their guilt and to give their readers a guilty conscience. Bound to one another by an awareness of their guilt, writer and reader may thus assess their positions, engaging themselves wholly in their situations and carrying their weight into the weight of their communities, the weight of the world" (10–11). For those on the margin, Trinh suggests, constructing a "we" implies a responsibility for representation. While Spivak only goes so far as to speak of "unlearning privilege," Trinh foregrounds the ethical entailments of her representative status.

At other moments she delights in the multiplicity of voices in writing, dividing herself into subject and object through a play of pronouns: "writing . . . is an ongoing practice that is concerned not with inserting a 'me' into language, but with creating an opening where the 'me' disappears while 'I' endlessly come and go" (35). She then breaks the boundary of that "i": "Taking in any voice that goes through me, I/i will answer every time someone says: I. One woman within another, eternally" (37). Pronouns are powerful tools for Trinh, who doubles the "I" in capital and lowercase, privileging the subject case (but multiple) "I" over the object "me." This mix of modes—metaphoric and metonymic—stymies attempts to categorize her and enacts her point that "Woman can only redefine while being defined by language" (44).

The visuals in her text—stills from her movies—illustrate her strategy of multiplication and a metonymic style of representation (Figure 1).

Offering multiple images rather than a single image breaks apart a process of metaphoric substitution. That we see the "native woman" with a child and without, calls into question a Western stereotype of non-Western women as primarily reproducers of masses of "others." The subject smiles directly into

FIGURE 1.

(Reprinted from *Woman, Native Other: Writing Postcoloniality and Feminism* p. 26 by Trinh Minh-ha T, Indiana University Press, © Copyright 1984 with permission from Trinh Minh-ha T, Moongift Films)

the camera, presumably held by Trinh (or perhaps an associate), indicating her apparent ease and pleasure in the process of being represented by another "other" suggesting perhaps a collaboration in the process of representation (see Bal). That she is shown in various "sizes," with child and without, looking into the camera and looking off, suggests subjects in context, in motion— not able to be caught or reduced through a single process of substitution.

Trinh's most effective strategy for moving between metaphoric and metonymic subjectivities is her frequent use of a broad ironic tone. In the following passage, she sarcastically rejects the position of authenticity, mimicking (but at the same time using) a voice of unreflective autobiography: "I am so much that nothing can enter me or pass through me. I struggle, I resist, and I am filled with my own self. [Here the tone shifts.] The 'personal' may liberate as it may enslave" (35). On the same issue, she asks: "How do you inscribe difference without bursting into a series of euphoric narcissistic accounts of yourself and your own kind?" Trinh wants to find her way between "navel-gazing and navel-erasing" (28).

Trinh is sensitive to the current seductions of fashionable otherness in academic circles, devoting the better part of a chapter to what she terms the "special" Third World woman issue. Parodying the title of a special issue of an academic journal, she points out how both the Western audience and the iconized postcolonial are complicit in dealing with otherness as a special issue: "Specialness as a soporific soothes, anaesthetizes my sense of justice; it is, to the wo/man of ambition, as effective a drug of psychological self-intoxication as alcohol is to the exiles of society" (88). The admonition is to be more sensitive to the systems of authorization, as well as the (very Western) myth of authenticity.

For Trinh, the relation to the collective is highly textualized but still there. Again we hear her mimicking one of the familiar voices of the American collective:

> A writing *for* the people, *by* the people, and *from* the people is, literally, a multipolar reflecting reflection that remains free from the conditions of subjectivity and objectivity and yet reveals them both. I write to show myself showing people who show me my own showing. I-You: not one, not two. (22, emphasis in original)

I hear in this passage a bold refiguration of the "subject," involving the group in its formation and complicating visibility as it is theorized in classical Western systems of representation.

Trinh is more at ease than Spivak in making common cause across differences. She accepts the alliance of nonwhite U.S. minorities with citizens of the older nonaligned nations who made up the original "Third World" group. She finds more threat in the colonialist creed of Divide and Conquer than she does in the threat of obscuring differences when such pacts are made. The radical dispersion of self through writing coexists in this text with a voice of collective solidarity. This coexistence in the rhetorical scene is articulated metonymically: "The process of differentiation . . . continues, and speaking nearby or together with certainty differs from speaking for and about" (101). "Difference does not annul identity. It is beyond and alongside identity" (104).

What strikes me as most apt in the specifically *post*colonial rhetoric of these two feminists is the tension here between metonymic and metaphoric representation—between a poststructural dispersal of subjectivity and an ethical commitment to analyzing communication in terms of the material realities of speakers and listeners. Postcolonial feminists dare to commit theoretical inconsistency, deploying a pragmatic rhetoric that suits their multiple locations. The principled resistance to the temptation to speak for India, for Vietnam, for women is joined with the principled impulse to put the voice of the "other" in play in First-World academic discourse. When we hear Spivak's speaking to (rather than for or about) and Trinh's speaking alongside, we hear an attempt to move between the two poles in the double session of representation.

For both writers, the metonymic operation of speaking alongside is not divided sharply from a rhetoric of substitution; they coexist, operating simultaneously. Practices of political representation cannot avoid the enactment of symbolic representation, the constant process of creating and recreating public images of difference. Actually appearing through symbolic representation entails access to public forums gained through (loosely defined) political processes. Both these writers are fully aware of their representational function: they do speak for the other. But they simultaneously recast images and frustrate any simple process of representation. As postcolonial subjects located in the metropolitan academic scene, both choose a complex construction of subjectivity in an ethical response to the exigencies of that placement.

These choices are consummately rhetorical, revealing a disruption of conventional assumptions about ethos and audience. Unlike the classical scenario, wherein the speaker constructs an ethos in relation to an audience—assuming it to be a group of which he was a member—the habitus of the postcolonial feminist is not shared by a Western academic audience.[13] The aim of this rhetoric is to open the distance between writer and audience rather than close it. Lunsford and Ede suggest a similar distancing in a recent self-critique of their earlier essay on audience, pointing out the "exclusionary tendencies of the rhetorical tradition" (174) in its assumption that the rhetor (and in their case, the student writer) would unproblematically seek to mold herself to the audience at hand. I believe these postcolonial feminist restructurings of ethos and audience might be helpful to teachers of writing and rhetoric. First, they illustrate through their elaboration of difference the power relations and assumptions about social similarity inherent in the classical model. Next, they might help us in developing strategies for our own speaking and writing that avoid reproducing unproblematically those older models, based on the assumption that speaker and audience will unquestionably share knowledge, goals, and habits. Finally, they might help us as we read student writing about the self to discover how students resist or refigure ethos and audience to characterize their own relations to the academy. I am not suggesting that students will consciously employ the complex tactics I have outlined in the writings of the two academic postcolonial feminists but rather that we might use Spivak's and Trinh's rhetorical gestures as guides for reading traces or symptoms of texts from students writing their own relations to institutional power. Imagining students capable of inscribing multiple selves could be an important reading posture for teachers concerned with subject construction in a postcolonial era.

I have proposed ways that the writings of Spivak and Trinh might contribute to rhetorical theory and to the reading practices of writing teachers.[14] The third subject of my analysis occupies a substantially different position in relation to composition studies in that (1) she was not a writer[15] and (2) her published account has appeared on reading lists for undergraduates across the country. As winner of the 1993 Nobel Peace Prize, Rigoberta Menchú Tum has gained international recognition as a spokesperson for her people. Given her chosen status as representative "other," her rhetorical task would appear to be quite the different from that of the postcolonial immigrant intellectuals analyzed above.

A REVOLUTIONARY SUBJECT

In the 1983 English translation of Guatemalan Indian Rigoberta Menchú Tum's *testimonio,* the construction of a subject appears in high relief from the opening lines:

> My name is Rigoberta Menchú. I am twenty-three years old. This is my testimony. I didn't learn it from a book and I didn't learn it alone. I'd like to stress that it's not only *my* life, it's also the testimony of my people. It's hard for me to remember everything that's happened to me in my life since there have been many very bad times but, yes, moments of joy as well. The important thing is that what has happened to me has happened to many other people too: My story is the story of all poor Guatemalans. My personal experience is the reality of a whole people. (1)

There appears to be no hesitation here to claim representative status—no hedging about subject positions or the problem of speaking for others. Menchú Tum tells the story of Indian peasants deprived of land, freedom, and life by an oligarchic government using the army to suppress any attempts by the Indians to seek justice and stop exploitive land grabs and cruel labor practices.[16] Literary critics identify a distinctive articulation of the speaking subject as a feature of the genre, *testimonio.* John Beverly's persuasive analysis places these accounts within the context of struggles for national autonomy: they are "novel or novella-length narratives told in the first person by a narrator who is also the real protagonist or witness of the events she or he recounts" (*Literature* 70). The claim of representation is at the center of these texts: "the situation of the narrator in *testimonio* must be representative (in both the mimetic and the legal-political senses) of a larger social class or group"; indeed, there is "an insistence on and affirmation of the authority of the subject" (Beverly, *Literature* 74, 76).

Neither the "deliverers," compilers, nor the critics of *testimonio,* however, are naive about the processes of textual construction involved in production of these accounts. Barbara Harlow, whose book *Resistance Literature* brings a number of these texts to the attention of Western readers, makes note of the ideological complexity of resistance organizations and national liberation movements (29). The involvement of a First-World intelligentsia in the collection of material complicates the question of authenticity further. Elizabeth Burgos-Debray, the compiler of Menchú Tum's *testimonio,* a Venezuelan social scientist living in Paris, documents the ways she constructed and adjusted the language in the oral account. In a recent visit to Miami University, Menchú Tum spoke about the caution she exercised in telling her story to Burgos-Debray. This caution involved presenting herself as a particular kind of subject, as well as withholding information about the Indian resistance fighters still at war in Guatemala at the time she was working for peace in Europe and Mexico.

Even though they acknowledge these mediations in the collection and production of *testimonios*, however, critics generally place more importance on the commonality of political goals between compiler and testifier. Beverly, for example, offers the examples of Margaret Randall, who assisted women in Cuba and Nicaragua through workshops in writing popular histories, and Nawal al-Saadawi, whose work with women in an Egyptian prison eventually led to the testimonial novel *Woman at Point Zero,* as examples of politically committed *testimonio* compilers ("Margin" 15, n. 8; 17, n. 11; see also Harlow). These relationships are forged out of "mutuality in struggle against a common system of oppression"; the compiling of the testimony under these conditions is specifically not, Beverly argues, "a reenactment of the anthropological function of the colonial or subaltern 'native informant' " ("Margin" 21).

The *testimonio,* nonetheless, still offers interpretive challenges on the issue of representation, even if they aren't exactly the same as those created by the particular national, educational, and class circumstances of the immigrant academic feminists.[17] For both Spivak and Trinh, the denial of authenticity is a necessary position for the diasporic intellectual, one which forces the first-world academic to notice the difference between another academic and a suppressed history of colonization. For Menchú Tum, the claim to authority—to the truth of her lived experience—is central to her project. There still remains a question about how to interpret the representational force of the strongly asserted "I" in the *testimonio* and how to understand the relationship with the reader. Does this mode of representation constitute a rhetoric of substitution?

Interpreters of *testimonio* answer that question by changing the terms. In the material and historical circumstances of a revolutionary struggle, the idea of one speaker "blocking out" another, as though subjects were individual, strongly differentiated units, gives way to the exigencies of communicating as a collective. The elite intellectual postcolonial feminists, working within a Western discourse tradition, needed to take apart individual subjectivity from the inside; Menchú Tum, on the other hand, comes from a strongly communal Indian village culture with a completely different understanding of the relation of the self to the community. Despite the first person of Menchú Tum's title, Lynda Marín notes that *testimonios* are marked by the "self-professed eschewal of the first person singular subject" in favor of a collective "we" (52).[18] Though these authors do specify their personal conditions, those details are less significant than the group struggle against state coercion. Their primary aim is getting out the reality of their collective experience to a metropolitan reading public, bringing to light experiences and events hidden in large measure from First World media. Doris Sommer, in an elegant reading of Rigoberta's continual reference to secrets about the community that cannot be revealed, claims that this strategy "defends us [First-World readers] from any illusions of complete or stable knowledge, and therefore from the desire to replace one apparently limited speaker for another more totalizing one" (57). Sommer goes on say that Menchú Tum "takes care not to substitute her community in a totalizing gesture. Instead, her singularity achieves its identity as an extension of the collective. The singular represents the plural, not because it replaces or subsumes the group, but because the speaker is a distinguishable part of the whole" (60–61). It is worth noting that Sommer's purpose in analyzing Menchú Tum is to distinguish the genre of *testimonio* from standard Western autobiography, a centuries-old locus for individuality: "Where autobiographies nurture an illusion of singularity [*sic*], assuming they can stand in for others, testimonies stand up among them" (61). John Beverly, similarly, attempts to redefine the terms through which subjectivity is expressed: "*testimonio* constitutes an affirmation of the individual self *in a collective mode*" ("Margin" 17). The oral delivery of *testimonio* and the political context of collective struggle combine to set aside figures of the "author" and "individual," and along with them, the problem of speaking for others as a gesture of substitution.

Looking at the *testimonio* from a rhetorical rather than a literary perspective actually makes it easier to imagine this shift. When we examined the postcolonial academic writers, the analysis was framed in terms of writing style. But for an orally produced text, the rhetorical category of ethos is more suitable. Sommer acknowledges the value of a shift to rhetoric: "while the autobiography strains to produce a personal and distinctive style as part of the individuation process, the testimonial strives to preserve or to renew an interpersonal rhetoric" (Sommer 65). The ethos/audience relation was redefined above for Asian postcolonial feminists to mark a difference and distance between rhetor and audience. In the case of Menchú Tum, *ethos* could signify the intense solidarity among members of the revolutionary group, as well as a powerfully rhetorical relationship to First-World readers.

Whereas the first two writers needed to disperse their subjectivity and representativeness for Western readers, Menchú Tum, as a subject of a nation still in struggle, had a much stronger interest—indeed, a life-or-death need—to engage the audience. Written for a metropolitan public, the *testimonio* creates a bond with its readers, "involv[ing] their identification—by engaging their standards of ethics and justice in a speech-act situation that requires response" (Beverly, *Literature* 78). The rhetoric of reading *testimonio* is cast as a movement from identification to persuasion, or "complicity." Sommer uses that term to spell out the psychological dynamics of subject-formation and audience address in the public event of *testimonio:*

> When the narrator talks about herself to you, she implies both the existing relationship to other representative selves in the community, and potential relationships that extend her community through the text. She calls us in, interpellates us as readers who identify with the narrator's project and, by extension, with the political community to which she belongs. The appeal does not produce only admiration for the ego-ideal, of the type we might feel for an autobiographer who impresses us precisely with her difference from other women, nor the consequent yearning to be (like) her and so to deny her and our distinctiveness. Rather, the testimonial produces complicity. Even if the reader cannot identify with the writer enough to imagine taking her place, the map of possible identifications through the text spreads out laterally. (65)

In this lateral movement, the represented community, testifier, and readers are found beside themselves.

Reading Menchú Tum against the two Asian feminists enables us to see a reversal of the movement from descriptive to transformative class. We are to understand from Menchú Tum that the class she represents is solidly constituted, already engaged in political action. Her task is to create that group as a descriptive class—to bring the Mayan Indians of Central America into view for a U.S. and Western European public. Because the two poles in the double session of representation are so closely connected for her group, there is a strong justification for the representational strategy she uses. Her goal is exactly the opposite of Spivak's: not "deidentification" but identification. My goal in making this contrast is not to value one mode of representation over another. It is, rather, to develop more supple instruments for recognizing and responding to diverse subjects in the absence of stable criteria for doing so. It has become standard for feminists (and others) to complain of poststructuralist theory that it robs nondominant groups of subjectivity before they've ever had a chance to have it. Gregory S. Jay raises a question about the terms of this dilemma: "it is not clear how the widely challenged classical schemas of representation can be replaced by a different representative system if there is no agreement about the 'unit' or basic element grounding the claim to representation [in the Enlightenment, the individual]" (15). Perhaps the rhetorical materials at use here might give us a way to describe subjectivities as something more multiple and diverse than "units," to discuss the question in terms less simply binary than presence or absence of a subject.

PEDAGOGY

The political reason we need something more complex than poststructural or postmodern critiques of the subject concerns the ways such arguments "travel." Criticisms of a representation of substitution—of "authentic voice" literature that makes claims to speak for others—from within nondominant groups line up disturbingly with the derision of a right-wing dogmatist like Dinesh D'Souza, who uses the evidence of Rigoberta Menchú Tum's differences from the Indians she represents as an excuse to dismiss her as a *"seemingly authentic Third World source"* (72, emphasis added). That Menchú Tum was able to move from the position of silenced subaltern to vocal victim of oppression provides D'Souza the opportunity to dismiss the account of her experience, to hear her instead as a mouthpiece for "Marxist and feminist views," and to focus his critical energies on the travesty of her displacement of Western classics in the Stanford University canon.

The difference between John Beverly's reading of Menchú Tum as an organizer, organic intellectual, and "foreign agent" to the West—i.e., as specifically not "the subaltern"—and D'Souza's reading is that the former is doing a sympathetic reading of representational strategies; the latter rejects Menchú Tum's account in favor of silence: i.e., he disqualifies her representative status so as to silence her. D'Souza's response recalls a stance I've encountered in some students who find reports from the margins so disturbing that their very claim to be heard is called into question (see Lu). This reaction takes shape as the skepticism on the part of an autonomous knower toward any truth claim: the response of a Kantian subject who, in rejecting the authority of teacher and text, overcomes "tutelage," the barrier to ascendance into full personhood, a rejection made all the easier if that narrative in some way calls into question the status of that very subject. Is it possible to distinguish between a silencing skepticism and a nuanced reading of representation?

It is our responsibility as teachers to try to mark out that difference. Through our choices of texts and every word we say about them we inevitably represent others to our students. Choosing different reading strategies for different texts is an exercise of power, but then, Rigoberta Menchú Tum is not Louis Bonaparte and neither are "we": teachers of writing, language, and literature in U.S. universities. Every pedagogical moment is a complex fusion of re-presentation, exercises of executive power, and transformation of consciousness. If we enter into that process relying solely on what Linda Alcoff calls the "retreat" response—claiming to speak only from our own narrow positions—we not only blind ourselves to the multiple functions of pedagogical discourse, but also lose opportunities for political effectivity (17–19).

Many of us believe that we have remade the teaching scene so as to avoid careless abuses of power. But we can't control the processes of representation—of metaphorical substitution. As those in nondominant positions well know, their voices are often heard as the voice of women, African-Americans, or lesbians despite disclaimers or qualifications. If, as teachers and scholars we retreated from the risk of representation, punctiliously refusing any occasion of speaking for others ourselves and vigilantly pointing out any instance of metaphoric substitution in others, we would avoid making a theoretical error. But, as Alcoff points out, "the desire to find an absolute means to avoid making errors comes perhaps not from a desire to advance collective goals but a desire for personal mastery, to establish a privileged discursive position wherein one cannot be undermined or challenged and thus is master of the situation" (22).

What is it we recognize? What parts of the whole do we "read"? What forms the links in the chains of association that lead us to act? Can we transform the modes of visibility through our teaching? Who is the "we" in these questions? By locating texts, including our own, in their different geopolitical contexts, teachers in U.S. universities can practice modes of writing and reading that allow us (students and teachers) to move collectively across the axes of metaphor/metonymy rather than speech/silence. And by enabling our students to write multiple versions of themselves informed by a knowledge of rhetoric in its political and figurative functions, we may give them access to their own experiences of conjunction and disjunction, of association and substitution. In doing this, we might more fully inhabit the meanings of the prefix to both figures, meta—which, in the poetic language of the Greek lexicon, places us "beside, alongside, among, in common with, with the help and favor of, in the midst of" others.

NOTES

I am grateful to my writing group at Miami University—Alice Adams, Lori Merish, and Victoria Smith—and to Andrea Lunsford for help with this essay. I also appreciate the valuable comments of others who read or heard earlier drafts: John Beverly, Laura Mandell, Kelly Oliver, Alpana Knippling Sharma, Scott Shershow, and Lester Faigley and his graduate students at the University of Texas at Austin.

1. In the Roof and Wiegman collection, see especially essays by Leslie Bow, Dympna Callaghan, and Sabina Sawhney.

2. See Mailloux for a related definition of rhetoric incorporating political effectivity and trope.

3. Chandra Talpade Mohanty offers a revealing critique of the ways some Western feminists have performed a similar operation on "Third World women" by beginning their analyses with the descriptive category of "woman" (59). In the research she cites, universal groupings such as "women of Africa" become "homogeneous sociological grouping[s] characterized by common dependencies or powerlessness" (59). Mohanty explains the ways resistance activities of Third World women—i.e., efforts toward representing themselves politically—are obscured by the assumption that they are "legal minors (read 'they-are-still-not-conscious-of-their-rights')" (72). Given Mohanty's endorsement of historical contextualization, it is odd that she ends her essay with the hope of moving beyond "the Marx who found it possible to say: They cannot represent themselves; they must be represented" (74)—a reference to Marx's "Eighteenth Brumaire" (see Marx 608). Marx is quite careful, in his analysis of the second phase of the French Revolution (1848–1851), to distinguish between a group of peasants who have historically resisted the oppressions of the old order (609) and those who, because of their geographic isolation and other circumstances of their mode of production, are "incapable of enforcing their class interest in their own name" (608). It is the latter Louis Bonaparte claims to represent. The danger to which Mohanty and Spivak point is assuming in advance of such careful analysis that a subordinated group cannot speak for themselves.

4. This definition doesn't presume to be the only or best definition of "metaphor"; in fact, it is a specialized definition associated with one strand of twentieth-century rhetorical theory. An anonymous reader of an earlier version of this essay objected to my use of metaphor in this way, arguing that the figure works through analogy and comparison rather than substitution, the point of an analogy depending on both terms being present to the mind rather than one standing in for or blocking out another. This reader objected that my use of "metaphor" to suggest substitution would not be helpful to language teachers struggling to help students understand how figures work. These comments led me to think about (among other things) the way all figures depend on the resonance between tenor and vehicle, and the way all figures distort or misrepresent. I ultimately decided to stay with this figurative analysis, including the definitions given above, because of a body of work I've encountered using the term in a similar way. Barbara Johnson summarizes this work, locating its contemporary origins with Roman Jakobson's famous study of aphasia. Johnson traces Jakobson's formulation of the metaphor/metonymy distinction from a linguistic construct to its use in designating hierarchies of genre poetry based on a principle of equivalence (narrative, on selection) through French structuralist and poststructuralist theory (DeMan's association of metaphor with necessity and metonymy with chance) and finally to the political implications of separating similarity from contiguity (153–58). This trajectory follows metaphor from privileged trope to "the trope of privilege" (158). See also Laclau and Mouffe, Ryan, and Sommer. One could say that this use of "metaphor" is itself a metaphoric act—substituting one partial definition of the figure for a fuller, more varied one.

5. Orignally titled *Mellamo Rigoberta Menchú. An Indian Woman in Guatemala,* before Menchú Tum married and changed her name.

6. My choice of three women as representative of postcolonial feminism performs the kind of metaphorical substitution I'm analyzing in the essay. I choose Spivak and Trinh because they revel in the act of writing, working over and through the problem of representation with a painful sensitivity I find appealing; Menchú Tum, because of the urgency of her situation. I choose them because I love to read them, each for different reasons. One of my purposes for writing this essay was to direct my responses away from a "conventional ethics of altruism" (Gunn 165) or an "uncritical hero-worship" (Sommer 69), and toward a "respect [that] is the condition of possibility for the kind of love that takes care not to simply appropriate its object" (Sommer 69).

7. Robert Con Davis and David S. Gross analyze Spivak's rhetoric in terms of *ethos,* raising some of the issues discussed below toward the end of pointing a direction for an ethical practice of cultural studies. They characterize Spivak's style in terms of "theatricality" (69) and imagine the voice of the subaltern as produced by a kind of "ventriloquism" (76).

8. In the analysis of Davis and Gross, the subaltern *ethos* does not refer to a particular group but rather to the impossibility of any discourse of the "other" available to the colonizer that has not been "defined by and related to the master discourse" (77).

9. Spivak differentiates her work from the "information retrieval" taking place in anthropology, political science, history, and sociology. She applies her critique of subaltern representation across these disciplinary boundaries, warning of potential for violence when historians et al. assume a consciousness of the subject under examination ("Subaltern" 298). Benita Parry takes issue with Spivak and others on this point, arguing that an over-scrupulous concern for such "violence" can have the effect of quelling efforts toward uncovering knowledge of colonized peoples and their resistant practices.

10. See Hennessy (96) for a discussion of a related theory: Pecheux's concept of "dis-identification." Hennessy defines it as the practice of *"working on* the subject-form": "critique, enacted in the disruption and re-arrangement of the pre-constructed categories on which the formation of subjects depends" (96).

11. In a survey of work at the borders of feminism and rhetoric, Lisa Ede, Cheryl Glenn, and Andrea Lunsford discuss women's alternative styles and the challenge by feminists of color to white feminists on issues of representation (420–8).

12. See Ede, Glenn, and Lunsford for a discussion of feminist alternatives to classical rhetorical arrangement (414–20).

13. See Jarratt and Reynolds for a related version of classical *ethos* through postmodern feminist theory.

14. Although this discussion of Spivak and Trinh is focused more on theorizing than pedagogy, I have assigned portions of Trinh's book to upper-division undergraduates in classes cross-listed with Women's Studies and English. I know at least one colleague who has used her chapter "Grandma's Story" with first-year composition students, and another who has taught Spivak in undergraduate feminist theory courses.

15. I use the past tense to indicate that Menchú Tum's literacy has changed in the fifteen years since she provided the oral account that led to the publication of her *testimonio*. In 1982, she had been studying spoken Spanish for three years. In 1997, she reported being almost finished with a new book, which I assume she herself is writing in Spanish.

16. The postcolonialisty of Guatemala is multi-layered. As Menchú Tum explains in her book, the Spanish conquest of Central America left as part of its legacy a three-layered society, with the indigenous Indian groups at the bottom, *ladinos*—Spanish-speaking assimilated *mestisos*—in the middle and upper-class descendants of the Spanish conquerors at the top. Although Menchú Tum does not emphasize the intervention of the U.S. government in the struggle for power in Guatemala, the role of the CIA in supporting the military government (even to the point of abetting the murder of U.S. citizens) in its deadly campaign during the 1980s to take land from the Indians and force them to work in extremely exploitative conditions on plantations is finally beginning to be documented by mainstream media (Krauss; Weiner).

17. Susan Morgan makes this point eloquently in her recent book on Victorian women writers in Southeast Asia, arguing (through the title) that *Place Matters*. She points out major differences among Singapore, Thailand, and India in their histories of contact with the West, its economies, and its social structures, and shows how those differences matter in our interpretations of colonial and postcolonial literatures.

18. Other examples of *testimonio* include Domitilia Barrios, *Let Me Speak* (Bolivia, 1978); Eugenia Claribel Alegría, *They Won't Take Me Alive* (El Salvador, 1998); and Elvia Alvarado, *Don't Be Afraid, Gringo* (Honduras, 1987).

WORKS CITED

Ahmad, Aijaz. *In Theory: Classes, Nations, Literatures*. London: Verso, 1992.

Alcoff, Linda. "The Problem of Speaking for Others." *Cultural Critique* (Winter 1991–92): 5–32.

Anderson, Benedict. *Imagined Communities: Reflections on the Origin and Spread of Nationalism*. London: Verso, 1983.

Bal, Mieke. "The Politics of Citation." *Diacritics* 21.1 (Spring 1991): 24–45.

Baumlin, James S., and Tita French Baumlin, eds. *Ethos: New Essays in Rhetorical and Critical Theory*. Dallas: Southern Methodist UP, 1994.

Brady, Laura. "The Reproduction of Othering." Jarratt and Worsham, 21–44.

Beverly, John. *Against Literature*. Minneapolis: U Minnesota P, 1993.

———. "The Margin at the Center: On *Testimonio* (Testimonial Narrative)." *Modern Fiction Studies* 35.1 (Spring 1989): 11–28.

Cixous, Hélène, and Catherine Clément. *The Newly Born Woman.* Trans. Betsy Wing. Minneapolis: U of Minnesota P, 1986.

Davis, Robert Con, and David S. Gross. "Gayatri Chakravorty Spivak and the Ethos of the Subaltern." Baumlin and Baumlin 65–89.

de Man, Paul. *Allegories of Reading.* New Haven: Yale UP, 1979.

D'Souza, Dinesh. *Illiberal Education: The Politics of Race and Sex on Campus.* New York: Vintage, 1991.

Ede, Lisa, Cheryl Glenn, and Andrea Lunsford. "Border Crossings: Intersections of Rhetoric and Feminism." *Rhetorica* 13.4 (Autumn 1995): 401–41.

Faigley, Lester. *Fragments of Rationality: Postmodernity and the Subject of Composition.* Pittsburgh: U Pittsburgh P, 1992.

Fanon, Frantz. *Black Skin, White Masks.* New York: Grove P, 1967.

Gunn, Janet Varner. "A Window of Opportunity: An Ethics of Reading Third World Autobiography." *College Literature* 19.3/20.1 (Oct. 1992/Feb. 1993): 162–69.

Harlow, Barbara. *Resistance Literature.* New York: Methuen, 1987.

Hennessy, Rosemary. *Materialist Feminism and the Politics of Discourse.* New York: Routledge, 1993.

Irigaray, Luce. *This Sex Which Is Not One.* Trans. Catherine Porter. Ithaca: Cornell UP, 1985.

Jakobson, Roman. "Two Aspects of Language and Two Types of Linguistic Disturbances." *Fundamentals of Language.* Ed. Roman Jakobson and Morris Halle. The Hague: Mouton, 1956.

Jarratt, Susan C., and Lynn Worsham, eds. *Feminism and Composition Studies: In Other Words.* New York: MLA, 1998.

——— and Nedra Reynolds. "The Splitting Image: Contemporary Feminisms and the Ethics of Ethos." Baumlin and Baumlin, 37–63.

Jay, Gregory S. "Knowledge, Power, and the Struggle for Representation." *College English* 56 (1994): 9–29.

Johnson, Barbara. "Metaphor, Metonymy, and Voice in *Their Eyes Were Watching God.*" *The Future of Difference.* Baltimore: Johns Hopkins UP, 1987. 155–71.

Krauss, Clifford. "Guatemala's War: Ideology Is the Latest Excuse." *The New York Times.* 9 April 1995. E.5.

Laclau, Ernesto, and Chantal Mouffe. *Hegemony and Socialist Strategy: Toward a Radical Democratic Politics.* London: Verso, 1985.

Landry, Donna, and Gerald MacLean. *Materialist Feminisms.* Cambridge: Basil Blackwell, 1993.

Lu, Min-Zhan. "Reading and Writing Differences: The Problematic of 'Experience.'" Jarratt and Worsham, 239–51.

Lunsford, Andrea A., and Lisa Ede. "Representing Audience." *College Composition and Communication* 47.2 (May 1996): 167–79.

Mailloux, Steven. *Rhetorical Power.* Ithaca: Cornell UP, 1989.

Mani, Lata. "Cultural Theory, Colonial Texts: Reading Eyewitness Accounts of Widow Burning." *Cultural Studies.* Ed. Lawrence Grossberg, Cary Nelson, and Paula A. Treichler. New York: Routledge, 1992. 392–405.

Marín, Lynda. "Speaking Out Together: Testimonials of Latin American Women." *Latin American Perspectives* 18.3 (Summer 1991): 51–68.

Marx, Karl. "The Eighteenth Brumaire of Louis Bonaparte." *The Marx-Engels Reader.* 2nd ed. Ed. Robert C. Tucker. New York: Norton, 1978: 594–617.

Menchú, Rigoberta. *I, Rigoberta Menchú: An Indian Woman in Guatemala.* Ed. Elizabeth Burgos-Debray. Trans. Ann Wright. London: Verso, 1984.

Mohanty, Chandra Talpade. "Under Western Eyes: Feminist Scholarship and Colonial Discourses." *Third World Women and the Politics of Feminism.* Ed. Chandra Talpade Mohanty, Ann Russo, and Lourder Torris. Bloomington: Indiana UP, 1991. 51–80.

Moi, Toril. "Feminism, Postmodernism, and Style: Recent Feminist Criticism in the United States." *Cultural Critique* (Spring 1988): 3–24.

Morgan, Susan. *Place Matters.* New Brunswick: Rutgers UP, 1996.

Parry, Benita. "Problems in Current Theories of Colonial Discourse." *Oxford Literary Review* 9.1–2 (1987): 27–58.

Roof, Judith, and Robyn Wiegman, eds. *Who Can Speak?: Authority and Critical Identity.* Urbana: U of Illinois P, 1995.

Ryan, Michael. *Politics and Culture: Working Hypotheses for a Revolutionary Society.* Baltimore: Johns Hopkins UP, 1989.

Sommer, Doris. "No Secrets: Rigoberta's Guarded Truth." *Women's Studies* 20 (1991): 51–72.

Spivak, Gayatri Chakravorty. "Can the Subaltern Speak?" *Marxism and the Interpretation of Culture.* Ed. Cary Nelson and Lawrence Grossberg. Urbana: U of Illinois P, 1988. 271–313.

———. "Feminism in Decolonization." *differences* 3.3 (Fall 1991): 139–70.

————. With Ellen Rooney. "In a Word: Interview." *differences* 1.2 (Summer 1989): 124–56.

————. *In Other Worlds: Essays in Cultural Politics.* New York: Routledge, 1988.

————. *Outside in the Teaching Machine.* New York: Routledge, 1993.

————. "The Political Economy of Women as Seen by a Literary Critic." *Coming to Terms: Feminism, Theory, Politics.* Ed. Elizabeth Weed. New York: Routledge, 1989. 218–29.

————. *The Post-Colonial Critic: Interviews, Strategies, Dialogues.* Ed. Sarah Harasym. New York: Routledge, 1990.

————. "Who Claims Alterity?" *Remaking History.* Ed. Barbara Kruger and Phil Mariani. Seattle: Bay P, 1989. 269–92.

Trinh, T. Minh-ha. *Woman, Native, Other: Writing Postcoloniality and Feminism.* Bloomington, Indiana UP, 1989.

Weiner, Tim. "A Guatemala Officer and the C.I.A." *The New York Times.* 26 March 1997. 6.

11

Rhetoric, Feminism, and the Politics of Textual Ownership

ANDREA ABERNETHY LUNSFORD

As a longtime advocate of collaboration and collabora-
tive writing and as a persistent critic of the kind of radical individualism reified by the "author construct," I might have been expected to welcome the
moves to dispersed authorship represented in so much of the postmodern
world. But I am not at all sanguine about these moves, for I believe now that
they signal not a challenge to the old ideology of authorship but rather its
appropriation for different and largely commercial ends. In the essay that follows, I hope to identify some alternatives to this appropriation and to explain
why embracing these alternatives is crucially important.

These changes in my understanding of the issues surrounding agency
and ownership (especially of language) have been very slow to evolve; they
began fifteen years ago when Lisa Ede and I were working on what we took to
be a fairly straightforward little essay called "Why Write . . . Together?" In it,
we argued that the concept of the lonely scribbler—the romantic concept of
the author as singular, originary, autonomous, and uniquely creative (in a
word, as "original")—effectively hid from view the largely collaborative
and highly dispersed nature of most creative endeavors, from art, drama,
literature, and film to scientific experimentation and discovery. In *Singular
Texts/Plural Authors* we explored further the deeply collaborative nature of
much professional and academic writing, and we noted some of the problems
attendant on continuing to try to fit the square peg of multiple, polyvocal creativity into the round hole of singular "authorship." We were responding to
work in composition studies that was revealing the collective nature of much
on-the-job writing, to the poststructuralist critique of the founding subject,
and to feminist activism in recovering the voices of women silenced by the
hegemony of romantic authorship—as well as to our own material conditions: we *wanted* to write together, but the academy (and especially our
department colleagues) didn't want us to.

We found supporters among women in many fields: in aesthetics and the

From *College English* 61 (1999): 529–44.

history of ideas from Martha Woodmansee, who has been arguing passionately since the early 1980s that our culture's obsession with the "author" of intellectual property that can be commodified and bartered in a capitalistic system has disenfranchised many, many creators—a great many of whom are women. In anthropology, we found scholars like Alma Gottlieb ("Beyond the Lonely Anthropologist: Collaboration in Research and Writing") and Elizabeth Lapovsky Kennedy ("In Pursuit of Connections: Reflections on Collaborative Work") reflecting not only on the ambiguous meaning of "collaborator" (after all, during the war collaborators were shot . . .) but on academic suspicions of all cooperative work. In the field of anthropology, Kennedy now notes that "it is unquestionably easier to do collaborative research and writing in the 1990s than it was in the 1960s"—and she credits three intellectual developments for managing such a change: "feminist scholarship, anticolonialist scholarship, and interpretive anthropology," all of which, she says, "present challenges to the traditional 'objective' report authored by the heroic anthropologist, the scientist of culture who works alone" (26).

We found support in many other fields as well, and for a (short) time it seemed to us possible that some kind of subtle but powerful rebalancing act might be possible: we would simply work with others to demonstrate the degree to which all discourse is produced socially, and growing recognition of this fact would break the hierarchical binary so firmly entrenched: solitary, original authorship = powerful, privileged, and good; collaborative, shared authorship = "uncreative," transgressive, and bad, very nearly a "crime" of writing.

I'm oversimplifying this narrative to make a point: during the '80s, we sensed a moment where change might be possible, change that would give voice to many women and members of other underrepresented groups, as well as to many means of cultural production not valued by modernist epistemologies or economies. It felt to us like a "postmodern moment" opening a space in which we could help work for change in the dynamics of intellectual property, of textual ownership, of the value structures surrounding certain kinds of cultural/textual production.

As with other such moments in the history of intellectual property, this one passed swiftly. Indeed, such a moment had occurred at the inception of intellectual property as we know it in copyright law today (in the early 1700s), when the "many hands" that produce a book were not hierarchized as they are today and when the "author" was not the solitary proprietary owner. Another moment seemed to occur with the 1798 edition of the collaboratively produced and anonymously published *Lyrical Ballads:* a moment in which language might be of and for the common people—the "folk" of the "middle and lower classes" as Wordsworth and Coleridge called them. In hindsight, this moment could have allowed for much greater democratization of language. But it passed swiftly, hardening into the Romantic iteration of originality and of individual proprietary ownership.

Certainly in retrospect, Lisa and I should have been more wary of this 1980s postmodern movement for change in understandings of intellectual property. In fact, we should have been wary of the term "property" itself, of the ways it has been raced and classed, as well as gendered; women and African Americans (and many Native Americans in the "new" world) were themselves thought of as property, their bodies commodified in many ways. From Latin *proprietas,* for ownership, "property" connotes exclusionary rights and possessions. Locke inscribed this view in his declaration that every man is entitled to "life, liberty, and property," and we can find that same concept enshrined in many discourses of Western government and religion from Locke's time to our own.

At the same time that Lisa and I were meditating on the metaphor of "property" and becoming more and more wary of "intellectual property" and all its baggage, other feminists were calling into question the supposed "death of the author"—the owner of intellectual property. Agreeing with Nancy Miller that this "death" does not "necessarily work for women," Linda Hutcheon puts it this way: "The current poststructuralist/postmodern challenges to the coherent, autonomous subject have to be put on hold in feminist and postcolonialist discourses, for both must work first to assert and affirm a denied or alienated subjectivity: those radical postmodern challenges are in many ways the luxury of the dominant order which can afford to challenge that which it securely possesses" (168). These cautions seemed compelling enough to suggest that the old economies of intellectual property—perhaps even the metaphor of property itself—should not be rejected out of hand if doing so once again disenfranchised many white women and most people of color. Perhaps ownership of intellectual property, and the "author" along with it, could be rehabilitated.

In fact, as many now recognize, during the three decades that literary theorists have been debating the notion of "authorship" and ownership of texts, the terms of the debate over intellectual property have shifted swiftly and dramatically. The "momentary space" I mentioned earlier, marked by challenges from poststructuralist theory, the electronic revolution, and women's (and particularly women of color's) modes of collaborative practice, has been closed up in the wake of a powerful appropriation of the "author" construct in the legal and corporate worlds. In the body of law governing copyright, the solitary and sovereign "author" holds sway: copyright cannot exist in a work produced as a "true collective enterprise"; copyright does not hold in works that are not "original" (which, as Peter Jaszi has demonstrated at length rules out protection for "nonindividualistic cultural productions, like 'folkloric' works, which cannot be reimagined as products of solitary, originary 'authorship'" [38]), and copyright does not extend to what the law sees as the "basic components" of cultural production (the rhythms of traditional musical forms, for example). What copyright law *does* protect is "author's rights," which have been repeatedly expanded during the last thirty years, and which have recently been expanded once again, effectively keeping a great deal of cultural material out of the public domain and further restricting the fair use of copyrighted works.

More interesting and alarming to me as a feminist and a rhetorician today, however, is the appropriation of the sovereign "author" construct by the corporate world, especially in cyberspace, where the largest single domain is now .com, with four and a half million hosts accounting for almost 25 percent of the Internet—and .com, the latest figures tell us, is growing by 52 percent annually, or at the rate of 18,000 new "hosts" per day. In this and other arenas, corporate entities now assume the mantle of the "author" who has clearly come back to life with a vengeance: look at Disney, at Microsoft, at the multinational corporations, even at *The New York Times,* which recently attempted to take copyright for everything printed in its pages, a move barely averted by the newspaper's writers. These large entities now claim "author's rights"—and they have squads of lawyers working around the clock to help them. (If you think you are an "author," think again—and check your contracts. In the last fifteen years, even the educational journals in our field have begun appropriating the copyright—in essence taking on "authorship" for themselves—and getting fees for our work when it appears in coursepacks, for instance.) I could, of course, cite further instances of the corporate and legal appropriation of the "author" construct and the use of it to shape intellectual property regimes that favor corporate interests. The trend has resulted in a kind of a "gold-rush" mentality to copyright and patent everything under the sun: Bill Gates is trying to corner the world's market of images; plastic surgeons in New York are trying to patent the faces they "produce"; scientists everywhere are patenting strings of DNA; Disney is working hard to extend the limits of copyright to over a hundred years because—horrors!—Mickey Mouse is coming out of copyright in 2003 and might become part of the cultural commons; and drug companies are moving to patent and copyright chemicals found in the plants of Third-World countries in order to process them and sell them as "cures"—at a great profit (for a fascinating related discussion, see Boyle). In this atmosphere, it's no wonder that the Italian government is trying to copyright the Tuscan landscape, that NBA players are trying to copyright certain moves, and that cartoons show children affixing copyright notices to their homework. Property indeed.

Perhaps most troubling of all, however, has been the move in legal and corporate worlds to apply the mantle of proprietary authorship to hardware and software. In spite of their wide public use and the fact that they are the products of a wholly collaborative process, computer programs (with a very few notable exceptions) are increasingly defined in the law as works of "originality" and "creative genius," that is, as works that fall within the expansive protection of copyright and author's rights. This latest move, seen in all the documents coming out of WIPO (the World Intellectual Property Organization), to my mind puts an end to the possibility for democratization of language and knowledge that cyberspace at one time seemed to promise. (Indeed, one of the postings on a listserv I read, CNI Copyright, had the subject fine "Fair Use Now Dead on the Internet.")

In short, while many have been debating the "death of the author" and theorizing about the possibilities of agency and subjectivity for silenced, muted, or disenfranchised groups, the horse is most definitely out of the barn.

While most of us watched from the sidelines, the old cloak of the originary author-genius has been (through an act of "theft" or "disguise" perhaps, to use Nancy Miller's terms) spruced up and donned by the corporate entrepreneurial interests—and the bigger, the more global, the better. Especially on the Internet, which Marc Andreessen (the twenty-four-year-old multimillionaire creator of Netscape) calls, in an understatement, primarily a platform for entrepreneurial activities.

In such an atmosphere, issues of "authorship" and intellectual property are getting really complicated. And given the complexity I've already conjured up, I won't even go into the ways we as academics perpetuate what I think of as the negative aspects of this authorial/entrepreneurial regime through our institutional policies, pedagogies, and practices. As a gesture toward this complicity, however, I can note a piece of a hypertext I worked on for the online journal *Kairos*, in which I said that "for a long time now, I have not felt a strong sense of individual ownership of any text I work on producing. . . . But I would be disingenuous indeed if I did not recognize the degree to which my position as a white tenured full professor gives me the luxury of this stand: were I a beginning assistant professor, much less a graduate student, I would have to acknowledge a major truth of our profession: individual ownership of intellectual property is the key to advancement" (Lunsford et al., "What Matters . . .?").

Rather than dwell on this complicity, however, which I think is fairly obvious, I want to ask instead how a feminist rhetoric can engage this complicated moment, and these complicated notions of ownership and intellectual property. What can we do in the face of the "land grab" or "gold rush" mentality that is currently driving legal, governmental, and corporate efforts to own and control more and more, to hedge off for their own benefit and profit most of the world's natural and intellectual resources? First and most obvious, I suppose, we can join 'em—taking on the mantle of entrepreneurial authorship whenever and wherever possible as one way to gain the agency and the presence of subjectivity long denied to women. Indeed, some feminist scholars have advocated such a move: if the tools of the master cannot dismantle the master's house, well, then, steal some new tools—and buy the house. I take this option seriously, especially given the vastly oppressive material conditions under which many of the world's women labor. And yet, given the history and ideology of this model of proprietary ownership, I am deeply troubled by this particular response.

A second response may be to hope for a shift in the values underlying the model of ownership, a shift (articulated by many in the digital world) that might redistribute "intellectual property" in new and beneficial ways. In composition studies, I've been especially encouraged by the *Computers and Composition* special issue on Intellectual Property guest-edited by Laura Gurak and Johndan Johnson-Eilola. Especially provocative in that issue are Carrie Shively Leverenz's "Citing Cybersources: A Challenge to Disciplinary Values," John Logie's "Champing at the Bits: Computers, Copyright, and the Composition Classroom," and Karla Saari Kitalong's "A Web of Symbolic Violence." In addition, two recent *CCC* essays also work at least indirectly toward new understandings of intellectual property. In one, Linda Adler-Kassner looks at models of ownership in terms of student writing, tracing two competing views (which she calls "democratic" and "individualistic"), and ends with a provocative overview of ways in which portfolio assessment and service learning courses work to move beyond limiting and individualistic agendas. In the other, Candace Spigelman discusses definitions and understandings of ownership among members of peer writing groups and argues for making the tensions in current students' conceptions of ownership central to the composition classroom.

Esther Dyson, author of *Release 2.0* and an influential member of the digerati (daughter of astrophysicist Freeman Dyson and sister of George, of "The Starship and the Canoe" fame), has argued for just such a shift in value, which, she insists, will no longer reside in "content" at all—not in the product, that is, of the originary genius. (Nicholas Negroponte apparently agrees, saying that the "content" of books may be "evolving toward being free" [Maney 2B]). Nor, says Dyson, will value reside in the producer of the content—the genius *him*self; nor even in the user of the content (Barthes's triumphant reader?). Rather, she claims, value will "lie in the relationships surrounding and nurturing the movement of content through networks of users and producers" (182–84). What Dyson predicts seems to me nothing less than the ultimate triumph of process over product, of networking over singularity. But this shift in value has, as I've just been arguing, already been appropriated as the province of the entrepreneur corporation or conglomerate—the entity that will "own" the efforts of those who, to use Dyson's words, nurture "the movement of content through networks of users and producers." In short, this particular response to the complicated set of issues surrounding debates over intellectual property may well lead only to a new kind of "work for hire" or "piecework." I don't need to point out that too many writing teachers have already been there, done that. So I am not optimistic about the potential of this second response.

We do have a third possibility, however: we can, as Nancy Miller suggests, try to articulate a new rhetoric of authorship, one that rejects the naïve construction of author as originary genius *or* as entrepreneurial corporate entity, without diminishing the importance of agency, and of difference, to the lives of working writers. (I might also mention many other scholars, such as Judith Butler, who eschews the "prediscursive I" or sovereign subject of modernism as well as the deterministic view of discourse that precludes the possibility of human agency.) My own hope is for more than that. I hope that, working together, feminist rhetoricians can create, enact, and promote alternative forms of agency and ways of owning that would shift the focus from owning to owning up; from rights and entitlements to responsibilities (the ability to respond) and answerability; from a sense of the self as radically individual to the self as always in relation; and from a view of agency as invested in and gained through the exchange of tidy knowledge packages to a view of agency as residing in what Susan West defines as the "unfolding action of a discourse;

in the knowing and telling of the attentive rhetor/responder rather than in static original ideas" (190).

Given the speed with which the traditional forms of ownership and intellectual property have been appropriated by global corporate and legal interests, however, such work is going to be exceedingly difficult. Nevertheless, I believe there are enactments, tracings of alternative forms of being and owning, already available to us. If we intend to create what Stanford public policy analyst Milbray McLaughlin calls a "new public idea" about intellectual property, we will have to work together on a number of fronts, for such public ideas are hard to invoke. Today, I can only gesture toward some of the work we may draw on to make such a new public idea possible—work that aims to create a "new idea" in the discourse of corporations, of technology, of politics, of law, and of cultural (including literary) production.

Let me turn first to the lion's den of the corporate world, where we might least expect to find alternative models of ownership or intellectual property available. I am only just beginning to learn about some of the efforts being made, particularly by and on behalf of the indigenous peoples' knowledge of plant biology that has been appropriated so stunningly and successfully in recent years. Some firms are trying to do business in a new way: Shaman Pharmaceutical, Inc., is publicly committed to sharing its profits with its "collaborators." Their "process is driven," they say, "by the science of ethnobotany, or how native peoples use plants. Shaman uses data provided by a network of ethnobotanists and physicians engaged in ongoing field research—in Africa, the South Pacific, Southeast Asia, and Central and South America—to provide initial direction. . . . Working with traditional healers of various rainforest cultures allows Shaman access to the largest in vivo laboratory in the world" (King and Carlson 136). Significantly, I think, Shaman is committed to sharing profits with *all* the communities with which they work, not just the ones that yield a marketable product. Further, they say that compensation plans will be arrived at collaboratively—with the Healing Forest conservancy, a nonprofit foundation established by Shaman, and representatives from communities Shaman works in—and that "payment" will include the support of land rights, "strengthening indigenous peoples' organizations and fostering communication . . . ; and promoting sustainable, ecologically sound development through local harvesting of products; and linking public health and welfare of indigenous cultures and tropical forests" (139). This model of intellectual property—with its accompanying version of agency—is one radically different from the traditional Western paradigm; the Shaman model creates a middle space between radically individual proprietary rights and the international public domain. In short, while I am not optimistic about corporate attempts at sharing—to put it mildly—such a model may offer an alternative to the copyright regime founded on the notion of the solitary, sovereign, and proprietary author.

I can see similar if more modest attempts among cyber-citizens like Esther Dyson, who gives away much of her "proprietary" knowledge as a way of gaining a wider audience for her views and of working collaboratively with others interested in the development of cyberspace. And she has some allies, among them Richard Stallman, one of the original MIT artificial intelligence hackers of the sixties. Stallman, known for his determined attempts to establish "copyleft," has founded the Free Software Foundation, which sells—and gives away—his software. As he puts it, "I *develop* free software . . . I do not necessarily distribute it for free. Free software is a matter of freedom, not price. Think of free speech, not free beer" (Benedek 46). What this means, I think, is that Stallman indeed "sells" his software (for about $60). But once a customer buys it, he or she is free to look at its source codes, figure out how the whole thing works, and modify it to meet personal needs—or, says Stallman, even give it away to friends. As readers will readily imagine, Stallman's generosity is seen as quirky if not mad by most of the computer industry, and Dyson—who is somewhat more conservative—is also viewed by some as overly generous. Nevertheless, their methods work toward a balance between protecting individual dignities and rights—especially those *not* protected by earlier regimes of intellectual property—and protecting the public good. Stallman's conception of software recently received a surprising show of support from browser pioneer Netscape when the company released the source code of Navigator, its immensely popular browser, to be freely copied and adapted by users and developers; Netscape CEO Jim Barksdale made this move to combat Microsoft's strategy of distributing its Explorer browser for free but then, as is typical in the software industry, keeping its code secret and proprietary.

And finally, if those working at the heart of computer technology today are actually going to articulate a new model of ownership and intellectual property, they will need the help of groups like Spiderwoman, a nonpartisan, online international community of (male and female) feminist web designers. This group, founded in 1995, was in the news for vehemently protesting a "Technology Summit" held in May 1997 by Bill Gates. The 103 guests invited to the "summit" came from all over the world and represented a wide variety of companies. But, as Spiderwoman was quick to point out, they did *not* represent women. Out of the 103 participants, Spiderwoman could find only one woman, AutoDesk CEO Carol Bartz. When Microsoft insisted that there were many women there—at least as many as three—Spiderwoman checked them out and found that one of the other two "many women" turned out to be not *Mary* but *Marvin* Runyan (<http://www.amazoncity.com/spiderwoman/webspinning/newsflash.html>).

In the realm of legal practice and theory, which I have associated primarily with the interests of Western corporate entrepreneurism, we can also find a few people questioning the link between copyright law and the "author construct" and searching for new ways to imagine the politics of ownership. Foremost among these I would name Pamela Samuelson, a member of the faculty of Berkeley's School of Information Management and Systems and winner of a 1997 MacArthur award. Even as she offers colleagues the codes she has developed for constructing the web site she teaches from at Berkeley—saying "Take my stuff, please!"—Samuelson is careful to say that she is by no means trying to achieve a world in which everything is shared or free. Rather, she wants to work with people from Silicon Valley who are trying to develop new technology—and new business models—and help them reconfigure copyright laws to fit the new models. While she acknowledges the complexity of the current copyright situation, she says her goal is actually simple: "to see that copyright laws do not infringe on the sharing of knowledge in society" (Krochmal). This goal may sound simple, but creating a new public idea from it will not be, even with women as formidably bright and determined as Pam Samuelson at work. According to John Perry Barlow, co-founder of the Electronic Frontier Foundation, she has "stood up against the entire weight of the commercial legal world" (and I would add the male wild west frontier atmosphere of the digital world) in trying to find an articulation of copyright law that will balance individual agency and rights with public good and with freedom of information (Krochmal). Perhaps not surprisingly, Samuelson's work, and that of the Electronic Frontier Foundation, is not widely known in English studies, where few have taken notice of—or acted to influence—the deluge of legislation related to expanding protection and limiting access to information. In fact, recent Congressional bills demonstrate an alarming move toward ever-greater control of knowledge by a select few. "The Digital Millennium Copyright Act," Public L. 105–304, became law in October 1998. Following vigorous and persistent work by members of the Digital Future Coalition (of which NCTE and many other academic groups are members), the WIPO legislation is not as hyperprotectionist as it was in earlier versions. Nevertheless, its current incarnation is still a far cry from responding to the needs of teachers and students and scholars, or from protecting the public good. In fact, while the bill makes vague general references to the concept of fair use, it does little to protect the fair use doctrine itself, especially in key areas such as educational photocopying or home taping. As a result, it could prepare the way for destroying a concept that has been crucial to the work of scholars and teachers. Especially troublesome are a number of sections tacked on to this bill, apparently late in the game and without debate. One of these additions incorporates (with very few changes) the substance of H.R. 2652, known as the "Collections of Information Antipiracy Act" when it passed the House of Representatives. In brief, this section seeks to expand protection of databases and database publishers in ways that will create strong disincentives for sharing data and, in turn, will be extremely harmful to scholars and teachers. Finally, a proposed revision of the Uniform Commercial Code, Article 2B, would create a new set of rights for "content providers," allowing them to claim that *any* use of their information, particularly in the case of digital access, constitutes the acceptance of a contract and thus enables them to control—and to charge for—any use of this information, whether in the public domain or not. While the language of the final Act was softened, and the most restrictive of the database protection material removed, these changes were made only at the very last moment after extensive and persistent lobbying. Even more troubling, this Congress passed (and the President signed into law on 27 October 1998) the Sonny Bono Copyright Term Extension Act, making the term for most works the life of the author plus seventy years. In celebrating the passage of this Act, Mary Bono perhaps unwittingly gave voice to what seems the contemporary rush to hyperprotection when she announced that copyright should be forever.

In spite of Mary Bono's oversimplifications, these legislative initiatives are complex and often cloaked in the most obscure legalese, but they are not impossible for teachers of reading and writing to understand. Moreover, they demand our action now, in letters, phone calls, and faxes to Senators and Representatives urging protection of fair use and of the public right to information. (The best source I know of for keeping up to date on unfolding legislation regarding intellectual property is the Digital Future Coalition Website: see <http://www.dfc.org>. Two other helpful sites are Dennis Karjala's home page <http://www.public.asu.edu/~dkarjala/> and the Conference on College Composition and Communication Intellectual Property Caucus site <http://www.ncte.org/cccc/cccc-ip>.)

Most of the contributors to the DFC website are lawyers, and like Samuelson they have done much to raise awareness about the ways in which contemporary legislative programs tend to appropriate the Romantic "author" agent for use by major corporate interests. Another legal scholar who is helping to think through the thicket surrounding agency, ownership, and political action is Lani Guinier, professor of law at the University of Pennsylvania and onetime nominee for head of the Justice Department's civil rights division. I cannot do justice to Guinier's elegant and complex envisioning of an agency beyond liberal individualism, one based on constantly shifting alliances and realliances, always in pursuit of more inclusive democratic possibilities. But I believe that the body of Guinier's work deserves a detailed and attentive reading from feminists and rhetoricians alike, particularly in terms of her (re)definition of authority. In an ingenious argument, Guinier steers a course between the individual and the group, between libertarian individualism and identity politics, situating authority in the *connections* a person makes among the discourses available to her and out of which can come what Guinier celebrates as a medley of component voices that is singular and plural at the same time. These medleys or coalitions are always momentary and shifting—and powerful. Though I know of no one who has pursued the possible connections between the work Samuelson is doing to (re)envision copyright and the both/and view of authority and voice articulated by Guinier, some immediate compatibilities seem apparent to me—and both offer to help create a new public idea about what it means to own and use language, about what it means to exercise agency far beyond the sphere of the radical individual self, about what it can and should mean, in Jacqueline Jones Royster's words, to operate ethically in a common space.

Finally, I want to call attention to the many women writers who are refiguring notions of textual production and ownership. Lisa Ede, Cheryl Glenn, and I wrote about some of these women in a *Rhetorica* essay in which we attempted to trace some of the many reciprocities between rhetoric and feminism and to name some of the ways in which women are literally rewriting the "rules" of rhetoric. Many readers will be familiar with Jackie Royster's and Shirley Logan's work on the models of shared linguistic power and collaboration embodied in the writing and speaking of many nineteenth-century African American women writers, and with Anne Gere's recent study of the women's club movement, groups that often understood "property" and language use in ways far different from those enshrined in the copyright tradition.

In addition, of course, we can find many examples of fiction, drama, and online writing today that call attention to collaborative writing practices, some of which may seem more transgressive of traditional rhetoric than others. In Kathy Acker's fiction, for example, the conventional crime of writing—plagiarism—is consciously deployed to call attention to what she sees as the current impossibility of "owning" language and to the need for alternative rhetorical practices for enacting multiple selves in discourse. I'm thinking here particularly of Acker's *Don Quixote: Which Was a Dream,* in which Acker interweaves shocking and intensely jarring language with word-for-word excerpts from Cervantes's canonical text. In his dissertation *The Author's Property,* John Logie looks carefully at Acker's appropriation of masculine discursive practices, showing how such an appropriation supplements traditional forms of authorship and resists linguistic ownership.

Playwright Anna Deveare Smith represents a related challenge to traditional notions of the rhetorical practice of authorship. In a series of dramas (including *Fires in the Mirror: Crown Heights, Brooklyn, and Other Identities* and *Twilight Los Angeles 1992: On the Road: A Search for American Character*), Smith uses the techniques of journalism—interviewing, tape-recording, transcribing—to capture the words and voices of those who then become "characters" in her one-woman plays. While some accuse Smith of "ventriloquism" and "unoriginality," others argue that her plays represent a kind of midwifery, an open acknowledgment of the weaving together of others' words characteristic to some degree of all writing. In terms of online discourse, we might turn not only to groups like Spiderwoman but to sites of electronic public discourse such as *Amazon City: Where She Is the Revolution* (<www.amazoncity.com>), noting the ways in which writers at this specifically gendered site appropriate and use the words of others—most often without attribution.

In this essay, however, I wish to focus on one particular woman, Gloria Anzaldúa, especially since I had a chance to conduct a lengthy interview with her. Let me begin with Anzaldúa's response to a question I asked about metaphors for writing. Without a pause, she said, "So, my composition theme . . . *Compustura* used to mean being a seamstress. [To me] *compustura* means seaming together fragments to make a garment you wear, which represents you, your identity in the world" (Lunsford 9). It is stitched together from "what's out there," what the culture and others give you, what you can take and use. This notion of writing, of language use, as a stitching, a seaming together of a garment (which echoes Anzaldúa's intricate discussions of making face/making soul) that is taken from "what is out there" and that is thus both yours and not yours seems to me to be very much in the spirit of what scholars like Guinier and Samuelson—and sometimes groups like Spider-woman and AmazonCity—are after. The result of such a refiguration would be to open up what Susan West calls the "authordoxy" to multiple voices, not just to those who are *author*ized to speak/write/be heard, and thus to enlarge and enrich the conversation for all and, incidentally, to refigure literacy as the ability to respond to a conversation already and always ongoing in a way that "invites the participation of others" (West 190). Anzaldúa's stinging critique of traditional literacy education and her own commitment to giving voice to multiple positionalities as well as to women's voices that have been muted or ignored indicates that she sees herself as already participating in such a refiguration.

Certainly much if not all of Anzaldúa's work seems to me to be highly collaborative, shared and stitched together in various ways, and so I asked her about this aspect of her knowledge-making and writing. She talked first about the children's books she has written and about her collaboration with artists:

> Well, at first it wasn't quite a straight collaboration, because I did the text first and then I gave it to the artist. But now I am doing a project for a middle-school girl readership, and there I will be working with the artist. But I also think that there is no such thing as a single author. I write my texts, but I borrow the ideas and images from other people. Sometimes I forget that I've borrowed them. I might read some phrase from a poem or fiction, and I like the way it describes the cold. Years and years go by, and I do something similar with my description, but I've forgotten that I've gotten it somewhere else. Then I show my text in draft form to a lot of people for feed-back: that's another level of co-creating with somebody. Then my readers do the same thing. They put all of their experience into the text and they change *Borderlands* into many different texts. It's different for every reader. It's not mine anymore. (19–20)

"Does that feel OK to you?" I couldn't help asking. "You don't feel possessive about your writing as your 'property'?" "No, I don't," was her response:

> I've always felt that way about writing. I do the composing, but it's taken from little mosaics of other people's lives, other people's perceptions. I take all of these pieces and rearrange them. When I'm writing I always have the company of the reader. Sometimes I'm writing with my friends in mind, and sometimes for people like you who teach writing. In writing, I'm just talking with you without your being here. This is where style comes in. Style is my relationship with you, how I decide what register of language to use, how much Spanglish, how much vernacular. It's all done in the company of others, while in solitude—which is a contradiction. (20)

Later in the conversation, Anzaldúa shifted the topic to "authority," saying, "When you get into reading and writing the 'other,' into assuming some kind of authority for the 'other'—whether you are the 'other' or you are the subject—there's a community involved. There's a responsibility that comes with invoking cultural and critical authority, and I think you could call that responsibility being open to activism and being responsible for your actions. No?" (26). In this last statement, Anzaldúa sums up for me the challenge facing rhetoricians, and particularly, feminist rhetoricians and compositionists today. How can we help to create a model of writing and ownership that encompasses both the subject and the larger community Anzaldúa speaks of? How can we best help to create a new public idea about intellectual property and the "ownership" of language? In short, how can we act in the face of the bitter battle already under way to control the future of all knowledge and all knowledge production, one that could lead us into a twenty-first century thoroughly imbued with destructive radical individualism and hypercompetition, with definitions of knowledge and language as commodities to be owned, bought, and sold, and with representations of human agency as limited and narrow?

In spite of the many forces at work, I am not entirely pessimistic about working for change, because of some of the encouraging work toward a new public idea described here, and especially because of the potential for new alliances among scholars and teachers committed to the kind of responsible activism Anzaldúa calls for. The first step of such activism, for those in English studies today, might be to lead the way in creating a contemporary grammar and vocabulary capable of recognizing—and re-valuing—rhetorical practices that until very recently have been defined, if not as writing "crimes," then certainly as suspiciously collaborative misdemeanors. Scholars of rhetoric and composition need to identify, theorize, and begin systematically practicing and teaching alternative forms of subjectivity and alternative modes of ownership.

WORKS CITED

Acker, Kathy. *Don Quixote: Which Was a Dream.* New York: Grove, 1986.
Adler-Kassner, Linda. "Ownership Revisited: An Exploration in Progressive Era and Expressivist Era Composition Scholarship." *CCC* 49.2 (May 1998): 208–33.
Amazon City: Where She Is the Revolution <www.amazoncity.com>.
Benedek, Emily. "Steal This Program: Richard Stallman's Campaign to Liberate Software." *Lingua Franca* August 1997: 45–48.
Boyle, James. *Shamans, Software, & Spleens: Law and the Construction of the Information Society.* Cambridge: Harvard UP, 1996.
Butler, Judith. *Gender Trouble: Feminism and the Subversion of Identity.* New York: Routledge, 1989.
CNI-Copyright. <http://www.cni-org/Hforums/cni-copyright/>.
Dyson, Esther. "Intellectual Value." *Wired* 3.07 (July 1995): 136+.
Ede, Lisa, and Andrea Lunsford. *Singular Texts/Plural Authors: Perspectives on Collaborative Writing.* Carbondale: Southern Illinois UP, 1990.
———. "Why Write . . . Together?" *Rhetoric Review* 1 (1983): 150–8.
Ede, Lisa, Cheryl Glenn, and Andrea Lunsford. "Border Crossings: Intersections of Rhetoric and Feminism." *Rhetorica: A Journal of the History of Rhetoric* 13 (1995): 401–42.
Gere, Anne Ruggles. *Intimate Practices. Literacy and Cultural Work in U.S. Women Clubs, 1880–1920.* Chicago: U of Illinois P, 1997.
Gottlieb, Alma. "Beyond the Lonely Anthropologist: Collaboration in Research and Writing." *American Anthropologist* 97:1 (1995) 21–26.
Guinier, Lani. *The Tyranny of the Majority: Fundamental Fairness in Representative Democracy.* New York: Free P, 1994.
Gurak, Laura, and Johndan Johnson-Eilola, guest editors. *Computers and Composition* Special Issue: Intellectual Property. 15:2 (1998).

Hutcheon, Linda. "Circling the Downspout of Empire: Post-Colonialism and Postmodernism." *Past the Last Post*. Ed. Ian Adam and Helen Tifflin. Calgary: U of Calgary P, 1990. 167–89.

Jaszi, Peter. "On the Author Effect: Contemporary Copyright and Collective Creativity. " Woodmansee and Jaszi, 29–56.

Kennedy, Elizabeth Lapovsky. "In Pursuit of Connections: Reflections on Collaborative Work." *American Anthropologist* 97.1 (1995): 26–33.

King, Stephen R., and Thomas J. Carlson. "Biological Diversity, Biomedicine, and Botany: The Experience of Shaman Pharmaceuticals." *Interciencia* 20 (May/June 1995): 135–9.

Kitalong, Karla Saari. "A Web of Symbolic Violence." *Computers and Composition Special Issue: Intellectual Property*. 15.2 (1998): 253–63.

Krochmal, Maurice M. "Fighting the Copyright Wars with a 'Genius Grant' in Hand." *CyberTimes Extra* (June 28 1997). <http://www.nytimes.com/library/cyber/week/062897/samuelson .html>; accessed 8/11/97.

Leverenz, Carrie Shively. "Citing Cybersources: A Challenge to Disciplinary Values." *Computers and Composition* Special Issue: Intellectual Property. 15.2 (1998): 185–200.

Logan, Shirley Wilson. *"We Are Coming": The Persuasive Discourse of Nineteenth-Century Black Women*. Carbondale, IL: Southern Illinois UP, 1999.

———. "When and Where I Enter: Race, Gender, and Composition Studies." *Feminism and Composition Studies: In Other Words*. Ed. Susan C. Jarratt and Lynn Worsham. New York, MLA 1998. 45–57.

———. *With Pen and Voice: A Critical Anthology of Nineteenth-Century African-American Women*. Carbondale, IL: Southern Illinois UP, 1995.

Logie, John. *The Author's Property: Rhetoric, Literature, and Constructions of Authorship*. Diss. Pennsylvania State U, 1999.

———. "Champing at the Bits: Computers, Copyright, and the Composition Classroom." *Computers and Composition* Special Issue: Intellectual Property. 15.2 (1998): 201–14.

Lunsford, Andrea A. "Toward a Mestiza Rhetoric: Gloria Anzaldúa on Composition and Postcoloniality. "*JAC. A Journal of Composition Theory* 18.1 (Winter 1998): 1–27.

Lunsford, Andrea, with Rebecca Rickley, Michael J. Salvo, and Susan West. "What Matters Who Writes? What Matters Who Responds? Issues of Ownership in the Writing Classroom." *Kairos: A Journal for Teachers of Writing in Webbed Environments* 1.1 (Spring 1996). Online <http:english.tta.edu/kairos/1.1/features/lunsford.html>.

Maney, Kevin. "Novel Trend Must Prove It's Got the Write Staff." *USA Today* 9 August 1998: 1B–2B.

McLaughlin, Milbrey, and Ida Oberman, eds. *Teacher Learning: New Policies, New Practices (The Series on School Reform)*. New York: Teachers College P, 1996.

Miller, Nancy K. "Changing the Subject: Authorship, Writing, and the Reader." *Feminist Studies/Critical Studies*. Ed. Teresa de Lauretis. Bloomington: Indiana UP, 1986: 102–20.

Royster, Jacqueline Jones, ed. *Southern Horrors and Other Writings: The Anti-Lynching Campaign of Ida B. Wells, 1892–1900*. New York: Bedford, 1997.

———. *Traces of a Stream: Literacy and Social Change Among African American Women*. Pittsburgh: U of Pittsburgh P, 2000.

Smith, Anne Deveare. *Fires in the Mirror: Crown Heights, Brooklyn, and Other Identities*. New York: Anchor, 1993.

———. *Twilight Los Angeles 1992: On the Road: A Search for American Character*. New York: Anchor, 1994.

Spigelman, Candace. "Textual Ownership in Peer Writing Groups. " *CCC* 49.2 (May 1998): 234–55.

West, Susan. "From Owning to Owning Up: Authorial Rights and Rhetorical Responsibilities." Unpublished manuscript.

Woodmansee, Martha. "The Genius and the Copy-Right: Economic and Legal Conditions of the Emergence of the 'Author.' " *Eighteenth Century Studies* 17 (1984): 425–48.

Woodmansee, Martha, and Peter Jaszi, eds. *The Construction of Authorship: Textual Appropriation in Law and Literature*. Durham, Duke UP, 1994.

12

Feminist Methods of Research in the History of Rhetoric: What Difference Do They Make?

PATRICIA BIZZELL

Ten years of scholarship in the history of rhetoric had to be accounted for when Bruce Herzberg and I undertook to prepare the second edition of our anthology of readings in rhetorical theory, *The Rhetorical Tradition*. It was first published in 1990 and the second edition is now in press. The past decade has seen a tremendous outpouring of work in the history of rhetoric, as researchers in classics, history, philosophy, and speech communication have been joined in unprecedented numbers by scholars from English studies and composition. Herzberg and I have, of course, attempted to reflect this new work in the changes we have made in our anthology. But in my opinion as co-editor, the most significant change in the second edition comprises the presence of women's rhetorics and rhetorics of color. I don't wish to suggest that I think the new book adequately represents these strands in Western rhetoric. But I wish to argue that their increased presence is significant for two reasons. I will explore these reasons primarily in terms of women's rhetorics here, although I believe that similar arguments could be made with respect to rhetorics of color, and as suggested below, there is considerable overlap. On the one hand, as Richard Enos contends in "Recovering the Lost Art of Researching the History of Rhetoric," feminist research in the history of rhetoric is perhaps the best current example of what humanistic scholarship in rhetoric can accomplish. On the other hand, feminist research in the history of rhetoric presents the most trenchant challenges to traditional scholarly practices, opening up exciting new paths not only in the material scholars can study, but also, and perhaps ultimately more significantly, in the methods whereby we can study it.

I

First, what has feminist research in the history of rhetoric produced? Preparing the second edition of *The Rhetorical Tradition* anthology puts me in a relatively good position to answer that question, because of my avowed agenda of

From *Rhetoric Society Quarterly* 30 (2000): 5–17.

representing women's rhetorics in that volume coupled with the anthologist's necessity of relying on already published scholarship. I felt that the state of scholarship in 1989, when the first edition of the book was sent to the printers, permitted me to include only the following: Christine de Pizan and Laura Cereta combined in a single unit, with two brief excerpts, within the Renaissance section; Margaret Fell and Sarah Grimké similarly combined, though with slightly longer excerpts, in what was then the Enlightenment section, covering the eighteenth and nineteenth centuries; and Julia Kristeva and Hélène Cixous also combined, with longer excerpts, in the twentieth-century section. This is not very many women. Furthermore, as many readers have pointed out, combining the women tends to imply a devaluation of their work, as if it were not important or substantial enough to stand on its own. And indeed, the only men presented in combination in the first edition are four nineteenth-century composition textbook authors, representing what is openly treated as a minor genre. The women are presented in combination because I felt the need to preface their work in every case with a rather lengthy headnote justifying their inclusion and providing hints for how to read these texts as rhetorical theory, since they usually do not resemble the kinds of theoretical texts written by men and familiar in the canonical tradition.

The explosion of feminist scholarship in the history of rhetoric over the last ten years has enabled the table of contents of the second edition of the anthology to look very different: first, no women are presented in combination. Second, every section of the book now contains at least one woman: Aspasia in the classical section; Christine de Pizan, with more excerpts, in the medieval section (where she really seems to belong); Madeleine de Scudéry, Margaret Fell, and Sor Juana Inès de la Cruz in the Renaissance section; Mary Astell in the eighteenth-century section; Maria Stewart, Sarah Grimké, Phoebe Palmer, and Frances Willard in the nineteenth-century section; and Virginia Woolf, Hélène Cixous, and Gloria Anzaldúa in the twentieth-century section. Adrienne Rich would have been included here as well if she had given us permission to reprint her work. From six women, we have gone up to thirteen, and moreover, what was the Enlightenment section in the first edition has been split into separate eighteenth- and nineteenth-century sections in large part because my co-editor and I felt that the advent of people of color and white women on the speaker's platform in the nineteenth century constituted a sufficiently significant change in the possibilities for rhetoric that the century—which in traditional histories is usually thought of as advancing little over the theoretical developments of the previous century—demanded its own section. Furthermore, this list is by no means exhaustive. It represents only those women on whom my co-editor and I felt sufficient research had been done to enable us to include them without tendentiousness.

The importance of this research is addressed by Enos. He is concerned to mount a defense of what he calls "the humanistic study of rhetoric" (8). He wishes to argue ultimately for improved graduate training in primary research methods, to correct a situation which, he says, "encourages students to passively respond to research rather than to actively produce it" (13). Lest anyone think that this line of argument identifies Enos as some sort of conservative old fogey in rhetoric scholarship, I want to point out that his position was anticipated, to some extent, by a more recent in-comer to the field of historical research, Linda Ferreira-Buckley, in her essay entitled "Rescuing the Archives from Foucault," which appeared as part of a discussion in a May 1999 *College English* forum, "Archivists with an Attitude." Moreover, and most radically given the state of scholarship only ten years ago, Enos concludes his essay by holding up as models of the kind of historical research he is calling for, feminist scholars Lisa Ede, Cheryl Glenn, Andrea Lunsford, and other contributors to Lunsford's collection *Reclaiming Rhetorica*. Interestingly, Ferreira-Buckley ends up in almost the same place, featuring among her approved examples the feminist work of Elizabeth McHenry, Jacqueline Jones Royster, and Susan Jarratt.

I mean to imply that feminist research in the history of rhetoric has indeed had a tremendous impact, if we find it cited as exemplary in two essays with ultimately rather different argumentative agendas—Enos calling for a sort of return to traditional research while Ferreira-Buckley openly advocates revisionist history while pointing out that "revisionist historians depend upon traditional archival practices" (581). If we think of the tasks of traditional research as discovering neglected authors, providing basic research on their lives and theories, and bringing out critical editions of their work, my survey of current work undertaken for the new edition of *The Rhetorical Tradition* anthology suggests that few, if any, other areas of research in the history of rhetoric have produced such rich results of this kind as feminist research.

II

Enos, however, misses an important implication of this new work in feminist research. As the "Archivists with an Attitude" forum shows us, historical research now, though relying on some traditional methods, must also raise new methodological questions. The problems that arise when the new wine is poured into old bottles can be seen in another *College English* exchange, that in the January 2000 issue between Xin Liu Gale and Cheryl Glenn and Susan Jarratt.

In "Historical Studies and Postmodernism: Rereading Aspasia of Miletus," Gale evaluates three scholarly works on the ancient Greek rhetorician Aspasia, comparing Glenn's and Jarratt's accounts, the latter co-authored with Rory Ong, with Madeleine Henry's book-length treatment. Gale favors Henry's work because, she says, Henry gives us "meticulous treatment of historical sources," "rather than eschewing the traditional historical method or twisting the male texts to suit her feminist needs" (379). Again and again, Gale uses the term "traditional" to characterize what she likes about Henry's approach. From these terms of praise, we may anticipate the terms of reproach used against Glenn, Jarratt, and Ong. They are continually accused of distortions and contradictions.

Gale's critique helpfully reminds us of the importance of traditional historical research methods in feminist scholarship. But Gale does not appreciate the extent to which Glenn, Jarratt, and Ong employ the traditional research methods she favors. As a glance at their bibliographies will reveal, their arguments are based in detailed scholarship every bit as "meticulous" and textually oriented as that which Gale praises in Henry, although Henry has the advantage of being more exhaustive because she gives Aspasia book-length treatment, as opposed to the limits of an essay or book chapter. Glenn, Jarratt, and Ong have all read the classical sources and secondary scholarship carefully. Indeed, their grasp on traditional methods may be seen in their replies to Gale, in which their defense takes the fundamentally traditional tack of accusing Gale of not reading their work carefully and not quoting from it responsibly. This exchange actually testifies to the importance of the position taken by Enos and Ferreira-Buckley that I described above, namely that people who are going to do research in the history of rhetoric do need training in traditional humanistic scholarly methods, even in this postmodern day and age.

At the same time, I think that none of the participants in this exchange adequately address the role of postmodern theory in feminist research methods. They do not adequately bring out just how revolutionary it has been. Gale acknowledges that all of the scholars she analyzes attest to the influence of postmodern theory on their work, but then she forgets about it in Henry's case in order to re-cast her as a more "traditional" researcher, and she forgets about it in the cases of Glenn and Jarratt and Ong in order to damn them for trying to do something that they explicitly said they were not trying to do, namely, to set up a new master narrative—what Glenn calls in her response a "mater narrative" (388)—to establish traditional sorts of truth claims against the truth claims of traditional rhetorical histories that leave Aspasia out. Hence for Gale, there is a deep "contradiction" in the work she attacks:

> ... on the one hand, we are asked to accept the post-modern belief that we are never able to obtain objective truth in history; on the other hand, we are asked to consider the reconceived story of Aspasia as a "truer" reality of women in history, a rediscovery of the obliterated "truth" independent of the existing historical discourse of men. (366)

But I would argue that this is a contradiction only if there is only one kind of truth, what Gale calls here the "objective" kind, which might be taken as the object of historical research. That is not the kind of truth that the scholars she attacks are seeking. Here, for example, is how Glenn characterizes her project in her reply:

> Writing women (or any other traditionally disenfranchised group) into the history of rhetoric ... interrogates the availability, practice, and preservation (or destruction) of historical evidence, [and] simultaneously exposes relations of exploitation, domination, censorship, and erasure. (389)

Similarly, Jarratt makes no bones about using what she calls an "intertextual interpretive method" that allows her to "take 'Aspasia' both as a rhetorical construct in Plato's text and as a real person" and to make a "speculative leap," as she says Henry does (I believe correctly), "that [allows] scholars to imagine women in relation to the practices of rhetoric, philosophy, and literary production so long considered almost completely the domain of men" (391).

Yet Gale does seem to be aware of this theoretical orientation in her opponents. In spite of accusing them of a contradiction involving objective truth, Gale does know that Glenn, Jarratt, and Ong are not after objective truth. In the same paragraph in which she identifies the contradiction, as quoted above, she notes that Glenn is working from a "postmodern conception of truth as relative and contingent" (366), and she similarly acknowledges Jarratt's and Ong's research premises. I guess that what Gale would say is that the contradiction is not in her argument, but in theirs. In other words, she contends that in spite of claiming that they are not after objective truth, they argue as if they were. But it is not clear exactly what they are doing to draw this attack from Gale. Yes, they argue as if they wished to persuade readers of the merits of their positions. But it seems to me we must allow any scholar to attempt to be persuasive, without thereby accusing him or her of closet foundationalism. Indeed, Glenn, Jarratt, and Ong might be expected to make more strenuous efforts to be persuasive than scholars who believe in objective truth would do, because their postmodern view of truths-plural-with-a-small-t suggests that only through persuasion do arguments get accepted as normative. They must be persuasive because they cannot count on their audience being moved simply by the clearly perceiving the Truth-unitary-with-a-capital-T in their arguments.

I believe that this tangle arises from Gale's not naming accurately what it is that bothers her in the work of Glenn, Jarratt, and Ong. I am moving here into the realm of speculation, and I want to be cautious about seeming to put words in Gale's mouth or to appropriate her arguments. But I am trying to tease out a subtle problem in feminist historiography. I suspect that what really bothers Gale is not that Glenn, Jarratt, and Ong neglect traditional methods of historical research, because they in fact share these methods with Henry, whom Gale approves. I don't think it really is that they are making unsupportable claims for new objective truths in their scholarship, because as Gale shows that she knows, they are not in fact making any objective truth claims—that is not the kind of truth they are interested in. What, then, is the problem? I believe that it has to do with the role of emotion in feminist historiography.

Gale begins to get at this problem in her complaints about the ways that Glenn and Jarratt define feminist communities. As I have noted, Gale is aware that the scholars she attacks are working from what she calls a "community relative view of truth" (370). Jarratt describes this view of truth as follows (mixing, as I have already suggested, what might be called traditional along with postmodern criteria):

> Does this history instruct, delight, and move the reader? Is the historical data probable? Does it fit with other accounts or provide a convincing

alternative? Is it taken up by the community and used? Or is it refuted, dismissed, and forgotten? (391)

But, says Gale in discussing Glenn's work, "all women do not belong to the same community, all women are not feminists, all feminists are not women, and even all feminists do not belong to the same community" (371). Gale makes a similar point when discussing Jarratt's work in her book *Rereading the Sophists:*

> If Jarratt has to attribute all the feminist characteristics to the First Sophists to include them in her feminist system, does she risk making the mistake of essentializing women? . . . [This move] may well raise questions such as how the resemblance between the Sophists and women would empower women and whether her feminist sophistic would create new exclusions, such as the exclusion of men. (377)

It seems that Gale is concerned about exclusions in the communities that Glenn, Jarratt, and Ong define as normative—indeed, a very legitimate concern.

The problem here, though, cannot exactly be that Glenn's, Ong's, or Jarratt's view of feminism is not inclusive enough. In her reply, for example, Jarratt states that Gale's "warning that my approach in this section of the book could have the effect of erasing differences among women is well taken" (392). Jarratt questions "the specter of a feminism that is One," and she praises the multiplicity of debate in feminist work and calls it to Gale's attention (392). This would appear to agree with Gale's own call "to invite other perspectives to correct our own partiality" (372). But Gale, it appears, wants closure never to be achieved, persuasion never to be accomplished, because she is afraid that the influence of any community values must be oppressive. She quotes Barry Brummett's caution in this regard, "'*Whose* community?'" as if this were a question that was unanswerable (371; emphasis in original). I would argue, on the contrary, that it is answerable by a process of debate and discussion, provisionally but persuasively—though indeed, the process may require the avowal of values and may not rely on supposedly value-neutral logical demonstration. I do not believe that humanistic knowledge can ever be established above debate. That is perhaps the ultimate epistemological question on which Gale and I disagree.

Therefore, I would redefine Gale's problem with the scholars she attacks as being one that arises when persuasion does not work. Glenn, Jarratt, and Ong have not drawn Gale in. I am wondering whether an important reason for her resistance is that she feels excluded not so much from their discourse or their arguments as from their emotions. Gale hears in this work expressions of feelings of solidarity that trouble her, as noted in her commentary on feminist communities above. Perhaps, she feels herself to be excluded from these feelings for reasons she does not discuss. It is notable to me that Gale is very sensitive to the emotions animating work she doesn't like. More than once, she calls Glenn's treatment of Aspasia "passionate" (365), a "personal 'truth'" (366), too "assertive" (366 *et passim*). Jarratt is also too emotional, it seems,

"intent on writing women into the history of rhetoric for the purpose of exposing male oppression and exclusion in order to liberate and empower women"
(375). In contrast, Henry's emotional valence as described by Gale is cool: she
is "meticulous," "painstakingly" "sifting, ordering, and evaluating evidence"
(379), and arriving at a conclusion that "may not be as exciting as Glenn's or
Jarratt's and Ong's" but that "commands respect" (381).

I think Jarratt is right on the money in her reply when she suggests that
Gale harbors "aversions to both rhetoric and feminism" (392). But of course,
Gale is under no compulsion to value either. My point would be, however,
that Gale should clarify the grounds for her attack. It really isn't that the scholars she censures have vitiated traditional research methods. They have
extended them in the service of feminist values and relied in part on rhetorical
ethos to promote their positions. What Gale really objects to, I suspect, are
these values, and she is not moved by the ethos. Let her be clear about that.
And this brings me to the methodological point that I do believe is raised by
this debate, namely the function of emotions in scholarly work. We perhaps
need more discussion of the part played in the setting of scholarly research
agendas and the constructing of scholarly arguments by our emotions about
our research topics—or subjects—and our imagined readers. Think, for
example, about the unexamined role of emotion in the fatuous debate
between Barbara Biesecker and Karlyn Kohrs Campbell over historical
research that focuses on individual figures. I believe we need a more thoroughly rhetorical discussion of these complications of research. Fortunately,
that discussion has already begun, and I will conclude by pointing to a few
examples.

III

We can now find feminist researchers in rhetoric openly discussing their feelings, both positive and negative, about their subjects of study. For example, in
her essay "Women in the History of Rhetoric: The Past and the Future," Christine Mason Sutherland has provided us with a nuanced discussion of the difficulties a twentieth-century believer in feminism and democracy encounters in
studying Mary Astell, an important eighteenth-century thinker on political
and religious questions and on women's rhetoric who was opposed to democratic forms of government and to many of the liberal tenets of the contemporary women's movement. Sutherland walks us through the ways the
researcher must negotiate her feelings about a woman whom she can admire
but not entirely agree with. A different example can be found in one of Vicki
Tolar Collins's first essays on women in Methodism, in which she tells how
she was mysteriously drawn to the work of Hester Rogers, first acquiring her
journal from Collins's elderly relative who thought Hester might be part of
the family, and then having a dream shortly after she began doctoral studies
that compelled her in the middle of the night to dig the book out of boxes as
yet unpacked from a move, read until dawn, and discover a research subject.
Interestingly, Collins chose to omit this moving story from the longer essay on

women and Methodism that she published later in Molly Meijer Wertheimer's collection *Listening to Their Voices:* did she fear that, being too personal, it might taint her scholarship in traditional eyes? And one more short example: in her essay on Ida B. Wells published in *Reclaiming Rhetorica,* Jacqueline Jones Royster repeatedly expresses her admiration for Wells, rather than simply recounting the facts of her life and analyzing her rhetorical practices. Royster observes that Wells practiced the rhetorical arts "with flair and style" (169), that she worked for a world "in which we, African American included, could all flourish" (173), and, in short, that "Ida B. Wells was a wonder, personally and rhetorically" (181).

I believe it is to Royster that we owe our most thorough theorizing of the role of emotions in feminist research to date. In her study of African American women's rhetoric and social action, entitled *Traces of a Stream,* Royster concludes with a chapter that addresses in detail the methodological questions I have raised here. She articulates an approach that frankly begins in her identification—she takes the term from Kenneth Burke—with the subjects of her inquiries (see 252, 272). On the one hand, this is a deeply personal identification, springing from a mutual African American heritage. As Royster says, "theory begins with a story" (255), and she shares her story of community allegiances and multiple experiences with extant archives on African American women, with colleagues on the scholarly journal *SAGE,* and with her students at Spelman College. At the same time, Royster pointedly rejects an essentialized notion of identity. She notes:

> There is a constancy in the need for negotiation, beginning with the uncomfortable question of how much I actually do share identities with the women I study and how much I do not. (271) . . . identity is not natural. It is constructed. I have indeed identified multiple connections between these women and myself, despite our not being perfectly matched. (272) . . . However, as full-fledged members of humanity, this work is not by necessity ours alone. Others can also have interests and investments in it that can be envisioned from their own standpoints, from their own locations. What becomes critical to good practice, however, is that these researchers—who are indeed outsiders in the communities they study—have special obligations that begin with a need to articulate carefully what their viewpoints actually are, rather than letting the researchers' relationships to the work go unarticulated, as is often the case with practices of disregard. (277)

What becomes critical, in other words, is the acknowledgment of the multiple functions of emotions and experiences in defining one's relationship to one's research, a departure from traditional methods that Royster calls "practices of disregard," which might be the practices that produce the emotional coolness I saw Gale preferring in Henry.

It follows from this acknowledgment of personal connection in Royster's theory that the scholar will care for the subjects being researched. Here is where emotional attachments come most clearly into the open. Royster notes that for students who learned about the history of African American women's rhetoric and social action, "the most frequent types of responses . . . were affective" (266), relating not only to how they felt about the women they studied but also to how they felt about their own lives as intellectuals. Royster observes that over the years of doing archival research herself, "I was developing a habit of caring as a rhetorician" (258)—note how this formulation links caring with disciplinary activity—"caring *as a rhetorician*" (emphasis added). Particularly for African American women engaged in such research, Royster argues, what she calls an "afrafeminist" methodology should "acknowledge a role for caring, for passionate attachments" (276)—there again is that passion that Gale detected, it seems somewhat disapprovingly, in the work of Glenn, Jarratt, and Ong.

Lest this kind of attachment lead to what Gale regards as merely "personal truth," however, Royster repeatedly emphasizes the necessity for feminist researchers to ground their work in the collective wisdom of their scholarly community and, importantly, in the community that they are studying. As Royster puts it:

> I recognize as valuable the perspectives of the scholarly fields in which I operate; simultaneously I respect the wisdom of the community with which I identify. I seek to position myself in academic writing, therefore, in a way that merges membership in two communities: the one I am studying and the ones in which I have gained specialized knowledge. (254) . . . [Afrafeminist scholars] speak and interpret *with* the community [of African American women], not just *for* the community, or *about* the community. (275; emphasis in original)

Royster makes explicit the discursive consequences of this orientation to multiple communities. Traditional academic discourse will not serve to express her research, but rather she must devise a kind of "academic writing" that mixes the cognitive and linguistic styles of her academic and African American communities—what I have called a "hybrid" form of academic discourse. Royster describes it this way:

> Critical to such methodological practices, therefore, is the idea that, whatever the knowledge accrued, it would be both presented and represented with this community [that is, the community being studied], and at least its potential for participation and response, in mind. This view of subjects as both audiences and agents contrasts with a presentation and representation of knowledge in a more traditional fashion. Typically, subjects [in traditional discourse] are likely to be perceived in a more disembodied way. . . . (274)

Clearly, this is an attempt to embody in discourse an answer to the question Gale rightly indicates as crucial for all postmodern historiography, namely, *whose* community is normative? Royster gives us more, and more specific, information on how she answers this question than any other researcher I have encountered. She does not rely on any unitary category of "women" to define her communities. Moreover, Royster is at pains to specify that even the values and perspectives of communities she holds dear cannot be allowed to hold uninterrogated sway over critical discourse. She continually stresses the need for cross-questioning among communities, not only, as noted above, between the academic community and the African American women's community (two which obviously overlap, in the person, for example, of Royster herself), but also between these communities and representatives of other standpoints who may be drawn to research in this area. As Royster says:

> . . . the need for negotiation is, therefore, not arbitrary. It is part and parcel of the consubstantial process. The need for negotiation is yoked to the need for a well-balanced analytical view that takes into account shifting conditions, values, and circumstances between human beings. (272)

Royster concludes her discussion by articulating a four-part "afrafeminist ideology" or what I would call "methodology," that organizes these insights. It is notable that the first element Royster mentions is "careful analysis" (279ff), by which she appears to mean the traditional "basic skills" of research for which Enos and Ferreira-Buckley call and which, I contend, Glenn, Jarratt, and Ong, as well as Henry, employ. To them, Royster adds three elements that bespeak the emotions and value commitments I have outlined in her theory above: "acknowledgment of passionate attachment" (280) to the subjects of one's research; "attention to ethical action" (280) in one's scholarship, which requires one to be rigorous in the traditional sense and at the same time "accountable to our various publics" (281); and "commitment to social responsibility" (281), which indicates the need not only to think about the social consequences of the knowledge we generate but also to use it ourselves for the greater common good.

In conclusion, I want to stress why Royster needs the new methodology that she theorizes so thoroughly in this book. She articulates the challenges that face her at the outset:

> The first and most consistent challenges have come hand in hand with the very choosing of the work itself, that is, with identifying myself as a researcher who focuses on a multiply marginalized group; whose interests in this group center on topics not typically associated with the group, such as nonfiction and public discourse rather than imaginative literature and literary criticism; and who is called upon by the material conditions of the group itself to recognize the necessity of employing a broader, sometimes different range of techniques in garnering evidence and in analyzing and interpreting that evidence. (251)

Later on, she explains how these challenges impacted her research methods:

> The project required that I learn something about history, economics, politics, and the social context of women's lives. For the first time, I had to spend more time considering context than text. I had to take into account insights and inquiry patterns from disciplines other than those in which I was trained. I had to take into account the specific impact of race, class, gender and culture on the ability to be creative and to achieve—not in

some generic sense, but in terms of a particular group of human beings who chose deliberately to write and to speak, often in public. (257)

As Royster notes, her techniques are "quite recognizably interdisciplinary and feminist" (257); she also characterizes them as a sort of ethnographic research in which she was unable to interview her subjects, because most of them were already dead (see 282). These techniques enabled her, as she says, to explore how "knowledge, experience, and language merge" in the lives of her research subjects (259). The point I wish to emphasize is that she thus generates scholarly knowledge that clearly could be developed no other way.

Have Royster, and other feminist scholars for whom she has now more completely articulated methodologies already in practice, departed radically from the rhetorical tradition? Yes, and no. No, because their work relies upon many of the traditional tools of research in the history of rhetoric. No, because the rhetors they have added to our picture of the history of Western rhetoric seem to me to be working within this tradition and enriching it, rather than constituting utterly separate or parallel rhetorical traditions. But yes, because in order to get at the activities of these new rhetors, researchers have had to adopt radically new methods as well, methods which violate some of the most cherished conventions of academic research, most particularly in bringing the person of the researcher, her body, her emotions, and dare one say, her soul, into the work. From my perspective as editor of an anthology called *The Rhetorical Tradition,* contemplating the major changes in scholarship over the last ten years, these new methods have made all the difference.

WORKS CITED

Biesecker, Barbara. "Coming to Terms with Recent Attempts to Write Women into the History of Rhetoric." *Philosophy and Rhetoric* 25 (1992): 140–61.

Bizzell, Patricia. "Hybrid Academic Discourses: What, Why, How." *Composition Studies* 27 (Fall 1999): 7–21.

———, and Bruce Herzberg. *The Rhetorical Tradition: Readings from Classical Tunes to the Present.* Boston: Bedford Books, 1990 (second edition, 2001).

Campbell, Karlyn Kohrs. "Biesecker Cannot Speak for Her Either." *Philosophy and Rhetoric* 26 (1993): 153–9.

Collins, Vicki Tolar. "Walking in Light, Walking in Darkness: The Story of Women's Changing Rhetorical Space in Early Methodism." *Rhetoric Review* 14 (Spring 1996): 336–54.

———. "Women's Voices and Women's Silence in the Tradition of Early Methodism." In *Listening to Their Voices: The Rhetorical Activities of Historical Women.* Molly Meijer Wertheimer, ed. Columbia: U of South Carolina P, 1997.

Enos, Richard. "Recovering the Lost Art of Researching the History of Rhetoric." *Rhetoric Society Quarterly* 29 (Fall 1999): 7–20.

Ferreira-Buckley, Linda. "Rescuing the Archives from Foucault." *College English* 61 (May 1999): 577–83.

Gale, Xin Liu. "Historical Studies and Postmodernism: Rereading Aspasia of Miletus." *College English* 62 (January 2000): 361–86.

Glenn, Cheryl. "Comment: Truth, Lies, and Method: Revisiting Feminist Historiography." *College English* 62 (January 2000): 387–9.

Jarratt, Susan. "Comment: Rhetoric and Feminism: Together Again." *College English* 62 (January 2000): 390–3.

———. *Rereading the Sophists: Classical Rhetoric Refigured.* Carbondale: Southern Illinois UP, 1991.

Lunsford, Andrea, ed. *Reclaiming Rhetorica: Women in the Rhetorical Tradition.* Pittsburgh: U of Pittsburgh P, 1995.

Royster, Jacqueline Jones. "To Call a Thing by Its True Name: The Rhetoric of Ida B. Wells." In *Reclaiming Rhetorica: Women in the Rhetorical Tradition.* Andrea Lunsford, ed. Pittsburgh: U of Pittsburgh P, 1995.

———. *Traces of a Stream: Literacy and Social Change among African-American Women.* Pittsburgh: U of Pittsburgh P, 2000.

Sutherland, Christine Mason. "Women in the History of Rhetoric: The Past and the Future." In *The Changing Tradition: Women in the History of Rhetoric.* Christine Mason Sutherland and Rebecca Sutcliffe, eds. Calgary: U of Calgary P, 1999.

A View from a Bridge: Afrafeminist Ideologies and Rhetorical Studies

JACQUELINE JONES ROYSTER

One key role for Black women intellectuals is to ask the right questions and investigate all dimensions of a Black women's standpoint with and for African-American women. Black women intellectuals thus stand in a special relationship to the community of African-American women of which we are a part, and this special relationship frames the contours of Black feminist thought. . . . While Black feminist thought may originate with Black feminist intellectuals, it cannot flourish isolated from the experiences and ideas of other groups. The dilemma is that Black women intellectuals must place our own experiences and consciousness at the center of any serious efforts to develop Black feminist thought yet not have that thought become separatist and exclusionary.

—PATRICIA HILL-COLLINS, *BLACK FEMINIST THOUGHT*

In resonance with this epigraph, my goal here is to share knowledge and experience, not about the literate practices of African American women as in the previous chapters but about my own standpoint as a researcher and scholar in the process of completing this book. The first and most consistent challenges have come hand in hand with the very choosing of the work itself, that is, with identifying myself as a researcher who focuses on a multiply marginalized group; whose interests in this group center on topics not typically associated with the group, such as nonfiction and public discourse rather than imaginative literature and literary criticism; and who is called upon by the material conditions of the group itself to recognize the necessity of employing a broader, sometimes different range of techniques in garnering evidence and in analyzing and interpreting that evidence. In declaring my interest in a non-mainstream academic area, I have benefited from an array of practices in rhetorical studies, literacy studies, and feminist studies. However, I have not been privileged to have a guide in identifying appropriate analytical frameworks for the use of such practices with my targeted group or in either choosing or developing a set of methodologies that were actually adequate to the task.

In forging ahead in uncharted territory, I have also had to confront

From *Traces of a Stream: Literacy and Social Change among African American Women* by Jacqueline Jones Royster. Pittsburgh: U of Pittsburgh P. 2000. 251–285.

directly, in the rendering of text, my own status as a researcher who identifies unapologetically with the subjects of my inquiries. In terms of my own invented ethos, within contexts that would position me otherwise because of the "marginality" of what I do, I have had to create proactive spaces rather than reactive spaces from which to speak and interpret. The task of creating new space, rather than occupying existing space, has encouraged in me the shaping of a scholarly ethos that holds both sound scholarly practices and ethical behavior in balance and harmony and that consistently projects this balancing in research and in writing.

As I have discussed in the essay "When the First Voice You Hear Is Not Your Own" (1995), despite my constructions of a proactive scholarly self, many who have responded to presentations of my research have resisted viewing my work in this way. They have consistently demanded, subtly and not so subtly, that I prove my worth and the worth of my subject matter using measures that seem to me to suggest the reader's or listener's own needs to contain, limit, and control both definitions of authenticity and rights to interpretive authority. For example, in the early days, when I explained my focus on nineteenth-century African American women, responses were often a statement of surprise, "Oh!" or statements of incredulity, "Were African American women really writing anything back then?" "How large a body of texts could we be talking about here?" "Who would have been their reading audience? After all, very few African Americans could read back then, right?" These responses were typically conveyed with more an intonation of declaration than inquiry. Such reactions suggest that the questioners expected me to fail in talking back to them, in making my case, rather than succeed in establishing my interests and viewpoint as reasonable and indeed valuable.

Further, whatever my counter-response, I have occasionally confronted a "so what?" factor, which seems to emerge in the guise of questions related to the saliency of evidence. In other words, given the source of the evidence I use (that is, the experiences and achievements of African American women), I have heard, between the lines, "How instructive could African American women possibly be in the grand scheme of things?" "How could the lives of *these* women possibly suggest anything important enough to notice that has not already been noticed by looking at others?"

Interpretations such as mine that take African American women into account as being not just redundant but valuable—or as agents of change rather than simple victims of oppression and dominance—seem particularly vulnerable to requests, even now in contemporary academic discourse, for comparisons with African American men, white women, and white men, comparisons in which the parameters of comparison are set by the other group.[1] My sense of the attitudes motivating such calls for comparison is that they arise all too often, still, not simply in the interest of comparative analyses (which have the potential to inform) but more from a belief that the marginal status of African American women in society requires that anything related directly to us is "naturally" inconsequential in larger interpretive frameworks. In effect, African American women are perceived to occupy positions, especially historically, of sociopolitical unimportance, which inevitably dictate that whatever point is made about such a low-status group gains credibility, validity, and reliability only as it can be redefined through the lives and contributions of others more credible, more legitimate, and more salient. The uniqueness of African American women's standpoint from such a view becomes a sign of weakness, not strength.

In other words, Charlotte Forten's story becomes secondary to Laura Towne's story. The significance of Anna Julia Cooper translates not by means of her own scholarship but through the master narratives of William E. B. DuBois or Alexander Crummell as preeminent African American male scholars. The political actions of Margaret Murray Washington or Amy Jacques Garvey become minor themes in accounts of their more highly esteemed husbands, Booker T. Washington and Marcus Garvey. The essayist traditions among African American women become absorbed and neutralized by our habits and practices in valuing Emerson, Thoreau, and their more recognizable progeny.

The mandates of this type of questioning have appeared to be in the interest of sustaining predominant views of material reality and resisting interpretations that might permit the emergence of alternative realities, such as the ones inherent in my research. From my point of view, I have operated, therefore, within systems of deep disbelief, which go beyond the doubts rooted in mere ignorance to those seemingly more deeply rooted in arrogance. Deep disbeliefs seem so ingrained they actually short-circuit a more inclusive knowledge-making process and limit the impact of challenges, however large or small, to predominant interpretive frameworks. The result is that researchers such as I have spoken, but we have not been believed, and our viewpoints have remained largely unacknowledged and unincorporated into predominant ways of knowing and valuing. The circles of people who are well informed about African American women and their work remain relatively small and specialized.

Over the years I have come to view the systems of deep disbelief as contending forces, as prevailing winds that push against scholarly proactivity and toward a continual reinscription of the status quo. My response has been to resist being circumscribed. Although I recognize that responding to disempowering sociopolitical mandates is unavoidable, I also recognize that responding only to these mandates would just as inevitably mean positioning myself as a defender of African American women's experience, rather than an interrogator of it. I prefer the latter since my own deep beliefs are keyed to the notion that African American women's achievements are fully capable of standing on their own merit, once that merit is articulated.

In a fundamental way, therefore, my response has been to define my own mandates. As a researcher and a scholar, I seek to develop scholarly practices that are theoretically sound, systematic, and generative. I recognize as valuable the perspectives of the scholarly fields in which I operate; simultaneously I respect the wisdom of the community with which I identify. I seek to position myself in academic writing, therefore, in a way that merges membership in two communities: the one I am studying and the ones in which I have gained specialized knowledge. A central task is to establish a sense of reciprocity between my two homes and to keep in the forefront of my thinking the sense that negotiations of these territories are ongoing.

My role as a researcher has been to look theoretically and philosophically at the data, to bring meaning to it. The very first order of business by necessity has been to establish an interpretive viewpoint that clearly places African American women at the center of our own story. The assumption is that viewpoint matters. As Anna Julia Cooper stated in 1892 , in *A Voice from the South,* "what is needed, perhaps, to reverse the picture of the lordly man slaying the lion, is for the lion to turn painter!" (1988: 225). In scholarly research and analysis, the question to be addressed is more than whether African American women occupy a passive position of object or an active position of subject. Rather, the question, at the level of interpretation, is how—as objects or subjects—we are placed on a landscape or within a material reality.

In this analysis, I rejected images of African American women that would position us interpretively as a mirror or a reflection of others, or as a room accessed by other people's doors and windows, or even as a backdrop against which other stories are told, invigorated, or clarified. Instead, this analysis positions African American women as the "lions" in a "lion's tale." My intent has been to consider African American women as the embodiment of our own dreams and aspirations, our own created and re-created selves, in a world with others, certainly, but without the need at critical points in the analytical process (that is, in the initial stages) to be filtered through the experiences of others, no matter how resonant or dissonant those experiences might be. In making such a commitment to creating a working space amid dualities, I believe I have acquired an understanding of both scholarly positioning and knowledge production in this arena from which advice to others might be abstracted. In choosing an appropriate mechanism for sharing advice in a more direct manner, however, without suggesting the notion of easy prescriptions, I realize once again that theory, like history, also begins with a story.

THEORY BEGINS WITH A STORY, TOO

My first archival project on African American women began without much fanfare in 1979 when I was named coordinator of the Spelman College centennial celebration. Over the next two years of preparation for the celebratory year of 1981, I had the good fortune of discovering women about whom I had previously known precious little or nothing, and about whom (I was quite certain) most others knew even less than I. I was so amazed by these women's stories of life and learning that I wanted to do more research. When the centennial celebration was over, I requested and was granted release time by the college to become in the fall of 1982 the first research associate of our new Women's Research and Resource Center.

The project I constructed focused on seven women from among the first graduates of Spelman, all of whom were missionaries, health-care providers, and/or teachers. My first opportunity to share my discoveries was in the form of a low-budget photodocumentary exhibit and an exhibit catalog, which I developed for the First National Conference on Black Women's Health, held in June 1983. The exhibit was entitled *Women as Healers: A Noble Tradition*. This project actually catapulted me into the world of Black feminist scholarship. Despite the title of the exhibit, however, the project actually pushed me in an identifiable way, not as a general researcher on African American women but as what I now refer to as an afrafeminist researcher in the field of rhetoric and composition.[2]

In setting up the lines of inquiry for the project, I chose women who were generally unknown in the annals of history but who were stellar in terms of their contributions to and impact upon the communities in which they lived and worked. My task was to consider factors such as race, gender, class, historical period, and cultural context as I tried to clarify and interpret their pathways to learning and achievement. As I became more knowledgeable of who they were, what they did, and how they did it, it became clearer to me that the lives of these women actually told quite a representative story among women of African descent, in terms of their collective quest for literacy and of the mechanisms whereby women who are marginalized in multiple ways might still find a means of participating in public domains and ways of working to make the world a better place.

With this insight I refined the task, which by this point had become a lifelong project. First, as I explained in the introduction of this book, I wanted to recover, flesh out, and reconstruct the ways in which women of African descent generally, and African American women in particular, came historically to acquire written language. I was even more curious, however, to figure out and document the texture of these women's lives and their patterns of behavior, not just in terms of their being hard-working people, which they certainly were, but more directly in terms of their being literate women who, regardless of their life's work, helped to form the first critical mass of college-educated women, many of whom demonstrated by their productivity as speakers and writers that they valued language well used.

My basic questions were: Under what circumstances did these women acquire literacy? What did literacy and learning mean to them? In what ways were they empowered to act in the world by their knowledge of language and how might it be useful in achieving particular rhetorical effects? Most of all, after they acquired these tools and abilities, what did they actually choose to do? What did their actions show evidence of? What differences did their actions make?

To answer these questions, I realized I had to operate quite differently as a researcher than I ever had before. I was no longer a person examining a literary text in terms of a theory of literary criticism, or even a person examining linguistic data in terms of a theory of language. Instead, I was looking at a collection of documents, various print and visual texts (photographs, for example), and other artifacts, the material evidence of lived experience, and I was trying to make sense of the lives of the people with whom these materials were connected. I saw it as my task to extend the base of specific details available on their lives, and to talk about this base in a useful way for our understanding of women's education in general and of their use of literacy for sociopolitical action in particular.

The project required that I learn something about history, economics, politics, and the social context of women's lives. For the first time, I had to spend more time considering context than text. I had to take into account insights and inquiry patterns from disciplines other than those in which I was trained. I had to take into account the specific impact of race, class, gender, and culture on the ability to be creative and to achieve—not in some generic sense, but in terms of a particular group of human beings who chose deliberately to write and to speak, often in public. This shift in analytical perspective toward a multi-lensed approach is in keeping with techniques that are now quite recognizably interdisciplinary and feminist.

I had set myself on a pathway that strikes me now as more transdisciplinary than interdisciplinary and more afrafeminist than feminist. By all accounts, my basic vision as a researcher was deeply affected, changing rather significantly the paradigm through which, from that time forward, I would draw meaning from women's experience. Before the shift, I had understood that there was much to know about these women because they were people of African descent. After the shift, I became conscious of how much *more* there was to know because these people were women and mostly poor, held certain cultural values, and can be placed at a particular point in time within a particular set of socioeconomic conditions. In this latter case, the women were all either employed outside the home or very actively involved in community service. In keeping with what Hill-Collins indicates in her analysis of Black women's experiences, the relationships of this group of women to material reality were unique.[3]

In becoming sensitized for the first time to a fuller understanding of this uniqueness, I conclude all these years later that I was developing the habit of caring as a rhetorician (as a researcher who centralizes the use of language), but I was constructing meaning with a transdisciplinary view in defiance of clearly rendered disciplinary boundaries. I pulled into my rhetorical schema a richly defined material world and brought texture to the conditions for learning and rhetorical action.

By coincidence, two other sets of activities supported the development of these transdisciplinary and afrafeminist habits. The first occurred in 1983 when I became a founding member of the editorial collective of *SAGE: A Scholarly Journal on Black Women* with Beverly Guy-Sheftall, Patricia Bell-Scott, and Janet Sims-Wood. We came together from across four disciplinary areas (American literature, sociology, history, and of course rhetoric and composition) to edit a semi-annual interdisciplinary journal focused on women of African descent.[4] By participating in this collaborative, I was privileged to read and to become intimately involved in knowledge production from across disciplinary boundaries, and to do so in ways that centralized the conditions, lives, and achievements of women of African descent wherever they might reside. I was required by this work to read more broadly than was my habit or training, and thus to think more comprehensively about women of African descent. My responsibilities as editor created systematic opportunities for me to participate in lively discussions around interdisciplinary issues. This work changed dramatically the terms by which I engaged with text. My perspectives for raising questions and perceiving details to be instructive were made clearer, more open-ended, and more inclusive, positively affecting both my research habits and my writing, that is, how I composed lives and drew meaning from written expression.

Essentially, as a researcher I used my linguistic training to center concerns within a conceptual frame that is rooted still in traditions of rhetorical criticism. Simply stated, I retained my interests in looking at who says what to whom under what circumstances and with what motives, intentions, impact, and legitimacy. From a more complex view, however, I became more curious about the ways in which knowledge, experience, and language merge, as African American women, through language, make decisions that have sociopolitical consequence. I became curious about how these women gain access to knowledge, construct new knowledge, and operate with a sense of agency. I became concerned with issues of authority, certification, validation, power, privilege, and entitlement. These concerns led me to pay closer attention to discourse communities and to constructions of voice and vision within those communities. I look now (as this book demonstrates) at the acquisition, uses, and consequences of literacy, at African American women's rhetorical expertise, at their use of language as a tool for living and working alone and in communities.

In reflection, I think it significant that at the same time as I was engaging in the intellectual work of my research project and with the *SAGE* editorial team, I was also teaching and coordinating the Spelman College Comprehensive Writing Program, a writing across the curriculum program that included a writing center. All three activities—research, editorial team activities, program administration—worked together in creating a generative environment in which I was able to discover new ways of being as a researcher and scholar. A remarkably synergetic dimension of this interface was that, at the same time as I was coming to understand that the convergence of gender, race, class, and ethnicity offered a provocative point of departure for considering historical issues of literacy and learning for African American women, I was also responsible for coordinating systems for developing the literate abilities of contemporary African American women through the activities of the Writing Program. One project in particular becomes instructive in demonstrating this point.

In 1985, I became the co-coordinator (with Beverly Guy-Sheftall, coeditor of *SAGE* and director of the Women's Research and Resource Center) of a new program we had created, the SAGE Writer/Scholars Internship Program.[5] It was a cooperative endeavor of the college Women's Research and Resource Center, the Comprehensive Writing Program, and *SAGE: A Scholarly Journal on Black Women.* By its very definition this program sought to support women who indicated a desire to work on their writing. It sought also to support the development of an intellectual pipeline that would carry forward the traditions of productivity and leadership that I had found so compelling in my work on nineteenth-century women. The program was supported during its first few years by the Fund for the Improvement of Post Secondary Education and then continued throughout the remainder of my tenure at Spelman with support from the United States Office of Education.[6] The goals of the project were various:

1. to introduce undergraduate women students to the process of writing as part of scholarly inquiry;

2. to provide opportunities for students to develop their critical and analytical skills and to demonstrate these through their writing;

3. to expose students to women of African descent who are writer/scholars and who would serve as mentors;

4. to provide opportunities for students to participate in the writing, editing, proofreading, and supportive research necessary for the production of a scholarly, interdisciplinary journal.

Fundamentally, the project was designed as an enrichment experience for students who had demonstrated academic excellence but who needed to build strength in scholarly writing as opposed to creative writing. In 1985, in the midst of the new attention being afforded African American women writers, we were acting against a prevailing image of African American women writers as writers of novels, short stories, poems, plays, and so on, rather than as writers of scholarly books, articles, and essays. Our intent was to shape the program by definitions of African American women as intellectual beings and not just creative beings.

In keeping with statistics at that time documenting the paucity of African American scholars across the nation, this program sought to encourage people with intellectual potential to rethink the territory of writing, and to consider graduate school rather than professional school. We sought to enrich their understanding of what it feels like to engage seriously, if not passionately, in research and scholarship, including scholarly publication. Students who participated in the program were generally self-selecting, based on their desires to enhance their critical skills and to know more about themselves as writers in a scholarly arena. Generally, they were quite active in several other classroom experiences and in extra-classroom work on and off the campus, such that a constant challenge for the program was finding times to schedule meetings. Over the years, the "culture" that emerged in the program encouraged me to name and respect this "busy-ness" as in keeping with the lives of African American women intellectuals.

Our administrative response was to adjust the definition of what "interning" with the program meant. Over the course of the project, we continued to offer an ever-growing array of experiences, as originally planned, but we developed an escalating sense of what we were really trying to do. We encouraged the students to be deliberative and selective about the level and intensity of their participation. We considered this process to be practice for the decision making and juggling we anticipated they would be doing for the remainder of their lives. In essence, we shifted from a sense of the program as an "internship," designed to extend experiences, to a clearer sense of it as a "mentoring" program, designed to help developing scholars think about what it means to be a writer/scholar.

The students responded variously. Typically over the course of a year, there was a small core of students who participated in almost everything. There were others who picked and chose. There were others who became occasional participants. Some students called themselves SAGE interns; some did not. All were welcome whenever they came. All were kept on the active roster and received announcements and updates about activities. Without a prescription for participation, however, our new challenge became finding ways to counteract our sense of disintegration in the program. We noted, though, that we were not the ones setting parameters; the students were. We came to see that we were not "structuring" an internship as such. We were helping students to engage in a particular kind of inquiry. We were advising them, directing them toward various and sundry opportunities for growth and inspiration, and offering ourselves to them as resources in support of particular needs that we all identified—together. We had placed the authority to shape, define, and measure in their hands. There were no grades. There was no credit. The idea was that, in as nonexclusive a manner as possible, we were nurturing intellectual potential and the students were developing it. This model—given the more structured ways in which such programs typically proceed—did not come automatically.

Very early in the project, I happened to ask the student interns two obvious questions: How many of you consider yourselves writers? How many consider yourselves scholars, intellectuals? The answers to the second question caught me off guard. I found (as I expected to find) that the interns were quite comfortable claiming themselves as writers, and as competent and capable people who expect to be successful. But in 1985 they were not so eager to claim and name themselves as scholars or intellectuals. I was surprised. Given the workings of gender, race, and culture in this country, though, I should not have been.

At this college in 1985, a women's college, there were no pedagogical or curricular structures in place to encourage these women to claim space as "intellectuals." We did not yet have, as a reflective model, the African American woman scholar who became president two years later. We did not have, as the writing program developed later, a Thinking Across the Curriculum project designed to raise intellectual development from tacit levels of understanding to conscious awareness and systematic attention. The "Life of the Mind" series had not yet begun, and at that point the Living-Learning Program did not operate as an extra-classroom experience to nurture relationships between faculty and other mentors and students. In effect, then, when the SAGE Writer/Scholars Internship Program began, there were no programs on the campus that directly "mentored" intellectual development.

There were internship programs of various sorts, but they were designed to broaden the horizon (as this program was originally intended to do) but not to nurture specifically intellectual potential.

In essence, campus discourse did not include, in any systematic way, talk about women of African descent as intellectuals. What we talked about and nurtured was an image of women as achievers, as creative and ingenious beings, as leaders—not really as thinkers, or scholars, or intellectuals. So, I should not have been surprised that the students in this program were able to talk about themselves as writers, as achievers, as academically talented, but were not so comfortable talking about themselves as scholars and intellectuals. Fortunately, times and images change, however. Shortly after 1985 the intellectual lives and actions of women in general and women of color in particular came to bolder relief across the landscape of higher education, and particularly through the research and scholarship in feminist studies.

At the inception of the internship program, however, I considered it very good fortune that I actually asked the students questions about these self-perceptions.[7] If I had not, we could have assumed too much about them and contributed unwittingly to a sort of stereotyping that could have been just as disintegrating to progress and development as the more negative stereotyping of women of African descent has been. Without such questions, I may not have given much conscious thought at all to the actual workings of education and literacy in people's lives. Having asked those questions, however, I was able to use the students' hesitations at that moment to inform and to energize how we went about operating the program. We became more conscious of the actual people before us and of the task at hand. This tidbit of information, this moment, became a window of opportunity that we used consistently to maintain clarity and direction.

One of our fundamental assumptions about how the program should work was intensified. We were much clearer about the need for change in the material conditions of the students' institutional lives—that is, changes in the cultural context of the institution and changes in their material relationships to academic work. We became more determined than ever to use the program as a testing ground. We felt the extra-classroom environment of the program could provide a lower-risk place to think about how to enhance learning and to operationalize learners. We were strengthened in our hopes that such efforts would be useful: in the classroom environment, in other activities of the Writing Program, and in institutional planning. We assumed also that—even though this project was designed especially for a specific group of students in a specific context—the experience still might have implications for other students, both marginalized and nonmarginalized.

Basically, we sought to enliven the intellectual atmosphere through a specific array of extra-classroom activities. We coordinated workshops on writing, thinking, and publishing; visits with mentors; trips to scholarly conferences. We encouraged students to submit manuscripts to *SAGE*. We encouraged students and faculty in joint research efforts. We structured dialogues on issues that impact upon our contemporary lives. We encouraged them to use their classroom experiences more boldly, to listen carefully, to read broadly, to question, to take authority and responsibility for themselves as learners. We urged them to be self-directed—to listen to the voices from within for what Howard Thurman, a noted theologian, called "the sound of the genuine" (1981). In actuality, we freed ourselves to structure a program we wish someone had structured for us as young women two decades before. The internship program became essentially a mentoring program, which recognized the advantages of joining hands collaboratively with other programs around the campus that sought to engage with students along complementary lines (by this point in time, the list of mentoring activities on the campus had grown exponentially).

With the interns, we were inspired to shape mentoring experiences based on the implications of questions such as the following: What sociocultural influences have shaped African American women to the extent that academically successful students would readily claim authority as learners and as creative writers but would be more reluctant to claim a comparable authority as scholars or intellectuals? What historical conditions and circumstances have given rise to how African American females feel about themselves and about scholarly achievement? What resonates about these conditions and circumstances in the lives of other women or people in general? How have those who have found degrees of comfort as writers, scholars, and/or intellectuals come to feel and operate as they do? What kinds of instructional practices have enhanced and hindered students who are well centered as intellectuals in terms of their comfort with the power and authority to write, to speak, to think, to learn, and to produce? How can students, female students, female students of African descent, assume the authority to speak, to think, to learn, to write, to claim anything? What is the genesis of authority? What are pathways to personal power and achievement?

These questions encoded the interface that I felt between my work with nineteenth-century African American women and my work with contemporary women. I was able to identify resonant patterns of engagement with issues of authority, agency, privilege, and entitlement across time. Moreover, seeing the continuity of African American women's mandates supported the shaping of my administrative style in the program in a way that I suggest now is very much in keeping with afrafeminist practices. From my point of view, this categorization of my administrative style gains integrity in two specific ways:

1. We relinquished our exclusive authority to define the program and our control of its sense-making with each act of listening to the students and responding actively to the material realities of their lives.

2. We centralized the notion of reciprocity in the roles and relationships that we were nurturing as mentors and participants each time that we shifted dialectically between program (that is, specialized perspectives) and participants (that is, the individual perspectives among this particular community of women).

In other words, the SAGE Writer/Scholars Internship Program, as we developed and refined it, was begun with a Black feminist standpoint, as the objectives indicate, and it grew stronger in this standpoint over time.[8] In pedagogical terms, I became more focused on what I thought it meant to help students gain authority and move productively toward intellectual empowerment. My strategies were designed to enhance the literate resources of young African American women who would potentially join the stream of their rhetorically productive ancestors. The impact of trying to carry out these strategies in terms of my own ideological development, however, is that I was led to two conclusions that now form constitutive parts of my ways of thinking and operating from an afrafeminist view: people who do intellectual work need to understand their "intellectual ancestry"; and people who do intellectual work need to understand power and how they are affected by it.[9]

People Who Do Intellectual Work Need to Understand Their Intellectual Ancestry

In the beginning, we thought of the SAGE Internship Program as a rather innocuous enrichment experience, but the time we spent on consciously structuring mentoring activities proved an ongoing strength. The central task became the structuring of specific experiences that might move these women toward a more concrete sense of their personal power as writers, scholars, and intellectuals. After all, each of them already had a claim to a history of academic success. We did not need to convince them they were competent and capable women. Instead, a critical task became helping them to broaden their definitions of their strengths—in ways that, at the time, women in general and women of African descent in particular did not habitually do so. Our task initially was to help them situate themselves within a community of women (especially women like themselves, that is, of African descent) and to help them see a historical continuum within which they were participating, consciously or not. Based on our own personal experiences as women scholars, we operated on the hypothesis that the students' pursuit of intellectual authority can be informed and sanctioned by their conscious and specific awareness of the historical conditions and circumstances of others like themselves. As Deirdre David (1987) terms it, "inventing and discovering intellectual ancestry" becomes an "informing event" (226).

Dialogue was a basic strategy. There was talk one-to-one, between the students and myself. There were periodic meetings for the full group, and conversations between the students and visiting mentors and faculty mentors about research, scholarship, life choices, life experiences. There were all manner of workshops, seminars, conferences, which formed a community of discourse wherein the students could participate actively. We talked and talked and talked in dialectical ways, with springboard resources and experiences and without them. We looked closely and critically at a broad range of issues that seemed to relate to what the students were observing, reading, writing, and also to how they were thinking, feeling, and believing. We encouraged them—always—to place their own sense of reality at the center and to question this sense of reality intensely, using various analytical frames without fear of accountability outside of their own accountability to themselves. The students benefited from this community. So did I.

The most frequent types of responses to the internship experience were affective. Generally, the students reported they had previously had little or no idea that African American women through the years had done all the things that they read about in the journal or that they learned about through internship-supported and -encouraged activities. The students particularly liked getting to know Beverly Guy-Sheftall and me better, since we were the faculty most centrally involved with the program, and getting to know other faculty who worked with us periodically. In these interactions they gained a more concrete appreciation of faculty as scholars, with intellectual lives of their own, over and above their previous recognition of faculty as teachers in classrooms. They were encouraged and inspired by the visiting mentors who participated in the program. The periodic opportunity to talk with other students who cared about the same issues, problems, and concerns as they cared about helped them to feel less "singular" or "different" as developing intellectuals—feelings they might have characterized earlier in the life of the program, as feeling alone and isolated. The change in vocabulary from "alone" and "isolated" to "singular" and "different" offers evidence of a change in awareness for both self and situation. They came to understand that their intellectual desires were not so singular or different. They belonged to a community. They also began to understand that their lives as African American women intellectuals ran a high risk of placing them in worlds that might indeed contribute to their feeling alone and isolated. They began to notice the systems and forces surrounding them, many of which are hostile.

An advantage during the formulation of this model was the growing body of scholarship across the disciplines on African American women. The students were able to use this type of scholarship to contextualize their own experiences and to be strengthened by the knowledge that others have gone before. With a combination of historical and contemporary mentors, we found that the students could identify specific torchbearers, pathfinders, heroines, women before them who have endured, who have soared, who have traversed, if not the same territory, at least similar paths. They could see what success looks and feels like and be energized and strengthened for their own struggles.

In addition to making use of this type of information, however, we found that the interns also needed the ability to contextualize their personal genesis as writers and scholars within the broad cloth of human experiences globally. We operated on the belief that students are in a much stronger position to fashion for themselves their own authority to speak, to write, to learn, and to produce when they can determine, not just the resonance of their own lives with others, but also the dissonance. The general result was that we developed a three-pronged approach as an operational model, determining that students need to:

1. reconstruct their pathways to the present point in time, to think specifically about how they have come to be as they are and to think, believe, and act as they do;

2. situate their experiences within the historical context of the lives of others like themselves, in this case the multidimensional lives of African American women generally; and then

3. examine the specifics of global conditions, circumstances, systems of oppression and privilege so that they can see more fully what possibility and productivity mean and often do not mean across communities.

Our assumption was that if students can take stock of the maze of material realities in various communities and cultures, taking into account both the ties that bind and the lines that divide people, then, perhaps, they can have a clearer sense of their own *psychic wholeness* and also of those factors that can contribute to fragmentation.[10]

PEOPLE WHO DO INTELLECTUAL WORK NEED TO UNDERSTAND POWER AND HOW THEY ARE AFFECTED BY IT

The second conclusion I drew from the internship program is that fleshing out intellectual ancestry reveals a need for students to articulate oppression and the making of victims in both personal and systemic ways.[11] Within models that traditionally operate in curricula and classrooms, the history, experiences, and achievements of marginalized people are, to a significant degree, imperceptible and uncredited. Marginalized students find ways of adjusting to these contexts, but sometimes their adjustments are more intuitive than conscious, making it more difficult upon occasion to maintain a positively defined sense of self and potential. My experiences have convinced me that students can more easily maintain balance when they understand power and how individuals, including themselves, are affected by it. This type of understanding is facilitated by the examination of conceptual models beyond Eurocentric, patriarchal ones (the examination of afrafeminist and feminist models, for example) and by the application of such models to varieties of human experiences.

In their explorations of power, authority, and privilege, feminist scholars (Lerner 1986; McIntosh 1988, for example) have been particularly helpful in clarifying factors and conditions that constitute systems of power and others that support the formulation of strategies for personal and group empowerment. Such research constantly reminds us that women in pursuit of learning, African American women in this case, are operating within instructional environments that are not designed for the personal benefit and interest of learners marginalized by race, class, or gender. This scholarship, therefore, echoes questions about whose knowledge is being privileged in schools and about whose interests are being served.[12] Fundamentally, these scholars question, as Lois Weis has done,

> [the] ideological analysis of the strategic implications of school knowledge, its silences, and its deletions of the self-affirming history of the oppressed. . . . The attempt to explicitly link knowledge to power also partially opened up a fecund ground of possibilities for the investigation

and exploration of school life around issues of the formation and constitution of racial and sexual identities and representations. . . . For writers
such as Baldwin and Shange, American schools are principal sites for the
production and naturalization of myths, half truths, silences and obfusca-
tions about the socially disadvantaged. (1988: 19–26)

Speaking to the dynamics of race, class, and gender, such analyses take
note directly of how these factors interact consistently as traditional patterns
of power, authority, and privilege are made manifest in curricula and in classrooms. These analyses also acknowledge complicity and resistance in how the
marginalized inevitably internalize prevailing values despite their needs to
resist these same values.

This type of dichotomous existence between margin and center was powerfully articulated in 1903 by W. E. B. DuBois in *The Souls of Black Folk* when he
talked about the *two-ness* of being Black *and* American. Bell hooks extended
our thinking in *Feminist Theory: From Margin to Center* (1984) when she focused
on the insights and resiliency that can be engendered by such thinking. On
one level, like the African American women who are the objects of my
research, marginalized students who are well centered in their personhood
seem to learn a type of multiconsciousness, a consistent awareness of otherness. They fashion multiconscious mechanisms (information, skills, strategies,
attitudes) that support academic work while simultaneously building up a
resistance against oppositional forces to positive and productive personal
development. Even in the face of opposition, they seem able to create for
themselves a proactive rather than a reactive vision of reality.[13] They see
sources of possible fragmentation and find a way to transcend them. Because
we are just beginning to document this type of transcendence,[14] empirically
documented patterns of proaction and reaction are yet to be established.

In working simultaneously with historical case studies and with contemporary students, I noticed that, when African American women define and
empower themselves, they often think and operate from the margins—in
opposition to central authority. They see, for example, what is marginalized or
ignored in their own lives, as well as in the lives of others. Dialectically, however, they think and operate from the center in resonance with that authority.
They are able to find and use their strengths, to bring their fully recognizable
selves into the focus of mainstream values and expectations. These women are
called upon to create a place of comfort in a stream that seems—by nature,
but more likely by design—to seek to drown, or, at the very least, to dilute
them. Typically, they fashion for themselves their own authority to speak, to
write, and to produce. Yet they also look at themselves, as DuBois says,
"through the eyes of others . . . measuring one's soul by the tape of a world
that looks on in amused contempt and pity" (1994: 45). What seems central to
creating a sense of *place*—that is, the space to be productive—seems to be an
informed understanding of power, authority, and privilege.

What I learned from this program as an administrator and teacher was
that the continuum of African American women's uses of literacy as professional women created learning occasions for the students, especially since

these professional arenas were often the ones in which the students envisioned themselves participating as leaders. I learned that making intellectual ancestry more explicit helped the students to a more visceral understanding of struggle—and (given the intent of this program) intellectual struggle. The students could see connections and disconnections between themselves and others and fashion within the context of their historical knowledge lines of authority, privilege, and entitlement.[15]

What I realized in terms of my own development, as we fashioned intellectual experiences for the interns and created a community of engagement for them, was that this work and the privilege of sharing culturally engaging experiences with the students were creating material connections for me as well. I was being nurtured and affirmed in my own ideological transformation. Being a codirector of the program, engaging in my research project on nineteenth-century women, working with *SAGE*, all contributed to my sense of ideology in action, and thereby to the dynamic evolution and transformation of my own ideology, an ideology that was manifesting itself at this point not only in my research and scholarship, but also, by means of the internship program, in my work as a teacher and administrator.

Within this highly charged context, I became more conscious of how my own authority as researcher, scholar, and teacher was transforming into the afrafeminist ideology that now shapes my professional practices. I view the African American women that I study (and by extension the varieties of students that I teach) as sentient beings who are capable of proactive engagement in the world. I deal consciously with the world as a place that is materially defined by social, economic, and political relationships. I continue to struggle in determining an appropriate place for myself in performing research. At the same time, however, I have become more comfortable with the notion that "place"—especially in the participant/observer roles I often take on—is continually negotiated and renegotiated, a process that offers peculiar challenges when (as in my case) many of my subjects are no longer living and the time frame for them is obviously the past.

There is a constancy in the need for negotiation, beginning with the uncomfortable question of how much I actually do share identities with the women I study and how much I do not. I share what I claim as a cultural heritage. I share in kind, though perhaps not in degree, some of their material realities. I do not share their time or place. I have known, for example, the oppression and domination of the segregated South, but not slavery or Reconstruction. I write about northern, mostly urban women, and I grew up in the rural South. I recognize the important cultural resonances that exist across African diasporic communities, but I understand also the existence of dissonance, especially as these distinctions become complicated by the passage of time and by cross-cultural fusions that I have experienced, and which they may have experienced differently. I am continually reminded, however, of two points. The first point, in keeping with Kenneth Burke's view of "identification," is the notion that identity is not natural. It is constructed. I have indeed identified multiple connections between these women and myself, despite our not being perfectly matched. The second point is that the need for negotiation is, therefore, not arbitrary. It is part and parcel of the consubstantial process. The need for negotiation is yoked to the need for a well-balanced analytical view that takes into account shifting conditions, values, and circumstances between human beings. This materiality for scholarly production and representation brings me recursively to two questions: What is an afrafeminist ideology? How does this viewpoint facilitate good practices in scholarship?

THE CONSTRUCTION OF AN AFRAFEMINIST IDEOLOGY

In "The Social Construction of Black Feminist Thought," an essay that preceded the book from which I draw the epigraph at the beginning of this chapter, Patricia Hill-Collins presents a compelling case for the emergence of a Black feminist standpoint. As she explains, she does not intend to suggest either a uniformly shared experience for all African American women or a uniformly articulated and recognized consciousness among us. Instead, she posits a plurality of experiences within an overarching concept that supports the idea that African American women have not passively accepted their domination or oppression but actively resisted it. She theorizes that these acts of resistance nourish the development of sensibilities among African American women as a variable group, sensibilities that form collectively a cultural worldview.[16]

In explaining this idea, Hill-Collins presents two interlocking characteristics of this standpoint. One is that African American women's political and economic status, as enacted through the paid and unpaid work we do, has provided us with a material reality that is unique. The second is that having a unique relationship to material reality inevitably shapes across a spectrum of political and economic conditions a comparably unique way of perceiving the world and ourselves in it. The relationships of African American women to the material world have yielded, at minimum, tacit perceptions of that world and the "places" we occupy. These perceptions, in turn, have enabled us to define ourselves in counterdistinction to the externally defined perceptions that have been assigned to us over the generations. Hill-Collins names this counterdistinction a Black feminist consciousness; I have been calling it an afrafeminist ideology.

In positing a theory of Black feminist consciousness, Hill-Collins acknowledges that making tacit connections between the "work" one does, paid and unpaid, and what one thinks, especially about self and possibility within the world, does not lead automatically to a clear theoretical articulation of this positioning as an intellectual standpoint, or as ideology. Quite the contrary. The expression of an afrafeminist ideology within a sociopolitical milieu set up to privilege other ideologies is inherently problematic. Societal apparatuses support other standpoints, which because of their places of power, prestige, and privilege are hegemonic. The central systems of belief, the predominant systems of practice, the master narratives of the social order do not invite the creation of counter-ideologies that would by their very existence have the potential to subvert prevailing authority or to resist domination.

Hegemonic systems by their very nature are set up to limit resources for resistance, to absorb the momentum generated by resistance, and to maximize the resources for resilience in maintaining the status quo.

In light of hegemonic systems that give rise to a hostile environment for the development of afrafeminist ideologies, my sense of the challenge to an afrafeminist theorist is twofold. On one hand, the task is basic. The challenge is to make overt connections, as Hill-Collins emphasizes, between the everyday understanding of African American women as they live their lives by whatever means and the specialized understanding that an African American woman intellectual might bring as she contextualizes these lives within meaningful frameworks. My goal as an afrafeminist researcher in rhetorical studies is to interrogate the literate practices of women of African descent in ways that enable me to find and collect data; to sort through, interrogate, and assess those data meaningfully; to draw implications that are well centered in the knowledge and experience of the group; and also to render interpretations that are recognizable by the group itself as meaningful, instructive, and usable.

On the other hand, the task is more complex. The challenge is not simply to operate well in terms of scholarly enterprises but to articulate an ideological view. Hill-Collins articulates this task as an identification of an overarching concept based on a collectivity of Black feminist standpoints. The purpose of fulfilling such a task is to use the concept, the ideology to enable action despite hostility. In intellectual pursuits, the effort is to assume a viewpoint that permits African American women to be imagined as embodied by our own values and beliefs; to root that viewpoint in both community knowledge (recognizing and valuing the specificity of the material context of African American women) and in specialized knowledge (recognizing and valuing the extent to which critical perspectives of that context become imperative). The idea is that afrafeminist theories permit Black women intellectuals to paint the contours of research and scholarship with a different brush and with a different scenario in mind. An afrafeminist approach, as an enabling site of operation for both thought and action, suggests in rhetorical studies a paradigm shift. The shift begins with a reconsideration of *who* the primary and secondary audiences of the scholarship are and *who*, even, the *agents* of research and scholarship include.

My intent in this book, for example, is to acknowledge and credit community wisdom and the roles that this knowledge might play directly and indirectly in affirming validity, reliability, and accuracy. My tendency has been to assign the women a point of view, authority, and agency in their intellectual work. The women emerge not just as subjects of research but also as potential listeners, observers, even co-researchers, whether silent or voiced, in the knowledge-making processes themselves. In contrast to their being the slates on which I write, I permit them to assume a *presence*. I think of them as real and not controlled by me. My job in analysis and interpretation is to account for their point of view and interests.

Critical to such methodological practices, therefore, is the idea that, whatever the knowledge accrued, it would be both presented and represented with this community, and at least its potential for participation and response, in mind. This view of subjects as both audiences and agents contrasts with a presentation and representation of knowledge in a more traditional fashion. Typically, subjects are likely to be perceived in a more disembodied way, that is, without allowing a central place of consideration for the material interests of the subjects in the knowledge-making. The differences here between approaches might be signaled by the contrasts between two questions: "How is this knowledge informative to or representative of the group on whose lives the knowledge is based?" in the first paradigm; and "How is this knowledge abstractable and relatable to larger meaning-making structures?" in the second. The first approach, which I claim not as exclusively afrafeminist but centrally so, assumes that the researcher has obligations to the community. The second, a more traditional approach, does not.

The contrast is one of values and assumptions. Afrafeminist models, in recognizing direct connections to lives and experiences of African American women, situate the intellectual work within the values and assumptions of this specific racialized and gendered group.[17] As African American women intellectuals doing this work, we are obligated, as are our counterparts within the community, to be holistic, to remember our connectedness in both places. We are free to do our own intellectual business, and at the same time we are also obligated to have that work respond to sociopolitical imperatives that encumber the community itself. We, like our sisters (the African American women whom we study), are accountable ultimately to the merging of the interests of mind, body, and soul as part and parcel of the wholeness of the knowledge-making enterprise, which includes accounting for our own social obligations as members of the group. We speak and interpret *with* the community, not just *for* the community, or *about* the community.

In other words, as participant/observers within the community, African American women intellectuals are accountable to those with whom and about whom we speak.[18] As I see the challenge, our work is expected by this view to recognize that research and scholarship have the potential to empower and disempower, that a primary site for the validation of knowledge is the community itself, and that there is an inherent expectation that knowledge carries with it a mandate for appropriate action, again, in the interest of the general welfare of the community, both narrowly and broadly defined, a mandate on which the research and scholarship quite literally rest.

Further, my view of afrafeminist thought is that African American women intellectuals as participant/observers are indeed the obvious originators of afrafeminist ideologies (as compared with nonmembers of the community), because of the very fact of our participant/observer status. We have deeply vested interests, which, by their very subjectivity, lay claim, not to biases as an abnormal condition but to biases as a normal condition and to levels of commitment to the work that such biases are likely to engender. Because of our potential as researchers with both insider knowledge and outsider knowledge, it seems obvious that we should be central to the formation and development of knowledge production in this arena. African American women intellectuals are the ones within intellectual circles who should generally care (and, I would venture to say, do generally care) the most. I suggest, then, that afrafeminist ideologies acknowledge a role for caring, for passionate attachments. In effect, the status of participant/observer suggests interests that cover a wide and deep range of caring. This range certainly includes our own reflexive interests as part of the group, but also it includes concerns centered as well in our disciplinary and transdisciplinary needs to know in keeping with typical scholarly practices and pursuits.

In positioning ourselves in this work as central players, African American women intellectuals are charged with creating *bridges* from which to speak and interpret, as compared with the *bridges* by which African American women in general have envisioned the world and operated within it.[19] This distinction relates more directly to the merging of specialized knowledge and community knowledge. As researchers and scholars who identify with the subjects of our scholarly gaze, Black women intellectuals occupy positions in the synergetic space at the in-between. From this bifocal standpoint, we have a primary responsibility for seeing, defining, naming, and interpreting our own reality within a sense-making schema and also for suggesting and taking appropriate actions in our own interests and in the interests of whatever alliances for progress and change across the sites and sources of knowledge-making that we may be able to forge.

In this latter regard, the second part of the epigraph at the beginning of this chapter becomes cautionary advice. I agree with Hill-Collins that afrafeminist ideologies cannot flourish in isolation from the ideas and experiences of others outside the group. A recurring question in ethnic and gender "studies," however, is whether researchers and scholars who do not share the identities of the subjects are capable of assuming an appropriate standpoint and of operating well. Is it possible, in this case, for someone who is not an African American woman to do good work in afrafeminist scholarship? I think most people would answer affirmatively, but the real question in this scenario is how is this so? In my estimation, the answers to such questions are multidirectional.

From one perspective, with special insider/outsider knowledge-making potential, African American women intellectuals are challenged to build bridges between afrafeminist insights within the group and the visions and experiences of others. The objective of such bridge-building is to maximize the interpretive power of various standpoints, by bringing all that we know together kaleidoscopically.[20] The assumption is that the whole of a kaleidoscopic view has greater interpretive power than a singularly defined view would have. The forging of knowledge-making coalitions and alliances, therefore, becomes an important dimension of a long-range developmental process for knowledge-making.

To restate the point, the work of making sense of the lives of African American women originates as a territory perfectly — if not naturally — suited to African American women. It is our work. However, as full-fledged members of humanity, this work is not by necessity ours alone. Others can also have interests and investments in it that can be envisioned from their own standpoints, from their own locations. What becomes critical to good practice, however, is that these researchers—who are indeed outsiders in the communities they study—have special obligations that begin with a need to articulate carefully what their viewpoints actually are, rather than letting the researchers' relationships to the work go unarticulated, as is often the case with practices of disregard. My view is that noncommunity scholars are called upon by their outsider status to demonstrate respect for the communities they study. They are obligated (by afrafeminist ideologies anyway) to recognize overtly, the ways in which their authority, as it may be drawn from dominant systems of power and privilege, intersects with the authority of others. They are obligated to hold themselves, rather than just their subjects, accountable for and responsive to disparities.

In other words, the intellectual work of afrafeminist scholarship is multidirectional. By the measure of this analysis, it originates with African American women intellectuals, and it can be extended and/or nuanced by the work of others. The idea is that scholarship can handle mutual interests, without setting aside the politics and privileges of "first voice" (Royster 1996). The concept of first voice acknowledges a need for scholarly practices to show a deliberate sense of both analytical and ethical regard. Given this dialectical expectation a persistent dilemma, however, continues along methodological lines. How do we clarify the distinctive roles of participant/observers, that is, those who speak and interpret as members of the community and those who speak and interpret as nonmembers? On what bases do those of us who are community members articulate our own locations in the research and in the rendering of scholarship? How do others engage likewise from their own locations? How do we each find "credible" places to stand? How do we develop methodologies that are both "credible" and accessible as touchstones for each other? In other words, what does it mean to do good work in researching the lives, conditions, and contributions of women of African descent and in interpreting that information in both insightful and respectful ways?

"WAYS OF DOING" IN AFRAFEMINIST SCHOLARSHIP

The actual articulation of an ideological perspective, as in my own case, may not be a task that can be done alone and in isolation. I suspect that ideology grows in the material world and in the company of others with similar interests and concerns (for example, in the ways I was enabled in my thinking and practices by the specificity of my work with the *SAGE* editorial team and, among other experiences, by my advisory role with the SAGE Interns). In other words, ideology formation, as a knowledge-making process, is socially constructed.

Moreover, as evidenced by the stories of African American women writers,[21] there is also a lively notion of apprenticeship, a sitting at the feet or by the side of others as we develop habits of seeing, doing, and in many cases, also of being. We find "teachers," "mentors," "guides," many of them indirectly rather than directly related to our specific goals, but who nonetheless have necessary advice and insights for us to complete our transformations. Octavia Butler, for example, enacts this need for "guidance" in her *Dawn* trilogy by illustrating that effective transformation is possible in the good and loving hands of others who assist in whatever ways the transforming subject needs the help.

In the case of the researcher who is more outsider than insider in relation to the community targeted for study, such guides are invaluable. With or without guides, however, it may be helpful to distinguish between the construction of personal identity (ways of being) and the articulation of research and scholarly methodologies (ways of seeing and doing) as we try to imagine a fuller spectrum of how participation in knowledge-making might optimally function. My sense is that, despite the coincidence of being or not being an insider, researchers and scholars still have systematic behaviors (habits of seeing and doing) in which they can engage that demonstrate a commitment to both scholarly and ethically responsible actions, such as those indicated in this explanation.

Setting aside the value of apprenticeship, my view of afrafeminism is very much definable in material terms. This approach embodies the notion that the mind, heart, body, and soul operate collectively and requires intellectual work to include four sites of critical regard: *careful analysis, acknowledgment of passionate attachments, attention to ethical action,* and *commitment to social responsibility.* From my perspective, these sites operate together to create a well-functioning whole with each site involving practices forged in light of critical ways of doing that are also capable of being touchstones for critical ways of being.

Careful analysis suggests typical concerns about scholarly behavior. I see the necessity of using systematically the vocabulary, theories, and methodologies of our field or fields of study, with attention to clarity, accuracy, and precision. In other words, it makes good sense to me that we should not discard the disciplinary views we have refined over the years, as they have helped us to draw out meaning in abstract and concrete terms. Instead, my view is that we can take supreme advantage of this specialized knowledge, merge it with the knowledge of the community, and then build interpretive frames that have more generative power, that is, the power to be dynamic and to have within their purview both general landscapes that speak to the whole and specific ones that account for varieties within the whole.

In other words, when I use a particular analytical model my caution is to make sure it is well rooted in the accumulated knowledge of the field and also useful in shedding light on the subject. Questions come in, however, through the application of the model. The opportunity for inquiry emerges at points where the subject of analysis exhibits characteristics that are likely to be specific rather than general, local rather than global, or outside the assumed and the valued. The imperative is both to use the framework and to interpret it. The act of both using and critically questioning the analytical framework makes it possible to notice both the predictable and the unpredictable and of taking note, thereby, of discrepancies and distortions between the expected and whatever might be unseen. By this process, I am suggesting that discrepancies and distortions can be perceived as normal rather than abnormal, and that the degree and extent of discrepancy and distortion often depend on the point of view. Paying attention to point of view clarifies the notion that any analytical framework reveals some characteristics and obscures others, a process that often opens up secondary questions: How can we make adjustments or refinements to the sight line and to the value system that sets the sight line? How can we see both more and differently? How can we engage in analysis in a more thorough way and develop interpretations that are more useful and meaningful?

An *acknowledgment of passionate attachments* reminds us that knowledge has sites and sources and that we are better informed about the nature of a given knowledge base when we take into account its sites, material contexts, and points of origin. My point here is that knowledge is produced by someone and that its producers are not formless and invisible. They are embodied and in effect have passionate attachments by means of their embodiments. They are vested with vision, values, and habits; with ways of being and ways of doing. These ways of being and doing shape the question of what counts as knowledge, what knowing and doing mean, and what the consequences of knowledge and action entail. It is important, therefore, to specify attachments, to recognize who has produced the knowledge, what the bases of it are, what the material circumstances of its production entail, what consequences or implications are suggested by its existence, and for whom the consequences and implications hold true.

Thus, *attention to ethical action* acquires considerable significance. This site suggests, on one hand, a scholarly mandate to be theoretically and methodologically sound, but on the other hand, it also indicates a need to sustain a sense of accountability. As researchers, scholars, and teachers, we are accountable to our various publics. We are challenged to think metacognitively about lines of accountability throughout the intellectual process. We see the importance of monitoring and measuring our methodologies from the beginning to the end of our actions. Based on this ongoing assessment, we recognize the need to negotiate working space and working relationships within this context of ongoing critical reflection. What also becomes clearer is the need to represent our work (whether in textual form or otherwise) in conscious regard of our ethical obligations.

In this paradigm, therefore, a *commitment to social responsibility* (and, I might add, social action) reminds us that knowledge does indeed have the capacity to empower and disempower, to be used for good and for ill. As researchers and scholars, we are responsible for its uses and, therefore, should think consciously about the momentum we create when we produce knowledge or engage in knowledge-making processes. Our intellectual work has consequences. I believe the inevitability of these consequences should bring us pause as we think not just about what others do but about what we are obligated to do or not do.

In being useful, however, ideology should be able to translate into action. In my own articulation of an afrafeminist ideology, I note the need for researchers and scholars to articulate their own ideological standpoints systematically, not simply as a personal or professional flag to wave at a convenient moment but in support of ideological clarity; in recognition of how our viewpoints are implicated in scholarly presentation and representation; and also in support of "humility," as we locate ourselves within the text as scholars, and thereby as people who have interpretive power. In addition to seeing one's own standpoint, however, I note also the need to look for the standpoints of others; to be sensitive to the importance of "location" as a specific scholarly value; and to be prepared, therefore, to reconstruct the standpoints of others as we analyze and interpret data, and construct a sense of audience or spectator. My sense of the advantage of such practices is that being able to articulate a standpoint ideologically makes use of an understanding of both self and others as both historical and sociopolitical beings and, more important, as people in specific relationships to power, privilege, authority, and entitlement.

To restate the idea, my use of an afrafeminist approach centralizes the need to develop and consistently enact a regard for material reality, which in turn shifts the inquiry toward a more multidimensional viewpoint. The imperative is to recognize that, by its very existence as a concept, *point of view* means that some things become visible while others are cast in shadow. We benefit, therefore, from an intentional shifting of perspectives. In my work, I have sought to demonstrate this commitment by triangulating types of evidence. See, for example, the attention I assign in chapter 2* to an examination of the formation of ethos, the context for action, and the rhetorical expertise of a given writer. I garner evidence from transdisciplinary sources; look diachronically, not just synchronically, at literate practices; and look across genres for resonances among a given writer's habits and concerns.

In other words, I consider myself to be operating ethnographically. What I find challenging, though, is using such an approach with historical subjects who can no longer be interviewed. Ethnography and historical subjects, in fact, make strange bedfellows. For me the combination has meant that the crisscrossing of available data becomes a necessity, not simply an option. The practice of merging sight lines, regardless of my inability to gather data as I would with contemporary subjects, is the key to what makes these practices fit within an ethnographic schema. The goal with historical subjects strikes me as the same. As a researcher I seek to reduce distortion by positioning various views in kaleidoscopic relationships to each other.

One type of evidence that gains authority in this type of triangulation of data is personal experience or, more accurately stated, the reporting of personal experience. The imperative in seeing and using reports of personal experience as evidence becomes a function of finding substantive and systematic ways to interrogate it and particularly to have a discriminating view of the behaviors that constitute it. In literacy studies, we have developed inquiry paradigms (such as the analytical model I posit in chapter 2) that permit an

---

*All references to chapters in this selection refer to Royster's *Traces of a Stream* from which this excerpt was taken.

exploration of the physicality of experience, and, in the case of rhetorical studies, permit us to examine in context specific behaviors related to literate production. The focus is on material culture, on (1) the researcher's capacity to be specifically attuned to the material context and (2) the conditions for meaning-making. Ethnographic methodologies, therefore, are useful, since interrogating experience and discriminating among specific behaviors demand typically that we make the familiar strange and the strange familiar. We need, as Clifford Geertz established, "thick" descriptions from which we develop the ability to see more of what is really there and what is actually going on.

In addition to embracing the disciplinary methodologies that are current in my field (such as trends and practices in rhetorical criticism, discourse analysis, ethnographic analysis, and so forth), I acknowledge, still, the need to be responsive both to the community that is the object of my scholarly gaze and to that community's own articulations of values, beliefs, and protocols. I look at and listen to what the women say and have said in writing over time. When I have the opportunity, I speak before contemporary African American women and listen to their responses to my work. I take their responses as advice, as wisdom to be consciously regarded as I make decisions about scholarly presentation and representation.

In recognizing the intersections of specialized and community knowledge, the afrafeminist paradigm that I am suggesting also makes room for the in-between, the liminal spaces where the threshold for new possibilities is high. New possibilities suggest there is a room in this viewpoint for imagination to enter and to find a useful place as an interpretive tool. In my work, the deliberated use of imagination has been eye-opening. In constructing a place for the imagination, I was able to traverse the cavernous space between the known, the unknown, and, in the case of African American women's history, quite probably the unknowable.

In offering these sample practices of how I manifest an afrafeminist ideology, I emphasize that I have encoded careful analysis, an acknowledgment of passionate attachments, attention to ethical action, and a commitment to social responsibility (and action) as touchstones. While I have discussed them as discrete points for consideration, I am aware there is nothing to indicate that these touchstones actually operate pristinely. Reinvoking the metaphor of the kaleidoscope, my sense is that these sites of regard merge and blend in various configurations as we take our intellectual work seriously, whatever our personal locations might be. The point is that afrafeminist ideologies, in my opinion, invite researchers and scholars to think of ourselves as whole in intellectual processes, rather than as disembodied, destabilized, or deconstructed. They permit wide-ranging choices because they centralize relationships to material reality, which inevitably reveals variations in context and condition. In these approaches similarity and generality matter; but simultaneity, specificity, and variability also matter.

In terms of the history of African American women's literacy, afrafeminist ideologies permit us to see the connections of these women's literate practices within the landscape of literate practices generally. In addition, however, they also permit us to see how these connections have been forged. We can see how these women with their unique voices, visions, experiences, and relationships have operated with agency and authority; defined their roles in public space; and participated in this space consistently over time with social and political consequence. Using this type of approach, with a group that by other lenses has been perceived as inconsequential, we have a provocative springboard from which to question what "public" means, what "advocacy" and "activism" mean, what rhetorical prowess means, even what "literacy" means. With this type of analysis, the ferreting out of actions and achievements in the alternative terrain are instructive for an interrogation of contemporary public discourses, debunking the myth that public discourse is a ground only for institutionally sanctioned voices. With African American women, we have a cautionary tale, one that speaks volumes for the historical habits and practices of rhetoric and composition.

These women's stories suggest that, as users of language, we construct ways of being, seeing, and doing in recognition of the materiality of the world around us and of who and how we are in our sundry relationships to it. Their work suggests that we should not automatically discount the discordant, revolutionary, or evolutionary voices of the unsanctioned or un-institutionally authorized. It also suggests that, in order to be generative in our interpretations of contemporary language practices, we need analytical models of discourse that are flexible enough to see the variability of the participants and their worlds, to draw meaning from the shifting contours of rhetorical negotiation across and within material relationships, and to imagine the possibility of building bridges. A basic advantage of more imaginative models, given the volatility of our contemporary era, is that we can see how connections are merging between private, social, and public space. We can understand the simultaneity of competing and conflicting agenda. We can think more carefully about what bridge-building—that is, coalition, alliance, codes of conduct and communicative practice in "public"—might more imaginatively mean as we solve complex problems. Most of all, we can imagine, as African American women have traditionally done, that the "public" arena is a place where negotiation can be with words rather than with weapons, and we can commit ourselves, as African American women writers have done, to turning our thoughts toward action in making a better world for us all.

NOTES

1. The problem of African American women's studies being treated as redundant was poignantly articulated in Hull, Bell-Scott, and Smith (1982).

2. See the next section for a more thorough explanation of the term *afrafeminist*. My sense here is that I operate with a Black feminist consciousness, supported by an ideological frame or worldview in which my awareness has been shaped by the experiences I cite in this chapter and others.

3. See the next section, "The Construction of an Afrafeminist Ideology," for a more detailed explanation of the unique relationships of African American women to the material conditions of work.

4. For an account of the founding of *SAGE*, see Royster (1995).

5. I chronicle my experiences with this program in similar fashion in Royster (1992, 1988). The collaboration for this project involved two people directly: Beverly Guy-Sheftall (director of the

Women's Center and cofounder/coeditor of *SAGE*) and myself (director of the Writing Program and senior associate editor of *SAGE*). However, we also received support through the years from the other members of the editorial team.

6. I left Spelman in 1992. The program, however, has continued to flourish and has been renamed the Bambara Writers Program in honor of African American woman writer Toni Cade Bambara.

7. In planning the program, I had administered an attitudinal survey to them about writing, but this instrument did not include questions related to their sense of "intellectual" self or to the "intellectual" dimensions of their lives. It focused mainly on writing and reading practices and their general attitudes concerning performance and abilities.

8. I acknowledge here the wisdom and experience of Beverly Guy-Sheftall in this collaboration. I credit much of my view of Black feminism to her, the more experienced Black feminist, and to the collegial relationships that developed from our work together on this and other projects. I benefited greatly from the consistency with which Beverly exercised a critical perspective on everything she came in contact with, and from the occasions that this intellectual companionship provided for me to exercise my own critical abilities more consistently.

9. See, for example, Chodorow (1978); Heilbrun (1981); O'Brien (1984); David (1987); Hansen and Philipson (1990); Haraway (1991).

10. For an explanation of "psychic wholeness," see Royster (1990). For a discussion of fragmentation, see Dubois (1994); and hooks (1984).

11. Examples of scholarship in this area include Hall and Sandler (1982); *SAGE* (Spring 1984); Solomon (1985); Hill-Collins and Anderson (1988); Pearson, Shavlik, and Touchton (1989).

12. Woodson (1990) raised similar questions.

13. See chapter 2 for a more extended discussion of the use of language in forging a proactive vision.

14. Examples of this type of scholarship include James and Farmer (1993); Wear (1993); and Kirsch (1993).

15. For an explanation of the concepts of "entitlement" and "privilege" as used here, see Coles (1977).

16. Compare this with my explanation (chapter 2) of how African American women's habits of action and belief have systematically supported uses of language and literacy. A significant difference between this chapter and chapter 2 is in the actual naming of the analytical approach I use in developing a theory of language and sociopolitical afrafeminist action. This chapter focuses on the approach. Chapter 2 is a demonstration of a theory that can emerge from such a standpoint.

17. My goal in this chapter is to explain how I have sought to make an afrafeminist approach manifest in my own work. My assumption is that this way constitutes one way of working, not the only way, and that there are other methodologies that would also be appropriate to this ideological view.

18. Interrogating the roles and practices of the participant/observer in research and scholarship is an area of considerable activity in several fields at the present time. For an example of how issues are being articulated and addressed in the field of rhetoric and composition, see Mortensen and Kirsch (1996).

19. See chapter 2 for my explanation of how experience, knowledge, and language converge in the lives of African American women to focus behavior and action.

20. See chapter 2 for an explanation of the use of a kaleidoscopic approach in knowledge construction.

21. hooks (1989) and Marshall (1981) are two examples of writers who discuss how young African American girls learn in the company of their "elders."

BIBLIOGRAPHY

African American Education

Pearson, Carol S., Donna L. Shavlik, and Judith G. Touchton, eds. 1989. *Educating the Majority: Women Challenge Tradition in Higher Education*. New York: American Council on Education.

Weis, Lois, ed. 1988. *Class, Race, and Gender in American Education*. Albany, State University of New York Press.

Woodson, Carter G. [1933] 1990. *The Miseducation of the Negro*. Trenton, N.J.: Africa World Press.

African American History

DuBois, W. E. B. [1903] 1994. *The Souls of Black Folk*. New York: Gramercy-Random.

Thurman, Howard. 1981. "The Sound of the Genuine." Centennial Founders Day Service, Spelman College, April 11.

African American Women's History and Culture

Butler, Octavia. 1987. *Dawn.* New York: Popular Library/Warner.
Chodorow, Nancy. 1978. *The Reproduction of Mothering: Psychoanalysis and the Sociology of Gender.* Berkeley: University of California Press.
David, Deirdre. 1987. *Intellectual Women and Victorian Patriarchy: Harriet Martineau, Elizabeth Barrett Browning, George Eliot.* Ithaca, N.Y.: Cornell University Press.
Hall, Roberta, and Bernice Sandler. 1982. *The Classroom Climate: A Chilly One for Women?* Washington, D.C.: Association of American Colleges.
Hansen, Karen V., and Ilene J. Philipson, eds. 1990. *Women, Class, and the Feminist Imagination.* Philadelphia: Temple University Press.
Haraway, Donna. 1991. *Simians, Cyborgs, and Women: The Reinvention of Nature.* New York: Routledge.
Heilbrun, Carolyn G. 1979. *Reinventing Womanhood.* New York: W. W. Norton.
Hill-Collins, Patricia. 1995. "The Social Construction of Black Feminist Thought." In *Words of Fire,* ed. Beverly Guy-Sheftall, 338–57. New York: New Press.
Hull, Gloria T., Patricia Bell-Scott, and Barbara Smith, eds. 1982. *All the Women Are White, All the Blacks Are Men, but Some of Us Are Brave: Black Women's Studies.* Old Westbury, Conn.: Feminist Press.
James, Joy, and Ruth Farmer, eds. 1993. *Spirit, Space and Survival.* New York: Routledge.
Kirsch, Gesa. 1993. *Women Writing the Academy.* Urbana, Ill.: National Council of Teachers of English.
Lerner, Gerda. 1986. *The Creation of Patriarchy.* New York: Oxford University Press.
Marshall, Paule. [1959] 1981. *Brown Girl, Brownstones.* Old Westbury, Conn.: Feminist Press.
McIntosh, Peggy. 1988. "White Privilege and Male Privilege: A Personal Account of Coming to See Correspondences Through Work in Women's Studies." Working paper no. 189. Wellesley, Mass.: Wellesley College, Massachusetts Center for Research on Women, ED335262.
O'Brien, Mary. 1984. "The Commutization of Women: Patriarchal Fetishism in the Sociology of Education." *Interchange* 15:43–60.
Royster, Jacqueline Jones. 1983. *Women as Healers: A Noble Tradition.* Atlanta: Spelman College.
———. 1990. "Perspectives on the Intellectual Tradition of Black Women Writers." In *The Right to Literacy,* ed. Andrea A. Lunsford, Helene Moglen, and James Slevin, 103–12. New York: MLA.
———. 1995. "Capping a Sage Stone: The Final Issue." *SAGE: A Scholarly Journal for Black Women* 9, no. 2 (Summer): 2–4.
Soloman, Barbara Miller. 1985. *In the Company of Educated Women: A History of Women in Higher Education.* New Haven, Conn.: Yale University Press.
Wear, Delese, ed. 1993. *The Center of the Web: Women and Solitude.* Albany: State University of New York Press.

The Essay and African American Women Essayists

Cooper, Anna Julia. [1892] 1988. *A Voice from the South, by a Black Woman of the South.* New York: Oxford University Press.
hooks, bell. 1984. *Feminist Theory: From Margin to Center.* Boston: South End Press.
———. 1989. *Talking Back: Thinking Feminist, Thinking Black.* Boston: South End Press.

Literacy, Language, and Rhetoric

Burke, Kenneth. 1966. *Language as Symbolic Action: Life, Literature, and Method.* Berkeley: University of California Press.
Coles, Robert. 1977. *Privileged Ones.* Boston: Little, Brown.
Geertz, Clifford. 1973. *The Interpretation of Cultures.* New York: Basic.
Mortensen, Peter, and Gesa E. Kirsch, eds. 1996. *Ethics and Representation in Qualitative Studies of Literacy.* Urbana, Ill.: NCTE.
Royster, Jacqueline Jones. 1988. "Reflections on the SAGE Women as Writer/Scholars Internship Program." *SAGE: A Scholarly Journal on Black Women* (Student Supplement): 4–6.
———. 1992. "Looking from the Margins: A Tale of Curricular Reform." In *Diversity and Writing: Dialogue Within a Modern University,* monograph 2, 1–11. Minneapolis: University of Minnesota Center for Interdisciplinary Studies of Writing.
———. 1996. "When the First Voice You Hear Is Not Your Own." *CCC* 47, no. 1 (February): 29–40.

Revisiting "Confronting the 'Essential' Problem"

JOY S. RITCHIE AND BARBARA DIBERNARD

Having just come back from our weekly early morning vigorous walk, full of talk about life and work, and drinking good coffee, we are revisiting the article Joy wrote as a result of her participant observation in Barbara's women's literature class in the fall of 1988. Although we realize that the essay has been read within composition for the questions about feminist theory and practice it raises, particularly the importance of helping students shift from a naïve to a more strategic use of essentialism, this morning we are talking about what this research has meant for our friendship, our teaching, and our professional lives.

The article documents the conflicts students experienced as they were challenged to think about their own status as women, about feminism, and about issues of difference. We realize that our students have changed as the world around them has changed; yet, the issues and conflicts present in the classroom in 1988 still exist. For example, the educational initiatives to promote "multiculturalism" have affected our students in different ways. We now find many students genuinely committed to issues of diversity: More heterosexual students know friends and family members who are lesbian or gay, and even our Midwest students have had more experience with people of different ethnicities and races. On the other hand, we encounter students who are cynical about multiculturalism and what they call "political correctness." Despite students' heightened sensitivity to these issues, most of them still believe in the American myth that "everyone can be whatever they want," that everyone has an equal opportunity. Many students still have not had opportunities to fully examine how all our lives are shaped by ideologies of race, class, gender, sexual orientation, and physical ability.

The past decade in literary and composition studies has seen a strong movement to engage students in cultural criticism by immersion in "theory." As we reread this article and thought again about the interactions in Barbara's class and numerous others we have taught since then, it reaffirmed to us that in rich interactive reading, writing, and discussions like those in this feminist classroom, students were already engaged and immersed in theory, examining the ideologies that surround their lives. The complex critical work the class engaged in reaffirms for us that theory is not limited to the writings of a select group of intellectuals and that reading what is traditionally defined as theory is not the only way to help students gain tools of analysis. Broadening our definition of theory is not enough. We must ask our students to recognize that this critical theorizing requires ethical action as the next necessary response.

Rereading "Confronting the 'Essential' Problem" also led us to reflect on what it has meant for our professional lives and friendship. The participation-observation study began a ten-year weekly conversation about teaching, feminist and cultural theory, pedagogy, and educational politics, inevitably interspersed with conversations about our aging parents, our partners/spouses, backpacking, birdwatching, and gardening. As we look back on this article, it affirms for us the value of projects that bring other people into our classrooms and create rich, productive collaborations that affect all aspects of our work. It is not overstating the case to say that our conversations have enabled us to survive as feminist academics.

Joy: I conducted the participant-observation study documented in "Confronting the 'Essential' Problem" because I had seen how influential Barbara's teaching had been for many graduate students, and I wanted to try to understand the connections I felt between feminist and composition pedagogy and theory. Although I knew from my previous experience that both the observer and the "observed" can be changed by the relationship that participant-observation makes possible, I could not have anticipated that it would have such far-reaching meaning for my life. The study certainly marks the beginning of my writing about feminism and composition, but its consequences for me extend far beyond my academic work alone. The ongoing conversations that began with this research pulled me back to what I think of as my feminist roots, somehow lost after I began my Ph.D. work, and encouraged me to reconnect my personal and professional identities as I have continued to evolve as a feminist teacher and scholar. From the first week of observing *and* participating with Barbara and her students as they wrestled with questions of identity and difference, I went back to my own classes with new questions and perspectives. My observation of her literature class prompted me to engage students in my writing and rhetoric classes in examining their own social locations and the material and rhetorical constructions of difference(s) they encounter. Barbara has listened to me as I have worked through my ideas and has supported me as I have encountered the conflicts these shifts in my teaching inevitably brought about. Barbara's friendship has changed me, because Barbara allowed me into her life through our friendship, allowed me to continue to see and attempt to more fully understand her struggles as a lesbian teacher, and allowed me to accompany her as she evolved as a teacher and took on new roles in the university. Being a participant-observer of her life also made me a more reflective observer of my own life and my beliefs as a feminist. Her growing activism in the university and in the community for lesbian, gay, and transgendered students and for people with disabilities has challenged me to continue to translate my academic feminism more actively into my life and to help students find ways to do so as well.

Barbara: When Joy asked to do a participant-observation study in my classroom, I was pleased—mostly, I think, because it seemed to be an external recognition of my teaching, always the heart of my intellectual life. However, I could not know then how life-changing the experience would be. To be able to discuss the dynamics of a particular class period with Joy was exhilarating. I would long to rush out of class to her office and ask her immediately, "What was going on there?" or "Why do you think the discussion took that turn?" Although we did have such conversations, even more important was Joy's observation that there was much conflict in the class within and between students, more than I would have liked to admit. One of the most central conflicts for me was that a lesbian student felt somewhat silenced. While I was out to this student and she to me, I was not yet willing to be out in class or very out about the inclusion of lesbian works. Seeing this reflected in Joy's article made me uncomfortable. It is not accidental that I used the feminist teaching group that Joy and I helped found to talk about these issues and to serve as commentators on an article I wrote in the summer of 1990, "Being an I-Witness: My Life as a Lesbian Teacher." It is also not accidental that, after years of agonizing over the decision, I came out in class for the first time in the spring of 1990 and by the next year was coming out during the first week of class to every class I taught in a letter introducing myself. For me, Joy was a companion on the journey, also an I-witness and an eye-witness. In the years since Joy sat in on my class, our friendship and conversations about teaching have challenged and emboldened me to push myself in my teaching even more—for example, by teaching writing by women with disabilities and including transgendered authors in my women's literature classes. It is also not accidental that I have written and published about both experiences. For me, there has been something powerful about having my work and my self named and visible. Although we were not collaborators on the original article, Joy and I have been collaborators ever since, accompanying each other on our journeys as feminist academics. Having a companion, knowing I was not alone, has made all the difference for me.

WORK CITED

DiBernard, Barbara. "Being an I-Witness: My Life as a Lesbian Teacher." *Private Voices, Public Lives: Women Speak on the Literary Life.* Ed. Nancy Owen Nelson. Denton, TX: U of North Texas P, 1995. 99–110.

PART THREE

Gender and Forms of Writing

Part Three: Introduction

LANCE MASSEY

As feminism established itself in composition, feminist scholars began investigating the ways that academic writing, both as taught in composition classes and as represented in our professional literature, privileged "masculine" ways of knowing and communicating. Academic discourse was shown to rely on agonistic rhetoric; valorize impersonal, universalizing logic; privilege fixed, closed meanings; and construct "the author" as a unified, solitary "I." Much of feminist composition has thus devoted itself to challenging these traditional forms of academic writing. The essays that follow represent some of the most interesting and important of these challenges.

Elizabeth Flynn draws on feminist theory to show that women and men write differently while making the larger argument that such feminist insights can shed light on composition's disciplinary problems. Flynn looks at four student essays—two by female writers and two by male writers—and finds that the essays written by women "are stories of interaction, of connection, or of frustrated connection" (275), while those written by men "stress individuation . . . and conclude by emphasizing separation rather than integration" (276). These differences, Flynn argues, suggest that contemporary process models are "better suited to describing men's ways of composing than to describing women's" (279). Since its publication, "Composing as a Woman" has been criticized for being too essentialist, for suggesting that all women share a common essence. In a reflection composed for this collection, Flynn addresses such arguments, maintaining that composition's historical moment in 1988 called for a clear, strong claim and asking that the essay be read in that context.

Andrea Lunsford and Lisa Ede also suggest a link between writing practices and gender. When they originally began their study of collaborative writing, they "expected (or, more accurately, hoped) to find that collaboration offered a mode that would serve a postmodern conception of writing" (284). What they found instead were multiple modes of collaboration, two of which—the "hierarchical" and the "dialogic"—interested them "as women and as collaborative writers" (284). The hierarchical mode, which they associate with the masculine, is writing that is often parceled out or delegated by a superior and usually signifies bureaucratic writing. It values efficiency, seeing "multiple voices" and "shifting authority" (284) as problems. The dialogic, or feminine, mode is writing that values fluidity of meaning, openness, and "creative tension" (285) and sees the writing process as producing rather than discovering knowledge. According to Lunsford and Ede, this dialogic mode has the potential to challenge "phallogocentric, subject-centered discourse" (287). Moreover, while such writing does not constitute a completely "new key" in composition, Lunsford and Ede suggest that our challenge is to "hear within that key the full texture of layered, polyphonic chords" (289).

Susan Jarratt notes early feminist composition's preference for expressivist pedagogy, which she would supplant with a social constructionist model in which conflict is not to be avoided but is, rather, an important means of articulating and debating the ethics of diverse discourse practices. Drawing on sophistic rhetoric, Jarratt suggests that expressivist composition instructors "spend too little time helping their students learn how to argue about public issues—making the turn from the personal back out to the public" (307). This public vision, moreover, helps students and feminist scholars alike "locate personal experience in historical and social contexts" (307), a process that inevitably produces awareness of difference and even conflict. In her reflective essay, Jarratt, like Flynn, addresses "misreadings" of "The Case for Conflict," noting that a teacher's job as she articulated it was not to be combative or confrontational but, rather, to "help writers excavate" their differences—a process she knew could lead to conflict.

In contrast to Jarratt, Catherine Lamb repudiates conflict in favor of a "maternal" view of argument that sees power "not as a quality to exercise on others, but as something which can energize, enabling competence and thus reducing hierarchy" (330). She says that adapting the oral strategies of negotiation and mediation, which are "cooperative approaches to resolving conflicts" (333), to writing can help us avoid the divisiveness of monologic argument, which emphasizes one's own interests and acknowledges opposition only to refute it. Monologic argument, she contends, while still a necessary part of composition, should be "a means, not an end," with the end of rhetoric being "a resolution of conflict that is fair to both sides" (326). The goals of Lamb's feminist rhetoric are to see knowledge as collaborative, cooperative, and constructed; to see written argument as a give-and-take process rather than a monologue; and to see power as "mutually enabling" (336).

Seeking her own enabling strategies, Lillian Bridwell-Bowles argues for the importance of experimental writing, both for students and for scholars. She contends that experimentation with new forms of expression for attitudes and thoughts that cannot be expressed in current forms allows rhetorical invention to be expanded and new meanings to be generated in academic discourse. Moreover, allowing students to write in nontraditional forms, perhaps mixing personal and academic voices or even writing entirely in questions, lets them develop a critical, "dialogical" relationship between formal academic knowledge and the diverse knowledges they bring to the classroom. Bridwell-Bowles narrates her own movement away from exclusively empiricist inquiry into more flexible, polysemous, humanistic modes in search of "a less rigid methodological framework, a writing process that allows [her] to combine hypothesizing with reporting data, to use patterns of writing that allow for multiple truths" (341). In doing so, she addresses the dilemma of the prison of patriarchal language, not by rejecting such language outright but by hypothesizing "powerfully diverse" theories of language that may, as yet, be unimaginable (345).

Terry Zawacki puts into practice many of the challenges posed by the essays in this section. In the "different voices" of reflective personal narrative and academic exposition, Zawacki questions the very distinction between personal and expository writing, enacting the resistance to conventional academic forms for which she calls and directly confronting the hegemony of expository academic writing. She asks, "Is it possible to challenge the traditional academic hierarchy which privileges expository prose by rejecting the distinction between personal writing and expository writing? By showing that genre boundaries themselves are as questionable as gender boundaries and that all writing is a means of creating a self, not for expressing a self that already exists?" (365). The language of this essay—simultaneously personal, academic, figurative, direct, literal, and metaphorical—supports Zawacki's argument that when we write we represent (our)selves and, perhaps more important, keenly demonstrates one of "the possibilities for representing a gendered self in writing" (365).

Finally, Donna LeCourt and Luann Barnes also advocate multivocal texts and explore how they can intervene in the "gendered power relations of academic discourse." Hypertext, they argue, offers a particularly good opportunity for writers to represent the multiple—especially the traditionally marginalized—positions a writer can adopt as well as explore how those positions are functions of context and community. As LeCourt and Barnes write, "hypertext . . . incites the writer's awareness of her multiplicity, thus making a feminist textual politic easier to enact" (371). While they acknowledge the "limitations for hypertext's ability to enact a textual politic, including its inability to escape the logocentricism of writing" as well as its inability to guarantee "an awareness of multivocality in a reader" (380–1), LeCourt and Barnes nevertheless contend that, with appropriate pedagogical support such as "continual peer review of the hypertexts [students] are creating" (381), hypertext carries the "potential for social change and personal empowerment" (382).

These essays speak and respond to—resonate and conflict with—each other and the others in this collection in complex ways. To many, for example, Ede and Lunsford's literal focus on writing with multiple authors will connect in more interesting ways to LeCourt and Barnes's claim that authors are *always* multiple than it does to Jarratt's endorsement of conflict. And how are we to understand Lamb's resistance to conflict and Jarratt's advocacy of it as *both* significant contributions to feminist composition when they occupy the same historical moment? How, that is, can we resolve the conflicts inherent in a tradition that repudiates divisive rhetoric even as it remains in many ways (and purposefully, necessarily) divided from the so-called mainstream of composition? These questions speak to a key tension that informs all politics of resistance and difference: How do we empower, when structures of power form precisely that which is to be resisted or altered? Does experimental, personal, multivoiced writing really support marginalized writers, or does it simply establish different exclusionary, elitist standards for writers to meet? What does it mean to write in ways that challenge, subvert, and liberate in a larger social context that so overwhelmingly privileges traditional forms of writing? These essays call for rereading and revision, not only of conventional conceptions of writing, but also of the inevitably partial and interested interpretations that helped shape this collection. As long as we commit ourselves to such rereadings, the conversations represented here will never be over, their histories never fixed.

14   *Composing as a Woman*

ELIZABETH A. FLYNN

I t is not easy to think like a woman in a man's world, in the world of the professions; yet the capacity to do that is a strength which we can try to help our students develop. To think like a woman in a man's world means thinking critically, refusing to accept the givens, making connections between facts and ideas which men have left unconnected. It means remembering that every mind resides in a body; remaining accountable to the female bodies in which we live; constantly retesting given hypotheses against lived experience. It means a constant critique of language, for as Wittgenstein (no feminist) observed, "The limits of my language are the limits of my world." And it means that most difficult thing of all: listening and watching in art and literature, in the social sciences, in all the descriptions we are given of the world, for silences, the absences, the nameless, the unspoken, the encoded— for there we will find the true knowledge of women. And in breaking those silences, naming ourselves, uncovering the hidden, making ourselves present, we begin to define a reality which resonates to *us*, which affirms *our* being, which allows the woman teacher and the woman student alike to take ourselves, and each other, seriously: meaning, to begin taking charge of our lives.

—ADRIENNE RICH, "TAKING WOMEN STUDENTS SERIOUSLY"

The emerging field of composition studies could be described as a feminization of our previous conceptions of how writers write and how writing should be taught.[1] In exploring the nature of the writing process, composition specialists expose the limitations of previous product-oriented approaches by demystifying the product and in so doing empowering developing writers and readers. Rather than enshrining the text in its final form, they demonstrate that the works produced by established authors are often the result of an extended, frequently enormously frustrating process and that creativity is

From *College Composition and Communication* 39 (1988): 423–35.

an activity that results from experience and hard work rather than a mysterious gift reserved for a select few. In a sense, composition specialists replace the figure of the authoritative father with an image of a nurturing mother. Powerfully present in the work of composition researchers and theorists is the ideal of a committed teacher concerned about the growth and maturity of her students who provides feedback on ungraded drafts, reads journals, and attempts to tease out meaning from the seeming incoherence of student language. The field's foremothers come to mind—Janet Emig, Mina Shaughnessy, Ann Berthoff, Win Horner, Maxine Hairston, Shirley Heath, Nancy Martin, Linda Flower, Andrea Lunsford, Sondra Perl, Nancy Sommers, Marion Crowhurst, Lisa Ede. I'll admit the term foremother seems inappropriate as some of these women are still in their thirties and forties—we are speaking here of a very young field. Still, invoking their names suggests that we are also dealing with a field that, from the beginning, has welcomed contributions from women—indeed, has been shaped by women.

The work of male composition researchers and theorists has also contributed significantly to the process of feminization described above. James Britton, for instance, reverses traditional hierarchies by privileging private expression over public transaction, process over product. In arguing that writing for the self is the matrix out of which all forms of writing develop, he valorizes an activity and a mode of expression that have previously been undervalued or invisible, much as feminist literary critics have argued that women's letters and diaries are legitimate literary forms and should be studied and taught alongside more traditional genres. His work has had an enormous impact on the way writing is taught on the elementary and high school levels and in the university, not only in English courses but throughout the curriculum. Writing-Across-the-Curriculum Programs aim to transform pedagogical practices in all disciplines, even those where patriarchal attitudes toward authority are most deeply rooted.

FEMINIST STUDIES AND COMPOSITION STUDIES

Feminist inquiry and composition studies have much in common. After all, feminist researchers and scholars and composition specialists are usually in the same department and sometimes teach the same courses. Not surprisingly, there have been wonderful moments when feminists have expressed their commitment to the teaching of writing. Florence Howe's essay, "Identity and Expression: A Writing Course for Women," for example, published in *College English* in 1971, describes her use of journals in a writing course designed to empower women. Adrienne Rich's essay, " 'When We Dead Awaken': Writing as Re-Vision," politicizes and expands our conception of revision, emphasizing that taking another look at the texts we have generated necessitates revising our cultural assumptions as well.

There have also been wonderful moments when composition specialists have recognized that the marginality of the field of composition studies is linked in important ways to the political marginality of its constituents, many of whom are women who teach part-time. Maxine Hairston, in "Breaking Our Bonds and Reaffirming Our Connections," a slightly revised version of her Chair's address at the 1985 convention of the Conference on College Composition and Communication, draws an analogy between the plight of composition specialists and the plight of many women. For both, their worst problems begin at home and hence are immediate and daily. Both, too, often have complex psychological bonds to the people who frequently are their adversaries (273).

For the most part, though, the fields of feminist studies and composition studies have not engaged each other in a serious or systematic way. The major journals in the field of composition studies do not often include articles addressing feminist issues, and panels on feminism are infrequent at the Conference on College Composition and Communication.[2] As a result, the parallels between feminist studies and composition studies have not been delineated, and the feminist critique that has enriched such diverse fields as linguistics, reading, literary criticism, psychology, sociology, anthropology, religion, and science has had little impact on our models of the composing process or on our understanding of how written language abilities are acquired. We have not examined our research methods or research samples to see if they are androcentric. Nor have we attempted to determine just what it means to compose as a woman.

Feminist research and theory emphasize that males and females differ in their developmental processes and in their interactions with others. They emphasize, as well, that these differences are a result of an imbalance in the social order, of the dominance of men over women. They argue that men have chronicled our historical narratives and defined our fields of inquiry. Women's perspectives have been suppressed, silenced, marginalized, written out of what counts as authoritative knowledge. Difference is erased in a desire to universalize. Men become the standard against which women are judged.

A feminist approach to composition studies would focus on questions of difference and dominance in written language. Do males and females compose differently? Do they acquire language in different ways? Do research methods and research samples in composition studies reflect a male bias? I do not intend to tackle all of these issues. My approach here is a relatively modest one. I will survey recent feminist research on gender differences in social and psychological development, and I will show how this research and theory may be used in examining student writing, thus suggesting directions that a feminist investigation of composition might take.

Gender Differences in Social and Psychological Development

Especially relevant to a feminist consideration of student writing are Nancy Chodorow's *The Reproduction of Mothering,* Carol Gilligan's *In a Different Voice,* and Mary Belenky, Blythe Clinchy, Nancy Goldberger, and Jill Tarule's *Women's Ways of Knowing.* All three books suggest that women and men have different conceptions of self and different modes of interaction with others as a result of their different experiences, especially their early relationship with their primary parent, their mother.

Chodorow's book, published in 1978, is an important examination of what she calls the "psychoanalysis and the sociology of gender," which in turn influenced Gilligan's *In a Different Voice* and Belenky et al.'s *Women's Ways of Knowing*. Chodorow tells us in her preface that her book originated when a feminist group she was affiliated with "wondered what it meant that women parented women." She argues that girls and boys develop different relational capacities and senses of self as a result of growing up in a family in which women mother. Because all children identify first with their mother, a girl's gender and gender role identification processes are continuous with her earliest identifications whereas a boy's are not. The boy gives up, in addition to his oedipal and preoedipal attachment to his mother, his primary identification with her. The more general identification processes for both males and females also follow this pattern. Chodorow says:

> Girls' identification processes, then, are more continuously embedded in and mediated by their ongoing relationship with their mother. They develop through and stress particularistic and affective relationships to others. A boy's identification processes are not likely to be so embedded in or mediated by a real affective relation to his father. At the same time, he tends to deny identification with and relationship to his mother and reject what he takes to be the feminine world; masculinity is defined as much negatively as positively. Masculine identification processes stress differentiation from others, the denial of affective relation, and categorical universalistic components of the masculine role. Feminine identification processes are relational, whereas masculine identification processes tend to deny relationship. (176)

Carol Gilligan's *In a Different Voice,* published in 1982, builds on Chodorow's findings, focusing especially, though, on differences in the ways in which males and females speak about moral problems. According to Gilligan, women tend to define morality in terms of conflicting responsibilities rather than competing rights, requiring for their resolution a mode of thinking that is contextual and narrative rather than formal and abstract (19). Men, in contrast, equate morality and fairness and tie moral development to the understanding of rights and rules (19). Gilligan uses the metaphors of the web and the ladder to illustrate these distinctions. The web suggests interconnectedness as well as entrapment; the ladder suggests an achievement-orientation as well as individualistic and hierarchical thinking. Gilligan's study aims to correct the inadequacies of Lawrence Kohlberg's delineation of the stages of moral development. Kohlberg's study included only male subjects, and his categories reflect his decidedly male orientation. For him, the highest stages of moral development derive from a reflective understanding of human rights (19).

Belenky, Clinchy, Goldberger, and Tarule, in *Women's Ways of Knowing,* acknowledge their debt to Gilligan, though their main concern is intellectual rather than moral development. Like Gilligan, they recognize that male expe-

rience has served as the model in defining processes of intellectual maturation. The mental processes that are involved in considering the abstract and
the impersonal have been labeled "thinking" and are attributed primarily to
men, while those that deal with the personal and interpersonal fall under the
rubric of "emotions" and are largely relegated to women. The particular study
they chose to examine and revise is William Perry's *Forms of Intellectual and
Ethical Development in the College Years* (1970). While Perry did include some
women subjects in his study, only the interviews with men were used in illustrating and validating his scheme of intellectual and ethical development.
When Perry assessed women's development on the basis of the categories he
developed, the women were found to conform to the patterns he had
observed in the male data. Thus, his work reveals what women have in common with men but was poorly designed to uncover those themes that might
be more prominent among women. *Women's Ways of Knowing* focuses on
"what else women might have to say about the development of their minds
and on alternative routes that are sketchy or missing in Perry's version" (9).

Belenky et al. examined the transcripts of interviews with 135 women
from a variety of backgrounds and of different ages and generated categories
that are suited for describing the stages of women's intellectual development.
They found that the quest for self and voice plays a central role in transformations of women's ways of knowing. Silent women have little awareness of
their intellectual capacities. They live—selfless and voiceless—at the behest
of those around them. External authorities know the truth and are all-
powerful. At the positions of received knowledge and procedural knowledge,
other voices and external truths prevail. Sense of self is embedded either in
external definitions and roles or in identifications with institutions, disciplines, and methods. A sense of authority arises primarily through identification with the power of a group and its agreed-upon ways for knowing.
Women at this stage of development have no sense of an authentic or unique
voice, little awareness of a centered self. At the position of subjective knowledge, women turn away from others and any external authority. They have
not yet acquired a public voice or public authority, though. Finally, women at
the phase of constructed knowledge begin an effort to reclaim the self by
attempting to integrate knowledge they feel intuitively with knowledge they
have learned from others.

STUDENT WRITING

If women and men differ in their relational capacities and in their moral and
intellectual development, we would expect to find manifestations of these differences in the student papers we encounter in our first-year composition
courses. The student essays I will describe here are narrative descriptions of
learning experiences produced in the first of a two-course sequence required
of first-year students at Michigan Tech. I've selected the four because they
invite commentary from the perspective of the material discussed above. The
narratives of the female students are stories of interaction, of connection, or of

frustrated connection. The narratives of the male students are stories of achievement, of separation, or of frustrated achievement.

Kim's essay describes a dreamlike experience in which she and her high school girlfriends connected with each other and with nature as a result of a balloon ride they decided to take one summer Sunday afternoon as a way of relieving boredom. From the start, Kim emphasizes communion and tranquility: "It was one of those Sunday afternoons when the sun shines brightly and a soft warm breeze blows gently. A perfect day for a long drive on a country road with my favorite friends." This mood is intensified as they ascend in the balloon: "Higher and higher we went, until the view was overpowering. What once was a warm breeze turned quickly into a cool crisp wind. A feeling of freedom and serenity overtook us as we drifted along slowly." The group felt as if they were "just suspended there on a string, with time non-existent." The experience made them contemplative, and as they drove quietly home, "each one of us collected our thoughts, and to this day we still reminisce about that Sunday afternoon." The experience solidified relationships and led to the formation of a close bond that was renewed every time the day was recollected.

The essay suggests what Chodorow calls relational identification processes. The members of the group are described as being in harmony with themselves and with the environment. There is no reference to competition or discord. The narrative also suggests a variation on what Belenky et al. call "connected knowing," a form of procedural knowledge that makes possible the most desirable form of knowing, constructed knowledge. Connected knowing is rooted in empathy for others and is intensely personal. Women who are connected knowers are able to detach themselves from the relationships and institutions to which they have been subordinated and begin to trust their own intuitions. The women in the narrative were connected doers rather than connected knowers. They went off on their own, left their families and teachers behind (it was summer vacation, after all), and gave themselves over to a powerful shared experience. The adventure was, for the most part, a silent one but did lead to satisfying talk.

Kathy also describes an adventure away from home, but hers was far less satisfying, no doubt because it involved considerably more risk. In her narrative she makes the point that "foreign countries can be frightening" by focusing on a situation in which she and three classmates, two females and a male, found themselves at a train station in Germany separated from the others because they had gotten off to get some refreshments and the train had left without them. She says:

> This left the four of us stranded in an unfamiliar station. Ed was the only person in our group that could speak German fluently, but he still didn't know what to do. Sue got hysterical and Laura tried to calm her down. I stood there stunned. We didn't know what to do.

What they did was turn to Ed, whom Kathy describes as "the smartest one in our group." He told them to get on a train that was on the same track as the original. Kathy realized, though, after talking to some passengers, that they were on the wrong train and urged her classmates to get off. She says,

I almost panicked. When I convinced the other three we were on the wrong train we opened the doors. As we were getting off, one of the conductors started yelling at us in German. It didn't bother me too much because I couldn't understand what he was saying. One thing about trains in Europe is that they are always on schedule. I think we delayed that train about a minute or two.

In deciding which train to board after getting off the wrong one, they deferred to Ed's judgment once again, but this time they got on the right train. Kathy concludes, "When we got off the train everyone was waiting. It turned out we arrived thirty minutes later than our original train. I was very relieved to see everyone. It was a very frightening experience and I will never forget it."

In focusing on her fears of separation, Kathy reveals her strong need for connection, for affiliation. Her story, like Kim's, emphasizes the importance of relationships, though in a different way. She reveals that she had a strong need to feel part of a group and no desire to rebel, to prove her independence, to differentiate herself from others. This conception of self was a liability as well as a strength in the sense that she became overly dependent on the male authority figure in the group, whom she saw as smarter and more competent than herself. In Belenky et al.'s terms, Kathy acted as if other voices and external truths were more powerful than her own. She did finally speak and act, though, taking it on herself to find out if they were on the right train and ushering the others off when she discovered they were not. She was clearly moving toward the development of an authentic voice and a way of knowing that integrates intuition with authoritative knowledge. After all, she was the real hero of the incident.

The men's narratives stress individuation rather than connection. They are stories of individual achievement or frustrated achievement and conclude by emphasizing separation rather than integration or reintegration into a community. Jim wrote about his "Final Flight," the last cross-country flight required for his pilot's license. That day, everything seemed to go wrong. First, his flight plan had a mistake in it that took 1½ hours to correct. As a result, he left his hometown 2 hours behind schedule. Then the weather deteriorated, forcing him to fly as low as a person can safely fly, with the result that visibility was very poor. He landed safely at his first destination but flew past the second because he was enjoying the view too much. He says:

Then I was off again south bound for Benton Harbor. On the way south along the coast of Lake Michigan the scenery was a beautiful sight. This relieved some of the pressures and made me look forward to the rest of the flight. It was really nice to see the ice floes break away from the shore. While enjoying the view of a power plant on the shore of Lake Michigan I discovered I had flown past the airport.

He finally landed and took off again, but shortly thereafter had to confront darkness, a result of his being behind schedule. He says:

The sky turned totally black by the time I was half-way home. This meant flying in the dark which I had only done once before. Flying in the dark was also illegal for me to do at this time. One thing that made flying at night nice was that you could see lights that were over ninety miles away.

Jim does not emphasize his fear, despite the fact that his situation was more threatening than the one Kathy described, and his reference to his enjoyment of the scenery suggests that his anxiety was not paralyzing or debilitating. At times, his solitary flight was clearly as satisfying as Kim's communal one. When he focuses on the difficulties he encountered, he speaks only of his "problems" and "worries" and concludes that the day turned out to be "long and trying." He sums up his experience as follows: "That day I will long remember for both its significance in my goal in getting my pilot's license and all the problems or worries that it caused me during the long and problem-ridden flight." He emerges the somewhat shaken hero of his adventure; he has achieved his goal in the face of adversity. Significantly, he celebrates his return home by having a bite to eat at McDonald's by himself. His adventure does not end with a union or reunion with others.

Jim's story invites interpretation in the context of Chodorow's claims about male interactional patterns. Chodorow says that the male, in order to feel himself adequately masculine, must distinguish and differentiate himself from others. Jim's adventure was an entirely solitary one. It was also goal-directed—he wanted to obtain his pilot's license and, presumably, prove his competence to himself and others. His narrative calls into question, though, easy equations of abstract reasoning and impersonality with male modes of learning since Jim was clearly as capable as Kim of experiencing moments of exultation, of communion with nature.

Joe's narrative of achievement is actually a story of frustrated achievement, of conflicting attitudes toward an ethic of hard work and sacrifice to achieve a goal. When he was in high school, his father drove him twenty miles to swim practice and twenty miles home every Tuesday through Friday night between October and March so he could practice for the swim team. He hated this routine and hated the Saturday morning swim meets even more but continued because he thought his parents, especially his father, wanted him to. He says, "I guess it was all for them, the cold workouts, the evening practices, the weekend meets. I had to keep going for them even though I hated it." Once he realized he was going through his agony for his parents rather than for himself, though, he decided to quit and was surprised to find that his parents supported him. Ultimately, though, he regretted his decision. He says:

> As it turns out now, I wish I had stuck with it. I really had a chance to go somewhere with my talent. I see kids my age who stuck with something for a long time and I envy them for their determination. I wish I had met up to the challenge of sticking with my swimming, because I could have been very good if I would have had their determination.

Joe is motivated to pursue swimming because he thinks his father will be disappointed if he gives it up. His father's presumed hold on him is clearly tenuous, however, because once Joe realizes that he is doing it for him rather than for himself, he quits. Finally, though, it is his gender role identification, his socialization into a male role and a male value system, that allows him to look back on his decision with regret. In college, he has become a competitor, an achiever. He now sees value in the long and painful practices, in a single-minded determination to succeed. The narrative reminds us of Chodorow's point that masculine identification is predominantly a gender role identification rather than identification with a particular parent.

I am hardly claiming that the four narratives are neat illustrations of the feminist positions discussed above. For one thing, those positions are rich in contradiction and complexity and defy easy illustration. For another, the narratives themselves are as often characterized by inconsistency and contradiction as by a univocality of theme and tone. Kathy is at once dependent and assertive; Joe can't quite decide if he should have been rebellious or disciplined. Nor am I claiming that what I have found here are characteristic patterns of male and female student writing. I would need a considerably larger and more representative sample to make such a claim hold. I might note, though, that I had little difficulty identifying essays that revealed patterns of difference among the twenty-four papers I had to choose from, and I could easily have selected others. Sharon, for instance, described her class trip to Chicago, focusing especially on the relationship she and her classmates were able to establish with her advisor. Diane described "An Unwanted Job" that she seemed unable to quit despite unpleasant working conditions. Mike, like Diane, was dissatisfied with his job, but he expressed his dissatisfaction and was fired. The frightening experience Russ described resulted from his failed attempt to give his car a tune-up; the radiator hose burst, and he found himself in the hospital recovering from third-degree burns. These are stories of relatedness or entanglement; of separation or frustrated achievement.

The description of the student essays is not meant to demonstrate the validity of feminist scholarship but to suggest, instead, that questions raised by feminist researchers and theorists do have a bearing on composition studies and should be pursued. We ought not assume that males and females use language in identical ways or represent the world in a similar fashion. And if their writing strategies and patterns of representation do differ, then ignoring those differences almost certainly means a suppression of women's separate ways of thinking and writing. Our models of the composing process are quite possibly better suited to describing men's ways of composing than to describing women's.[3]

PEDAGOGICAL STRATEGIES

The classroom provides an opportunity for exploring questions about gender differences in language use. Students, I have found, are avid inquirers into their own language processes. An approach I have had success with is to make the question of gender difference in behavior and language use the subject to be investigated in class. In one honors section of first-year English, for instance, course reading included selections from Mary Anne Ferguson's *Images of Women in Literature,* Gilligan's *In a Different Voice,* Alice Walker's *Meridian,* and James Joyce's *A Portrait of the Artist as a Young Man.* Students were also required to keep a reading journal and to submit two formal papers.

The first was a description of people they know in order to arrive at generalizations about gender differences in behavior, the second a comparison of some aspect of the Walker and Joyce novels in the light of our class discussions.

During class meetings we shared journal entries, discussed the assigned literature, and self-consciously explored our own reading, writing, and speaking behaviors. In one session, for instance, we shared retellings of Irwin Shaw's "The Girls in Their Summer Dresses," an especially appropriate story since it describes the interaction of a husband and wife as they attempt to deal with the husband's apparently chronic habit of girl-watching. Most of the women were sympathetic to the female protagonist, and several males clearly identified strongly with the male protagonist.

The students reacted favorably to the course. They found Gilligan's book to be challenging, and they enjoyed the heated class discussions. The final journal entry of one of the strongest students in the class, Dorothy, suggests the nature of her development over the ten-week period:

> As this is sort of the wrap-up of what I've learned or how I feel about the class, I'll try to relate this entry to my first one on gender differences.
>
> I'm not so sure that men and women are so similar anymore, as I said in the first entry. The reactions in class especially make me think this. The men were so hostile toward Gilligan's book! I took no offense at it, but then again I'm not a man. I must've even overlooked the parts where she offended the men!
>
> Another thing really bothered me. One day after class, I heard two of the men talking in the hall about how you just have to be really careful about what you say in HU 101H about women, etc. *Why* do they have to be careful?! What did these two *really* want to say? That was pretty disturbing.
>
> However, I do still believe that MTU (or most any college actually) does bring out more similarities than differences. But the differences are still there—I know that.

Dorothy has begun to suspect that males and females read differently, and she has begun to suspect that they talk among themselves differently than they do in mixed company. The reading, writing, and discussing in the course have clearly alerted her to the possibility that gender affects the way in which readers, writers, and speakers use language.

This approach works especially well with honors students. I use somewhat different reading and writing assignments with non-honors students. In one class, for instance, I replaced the Gilligan book with an essay by Dale Spender on conversational patterns in high school classrooms. Students wrote a paper defending or refuting the Spender piece on the basis of their experiences in their own high schools. I have also devised ways of addressing feminist issues in composition courses in which the focus is not explicitly on gender differences. In a course designed to introduce students to fundamentals of research, for instance, students read Marge Piercy's *Woman on the Edge of Time* and did research on questions stimulated by it. They then shared their findings with the entire class in oral presentations. The approach led to wonderful papers on and discussions of the treatment of women in mental institutions, discrimination against minority women, and the ways in which technology can liberate women from oppressive roles.

––––––––

I return now to my title and to the epigraph that introduces my essay. First, what does it mean to "compose as a woman"? Although the title invokes Jonathan Culler's "Reading as a Woman," a chapter in *On Deconstruction,* I do not mean to suggest by it that I am committed fully to Culler's deconstructive position. Culler maintains that "to read as a woman is to avoid reading as a man, to identify the specific defenses and distortions of male readings and provide correctives" (54). He concludes:

> For a woman to read as a woman is not to repeat an identity or an experience that is given but to play a role she constructs with reference to her identity as a woman, which is also a construct, so that the series can continue: a woman reading as a woman reading as a woman. The noncoincidence reveals an interval, a division within woman or within any reading subject and the "experience" of that subject. (64)

Culler is certainly correct that women often read as men and that they have to be encouraged to defend against this form of alienation. The strategy he suggests is almost entirely reactive, though. To read as a woman is to avoid reading as a man, to be alerted to the pitfalls of men's ways of reading.[4] Rich, too, warns of the dangers of immasculation, of identifying against oneself and learning to think like a man, and she, too, emphasizes the importance of critical activity on the part of the woman student—refusing to accept the givens of our culture, making connections between facts and ideas which men have left unconnected. She is well aware that thinking as a woman involves active construction, the recreation of one's identity. But she also sees value in recovering women's lived experience. In fact, she suggests that women maintain a critical posture in order to get in touch with that experience—to name it, to uncover that which is hidden, to make present that which has been absent. Her approach is active rather than reactive. Women's experience is not entirely a distorted version of male reality, it is not entirely elusive, and it is worthy of recuperation. We must alert our women students to the dangers of immasculation and provide them with a critical perspective. But we must also encourage them to become self-consciously aware of what their experience in the world has been and how this experience is related to the politics of gender. Then we must encourage our women students to write from the power of that experience.

NOTES

1. I received invaluable feedback on drafts of this essay from Carol Berkenkotter, Art Young, Marilyn Cooper, John Willinsky, Diane Shoos, John Flynn, Richard Gebhardt, and three anonymous *CCC* reviewers.

2. The 1988 Conference on College Composition and Communication was a notable exception. It had a record number of panels on feminist or gender-related issues and a number of

sessions devoted to political concerns. I should add, too, that an exception to the generalization that feminist studies and composition studies have not confronted each other is Cynthia Caywood and Gillian Overing's very useful anthology, *Teaching Writing: Pedagogy, Gender, and Equity*. In their introduction to the book, Caywood and Overing note the striking parallels between writing theory and feminist theory. They conclude, "[T]he process model, insofar as it facilitates and legitimizes the fullest expression of the individual voice, is compatible with the feminist re-visioning of hierarchy, if not essential to it" (xiv). Pamela Annas, in her essay, "Silences: Feminist Language Research and the Teaching of Writing," describes a course she teaches at the University of Massachusetts at Boston, entitled "Writing as Women." In the course, she focuses on the question of silence—"what kinds of silence there are; the voices inside you that tell you to be quiet, the voices outside you that drown you out or politely dismiss what you say or do not understand you, the silence inside you that avoids saying anything important even to yourself, internal and external forms of censorship, and the stress that it produces" (3–4). Carol A. Stanger in "The Sexual Politics of the One-to-One Tutorial Approach and Collaborative Learning" argues that the one-to-one tutorial is essentially hierarchical and hence a male mode of reaching whereas collaborative learning is female and relational rather than hierarchical. She uses Gilligan's images of the ladder and the web to illustrate her point. Elisabeth Daeumer and Sandra Runzo suggest that the teaching of writing is comparable to the activity of mothering in that it is a form of "women's work." Mothers socialize young children to insure that they become acceptable citizens, and teachers' work, like the work of mothers, is usually devalued (45–46).

3. It should be clear by now that my optimistic claim at the outset of the essay that the field of composition studies has feminized our conception of written communication needs qualification: I have already mentioned that the field has developed, for the most part, independent of feminist studies and as a result has not explored written communication in the context of women's special needs and problems. Also, feminist inquiry is beginning to reveal that work in cognate fields that have influenced the development of composition studies is androcentric. For an exploration of the androcentrism of theories of the reading process see Patrocinio P. Schweickart, "Reading Ourselves: Toward a Feminist Theory of Reading."

4. Elaine Showalter, in "Reading as a Woman: Jonathan Culler and the Deconstruction of Feminist Criticism," argues chat "Culler's deconstructionist priorities lead him to overstate the essentialist dilemma of defining the *woman* reader, when in most cases what is intended and implied is a *feminist* reader" (126).

WORKS CITED

Annas, Pamela J. "Silences: Feminist Language Research and the Teaching of Writing." *Teaching Writing: Pedagogy, Gender, and Equity*. Ed. Cynthia L. Caywood and Gillian R. Overing. Albany: State U of New York P, 1987. 3–17.

Belenky, Mary Field, et al. *Women's Ways of Knowing: The Development of Self, Voice, and Mind*. New York: Basic Books, 1986.

Britton, James, et al. *The Development of Writing Abilities*. London: Macmillan Education, 1975. (11–18).

Caywood, Cynthia L., and Gillian R. Overing. Introduction. *Teaching Writing: Pedagogy, Gender, and Equity*. Ed. Cynthia L. Caywood and Gillian R. Overing. Albany: State U of New York P, 1987. xi–xvi.

Chodorow, Nancy. *The Reproduction of Mothering: Psychoanalysis and the Sociology of Gender*. Berkeley: U of California P, 1978.

Culler, Jonathan. *On Deconstruction: Theory and Criticism After Structuralism*. Ithaca: Cornell UP, 1982.

Daeumer, Elisabeth, and Sandra Runzo. "Transforming the Composition Classroom." *Teaching Writing: Pedagogy, Gender, and Equity*. Ed. Cynthia L. Caywood and Gillian R. Overing. Albany: State U of New York P, 1987. 45–62.

Gilligan, Carol. *In a Different Voice: Psychological Theory and Womens Development*. Cambridge: Harvard UP, 1982.

Hairston, Maxine. "Breaking Our Bonds and Reaffirming Our Connections." *College Composition and Communication* 36 (October 1985): 272–82.

Howe, Florence. "Identity and Expression: A Writing Course for Women." *College English* 32 (May 1971): 863–71. Rpt. in Howe, *Myths of Coeducation: Selected Essays, 1964–1983*. Bloomington: Indiana UP, 1984. 28–37.

Kohlberg, Lawrence. "Moral Stages and Moralization: The Cognitive-Developmental Approach." *Moral Development and Behavior*. Ed. T. Lickona. New York: Holt. 1976. 31–53.

Perry, William G. *Forms of Intellectual and Ethical Development in the College Years.* New York: Holt, Rinehart & Winston, 1970.

Rich, Adrienne. "Taking Women Students Seriously. " *On Lies, Secrets, and Silence: Selected Prose, 1966–1978.* New York: W.W. Norton, 1979. 237–45.

——. " 'When We Dead Awaken': Writing as Re-Vision." On *Lies, Secrets, and Silence: Selected Prose, 1966–1978.* New York: W.W. Norton, 1979. 33–49.

Schweickart, Patrocinio P. "Reading Ourselves: Toward a Feminist Theory of Reading." *Gender and Reading: Essays on Readers, Texts, and Contexts.* Ed. Elizabeth A. Flynn and Patrocinio P. Schweickart. Baltimore: Johns Hopkins UP, 1986. 31–62.

Showalter, Elaine. "Reading as a Woman: Jonathan Culler and the Deconstruction of Feminist Criticism." *Men and Feminism.* Ed. Alice Jardine and Paul Smith. New York: Methuen, 1987. 123–7.

Stanger, Carol A. "The Sexual Politics of the One-to-One Tutorial Approach and Collaborative Learning." *Teaching Writing: Pedagogy, Gender, and Equity.* Ed. Cynthia L. Caywood and Gillian R. Overing. Albany: State U of New York P, 1987. 31–44.

15 Rhetoric in a New Key: Women and Collaboration

ANDREA ABERNETHY LUNSFORD
AND LISA EDE

Stories, Carolyn Heilbrun has recently reminded us in *Writing a Woman's Life*, are powerful. They enable us to explore, try out, and sometimes to embody, new ways of seeing, doing, and being. Far from recounting mere anecdotal evidence, stories tell us what is imaginable, possible, or—in Geertz's terms—commonsensical in our culture. In this brief essay, we wish to tell a number of stories about a phenomenon that we have come to call collaborative writing. These stories point, we think, to the possibility of a new rhetoric, a rhetoric in a new key that rejects what Toril Moi has called "the model of the author as God the Father of the Text" (62) for a dialogic or polyphonal model of communication. These stories only *point* to this new rhetoric, however. Rather than telling a single narrative, these stories as a group function in a Burkean perspective-by-incongruity fashion to point to a site of struggle, a site we see also as one of opportunity.

Any story we tell, of course, is necessarily a version of our own story, and that story, as it relates to our work on collaborative writing, is a long and in some ways unsettling one to us. Our interest in collaboration grew directly out of our personal experience as long-time friends and coauthors, piqued by our surprised realization that coauthorship was not valued in our own departments of English. At the time, we did not associate this devaluation of a mode which seemed important and productive to us with the phallologocentric nature of the academy; we were merely irritated. And so we set out, rather naively, to "prove" how unreasonable this devaluation was. We would simply collect enough empirical "information" to demonstrate that collaborative writing is a feature of much contemporary discourse—and, voilà, the importance and efficacy of collaborative writing would be "obvious." In fact, we went on to gather such data, the story of which we have published in two earlier *Rhetoric Review* essays.

In the six years since we began what we originally thought of as a fairly straightforward data gathering project, we have come to situate the issue of

From *Rhetoric Review* 8 (1990): 234–41.

collaborative writing in a much broader historical, political, and ideological context and to contemplate the ways in which our society locates power, authority, authenticity, and property in an autonomous, masculine self. It was not hard to find provocative discussions of this phenomenon all around us—in literary and feminist theory, of course, but also in fields as diverse as anthropology, psychology, and library science. But while the "author" as construct was revealed, challenged, declared dead, and so on, people continued authoring—most often as solitary writers who signed single names to their texts.

Our interest in collaboration at this point took on the typical characteristics of a binary opposition: Against the solitary, sovereign author-ity of the single writer, we would investigate the multivoiced power of collaborative writers. And so as we began our study of collaborative writers in seven major professions, we expected (or, more accurately, hoped) to find that collaboration offered a mode that would serve a postmodern conception of writing.

What we found, however, was not **A** mode of collaborative writing but a number of modes, each deeply embedded in specific political, social, and ideological contexts. From this variety of modes, we eventually identified two that are particularly interesting to us as women and as collaborative writers. These modes we have come to call the hierarchical mode and the dialogic mode. In our research the hierarchical mode of collaborative writing emerged early on; it is a widespread means of producing texts in all the professions we studied. This form of collaboration is linearly structured, driven by highly specific goals, and carried out by people who play clearly assigned roles.

These goals are most often designated by someone outside of and hierarchically superior to the immediate collaborative group or by a senior member or "leader" of the group. Because productivity and efficiency are of the essence in this mode of collaboration, the realities of multiple voices and shifting authority are seen as problems to be overcome or resolved. Knowledge in this mode is most often viewed as information to be found or a problem to be solved. The activity of finding this information or solving this problem is closely tied to the realization of a particular end product. This mode of collaborative writing is, we would argue, typically conservative. It is also, need we say, a predominantly masculine mode of discourse.

Along the highways and byways of our research and reading roads, however, we began to catch glimpses, perceive traces, of another mode of collaboration, one we came to call dialogic. This mode is not as widespread in the professions we studied as the hierarchical mode and, in fact, its practitioners had difficulty describing it, finding language within which to inscribe their felt realities. This dialogic mode is loosely structured, and the roles enacted within it are fluid; one "person" may occupy multiple and shifting roles as the project progresses. In this mode the process of articulating and working together to achieve goals is as important as the goals themselves. Those who participate in dialogic collaboration generally value the creative tension inherent in multivoiced and multivalent ventures. What those involved in hierarchical collaboration see as a problem to be solved, these individuals view as a strength to be capitalized on and emphasized. In dialogic collaboration this group effort is seen as essential to the production—rather than merely the recovery—of knowledge and as a means of individual satisfaction within the group. This mode of collaboration, we argue, is, potentially at least, deeply subversive. And because our respondents had no ready language with which to describe such an enterprise, because many of those who tried to describe it to us were women, and because this mode of collaboration seemed so much the "other"—we think of this mode as predominantly feminine.

At present, our thinking about the nature and implications of hierarchical and dialogic collaboration is tentative and preliminary. We have found this way of viewing collaborative writing provocative and clarifying, yet we are aware that there are not only questions we have not answered but questions we have not even thought to ask. And we know that we need to "converse" or collaborate with many others—French and Anglo-American feminists, educational and political analysts, critical theorists, as well as (we would want to emphasize) those who collaborate regularly on the job or in their research or creative writing—before we can present a full, complex picture of these modes of collaboration.

For now, however, we want to tell our story but, as Emily Dickinson does, "tell it slant," by pointing up a persistent but not very surprising irony revealed in our research: The two professional fields in our study most populated by women—the Society for Technical Communication, of which 62 percent are women, and the Modern Language Association, of which 46 percent are women—are generally not enacting the dialogic mode of collaboration. Let us look briefly at what our study revealed about collaborative writing among members of these two professional groups.

The Society for Technical Communication members who responded to our call for information described a collaborative process that is very often hierarchical. Typically, a document begins with the technical writer, who produces it after consultation with various information sources within the organization. The document then travels in a rigidly linear way, through level upon level of bureaucratic authority. We have many stories we could tell to illustrate what is a fairly standard mode of collaboration experienced by technical writers. One such story emerged as we were testing one of our survey instruments with technical writers at the Environmental Protection Agency. The writers, who work in a strongly bureaucratized and thus deeply hierarchical context, indicated in their responses that they experienced dissatisfaction with collaborative writing in proportion to their sense of loss of control over the documents they were charged with initiating and "authoring."

A similar story emerged in an ethnographic study of a collaboratively produced document in a very large insurance firm undertaken by one of our graduate students (Cross, 1988). This document, a report to stockholders originally written by a technical writer, went through the same kind of upward series of steps, being altered and criticized at every step. At the end of this process, the report was so unsatisfactory to the chief officer who was to sign it that the whole project was scrapped—at great cost of time and money. In this instance the hierarchical mode turned out to be not only unsatisfactory to the technical writer and to the senior officer but inefficient and unproductive as well. Most often, though, our data indicate that collaborative writing in the hierarchical mode is perceived as efficient and productive if sometimes unsatisfying—and that it is embraced by technical writers as essentially unproblematic and as "the way things are."

The Modern Language Association, 46 percent of whom are women, did not in their responses to us embrace ANY concept or mode of collaboration but rather seemed suspicious of work that was produced in concert with others, saying that almost all their writing was done alone, the sole exception being writing they did to secure grants. Of course, we hardly need demonstrate that the humanities in general and English in particular valorize and reward single authorship and disregard collaboratively produced texts. Even those few scholars in our field who do write collaboratively fail to connect their own collaborative practices with larger theoretical, political, or pedagogical issues. But if we need to remind ourselves of the power of this particular authorial construct and its power in our own sphere, we can offer numerous exempla:

> A prestigious English department decided to withdraw its undergraduate poetry prize when the anonymous "author" of the winning poem turned out to be three undergraduate collaborators.

> Two women who petitioned and were granted permission to conduct collaborative research on a dissertation project were later told they would have to produce two separate and "different" dissertations.

> At a large research institution, a woman who often writes collaboratively was tenured and promoted to associate professor—but warned that her promotion to full professor would be contingent on producing single-authored books and articles.

> A well-known feminist scholar, whose work is collaboratively written, stated that she can draw no compelling pedagogical implications from her practice. The classroom structure of teacher-lecturer giving information to student-listeners seems perfectly efficient and reasonable to her.

> Those who work on collaborative projects "cannot apply for grants from the NEH under the fellowship program available for single authors," but must instead apply only under "Research Programs" and hence compete with universities and other large institutions. (See, for example, Smith, 1987.)

We could go on with such stories of our own profession's antipathy toward collaboration in spite of the challenges posed by poststructuralist and feminist critiques. But you know these stories—and many other ones as well—yourselves.

Given that the dialogic mode of collaborative writing can be discerned or glimpsed at work in certain places, the major issue for us then becomes to what extent such a mode represents the possibility of subverting traditional phallogocentric, subject-centered discourse—for a rhetoric, if you will, in a new key. As we have studied this question, we have found responses in some likely—and other unlikely—places. Particularly important to realizing what we call a dialogic mode of collaborative writing is work in women's studies. We are thinking here particularly of books such as Carol Gilligan's *In A Different Voice* and Belenky, Clinchy, Goldberger, and Tarule's *Women's Ways of Knowing*—works that challenge and subvert conventional western conceptions of the self. We could also point to work women are doing in sociology, especially that of Laurel Richardson, on the nature of teaching styles and the relations of those styles to traditionally masculine and univocal concepts of self. Psychologists such as M. Brinton Lykes are also helping to articulate a view of the self as ensembled or social, rather than autonomous and independent.

In practice we see the dialogic mode of collaboration enacted in interesting and subtle ways. We hear echoes of this mode, for instance, in a series of prefaces and acknowledgements to recent books. Read together, these strongly personal statements stand as a powerful challenge to and indictment of the concept of a single-authored, authoritative, univocal text. Let us cite here only a few of the many we have collected, almost all of which, by the way, are by women:

> From Dale Spender's *Man Made Language* (xv–xvi)—"there is an assumption I wish to challenge: it is that people sit in garrets and write books on their own. I sat in the Women's Resources Center at the University of Utah in Salt Lake City, and I was *not* on my own. . . . While this book may represent a 'sum total,' its many parts have been shaped . . . by many different people. . . . Not in isolation in a garret did this book come into existence, but in the co-operative and dynamic context of women's struggle. . . ."

> From Belenky, Clinchy, Goldberger, and Tarule's *Women's Ways of Knowing* (ix)—"As we steeped ourselves in the women's recorded and transcribed words we found ourselves drawing ever closer to their frames of mind. We emerged from this long process with an extraordinary sense of intimacy and collaboration with all the women. . . . So, too, during our work together, the four of us developed . . . an intimacy and collaboration which we have come to prize. We believe that the collaborative, egalitarian spirit so often shared by women should be more carefully nurtured in the work lives of *all* men and women. *We* hope to find it in all our future work."

> From Shirley Brice Heath's *Ways with Words* (ix)—"Those to whom the greatest acknowledgement of gratitude is due for help writing this book are the community members of Roadville and Trackton, and the school, mill, and business personnel of the Piedmont Carolinas with whom I lived and worked for nearly a decade."

> From Bellah, Madsen, Sullivan, Swidler, and Tipton's *Habits of the Heart* (xi)—"The people who let us into their homes and talked to us so freely during the course of our study are very much part of the authorship of this book."

And from Karen Burke LeFevre's *Invention as a Social Act* (xiii)—"In the chapters . . . that follow . . . I attempt to identify those points at which the voices of others—those necessary others whose words I have read, and those with whom I have spoken and thought and worked—are particularly evident."

These and other statements are provocative—and, to us at least, moving. But it's important to note that these assertions about the importance of collaboration are marginalized by appearing in prefaces or acknowledgements, rather than in the bodies of texts. Though many writers are convinced of the crucial importance and benefits of collaboration, then, they generally have not yet found ways to incorporate these concerns in the body of their texts, which as a rule do not challenge the conventions of single-authored documents.

Other scholars are helping us reenvision authorship along the lines of what we are calling a dialogic collaborative mode, one that radically subverts the status quo. We think particularly here of Karen LeFevre's studies (1988) of Frances Steloff, of the famed New York Gotham Book Mart, studies which have done much to illuminate a scene of writing and publishing in which Steloff's voice is a crucial and integral part not of a series of monologic individual productions but of a creative polylogue. LeFevre's work helps us to see "authorship" in this case as grounded not in individual writers (such as Hart Crane and e. e. cummings, to name two who were members of this circle) but in dialogic and relational acts. Still others show us that the dialogic mode of collaboration we are trying to bring into focus has a history or, more appropriately, a herstory. We see traces of it in the women's writing groups described in Anne Gere's study (1987), and we see it powerfully revealed in Jackie Jones Royster's chronicling of the tradition of black women writers.

Primarily through the work of women, then, we have found evidence of a dialogic mode of collaboration, one that allows a contextualized, multivocal text to appear. This mode, this "new key," as Langer says in her preface to *Philosophy in a New Key* is not one which alone we have struck. "Others," she says, "have struck it, quite clearly and repeatedly" (viii). It is a key, we would argue, that has been and is being struck clearly and repeatedly by many of the women and a few men we have mentioned, but which has not often been heard—by our professional organizations, by our institutions, by the culture within which we are all so deeply inscribed. Our challenge, then, is not to *strike* a new key but to hear within that key, the full texture of layered, polyphonic chords—and to create institutional and professional spaces within which those chords may be played and echoed.

WORKS CITED

Belenky, Mary Field, et al. *Women's Ways of Knowing.* New York: Basic Books, 1986.
Bellah, Robert, et al. *Habits of the Heart.* Berkeley: U of California P, 1985.
Cross, Geoff. "An Ethnographic Exploration of Editor-Writer Revision at a Midwestern Insurance Company." Diss. The Ohio State University, 1988.
Ede, Lisa, and Andrea Lunsford. "Why Write . . . Together?" *Rhetoric Review* 1 (January 1983): 57–68.
———. "Why Write Together: A Research Update." *Rhetoric Review* 5 (Fall 1986): 71–84.

Gere, Anne Ruggles. *Writing Groups: History, Theory, and Implications*. Carbondale: Southern Illinois UP, 1987.

Gilligan, Carol. *In a Different Voice: Psychological Theory and Women's Development*. Cambridge, MA: Harvard UP, 1982.

Heath, Shirley Brice. *Ways with Words: Language, Life, and Work in Communities and Classrooms*. Cambridge: Cambridge UP, 1983.

Heilbrun, Carolyn. *Writing a Woman's Life*. New York: Norton, 1988.

Langer, Suzanne. Preface to *Philosophy in a New Key*. New York: The New American Library, 1942.

LeFevre, Karen Burke. *Invention as a Social Act*. Carbondale: Southern Illinois UP, 1987.

———. "Studying Writers in Literacy Communities: A Social Perspective." CCCC Convention, St. Louis, March 17–19, 1988.

Lykes, M. Brinton. "Collective Action and the Development of Social Individuality in Women." The Annual Convention of the American Psychological Association, Toronto, August 24–28, 1984.

Moi, Toril. *Sexual/Textual Politics: Feminist Literary Theory*. London: Methuen, 1985.

Richardson, Laurel, et al. "Down the Up Staircase: Male and Female University Professors' Classroom Management Strategies." *Feminist Frontiers*. Ed. Laurel Richardson and Verta Taylor. New York: Random, 1983.

Royster, Jacqueline Jones. "Contending Forces: The Struggle of Black Women for Intellectual Affirmation." Columbus, Ohio, March 1, 1989.

Smith, Nicolas D. "Collaborating Philosophically." *Rhetoric Society Quarterly* 17 (Summer 1987): 247–62.

Spender, Dale. *Man Made Language*. London: Routledge and Kegan Paul, 1980.

———. "Studying Writers in Literacy Communities: A Social Perspective." CCCC Convention, St. Louis, March 17–19, 1988.

16 Feminism and Composition: The Case for Conflict

SUSAN C. JARRATT

- Heterosexual male students read aloud personal narratives about sexual conquest; women and other male students remain silent.

- White male students write fictional narratives in which a white male protagonist commits violence against a female teacher; the female teachers are unsure how to comment on the papers.

- The blatant sexism in a white male student's reading of a novel is overlooked as his essay is included in a book of model essays for new students because of its honest voice.

- A female student reports two years later that she now feels resentment at having been "manipulated into a position of vulnerability" in a student-centered composition class whose instructor was male.

These incidents and others like them—having floated about uneasily in my memory over the last few years—coalesce finally as a question about the relation between feminism and composition. The question especially concerns the kind of composition class that places a high priority on establishing a supportive and accepting climate in which students write primarily about personal experiences. The relation between feminism and composition studies has recently received some careful and productive attention.[1] While I see the powerful potential of the connections between the two realms, my question arises from a less promising tendency that they share: a strong resistance to conflict. Certain advocates of feminism and some composition teachers decline to contend with words. Some feminists vigorously reject argument on the grounds that it is a kind of violence, an instrument specific to patriarchal discourse and unsuitable for women trying to reshape thought and experience by changing forms of language use. For some composition teachers, creating a supportive

From *Contending with Words: Composition and Rhetoric in a Postmodern Age.* Ed. Patricia Harkin and John Schilb. New York: MLA, 1991. 105–23.

climate in the classroom and validating student experience leads them to avoid conflict. This stance toward conflict, while it diminishes the power difference between teacher and student, leaves those who adopt it insufficiently prepared to negotiate the oppressive discourses of racism, sexism, and classism surfacing in the composition classroom. Such discourses arise in classes aimed specifically at exposing attitudes toward class, race, and gender (see Ellsworth) but also in classes not necessarily concerned with those issues: for example, in "student-centered" courses, where the instructor allows students a wide range of choice in writing topics. Further, those who avoid conflict minimize unforeseen possibilities for using argument to reconstruct knowledge available to both teacher and student.

First, I review feminist opposition to conflict, especially Sally Miller Gearhart's passionate distillation of the position. Next, I point out similarities in this feminist stance to a particular style of composition teaching. Finally, I argue for a rhetoric historically grounded in the practice of the first Sophists and revived today in overtly confrontational feminist pedagogies as a progressive mode of discourse in the composition classroom.

THE FEMINIST CASE AGAINST ARGUMENT

Feminists have been exploring the political significance of forms of discourse from the beginning of the "second wave" in the seventies. Some theorists condemn conventional academic discourse as the product of a hierarchical, male-dominated system of logic and learning that is oppressive to women (Cixous and Clément; Spender; Lewis and Simon; and many others).[2] In "The Womanization of Rhetoric" Gearhart insists on the material consequences of discourse practices. She speaks with the same tone of urgency and conviction I've heard in conversations and meetings with women who share her view. Gearhart vigorously rejects argument on the grounds that "any intent to persuade is an act of violence" (195). Writing from within a department of speech communication, Gearhart extends her attack on speech and writing even to education as "itself an insidious form of violence" (195). Any attempt to change another person is the expression of a "conquest/conversion mindset," a species feature that Gearhart claims evolved sometime after an earlier golden age when human beings lived in harmony with the earth (196–97). She speculates that this mindset may have developed simultaneously with the birth of language itself.

Despite Gearhart's sometimes extreme claims—"the difference between a persuasive metaphor and a violent artillery attack is obscure and certainly one of degree rather than kind" (197)—the problems troubling her are real and global. Gearhart despairs of the thoughtless destruction of humans, animals, and the earth itself—the product of centuries of male domination—leading us "pell-mell down the path to annihilation" (196). Her sociobiologic reading of a sex-specific tendency to violence resembles Walter J. Ong's in *Fighting for Life: Contest, Sexuality, and Consciousness,* as does her recommendation for change: the "womanization" of rhetoric. Gearhart suggests a shift from a speaker-oriented delivery of truth to a more peaceful context for communication. In her model, no participant seeks to inform or persuade another, but somehow differences are expressed. These communication situations may involve "learning" and "conflict encounter," but each participant must be willing "on the deepest level to yield her/his position entirely to the other(s)" (199).

It's too easy a game to point out the inconsistencies and contradictions in Gearhart's argument (for it is clearly that): decrying the intention to change while calling for change; arguing that arguments are violent. A more generous reading would focus on the distinction she draws between a "male chauvinist" model of speech and a dialogic context for exchange of ideas— a field of communication Gearhart describes as a womblike matrix (199). Like the compositionists of the sixties and seventies who sought to shift the center of the class from teacher to student, to let students write about their experiences, to realign power in the classroom, Gearhart wants to replace an authoritarian model of education with a nurturing atmosphere for human interaction (200). The teacher becomes "co-creator and co-sustainer" of the communication possibilities. These admirable goals aim at real problems still with us.

But problems with Gearhart's proposal arise in the details of the communication context she envisions. She demands that "persons involved feel equal in power to each other" but doesn't explain how, for example, a black student in an all-white class can attain that feeling of equality. Apparently, communication for all is impossible without it. Gearhart acknowledges that communication is difficult and must be worked at, but she provides only the most general suggestions for handling cases when "genuine disagreements" arise (198). And these suggestions come right out of the rhetoric she so violently rejects:

> Some unity will have to occur there of personality differences with the principled advocacy of positions; some techniques of interpersonal clarification and openness will have to blend with the use of good reason in the controversy. (199)

In calling for "principled advocacy of positions," Gearhart redefines rhetoric in a way that differs from her earlier narrow view but that remains quite consistent with a number of classical formulations (e.g., those of Cicero, Quintilian, Augustine). The use of "good reason" relies on a standard of judgment at least as gendered as the rhetoric Gearhart rejects.[3] Those who have enjoyed positions of power in the field of discourse within which Gearhart dwells— namely, white men—have for centuries been responsible for normalizing "reason," with very little interference from other groups. And she provides no method to adjudicate differences about what constitutes "good reason," should they arise. Finally, perhaps the most revealing element in her formula for handling conflict is the implication that difference occurs on the personal level: differences in "personality" can be resolved through "interpersonal" techniques. Despite her identification with feminism, Gearhart fails to anticipate the emergence of differences among groups. She applauds rhetoric's recent turn to an awareness of audience (a singularly ahistorical reading), but she's clearly working on the model of one individual speaking to another.

Gearhart recommends the rediscovery of rhetoric's historical connection with ethics (200), particularly as a corrective to the current social-science orientation of communication theory. But for her that ethical imperative is enacted through a simple inversion, in which persons using the conquest model of speaking and teaching become vessels "out of whose variety messages will emerge" (201). Even if we grant some scope for change through human agency, Gearhart's model pays no attention to the power of institutions to reproduce ideology (see Althusser, *Lenin*) or of discourses in Foucault's sense that speak through members of a culture. While she contributes to a discourse of difference, an important moment in feminism's challenge to a male-dominated status quo,[4] Gearhart does not account for the way other struggling voices can be drowned out, despite the good intentions of the instructor, in specific communication contexts where the dominant discourse is well represented.

COMPOSITION WITHOUT CONFLICT

Gearhart's rejection of rhetoric reminds me of the attitude toward conflict I see in composition teachers trained in or converted to student-centered writing pedagogies. Though I haven't done a systematic study comparing approaches, I have spent many hours working with graduate-student teachers schooled in a program based on works like Peter Elbow's *Writing Without Teachers* and Donald M. Murray's *Write to Learn*. James A. Berlin's analyses of these composition theorists, whom he calls "subjective" or "expressionist," emphasize their interest in self-discovery and the assumption of common human experiences and values underlying their practices (*Rhetoric and Reality* 145; "Rhetoric and Ideology" 484–87).

At their inception, these pedagogies created productive conflict at the institutional level by encouraging students to write about what mattered to them and by challenging an institution of literary studies unresponsive to students' lives. The pedagogies encouraged teachers, through example and practical advice, to loosen their grip on a stiff, academic language taught largely through error-identification and to experiment with alternative styles. In classes and in books guided by these theories I find an intense and genuine desire to break down the barriers between teacher and student, between distant, academic discourse and personally meaningful writing. Teachers who follow these theories nurture rather than act as authority figures. Indeed, the two books cited above have no teachers—only readers, who are most often sympathetic and committed.

Removing the teacher from the center of the classroom—away from the authoritative position as the source of knowledge—is a postmodern move, in the sense that the teacher was taken as the locus of a Truth. But the transformative potential of expressive pedagogy has to be evaluated in the light of the broader political implications of the theory. Berlin has effectively identified the cooptive potential of the emphasis on the individual in expressive pedagogy ("Rhetoric and Ideology" 487). In my experience at a midwestern state university, affirming the voice of a white, middle- or upper-middle-class student often involves teachers in rationalizing a future in corporate anonymity, in endorsing the clichés of competitive self-interest that perpetuate a system of racism, sexism, and classism still very much a part of American culture. The complexities of social differentiation and inequity in late-twentieth-century capitalist society are thrown into the shadows by the bright spotlight focused on the individual. Consider the epigraphs opening Murray's *Write to Learn:* from Jane Austen, "I must keep to my own style, and go on in my own way"; from e. e. cummings, "To be nobody-but-yourself—in a world which is doing its best, night and day, to make you everybody else" (1).

Paradoxically, when groups do work together in these pedagogies, the ideal is homogeneity, another way of avoiding confrontations over social differences. In *Writing Without Teachers,* Elbow describes a group of seven to twelve committed writers, best if they're "people who have a lot in common" (79). Murray brings the reader into his text *Write to Learn* only on page 195, and then his advice about reading and readers assumes a commonality of experience. Reading as a writer means "reading unwritten texts," like an archaeologist unearthing potential meanings. The reader intuitively fills in the spaces because of an unspoken empathy with writers and their texts. Although conflict is anticipated, it usually occurs because of a lack of clarity in the message—fog or static, in Elbow's terms (127–32). Conflict is a matter of each reader's experience, personal quirks that can't be second-guessed by the writer; the writer's control over the text is paramount (104–5). This vision of communication fails to acknowledge fundamental clashes in values that underlie issues of style, effect, and meaning. How would those differences be negotiated in Elbow's writing group? They wouldn't, because the group is essentially value-free. His advice to readers includes "Never quarrel with someone else's reaction" and "No kind of reaction is wrong" (95). Both writers and readers are "always right and always wrong" (100, 106). Elbow encourages, even demands, uncensored accounts of the experience of reading and self-evaluations of writing. But this view assumes that the writer will be able to do whatever he or she wishes with the responses because of the equality of all group members (126). In our society, men and women, blacks and whites, rich and poor are positioned in "antagonistic and asymmetrical relation," as the feminist theorist Teresa de Lauretis has observed (*Technologies* 38). Because those structural differences pervade the writing classes most of us teach, our students can't merely accept or reject such responses on an equal basis, because of the material realities in our society in which such responses are grounded. Such inequities often make the attempt to create a harmonious and nurturing community of readers an illusory fiction—a superficial suturing of real social divisions.

Although the expressionists are displacing authority and thus enacting a feminist goal, expressive pedagogy presents problems for women and for feminism. Consider, for example, the heavily gendered language with which Peter Elbow instructs the reader of student writing in *Writing Without Teachers*. Working against the standard teaching and writing practices of the literary criticism he inherited, Elbow encourages participants in the "believing game" to give up the aggressive, combative, argumentative rigidity required for the "doubting game" (178–79).[5] In so doing, they leave themselves open — but not to "force-feeding" or "rape," Elbow assures us (185); nor will they go "intellectually soft and limp" (181). Rather, Elbow advises, following Conrad, "In the destructive element immerse"; give yourself over to the alien — what threatens to poison or infect (186–87). *Writing Without Teachers* is truly a revolutionary text in its feminization of the male writing teacher. But female readers — teachers or students of composition — are positioned differently in relation to these instructions.[6] Demanding that our female students listen openly and acceptingly to every response from a mixed class can lead to a discursive reenactment of the violence carried on daily in the maintenance of an inequitable society (de Lauretis, *Technologies* 34). Advising a female student to "swallow" without reply a conventional male reaction to a woman's experience has serious consequences. Similar problems occur when a female teacher takes a nurturing role in a class of men and women — replicating the traditional female role in our culture. A female teacher who takes a position of uncritical openness toward the male student, especially if social-class differences also apply, invites the exercise of patriarchal domination to which every man in our society is acculturated. Because most high school teachers are women and may be seen as maternal figures, the role of the supportive, nurturing composition teacher repeats that childish pattern and puts the teacher at a disadvantage in any attempt to assert a counterhegemonic authority as a woman.[7] A third problem is that of the female student whose male composition teacher encourages her to make a deep and serious self-examination of personal experience. How is the female student to resist an exposure she feels unwilling but obligated to make under the rules of the institution and the culture? These are the problems surfacing in the incidents I cited in the opening of this essay.

I can hear those who use expressivist methods objecting that none of these scenarios would occur in the classroom of a sensible and sensitive teacher: one who would intervene in an objectionable discourse from a male student, who would simply take on a stronger role as a woman with male students testing the limits of the supportive setting, who would never demand a self-revelation from a resisting student. I am confident that many teachers, male and female, intuitively negotiate such situations with sensitivity to the complexities of gender, race, and class differences. But we can't always control the ways discursive power works in our classes. We can't force female students to speak out against men, or students of color to speak out against whites. We can't always undo the institutional authority of our roles through our instructions and assurances. Despite the efficacy of intuitive responses, I contend that we need more, especially in the area of teacher training. We need a theory and practice more adequately attuned than expressivism is to the social complexities of our classrooms and the political exigencies of our country in this historical moment.

FEMINIST ADAPTATIONS OF EXPRESSIVIST COMPOSITION

Some feminists find the work of the expressionists much less troublesome than I do. They agree with Elbow and Murray that the writing teacher should be, above all, nurturing and the writing class, above all, nonconflictual. Elisabeth Däumer and Sandra Runzo elaborate the parallel between the mother and the teacher of writing. Citing the "distinctly female perspective in the works of Janet Emig and Ann E. Berthoff," they create a genealogy for feminist composition theory, emphasizing the supportive context within which students can best learn to write and endorsing the idea of "drawing on maternal practice and the values it cultivates" (48, 50). While they acknowledge the downside of that model—the exploitation of women through the devaluation of women's work and the socializing burden placed on mothers—they keep it as their ideal for the composition teacher. Rather than turn that ambivalence about mothers into a complication of the teacher's role, they direct it toward the pedagogical choices of the teacher-mother. Instead of asking if the teacher should be like a mother or, as Margo Culley et al. do, how we can understand and make the best of the psychological dynamics at work when a woman teaches, the question Däumer and Runzo ask becomes, What does the mother teach? The answer is women's texts. Rejecting an approach to writing embodying a masculine ethic of "aggression and adversarial relationships," they advocate a class in which women write about personal experiences after reading women's autobiography, history, and fiction. Despite the emphasis on women's experience, Däumer and Runzo claim that reading and writing assignments "can easily be modified to include men" (47). What appeals to me about this pedagogy is the opportunity it provides for women's growth in such a composition class. What disturbs me is the easy assumption that male students would have no problem fitting into such a class and the absence of any reference to the psychological complexities around the conjunction of mothering and teaching.[8] Under such circumstances—which the authors acknowledge as the norm—I think we need a more rhetorical composition theory, one providing a model of political conflict and negotiation.

Carol A. Stanger addresses the possibility of gender-related conflicts in the composition classroom more directly. She argues for sex-linked language difference, traces a history of the suppression of women's writing, and seeks the most efficacious mode of composition teaching for encouraging female students to write (32–34). Using a hypothetical student as an example, Stanger contrasts an authoritarian form of one-on-one tutoring with Kenneth Bruffee's collaborative method of reader response. She finds collaboration preferable for drawing out women writers in the group through a dialogue between male and female language:

> Although we would expect that male language would dominate, the new social structure of the peer learning group, the lack of a patriarchal presence "teaching," and the presence of strong and vocal women in the group can combine to give women's language the power to surface and replace men's language. (42)

Stanger does not guarantee that collaboration works for the woman writer, but she has strong confidence in the possibility of a transcendent, "oceanic" group experience mirroring the experience of "perfect oneness with the mother, a primary intimacy" (40). Again the feminist composition class becomes founded in the maternal, though the teacher is not placed directly in the mothering role. If indeed this transcendent experience comes about—although I can't say I've witnessed it in years of what I considered successful collaborative work in my writing classes—students will most likely see the teachers as the source of this maternal intimacy, since teachers initiate the groups, presumably control the larger process, and ultimately give the grades. Anticipating such a positive response to teacher as mother naively ignores the deep ambivalence toward and repression of the mother in our culture. But what of the occasions when conflicts do arise? Stanger relies on Carol Gilligan's reading of the differences between men's and women's socialization on questions of moral value. While male students fight for the "right" answer, female students seek compromise, and thus the group reaches consensus (41). Doesn't that suggest that the women probably give in to the men's positions? Because consensus is necessary for the pedagogy to work, Stanger can only hope that it includes women's as well as men's voices. Like Elbow, she puts a high priority on placing power in the voices of the students, on shifting power from teacher to students who are undifferentiated by gender—not to mention class or race.

Even when teachers announce the desire to create a particular climate, they can't neutralize by fiat the social positions already occupied by their students. I believe we need to supplement the note of hope sounded in Stanger's essay with a more open acknowledgment of gender, race, and class differences among students and with a pedagogy designed to confront and explore the uneven power relations resulting from these differences. It's not a question of throwing out the innovations of teachers like Elbow and Murray or of shutting down the voices and personal experiences of students; rather, it's a question of relocating those practices and interests in a different theoretical context—getting a larger sense of what produces them and of what the writing based in them should do. It is a question of metaphorically breaking down the classroom walls to examine the ways the infrastructures of society have created those experiences. While these early mappings of feminist pedagogy deserve praise, we must work to strengthen the goal of displacing teacher authority with a more carefully theorized understanding of the multiple forms of power reproduced in the classroom. Differences of gender, race, and class among students and teachers provide situations in which conflict does arise, and we need more than the ideal of the harmonious, nurturing composition class in our repertory of teaching practices to deal with these problems.

CONFLICT IN HISTORICAL RHETORIC

A leap back to classical rhetoric can give us a perspective on the political implications of suppressing conflict that may be hard to get at close range. Plato and Aristotle condemn the Sophists for eristic argumentation—that is, a competitive contentiousness allegedly engaged in for its own sake. It is this kind of argument feminists and compositionists reject. Both philosophers replace the sophistic *techne* with more respectable alternatives: for Plato, dialectic; for Aristotle, invention. In each case, the objective method masks the political implications of its appropriation by an interested party. In other words, Plato's metaphysical goals underlie Socrates's questioning in many dialogues but are not themselves brought under examination. Pure scientific knowledge and dialectic differ from the informal logic of rhetorical invention in Aristotle's theory, but such divisions themselves are not matters for rhetorical argument. Both Plato and Aristotle assume that, for any audience in possession of full knowledge, rhetoric would not only lack conflict, it would be unnecessary. That is, each idealizes an audience completely in harmony about fundamental assumptions, even though each acknowledges the persistence of conflict in real human affairs. This understanding fits the ideal political arrangement envisioned by both philosophers: rule by a small, homogeneous group of aristocrats.

In contrast, the first Sophists place at the center of their practice *dissoi logoi*—conflicting views about an issue. Their theory assumes that knowledge is always constructed socially and that public action is guided by informed debate among members of a democratic community (Jarratt, *Rereading*). Conflict is central to their theory of rhetoric and democratic politics. Only through recognition of and argument over differences can conflict be resolved into *homonoia*, like-mindedness. If we can make the same kinds of assessments about contemporary composition pedagogy, then conflict—the place it holds in theory and practice and the ends toward which it is employed—can serve as a measure of the political effect of a discourse practice.

MOVING TOWARD RHETORIC

Here I wish to examine two pedagogies moving toward a more politically efficacious use of argument: one offered by the feminist philosopher Joyce Trebilcot in "Dyke Methods or Principles for the Discovery/Creation of the Withstanding" and the other by a more rhetorical Elbow than we saw earlier. Trebilcot, at first glance, appears to be laying out a discourse scenario similar to Gearhart's radical rejection of conflict. But a closer look shows that Trebilcot refines Gearhart's case for nonconflict because she takes into account different situations—places where the rules of nonconflict hold and places where they are debilitating. The methods her essay title refers to apply only when women are speaking together in "safe spaces":

> The principles are not intended to be used in situations that are predominantly patriarchal, that is, when getting something from men is at stake, as when one is working in the patriarchy for money, doing business with men and male-identified women, etc. In these contexts I find that it is usually most effective to operate according to patriarchal ideas of knowledge and truth. (3)

Trebilcot, a philosopher, seeks to establish methods of using language to account for reality without participating in the "domination inherent in the patriarchal idea of truth." Like Gearhart, she refuses, when talking with other women, to engage in persuasion: I speak only for myself. I do not try to get other wimmin to accept my beliefs in place of their own" (1).

While Gearhart approaches the issue from a global and historical perspective, Trebilcot arrives at her principles out of personal anger against control. In male-dominated discourse, she often sees herself and other women either excluded or misrepresented. Like the expressionists, Trebilcot wants to unweave the fabric of discourse, separating out the single thread that is hers. Or, in terms of another figure, she wants her voice to sound alone rather than be submerged in the flood of male voices either drowning her out or pretending to sing her part for her. But she is not unaware of a Bakhtinian heteroglossia always present in any discourse: "pure wimmin's spaces can't exist—we are interlarded everywhere with patriarchy" (10). The purpose of Trebilcot's "principle of nonpersuasion" is to avoid, in communication with like-minded women, the exercise of male power and control she experiences in the "truth industry—heteropatriarchal science, religion, scholarship, education media"— and to promote serious respect for the differences among women (7).

Through the dialogic construction of her article, a result of arguing both with herself and with commentators on her work, Trebilcot anticipates and answers a number of objections critics might raise about her principles. She agrees that discourse can persuade even when it isn't intended to, that power relations influence how discourse works, and that her claim to a single voice denies the working of a community. I find the last of these issues the most intriguing because of the way she defines nonpersuasive communication and describes her experience of discourse. When "wimmin" meet to talk in nonhierarchical and noncompetitive communication situations, they tell stories— past, present, and future—and plan action. In a telegraphic way, Trebilcot proposes a version of sophistic rhetoric, the art of representing the past and present so as to suggest a course of action for the future. Trebilcot's definition elides the process of coming to agreement about the particular course of action to be taken, but she does explain that if anyone in a group of compatible women disagrees with a plan, it is dropped (9).

But persuasion of some kind must be going on in the space between telling stories—necessarily different stories—and planning action, even in a group of like-minded people. Further, I think that for pedagogical purposes—that is, as a model for the language of the classroom—it is more productive to bring out and examine the contradictions and conflicts being resolved in that space than to overlook them or minimize their significance. The same kind of sharp dichotomy between argument and agreement appears in Elbow's essay "Methodological Doubting and Believing: Contraries in Inquiry." Seeking to shift the balance in intellectual inquiry away from the critical process of attacking propositions with rigid logical instruments, Elbow argues for the "believing game"—the process of granting provisional assent in order to expand mental abilities and arrive at valid judgments. In this essay (a later version of the appendix to *Writing Without Teachers*), Elbow openly acknowledges the gender associations of the two poles: "Believing invites behaviors associated with femininity: accepting, saying Yes, being compliant, listening, absorbing, and swallowing . . . being mute or silent" (266). Indeed, he links his project with feminist theory, because both attempt to emphasize experience and assent, "processes that have been undervalued in a culture deriving its tradition from methodological doubt and male dominance" (266). With Trebilcot, Elbow shares a conviction that storytelling can help listeners envision new worlds (277–78). Like the Sophists, he questions the rules of noncontradiction (279). His plea for believing sounds, at times, like the Sophists' way of making the worse case better. In positive terms, this practice means imagining the unimaginable; he advises storytelling as an aid to this kind of imagining (277–78). In short, Elbow's essay makes a major contribution toward providing a rhetorical foundation for the expressive composition class.

I find his theoretical formulation of the believing game troubling, however, in its reliance on authority for validity and in its silence on the issue of social differences in the practice of believing. While Elbow defends the believing game as a way to ensure that minority opinions are given power against those of the majority, how can that guarantee work when the "proof" of a belief is its acceptance by "a respected group of authorities" who endorse it through participation (266, 267)? Elbow's criterion is open to the same criticisms as Stanley Fish's "interpretive community," which Elbow offers as a parallel to his own model (see Fish, *Is There a Text*). Those educated readers who make up an interpretive community reflect the dominant group and crowd out marginal voices. Aristotle also evaluates the legitimacy of a deduction in terms of its "reputability": it is judged by whether the majority, all, or the most notable of men accept it (*Topics* 100a–b). If it isn't "reputable," it's "contentious." Elbow seems more concerned with the possible corruption of the reputable, the commonsensical, than with the silencing of marginal voices. He counters a charge of mental promiscuity or laxness, the seduction of the thinker into some sort of fringe belief such as "Moonie-ism," but never brings up the much more common problem of what happens to a woman's voice in a group of men or a black voice in a group of whites (283). A gender-sensitive reading of Elbow's rhetoric of belief shows it to be the feminization of a masculinist discourse of logic. That is, if taken to heart by a man, it would really help a male listener experience a female discourse. But for a female listener, the effect is much different. In Lacanian terms, Elbow is taking the position of castration, but because woman is already castrated in patriarchal discourse, placing a female reader in the position of castration (like Jane Gallop does, in *Reading Lacan*) is doubly disempowering (Moi, "Feminism" 15). Elbow advises us to overcome our "archetypal fears" of becoming "the large opening into which anything can be poured—force-fed, raped" (283–84). Though he wishes to offer all readers a way of gaining more control over their minds, because "compulsive doubters [are] more dominated by unaware beliefs than other people are" (284), this loaded language positions its gendered readers differently. Only read Elbow's rhetoric of surrender as a female subject, which I must do, and that positioning becomes frighteningly clear (285). An attitude of complete receptivity, of openness to "any view or hypothesis that a participant seriously wants to advance" (260), still puts a woman, I believe, in a dangerous stance.

Like Trebilcot, Elbow repudiates argument. But he goes much further in describing the process by which the listener participates in a belief. In citing the sophomore who petulantly asserts that argument is pointless, Elbow accepts a definition of argument like Aristotle's use of the eristic for the Sophists. Sometimes translated as "wrangling," eristic discourse is competitive, the point being, as Elbow says of argument, to defeat the opponent. But the Sophist Prodicus in Plato's *Protagoras* provides a synonym and thus an alternative for wrangling: "I . . . would beg you Protagoras and Socrates, . . . that you will dispute *(amphisbetein)* with one another and not wrangle *(erizein)*, for friends dispute with friends out of good will, but only adversaries and enemies wrangle" (337b).[9] In place of "eris-ize"—to behave like the Eris, the goddess of discord—Prodicus offers a word meaning loosely to "go both ways." The noun form in fact refers to a serpent that can go forward or backward (Liddell and Scott 45). This ability to move into different positions, paradoxically, seems more consistent with the positive pole of both Trebilcot's and Elbow's oppositions. The kind of argument they reject is a one-sided, combative form of discourse: one that completely shuts out any opposing view. In both these formulations, then, conflict has a place—can be strategically deployed—though it is de-emphasized in favor of "believing" (Elbow) and of the "principle of nonpersuasion" (Trebilcot 5).

PRODUCTIVE CONFLICT IN FEMINIST COMPOSITION PEDAGOGY

For pedagogies most fully engaged in issues of gender, race, and class—pedagogies in which conflict is central—I turn to the research of Kathleen Weiler and the radical black feminism of bell hooks. Weiler's work gives a feminist turn to the critical pedagogy of Paulo Freire, Henry Giroux, and others. Where the male theorists have focused largely on the issue of class, Weiler broadens the venue of critical pedagogy with special attention to gender. Her book *Women Teaching for Change* is particularly interesting for writing teachers because it uses personal narratives as a research methodology (see the chapter "The Dialectics of Gender in the Lives of Women Teachers" 73–100) but also because it moves beyond the supportive context of personal experience in an examination of classroom discussions in which gender, race, and class create conflicts among students and teachers. Weiler grounds her study in an analysis of schools as places where culture is both reproduced and produced. Though educational institutions enforce the power and control of the existing social order, they also allow students and teachers to challenge, oppose, and resist those forces. Her project, then, given that potential, is to work toward "a more fully developed theory of gender in an examination of the lived experiences of teachers and students in schools" (24),

Weiler observed feminist high school teachers in a range of subjects, including composition, who work with students of different classes, races, and genders (130). Like many composition teachers brought up on Elbow, Murray, and Ken Macrorie, these teachers:

> expand the limits of discourse by directly addressing the forces that shape their students' lives ... attempt[ing] to legitimize their students' voices by acknowledging their students' own experiences and by calling for their students' own narratives. (131)

But these teachers go farther than creating a nurturing, student-centered classroom:

> [R]elated to the expansion of discourse, is their own presentation of themselves as gendered subjects with a personal perspective on issues of gender and race. They are overtly political in their presentation and both will use personal anecdotes and will challenge and engage students on these topics. (131)

In foregrounding their membership in a class, race, and gender, these teachers either conflict with or affirm their students' identities. They create a classroom in which personal experience is important material but openly acknowledge that differences exist and cause conflicts. The negotiation of those conflicts becomes the subject of the dialogue Weiler quotes and comments on. Not all the discussions Weiler relates show teachers smoothly mediating the conflicting positions of their students. In one example, a working-class girl, questioning the morality of the rape victim who left her children at home to go to a bar, is silenced by middle-class feminist students (138). In another, the contribution of a black boy, who wants to discuss a segment of *The Autobiography of Malcolm X* in terms of racism, is passed over by his white teacher, who is making a point about socialization (140). The point of Weiler's account is not to showcase exemplary teachers but rather to capture and analyze the highly complex collisions of gender, race, and class in the classroom. She expresses no aim to rid the classroom of conflict because it is "always a site of conflict, and will be a site of conflict for the feminist or critical teacher ... just as much as it will be for a traditional or authoritarian teacher" (137) or, I would add, even for the composition teacher seeking a nurturing environment for a heterogeneous group of students writing about personal experiences. Recognizing the inevitability of conflict is not grounds for despair but the starting point for creating a consciousness in students and teachers through which the inequalities generating those conflicts can be acknowledged and transformed (144–45).

The teacher's role in the writing classroom, in a feminist critical pedagogy, varies greatly depending on the makeup of the class in relation to the teacher's subjectivity. Beyond recognizing the institutional power of teachers—the political intervention staged by expressionists—a teacher would recognize, for example, an unequal positioning if she or he were the product of a working-class background but teaching in an elite school. A black man teaching all white students would face a much different situation. In the polyphony of voices, not all will or should sound equally. Ira Shor, using Freire, explains how the teacher, even while creating a "loving matrix" for dialogue, may sometimes need to take on an adversarial role against an abusive student or to voice an unrepresented view in the dialogue (*Critical* 95, 102). As Moi asks, "What dogmatism says that it is *never* feminist to speak with authority?" ("Feminism" 15).

An eloquent and powerful example of how, even among women, voices differ, hooks speaks directly to the issue of conflict in the title of her recent collection of essays, *Talking Back.* While the stereotype of women's speech under patriarchy is that it is silenced, hooks remembers women's voices as strong and angry in her experience as a child in a southern black family and community. She was silenced not by men but by the adult women in her family who tried to socialize her as a female child into using the right kind of speech (6). Her account runs counter to the assumptions of feminist compositionists cited earlier whose primary aim is to make a space for the voices of women (Däumer and Runzo) or for an essentialized "women's speech" in dialogue with men's (Stanger). For black women, hooks explains, the "struggle has not been to emerge from silence into speech but to change the nature and direction of our speech, to make a speech that compels listeners, one that is heard" (6). Perhaps the nurturing, nonconflictual composition classroom could aid in this enterprise, but perhaps not. hooks's revolutionary feminist pedagogy rejects an exclusive focus on personal experience as a simple inversion of the older pedagogy of domination against which compositionists reacted in the sixties and seventies (52). I agree with hooks that "[t]his model must be viewed critically because a class can still be reinforcing domination, not transforming consciousness about gender, even as the 'personal' is the ongoing topic of conversation" (52). The incidents recounted in the opening of this essay are examples of domination in the context of classroom conversations about the "personal."

Using her favorite teacher as a model, hooks endorses a pedagogy grounded in "an oppositional world view"—essential for blacks in a white, racist society (49). Her teachers, almost all black women, "offered . . . a legacy of liberatory pedagogy that demanded active resistance and rebellion against sexism and racism" (50). hooks's analysis of the current educational climate, oddly similar to a picture of the sixties, calls up a different pedagogy in response. Students today, she writes, "suffer from a crisis of meaning, unsure about what has value in life," and they long for a context where their subjective needs can be integrated with study" (51). But rather than the safe and nurturing classroom, hooks recommends a class wherein "the primary focus is a broader spectrum of ideas and modes of inquiry, in short a dialectical context where there is serious and rigorous critical exchange" (5 I). In this frank description, she marks very pointedly the difference between her pedagogy and the one under critical examination here:

> Unlike the stereotypical feminist model that suggests women best come to voice in an atmosphere of safety (one in which we are all going to be kind and nurturing)., I encourage students to work at coming to voice in an atmosphere where they may be afraid or see themselves at risk. The goal is to enable all students, not just an assertive few, to feel empowered in a rigorous, critical discussion. Many students find this pedagogy difficult, frightening, and very demanding. They do not usually come away from my class talking about how much they enjoyed the experience. (53)

While this account may make advocates of the expressive school uneasy, I suggest that we need now to reassess the criteria by which we evaluate success in the writing class. We must again take a political pulse to determine the effects of our practices and to reconsider strategies. The expressivist focus on student experiences and concerns is an important starting point for feminist pedagogy. But my double concern about those feminist compositionists who advocate such pedagogies is not only that they are positioned unequally in the expressivist discourse but also that they spend too little time helping their students learn how to argue about public issues—making the turn from the personal back out to the public. As Gayatri Chakravorty Spivak points out, a mere inversion of the public-private hierarchy succeeds only in a more rigid division of the two realms. Just as "the so-called public sector is woven of the so-called private, the definition of the private is marked by a public potential, since it *is* the weave, or texture, of public activity" (103). My hopes are pinned on composition courses whose instructors help their students to locate personal experience in historical and social contexts—courses that lead students to see how differences emerging from their texts and discussions have more to do with those contexts than they do with an essential and unarguable individuality. I envision a composition course in which students argue about the ethical implications of discourse on a wide range of subjects and, in so doing, come to identify their personal interests with others, understand those interests as implicated in a larger communal setting, and advance them in a public voice. Such a content for composition would replicate closely the Sophist Protagoras's identification of the subject of rhetoric: "prudence in affairs private as well as public." Through this course, the student will "learn to order his own house in the best manner, and he will be able to speak and act most powerfully in the affairs of the state" (Plato, *Protagoras* 318e–319a).[10]

Feminists are arguing the argument issue, and some of the most prominent voices are advocating a specific alignment of rhetoric and feminism. Examining the ways some feminist theorists discover a productive tension in the differences among feminists' positions, I have argued elsewhere for the parallel positioning of women and sophistic rhetoric against philosophy in the Western intellectual tradition ("First Sophists"), a view Patricia Bizzell extends in a reevaluation of the goals of cultural literacy. The discursive method driving both feminist and sophistic ways of negotiating change through discourse is argument. In both the prephilosophical fifth century, B.C., and in the current postmodern antifoundational context, rhetorical positions stand temporarily as grounds for action in the absence of universally verifiable truth (Jarratt, *Rereading;* Bizzell, "Beyond Anti-Foundationalism"). When we recognize the need to confront the different truths our students bring to our classes—not only through self-discovery but in the heat of argument—feminism and rhetoric become allies in contention with the forces of oppression troubling us all.[11]

NOTES

1. Elizabeth Flynn astutely identifies composition as the "feminization" of the field of literary studies. Using Carol Gilligan's *In a Different Voice,* Flynn demonstrates a gendered reading of student narratives in a first-year writing class. In Cynthia L. Caywood and Gillian R. Overing's collection, *Teaching Writing: Pedagogy, Gender, and Equity,* a number of the essays build on the inherently similar goals of a student-centered writing class and a particular style of feminist pedagogy (e.g., Stanger; Däumer and Runzo).

2. See Catherine Clément, however, for a defense of women's use of a hegemonic, logical discourse (Cixous and Clément). Jane Tompkins creates a mixed discourse in "Me and My Shadow," encasing a conventional critique of another woman's work within a sympathetic, personal narrative about a woman's experience of academic life.

3. Elizabeth Ellsworth criticizes the "rationalist assumptions" she finds underlying critical pedagogy (4–5).

4. The feminist theorist Toril Moi defines *difference* as one of three positions emerging historically since the late sixties in the international women's movement ("Feminism" 5).

5. Peter Elbow's most rhetorical statement on writing occurs in his "Appendix Essay: The Doubting Game and the Believing Game—An Analysis of the Intellectual Enterprise," an elaborated version of which appears in *Embracing Contraries.*

6. Barbara Johnson makes a similar observation about Paul de Man's pedagogical posture of "self-resistance":

> [T]he question *can* be asked why de Man's discourse of self-resistance and uncertainty has achieved such authority and visibility, while the self-resistance and uncertainty of *women* has been part of what has insured their lack of authority and their invisibility. It would seem that one has to be positioned in the place of power in order for one's self-resistance to be valued. Self-resistance, indeed, may be one of the few postures remaining for the white male establishment. (45)

7. Margo Culley et al. explain the double bind for the women in the academy in terms of the psychological dynamics of the family. On the one hand, the child, needing the mother for nurturance, ultimately comes to resent her power and the child's own dependence. On the other hand, in the role of "father" as an intellectual in the academy, a woman "betrays [her] body's traditional significance." As women academics, "our maternal power is feared, our paternal authority is mistrusted" (14).

8. A collaborative inquiry in feminist pedagogy at Miami University, based on students' responses on teacher evaluations, indicates that a focus on women's issues in composition classes can create problems for both male and female students (Bauer et al.). In "Pedagogy of the Oppressors?" John Schilb describes the feminist pedagogy he arrived at through his experiences teaching women's studies to "mixed" classes, most of whose members "routinely oppose [his] values" (253). See also Margo Culley et al. on nurturance.

9. The Sophist Protagoras himself demonstrates goodwill and flexibility in the dialogue, using both *mythos* (storytelling) and *logos* (laying out a case) to make a successful argument against Socrates that virtue can be taught.

10. I maintain the gendered language of the original because of its historical accuracy but assume that its contemporary application will be understood as gender inclusive.

11. I'd like to thank Dale Marie Bauer, Sara Farris, Peter W. Rose, and John Schilb for helpful comments on an earlier draft of this essay.

WORKS CITED

Althusser, Louis. "Ideology and Ideological State Apparatuses." Althusser, *Lenin* 127–86.

———. *Lenin and Philosophy and Other Essays.* Trans. Ben Brewster. New York: Monthly Review, 1971.

Aristotle. *The* Rhetoric *and* Poetics *of Aristotle.* Trans. Rhys Roberts *(Rhetoric)* and Ingram Bywater *(Poetics).* New York: Modern Library, 1984.

———. *Topics.* Trans. W. A. Pickard-Cambridge. *The Complete Works of Aristotle: The Revised Oxford Translation.* Vol. 1. Ed. Jonathan Barnes. Princeton: Princeton UP, 1984. 167–277. 2 vols.

Bakhtin, Mikhail. *The Dialogic Imagination.* Trans. Caryl Emerson and Michael Holquist. Ed. Holquist. Austin: U of Texas P, 1981.

Bauer, Dale Marie, et al. "Feminist Pedagogy." Unpublished ms., 1988.

Berlin, James A. "Rhetoric and Ideology in the Writing Class." *College English* 50 (1988): 477–94.

———. *Rhetoric and Reality: Writing Instruction in American Colleges, 1900–1985.* Carbondale: Southern Illinois UP, 1987.

Bizzell, Patricia. "Beyond Anti-Foundationalism to Rhetorical Authority: Problems Defining 'Cultural Literacy.'" *College English* 52 (1990): 661–75.

Bruffee, Kenneth A. "Collaborative Learning and the 'Conversation of Mankind.'" *College English* 46 (1984): 635–52.

Caywood, Cynthia L., and Gillian R. Overing, eds. *Teaching Writing: Pedagogy, Gender, and Equity.* New York: State U of New York P, 1986.

Cixous, Hélène, and Catherine Clément. *The Newly Born Woman.* Trans. Betsy Wing. Minneapolis: U of Minnesota P, 1986.

Culley, Margo, and Catherine Portuges, eds. *Gendered Subjects: The Dynamics of Feminist Teaching.* Boston: Routledge, 1985.

Culley, Margo, et al. "The Politics of Nurturance." Culley and Portuges, 11–20.

Däumer, Elisabeth, and Sandra Runzo. "Transforming the Composition Classroom," Caywood and Overing, 45–62.

de Lauretis, Teresa. *Alice Doesn't: Feminism, Semiotics, Cinema.* Bloomington: Indiana UP, 1984.

———. *Technologies of Gender.* Bloomington: Indiana UP, 1987.

Elbow, Peter. "Appendix Essay: The Doubting Game and the Believing Game—An Analysis of the Intellectual Enterprise." Elbow, *Writing* 147–91.

———. *Embracing Contraries.* New York: Oxford UP, 1986.

———. "Methodological Doubting and Believing: Contraries in Inquiry." Elbow, *Embracing Contraries* 254–300.

———. *Writing Without Teachers.* New York: Oxford UP, 1973.

Ellsworth, Elizabeth. "Why Doesn't This Feel Empowering? Working Through the Repressive Myths of Critical Pedagogy." Tenth Annual Conference on Curriculum Theory and Classroom Practice. Dayton, 26–29 Oct. 1988.

Fish, Stanley. "Anti-Foundationalism, Theory Hope, and the Teaching of Composition" and "Interview with Stanley Fish." *The Current in Criticism.* Ed. Clayton Koelb and Vergil Lokke. W. Lafayette: Purdue UP, 1987. 65–98.

———. *Is There a Text in This Class?* Cambridge: Harvard UP, 1980.

Flynn, Elizabeth. "Composing as a Woman." *College Composition and Communication* 39 (1988): 423–35.

Freire, Paulo, and Donaldo Macedo. *Literacy: Reading the Word and the World.* S. Hadley: Bergin, 1987.

Gallop, Jane. "The Immoral Teachers." *Yale French Studies* 63 (1982): 117–28.

———. *Reading Lacan.* Ithaca: Cornell UP, 1985.

Gearhart, Sally Miller. "The Womanization of Rhetoric." *Women's Studies International Quarterly* 2 (1979): 195–201.

Gilligan, Carol. *In a Different Voice: Psychological Theory and Women's Development.* Cambridge: Harvard UP, 1982.

Giroux, Henry. *Theory and Resistance in Education: A Pedagogy for the Opposition.* S. Hadley: Edward Arnold, 1978.

Graves, Richard L., ed. *Rhetoric and Composition: A Sourcebook for Teachers and Writers.* Upper Montclair: Boynton, 1984.

hooks, bell. *Talking Back: Thinking Feminist, Thinking Black.* Boston: South End, 1989.

Jarratt, Susan C. "The First Sophists and Feminism: Discourses of the 'Other.'" *Hypatia* 5 (1990): 27–41.

———. *Rereading the Sophists: Classical Rhetoric Refigured.* Carbondale: Southern Illinois UP, 1991.

Johnson, Barbara. *A World of Difference.* Baltimore: Johns Hopkins UP, 1987.

Lewis, Magda, and Roger I. Simon. "A Discourse Not Intended for Her: Learning and Teaching Within Patriarchy." *Harvard Educational Review* 56 (1986): 457–72.

Liddell, H. G., and Robert Scott. *A Lexicon, Abridged from Liddell and Scott's Greek-English Lexicon.* Oxford: Clarendon P, 1983.

Moi, Toril. "Feminism, Postmodernism, and Style: Recent Feminist Criticism in the United States." *Cultural Critique* 9 (1988): 3–22.

———. *Sexual/Textual Politics: Feminist Literary Theory.* London: Methuen, 1985.

Murray, Donald M. "Teach Writing as a Process Not Product." Graves, 89–94.

———. *Write to Learn.* 2nd ed. New York: Holt, 1987.

Ong, Walter J. *Fighting for Life: Contest, Sexuality, and Consciousness.* Amherst: U of Massachusetts P, 1989.

———. *Orality and Literacy: The Technologizing of the Word.* London: Methuen, 1982.

Plato. *Phaedrus. The Collected Dialogues of Plato.* Trans. R. Hackforth. Ed. Edith Hamilton and Huntington Cairns. Princeton: Princeton, UP, 1961. 475–525.

———. *Protagoras.* Trans. B. Jowett. Ed. Gregory Vlastos. Rev. Martin Ostwald. Indianapolis: Bobbs, 1956. 475–525.

———. *Theaetetus and Sophist.* Trans. Harold North Fowler. Cambridge: Harvard UP, 1961.

Schilb, John. "Pedagogy of the Oppressors?" Culley and Portuges, 253–64.

Shor, Ira. *Critical Teaching and Everyday Life.* Boston: South End, 1980.

———, ed. *Freire for the Classroom.* Portsmouth: Boynton, 1988.

Spender, Dale. *Man Made Language.* London: Routledge, 1980.

Spivak, Gayatri Chakravorty. *In Other Words: Essays in Cultural Politics.* New York: Methuen, 1987.

Stanger, Carol A. "The Sexual Politics of the One-to-One Tutorial Approach and Collaborative Learning." Caywood and Overing, 31–44.

Tompkins, Jane. "Me and My Shadow." *New Literary History* 19 (1987): 169–78.

Trebilcot, Joyce. "Dyke Methods or Principles for the Discovery/Creation of the Withstanding." *Hypatia* 3 (1988): 1–13.

Weiler, Kathleen. *Women Teaching for Change: Gender, Class, and Power.* S. Hadley: Bergin, 1988.

17   *Beyond Argument in Feminist Composition*

CATHERINE E. LAMB

Current discussion of feminist approaches to teaching composition emphasizes the writer's ability to find her own voice through open-ended, exploratory, often autobiographical, writing in which she assumes a sympathetic audience. These approaches are needed and appropriate: they continue to show us the richness and diversity of women's voices. My intent in this essay is to suggest a means by which one can enlarge the sphere of feminist composition by including in it an approach to argument, ways to proceed if one is in conflict with one's audience—in other words, the beginning of a feminist theory of composition. The place to start is not with particular forms—those close off options too easily—but by understanding the range of power relationships available to a writer and her readers. One then determines which are consistent with the emphasis on cooperation, collaboration, shared leadership, and integration of the cognitive and affective which is characteristic of feminist pedagogy (Schniedewind 170–79). This line of exploration has taken me to the study of negotiation and mediation, and how these well-established forms of oral discourse can be adapted for a feminist composition class. Argument still has a place, although now as a means, not an end. The end—a resolution of conflict that is fair to both sides—is possible even in the apparent one-sidedness of written communication.

BROADENING THE SCOPE OF FEMINIST MODES OF DISCOURSE

Much has now been written about women writing and feminist modes of discourse. To illustrate representative approaches, I have selected two essays that have appeared recently in composition journals—one by Elizabeth Flynn describing patterns in women's narratives; the other by Clara Juncker playing out some of the implications if one applies French feminists' theories in the classroom, especially those of Hélène Cixous. Neither pretends to be an exhaustive treatment of the subject. However, because both deal in the content

From *College Composition and Communication* 42 (1991): 11–24.

and form that we have come to associate with the broad topic of women and writing, one could quite easily get the idea that these are the only areas in which feminist composition has a contribution to make.

In "Composing as a Woman," Elizabeth Flynn uses what we know about gender differences in social and psychological development to interpret the content of narratives her students wrote. The four essays she uses, two by women and two by men, are not meant to be definitive proof that women write one way and men another, but rather to show that the connections between psychological theory and narrative content are there and may illuminate each other. Her findings are not surprising: women write "stories of interaction, of connection, or of frustrated connection"; men write "stories of achievement, of separation, or of frustrated achievement" (428). This essay and one which followed it fourteen months later, "Composing 'Composing as a Woman': A Perspective on Research," emphasize the open-ended, provisional nature of Flynn's thinking—another quality that has come to be associated with (and prized in) feminist composition.

What I have learned from Flynn's essay and others like it helps me when I am working with women students and reading some literature by women. I need something else, though, if I am to develop a comprehensive approach to feminist composition, guidelines that could be used throughout a course, including the emphasis I used to give argument as a mode in which one's goal is to persuade another to one's point of view. I would also like to be as free as possible from the charge of essentialism, to which an essay like Flynn's is vulnerable. A feminist composition class could easily be a place where matriarchal forms are as oppressive as the patriarchal ones once were, even if in different ways.

Clara Juncker's essay "Writing (with) Cixous" is quite a different piece, written in the exuberant manner of the theorists whose work she is describing. Like them, she is much less interested in women as gendered beings possessing certain characteristics (a possible extension of Flynn's argument) than she is in "woman" as a feminine linguistic position from which to critique phallogocentrism, "the fantasy of a central, idealized subject and the phallus as signifier of power and authority" (425). If this order is dislocated, students may be able to find their own voices on the margins. Playing with language, as well as stressing pre-writing and revision, can sensitize students to the open-endedness of writing. And if they read material sufficiently outrageous, they are more likely to empathize with otherness, whether "racially, politically, sexually, herstorically" (433).

With Flynn's essay, in spite of its value, I see its potential for reductiveness. My concerns with Juncker's essay are theoretical and practical in a different way. I admire the energy in her essay and, having heard her read a shortened version of it at CCCC in 1988, I don't doubt she is able to convey the same to her students. But after the disruptions, then what? I can imagine an essay written this way that is every bit as combative as the masculinist discourse we are seeking to supplant. Further, how can students take these forms and use them in other classes or in the world of work? If we are serious about the feminist project of transforming the curriculum and even affecting the way students think, write, and act once they leave us, we need an approach to teaching composition that is more broadly based and accessible to our students.

Without such a framework, we are also left battling the dichotomies that Cynthia Caywood and Gillian Overing identify in the introduction to their anthology *Teaching Writing: Pedagogy, Gender, and Equity.* Noting that "the model of writing as product is inherently authoritarian," they continue, "certain forms of discourse and language are privileged: the expository essay is valued over the exploratory; the argumentative essay set above the autobiographical; the clear evocation of a thesis preferred to a more organic exploration of a topic; the impersonal, rational voice ranked more highly than the intimate, subjective one" (xii). I don't know anyone who would deny that these dichotomies exist and are evaluated in the manner described. Neither do I deny the value of continuing to emphasize and explore the potentials of the categories in the second half of each of these dichotomies, as do Flynn and Juncker, along with the contributors to this anthology. We need as well, however, to consider a feminist response to conflict, at the very least to recast the terms of the dichotomy so that "argumentation" is opposed not to "autobiography" but, perhaps, to "mediation."

One half of the problem I am addressing is the narrow range of feminist composition as defined so far. The other is its incompatibility with the values of what I am calling here "monologic argument," the way most (all?) of us were taught to conceptualize arguments: what we want comes first, and we use the available means of persuasion to get it, in, one hopes, ethical ways. We may acknowledge the other side's position but only to refute it. We also practice what we were taught. Keith Fort, in a 1975 essay that uses language we have come to expect in feminist critiques, sees stating a thesis as a competitive act, a way to claim mastery over the subject matter. Similar competition may be generated between the reader and the text (179).[1] More recently, Olivia Frey demonstrates that the antagonism in our writing is much more overt than Fort implies. Using a sample that included all the essays published in *PMLA* from 1975 to 1988 as well as articles in a variety of other professional journals, she found some version of the "adversarial method" in all but two of the essays she examined (512). We have uncritically assumed there is no other way to write—at least that attitude was present in much of the discussion about ways to respond to conflict at the 1990 Wyoming Conference on English. Even a text like Gregory Clark's *Dialogue, Dialectic, and Conversation,* which does a superb job of laying out the theory for a cooperative, collaborative approach to writing and reading that is consistent with much of what I shall present later in this essay, sees the act of writing as by definition authoritarian in an even broader sense than do Caywood and Overing. Thus, it is the reader, not the writer, who has the primary responsibility for how a text functions in a community (see especially 49–59). Ideally, wouldn't we want the reader *and* the writer to share that responsibility?[2]

If we as teachers pass on without reflection what we have been taught and ourselves practice concerning argument, whether the rest of our pedagogy intends it or not, we are contributing to education as "banking," Paulo Freire's metaphor for education that is an act of "depositing" information into students who are only to receive and have no say in what or how something is taught (58–59). We are doing so because we are teaching students to form "banking" relationships with their readers, resisting dialogue, which, for Freire, means they are precluded from any possibility of naming the world, the essential element of being human (76). One of my first-year students this past year knew at some basic level what Freire was talking about when he described himself as a writer at the beginning of the semester: "For myself writing as a whole is not very important. . . . I would much rather interact with someone by voice rather than writing. Writing is one-sided where no argument or opinion from others can be intervened."

In my discussion thus far of monologic argument, I have intentionally avoided associating it with classical rhetoric, especially Aristotle's. While the connections can surely be made and have been for more than two thousand years, recent scholarship is much more likely to explore ways in which both Plato and Aristotle comment on the social, dialogical context in which knowledge is acquired and exchanged. (See, for example, chapter 2 in Clark, "Rhetoric in Dialectic: The Functional Context of Writing.") Here, I wish only to remind readers of some of those connections without discussing them in detail. The feminist alternatives I am advocating do not follow necessarily, but they are clearly consistent with them. With respect to Plato, what is most important is the example of his dialogues themselves illustrating the dialectic he is advocating, even though the goal, immutable truth, may not be one we share. In the *Phaedrus,* Socrates criticizes writing (in writing), seeing it as something static which inhibits dialectic (95–103). However one interprets his condemnation,[3] the dissonance resulting from an attack on writing itself, also made directly by Plato in *Letter VII* (136), contributes to the dialectic. Aristotle is much more explicitly connected to monologic argument, especially if one stops at his definition of rhetoric as no more than dealing with "the available means of persuasion," a set of techniques to be used. Andrea Lunsford and Lisa Ede have refuted the contradictory claims that Aristotelian rhetoric overemphasizes the logical and is manipulative ("On Distinctions"), making use of William Grimaldi's work on Aristotle. Grimaldi maintains that in Aristotle's *Rhetoric* one person is speaking to another *as a person;* the rhetor's task is to put before the audience the means by which the audience can make up his or her mind, but it is then up to the audience to decide. The enthymeme is most often cited by these writers and others as illustrating Aristotle's recognition of the proper use of both reason and emotion. The speaker, in constructing an enthymeme, must take the audience into account since it is the audience who supplies the unstated premise. As Lloyd Bitzer says, the audience in effect persuades itself (408).

A FEMINIST THEORY OF POWER

While it is helpful to view Plato and Aristotle in the ways I have just summarized, neither provides ways to get to concrete alternatives to monologic argument. Considering writer/reader relationships in the context of a feminist theory of power allows us to see more clearly the disjuncture between mono-logic argument and the modes of discourse advocated by Flynn and Juncker. It also provides a framework for evaluating any alternatives to resolving con-flict. Because the emphasis is on values available to men as well as women, essentialist aspects of this approach are minimized.

In an earlier essay, I note that we understand power in a common-sense way as "the ability to affect what happens to someone else" (100). Monologic argument fits in here easily. There are, however, a number of feminist theorists who view power not as a quality to exercise on others, but as something which can energize, enabling competence and thus reducing hierarchy.[4] More than thirty years ago, Hannah Arendt, in her discussion of "action" in *The Human Condition*, showed us what this use of power might look like. She wrote about the *polis* in classical Greece, in which rhetoric as a spoken art, and therefore argument, would have functioned to maintain the *polis* as she describes it. Its essential character is not its physical boundaries, but "the organization of the people as it arises out of acting and speaking together, and its true space lies between people living together for this purpose" (198). Power maintains this space in which people act and speak: no single person can possess it (as an individual can possess strength). It "springs up" when people act together and disappears when they separate. This sort of power is limitless; it can, therefore, "be divided without decreasing it, and the interplay of powers with their checks and balances is even liable to generate more power" (200–1). I am reminded here of Bakhtin's familiar image of the carnival as the place where hierarchy is suspended and with it the distance between people (e.g., *Problems of Dostoyevsky's Poetics* 122–26). The image is much less dignified than Arendt's idealized description of the *polis*, but the impulse that drives and sustains them is, I believe, the same.

In discussing Dostoyevsky's world view, Bakhtin says its governing prin-ciple is "To affirm someone else's 'I' not as an object but as another subject" (10). Some feminist theorists contribute to articulating how such a relationship might develop through insights gained from studying women's experience. They are arguing from what has come to be called a "feminist standpoint," defined by Sara Ruddick as "a superior vision produced by the political conditions and dis-tinctive work of women" (129). The superiority of the standpoint derives from the manner in which it is acquired. An oppressed group, in this case, women, gains knowledge only through its struggle with the oppressor, men, who have no need to learn about the group they are oppressing. With this experience, women's knowledge has at least the potential to be more complete than men's (Harding, "Conclusion" 184–85). There are, admittedly, dangers in using stand-point theory: It can imply the moral superiority of women, easily become essen-tialist,[5] and ignore the reality that many of the qualities we ascribe to women can just as accurately be called non-Western—possibilities that my anthropolo-gist friends have pointed out to me and that Harding notes in a later essay ("Instability" 29–30). I continue to use this approach, however, because of the teaching power of concrete experience reflected on, to which the success of a book like Belenky et al.'s *Women's Ways of Knowing* is eloquent testimony.

The most complete feminist discussion of the thought and action which makes possible the use of power described above, in individual relationships as well as those between nations, is Sara Ruddick's *Maternal Thinking*. Ruddick deliberately uses "maternal" because women still have most of the responsibility for raising children; mothering work, she says, can be done as well by men as by women (xi). One need not be a biological parent either. I want to summarize the main features of maternal thinking and then apply them to writer/reader relationships. (They are also readily applicable to teacher/student relationships—but that is another essay. One of the pleasures of teaching this approach to conflict resolution is that it invites attention to the congruence between what and how one teaches.) Central to the idea and experience of maternal thinking is "attentive love, or loving attention" (120). Loving attention is much like empathy, the ability to think or feel as the other. In connecting with the other, it is critical that one already has and retains a sense of one's self. The process requires, ultimately, more recognition and honoring of difference than it does searching for common ground. The vulnerability of the child, combined with the necessity for it and the mother to grow and change, place apparently contradictory demands on the relationship. On the one hand, maternal work requires an attitude of "holding," in which the mother does what is necessary to protect the child without unduly controlling it. On the other hand, she must continually welcome change if she is to foster growth (78–79, 89–93, 121–23).

In the second half of her book, Ruddick shows how maternal thinking can be applied to conflict resolution more generally. One begins by recognizing that equality often does not exist in relationships; even with this reality, individuals or groups in unequal relationships do not have to resort to violence to resolve conflicts. Making peace in this context requires both "giving and receiving while remaining in connection" (180–81). In *Composing a Life*, a discussion of the shaping of five women's lives, Mary Catherine Bateson reflects on these asymmetrical, interdependent relationships and how ill-prepared we are to function in them. Typically, we value symmetrical relationships—buddies and colleagues—which happen also to promote competition. Instead of honoring difference, which makes interdependence possible (both are qualities which "loving attention" cultivates), we want to reduce difference to inequality (102–6).

Monologic argument, even at its best, inevitably separates itself very quickly from the qualities I have just described because of its subject/object, I/it orientation. As I shall demonstrate later, where we still need this kind of argument is at the early stages of resolving a conflict, where both parties need to be as clear as possible about what they think and feel. Our students need to learn it for their survival in other contexts, and, more fundamentally, as part of the process of becoming adults. It promotes differentiation, the sense of self that Ruddick says must precede maternal thinking or integration more generally. This essay is itself a kind of monologic argument because I am asking readers to consider a different (and better, I believe) approach to resolving conflicts in writing. For any change to occur, however, readers first need to know what it is I am proposing.

At this point, readers might be thinking of Rogerian argument as an alternative to monologic argument. In it, the writer goes to great lengths to show the audience that he understands their point of view and the values behind it. The hope is that the audience, feeling less threatened, will do the same. My experience using Rogerian argument and teaching it to my students, is that it is feminine rather than feminist. It has always been women's work to understand others (at Albion, it is women, not men, who sign up for The Psychology of Men); often that has been at the expense of understanding self. Rogerian argument has always felt too much like giving in. (In "Feminist Responses to Rogerian Argument," Phyllis Lassner makes these points and others about the difficulties of using Rogerian argument, and the hostilities it may arouse in users, especially if they do not yet have a clear sense of self.)

MEDIATION AND NEGOTIATION AS ALTERNATIVES

What we need as an alternative to the self-assertiveness of monologic argument is not self-denial but an approach which cultivates the sense of spaciousness Arendt describes in the working of the *polis*. My very brief comments on Plato and Aristotle were intended as another way of saying they are concerned with knowledge as something that people do together rather than something anyone possesses (Gage 156). In a reversal of Bacon's dictum, we could say that Arendt's notion of power makes possible knowledge realized this way. We are ready now to apply this relationship of knowledge and power more specifically to a conflict situation. In it, both parties can retain the interdependence that permits connectedness while also going through the giving and receiving necessary if they are to resolve their conflict. The result is a paradoxical situation where the distance between writer and audience is lessened (as they explore the dimensions of the conflict together) while the "space" in which they are operating has enlarged because they see more possibilities (Lamb 102–3). Jim Corder, in "Argument as Emergence, Rhetoric as Love," also asks us to visualize the writer/audience relationship in terms of physical space. Argument, he says, is too often a matter of "presentation" and "display." Instead, it should just "be." Rather than objectifying the other, we need to "emerge" toward it. In a corollary to the idea of creating more space in which writer and audience can operate, he says we should expect to have to "pile time" into our arguments: we can do so by relying less on closed, packaged forms and more on narratives that show who we are and what our values are (26–31).

When I read Fisher and Ury's *Getting to Yes*, a layperson's version of how the process of negotiation works, I saw that here were some new (to me, as a composition teacher) ways of thinking about argument and conflict resolution. I later attended a seminar on mediation and have mediated cases of sexual harassment at Albion, as one of the people designated by the College to hear these complaints. What quickly became apparent, in both negotiation and mediation, is that the goal has changed: it is no longer to win but to arrive at a solution in a just way that is acceptable to both sides. Necessarily, the conception of power has changed as well: from something that can be possessed and used on somebody to something that is available to both and has at least the potential of being used for the benefit of both. When negotiation and mediation are adapted for a writing class, talk is still central for either process. Writing marks critical stages but cannot occur without conversation that matters, before and after. With all of the currently fashionable and often obscure discourse about writing as dialogue, here is a simple, concrete way of actually doing it.

Central to understanding this broadened and re-focused "practice" of power—how it creates more space and the possibility for loving attention—is articulating the place of conflict in it. As a culture, we learn much more about how to repress or ignore conflict than how to live with and transform it. When we practice and teach monologic argument as an end, we are teaching students that conflict can be removed by an effort that is fundamentally one-sided. Morton Deutsch, in *The Resolution of Conflict,* reminds us that conflicts arise in order that tensions between antagonists might be resolved. They can be healthy ways of finding a new stability and of clarifying values and priorities (9), especially if both parties participate in the resolution in ways that are mutually satisfactory. Negotiation and mediation are *cooperative* approaches to resolving conflicts that increase the chances of these goals occurring. They focus on the future, not the past (as does the law), and seek to restore trust between the two parties. A win-lose orientation encourages narrowness and a wish to use resources only for the goal one has already identified. Deutsch notes that the outcomes of a cooperative approach are those which encourage creative problem-solving: "openness, lack of defensiveness, and full utilization of available resources" (363). Negotiation and mediation are also *collaborative,* with both parties using the process to identify interests and outcomes they share. (See Clark, xvi, for distinctions between cooperation and dialogue on the one hand and collaboration and dialectic on the other.) Finally, both cooperation and collaboration are facilitated by negotiation and mediation as *structured* forms of conflict resolution. The point is important, for the guidelines which provide the structure are the mechanism whereby space between the two parties can be increased, making it possible for the distance between them to lessen as they move toward each other.

Negotiation as it is described in *Getting to Yes* begins with a recognition that focusing on the particularities of the *positions* of both parties will get them nowhere. Instead, identifying underlying *interests or issues* is a way to get at root causes of the problem as well as seeing where there might be common ground. The parties brainstorm a number of possible solutions, evaluating them using criteria both sides can accept. For Fisher and Ury, the ideal outcome is to reach a solution to which both sides can unequivocally answer "yes." Mediation extends and elaborates the process of negotiation with the introduction of an impartial third party. The nature of the outcome is still the responsibility of the disputants, as is carrying out the settlement. The parties in a dispute often appeal to a mediator when they believe they cannot resolve the conflict themselves. The presence of a mediator is also extremely valuable if there is a power imbalance between the two parties, as with, in my experience, cases of sexual harassment involving a student and professor. One of the mediator's main functions, especially at the beginning, is collecting information: What are the problems for each side? What are the interests these problems reflect? Where are the areas of agreement? What are the outcomes each side wants? The mediator's goal is a written agreement, which all parties sign, consisting of concrete statements describing actions both parties will take to resolve the conflict.[6]

I am not yet prepared to recommend one process of conflict resolution over the other in a composition classroom. Mediation may be somewhat more accessible because the roles of negotiator and disputant are separate. I have also taught both only in upper-level writing courses, negotiation in Advanced Expository Writing and mediation in Technical Writing. (I originally used mediation in Technical Writing because a good mediation agreement is also a model of good technical writing: its function is instrumental, and it must be straightforward, concrete, and unambiguous.) In both courses, the pedagogy is feminist, but only in the expository writing class do I use the theoretical orientation I describe in this paper as a guiding principle for the entire course. Here, I shall describe my use of mediation first to show how the roles operate separately. It also illustrates how a traditional-looking, writing-as-product piece of discourse actually functions quite differently because of the context out of which it comes.

Students work in groups of three, deciding what problem they will work with and who will take what role. Projects come from their reading or current college issues. Last semester, they were as disparate as mediating a property settlement between Donald and Ivana Trump and a dispute between the Inter-Fraternity Council and the administration at Albion College over the social function fraternities serve on campus. Much of the training for being a mediator (or a disputant) goes on in role plays. Of the many skills a mediator needs, I concentrate on just a few: getting as complete a picture as possible from both sides, separating the facts of the situation from the issues, and getting the parties they are working with to come up with as many options as possible in the process of arriving at a solution.

The first piece of writing is one they do individually after they have met several times as a group. If they are one of the disputants, they write a memo to the mediator in which they explain the problem as they see it, including an attempt to separate the immediate ways in which the problem has exhibited itself from the underlying issues or interests. They gain more from the experience if they are willing to take on a role opposite from their own actual position: a fraternity member representing the administration; or a woman playing a man whose spouse has just been offered a high-paying position hundreds of miles away—accepting it would mean serious disruptions in the family and in his career. If a student is the mediator, he or she writes a memo to a supervisor, summarizing the issues for both parties as they appear at that point. Here, all three are using the analytical skills we associate with mono-logic argument, although not with the goal of persuasion. The memos are part of what will give the mediator a sense of the dimensions of the conflict. For the disputants, they act to "pile time." All of these actions encourage maternal thinking, which is especially desirable between the mediator and both dis-putants; one hopes it also occurs between the disputants by the end of the process. The second piece of writing is the mediation agreement itself, which all three prepare together. Here are two of ten clauses in an agreement the Inter-Fraternity/administration group reached to resolve their differences:

1. Fraternities agree to restrict the number of house parties to two per semes-ter for the spring 1990 and fall 1990 terms.

2. The administration agrees to begin free shuttle services to cities (Ann Arbor and Lansing) to widen the available social possibilities.

All these pieces of writing in the mediation process are products and not, as will be seen in the discussion of negotiation, a record of a process. Because of the interaction that must occur, particularly when the agreement is being developed, and because everyone involved is both writer and audience, I am not willing to accept Caywood and Overing's judgment that "writing as prod-uct is inherently authoritarian." The group's inventing has quite literally been a collaborative, social act, as Karen LeFevre has urged us to see invention more generally (see especially 35–40). Developing and carrying out a media-tion agreement is clearly an illustration of what Arendt is getting at when she describes how power works, a point LeFevre also makes. The mediator and disputants, acting together in good faith, can move beyond the conflict that divides them. They are likely to have the experience described by one of the professionals Andrea Lunsford and Lisa Ede interviewed for their book on collaborative writing, *Singular Texts/Plural Authors:* "Working with someone else gives you another point of view. There is an extra voice inside your head; that can make a lot of difference" (29). If, however, one disputant pulls out, or the mediator gives up her neutrality, the energizing power is gone.

When I teach negotiation, it, like mediation, comes in the second half of the course when students trust me and one another and are accustomed to working in groups on various projects. Many of the features of teaching medi-ation (sources for topics, how to do the training, using writing in different ways at various stages of the process) apply as well to negotiation. Students work in pairs, selecting an issue of some substance in which they are both interested and which will require outside research. Individually, they each write a paper in which they take a contrasting position on the issue. I expect a monologic argument in the best sense of that term. Students see they cannot hope to negotiate a solution with integrity unless they are first clear about the characteristics and values of the viewpoint they are presenting, especially crit-ical if it is one with which they do not agree. When the students have finished the first paper, I meet with the pairs to discuss their arguments. Sometimes, students on their own will take the initiative to begin negotiating a resolution during the conference, ignoring me. We can all then see the process occurring; their next essay, which they write together, is a record of it. They have little trouble differentiating the effect of reading it, its greater sense of spaciousness, from the much more linear effect of reading a monologic argument. The most common form of resolution is some kind of compromise, for example, merit pay for teachers, with the conditions limiting its application making it acceptable to its opponents. (The dynamics of power between the students working together are something I have not yet tried to identify in any systematic way. My impression, from anecdotal evidence, is that most pairs function in a fairly egalitarian way. Of course, they also know that's what I want to hear them say.)

Taking together my discussion of mediation and negotiation, these several features of a feminist alternative to monologic argument are apparent: (1) Knowledge is seen as cooperatively and collaboratively constructed (what the groups have created has come out of the relationships among their members). (2) The "attentive love" of maternal thinking is present at least to some degree (or they would not have been able to come up with a solution acceptable to both of them). (3) The writing which results is likely to emphasize process. (4) Finally, overall, power is experienced as mutually enabling.

These forms, along with the contexts in which they are produced, may also be ways to respond to Lunsford and Ede's call for written discourse which reflects dialogic collaboration in the texts themselves (*Singular* 136). They will not necessarily be of interest to all feminists. Sandra Gilbert and Susan Gubar, among the best known feminist collaborators, have said in a public discussion that they do not see any particular value to writing in a way that would reflect their collaboration and, by extension, more overtly invite the reader into the text. For those of us who *are* interested, these forms show how the writing of a text need not be "an inherently unethical act" (Clark 61), saved only by its readers and their responses. The forms are expressions of writer/reader relationships which reflect an understanding of power consistent with feminist values. As we use them, the forms themselves will change to mirror our evolving understanding of what we are constructing. We *can* move beyond argument. It may not even be foolish to hope for a time when wanting to do so is beyond argument.

NOTES

1. Fort's essay is cited by William Covino in *The Art of Wondering*. Fort's solution for the critical essay is to recommend "process criticism," where one might explore the correctness of a particular thesis rather than begin with it and show only how the work being analyzed fits. Fort notes that, to some extent, such essays are about the *process* of criticism; in the same way, the form I have students use when they are using negotiation as an alternative to argument is about the process of negotiation.

2. S. Michael Halloran works under assumptions similar to Clark's in "Rhetoric in the American College Curriculum: The Decline of Public Discourse." He is arguing for returning the practice of teaching public discourse to our teaching of rhetoric (a goal I support, as does Clark, for the ways it would reinforce the social function of writing). Although the form of the discourse is not his major concern, the examples he gives all assume a debate model of interaction.

3. For examples of the range of interpretations possible, see Ronna Burger, *Plato's Phaedrus,* in which she argues for Plato's developing a "philosophical art of writing"; Jasper Neel, on the other

hand, in *Plato, Derrida, and Writing,* argues that Plato is not using writing but trying to "use it up," appropriating both Socrates's voice and then his means of expression (1–29). Walter Ong, in *Orality and Literacy,* is more relaxed. He notes that Plato's criticisms of writing are the same that were made with the advent of printing and now of computers (979).

4. In addition to the theorists discussed in this essay, I also refer to Jean Baker Miller, *Toward a New Psychology of Women,* and Elizabeth Janeway, *Powers of the Weak.* Another important source is Nancy Hartsock, *Money, Sex, and Power.*

5. I invite readers to consider whether Ruddick's approach as I go on to summarize it is essentialist. Perhaps in the final analysis it is, although in her book she goes to considerable lengths to discuss varieties of mothering experiences. The potential oppression of any essentialist features is also reduced because the process she describes is available to men as well as women and has as its hallmark a deep respect for the other as person.

6. I have taken this very abbreviated description of the mediation process from Christopher Moore, *The Mediation Process,* and from the *Mediator Training Manual for Face-to-Face Mediation* (Boston: Department of Attorney General, 1988), used at the Mediation Institute taught each spring at the University of Massachusetts at Amherst by staff of the Mediation Project.

WORKS CITED

Arendt, Hannah. *The Human Condition.* Chicago: U of Chicago P, 1958.

Bakhtin, Mikhail. *Problems of Dostoyevsky's Poetics.* Trans. and ed. Caryl Emerson. Theory and History of Literature 8. Minneapolis: U of Minnesota P, 1984.

Bateson, Mary Catherine. *Composing a Life.* New York: Atlantic Monthly, 1989.

Belenky, Mary Field, et al. *Women's Ways of Knowing.* New York: Basic Books, 1986.

Bitzer, Lloyd F. "Aristotle's Enthymeme Revisited." *Quarterly Journal of Speech* 45 (Dec. 1959): 399–408.

Burger, Ronna. *Plato's Phaedrus.* University, AL: U of Alabama P, 1980.

Caywood, Cynthia L., and Gillian R. Overing. Introduction. *Teaching Writing: Pedagogy, Gender, and Equity.* Albany: State U of New York P, 1987. xi–xvi.

Clark, Gregory. *Dialogue, Dialectic, and Conversation.* Carbondale: Southern Illinois UP, 1990.

Corder, Jim W. "Argument as Emergence, Rhetoric as Love." *Rhetoric Review* 4 (Sept. 1985): 16–32.

Covino, William. *The Art of Wondering.* Portsmouth: Heinemann, 1988.

Department of Attorney General. *Mediator Training Manual for Face-to-Face Mediation.* Boston: Department of Attorney General, 1988.

Deutsch, Morton. *The Resolution of Conflict.* New Haven: Yale UP, 1973.

Fisher, Roger, and William Ury. *Getting to Yes: Negotiating Agreement Without Giving In.* New York: Penguin, 1983.

Flynn, Elizabeth A. "Composing as a Woman." *College Composition and Communication* 39 (Dec. 1988): 423–35.

———. "Composing 'Composing as a Woman': A Perspective on Research." *College Composition and Communication* 41 (Feb. 1990): 83–91.

Fort, Keith. "Form, Authority, and the Critical Essay." *Contemporary Rhetoric.* Ed. W. Ross Winterowd. New York: Harcourt, 1975. 171–83.

Freire, Paulo. *Pedagogy of the Oppressed.* Trans. Myra Bergman Ramos. New York: Seabury, 1970.

Frey, Olivia. "Beyond Literary Darwinism: Women's Voices and Critical Discourse." *College English* 52 (Sept. 1990): 507–26.

Gage, John. "An Adequate Epistemology for Composition: Classical and Modern Perspectives." *Essays on Classical Rhetoric and Modern Discourse.* Ed. Robert J. Connors, Lisa S. Ede, and Andrea A. Lunsford. Carbondale: Southern Illinois UP, 1984. 152–69, 281–84.

Grimaldi, William M. A. *Aristotle, Rhetoric I: A Commentary.* New York: Ford ham UP, 1980.

Halloran, S. Michael. "Rhetoric in the American College Curriculum: The Decline of Public Discourse." *PRE/TEXT* 3 (1982): 245–69.

Harding, Sandra. "Conclusion: Epistemological Questions." *Feminism and Methodology.* Ed Sandra Harding. Bloomington: Indiana UP, 1987. 181–90.

———. "The Instability of the Analytical Categories of Feminist Theory." *Signs* 11 (1986). Rpt. in *Feminist Theory in Practice and Process.* Ed. Micheline R. Malson et al. Chicago: U of Chicago P, 1989. 15–34.

Hartsock, Nancy. *Money, Sex, and Power.* Boston: Northeastern UP, 1983.

Janeway, Elizabeth. *Powers of the Weak.* New York: Knopf, 1980.

Juncker, Clara. "Writing (with) Cixous." *College English* 50 (April 1988): 424–36.

Lamb, Catherine E. "Less Distance, More Space: A Feminist Theory of Power and Writer/Audience Relationships." *Rhetoric and Ideology: Compositions and Criticisms of Power.* Ed. Charles W. Kneupper. Arlington: Rhetoric Society of America, 1989. 99–104.

Lassner, Phyllis. "Feminist Responses to Rogerian Argument." *Rhetoric Review* 8 (Spring 1990): 220–32.

LeFevre, Karen Burke. *Invention as a Social Act.* Carbondale: Southern Illinois UP, 1987.

Lunsford, Andrea, and Lisa Ede. "On Distinctions Between Classical and Modern Discourse." *Essays on Classical Rhetoric and Modern Discourse.* Ed. Robert J. Connors, Lisa S. Ede, and Andrea A. Lunsford. Carbondale: Southern Illinois UP, 1984. 37–49, 265–67.

———. *Singular Texts/Plural Authors: Perspectives on Collaborative Writing.* Carbondale: Southern Illinois UP, 1990.

Miller, Jean Baker. *Toward a New Psychology of Women.* Boston: Beacon, 1975.

Moore, Christopher. *The Mediation Process.* San Francisco: Jossey-Bass, 1987.

Neel, Jasper. *Plato, Derrida, and Writing.* Carbondale: Southern Illinois UP, 1988.

Ong, Walter. *Orality and Literacy.* New York: Methuen, 1982.

Plato. *Phaedrus and Letters VII and VIII.* Trans. Waiter Hamilton. London: Penguin, 1973.

Ruddick, Sara. *Maternal Thinking.* Boston: Beacon, 1989.

Schniedewind, Nancy. "Feminist Values: Guidelines for Teaching Methodology in Women's Studies." *Freire for the Classroom.* Ed. Ira Shor. Portsmouth: Heinemann, 1987. 170–179.

18

Discourse and Diversity: Experimental Writing Within the Academy

LILLIAN BRIDWELL-BOWLES

In classes ranging from "Advanced Expository Writing" and "Women and Writing" at the undergraduate level to "Gender, Language, and Writing Pedagogy" and "Classical and Contemporary Rhetoric" at the graduate level, I have invited students to imagine the possibilities for new forms of discourse, new kinds of academic essays. I do this because I believe that writing classes (and the whole field of composition studies) must employ richer visions of texts and composing processes. If we are to invent a truly pluralistic society, we must envision a socially and politically situated view of language and the creation of texts—one that takes into account gender, race, class, sexual preference, and a host of issues that are implied by these and other cultural differences. Our language and our written texts represent our visions of our culture, and we need new processes and forms if we are to express ways of thinking that have been outside the dominant culture. Finally, I believe that teaching students to write involves teaching them ways to critique not only their material and their potential readers' needs, but also the rhetorical conventions that they are expected to employ within the academy.

Work in composition has been expanded enormously by theories of cognitive processes, social construction, and by the uses of computers and other forms of technology, yet, as Adrienne Rich writes, "we might hypothetically possess ourselves of every recognized technological resource on the North American continent, but as long as our language is inadequate, our vision remains formless, our thinking and feeling are still running in the old cycles, our process may be 'revolutionary,' but not transformative" (Rich 247–48). David Kaufer and Cheryl Geisler argue that "freshmen composition and writing across the curriculum have remained silent about newness as a rhetorical standard, as a hallmark of literacy in a post-industrial, professional age." They do not believe that "this silence can be justified on either intellectual or pragmatic grounds . . ." (309). Others among the composition community (e.g., Calderonello) have also called for challenges to traditional essays.

I am skeptical about whether simply changing the surface of our aca-

From *College Composition and Communication* 43 (1992): 349–68.

demic language can give us Rich's "dream of a common language," but I have decided to start where I know how to start—and that is with tinkering on the surface. I have experimented with new forms to match my own changing scholarship, work that has become more and more cross-disciplinary. Just as I have moved from lines of inquiry exclusively based in social science and empiricism to those that are more oriented in humanistic, feminist, and liberation theories, so must my language change. Experiencing what my colleague Lisa Albrecht described as my "own personal paradigm shift," I have sought alternatives—a more personal voice, an expanded use of metaphor, a less rigid methodological framework, a writing process that allows me to combine hypothesizing with reporting data, to use patterns of writing that allow for multiple truths, what Dale Spender has called a "multidimensional reality," rather than a single thesis, and so on.

This ongoing process has made me realize that students may need new options for writing if they, too, are struggling with expressing concepts, attitudes, and beliefs that do not fit into traditional academic forms. To give them permission to experiment, I simply tell them that they need not always write the "standard academic essay" and encourage them to write something else. Many continue to write in familiar forms, and I do not require that they do otherwise. They may need to adopt the standard conventions before they can challenge or criticize them (see Bizzell for an account of this position). But increasing numbers of students take me up on my option and learn ways of critically analyzing rhetorical conventions at the same time that they are being introduced to traditional academic discourse communities.

When one attempts to write outside the dominant discourse, one often has to begin by naming the new thing. I have used various terms for our experiments, including "alternative" and "feminist," but recently we have been using the term "diverse discourse." "Alternative discourse" does not allow us to reform thinking, to imagine the possibility that writing choices that are now marginal could someday be positioned alongside, or in place of, the dominant ones. "Feminist discourse" has been my sentimental favorite because feminist theory gave me, personally, new ways of thinking and writing, but many students still feel excluded by this term. I am careful to say here, and in my classes, that even though I use feminist texts as my inspiration, students should feel free to read them as metaphors for their own attempts to write outside a dominant culture, however they define their positions. If they are not attempting to write outside established conventions, I invite them to consider how others might feel the need to do so.

In this essay, I will provide a rationale for this experimentation with diverse discourse, examples of the readings that inspire me and students in my classes, and samples of student essays.

WHY THE NEED FOR EXPERIMENTS? OR, WHAT IS YOUR PROBLEM?

Old patterns of argument, based on revealing a single truth (a thesis), using all the available means of persuasion, run counter to new theories of socially constructed knowledge and social change. Sally Miller Gearhart goes so far as to say that "any intent to persuade is an act of violence" (195). She wants to see communication in a more holistic way, as a "womb" or a "matrix . . . within which something takes form or begins" (199–200). She wants an entirely different rhetorical perspective:

> We are not the speaker, the-one-with-the-truth, the one-who-with-his-power-will-change-lives. We are the matrix, we are she-who-is-the-home-of-this-particular-human-interaction, we are the co-creator and co-sustainer of the atmosphere in whose infinity of possible transformations we will all change. (200)

Susan Meisenhelder also describes rhetorical aggression in her analysis of warlike, pugilistic, and phallic metaphors in writing. I hardly think that all forms of argumentation are passé. What do we do when we describe our positions on issues of social change, when we see a position as clearly "wrong," morally, ethically, socially? Obviously, argumentation has a place (even in this essay), but it need not be the only form our scholarly writings take.

Donald Murray, a familiar and respected member of the composition community, appears to support another contested convention when he argues for a distinction between "academic voice" and "personal voice." They are clearly separate for him. According to Murray, academic writing should appeal to reason, maintain a distanced and detached tone, cite outside authority, and be written in response to previous academic writing: "scholarly knowledge is built in increments of small additional bits added to previous knowledge" (189). Others, who might not make such clear distinctions, pass along similar, conventional academic wisdom for other reasons. Patricia Bizzell, a progressive member of the composition community, argues that students who are politically oppressed must master conventions of academic discourse in order to succeed, but she defines them significantly more broadly. Many students believe that academic "standard" language is the key to their success, perhaps even the key to their very survival, and I try not to debate this point, even though I question whether this key is sufficient for survival and success. We may agree on its necessity, but not on its sufficiency. I also believe that linguistic and rhetorical flexibility may help students to write better conventional prose.

In addition, I know that there are positions other than accommodation to or rejection of the dominant patterns of discourse. Min-zhan Lu takes such a position when she writes about her concern for students in composition classrooms, particularly in the light of her own personal struggle to mediate between the voices of home (English in a Chinese home) and school (Standard Chinese, the official language of New China):

> When composition classes encourage students to ignore those voices that seem irrelevant to the purified world of the classroom, most students are often able to do so without much struggle. . . . However, beyond the classroom and beyond the limited range of these students' immediate lives lies a much more complex and dynamic social and historical scene. To help these students become actors in such a scene, perhaps we need

to call their attention to voices that may seem irrelevant to the discourse we teach rather than encourage them to shut them out. . . . We might encourage students to explore ways of practicing the conventions of the discourse they are learning by negotiating through these conflicting voices. We could also encourage them to see themselves as responsible for forming or transforming as well as preserving the discourse they are learning. (447)

Geoffrey Chase (15), employing the theories of Giroux and Freire, also proposes that students can resist the conventions of academic discourse, analyzing and challenging them, not for the sake of mere opposition, but in order to work for social change. On the other hand, I also know that conventional academic discourse can be used in the service of reform.

For a variety of reasons, then, many students welcome the opportunity to critique academic discourse. Instead of adopting prior knowledge in an uncritical way, they establish a dialectical relationship with much previous knowledge; they sometimes take a position apart from the established academy. As one student put it, "People like yourself, Robin, Ellen, and others send us the message that WE DO NOT HAVE TO BE COOKIE-CUTTER SCHOLARS. In fact, some of us gave up BAKING long ago and we ARE the products of 20 years of feminist theory . . . unlike the traditional angel of the house, we have left the kitchen (KP duty and all) and have a LABORATORY of our own . . . in which we are creating new forms" (Olano, "Letter," 5).

Any departure from the norm is accompanied by fear, however, and some students are afraid to go too far. Pamela Olano goes on to say that she and her peers:

all have a morbid curiosity about what it is we ARE creating . . . and I can sense a desire to control the unknown . . . to make it "look like" something familiar. . . . This is heady stuff . . . and frightening stuff to fledglings just learning to fly (doctoral students . . . particularly women who are not sure as to their "welcome" into the fold). . . . Sometimes I think the academy and the educational system have done their jobs too well. We (men and women) arrive here believing that there is AN ANSWER KEY (like the one in the back of the teacher's edition), . . . then we run up against the UNDERGROUND that whispers "try it another way." We may in fact resist the voices we hear, but eventually we step off the limb . . . we write in a new voice, we experiment, we return to the limb. (Olano, "Letter," 5–6)

Perhaps with time, poststructuralist revolutions in thinking about our culture will influence our language so much that we will come to see personal writing, nonlinear patterns of organization, writing that contains emotion, writing that closes the gap between subject and object, writing that does something "with" and not "to" the reader, and all the other possibilities yet to come as having equal status with carefully reasoned, rational argument.

For now, however, writing in any of these ways clearly suggests "Other," and I have tried to explore ways that Other voices could be read and heard in my classes, ways that the Other could be celebrated. I have also included readings that show how successful writers and academics have shared concerns similar to Olano's above.

The Essentialist Problem and Feminist Discourse

Because I often use the term "feminist discourse" and readings from feminist theory are the starting point of my classes, I have to work very hard not to predispose students toward a construction of discourse that invokes the "essentialist" problem so carefully outlined by Joy Ritchie. I do not want to promote the idea that women, left to their own devices, would *all* write in a certain way and that this writing would always be different from *all* men's writing, but neither do I exclude the possibility that there might be significant, socially inherited and constructed contrasts between *many* women's and men's ways of thinking, their experiences, and their language. Of course, these differences have to be further integrated with race, class, and other differences if we are to fully understand the ways women use language.

I like Carolyn Heilbrun's 1988 discussion of "feminist" with regard to her own and others' writing, and her interpretation of Nancy Miller's definition of "feminism": "a self-consciousness about women's identity both as inherited cultural fact and as a process of social construction" (18). Heilbrun comments, "It is hard to suppose women can mean or want what we have always been assured they could not possibly mean or want" (18). An awareness of the ways our cultural inheritance, embodied largely in language, has limited our vision suggests the need for new ways of writing and the need for experimentation in academic settings.

All of this is complicated, of course, because we are working within a patriarchal, racist, and classist culture and using a patriarchal, racist, and classist variant of language to try to define something outside the culture. It may not be possible to create a feminist discourse with the "father's tongue" (Penelope) or the "master's tools" (Lorde, "Master's"). As Gauthier has put it, "Perhaps if we had left these pages blank, we should have had a better understanding of what feminine writing is all about" (162). Indeed, silence is a major topic in nearly all feminist theories.

While I have found no simple solutions to many of these problems, I must go on using language. My pragmatic approach is to discuss them directly with students and to invoke an experimental, open attitude. One student speaks for others when she says that an experimental approach is a way of proceeding: "I have said that I find this concept [feminist discourse] stimulating. By that I mean that it works for me as an inspiration, as a metaphor, as an idea fostered by an outrageous, free-roaming imagination." She writes this, even though she herself cannot write her way out of patriarchal language: "And I, at least, can't see how we are to get out of the straitjacket of patriarchal discourse. I have begun to feel as I have grappled with these wonderful ideas that the realization of a woman's voice, the demolition of the straitjacket, is an impossible project" (Ripoll). I responded to her conclusion, and others like it, by saying that I can at least hypothesize the existence of a powerfully diverse theory of discourse, even if I cannot as yet define it or create it.

Reading as an Inspiration for Writing

As a way of beginning, I provide students with dozens of readings and excerpts from feminist scholars and writers who hypothesize diverse forms of discourse. I often begin with Virginia Woolf, who begs us to preserve differences: "It would be a thousand pities if women wrote like men. . . . Ought not education to bring out and fortify the difference rather than the similarities? For we have too much likeness as it is" (91–92). Adrienne Rich captures the essence of so many problems with women and language; here she describes feelings common to many women students and academics: "Listen to a woman groping for language in which to express what is on her mind, sensing that the terms of academic discourse are not her language, trying to cut down her thought to the dimension of a discourse not intended for her" (243–44). Other texts that are invaluable for providing a theoretical background are Dale Spender's *Man Made Language* and Julia Penelope's *Speaking Freely: Unlearning the Lies of the Fathers' Tongue,* and essays by Susan Meisenhelder and Sally Miller Gearhart.

The French feminists also give us many tantalizing texts to consider when we allow ourselves to write—or to imagine writing—outside patriarchal, phallocentric discourse. From Julia Kristeva:

> How can we conceive of a revolutionary struggle that does not involve a revolution in discourse (not an upheaval in language as such, but rather a theory of this very upheaval)? (140)

From Helene Cixous, on *"écriture féminine"*:

> Most women are like this: they do someone else's—man's writing, and in their innocence sustain it and give it voice, and end up producing writing that's in effect masculine. Great care must be taken in working on feminine writing not to get trapped by names: to be signed with a woman's name doesn't necessarily make a piece of writing feminine. It could quite well be masculine writing, and conversely, the fact that a piece of writing is signed with a man's name does not in itself exclude femininity. It's rare, but you can sometimes find femininity in writings signed by men: it does happen. (qtd. in Moi 108)

From Moi, writing about Kristeva and Helene Cixous:

> The speaking/writing woman is in a space outside time (eternity), a space that allows no naming and no syntax. In her article "Women's Time," Julia Kristeva has argued that syntax is constitutive of our sense of chronological time by the very fact that the order of words in a sentence marks a temporal sequence: since subject, verb, object cannot be spoken simultaneously, their utterance necessarily cuts up the temporal continuum of "eternity." Cixous, then, presents this nameless pre-Oedipal

space filled with mother's milk and honey as the source of the song that resonates through all female writing. (114)

Though difficult to read in the ways we typically read discursive prose, French feminist theories have been interpreted in ways that students and I have found meaningful by Toril Moi (as in the passage above), Susan Suleiman, Clara Juncker, Robert de Beaugrande, Ann Rosalind Jones, and Elaine Marks and Isabelle de Courtivron. Suleiman, describing Cixous's dream of writing, says that it would "break open the chains of syntax, escape the repressiveness of linear logic and 'story-telling' and allow for the emergence of a language 'close to the body.' This language, linked, for Cixous, to the voice and the body of the mother, would allow the 'wildness' of the unconscious to emerge over the tame reasoning of the superego of the Law" (Suleiman 52).

When I read many of the texts I have mentioned so far, I am filled with optimism about the possibilities for a liberating discourse, one that contains changes in the deep structure, as well as obvious alterations in the surface structure. Though I cannot define it, with feminist discourse (or "diverse" or "experimental" discourse) I have a name for what I seek, and that gives me hope. But it is easy to understand a pessimistic perspective. Despite some positive connotations offered by theorists such as Elizabeth Flynn, we can certainly conjure up the negative connotations for "writing like a woman." This negative semantic space is sometimes at the heart of what bothers my students when we use the term "feminist discourse." Our heads are filled with negative images of what it means to think, write, drive, throw a ball—anything—"like a woman." Irigaray is direct on this: "They have left us their negative(s)" (207).

There is perhaps no more discouraging treatise on women's language than Otto Jespersen's chapter entitled "The Woman" in his "seminal" book written in 1922, during the genesis of modern linguistics. A sampling:

> Men will certainly with great justice object that there is a danger of the language becoming languid and insipid if we are always to content ourselves with women's expressions, and that vigour and vividness count for something. . . . [T]he vocabulary of a woman as a rule is much less extensive than that of a man. . . . [W]oman is linguistically quicker than man: quicker to learn, quicker to hear, and quicker to answer. A man is slower: he hesitates, he chews the cud to make sure of the taste of the words, and thereby comes to discover similarities with and differences from other words, both in sound and in sense, thus preparing himself for the appropriate use of the fittest noun or adjective. (247, 248, 249)

Many students are shocked to see the biases in the foundational texts of linguistic "science."

Carolyn Heilbrun provides additional evidence of the powerful lenses through which participants in our culture view women and their writing. She claims that the bonds for women writers are so great that they have suffered from "autobiographical disabilities," unable even to tell their own stories.

Before May Sarton's rewrite of her autobiography, in which she attempted to tell the truth about what she had written earlier, most women's stories about themselves are facades, according to Heilbrun, artifices built of what the culture expects of them, including acquired modesty and humility. About Eudora Welty's autobiography, Heilbrun writes, "[I]t is nostalgia, rendered with all the charm and grace of which she is capable, that has produced this autobiography, that same nostalgia that has for so many years imprisoned women without her genius or her rewards" (15). This nostalgia, according to Heilbrun, is a mask for the kind of anger and true emotion that many women suppress when they write.

Because some students, for all these reasons, cannot bring themselves to describe their work as "writing like a woman," I invite them to experiment with what it means to apply feminist theories about difference and diversity to language, hence, our working title for their work: "diverse discourse." Of course, there are other objections to using alternative forms: "it's not scholarly," "it's not objective," "it's too emotional." The discussions of negative writing associated with women provide an occasion for analyzing responses to all kinds of "other" texts. (See Joanna Russ's depressing but informative catalog of the ways women's writing has been positioned as inferior.)

PROFESSIONAL SAMPLES OF DIVERSE DISCOURSE

Not all of the feminist theorists I have quoted write in experimental modes. So we often search beyond feminist discourse theories for samples that can serve as catalysts for our writing experiments. Such writing provokes lively class discussion and, while I don't require students to write in experimental modes, their readings and discussions prompt many students to try their own experiments with writing. (See the section on "Student Samples" later in this essay.)

Personal/Emotional Writing

Samples of "personal narrative" and "emotional writing" are plentiful in the recent writing of feminist scholars, but it was not always so. Personal journals and diaries have always been an outlet for women and men, but they did not cross over into prestigious academic journals as scholarship. Jane Tompkins describes the price a feminist literary scholar has to pay for violating the expectations of the community of literary critics. Responding to a scholarly article by Ellen Messer-Davidow on philosophy and feminism, Tompkins feels split between the public and the private. She wants to write as a respectable scholar and also as a woman sitting in her stocking feet looking out the window at a red leaf and feeling rage like an "adamantine, a black slab that glows in the dark" (177). She writes with both voices and comments on her ambivalent feelings:

> One is the voice of a critic who wants to correct a mistake in the essay's view of epistemology. The other is the voice of a person who wants to

> write about her feelings. (I have wanted to do this for a long time but have felt too embarrassed.) This person feels it is wrong to criticize the essay and even beside the point, because a critique of the kind the critic has in mind only insulates academic discourse further from the issues that make feminism matter. That make *her* matter. The critic, meanwhile, believes such feelings, and the attitudes that inform them, are soft-minded, self-indulgent, and unprofessional. (169)

This essay evokes discussions of being silenced. We have many stories to tell each other about the ways we have been embarrassed to write truthfully. Other outstanding examples of the interweaving of personal and academic voices are Patricia Williams's *The Alchemy of Race and Rights,* Toni McNaron's *I Dwell in Possibility,* and Gayle Graham Yates's *Mississippi Mind: A Personal Cultural History of an American State.*

Breaking the Boundaries of Textual Space

Another of my favorite texts is Judy Chicago's *The Birth Project,* an account of her desire as an artist to produce images of childbirth in designs stitched by women needleworkers. She chose to work in a unique way, designing multiple images and employing women working in collectives across the country to execute her designs. On a typical double-page spread from her book (154–55), we find multiple voices speaking to us from the pages. In column one we read excerpts from her personal journal during the project. Columns two, three, and four contain excerpts from a stitcher's journal. In the fifth column, Judy Chicago comments retrospectively on the project, and the journal continues in the final column. Each writer has a different perspective on the project. In fact, Chicago often discusses their differences and the difficulties they had as feminists trying to work together on a project that demanded so much of each of them. Many students find this work helpful as they try to weave together papers that preserve their own voices alongside the voices of others who disagree with them or the voices of authorities who might drown out their own.

Language Play

If my students and I were fluent readers of French, we could turn to Cixous, Irigaray, and Kristeva for many examples of language play, but because we all are not, I have found that Mary Daly's *Gyn/Ecology* serves very well for English examples. From the title page to the last page, Daly emphasizes that we must "dis-spell" the "spooks of grammar," lexicon, and rhetoric with our own language constructions. She plays with diction, spelling, punctuation and other orthographic conventions to develop a style that signals at every turn that she means something other than what is typically meant. For example, she reinvests terms such as "crone," "hag," and "spinster" with positive semantic features. She notes with irony that Noam Chomsky was "genuinely puzzled and intrigued" by the possibility that there might be connections between "Language and Freedom" when he was asked to speak on this topic (328). Daly argues that "to break the spell ... Croneographers should remind our Selves that the Newspeak of Orwell's negative utopian tale is patriarchal Oldspeak" (330). So that we can break the bonds of language, we must invent new terms, new constructions, new rhetorics:

> This applies to male-controlled language in all matters pertaining to gynocentric identity: the words simply do not exist. In such a situation it is difficult even to imagine the right questions about our situation. Women struggling for words feel haunted by false feelings of personal inadequacy, by anger, frustration, and a kind of sadness/bereavement. For it is, after all, our "mother tongue" that has been turned against us by the tongue-twisters. Learning to speak our Mothers' Tongue is exorcising the male "mothers." (330)

Daly inspires a "serious playfulness" in the writing of many students. Whether or not we can ever find a language other than the "male Mother tongue" is a topic of much discussion in my classes. Those who are not prepared to use experimental language in their writing often find acceptable models in analyses of male discourse such as those written by Penelope and Spender.

Not the Mythic White Women

Along with constructions of "Other" based on gender, we also consider additional sources of difference for our experimental papers. Even if we are female, we are not writing as "THE Mythic Woman," typically "THE Mythic WHITE Woman," as in much early feminist work. (See bell hooks for an extended discussion of this problem.) We write as individuals participating in various discourse communities. We are social beings, from different racial and ethnic communities, not just two-dimensional versions of "Woman" [or of "Man," trying to "write like a woman"]. Moi, in her critique of Cixous, writes, "Stirring and seductive though such a vision is, it can say nothing of the actual inequities, deprivations and violations that women, as social beings rather than as mythological archetypes, must constantly suffer" (123). Rich reminds us that any new theory of "feminist discourse" will have to preserve the differences among women as well as men: "Women both have and have not had a common world. The mere sharing of oppression does not constitute a common world" (203).

Breaking Out of Linguistic Prejudice

Throughout the collection of essays *Bridges of Power: Women's Multicultural Alliances*, edited by Lisa Albrecht and Rose M. Brewer, we find the tension between common ground (oppression) and difference (race, class, sexual preference) in women's experiences. Audre Lorde, for example, writing of women of the Black Diaspora, does not assume that women will always share common ground. Differences across languages set up many cultural barriers. She writes, "One of the problems is, we for the most part are very provincial in North America, and we believe that English is the end of all languages. One of the things we need to, I think, start to do as we begin to experience our sisters, is to expose ourselves, open ourselves to learning other languages, so that we can in fact communicate, not only in translations" ("African-American" 208–09).

Gloria Anzaldua, also represented in *Bridges of Power*, illustrates cross-linguistic tensions. When she writes in English, Anzaldua blends Spanish and Nauhtl terms to make the point that something very important to her is lost in translation. A sampling:

> Oh, white sister, where is your soul, your spirit? It has run off in shock, *susto,* and you lack shamans and *curanderas* to call it back. *Sin alma no te puedes animarte pa'nada.* Remember that an equally empty and hollow place within us allows that connection, even needs that linkage. (229)

Even within Spanish, she needs language she does not have and invents the term "lesberadas," prompted by the word "desperado." Once we share languages, as Lorde would have us do, we can begin to understand some of the common ground of patriarchal oppression and how it is reflected in each language, but we need to retain our differences as well.

Class Barriers

Other factors, beyond gender, race, and mother tongue, create differences and influence our language. My students and I have just begun to explore the influence of class in this context. Clearly it is a powerful determinant of success and failure within academia and a restrictive force in our linguistic freedom. Standard Written English, with its roots in prestige dialects, does not allow our class roots to show. Our fear of revealing class identities that diverge from the middle restricts our writing options. Writing classes often serve as a gatekeeper, protecting the academy from the infelicities of "errors" generated by differences among dialects that derive from social, racial, and ethnic differences.

Mike Rose's book *Lives on the Boundary* poignantly tells the story of his own fears and his students' fears of being outsiders, mirrored in his response to the image of the medieval goddess of grammar, "Grammatica," represented as "severe, with a scalpel and a large pair of pincers. Her right hand, which is by her side, grasps a bird by its neck, its mouth open as if in a gasp or a squawk" (1). Rose writes, "And it's our cultural fears—of internal decay, of loss of order, of diminishment—that weave into our assessments of literacy and scholastic achievement" (7). The academy does not yet have room, except in the rarified atmosphere of "creative" writing, for dialects that differ from "Standard" Written English.

Lives on the Boundary has inspired several of my graduate students to write their ethnographic dissertations in a style that is truer to themselves—and far more interesting to me and to the other members of their committees than some of the pseudo-ethnographies that have sprouted up in composition studies in recent years. They draw courage from Rose's candid discussions of his own working-class history.

Sexual Orientation

Sexual orientation is another powerful source of difference, and orientations other than the "presumed" heterosexual are only now becoming somewhat "safe" topics for discussion in the context of writing classes. This lack of safety is indeed troublesome, given the myth of the academy as the open market-place of ideas vs. the reality of homophobia and violence against gays and lesbians within the academy. Until very recently, very little had been published on the connections between sexual orientation and writing. In some prelimi-nary work on this question, I turned up only one source on the topic of gay and lesbian writing in our university's library: Mark Lilly's edited collection entitled *Lesbian and Gay Writing*. More careful studies of feminist, gay, and lesbian scholarship (e.g., Olano's "Lesbian Feminist Literary Criticism: A Sum-mary of Research and Scholarship") reveal a growing body of work in specialized journals. The topic is not safe enough obviously; while gay and lesbian students in my classes have written about the connection between their sexual orientation and their writing, they chose not to give me permis-sion to include samples of their writing in this essay.

Different Composing Processes

Finally, I also encourage students to consider alternative processes for writing their essays. Lisa Ede and Andrea Lunsford's book *Singular Texts, Plural Authors* provides support for the idea of collective, collaborative writing processes. To this I also add many examples of my own from business and industry, as well as from academia. I also share some of the personal difficul-ties I have experienced as a co-author doing an unequal share of the work, especially when there were inequities of power in these situations, or as an academic whose co-authored works were not valued as highly as those of col-leagues who choose to work alone. We talk about these as a way of commit-ting ourselves to another "diverse" approach to writing.

The Invigorating Search for Materials

One of the antidotes to the problem of "essentialism" noted earlier is to ana-lyze the differences among women, among men, and between women and men, as well as their shared experiences. Analyses of race, class, gender, lan-guage, and sexual preference allow possibilities for all writers who want to create their own divergent, alternative discourses. They extend our thinking beyond earlier feminist analyses of language and discourse. In this section I have shared but a few of the samples that I have been collecting for the pur-pose of generating more critical readings of patriarchal discursive practices. I have found that searching for language and writing that I can use in these ways has reinvigorated me as a reader, as well as a teacher and a writer.

STUDENT SAMPLES OF DIVERSE DISCOURSE

The following examples of student writing represent a range of experiments that students in my classes have produced, inspired by their readings of alternative discourse and their desire to produce something unconventional. Even in the "safe" space that I work to construct within my classrooms, the signs of student insecurity with experimentation reflect my own. On the one hand, they know that they will write for other teachers, other professors, who are not receptive to these challenges to convention. On the other, they often wonder about the value of conventional writing to reflect their own realities.

Toying with Academic Writing

Many students choose to put themselves back into their learning and experiment with personal voice in academic writing, echoing, for example, Tompkins' dialogue with herself. One undergraduate woman, writing her summa thesis "under my direction" (in quotes for reasons that unfold below), chose to taunt academic discourse. In "Something Like a Preface" she writes,

> I began this project with the intent to write a paper on whether or not there is such a thing as "feminine writing," and if there is, how it differs from the enigma of "masculine writing." It sounds impressive anyway when people ask you what you're up to: *summa thesis*. . . . In any case, it's a paper that by definition "crowns the undergraduate student's work in the University of Minnesota English Department" (and here she cites our handbook). Crowns, no less. It's a coronation of sorts, then, with the king and queen waiting anxiously in the wings.
>
> But hold the horns. This prom won't promenade without a pepfest. (At least, none of the ones I ever attended in high school did.) Indeed, a pepfest is absolutely mandatory. But this is a *summa thesis* (need I remind you). We can't just have sophomores bellowing "JUNIORS!" and juniors indignantly bellowing "SOPHOMORES!" right back across the gymnasium floor. In fact, we can't have sophomores and juniors at all (this is a *summa th . . .*). Instead, psychoanalysts, linguists, sociologists, and English professors from around the world have gathered for a pepfest of the magnanimous kind, a stadium of scholars with flags and whistles, hats and cheers, and lips marching in rhythmic unity. . . . (Schubert 1)

In this passage, Schubert reveals her impatience with the view that she has to please her "masters" and be blessed by those in authority for her work. She also suggests that she cannot write in language that is more immediate to her experience (pepfests). She is supposed to take on the mantle of objectivity. Her paper goes on to reveal very serious scholarship, but the tone throughout is playful and irreverent. The "Review of the Literature" is called "Ancient History" and reveals how irrelevant she finds much that she read about women's voices. At the same time, she lets the reader know when she approves of her reading and by what criteria she makes these judgments. The section in which she comments on what she has read and applies it to people she has known, herself included, is entitled "Unleashed and Raging." She lets her anger shine through the prose, instead of politely maintaining distance as she has been taught to do in academic prose. I responded to her shifts in tone with high praise, but I was not entirely sure what my colleagues would say about it. I should have had more confidence because this paper won the award for the best undergraduate essay of the year in the Women's Studies Department and satisfied the English Department's requirement for a crowning achievement. I suspect that one of the reasons it was accepted, beyond its insightfulness, was that it was novel, and I have wondered what would happen if more students wrote like this.

The Risks in Challenging Conventions

Another student, at the graduate level, is more fearful about her audience when she writes a paper about her struggles with "feminist reading and writing":

> I still fear that it will lack coherence to any reader excluding me, and maybe me, too. . . . This is probably why I feel some discomfort in displaying it to any audience outside of myself. "Nonsense" they'll think, "What jibberish she's written! And a graduate student in English! . . ." I imagine my readers saying "Is it too confessional? Too reflective?" (Anonymous)

Even though her classmates and I were the only readers who would see this paper without the writer's permission,[1] she was still hesitant to leave behind the objectivity and distance that had served her well as an undergraduate. Throughout the essay, she weaves concerns with audience into challenging questions about the material she has read. It truly is "private writing," or "writer-based prose" in the jargon of composition, but as I had told her earlier, that was what the course was about: making external knowledge personal. I encouraged her to think that "writer-based prose" is not always just a "phase" that we have to go through to get to something better, that not all academic writing has to be "reader-based." At the end of the course, she still held the view that academic writing should be public and not private, but she said she had learned something from the experiment.

Another female student, writing in a course in rhetoric, revealed an awareness of herself as a reader with gender and class as she reacted to one of the textbooks used in the course. In the paper excerpted below, she refuses to be left out of the discourse of rhetoric and ultimately proposes a revisionist's view of *Phaedrus*. Powerfully aware of the restricted view of culture and class revealed in classical rhetoric, she describes some of her reasons for rejecting these traditions:

> I was doing fairly well as a reader of George Kennedy's *Classical Rhetoric* although I knew that the world he would describe, and respectfully so,

would render me invisible; I agreed to read what the Boys were doing back then, just one more time. But my self "the reader" slips so easily into that imagination: I must have begun to indulge in his account by injecting myself into that past life, by imagining myself at least somewhere in fifth century [B.C.] Athens. . . . The Greek harmony is brought to, say, undergraduates, and held up as a sublime romance, especially according to modern day middle class standards. . . . From whence comes the armless, legless, headless, marble Greek woman[?] Yet marble women can read noncontextually, so like I said, I was doing well, participating in the fantasy. . . . Though I must have known, at some level, that I was not in this course, nor would have been my father. . . . (Bock 1)

Another student, a man, also felt estranged from the readings in a course focusing on feminist analyses of language. He wanted to find a way to connect the theories to his life, so he talked to his friends and family about them. He introduces himself this way: "I work as a bartender, a stereotypical position of a man who tells dirty jokes, listens to one's problems and gives advice" (Anonymous). He writes a one-page introduction which he calls a "resonating core" and then juxtaposes excerpts from the course readings alongside commentaries about these quotes from regulars at the bar, family members, and friends. The title of the paper is "What the hell are you taking a class like that for???" I believe writing this paper allowed him to process his own personal struggle with that very question.

These few examples illustrate some of the ways students have chosen to put themselves back into their writing. To do so is a risk, and it is not surprising that so many of them write about their fears. Neither is it surprising that some students preferred that I not mention their names in this section.

Writing without an Argument

One of the men in a graduate class was "persuaded" by Sally Miller Gearhart's essay, "The Womanization of Rhetoric," that argument may not be a mode he wants to adopt in all of his academic writing. Gearhart indicts the discipline of rhetoric because of her belief that "any intent to persuade is an act of violence" (195). The intention to change others, she writes, embodies a "conquest model of human interaction." At least for the week's writing assignment, he chose to write his entire essay as a series of questions. Here is his introduction: "I make no claims to be an expert on the subject [feminist criticism], or even to have a cursory knowledge. I believe I can contribute more by adding questions to the discussion than by asserting opinions or viewpoints. . . . What if questions were answered simply with questions? Imagine the difference in tone!" He then proceeds to ask 58 questions, not in list form, but as continuous prose. An excerpt:

Does a voice that tries "to please all and offend none" boil down to the same as Gearhart's voice that refuses to conquer? Is a voice that refuses either to please or offend a strong voice? What is a strong voice? What does Peter Elbow mean by a voice so strong it scares others? What is

"Writing with Power"? Is that what feminist rhetoric is attempting? Is powerful feminist rhetoric a contradiction? An oxymoron? Can the rhetoric of consensus building permit strong, powerful, *individual* voices? Can it permit a strong, powerful, *collective* voice? How is this achieved? If it is achieved, does it contradict the ideology that set it in motion? (Maylath 2)

In contrast to the writers above, he takes his own opinions out of the paper, except as his questions reveal an underlying position. He could have easily developed a tightly reasoned argument against some of the readings, for he did not agree with all of them. Instead, he chose to think in a new way, to allow himself to ask questions instead of answering them. In the end, he asks, "How do I end this paper???" How, indeed, would he? My hope is that he has not.

Experiments with Form

Many students have experimented with ways to weave their writing together with external sources. With the advent of word-processing packages that make it simple to vary font styles and sizes, as well as to arrange the page horizontally and in columns, my students have been imitating layouts like those in Judy Chicago's *The Birth Project.* Figure 1 shows a page from a paper written by Tania Ripoll, a student in my Feminist Language and Writing Pedagogy seminar. She uses two columns, lining up the excerpts she finds interesting in one column and commenting on them in the other. In a memo she wrote to students in another class who were reading her paper, she asks, "Does the format work? Since much of the content of the paper is a rejection of linearity as a patriarchal construct, evidently the form had to be adjusted also. How superficial does it seem?" (Ripoll 2).

Another student decided that she would likewise include a long series of quotes from her readings because:

> there is an obvious interconnection between all the readings, something I've never experienced so profoundly in my studies; and, most wondrous of all, these writings, these words, are connected to me. They speak to me and for me, in one voice but many. A poly/mono-centered discourse. A collection of interconnected voices. A peaceful cacophony. (Anonymous)

She arranges these quotes—from writers such as Deborah Cameron, Helene Cixous, Mary Daly, and Dale Spender—in the form of a reader's theatre script. Her own ideas are given equal weight as she includes her own name in the cast of characters, the "Voices in Order of Appearance."

Another experiment with form in which students seem to be taking new directions is the addition of a great deal of visual material to their writing. This is easier now that graphics can be easily integrated into word-processed documents. In fact, the advent of icon-driven computers with integrated graphics packages may be a causal factor in this development. These graphics show up frequently in technical writing classes and they are increasingly present in classes in writing for the arts and in the writing in design disciplines. In

FIGURE 1   Excerpt from Tania Ripoll's "Women's Voices?"

OF WHY PATRIARCHAL LANGUAGE IS INADEQUATE

If we keep on speaking the same language together, we're going to reproduce the same history. Begin the same old stories all over again. Don't you think so? . . . The same . . . Same . . . Always the same. . . . If we keep on speaking sameness, if we speak to each other as men have been doing for centuries, as we have been taught to speak, we'll miss each other, fail ourselves. (Iragaray (2), 205)

According to Starhawk, the concept of god as separate from its creation is expressed in the grammatical structure of the indo-european languages, where the subject is separated from the object. (Solomonsen, 49)

If discourse is reflective and productive of culture, and we as feminists are engaged in the creation of a new culture, the inadequacy of patriarchal discourse for the expression of our culture is obvious.

All dogmatism is seen to be based on the belief in language as being identical to reality, the sign representing its referent. (Salomonsen, 46)

. . . the hunger unnamed and unnameable, the sensations mistranslated. (Rich (1), 248)

. . . a language in which everything, verbs and subjects, was masculine. And so, having lost their minds, women believed they could be men, equal their masters in adopting their grammar syntax, (Gauthier (1), 162)

It is nevertheless interesting to look closely at patriarchal discourse. In order to see in more detail what characterizes it. I don't believe that feminist discourse can articulate itself in opposition to patriarchal discourse, aiming/claiming to be everything that patriarchal discourse is not; we would then still operate within limits dictated by patriarchy. In patriarchy's own dichotomous pattern. If patriarchal discourse cannot show us how our voice must be, however, it can show us what it can't be—as well as further demonstrate why we can't use its tongue for our own ends.

The problems with patriarchal discourse are, not surprisingly, deeply structural. It is a clearly linear discourse, structured as it is on the basis of chronologically articulated words (Moi, 114, on classes in landscape architecture, for example, I have found consistent use of drawings and graphics integrated with text. One student included elaborate drawings of Loring Park in Minneapolis, accompanied by her verbal notations in her class journal. These drawings and commentaries eventually became part of a new design and of a report on the design submitted to a jury of landscape architects for a course evaluation. Periodically, throughout the journal she would pause to think only in words, wondering at one point, "What does Loring Park Mean?" and then listing all of her possible interpretations. But on most pages, the interplay between visual and verbal images was essential to her process of treating a design that conveyed her sense of the place. These combinations of the verbal and visual illustrate yet another way of avoiding the logocentrism discussed in so many of our readings. In an increasingly iconic culture, students need experience in combining visual images with verbal images in appropriate ways. While this practice is commonplace in many fields, too many writing classrooms have ignored the role of visual symbols in communication.

Differences in Ways of Working

Students in writing classes across the country have begun to explore the possibilities of writing collaboratively, challenging the notion that the individual author must possess all the knowledge, both of content and form, necessary to write well. One of many such collaborative groups in my class was led by a deaf woman and her interpreter who showed the hearing women examples of signs from American Sign Language that they considered sexist. Not only were the students challenged to exchange their written words in cooperative ways, but they also had to learn new ways of sharing their spoken words, all the while self-conscious that the signs and language they were using constrained their meanings.

Diverse Discourse for Me as a Teacher and a Scholar

I want to end this essay by saying again how invigorating experimentation is for me as a reader, as a writer, and as a teacher. I have read and written more and taught with more enthusiasm as students and I have struggled with genuine questions to which I have no clear answers. They and I have questions and responses, if not answers. In many of my classes, I have felt the balance of power shifting; students have been my teachers in a very real sense, and I theirs, when it was appropriate, which was not always. About my reading and my writing and my teaching, I have felt that I was encountering my work as Gloria Anzaldua describes hers: "an assemblage, a montage, a beaded work with several motifs and with a central core, now appearing, now disappearing in a crazy dance" (66). I find this work much more satisfying than the traditional academic scholarship, social-scientific research on writing that I have been producing. Inter- and cross-disciplinary methods seem much more appropriate for the questions that concern me. A challenge in my future work will be to find ways to integrate this past work with my ways of working now.

I also realize that in many ways I am not like my students and younger members of the profession. I can afford the luxury of experimentation because I am a tenured and reasonably secure member of the profession. Given the era when I was establishing my career, I had no rhetorical choices (or thought I had none). I had to write in conventional language, in traditional rhetorical patterns, using accepted research methodologies, if my research articles were to be published. "I" could not be in them at all. For these reasons, I am sympathetic to those who do not feel that they can take risks. But another part of me wants to use the security I have to open doors for others, to consider new possibilities.

I know that this experimentation is important for many students. One former student and composition instructor wrote, in response to this essay:

> In fact, what does go on in freshman composition classes? I would suggest that many of thew classes are HOT-BEDS of student resistance. The new crop of scholars . . . [has] been exposed to feminism in "changed forever" ways. Whether we are resisting the theories or espousing them is really immaterial. . . . We are ENGAGED in conversation about them and that creates NEW MEANINGS. . . . Meaning about writing, reading, multi-dimensional realities. (Olano, Letter 4)

The real change for me does not lie on the surface of language at all, where I have chosen to begin, but in the deep structure where language and culture interact. In these places, I treasure the new meanings that I and many others have discovered.

NOTE

1. This student has given permission to quote from her essay, so long as she remains anonymous. Several others gave permission to be quoted anonymously; no student cited anonymously is cited more than once. Others gave permission to me to use their names, and they are cited in the text.

WORKS CITED

Albrecht, Lisa, and Rose M. Brewer, eds. *Bridges of Power: Women's Multicultural Alliances.* Philadelphia: New Society Publishers, 1990.

Anzaldua, Gloria. "Bridge, Drawbridge, Sandbar or Island: Lesbians-of-Color Hacienda Alianzas." *Bridges of Power.* Albrecht and Brewer, 216–31.

Beaugrande, Robert de. "In Search of Feminist Discourse: The 'Difficult' Case of Luce Iragaray." *College English* 50 (Mar. 1988): 253–72.

Bizzell, Patricia. "College Composition: Initiation into the Academic Discourse Community." *Curriculum Inquiry* 12 (1982): 191–207.

Bock, Mary. "How Do Western Homosociality and Heterosexuality Fit Together? An Invincible Rhetoric for a Vulnerable Cultural Tension." Unpublished manuscript, n.d.

Calderonello, Alice. "Toward Diversity in Academic Discourse: Alice, Sue and Deepika Talk About Form and Resistance." *ATAC Forum* 3.1 (Spring/Summer 1991): 1–5.

Cameron, Deborah. *Feminism and Linguistic Theory.* New York: St. Martin's, 1985.

Chase, Geoffrey. "Accommodation, Resistance and the Politics of Student Writing." *College Composition and Communication* 39 (Feb. 1988): 13–22.

Chicago, Judy. *The Birth Project.* Garden City: Doubleday, 1985.

Cixous, Helene, and Catherine Clément. *The Newly Born Woman.* Trans. Betsy Wing. Minneapolis: U of Minnesota P, 1986.

Daly, Mary. *Gyn/Ecology: The Metaethics of Radical Feminism.* Boston: Beacon, 1978.

Ede, Lisa, and Andrea Lunsford. *Singular Texts, Plural Authors: Perspectives on Collaborative Writing.* Carbondale: Southern Illinois UP, 1990.

Flynn, Elizabeth A. "Composing as a Woman." *College Composition and Communication* 39 (Dec. 1988): 423–35.

Gauthier, Xaviere. "Existe-t-il une écriture de femme?" *New French Feminisms.* Marks and de Courtivron 161–64.

Gearhart, Sally Miller. "The Womanization of Rhetoric." *Women's Studies International Quarterly* 2.2 (1979): 195–201.

Heilbrun, Carolyn G. *Writing a Woman's Life.* New York: Ballantine, 1988.

hooks, bell. *Ain't I a Woman: Black Women and Feminism.* Boston: South End, 1981.

Irigaray, Luce. *This Sex Which Is Not One.* Trans. Catherine Porter, Ithaca: Cornell UP, 1985.

Jespersen, Otto. *Language: Its Nature, Development and Origin.* London: G. Allen & Unwin, Ltd., 1922.

Jones, Ann Rosalind. "Writing the Body: Toward an Understanding of l'Écriture feminine." *The New Feminist Criticism: Essays on Women, Literature, and Theory.* Ed. Elaine Showalter. New York: Pantheon, 1985. 361–77.

Juncker, Clara. "Writing (with) Cixous." *College English* 50 (April 1988): 424–36.

Kaufer, David S., and Cheryl Geisler. "Novelty in Academic Writing." *Written Communication* 6: (Jul. 1989): 286–311.

Kristeva, Julia. "La femme, ce n'est jamais ça." Marks and de Courtivron 137–41.

Lilly, Mark, ed. *Lesbian and Gay Writing: An Anthology of Critical Essays.* Philadelphia: Temple UP, 1990.

Lorde, Audre. "African-American Women and the Black Diaspora." Albrecht and Brewer 206–9.

———. "The Master's Tools Will Never Dismantle the Master's House." *This Bridge Called My Back: Writings by Radical Women of Color.* Ed. Cherrie Moraga and Gloria Anzaldua. Boston: Persephone, 1981. 98–101.

Lu, Min-zhan. "From Silence to Words: Writing as Struggle." *College English* 49 (Apr. 1987): 437–47.

Marks, Elaine, and Isabelle de Courtivron. *New French Feminism: An Anthology.* New York: Schocken Books, 1981.

Maylath, Bruce. "A Question, Please?" Unpublished manuscript, n.d.

McNaron, Toni A. H. *I Dwell in Possibility: A Memoir.* New York: The Feminist Press at CUNY, 1992.

Meisenhelder, Susan. "Redefining 'Powerful' Writing: Toward a Feminist Theory of Composition." *Journal of Thought* 20 (Fall 1985): 184–95.

Messer-Davidow, Ellen. "The Philosophical Bases of Feminist Literary Criticisms." *New Literary History* 19 (Autumn 1987): 65–103.

Moi, Toril. *Sexual/Textual Politics.* London: Methuen, 1985.

Murray, Donald M. *Write to Learn.* 2nd ed. New York: Holt, 1987.

Olano, Pamela. "Lesbian Feminist Literary Criticism: A Summary of Research and Scholarship." *Women's Studies Quarterly* 19 (Fall/Winter 1991) 174–79.

———. Letter to the author. 11 Nov. 1990.

Penelope, Julia. *Speaking Freely: Unlearning the Lies of the Fathers' Tongue.* New York: Pergamon, 1990.

Rich, Adrienne. *On Lies, Secrets and Silences: Selected Prose 1966–78.* New York: Norton, 1979.

Ripoll, Tania. "Women's Voices?" Unpublished manuscript, n.d.

Ritchie, Joy S. "Confronting the 'Essential' Problem: Reconnecting Feminist Theory and Pedagogy." *Journal of Advanced Composition* 10 (Fall 1990): 249–73.

Rose, Mike. *Lives on the Boundary: A Moving Account of the Struggles and Achievements of America's Educational Underclass.* New York: Penguin, 1989.

Russ, Joanna. *How to Suppress Women's Writing.* Austin: U of Texas P, 1983.

Schubert, Lisa. "The Thing I Came For. . . ." Undergraduate thesis. U of Minnesota, 1990.

Spender, Dale. *Man Made Language.* 2nd ed. London: Routledge, 1985.

Suleiman, Susan Rubin. "(Re)writing the Body: The Politics and Poetics of Female Eroticism." *Poetics Today* 6 (1985): 44–55.

Tompkins, Jane. "Me and My Shadow." *New Literary History* 19 (Autumn 1987): 169–78.

Williams, Patricia J. *The Alchemy of Race and Rights.* Cambridge: Harvard UP, 1991.

Woolf, Virginia. *A Room of One's Own.* San Diego: Harcourt, 1929.

Yates, Gayle Graham. *Mississippi Mind: A Personal Cultural History of an American State.* U of Tennessee P, 1990.

19 Recomposing as a Woman—
An Essay in Different Voices

TERRY MYERS ZAWACKI

I learned to garden from my mother. Every year it was the same—Mom watched while Dad prepared the plot for vegetables. Dad wanted perfectly straight, even rows; he hammered in small stakes to mark the beginning and end of the row. Next he stretched a string between the stakes until it was taut. Then, guided by the string, he hoed the row. He measured off a foot or two between rows and then repeated the process of staking and stretching string.

Mom waited until Dad had done all of his planting before she sowed flower seeds in the spaces he had left her on the borders of the garden and the edges of the yard. She loved flowers which could be relied on year after year and didn't mind where they were planted—red, orange poppies with black centers, tall sunflowers sharing the narrow space between our driveway and the neighbor's garage with daylilies at their shoulders and violets at their feet, feathery purple asters, scarlet irises, and rainbows of marigolds and zinnias. I remember her delight whenever she discovered that flowers she had planted in one space had somehow made their way to other spots about the yard or planted roots in neighbors' yards.

Today I will write, I have promised myself. It's early morning and I have brewed a large pot of coffee. I pour my first cup and then reward myself for getting started at this hour with a leisurely walk along the wildflower beds which meander around the perimeter of my wooded acre of property. The "money" plants with their purply-pink clusters of flowers dominate the beds this time of year. I worry that they are taking over, especially when I don't see any sign of the Oriental poppies which have always sprung up alongside them. I do notice with pleasure that the purple thistle I dug up from a friend's farm in Culpeper last summer has reseeded itself and lies in great healthy clumps throughout the upper beds. I am never sure what will appear from

From *College Composition and Communication* 43 (1992): 32–38.

season to season—so far this month the hollyhocks, which I thought had died of rust last summer, are bushy with foliage but only one foxglove has come up in a place where there had been many. I like my gardens to surprise me, for flowers to grow where they were not planted, escaping their borders, refusing to be orderly. Marigolds sprout even on the edges of my woods. Black-eyed Susans wander here and there. Seeds blow; roots travel underground. The connections can't always be seen, yet I can tell, when I stop to think about it, how each connects to each.

These same qualities are, I think, what attract me to the personal essay. I like its openness, how it pulls from here and there, observing, reflecting, moving through disconnections to make connections. Unlike the traditional academic essay, the personal essay does not rely on positions staked out in advance, on straight arrangements and tightly connected points leading to a single conclusion. Differences can be cultivated in the personal essay—there is room to talk and room to listen. This is a friendly conversation, a process of composing and recomposing as other voices join in and the writer responds. "I've been thinking about these things for a while," the writer seems to say, "and I'd like to hear what you've been thinking."

"Our primary goal in this course is that students will be able to construct rational, organized arguments," my colleague said as she described a new course being designed to fill a lower-level general education requirement. After the meeting, I asked her why we have to focus solely on teaching students to write arguments. I suggested that a new course, especially a freshman-level course, might be a good place to present alternatives to traditional academic discourse and to recognize other ways of knowing and writing about what we know. "What alternatives are there?" she demanded with surprise and some annoyance.

I was annoyed at her annoyance, but I must admit that I wasn't too sure about the alternatives even though I write personal essays and had been reading the articles appearing regularly in the journals on valuing the personal essay as a mode of inquiry in the academy. I'd been particularly interested in articles about the link between the personal essay and feminine forms of knowledge and expression, such as those described by Mary Belenky and her co-authors in *Women's Ways of Knowing*. What would a personal-academic essay sound like, I wondered. What subject matter might it contain? Many of the women Belenky and her co-authors interviewed talked about their efforts to find a voice in the academy by "weaving together strands of rational and emotive thought" and by blending knowledge they "intuitively" felt was important with what they learned from others (135). One woman described it as letting "'the inside out and the outside in'" (135). Elizabeth Flynn suggests in "Composing as a Woman" that some of her women students moved "toward the development of an authentic voice" when they discovered that external voices and truths were not "more powerful" than their own (429).

When I mentioned to my colleague my interest in the personal essay and the parallels between it and the way women construct knowledge, she grimaced. I can understand why. It's risky to talk about women writing their gender and to suggest that some voices are more natural or authentic than others because they come from somewhere inside the self. There are dangers too in saying that certain forms of writing might somehow represent women's ways of constructing knowledge better than other forms. Women's lives are always already being read into texts as if to say that women can write only from the perspective of their own personal experience, whereas men can transcend narrow self-interests and "write" the world. Yet we may have to risk focusing on gender difference if we want to hear voices which have been marginalized or silenced by our insistence on rational argument as the prevailing mode of discourse in the academy.

Especially worrisome is the possibility Keith Fort suggests in "Form, Authority, and the Critical Essay" that the form itself, by limiting the attitudes that may be expressed, also controls the attitudes. "In general," Fort writes, "we cannot have attitudes towards reality that cannot be expressed in available forms." If we are only allowed to express ourselves in the form of the standard critical essay, then "we can only have an attitude that would result in the proper form" (174). The critical essay "conditions students to think in terms of authority and hierarchy" (178) and to write in a spirit of competitiveness. If we privilege other ways of knowing and representing the world, what new forms will emerge?

———

Instead of writing I have spent the afternoon digging compost into a small area of the garden I've reserved for tomatoes. The compost comes from a pile which lies about three feet into the woods behind one of the shady perennial beds. The pile starts with leaves and grass clippings, and to that I add peelings, cores and seeds, coffee grounds, wood ash, even shredded newspapers. Last year plants I couldn't identify but which looked like tomatoes grew up in a patch of sun on the edge of the compost pile. Small yellow-spotted beetles ate all but one, which grew until its large ungainly stalk flopped over onto the hostas in the flower bed. Finally I decided to pull it out. Tiny potatoes scattered around me; the potato peelings had rooted in the compost.

———

"Often nothing tangible remains of a woman's day," Virginia Woolf writes in "Women and Fiction." The food she prepares has been eaten and the children are reared and have gone out into the world. "Where does the accent fall?" Woolf asks, as she wonders what subject matter a woman novelist can write about. As a woman's attention is "directed away from the personal centre which engaged it exclusively in the past to the impersonal," she will no longer be content to "record with astonishing acuteness the minute details which fall under (her) own observation" and will learn instead to look beyond personal relationships to the wider questions of "destiny and the meaning of life" (82–83). When a woman is able to do this, Woolf says, the novel will no longer be "a dumping ground for the personal emotions" (84).

What interests me most about Woolf's analysis of how women's writing will change as they go out into the world is her statement earlier in the essay that a woman can write as she wishes to write only if she "has the courage to surmount opposition" (81). Men have decided upon the conventions and have established the values which will prevail. A woman will find, Woolf writes, that:

> she is perpetually wishing to alter the established values — to make serious what appears insignificant to a man, and trivial what is to him important. And for that, of course, she will be criticized; for the critic of the opposite sex will be genuinely puzzled and surprised by an attempt to alter the current scale of values, and will see in it not merely a difference of view, but a view that is weak, or trivial, or sentimental, because it differs from his own. (81)

By the end of her essay, though, Woolf seems to have come around to the view that women must embrace male values if they are to practice "the sophisticated arts . . . the writing of essays and criticism, of history and biography" (84). Woolf wrote this essay in 1929; though she was writing about the woman novelist who was only beginning to live outside of her home "and her emotions" (79), her observations about the established scale of values and the genuine puzzlement over attempts to change those values still apply to women trying to use alternative voices in the academy. Where might the accent fall? Where do we dare to place it? What can we safely teach our students in composition classes designed to prepare them for college writing?

———

In "Pedagogy of the Distressed," Jane Tompkins describes a feminist theory course she taught with the objective of getting "'out there' and 'in here' together." She wanted the students to "feel some deeper connection between what they were working on professionally and who they were, the real concerns of their lives" (658). Her inspiration for teaching the course in this personal way, Tompkins writes, was her desire to "break down the barrier between public discourse and private feeling, between knowledge and experience" (658). When I read Tompkins' essay, I can't help thinking about the authority that Tompkins has, because she is "Jane Tompkins," to challenge boundaries. "I am not Jane Tompkins," Olivia Frey writes at the end of "Beyond Literary Darwinism: Woman's Voices and Critical Discourse," to explain why she feels the need to use "the adversary method" to convince the profession to open up to alternative forms of writing (524). Frey hopes that "the brave experimenters will make a difference" because "if some of us do not use the adversarial method, or if we explore ideas without reaching any conclusions, or if we get personal in our essays about literature," we may be able to "stand knowledge on its head" (521–22). The final "poignant" irony for Frey, though, is that we will succeed because of the adversary method (524).

Last semester my student Alex told me that he really disliked Tillie Olsen's "Silences." "She's arguing for something, but she's just not coming across as very assertive," he said. "It bothers me that she uses all these quotes from other people to make her point, whatever her point is," Alex went on. "Why didn't she just use her own words?" When I went back to reread Olsen's essay in light of Alex's observations, I found myself distracted by her constant use of parenthetical explanations and asides. I too wanted Olsen to get to the point, or at least to stop interrupting herself. Until I read:

> How much it takes to become a writer . . .: how much conviction as to the importance of what one has to say, one's right to say it. And the will, the measureless store of belief in oneself to be able to come to, cleave to, find the form for one's own life comprehensions. Difficult for any male not born into a class that breeds such confidence. Almost impossible for a girl, a woman. (27)

How can I teach myself and my students to be more receptive to prose which does not get directly to the point, which seems tentative and unsure?

———

In a 1990 CCC's talk, "Academic Conventions and Teacher Expectations: A Feminist Perspective," Pat Sullivan pointed out that to be successful in the academy women have learned "to argue like men" and, perhaps "more alarming," to read women's discourse with those same expectations. Sullivan gave the example of a graduate student whose thesis she was directing—a woman who was having a great deal of difficulty writing in a direct and logical fashion because she was letting her sources voice multiple views. The student was mediating among the voices without coming to any final conclusions. Sullivan admitted that she helped the student to revise the paper until she "got it right." Only now, Sullivan said, does she realize that she did not know how to "hear" the woman's discourse. We must learn, she said, to listen for the differences in women's and men's discourse in order to help women writers compose themselves as they write.

As much as I want to learn to hear differences in my women students' writing, I still have questions about what Sullivan means when she says we (does she mean both men and women?) must listen for differences. Should we listen as "women" listening? (Can women listen as "other" than women?) If we listen as women, what will we hear that will help women to compose themselves? From what position might men "listen" to women's writing? If we as women (or we as men) listen with the expectation of discovering differences, what differences will appear? It seems to me that what Sullivan is talking about is not how women compose themselves when they write but rather how we must construct ourselves as readers when we read women's writing.

Instead of trying to discover what makes a written voice distinctly a woman's, or a man's, I want to focus on how language can be manipulated to make readers believe that there is a gendered self contained in the margins. In the opening paragraphs of this essay, I describe my mother's and father's differing approaches to planting their garden and my own pleasure in discovering flowers which have taken root in unpredictable places. These paragraphs seem to say that I am writing about gardens because they matter to me personally; they also suggest that there might be naturally feminine and masculine ways to compose gardens. But the truth is I want to see how descriptions of my garden might work in an academic essay, and I think gardening styles are more a matter of personal preference and who's in charge of the planning and planting than a reflection of gender. (Still, my mother continued to plant in straight evenly spaced rows years after my father died and explained to me many times the value of arranging a garden symmetrically. "Vegetables like plenty of space. They want to be at least six inches apart." "Flowers don't look right when they go every which way." Part of her advice was common sense—vegetables and flowers do like lots of room—but the other part, it seems to me, was her belief that my father's way was the right way to compose a garden.)

Is it possible to challenge the traditional academic hierarchy which privileges expository prose by rejecting the distinction between personal writing and expository writing? By showing that genre boundaries themselves are as questionable as gender boundaries and that all writing is a means of creating a self, not for expressing a self that already exists? If I situate myself in the context of other voices, if I write about experiences and feelings, if I choose not to get to the point, it's not because I am a woman, but rather because I want to discover the possibilities for representing a gendered self in writing.

––––––––––

In my first version of this essay, I closed with another, rather lengthy, gardening story. I wrote about tracing the roots of the oldest flowers in my garden to the family members and friends who had given them to me. (E.g., "The pink fringed poppies come from seeds my father sent me shortly before he died. 'Beautiful and hardy,' he had jotted on the envelope. 'Plant them before the first frost.'") I described how each transplanted flower changed the composition of the garden and seemed itself to change as it found its place among the others. ("The lamb's ears from my brother's Illinois garden have established themselves and are wandering gently around the yellow buttercups. In contrast to the sprightly buttercups, they look even more soft and subdued.") I ended by promising myself that next week I would spend time weeding and redigging borders. ("Though I like the flowers to grow at will, I also like the appearance of a neat deeply dug border.") The truth is I do like borders—they are not synonymous with boundaries—in my garden and in my writing; it's the margins I want to escape.[1]

NOTE

1. I want to thank Laura Brady and Cindy Herman, friends and colleagues, whose voices, though not "heard" in the text, were central to the conversation. As they read and responded to seemingly endless drafts, we found that each revision became a new conversation as the essay recomposed itself.

WORKS CITED

Belenky, Mary Field, Blythe McVicker Clinchy, Nancy Rule Goldberger, and Jill Mattuck Tarule. *Women's Ways of Knowing.* New York: Basic, 1986.
Flynn, Elizabeth A. "Composing as a Woman." *College Composition and Communication* 39 (Dec. 1988): 423–35.

Fort, Keith. "Form, Authority, and the Critical Essay." *Contemporary Rhetoric.* Ed. W. Ross Winterowd. New York: Harcourt, 1975. 171–83.

Frey, Olivia. "Beyond Literary Darwinism: Women's Voices and Critical Discourse." *College English* 52 (Sept. 1990): 507–26.

Olsen, Tillie. *Silences.* New York: Delacorte, 1965.

Sullivan, Pat. "Academic Conventions and Teacher Expectations: A Feminist Perspective." CCCC Convention. Chicago, March 1990.

Tompkins, Jane. "Pedagogy of the Distressed." *College English* 52 (October 1990): 653–60.

Woolfe, Virginia. "Women and Fiction." *Granite and Rainbow.* Ed. Leonard Woolfe. New York: Harcourt, 1958. 76–84.

20 Writing Multiplicity: Hypertext and Feminist Textual Politics

DONNA LECOURT AND LUANN BARNES

Although hypertext has generated a considerable body of work on how it alters traditional textual dynamics, feminist discussions have primarily been limited to the use of discussion technologies (e.g., Flores, 1990; Jessup, 1991; Selfe, 1990). The few references to gender and hypertext have primarily been cautionary ones. Carolyn Handa (1990), for example, expressed concern that "from . . . a female point of view," the focus on reader control might seem like yet another way to silence an author (p. 177). Similarly, Joel Haefner (1995) noted that although almost all his students, male or female, found their collaboratively written personal hyperessay "an attack on their selves," the way reactions were "expressed was clearly gendered" (p. 7). The women students, in particular, invoke metaphors of rape, discuss a lack of respect for emotions and private thoughts, and resent the "invasion of privacy" (p. 7) opening up their personal writing to the interventions others caused.

Although these concerns that female students might find hypertext a threatening textual environment are not insignificant, there remains another story of feminism and hypertext yet to be told. This story, rather than bemoaning the death of the author, would celebrate its potential to disrupt the assumption that a text *should* have a unified voice. It is precisely because hypertext *does not* allow for the expression of an authentic feminine experience that hypertext might have significant potential for the feminist writing teacher. Exploring such potential, however, means shifting the conversation from one wherein the expression of self is a means to political transformation to one wherein gendered politics are inseparable from textuality. Such a textual politic presumes that textuality itself is the problem to be addressed: that social transformation is best executed by disrupting the gendered nature of writing. Because these forms of feminist intervention, or textual politics, rely on deconstructing text and creating new forms of textual space, they seem ideally suited for the differently ordered writing of hypertext, which alters

From *Computers and Composition* 16 (1999): 55–71.

reader-writer relationships and allows for expression of multiple positions. Expressing multiplicity in this way not only validates feminine experience but also politicizes the nature of textuality itself, calling attention to the way discursive contexts attempt to silence alternative perspectives.

In this article, then, we explore the relationship between a feminist textual politic and hypertext, particularly in terms of how it might address the gendered nature of writing in the classroom. In particular, we propose to investigate hypertext's potential for realizing two key feminist interventions: (a) the disruption of the contexts and communities that force the author to accede to masculine ways of knowing, and (b) the deconstruction of the author as a single, unified self who suppresses alternative perspectives and gendered ideologies. We conduct this investigation both theoretically and materially, via our experiences writing hypertexts. Although we are enthusiastic about the possibility for hypertext to realize a feminist politic, this essay is not yet another celebration of hypertext's potential; instead, we would characterize our investigation more appropriately as restrained enthusiasm. As is frequently the case, our practical experiences as authors of hypertexts tempers an unqualified celebration of its theoretical potential. Based on these experiences, we conclude by suggesting how the limitations we highlight might be addressed in a feminist composition classroom.

Feminist Textual Politics: Interrogating Context and Self

To see writing as a form of politics, we must first understand the ways text production can be gendered. Feminist theory provides two ways into this issue: the effect of context and community on producing a certain type of gendered "I" for a text, and the political ramifications of producing a single "I" for a text in any context. In both these articulations, the key problem of textuality becomes associated with the type of voice, authority, and logic that writing produces.

From the perspective of social construction, the act of writing creates a single position for the writer, a position more often aligned with the context out of which it was created than with the writer's position in culture. Thus, the problem of gender and textuality is characterized primarily in terms of context and community. For example, Janis Tedesco (1991) argued that rather than seeing gendered positions as reflected *in* text (i.e., where the textual "I" is seen as an accurate reflection of the writer's feminine self), we should look at how writing contexts create gendered positions. These positions are perhaps best understood through Janis Haswell and Richard Haswell's (1995) concept of gendership. *Gendership* refers to "the image of the writer's sex interpretable from text and context. It can be conceived of as the gender dimension to the 'authorial personality' intended by the writer, or the gender dimension of the 'implied author' imagined by the reader" (p. 226). Seen this way, gender becomes inextricable from the rhetorical act of meaning-making; it forms a part of *ethos*, "a strategy of self-presentation" in response to a given discursive context (p. 232). The construction of this self is not autonomous; instead, the writer's interpretation of a context, and the contexts themselves, invoke assumptions about how authority and voice can be constructed in a given text. This interpretation and the different "regression or adaptations of gendered ways of knowing" that the context inspires results in the gendered self we read on the page (Tedesco, 1991, p. 250).

This interpretation of context, further, emerges from the writer's location in a community. It is primarily through the mechanism of readers— considering their needs, their expectations about genre, text, and voice, and their assumptions about knowledge within a given discourse community's context—that discursive contexts inscribe a particular gendership for a given text. In seeking to communicate within a given discourse, writers invoke the discursive norms of that community, thus creating a voice for the text, which will be aligned with such norms. When we link this construction to the masculine ways of knowing encouraged by academic genres (e.g., Bleich, 1989; Farrell, 1979; Kraemer, 1990; Lamb, 1991), teaching academic discourse seems to require that students construct masculine textual selves in response to academic contexts. Although a writer could ignore these contextual demands to speak a more authentic feminine self, such a feminist intervention ignores the situationally dependent nature of writing on which both readers and writers *must* rely for communication. As Don Kraemer (1990) noted, these shared discursive norms cannot be completely ignored if the writer desires a text to be read and taken seriously.

Rather than creating *safe* spaces for alternative writing, then, social feminists argue for a direct intervention into the ideology of writing spaces: what we are calling a textual politic. Such a politic attempts to allow other positions to be spoken by overtly politicizing the writing space for the writer and reader. In such a politic, writers are encouraged to inquire into how "specific acts of reading and writing" result in different gendered positions within text (Kraemer, 1990, p. 315). Becoming aware of this gendering process encourages the writer to express silenced or marginal positions by highlighting for the reader how such positions have been silenced by discursive norms. For many, multivocal texts become the best means of creating this space for alternative voices (e.g., Batson, 1989; Belanoff, 1990; Zawacki, 1992). A text that speaks multiple positions, in these arguments, also seeks to expose to the reader how "genre boundaries themselves are as questionable as gender boundaries and that all writing is a means of creating a self, not expressing a self that already exists" (Zawacki, 1992, p. 37). Thus, the writer seeks not only to create a space for her difference but also to highlight the textual silencing of difference for her reader such that a reader cannot reinvoke normalized assumptions about text to dismiss her attempt to speak alternatives.

Postmodern feminists describe the function of multivocal texts in remarkably similar ways, although in the service of a much different function. Rather than locate their textual politic only in a concern for the writer (i.e., her ability to express silenced, gender positions), these feminists see multivocal texts as cultural interventions into the power relations embedded in the production of knowledge and communication. For Donna Haraway (1991) and bell hooks

(1990), for example, the value of disrupting the univocality of the writing subject lies in exposing the ideology of text so that the means of constructing authority become apparent. As Haraway put it in an interview with Gary Olson (1996), cyborg writing works against the type of "authoritative writing practices that try hard to produce the masterful 'I,' a particular authority position that makes the viewer forget the apparatus of the production of that authority" (Olson, 1996, p. 5). In much the same way as hooks (1990) recommended that all positions be acknowledged as positions open to interrogation—whether from the center or the margin—Haraway (1991) argued that all claims of position, even "speaking as woman" or "woman of color," acknowledge the specificity of their authorization (p. 157). Acknowledging such a specificity serves a dual function for Haraway and hooks.

First, making the politics of location explicit works against the phallocentric assumption that truth and meaning transcend contexts. Particularly within academic discourse, the voice constructed in writing is associated with a position of authority that claims its perspective as all-encompassing. Such a voice, however, reinvokes the logic of phallocentrism by claiming its perspective as the *only* way of seeing the world. Presuming such a singular truth, these theorists contend, is one of the chief ways by which alternatives are silenced and current ideologies maintained. As Luce Irigaray (1977/1985) explained, silencing the multiplicity of meaning and the multiple positions all subjects occupy is what allows power relations to remain intact. By ensuring that meaning and subject positions are univocal, we reproduce phallocentric means of achieving authority in text, suppressing difference in favor of replicating texts that privilege the singularity of meaning. Thus, highlighting the locatedness of positions—making apparent to readers the contexts from which one speaks and writes—becomes a form of intervention. The politics of this intervention lies in the text's consistent reminder that no knowledge is produced outside of a given location; hence, no text can speak without recognizing its situatedness in culture. As such, these texts participate in the project of deconstructing phallocentricism by continually "suspending its pretension to the production of truth and meaning that are excessively univocal" (Irigaray, 1977/1985, p. 78).

Writing multivocal texts also serves a second function: to remind the writer of the contradictory and fragmented nature of her own positions. When we write as if we were a stable being who can stand outside discourse, we undercut our own recognition of our multiple positions and the power of that multiplicity. That is, the act of writing reflects our *selves* back to us in similar ways; we learn to see ourselves as unitary subjects and to silence feminine perspectives because they might contradict such unity. We risk, in short, accepting a definition of self that has been formed by the patriarchy. Thus, for postmodern theorists, the power for change resides in recognizing the partiality of our own knowledge and the multiple ways we interact with the world. Only by recognizing our multiplicity and attempting to communicate these positions might we begin to form new alliances with our cultural others rather than speaking for them. Acknowledging the partiality and multiplicity of the subject allows one to write from a variety of positions simultaneously in such a way that the subject is "able to join with another, to see together without claiming to be another" (Haraway, 1991, p. 193). The "death of the subject" in this light has "more to do with the end of some speaking for others than the end of liberatory struggle" (Lather, 1992, p. 132).

Helping students enact liberatory struggle is where feminist politics and pedagogy meet. For pedagogy, the goal is to imagine how new forms of being can be constructed and marginalized voices expressed in public, textual forms. These forms not only create alternative routes to voice for students but also attempt to expose the ideology of academic textuality, which seeks to silence perspectives contrary to its ideology. Through engaging in writing a multivocal text, both the silencing of the feminine in academic contexts and its claims to authoritative knowledge supported by its genres and contexts become open to interrogation. The hope is that through such investigations students will not only interrogate but also resist the discursive authority they are invited to claim, reminding them of the partiality of their knowledge and thus opening up new possibilities for communicating and forming alliances with their cultural Others.

The Promise of Theory: Feminist Textual Politics and Hypertext

Although we obviously find much value in feminist textual politics for the classroom, the difficulty of such a pedagogy lies in finding ways not only to investigate the gendered nature of academic discourse's contexts but also to provide venues for writing the multiple "I" key to a critical, feminist text. This is where employing hypertext in such a classroom may be particularly help-ful. We are not recommending that hypertext replace more traditional forms of writing in the classroom. Instead, hypertext might help students inquire into the nature of textual production itself by allowing students to speak multivocally. As Johndan Johnson-Eilola (1994) claimed, "hypertextually-influenced education might well be disruptive, but therein lies its value: theo-rists, teachers, and students may take the potentially rupturing influence of hypertext as an opportunity for close consideration of unquestioned assump-tions" (p. 216). From a feminist standpoint, those unquestioned assumptions are inextricable from the ways in which academic contexts create a gendered ideology of text. In fact, what hypertext is purported to disrupt are precisely those textual elements — reader considerations, genre assumptions, and the ideology of a unified "I" — that feminists indict as the primary mechanisms by which such a gendered ideology is produced (Bolter, 1991; Landow, 1992; Lan-ham, 1993; Slatin, 1990).

In this light, hypertext potentially disrupts many ideological mechanisms of text production. Most significantly, hypertext also incites the writer's awareness of her multiplicity, thus making a feminist textual politic easier to enact. Because the *voice* of a text is decentered, theorists tell us, the author becomes similarly dislocated. George Landow (1992), for example, asserted that the author of hypertext is more accurately a "decentered network of codes" than the unified "I" of print (p. 73). Bolter (1991) suggested that writing hypertext could possibly help create an awareness of this multiple consciousness by revealing the writer to herself in a different way (p. 233). Similarly, Catherine Smith (1994) explored the opportunities writing hypertext offers for discovering new forms of personal knowledge. By serving as a heuristic for "thick cognition" — acts of thinking that employ "the thinker's multiple physical, social, cultural, and historical life worlds" (p. 265) — hypertext encourages the writer to reassess her own cultural positions. In each of these statements, hypertext seemingly allows, indeed forces, a writer to become more aware of her multiplicity: the precursor to enacting a feminist textual politic.

Further, hypertext seems ideal for the ways in which this politic is enacted by allowing each voice to speak from its own unique location in culture. As many have noted, one of hypertext's chief benefits is how easily it allows for collaborative writing, and thus the ability to communicate multiple voices (e.g., Landow, 1992; Winkelmann, 1995). In collaboratively written texts, the voices of an individual author can presumedly be presented in such a way that each can be seen as equally authoritative in creating meaning. In short, the lack of conventional hierarchical structures, which can be so frustrating for readers (see Charney, 1994), provides writers with the opportunity to authorize multiple perspectives equally. This ability to equitably present perspectives also calls attention to the partiality of each voice and its links to the cultural contexts in which it was constructed. As Stuart Moulthrop (1994) argued, hypertext makes obvious "the designation of place or occasions" for speaking (p. 301), rather than the *logos* of a unitary meaning and all-knowing subject, thus calling the reader's attention to the partiality of all knowledge.

What all these observations seem to point to, then, is how ideal hypertext may be for a feminist textual politic. Hypertext's ability to disrupt academic discursive norms and reader expectations, combined with its potential to make writers aware of their multiplicity, seemingly provides the critical sense about self and discourse such a politic demands. Further, its ability to emphasize the location of each voice might also make the more conventional grounds of authority apparent to readers in ways that call such an ideology into question. In this way, hypertext serves a disruptive function for both the writer and the reader, calling attention to the politics of textuality in which both are immersed. Thus, although hypertext may not yet exist as an academic genre to be resisted (although it is quickly becoming so), its own conventions provide the opportunity for highlighting academic genres' ideology, while simultaneously encouraging the writer to construct other positions from which to write.

WRITING THE TEXTUAL FEMININE IN HYPERTEXT

Yet, the question remains whether hypertext's promise can be enacted. In this section, we analyze Luann Barnes' (1997) attempt to construct such a text for a class to highlight how hypertext does, in fact, aid the writer in realizing such goals.[1] Not surprisingly, however, hypertext does not obviate all the difficulties involved in critically interrogating academic contexts nor in speaking the locatedness of multiple subject positions. Both the context in which such hypertexts are situated and the nature of hypertextuality itself ultimately interfere with the writer's attempt to completely realize the textual intervention for which the theory calls.

RESPONDING TO CONTEXT: CONSTRUCTING GOALS

From a writer's point of view, one key difference between functional and experimental hypertexts is the degree to which context and readers affect what she produces. Functional texts (e.g., electronic encyclopedias, educational web sites) highlight context and readers' needs to a significant degree, much like technical writing in print. Experimental texts (e.g., Joyce's "Afternoon"), on the other hand, seek to enact a writer's more personal goals, thus creating contexts (or breaking them), leaving the reader free to interpret the textual action in ways other than the writer intended. Hypertexts written along the lines we suggest here, however, fit neither category easily. They are partially functional in that they must respond to the context of the classroom, academic discourse, and a teacher-reader, yet experimental in their attempt to voice the multiplicity of the author and defer the assertion of a single, univocal meaning for the reader. As a result, the success of such texts lies equally in their ability to disrupt the context to speak from other subject positions and in exposing the mechanisms by which such positions would be silenced so that the text is not seen as a failure or an inability to write academic discourse.

Barnes' text is ideal for examining both these aspects of a feminist textual politic. It was originally produced for a graduate class—Gender and Genre—without any consideration of this article, conceived later. As such, the text had to respond to the context of the class and acknowledge its own embeddedness within academic discourse. Part of the goal of the class, which in turn shaped the goal of this project, was to interrogate textual and cultural constructions of gender and genre. By explicitly foregrounding the role of text in gendered representation, this class set up a context wherein an examination of a writer's relationship to textual production was an appropriate response to the seminar paper requirement. Recognizing that she was writing within an academic context for a class about *genre,* Barnes became interested in the effect of academic discourse on gendered representation. As she reflected at the time in her journal, she was intrigued by how academic genres work to create a shared context for writer and reader, and thus an environment in which to communicate. With different genres come different reader expectations and along with them different scripted responses, making certain genres more disposed to allowing certain subject positions to be spoken. Her conviction that academic writing proscribed a single voice combined with her assumption that maintaining multiple subject positions was a key feminist act led her to hypertext:

> I wanted to experiment with different genres to see if opposing genres would allow different voices to emerge. The possibility of hypertext to

create a multivocal text resides in its ability to juxtapose academic writing with that of multiple personal narratives, to allow the existence of multiple genres simultaneously in the same text. By both blurring genres and making them collide, never allowing a reader to be totally comfortable with a single genre, a hypertext writer can make a reader see genre as artificial and subject positions as dynamic. I hoped ultimately to encourage the interrogation of text rather than the pursuit of stable meaning. I had also embraced the idea of the multiple self and the importance of maintaining multiple subject positions. At the outset, hypertext seemed an ideal vehicle for speaking from other subject positions in an academic context, specifically in the context of a graduate seminar paper that, in most cases, demands a unified argument. By disrupting the academic genre, I hoped to give voice to multiple subject positions and expose the fallacy of a unified self. In a way this was my attempt to show what drives logical choices, but does not end up in a final text. It is through the multiplicity of genres that I hoped multiple voices would be able to emerge.

Although this reflection is after the fact, her journal noted that she was motivated primarily by a frustration with the exclusion of emotion from aca-

FIGURE 1.   The Fabric of Voices

(Reprinted from *Computers and Composition* Vol. number 16, Donna LeCourt and Luann Barnes, "Writing Multiplicity: Hypertext and Feminist Textual Politics." Page No. 62, © Copyright 1999 with permission from Elsevier Science)

FIGURE 2.   Overvoice in Emotions Path

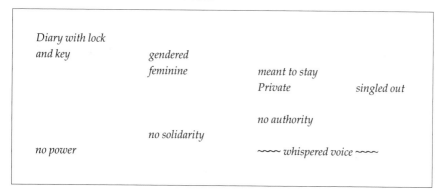

demic spaces. As a result, the initial idea was to resituate a text within a context, in a sense to put back some of the voices silenced in the production of an
academic text, but to do so in a way that called attention to academic discourse's attempt to silence them. In this way, Barnes sought to create new
spaces in academic contexts for alternative voices by exposing how knowledge is situated in multiple locations and thus expressed in multiple voices. In
short, she ought to enact a textual politic, even though she did not put it in
these terms at the time.

Beginning with how a single published text had generated multiple academic and personal texts over a four-year period, she wanted to highlight her
growing realization that each text was different because each was written
within a different historic context, and that these changing contexts also
revealed different subject positions. This published text and its multiple
responses became the point of origin for the hypertext: the initial conflict that
made the "borders" of some of her personal subject positions more apparent.
From here the text began to incorporate more voices and positions—academic, daughter, emotional female, programmer—as well as ones linked to
the genres in which she was writing: poetry, journals, music. As the text progressed, however, labels for positions became impossible: *I struggle giving
them labels. Some I can but others defied labels and just stayed random voices suspended in the text. Is this multivocality if I can't name my subject positions? I think so*
(*Fabric*, Gender Journal Path).

DESCRIPTION OF *THE FABRIC OF VOICES*

The final text is arranged somewhat hierarchically. Because the initial goal
was to represent and clarify multiple voices, the text attempts to construct this
representation structurally for the reader. The opening screen is neat and
orderly, complete with title and discrete categories for voices. Although such
an organization seems linear, the opening screen also tries to counter this
assumption by breaking convention. The title is in the bottom right corner, not
top left, and the categories are represented by icons: overvoice (figure), academic voice (books), programmer voice (binary notation), journals (paper &

brush), emotions (random lines), and other voices (computer.) Labels only appear when the mouse is passed over the icon, making only one label visible at a time. The icons represent both single voices and groups of voices, which may not be clear to a reader at first glance. The overvoice mediates and interrogates the other voices, offering a reader an explanation for the project and help with navigation. The structure is initially hierarchical with subcategories within the categories represented on the opening screen. For instance, the category of journals leads a reader to a screen that lists home journal, gender journal, and programmer's journal.

Both Barnes' ability and desire to maintain such a clear organization, however, changed as the text became more complex. Thus, as a reader progresses through the text, the voices blur and merge. The overvoice that begins as academic is subverted by stylistic features, sentence fragments and other syntax unbecoming of a truly academic voice. As in the example previously mentioned, the overvoice frequently speaks in fragments. Similarly, all the academic texts stay in a rigid hierarchy, but embedded within those texts are contextual links that jump genre boundaries without warning. For example, within the academic voice path, a reference to "anglo" in a seminar paper jumps to the gender journals and an author's name sends readers to another site in the internet, while another link within the same paper sends the reader to a poem. Organizationally, the hypertext is designed to keep readers jumping from voice to voice rather than remaining in a single path, unless the reader decides only to employ the BACK button.

Overall, the final text, then, gives the reader a firm sense of direction and structure in the initial levels, yet begins to subvert those expectations as one moves further into the text where the reader-text interaction is more similar to that found in experimental hypertexts. This subversion is somewhat limited, however, by the inclusion of a home icon, which can return the reader to the opening, overview screen from any point in the text.

FEMINIST TEXTUAL POLITIC OR EXPERIMENTAL HYPERTEXT?

A Fabric of Voices clearly succeeded in producing a multiple text, yet, the question remains whether or not it engages in a feminist textual politic for which multiplicity as deconstructive play is simply not enough. Instead, the text should allow the writer to recognize and work against the subject positions academic discourse inscribes and help her become more aware of her own multiplicity as well as the partiality and specificity of her subject positions. Further, the textual product should help readers acknowledge the ideological nature of the context and recognize the multiple voices as expressing a certain politics of location. By presenting the reader with multiple perspectives, which the organization refuses to reconcile, embedding contradictions antithetical to linear argument, and calling attention to academic structures through organization, style, and emotive content, *Fabric* seems to disrupt the academic context for both writer and reader in ways a feminist textual politic recommends. As the analysis of the text and Barnes' process later reveals, however, the extent to which writing this hypertext served these functions for writer and reader is limited to the parts of discursive context Barnes was *allowed* to examine and how much hypertext was able to disrupt normalized ways of meaning-making.

Interrogating the Context of Academic Discourse

Although hypertext aided in Barnes' attempt to engage critically the academic context's assumptions about genre, proof, style, and persona, other aspects of the context remained hidden from critical interrogation. Probably the most intriguing of these aspects is how her concern for a reader reinvokes academic forms of authority because of hypertext itself. Although Barnes was critically aware of the many expectations of the readers about academic writing and sought to work against them, she expressed concern, instead, with her readers' unfamiliarity with hypertext:

> I spend at least eight hours a day immersed in the writing of hierarchical "functional" hypertexts geared towards assisting students in the writing of phallocentric academic texts. I set out to disrupt the hierarchy and cohesive demands of an academic text, but my sensitivity to reader disorientation in reading unstructured hypertexts went unquestioned.

It is this concern that resulted in the structure for the text and the inclusion of the overvoice. Although Barnes added the overvoice and structure so that readers would not get lost in the hypertext, she also quickly reinvoked academic means of achieving authority by perceiving a need for these devices. Considering this need as resulting from the unique demands of hypertext, however, kept Barnes from seeing their connection to academic discursive norms.

The overvoice serves many functions within the text: It is the voice that defines hypertext and guides a reader; it offers definitions of multivocality, and most importantly, it mediates among the other voices. In short, it attempts to control the reader in ways an academic text usually does more subtly. Because of Barnes' concern with reader disorientation, the overvoice spends much time on the initial levels reminding readers of her goal of multivocality:

> I wonder if I am forcing the perception of multivocality on a reading by proclaiming that this is a *multivocal* text, because that is what I am trying to accomplish? Or is it a plea to the reader to try and make my experiment successful? (*Fabric,* Overvoice Path)

Much like a thesis statement, then, Barnes accedes to academic context's demands that she express an intent that can, in fact, contain what follows. Similarly, the almost linear organization of the opening screen, which provides an overview (essay map?) with clear labels of voices (subtitles?) and explanations of hypertext's functions (cohesive devises?), as well as the semi-hierarchical organization of the top levels (an outline?), remind us that this text does conform to many academic expectations about how coherence is achieved.

Although Barnes included these academic conventions to address the potential confusion hypertext could cause, it is extremely significant that she refers back to academic means for achieving coherence. Within this context, such a response is, after all, only natural. Upon reflection, Barnes realized that such devices invoked tacit desires that had little to do with the hypertext environment and everything to do with communicating clearly to her audience. Rather than allowing meaning to be consistently deferred, she wanted her readers to find the text accessible. Her familiarity with academic discourse made it impossible to avoid trying to foreground her intent in such a way that she could ensure that the hypertext was read correctly.

On one level, Barnes did not want her class members and instructor to misinterpret the purpose of the text. This concern emerged from her desire to control the authority they would grant the text and her thoughts:

> Again, the difficult part will be to deflect the censorship of the academic voice, the one I must say is privileged even in my attempts to subvert it. Luce Irigaray said that "she is multiple in her language and is often accused of being incoherent." Here I feel freed from the need to be coherent. Perhaps not. (*Fabric*, Gender Journal Path)

On another level, concerns for the reader were also inextricable from the textual politic Barnes was trying to enact. If the text was to serve its political function, it must be understood:

> As a writer I struggle to make it meaningful for a reader, worried that the disruption of the text will make a reader walk away from the text. And without a reader, does a text exist? As a feminist I want the text to be disruptive in terms of not allowing stable contexts which force the author/reader to accede to masculine ways of meaning making, but even the feminist does not want the text to be totally inaccessible. If the text is inaccessible it does not serve a political purpose because "male ways of knowing" go unquestioned. This need to explain also highlights the fact that voices can be silenced in hypertext just by readers missing certain links.

This concern for readers, in terms of both structure and content, cannot be attributed solely to the academic context but again emerges from a potential problem with hypertext. Although in a multivocal print text a writer can ensure all voices will be read, hypertext's ability to grant this control to the reader raises the potentiality that many paths, and the positions they express, will never be heard. Although hypertext allowed Barnes a venue for expressing these voices, the disruptions that allow for such alternative means of achieving voice also led her to replicate academic textual conventions to ensure the reader would recognize the critique of such conventions.

These tensions between meeting the demands of readers to get heard while attempting to deconstruct the means by which such voices are authorized result in a text that accedes to an academic context in some ways (structural devices, textual references, and thesis statements) while disrupting them in others (multiple positions, calling attention to academic forms of authority, etc.). Context, while disrupted, is not escaped. In seeking to call a reader's attention to the ideological nature of that context, the writer, it seems, becomes subject to normalizing influences created by *hypertext*—ironically, the form of textuality that also obviates many other academic discourse norms.

Similarly, the political act of mobilizing silenced voices and making multiple locations apparent in a context, which normally calls for a single, unified "I," has both disruptive and normalizing influences. The disruption of the academic context and benefits for the writer in speaking what is silenced are apparent, yet it is equally important to note that the choice of these voices is not free of contextual influences. The more academic roles—programmer, student, and technical writer—are most obvious here; however, the limited choices that are acceptable can be seen in other positions as well. Although these subject positions, which speak emotive content, invoke authority from private spaces like family and experience, or attempt to engage in multiple genres usually marginalized in academic arguments, these voices are not marginalized within academic discourse. Personal experience, for example, is highly acceptable in certain forms of writing, including, significantly, feminist writing. Similarly, the emphasis on emotions invokes acceptable definitions of gender within the academy. The multiple genres (e.g., poetry, journals) are all acceptable within the discourse as well. In short, the positions spoken in *Fabric,* while usually silenced in the genre of seminar paper, are not unacceptable within other genres of academic discourse:

> I look back on all the separate ideas grouped in tidy little paragraphs and separated by spaces, and wonder if I have really accomplished what I set out to do. Was I able to override the academic voice at all? I am also amazed at, as much as was going on in my head, how little made it to paper. . . . The last minute trepidation of whether I really want to take the risk. (*Fabric,* Home Journal Path)

The risk, of course, is real. Venturing too far outside academic and cultural acceptability risks not only not being read but also the material results of grades, authority with the graduate students with whom she works as a programmer, and her colleagues, teachers, and supervisors within the department. (The teacher for Gender and Genre, not incidentally, was the chair of the department.) As such, even hypertext cannot escape the mechanism of *ethos* orchestrated by the academic context. Knowing that others would eventually read this text constructs a concern that Barnes not be seen as inappropriate; such a concern for self-presentation is difficult to resist, particularly for students.

The Multiplicity of the Subject

Fabric of Voices obviously manages to speak the multiple subject in that it explicitly engages many of Barnes' subject positions—daughter, poet, feminist, technical writer, student, programmer, and others she couldn't name— even if it restricts the choice of voices to acceptable, academic positions. Further, the final product engages many political ends multivocality is meant to achieve by explicitly foregrounding what contexts with which such positions were associated and deliberately juxtaposing those positions. The deeper levels, in particular, make it almost impossible for a reader to avoid being jumped from position to position, each of which comments on the other. One of the most obvious ways in which this multivocality questions academic contexts is the references path labeled other voices, which is presented in lower case as a way to minimize the importance of outside references. Academic means of achieving authority through textual references are separated from more personally located voices, calling attention to the way references are usually *spoken over* by an author. Thus, *Fabric* illustrates clearly how amenable hypertext is to enacting this politic for the *reader*. However, the role hypertext played for the *writer's* ability to access such multiplicity and write the voices that emerged remains to be interrogated.

What Barnes discovered in writing *Fabric* was that hypertext did not ameliorate many difficulties in producing such a text, particularly in the creation of the content. The necessity of constructing a unified self to produce text became extremely relevant as Barnes discovered that no matter what method she employed she could not escape the need to construct a unified voice:

> I tried multiple writing methods (electronic, pen and paper, sketches, flow charts), as a way to create different contexts, in an attempt to allow multiple voices to emerge in the writing process. I also started to experiment with place—to see how that defines who I am and how I write. The first part of the gender journal I carried diligently back and forth on disk. After that I decided to split it into gender journal and home journal. One segment of the journal I kept at home, where I feel I am gendered differently than I am gendered at the university. It is a safer space where I don't feel under the scrutiny that I am at the university. It is at home that I do most of my musing—reflecting forwards and back—on the happenings of the day and how they weave into my textuality—my fabric of stories. It is there that I feel freed from the need to be coherent and had hoped to be able to invoke a multivocal context. But all my attempts to write a multivocal text simultaneously only became random disjointed thoughts and not the expression of multiple voices.

Constructing voice resulted, not surprisingly, in referring back to a presumedly shared, discursive context with the reader and the exigencies it produced as well as the unification of self Irigaray (1977/1985) argued is impossible to avoid when producing the most basic linguistic structures. Each path/voice had to be written separately: *What I found was that I was only able to invoke a single context with any consistency, and multiple voices cannot exist within a single context. One can only write with one voice, and that voice silences all others.*

As a result, the writing process and the unification of self it orchestrates remained unchanged, and further, unquestioned when producing the content. The tension between opposing voices was too uncomfortable and too disruptive to the flow of text production, particularly for a writer so familiar with the types of cohesion and authorial voice required by academic discourse. As a result, Barnes realized during the process that she was continually acceding to phallocentric means for achieving voice in text, and yet could not avoid doing otherwise: *What I initially saw as getting into the "groove" of writing was in fact forcing me into a male subject position in order to invoke a stable unified "I." Anything less, though, was just too uncomfortable.*

Barnes' experience suggests that even when writing for hypertext, univocality and linearity are impossible to escape. The thinking involved may be engaged in making multiplicity apparent, but the production of language forces the text to be written one word at a time with a single context in mind. When it came to creating links, however, hypertext's benefits for enacting the multiplicity of self were much more apparent. The political goals of becoming more aware of the locatedness of positions and how they interact was only realized in the linking process. Most importantly, Barnes is convinced that many of these interactions, and the critical awareness they produced, would not have been possible without hypertext:

> A multiple self did not emerge until I created the hypertext document, in other words, until I started connecting the multiple linear texts—each reflecting a single voice. This is where conflicts in subject positions began to become more apparent. In tying together a common theme of hypertext I connected the programmer of functional hypertexts with the feminist, and only when those two voices were next to each other did I notice the clash in some of their ideologies. These were voices that, up to this point, I thought were primarily in agreement. When I took the personal narrative out of the seminar paper and let it stand alone, I realized that the academic voice was trying to explain away the emotional reaction I had to the poetry reading. Instead, I let that angry voice tell the academic that it was not OK be to named as an other by a fellow Chicano graduate student in his attempt to name himself. These clashes of subject positions were not apparent when involved with writing in a single voice, even as I considered how they might work together.

The realizations creating links orchestrated suggests that hypertext may be one of the best ways to create an unstable context and access the multiple self, as the theory asserts. For Barnes, at least, many critical benefits for voicing subjugated positions and understanding the historical specificity of those voices—and thus their limitations for expressing her self and speaking of and for the Other—would not have been possible without the ability to create connections in the text. Although such connections could certainly be made in print text as well, the ease and, indeed necessity, of creating multiple links is only possible in hypertext. Multivocal print texts allow the writer to juxtapose one position with another, while hypertext allows any number of positions to be put into conversation with each other. The only problem hypertext cannot avoid, however, is how programming interferes with its infinite potential for linking. Programming, after all, is nothing more than writing in a computer language and can only be accomplished one task at a time, confining the writer, as in print, to focusing only on one juxtaposition at a time. The linearity of such a task exposes the potential for hypertextual writers to reproduce binary oppositions rather than a multivocality of self.

The need to continually engage in these oppositions, however, need not undercut hypertext's potential; instead, it is probably best to characterize the programming task as a deferral of multivocality. Once links are created, the writer as reader of her text finds her self reflected back to her in ways that enact a multiplicity she cannot engage either when producing content or programming links. Just as significantly, it expresses that self to other readers in ways that hide the unification of the subject the process of writing made inescapable: *Even in terms of programming, I waited to determine the multivocality of the text through the reading process, not the writing or programming processes.*

IMPLICATIONS FOR PEDAGOGY

Our analysis highlights many limitations for hypertext's ability to enact a textual politic, including its inability to escape the logocentrism of writing, its immersion within a discursive context, and the new mechanisms of reader-control it introduces. The reader issues resulting from the hypertextual environment are arguably the most troubling. As Barnes' continual concern with reader dislocation reveals, the disruptive potential of hypertext alone will not create an awareness of multivocality in a reader. Rather, readers ultimately can subvert the multivocality and fragmentation with their need to create a cohesive narrative. The reader's location within a discursive context is perhaps the most difficult to mediate when trying to enact such a politic, particularly for students whose negotiation of that context is inseparable from its material effects on their lives (i.e., grades, graduation). What Barnes' process and product highlight, further, is that simply writing hypertexts focused on multiple voices will not achieve the goals of a feminist politic in themselves. As Patricia Webb (1997) argued, merely engaging in the seemingly disruptive practice of computer-mediated communication (CMC) does not lead to a new perception of self and writing; instead, it is more likely that students will reproduce humanist concepts of self and author. We are convinced that without the foregrounding of gender and genre relations and Barnes' background in considering the gendered nature of academic discourse, the process of writing hypertext would have been much less beneficial. Further, many ways in which she acceded to an academic context in the hypertext were made available only by our dialogic questioning of the text.

Thus, writing such texts in the composition classroom cannot be separated from a pedagogy that highlights the gendered nature of textual production in other ways. One way to work against the normalizing effects of the discursive context that still surface in hypertext, for example, may be to engage students in continual peer review of the hypertexts they are creating. As our theoretical premises assert, other students will bring more positions to such an interrogation than the author alone can do. Yet, with this suggestion, we are *not* arguing in favor of collaborative writing; the benefits of writing a multivocal hypertext cannot be realized unless they engage the single author in an interrogation of her positions. Similarly, attempts to investigate positionality itself, through autobiographical writing, the reading of published literacy narratives on potential conflicts with academic discourse, or other means, must precede the writing. Although hypertext can highlight the interactivity of multiple positions, it cannot in itself create an awareness of those positions.

Hypertext's inability to invoke a feminist politic on its own, however, does not undercut its value for pedagogy. Although Barnes is hesitant about whether her text actually performs such a politic for the reasons cited previously, its chief value lay in the process of the attempt. Defining the academic context and learning how it defines her initiated a process of discovery difficult to attain in any other way. This process not only made the mechanisms of discursive authority more apparent; it also led to a greater understanding of her positions and the critical potential juxtaposing those perceptions provided her for seeing the world and her positions within it:

> Each time my relation to the academic context changed (student, writer/ programmer, collaborative author) I was able to see how I had acceded to that context in ways I was previously unaware. I consciously chose voices that I knew would conflict, but also discovered further conflicts between positions I previously thought were in agreement.

Such reflections, for us, point to an obvious value for using such writing in the composition classroom. Much of what we attempt as feminist teachers can be realized by engaging in such experimental writing: a place for marginalized voices, an interrogation of power relations, an awareness of the gendered nature of academic discourse, and, most importantly, an insight into self and its relation to others. Perhaps the primary reason to encourage such writing, however, lies in its potential for social change and personal empowerment. Whether the texts produced for class actually enact a textual politic seems less important than what students may learn in the process—the need to interrogate the discursive grounds of achieving authority such that they can write differently in the other contexts which would silence both their alternative voices and the challenges those voices might make to the context's ideology.

NOTE

1. Because our primary goal in this essay is to investigate how writing such texts might make it possible for the student *writer* to revise the grounds on which textual authority is achieved, our analysis focuses primarily on Barnes' perceptions during the writing process and our interrogation of both the process and product. By foregrounding the results of producing a feminist hypertext for the writer, that is, we hope to gain insight into the potential benefits for using such writing in the composition class for our female students. Further, arguing from such personal experience seems the most appropriate way to investigate the material relations of a theory which presumes all experience and knowledge to be situated in the specificity of bodies and local cultural interactions.

WORKS CITED

Barnes, Luann. (1997). *The Fabric of Voices.* [Online, WWW]. Available: <http://www.colostate.edu /Depts/WritingCenter/assignments/e630d/voices/home.htm>.

Batson, Lorie Goodman. (1989). Defining ourselves as woman. *Pre/Text, 10,* 117–9.

Belanoff, Pat. (1990). The generalized other and me: Working women's language and the academy. *Pre/Text, 11,* 59–73.

Bleich, David. (1989). Genders of writing. *Journal of Advanced Composition, 10,* 305–20.

Bolter, Jay David. (1991). *Writing space: The computer, hypertext, and the history of writing.* Hillsdale, NJ: Erlbaum.

Charney, Davida. (1994). The effect of hypertext on processes of reading and writing. In Cynthia L. Selfe & Susan Hilligoss (Eds.), *Literacy and computers: The complications of teaching and learning with technology* (238–63). New York: Modern Language Association.

Farrell, Thomas J. (1979). The female and male mode of rhetoric. *College English, 40,* 909–21.

Flores, Mary J. (1990). Computer conferencing: Composing a feminist community of writers. In Carolyn Handa (Ed.), *Computers and community: Teaching composition in the twenty-first century* (106–17). Portsmouth, NH: Boynton/Cook.

Haefner, Joel. (1995). *Towards a rhetoric of the hyperessay.* Paper presented at the Conference on College Composition and Communication. Washington, DC, March 23–25. (ERIC document: ED390 048).

Handa, Carolyn. (1990). Politics, ideology and the strange, slow death of the isolated composer: Or, why we need community in the writing classroom. In Carolyn Handa (Ed.), *Computers and community: Teaching composition in the twenty-first century* (pp. 160–184). Portsmouth, NH: Boynton/Cook.

Haraway, Donna J. (1991). *Simian, cyborgs, and women: The reinvention of nature.* New York: Routledge.

Haswell, Janis, & Haswell, Richard. (1995). Gendership and the miswriting of students. *College Composition and Communication, 46,* 223–54.

hooks, bell. (1990). *Yearning: Race, gender and cultural politics.* Boston: South End.

Iragaray, Luce. (1985). *This sex which is not one.* (Catherine Porter with Carolyn Burke, Trans.) Ithaca NY: Cornell. (Original work published 1977)

Jessup, Emily. (1991). Feminism and computers in composition instruction. In Gail E. Hawisher & Cynthia L. Selfe (Eds.), *Evolving perspectives on computers and composition studies: Questions for the 1990s* (pp. 336–55). Urbana, IL: National Council of Teachers of English.

Johnson-Eilola, Johndan. (1994). Reading and writing in hypertext: Vertigo and euphoria. In Cynthia L. Selfe & Susan Hilligoss (Eds.), *Literacy and computers: The complications of teaching and learning with technology* (pp. 195–219). New York: Modern Language Association.

Kraemer, Don. (1990). No exit: A play of literacy and gender. *Journal of Advanced Composition, 10,* 305–20.

Lamb, Catherine. (1991). Beyond argument in feminist composition. *College Composition and Communication, 42,* 11–23.

Landow, George. (1992). *Hypertext: The convergence of contemporary critical theory and technology.* Baltimore: Johns Hopkins.

Lanham, Richard. (1993). *The electronic word: Democracy, technology, and the arts.* Chicago: University of Chicago Press.

Lather, Patti. (1992). Post-critical pedagogies: A feminist reading. In C. Luke & J. Gore (Eds.), *Feminisms and critical pedagogy* (pp. 120–137). New York: Routledge.

Moulthrop, Stuart. (1994). Rhizome and resistance: Hypertext and the dreams of a new culture. In George Landow (Ed.), *Hyper/Text/Theory* (pp. 299–319). Baltimore: Johns Hopkins.

Olson, Gary. (1996). Writing, literacy, and technology: Toward a cyborg writing. *Journal of Advanced Composition, 16,* 1–26.

Selfe, Cynthia L. (1990). Technology in the English classroom: Computers through the lens of feminist theory. In Carolyn Handa (Ed.), *Computers and community: Teaching composition in the twenty-first century* (pp. 118–139). Portsmouth, NH: Boynton/Cook.

Slatin, John. (1990). Reading hypertext: Order and coherence in a new medium. *College English, 52,* 870–83.

Smith, Catherine. (1994). Hypertextual thinking. In Cynthia L. Selfe & Susan Hilligoss (Eds.), *Literacy and computers: The complications of teaching and learning with technology* (264–81). New York: Modern Language Association.

Tedesco, Janis. (1991). Women's ways of knowing/women's ways of composing. *Rhetoric Review, 9,* 146–56.

Webb, Patricia. (1997). Narratives of self in networked communications. *Computers and Composition, 14,* 73–90.

Winkelmann, Carol L. (1995). Electronic literacy, critical pedagogy, and collaboration: A case for cyborg writing. *Computers and the Humanities, 29,* 431–48.

Zawacki, Terry Myers. (1992). Recomposing as a woman—An essay in different voices. *College Composition and Communication, 43,* 32–38.

Contextualizing "Composing as a Woman"

ELIZABETH A. FLYNN

Ideas that challenge received wisdom often need to be expressed with a minimum of qualification in order to overcome the considerable resistance that might accompany their introduction. Qualification usually comes later, after the ideas have circulated and been responded to. Thomas Kuhn's *The Structure of Scientific Revolutions* (1962) is a case in point. Kuhn explains in the preface to the first edition of the book that his exposure to the history of science radically undermined some of his basic conceptions about the nature of science and the reasons for its special success (v). The result was his development of the importance of "paradigms," "scientific achievements that for a time provide model problems and solutions to a community of practitioners" (vii). Kuhn is primarily interested, however, in those anomalous moments when the paradigm is disrupted and a revolution results (ix). Given that his conception of how scientific change occurs challenged existing explanations, he needed to make the strongest case possible. In a postscript to the second edition of the book written seven years later, however, he responds to his critics and refines his position. He acknowledges that the boundaries that separate scientific communities are considerably less rigid than he originally suggested (177) and that the change brought about by revolutions need not be large and need not be accompanied by crisis (181).

"Composing as a Woman" (1988), while hardly the equivalent of Kuhn's *The Structure of Scientific Revolutions*, was, like Kuhn's work, written at a transitional moment. It looks back to the time when feminism and composition studies had not yet engaged each other, and it looks forward to the emergence of feminist composition. Work that the essay draws on—Nancy Chodorow's *The Reproduction of Mothering*, Carol Gilligan's *In a Different Voice*, and Belenky, Clinchy, Goldberger, and Tarule's *Women's Ways of Knowing*—was written at a similar moment. Explanations of psychological and intellectual development by male researchers had ignored important differences between the processes of males and females because they had focused exclusively on the development of males. Chodorow, Gilligan, and the *Women's Ways of Knowing* collective needed to make clear that attending to women's different processes changes traditional findings in important ways. And they needed to establish that significant differences do exist. Qualification of their basic claim would have weakened their position and invited dismissal of their ideas.

Like Chodorow, Gilligan, and the *Women's Ways of Knowing* collective, I was introducing a relatively new idea into composition studies, the idea that the composing processes of male and female students may differ in important ways. To make the point, I selected especially good examples that demonstrated the usefulness of feminist work in other fields to the study of composition. Although the qualifications I provided have often been overlooked, I did make clear that my findings were provisional, that there were similarities as well as differences between the male and female writers, and that some student writing exhibited characteristics that contradicted the dichotomous descriptions I provided. I nevertheless was primarily interested in establishing, if only tentatively, that it would be productive for researchers in the field to attend to differences between male and female writers.

Fifteen years later we are at a considerably different moment within feminist studies in general and feminist composition in particular. The legitimacy of feminist approaches no longer needs to be established. They have been embraced to a greater or lesser degree in most fields in the humanities and the social sciences, and important work is being done in areas such as the sciences, law, and engineering. Within composition studies, feminism has emerged as an important area of inquiry, and numerous single-author and multiple-author books, journal articles, and book chapters have appeared in recent years. The biannual Feminism(s) and Rhetoric(s) conference has increased in size and significance, and numerous junior scholars are exploring rhetoric and composition from a feminist perspective. Some of this work continues to focus on differences between male and female writing strategies. As often, though, it challenges or qualifies the claims of earlier work, thereby providing refinement and the development of new research directions.

My recent work has moved far beyond the research questions addressed in "Composing as a Woman." For instance, in my book, *Feminism Beyond Modernism,* I defend postmodern feminism and distinguish it from modern and antimodern feminisms. A postmodern feminist approach, I argue, challenges conceptions of gender as an essence or a fixed category, seeing it, instead, as a dynamic process. I point out some of the limitations of modern feminist emphases on equality between men and women and of antimodern emphases on differences between men and women. Portions of the book are substantially reworked versions of essays I published in the 1990s. In some ways, however, "Composing as a Woman" has overshadowed these essays. It continues to be reprinted (this, I believe, is the seventh reprinting), and with each reprinting the disparity between the historical moment that gave rise to it and the present historical moment increases.

This is a good time, therefore, to point out some of my present discomfort with the essay. I must confess that even when I was writing "Composing as a Woman" I felt uneasy about dichotomous representations of the differences between males and females in the work I was drawing on and about assumptions that women's traditional roles were reproduced easily and readily because daughters identified with and emulated their mothers. In my family, class differences intersected gender differences in complex ways, and the accounts of neither Chodorow, Gilligan, nor the *Women's Ways of Knowing* collective seemed adequate to explain the conflicts between my parents or between my mother and me. My students, too, have made it clear that the families they come from often depart from the traditional nuclear family in which the mother is the primary parent. Many are raised by single parents, or their mothers work outside the home. I don't regret publishing "Composing as a Woman" when I did. But I hope, as it continues to be republished, that it will be seen in its historical context. It was important, in the late 1980s, to make a strong case for differences between men and women, even if we would later need to qualify, refine, and even contradict those claims.

WORKS CITED

Belenky, Mary Field, Blythe McVicker Clinchy, Nancy Rule Goldberger, and Jill Mattuck Tarule. *Women's Ways of Knowing: The Development of Self, Voice, and Mind.* New York: Basic Books, 1986.

Chodorow, Nancy. *The Reproduction of Mothering: Psychoanalysis and the Sociology of Gender.* Berkeley, U of California P, 1978.

Flynn, Elizabeth A. *Feminism Beyond Modernism.* Carbondale: Southern Illinois UP, 2002.

Gilligan, Carol. *In a Different Voice: Psychological Theory and Women's Development.* Cambridge: Harvard UP, 1982.

Kuhn, Thomas S. *The Structure of Scientific Revolutions.* 1962. 2nd ed. Chicago: U of Chicago P, 1970.

Reflections on "Feminism and Composition: The Case for Conflict"

SUSAN C. JARRATT

This essay, now more than a decade old, was written from within the context of a thoroughly expressivist composition community. That situation dictated the need to recognize the possibilities inherent in "conflict" in a situation in which they were ignored or suppressed. The times and customs of compositionists—both at my home institution and elsewhere—are quite different now. Cultural studies, critical and feminist pedagogy, and multiculturalist approaches, all of which foreground social differences and therefore potential conflict, have been taken up with enthusiasm; discussions of their theories and practices fill our journals and book lists. It seems less necessary now to point out the existence of conflicts among positions in the composition classroom, but it is still important to figure out how to analyze them and use them in pedagogically productive ways.

Perhaps the most common misreading of the essay comes in the form of an expression of distress from graduate student teachers in training (most often women) who say that they don't want to create conflict in their classrooms—that they are not conflictual people and would be uncomfortable fostering conflict. They read the essay as encouraging them to be contentious in the classroom. They seem to have generated an image of a combative and confrontational teacher out of the discussion of "conflict." I had (and still have) a somewhat different image in mind. The idea was rather to point out that the differences students bring into the classroom are differences that undergird our culture, forming an ever-shifting and unstable foundation, the girders of which will stick up at odd angles in our students' writing, no matter what the topic. The teacher can be ready to help writers excavate those foundations by means of rhetorical resources. And this process will not be a smooth one; we will bump into each other along the way. The more adept we are at understanding how language works at those junctures, the better composition teachers we will be.

Over the years since I wrote this piece, I have found that students are somewhat more resilient—less breakable—than I believed them to be. Some of them—male and female—are adept and enthusiastic arguers; others are less willing to jump into a class discussion, but their writings show that they are following along in their heads, constructing their own responses, and processing them through writing. On the other hand, we live now in a media wasteland so far as argumentation is concerned. Talk shows (really shouting shows), talk radio (often hate-talk radio), and the incredible poverty of political discourse in which we are awash do not provide good examples of productive conflict for students to learn from. But that is all the more reason to keep making the case for conflict, informed by feminist pedagogical principles and strong rhetorical theory.

PART FOUR

Gender, Teaching, and Identity

Part Four: Introduction

FAYE SPENCER MAOR

Early work in feminism and composition often centered on notions of identity as it relates to gender. Questions like how women write and how being female affects work in the composition classroom were subjects of discussion. Composition teachers and scholars asked these questions in response to the students they encountered. Needless to say, feminism has been, and must continue to be, concerned with these issues, but just as important is how we define ourselves as teachers and as feminists. The conversation must include discussions of teacher identity.

The essays in this section shift the focus of discussion from student to teacher and complicate notions of identity and gender. Beyond gender, what other "differences" influence teachers, differences often characterized by teachers' races, genders, and ethnicities? Further, how does technology, when used in the classroom, affect that "difference," and how is this "difference" represented? In "On Becoming a Woman: Pedagogies of the Self," Susan Romano suggests that technology does not create the "safe spaces" for women that it was once thought to do. She shows how "gender issues pervade classroom discourse" and argues that students will invite the discussion of gender online, often using the anonymity and masks of online discussion to address gender issues in ways not seen in traditional classroom settings. Compositionists must rethink their belief in the "benevolence of online discourse," Romano concludes.

Equal representation of varied, multicolored, and multipositioned voices is a desire of feminist work; however, exactly what that means, and how it can be achieved, is not always clear. This is especially true when the word *feminism* itself may lead to a rejection of the instructor as a feminist and her desire to create a feminist classroom. Dale Bauer, in "The Other 'F' Word," argues that students' desire for a politically and socially "neutral" classroom leads to resistance and sometimes rejection of the feminist teacher and her efforts to achieve feminist goals. Bauer questions how students can be engaged in feminist dialogue and realize the benefits of such an engagement when the desire for a neutral classroom is so strong. The term *feminism* is often resisted by students, and that resistance is often reflected in negative comments on course evaluations, which in turn can have an impact on the teacher's presence in the classroom. How does the feminist teacher overcome these attitudes? Further, for some researchers, "feminism" might be overshadowed by other parts of their identity.

For example, Shirley Wilson Logan, in "'When and Where I Enter': Race, Gender, and Composition Studies," says nineteenth-century African American women often exerted feminist causes in their work for the race, under the umbrella of race progress. The women Logan discusses saw their work for the race as an expression of their feminism. Logan's essay grounds the work of African American women in a history of activism for literacy, racial uplift, and political power. In this essay, Logan quotes nineteenth-century activist and literacy worker Anna Julia Cooper, who argues women's work in the public sphere is necessary in bringing the "feminine side of truth" to the issues affecting African Americans. Given this history, what issues of identity and race arise for African American women working in predominantly white writing classrooms? How does this history affect pedagogy?

One answer to that question might be that the African American feminist teacher has had to cross traditional and untraditional lines when she finds herself in a predominantly white classroom. In "Participatory Rhetoric and the Teacher as Racial/Gendered Subject," Cheryl Johnson grapples with the effects of teaching African American literature, as an African American teacher, to predominantly white students. Johnson talks about the lines she had to contemplate crossing, as well as the lines her students crossed, because of who she was and what was being read. She argues that students not only read the texts but also read the instructor (her embodiment of race and gender, in particular) and that those readings affect and complicate her role as professor. How do race and gender construct/influence pedagogy and the ideology of African American literature? Some eight years later, in "Masks and Other Drapings: A Reconsideration (or Reconciliation?) of 'Participatory Rhetoric and the Teacher as Racial/Gendered Subject,'" Johnson reflects that although she still finds herself wearing masks and conducting rituals as a black woman in a predominantly white classroom, the costuming and fanfare have gotten lighter and a little easier to wear.

Experience can, and perhaps should, be used more critically in the feminist classroom, suggests Min-Zhan Lu in "Reading and Writing Differences: The Problematic of Experience." She asks students and teachers to examine the political uses and abuses of personal experiences in reading and writing about differences. No longer can we use personal experiences solely as criteria to address and separate issues of gender, race, and class, she argues. As feminist teachers, Lu says, we must find better ways of using personal experience critically, and she offers ways of getting at the analytical possibilities of experience.

Clearly, the experiences and history that each of us brings to the composition classroom differ, but for women teaching in the academy, one issue is often shared—the issue of authority. The seven authors of "A Symposium on Feminist Experiences in the Composition Classroom" provide seven different perspectives of how feminist writing teachers encounter and cope with issues of authority. The writers suggest that, generally, notions of authority are not associated with women and that female composition teachers' authority is further complicated by composition theories that call for student-centered process pedagogies. Unique problems arise for women composition instructors when these pedagogies seek to decenter the classroom. In our efforts to make the classroom a "safe space," are we really marginalizing female teachers? Should classrooms be "safe spaces"?

Likewise, Michelle Payne wrestles with issues of authority in "Rend(er)-ing Women's Authority in the Classroom." She argues that the teacher's identity, formed by personal history, experience, gender, and race, can create a "conflicting internal dialogue" about what and how authority should be shaped. There are times, she suggests, when the teacher wants to, or feels she should, direct and instruct students explicitly. She encourages composition teachers to question pedagogies that suggest they always decenter authority and create an egalitarian classroom in hope of reaching "all" students. She cautions that "romanticizing" students can silence our own experiences as multidimensional teachers and individuals. Instead, she suggests, our experiences as racial and gendered individuals can be a valuable resource in the classroom.

For the gay and lesbian teacher of composition, there are many dilemmas. What impact does coming out in the classroom have? Mary Elliott explores these dilemmas in "Coming Out in the Classroom: A Return to the Hard Place." What effect does a pedagogy of disclosure and visibility have on heterosexual, as well as gay or lesbian, students? How can "coming out" be used as a pedagogy? For example, a pedagogy of disclosure and visibility may be liberating for gay and lesbian teachers, but for some gay and lesbian students it may cause withdrawal or discomfort. For other students, a teacher's coming out in the classroom might create pressure for them to make revelations about themselves that they are not ready, able, or willing to make. What effect does this type of pedagogy have on heterosexual students, and how does the instructor balance all of the potential reactions, objections, and protests to her or his teaching and classroom?

And how do students respond to and perceive teachers of different sexual orientations? In "Bi, Butch, and Bar Dyke," Michelle Gibson, Martha Marinara, and Deborah Meem offer three "theorized narratives" that explore how they "experience and perform" their multiple identities. (70) Marinara reflects on her statuses as bisexual and working class to argue for a "flexible identity" that can inhabit multiple "useful political positions." (79) Meem also writes of her multiple identities, noting how her butch lesbian persona can actually function as a privileged identity category. Finally, Gibson narrates her performance as "a femme lesbian, a survivor of family violence, and a recovering mental patient" (85) in an academic reappointment evaluation. Such conscious performance, she writes, can "transform the public spaces we inhabit from oppressive realms into inclusive realms." (92)

Issues of gender and identity, as they relate to the teacher, contain much uncharted territory. The essays in this section grapple with many of them but leave much more to be explored. Further work is needed to probe and complicate the work begun here. How do classroom practices change when an African American gay/lesbian teacher walks into a classroom in which she is the minority? What should she do differently? Will coming out in the classroom aid or hinder learning? Can technology really help erase gender bias, or does it create a different space for the same problems? Should we, and can we, use the site of difference, the site of conflict, to effectively release student and teacher voices?

The essays presented here have been, and will be, influential in the conversation of feminism, composition, race, gender, and identity. Ethnic minorities, gays, lesbians, white men, and women have been participating in this conversation and will continue to, just not always in the ways we might expect. We must always look for the conversations that will aid in expanding and clarifying our positions and ideologies as feminists and literacy workers.

21 The Other "F" Word: The Feminist in the Classroom

DALE M. BAUER

EVALUATING FEMINIST TEACHERS

The best of our writing is entangled in the messiness of our experience.

—NINA AUERBACH

In just about half of a colleague's teaching evaluations (twelve of twenty-six evaluations) from two first-year composition and introduction to literature sections, she read objections to her feminist stance, especially her discussions of feminism and pedagogy. Most of the objections came from students who insisted that the classroom ought to be an ideologically neutral space free from the instructor's interests and concerns. The following samples, copied verbatim, suggest the drift of the students' complaints:

> I feel this course was dominated and overpowered by feminist doctrines and ideals. I feel the feminist movement is very interesting to look at, but I got extremely bored with it and it lost all its punch & meaning because it was so drilled into our brains.

> I also think you shouldn't voice your "feminist" views because we don't need to know that—It's something that should be left outside of class.

> I found it very offensive that all of our readings focused on feminism.

> Feminism is an important issue in society—but a very controversial one. It needs to be confronted on a personal basis, not in the classroom. I didn't appreciate feminist comments on papers or expressed about a work. This is not the only instructor—others in the English Dept. have difficulties leaving personal opinions out of their comments.

As one of those other instructors who have "difficulties" leaving that other "f" word, feminism, out of my classroom, I am troubled by the easy separation

From *College English* 52 (1990): 385–96.

these students insist upon between the private or personal and the public space. Precisely because they insist on this separation, our first task should be to show how the personal is public. Perhaps the last quote is the most telling: feminism is a social issue; the classroom, however, is removed from society. Social issues are not to be publicized, either to know the issues, to engage them, or to challenge the issues in the process. Rather, established truth, as Paulo Freire has told us, is to be banked. The students fear more than anything a perceived intellectual bankruptcy in the classroom. For this student, the classroom is a place of absorption, but it should not be a social arena.

Another student articulates a fear of gendered subjectivity:

> My professor has one distinct and overburying [*sic*] problem. She is a feminist and she incorporates her ideas and philosophy into her grading scale. If you do not make women sound superior to men or if you make women sound inferior, despite the belief of the writer, she will grade lower. I think the University should investigate this class and compare the scores of the males in the class with the females. It is my belief that among males that we are getting lower grades because of our sex.

The instructor in a personal note to me glossed this evaluation as follows: "The closest I can come to 'mak[ing] women sound superior' is to require that all essays be written in inclusive language." This evaluation is striking for two reasons. First, the metaphor of detection and investigation, of eradicating gender difference in the classroom, indicates many students' beliefs about classroom neutrality. Second, and perhaps more important, it represents the fear of gender issues invading the public world of the classroom during an era in which it is necessary for most students to insist on rationalizing intellectual labor. For most feminists, there is no separation between the outer world and the inner word, let alone between politics and intellectual work.

This second issue concerns feminism as a topic of intellectual and academic value. In the students' complaints, I hear a suggestion, echoed by some of my colleagues, that feminism is not a discipline, that gender issues are based on perspectives unsuitable for the labor of the intellectual. Consider the following student comment: "I think works should be more well-rounded without a continual stress on feminism." "Well-rounded" and balanced are set off against "feminism"—that locus of imbalance, fanaticism, eccentricity. "Continual stress" comes out of the perception of aggravation. The irony in the student comments, however, arises from a cultivated distance from the authority in the classroom, here an authority identified with an alien, radical, and threatening political position. On this point, I am persuaded by Suzanne Clark's articulation of literary studies as part of the continuum of rhetorical studies: "Feminist writing . . . breaks down the distances established by irony and provokes rhetorical responsiveness—the dialectic of resistance and identification that can then lead to critical thinking" (10; see Paine's definition of critical thinking 538–39).

How can a feminist rhetoric constitute this dialectic in the classroom? In the student comments I quoted above, there is an often overwhelming insistence on individualism and isolation; they also insist on the alienated work of the classroom, even if the professor holds forth the goal of collaborative learning in contrast to a traditional sense of knowledge as mechanized or routinized labor (see Paine 559). The students (responding here to feminism) labor at developing a critical distance to avoid participating in "the dialectic of resistance and identification" crucial not only to teaching and critical thinking, but also to political responsibility. Interrogating her students on the understanding of indoctrination, Gayatri Spivak addresses this problem in her recent book, *In Other Worlds*. She challenges her students' acceptance of the split between "moral speculation" and decision making. Spivak sees this separation as rendering them "incapable of thinking collectively in any but the most inhumane way":

> Suppose an outsider, observing the uniformity of the moves you have all sketched in your papers, were to say that you had been indoctrinated? That you could no longer conceive of public decision-making except in the quantified areas of your economics and business classes, where you learn all about rational expectations theories? You *know* that decisions in the public sphere, such as tax decisions, legal decisions, foreign policy decisions, fiscal decisions, affect your *private* lives deeply. Yet in a speculative field such as the interpretation of texts, you feel that there is something foolish and wrong and regimented about a public voice. (99)

What Spivak notes as the public-private split in the academy is fostered by the teaching of decision-making policy as a science, as corporate policy. Decision making in the realm of ethics and values (the stuff of the humanities classroom) is still conceived as intensely intimate, insular, isolated from what we see as the public voice of politics, business, and multinational capitalism.

Why this resistance to collective moral and ethical rhetoric? How do we move ourselves out of this political impasse and resistance in order to get our students to identify with the political agenda of feminism?

My response, like Ira Shor's and Freire's, is to foreground dialogics in the classroom. This strategy uses one kind of mastery, feminist and dialogic in practice, against another, monologic and authoritarian. I am working from the notion that the classroom is a place to explore resistances and identifications, a place also to explore the ambiguous and often ambivalent space of values and ethics. That is not to say that we return to the politics of the personal, a politics often mired in contradiction and confusion. The contradictions that the feminist encounters in the classroom — as outlined in *Gendered Subjects,* for instance, by the collaborators on "The Politics of Nurturance" — reveal the internalized patriarchal structures and our resistances to them (see Pheterson's definitions of internalized oppression and domination 141).

Consider the collective claim about ambivalence in "The Politics of Nurturance": "As a result of our successes in the system, we are more deeply and passionately ambivalent about the intellectual life than our students can be" (13). I focus on this sentence because I sense that our students are often more deeply ambivalent about commitment than we, their instructors, are — in part because we realize that commitment is the only survival tactic and in part because we have more experience in dealing with confusion about several, often contradictory, allegiances. My students seem often quite unambiguously committed to "the system"; their ambivalence is buried deeply, already reconciled. In recognizing their unacknowledged ambivalence, feminists must teach a way not of reconciling this division but of fostering the critical urgency born out of it.

Fostering that ambivalence does not mean leaving students in a void or teaching critical thinking without a critical alternative to dominant social norms. In effect, we teach ethics as a kind of counter-indoctrination, a debriefing, to privatizing personal ethics. One of my own evaluations in a first-year composition course brought the lesson home: "[The teacher] consistently channels class discussions around feminism & does not spend time discussing the comments that oppose her beliefs. In fact, she usually twists them around to support her beliefs." In my defense, I would say, following Charles Paine (563), that we must accept our own roles as rhetoricians. On the student's behalf, I would argue that his or her recognition of the rhetorical agenda of the class—to foreground feminism as a classroom strategy—is sophisticated and aware. That is, the teacher is responsible for clarifying the agenda of the classroom, the student for challenging that agenda. Each agent—whether teacher or student—is responsible as citizen for ethical choices, although those choices often involve contradictory positions. Because agency involves a complex intersection of historically conditioned practices, discourses, and customs or habits, choice is never unambivalent or easy or unmediated. Students may ask, is it possible—or even desirable—to occupy an unambivalent position, to assume an identity without crisis? Gender complicates one's position, and this gendered mode of identifying is political: it rejects biological essence in favor of rhetorical choice. Gender identification, then, becomes a set of choices that signify the marking or signing of one's body in the world. The ambivalent space of this signing (a double participation in the imaginary and the symbolic) should not always be read negatively. Rather than opposing the public and private voices or opposing masculine and feminine, we need to see how to negotiate that opposition in order to speak a multiplicity of voices into the cultural dialogue.

With this in mind, I dispute the analysis of the feminist teacher's position the authors of "The Politics of Nurturance" offer. They suggest that the feminist teacher is nurturer, mother:

> Our students see us as something more, or certainly something other, than simply their teachers. We are, inescapably, also their mothers— necessary for comfort but reinforcing a feared and fearful dependency if such comfort is too easily accepted. But we are also, in part, their fathers—word-givers, truth-sayers—to the extent we incorporate what Dinnerstein calls the father's "clean" authority in our female bodies. (14)

This distinction between mother and father roles, like the one between public and private invoked in the student evaluation comments, belies the positive

ambivalence students feel about the confusion of familial roles and authoritative spaces which occurs in the feminist classroom. The Oedipal model
doesn't hold up.

While the feminist classroom is not "the place where the cultural split
between mother and father may be healed" (18), the authors' strategy to articulate the unconscious is nevertheless on target. For the feminist classroom is
the place where the cultural split can be investigated for its effect in the conscious and unconscious processes which make ambivalence a part of radical
pedagogy. This is why I find Gregory Jay's "The Subject of Pedagogy: Lessons
in Psychoanalysis and Politics" useful in determining the unconscious processes of resistance (and, by implication, identification) in teaching: "There is a
'pedagogical unconscious' . . . informing the educational performance, and
what we resist knowing is intricately tied to our constitution as social subjects" (789). Where there is no ambivalence, there is no dialogue (see Fine,
"Silencing" 165). Where there is no dialogue, there is no dialectic of resistance
and identification.

One way to tap into this urgency is to offer something else in the place of
the resistance that critical pedagogy offers. It is not enough to foster critical
thinking; we need to suggest something in the place of what we tear down
when we ask students to resist cultural hegemony (see Bizzell and Clark). Cultural optimism, what Henry Giroux criticizes as the pedagogy of "positive
thinking" (123–25), is too broad; nonetheless, we need an antidote to cultural
criticism's and critical pedagogy's negativity.

In short, I would argue that political commitment—especially feminist
commitment—is a legitimate classroom strategy and rhetorical imperative.
The feminist agenda offers a goal toward our students' conversions to emancipatory critical action (see Paine 564).

PRIVATE INTO PUBLIC DISCOURSE: A RHETORIC OF CONVERSION

> To refuse the task of building a critical language is to refuse to re-invent oneself
> collectively outside the atomized and privatized self and liberal (possessive)
> individualism of the dominant culture.
>
> —PETER MCLAREN AND MICHAEL DANTLEY

Nina Auerbach's "Engorging the Patriarchy" is one narrative of conversion or,
rather, "unconversion" into feminist agency. This conversion emerges from a
rejection of the authoritative word—the word of former Governor Reagan's
mandate to the Cal State System where Auerbach first taught after graduate
school—to be "drearily functional and nothing more" (233). Auerbach sees
her first years as an assistant professor as a period in which she was "*un-
converted*—into a loss of faith—forced to see (and sometimes to implement)
the ways in which books betrayed experience" (233). Her realization is a matter of transforming the outer word—what she resists in the dominant culture,
in Reagan's California—into an internally persuasive word which "converts"
her into feminism. The process of turning the outer word (that is, received

cultural and social opinion) into an inner speech (her political self-declaration) is even clearer in Auerbach's following claim: "I became a feminist critic at the University of Pennsylvania because my department assumed I already was one" (234). This may seem backward, but this is more often the case than not: we do not declare ourselves feminist critics and then change our critical orientation to the world. Rather by virtue of our ideologies, our words, we are marked and judged by the community around us as feminists. Similarly, we do not transform students and then change their critical orientation to the world. Rather, the process of self-identification is more complex and more fruitful than an easy declaration of their resistance to hegemony.

I use Auerbach's confession as a paradigm for the pedagogical model to break down resistances and offer identifications in the classroom (see Emerson 33). The question is, how do we make the word respond to our own intentions in a feminist pedagogy? How do we make our authority as feminist rhetors available to our students for their language and thus contravene their resistance? In asking our students to deconstruct dominant ideology, "we exercise authority over them in asking them to give up their foundational beliefs, and at the same time, we give them nothing to put in the place of these foundational beliefs because we deny the validity of all authority, including, presumably, our own" (Bizzell 14). So goes Pat Bizzell's argument for the current trend in critical studies. But a feminist—or identificatory—rhetoric is an appropriate form of classroom authority, a conception of authority designed to promote "collective participation in the rhetorical process" (Bizzell 16, 18). At the base of this is the conviction that all signs are social; all language, therefore, is ideologically charged and can unite us rather than divide us socially. Language has a material reality that goes beyond individual differences and is culturally shared, although every shared language means negotiation and commitment. We are in line, then, in the classroom to negotiate the gap of understanding between our students' experience and our own, a gap which often seems insurmountable (Emerson 36–37). Negotiating this stance is often the hardest for the feminist rhetor. But it's clear that there is no way not to accept this authority; anything less ends up being an expressivist model, one which reinforces, however inadvertently, the dominant patriarchal culture rather than challenges it.

My emphasis on feminist rhetoric relies on Kenneth Burke's formulation of education as persuasion. Advocates of radical pedagogy often use the term "identification" without understanding its rhetorical base or, more important, how to employ identification in the classroom. Burke's *Rhetoric of Motives* provides this compelling political (indeed, personal) identification with an ideological stance: "In accordance with the rhetorical principle of identification, whenever you find a doctrine of 'nonpolitical' esthetics affirmed with fervor, look for its politics" (28). Why not apply this claim to the pedagogical situation itself? Whenever we hear students or colleagues affirming the "'nonpolitical' esthetics" of the classroom, look for its political consequences. For Burke, education is persuasion; making a rhetorical identification possible with the position (even of difference and conflict) from which we speak. Burke distin-

guishes between realistic and idealistic identifications. In realistic identification, persuasion compels social action. The idealistic identification occurs
when the powerful identify with someone less powerful. Feminists yearn for
the latter—when we can hope for a change in patriarchal attitudes—but
work within the former, a realistic identification with those oppressed. Like
Burke, I hold out for the magic of the idealistic identification, but I work in the
classroom and in criticism for the realistic identification.

In "Identification and Consubstantiality," Burke puts the case for an
ethics of motives based on the rhetoric of identification:

> A is not identical with his colleague, B. But insofar as their interests are
> joined, A is *identified* with B. Or he may *identify himself* with B even when
> their interests are not joined, if he assumes that they are, or is persuaded
> to believe so. . . . Similarly, two persons may be identified in terms of
> some principle they share in common, an "identification" that does not
> deny their distinctness. (20–21)

Burke rightly suggests that division is implied in identification since without
it there would be no need for the rhetorician to work to achieve community.
Again, Burke's *Rhetoric of Motives:* "But put identification and division
ambiguously together, so that you cannot know for certain just where one
ends and the other begins, and you have the characteristic invitation to rhetoric" (25). Burke goes on to label rhetoric as a *"body of identifications"* —a multiplicity of situations, stances, positions (26). It is up to the ideological critic,
therefore, to show how these positions contradict each other and, in practical
terms, demand a choice. "Belonging" is rhetorical (28). In this sense, we can
think of feminism as a rhetorical criticism, an act by which we teach students
how to belong, how to identify, as well as how to resist.

Finally, Burke writes about the relationship of identification as an awareness of contingent joining and separating with another. Thus, Burke implies
that identification allows for another voice to be in sync but not to erase difference: "to begin with *identification* is . . . though roundabout, to confront the
implications of *division.* . . . If men were not apart from one another, there
would be no need for the rhetorician to proclaim their unity" (22). The implications of this claim are at least twofold for feminist criticism: the feminist can
work toward social change by suggesting identificatory readings rather than
(or only) resisting ones (as I will discuss later). Opposition creates the necessity of rhetoric, of resistance and identification. Burke argues that political
conditions call for a powerful identification with others, but those same conditions escalate "the range of human conflict, the incentives to division. It would
require sustained rhetorical effort, backed by the imagery of a richly humane
and spontaneous poetry, to make us fully sympathize with people in circumstances greatly different from our own" (34). Burke's humanism aside, his
argument brings to the fore the divisiveness of a culture which we, as radical
teachers of English, try to overcome.

When we ask our students to identify with a political position offered
in class or to identify with us as the most immediate representative of that

political stance, we are asking them to give allegiance to an affinity or coalition politics that often competes with or negates other allegiances they have already formed (see Alcoff 423, 431). We ask them to recognize identity—and politics—as social constructions. But without that critical tension between internally persuasive words and externally authoritative rhetoric, we have no hope, nor offer any, for radical social change. Thus, paradoxically, I affirm the students voicing their concerns against feminism in their teaching evaluations; that voicing shows that their feminist teachers (who bravely offered their evaluations for my study) brought their students into some conflict with their previously held norms. In short, there is no natural or essential identification, but only one forged from rhetorical situations and political awareness. In that case, in the classroom, we are not presenting objective categories of political affiliation but a rhetorical context of modes or bodies of identifications.

In teaching identification and teaching feminism, I overcome a vehement, even automatic, insistence on pluralistic relativism or on individualism. I teach how signs can be manipulated, appropriated, and also liberated. Coming to consciousness of any kind is the recognition of the social signs we all internalize and inherit, inevitably against our will. As Auerbach explains, her coming to consciousness as a feminist meant for her becoming aware of the ideological signs she represented for others. Feminism, then, proved to be both social (her interaction with her colleagues "marking" and "de-signing" or, better yet, "re-signing" her to her oppositional stance) and psychological, since her internally persuasive voice resulted in her rejection of another social category: the "good" mother and caretaker/teacher.

Auerbach uses her social de-signation as feminist in order to open up the question of cultural politics with her students. She works, then, from the notion that there is no individual stance that would be alien to her but that the classroom is thoroughly social, a locus of many voices, often conflicting, always in flux. In her words:

> No doubt all beginning teachers identify with their students rather than with their colleagues, and I did too. Trying to negotiate the den of vipers which the Cal State English Department looked like to me at that time, I saw myself in my students, and I saw myself for the first time. . . . Like my students, I tried to learn to be blandly affable and to keep my mind in the closet, my unorthodox scholarly writing a secret. . . . I was converted into subservience. (233)

The "answers" about feminism don't come from "within," but, as Auerbach notes, we designate ourselves through our dialogue with others and with ourselves. In advancing the dialogue within herself, Auerbach hopes to affect the one with her students.

Whose signs we articulate as part of our internally persuasive speech make all the difference. As I see it, the dialogue in the feminist classroom helps clarify the contradictions between what we all have internalized as part of a patriarchal unconscious and a resistance to those assumptions. As feminist rhetors, we supply an authoritative word about potential sites of identification and of resistance to patriarchy.

Ultimately, we don't think "feminism" until we have the sign-system to do so. Our task, then, is to make this speech readily available and heard — sometimes over and against the social objections of others. As Pat Bizzell argues in "Beyond Anti-Foundationalism to Rhetorical Authority: Problems Defining 'Cultural Literacy,'" we need the oratorical perspective of feminism, what she aligns with the anti-foundationalist theoretical concerns of English studies. We have nothing to study but the matter of persuasion, in other words ideologies, the kind of value orators have always dealt with (664). I want to advocate feminism as a matter of persuasion, as a "rhetorical turn."

NARRATION AND SOCIAL CHANGE

So far, critical pedagogy has generally slighted the problem of identification; excellent studies like Giroux's, McLaren's, Weiler's, and Shor and Freire's are filled with narratives of students' resistance to hegemonic forms. There are few or no narratives about the identification students have with, say, anti-racist, antisexist, or antihomophobic politics. The process comes down to articulating social change in the literature classroom so that it strikes a middle ground between optimism and pessimism. The feminist teacher must offer a language of resistance and identification: both are confessional forms — direct addresses — designed as rhetorical invitations to the reader. They invite participation in narratives, in the literature we teach (see Warhol).

How do we draw out and discuss those resistances to theory, to feminism? I do so by compelling students to work through them in literature by confronting fears and values mediated by the form of fiction. Let me explain how I use Pat Barker's *Blow Your House Down* (1984) as one example of breaking down cultural stereotypes. This novel about working-class British women, many of whom have turned to prostitution because of the 1974 coal strike and the failing British economy, is ostensibly a detective/murder mystery, but it eventually explodes our expectations about the genre as well as about violence against women. A prostitute-killer is loose, and the first three sections of the novel, each one from the perspective of a different woman, detail responses to arbitrary violence against women. In the first, Brenda explains how she became a prostitute when her first husband left her and how difficult it is to give up life on the streets: "It was hard to say really why you stuck with it. Money, friends, habit — and of course it was easy, if you were ever short, if you ever needed anything, it was always there" (63–64). Kath's section, the second, leads up to her murder, after Kath has lost her boys and daughter to the social welfare system. In the third part, Jean avenges that murder, along with the murder of Carol, her own lover.

Each section also raises questions about these women's relations to their clients, to the dole, to dominant cultural morality, to capitalism in general. The final section, Maggie's, begins with another act of random violence, this time against a "respectable" woman who works in a chicken factory rather than on the streets. Like Maggie, the students must come to terms with a violence against women which is random and senseless and which finally makes the victim more victimized by the neighbors and the police than by the assailant.

She is suspected of "asking for it," if only because she takes a shortcut home from work on Friday night after her weekly drink with her colleagues: "you needed a drink, you needed something to swill the blood and guts away, and make you fit to face the world" (177). Another sort of victimization occurs in the novel: like the prostitutes, Maggie is "cut"—interrogated about the events of the attack and then shunned by her neighbors. Maggie comes to feel as though her neighbors were, in her terms, "enjoying it too": "They read the papers, they tried to read *between* the lines, and the same questions were there. *What does he do to them? How much did he do to her?* It was all very exciting, having a victim living in the same street" (193). The spectacle of violence perpetuates the rationalization of that violence.

This is a confusing novel for many students, in part because of the explicit economics of prostitution (there is no point of view from which the sexual encounters that occur appear anything other than economic and quotidian). But the students are willing enough to accept the violence against the prostitutes since part of their job, the students reason, is an acceptance of risk. What they are not prepared to accept is the violence against Maggie, the wife and mother, whose shortcut home endangers her life. Maggie has not "asked for it," nor is Maggie's profession morally suspect. Because of this rupture of generic and moral expectations, the students are led to question their assumptions about violence against women. There is no rationale or logic to violence; the only logic behind violence, they learn, is patriarchal power.

Barker historicizes that violence; her novel calls into question women's expectations of violence both in the home and outside of it. The women debate what to do about the recent prostitute killings going on:

> And there were all sorts of ideas flying around. "Always get out of the car." "Never get out of the car." "Take the numbers." "Work in pairs." "Don't bend down." "Don't turn your back." "Don't suck them off." Load of rubbish. I never did any of it. I did start carrying a knife and then I thought well, you dozy cow, you're just handing him the weapon. So after that I didn't bother. (17)

In rehearsing the contradictory advice about dealing with violence on the streets where she works, Maureen reveals the mystification of male violence, no less frightening because it is random and aleatory.

After her attack, Maggie's heterosexual marriage is no longer a safe place, nor is the master bedroom. She comes to expect violence from Bill in the same way that the prostitutes anticipate it on the streets. As Elaine says, "'the way I look at it, if you're living with a bloke he's gunna hit you about something'" (105). Maggie's experience of violence leads her to a rejection of the alienated work in the chicken factory and a moral confusion, one of the only positive effects of her encounter with what Barker terms the "abyss" of violence:

> Their own bedroom. She knew every mark on the wallpaper, every creak of the floorboards, every bump and sag in the mattress. It ought to've been completely safe, but it wasn't. She found herself listening for Bill's footsteps on the stairs.

> This was something she couldn't understand. As long as she could *see* Bill, as long as he was in the same room with her, she was alright. But if he was behind her, or in a different part of the house, she started to worry. It wasn't fear exactly, but she needed to know what he was doing. . . .
>
> But she was left with a feeling that the road back to "normal" might be longer than she had wanted to believe. (186)

Maggie also comes to understand that her middle-class notions about violence—that it happens only to women who provoke men, women who work on the streets—are illusory. Both Jean's and Maggie's sections suggest what happens when women cannot comprehend violence according to "rational" categories. Violence, in Barker's text, is not a masculine construction; rather, it is symbolic, available to both men and women and destructive to both. Barker provides a middle-class audience with an identificatory model in Maggie, a model to explore in class discussions of ethics.

Because this text raises so many questions about class and gender, it opens up as topics of discourse values and assumptions which have been naturalized in dominant culture. These classes, indeed perhaps feminist pedagogy and rhetoric in general, end ambivalently: these disrupted values or assumptions are not occasions for reconstituting consciousness into clear categories of good faith feminism and bad faith—or, worse, good and bad politics. Having access to a common language is only a first step; speaking languages of difference is another.

My final appeal is to Kenneth Burke's *Rhetoric of Motives* and the call for rhetorical criticism:

> Education ("indoctrination") exerts such pressure upon [the student] from without; [students complete] the process from within. If [they do] not somehow act to tell [themselves] what the various brands of rhetorician have told [them], [the] persuasion is not complete. Only those voices from without are effective which can speak in the language of a voice within. (39)

As feminist rhetors, our task is to make compelling the wider implications of the feminist dialogue in the classroom. Because my voice in the classroom is one in competition with other voices speaking for the students' allegiance, the most pernicious voice that reinforces the split between public and private, I would do well to be aware of the rhetorical situation of the classroom—of the necessity for a mastery that is not oppressive, of an authoritative voice that is not the only authority.

WORKS CITED

Alcoff, Linda. "Cultural Feminism versus Post-Structuralism: The Identity Crisis in Feminist Theory." *Signs* 13 (Spring 1988): 405–36.

Auerbach, Nina. "Engorging the Patriarchy." *Historical Studies and Literary Criticism.* Ed. Jerome J. McGann. Madison: U of Wisconsin P, 1985.

Barker, Pat. *Blow Your House Down.* New York: Ballantine, 1984.

Bizzell, Patricia. "Beyond Anti-Foundationalism to Rhetorical Authority: Problems Defining 'Cultural Literacy.'" *College English* 52 (1990): 661–75.

Burke, Kenneth. *A Rhetoric of Motives.* New York: Prentice, 1950.

Clark, Suzanne. "Feminism, Poststructuralism, and Rhetoric: If We Change Language, Do We Also Change the World?" CCCC paper. March 16, 1989.

Culley, Margo, Arlyn Diamond, Lee Edwards, Sara Lennox, and Catherine Portuges. "The Politics of Nurturance." *Gendered Subjects.* Eds. Margo Culley and Catherine Portuges. Boston: Routledge & Kegan Paul, 1985: 11–20.

Emerson, Caryl. "The Outer Word and Inner Speech: Bakhtin, Vygotsky, and the Internalization of Language." *Bakhtin.* Ed. Gary Saul Morson. Chicago: U of Chicago P, 1986: 21–40.

Fine, Michelle. "Sexuality, Schooling, and Adolescent Females: The Missing Discourse of Desire." *Harvard Educational Review* 58 (February 1988): 29–53.

———. "Silencing in Public Schools." *Language Arts* 64 (February 1987): 157–74.

Giroux, Henry. *Schooling and the Struggle for Public Life.* Minneapolis: U of Minnesota P, 1988.

Jay, Gregory S. "The Subject of Pedagogy: Lessons in Psychoanalysis and Politics." *College English* 49 (November 1987): 785–800.

McLaren, Peter, and Michael Dantley. "Leadership and a Critical Pedagogy of Race: Cornel West, Stuart Hall, and the Prophetic Tradition." *Journal of Negro Education,* 59 (1990): 29–44.

Paine, Charles. "Relativism, Radical Pedagogy, and the Ideology of Paralysis." *College English* 51 (October 1989): 557–70.

Pheterson, Gail. "Alliances between Women: Overcoming Internalized Oppression and Internalized Domination." *Reconstructing the Academy: Women's Education and Women's Studies.* Eds. Elizabeth Minnich, Jean O'Barr, and Rachel Rosenfeld. Chicago: U of Chicago Press, 1988: 139–53.

Shor, Ira, and Paulo Freire. *A Pedagogy for Liberation: Dialogues on Transforming Education.* South Hadley, MA: Bergin & Garvey, 1987.

Spivak, Gayatri Chakravorty. *In Other Worlds.* New York: Methuen, 1988.

Warhol, Robyn R. *Gendered Interventions.* New Brunswick: Rutgers UP, 1989.

Weiler, Kathleen. *Women Teaching for Change: Gender, Class, & Power.* South Hadley, MA: Bergin & Garvey, 1988.

22

A Symposium on Feminist Experiences in the Composition Classroom

JILL EICHHORN, SARA FARRIS,
KAREN HAYES, ADRIANA HERNÁNDEZ,
SUSAN C. JARRATT, KAREN POWERS-STUBBS,
AND MARIAN M. SCIACHITANO

INTRODUCTION: FEMINIST SOPHISTICS PEDAGOGY GROUP

Marian M. Sciachitano

The essays that follow are a result of a collaboration beginning with Feminist Sophistics, a three-week graduate seminar held at Miami University of Ohio and highlighted by a national conference in June of 1990. The project grew at the confluence of two disciplines: feminist pedagogy and sophistic rhetoric (see Bauer and Jarratt). Following the seminar and conference, the seven of us formed a feminist pedagogy research group to pursue the relation between feminism and composition teaching—two of the most politically active fields in the academy in the last two decades. In the fall semester following the Feminist Sophistics seminar, we met every two weeks in an ongoing collective effort to create new spaces of discourse in the academy. As feminist writing teachers, we find ourselves teaching in the margins of a still male-dominated academy which often doesn't speak to feminist concerns. Our group is an attempt to seriously engage with others' narratives, histories, and visions of the "not yet."

We structured our work around the teaching of Miami University's required first-semester writing course and offer accounts from the five of us who taught the course in the fall of 1990 and reflections from the other two members of the group. We speak here both as a collective and in our seven different voices. Unlike the consciousness-raising groups of the women's movement in the early seventies, we offer these accounts not as sharing for sharing's sake, as confessional, as the celebration of any and all narratives, or as a simple exchange of practitioner's lore. Rather, our teaching narratives serve to reclaim and construct us as women with agency in the composition classroom and academy.

From *College Composition and Communication* 43 (1992): 297–322.

The group collaborating in this symposium consists of seven heterosexual women, including two women of color—an Asian American and an Argentine national. We range in age from late twenties to early forties and in teaching experience from first-time teacher to more than fifteen years of high-school and college-level teaching experience combined. Six group members are graduate students at various stages in their MA or PhD studies (three composition/rhetoric majors, two American literature majors, and one educational leadership major), while the seventh is a tenured professor of composition and rhetoric. Many of us are non-traditional students and faculty in the sense that we are either older women making a gradual return to school after family/work commitments, or we are younger women coming out of socioeconomic, racial, cultural, or geographic backgrounds where we may be the first one in our families to pursue a graduate degree or academic career. Five group members are married, one is single, and one is a divorced, single parent. Two have children attending high school and/or college, while two others have recently become first-time mothers. While there are many differences among us, we formed a collaborative inquiry group because we all consider ourselves feminist writing teachers committed to developing theories and practices of pedagogy responsive to gender and other differences: race, culture, class, and sexual preference.

As we explore the ways we have been named, inscribed, objectified, exoticized, silenced, and coopted by male-dominated discourses, we simultaneously engage in the articulation, negotiation, and collective re-vision of our gendered, racial, and class locations. Historically, feminist work has stressed the importance of located personal accounts and the intertwining of theory and practice. Ever since the second wave of feminism, feminist researchers in many fields have been "generating and refining more interactive, contextualized methods" of doing feminist work (Lather 72). Because we are trying out a new approach to research, we realize, along with Elizabeth A. Flynn, that our process may not appear to be composition research as we have known it ("Composing 'Composing'" 83–84). In the essays that follow, we offer individual teaching narratives, written out of our personal experiences in the composition classroom and processed through our collective reflections, to be read in terms of two key problematics: difference and authority.

One difference we explore, among a multiplicity of differences, is that as feminist graduate students and faculty who teach composition we do not experience the same authority in the classroom as white male, middle-to-upper-class graduate students and faculty. We have discovered, with Susan Stanford Friedman, that "both our students and ourselves have been socialized to believe . . . that any kind of authority is incompatible with the feminine" (207). And furthermore, we acknowledge that we live "in a culture that has negated or trivialized woman's intellect and authority" (207). The very field of composition itself continues to reinforce and perpetuate these cultural assumptions through the "feminizing of composition." As Sue Ellen Holbrook explains, "Saturated by women practitioners, focused on pedagogy, allied with education departments and school teaching, conceived as having a 'service' and elementary place in the curriculum, and pervaded by para-professionalism, composition has become women's work. And so it will remain—disproportionately the work of women and work of lesser value—as long as these conditions remain" (211).

In a recent update, Bernice Resnick Sandler, famous for her reports on the "chilly climate" for women—Black and Latin as well as white women—inside college classrooms, reports that women faculty still do not experience the same respect from their male and female students as do men faculty. For instance, on an overt level, women faculty are more likely to be asked about their credentials: "Do you have a doctorate?" "I can't believe you're a professor" (7). On a more subtle level, "women faculty may be more likely to be called 'Miss,' 'Ms.,' or 'Mrs.' rather than 'Professor' or 'Dr.'" (8). These findings indicate in an everyday way the difficulties of establishing authority for any female teacher; for the feminist teacher, one who is questioning accepted beliefs about gender, race, or sexual orientation in the classroom, the challenge deepens. Establishing authority as feminist writing teachers is made even more problematic by some student-centered composition theories which seek to radically displace teacher authority in general. Though we acknowledge the liberatory potential of calling institutional authority into question and revaluing student experiences, some of us question whether a pedagogy which fails to examine multiple power relations can create the best conditions for female teachers who have yet to experience all "authorizing voice" in the classroom (Bauer 395).

Taking up a feminist politics of location in the classroom, as Adrienne Rich has observed, means taking differences seriously. It also means taking the responsibility to construct critical classroom spaces "where [we and our] students can come to see ambivalence and differences not as obstacles, but as the very richness of meaning-making and the hope of whatever justice we might work toward" (Lather 145). Tensions and conflicts—"rhetorics of dissensus" (Trimbur)—are bound to arise, but we must remind ourselves that in a radically democratic society they reflect actual social, political, and material realities which students and teachers experience in our everyday lives (Weiler 144–45). It's important for us not to deny or refuse to acknowledge these differences and contestations when they arise. While some critics fear that feminist pedagogies of difference are "authoritarian" (see Giroux 74–75), Kathleen Weiler reminds us that the "classroom is always a site of conflict, and will be a site of conflict for the feminist or critical teacher trying to create a counterhegemonic vision just as much as it will be for a traditional or authoritarian teacher" (136–37). As feminist teachers of writing we want to question those pedagogical models which privilege only an atmosphere of safety or a completely maternal climate (Flynn, "Composing as a Woman" 423; Hunter 233–34; Jarratt 113). While these models might be useful up to a point, when it comes to a gendered space, we ask, How can we teach for radical change if we don't challenge our students' androcentric readings of literary texts or their classist, sexist, racist, and homophobic discourses as they arise in journals, essays, and class discussion? Does challenging these readings and writings necessarily mean denying student subjectivities? Can there be a truly "safe space," in or out of the classroom? Should there be? Is there in our desire for a safe space also a refusal to recognize that our different locations—as men or women, as Anglos or people of color, as faculty or as graduate students—are and have always been unequal?

Collaborating for authority in the academy has meant that the seven members of this feminist inquiry group have embraced our marginality "as a site of resistance—as a location of radical openness and possibility" (hooks, *Yearning* 153). In the narrative accounts which follow, we articulate that space of openness and possibility as we confront differences and problems of authority in writing classrooms.

CREATING SPACE FOR DIFFERENCE IN THE COMPOSITION CLASS

Karen Hayes

I began teaching first-year composition in the fall of 1990 as a new convert. For the first time, I had begun to understand the concept of "difference" in the classroom as something to be promoted, rather than suppressed or politely ignored. For many writing teachers, this is a familiar value; this was not the case for me. I had been away from college campuses for twelve years before returning to graduate school; when I left, I took with me an idea of the academic classroom as a polite, somewhat reserved place, where scholars exchanged insights and ideas, sometimes disagreeing, but always with an understanding that common ground underlay their work. I liked that image—I cherished it, in spite of the fact that I always felt a little excluded from these well-mannered exchanges. I was suspicious of any conflict, and one of my major goals in any discussion was that everyone depart as good friends. I returned to the academic world to find dispute and diversity more popular than politeness and common ground, and I wasn't completely happy about the change. I might have asked the plaintive questions Lex Runciman asked: "why not sameness, for once: why not consensus?" (157).

Linda Brodkey speaks in her short essay, "Transvaluing Difference," of her own education, remembering an encounter in fifth grade with a Carl Sandburg introduction to a book of photography called *The Family of Man*. She was, she writes, a believer in consensus, and in the "universal human condition." It was not until her experience in the Peace Corps that she began to realize that differences in cultures and individuals were more than superficial, began:

> to realize along with the others that where you were born, to whom, and under what circumstances makes a difference, and to wonder whether focusing on similarities wasn't distracting me from noticing the consequences of difference, namely inequity. (599)

I too learned about the "universal human condition." For me, the outstanding image is a jigsaw puzzle of a Norman Rockwell painting in which representatives of all sorts of human existence stand together before a wall on which are inscribed great words of many religious traditions. It was a beautiful picture and a really hard puzzle, and I spent a lot of time with it at age 10 or 11. I learned the lesson of universality well, and I'd be dishonest if I didn't admit that I still believe there to be many, many less valuable ideas in the world than the "tolerance" and "diversity" Brodkey writes against. Like her, however, I have come to view tolerance as an inadequate response to human difference. She found her turning point in the Peace Corps; mine was a post-college move from the suburbs to a tiny farm village in northwestern Ohio. I didn't need a passport or inoculations, but I experienced a genuine culture shock, enough to make me begin to seriously examine many of my assumptions.

That process of examination eventually brought me back to graduate school, where I encountered scholar after scholar promoting this concept of difference, and the way they said it you could almost see the quotation marks hovering in the air. This was Difference with a capital D, and gradually their theories began to give me a vocabulary for what I had begun to learn from my own experience. I read Elizabeth Flynn, Adrienne Rich, bell hooks, Patricia Bizzell, Peter Elbow—all seemed to be insisting on the need for something other than consensus, for the creation of space for students' differences. I remembered that uncomfortable feeling I'd had in those genteel classrooms of my undergraduate days, realizing that I had sometimes suppressed my own ideas in my need to come to agreement with others. I began to claim my own difference—not only as a woman in the male system of the academy, but as an older-than-average graduate student, a mother, a person of faith in a secular environment. I found myself standing happily apart from others, willing to tell them, "Yes, but from here, it all looks like this. . . ." And when I heard feminist teaching advocated as a means for creating this kind of space for students in composition classes, I listened; and I thought, maybe they are right.

So I approached my two composition sections that fall ready to try something new. As part of a feminist project, I was committed to using certain teaching methods and to reporting various classroom happenings; I told my students this from the start. They seemed to have no objections; actually, I later learned, they just weren't paying much attention.

A few weeks into the term, I asked the students to make a journal entry in response to the question, "What is feminism?" I hoped to elicit some definitions as well as some discussion; I certainly didn't expect the firestorm of response students produced, though perhaps I should have. Our discussion took place the week after reporter Lisa Malone's experience in the locker room of the New England Patriots football team. Some students wrote angry criticisms of her (or any woman's) presence in such male preserves. Others confused "feminism" with "femininity," describing such images as a "string of pearls against a clavicle bone." While some responses included agreement with feminist goals of on-the-job equality, many included some allusion to "man-haters." Each entry was read aloud, and vehement (though often uninformed) discussion followed. I left both classes that day wondering whether there was any way at all to address women's issues in such a climate; even students sympathetic to feminist concerns often seemed threatened by what they perceived to be the "radical" stance of activists.

What I would like to emphasize here is the difference that emerged between my two sections in their acceptance of what I had to say about feminism. Both classes were randomly selected first-year students, both met twice a week, both had the same syllabus. Students made similar evaluative comments at the end of the semester. I can't say that section DA members emerged from my course as a group of 24 committed feminists, while GA students remained unchanged. The difference I noted was much less pronounced—but still there.

It came out most clearly during a DA class discussion of a recently adopted university policy known as the "diversity statement," a short paragraph indicating that no group of society was unwelcome at the university and upholding the institutional responsibility of making this claim a reality. Class reaction to the statement was rather predictable at first, with many students cynically maintaining that there was no diversity—that everyone here was the same. Eventually an extremely outspoken male student I'll call Al moved on to claim that not only was everyone here the same, but everyone here (and by implication everywhere else in twentieth-century life) was treated with impeccable fairness, except that white men suffered from the current over-attention to minorities. Attempts to address differences were, to use his term, "stupid." At our university, like many others, there is a large group of students for whom this is party line. On the main campus of Miami, nearly all our students are white, nearly all are age 18–22, nearly all come from fairly wealthy backgrounds. It's not unusual to hear comments like Al's. What was unusual was what happened next. Students began to stir in their seats and they began to speak of their own differences: two Asian-American students asserted that they had indeed felt prejudice and that their backgrounds were not the same as their mostly Midwestern classmates'. A Moslem, who before the term began had asked to be called "Sein" instead of "Hussein," spoke up about popular images of members of his faith as crazed followers of demagogues. An Indian-American student commented on the sudden "difference" he had felt while traveling in Great Britain. These students were American citizens, graduated only months before from Midwestern high schools, and had apparently never established themselves in classmates' eyes as "different" in any way. They had been treated as "honorary whites," so to speak, and their classmates had felt free to say things like, "Moslems enjoy killing Jews," without acknowledging their presence at all—without acknowledging their insult to one they thought of as a friend.

The credit for the class's outspokenness that day goes to Al, that extremely vocal student I mentioned. He is the source of the comment about Moslems, as well as a remark about gays deserving to die because "they brought us AIDS" and a carefully reasoned argument that men deserved to be paid more than women because of men's superior physical strength. This student was invaluable. What he said foregrounded difference in a way I never could have accomplished alone. Students listening to my feminist statements in DA could not deny that here, indeed, was difference, that I was holding a position different from that of the most outspoken (male) member of the class. Al was so outrageous that I could and did flatly state that I disagreed with and was actually offended by his remarks. I believe that other students, especially females, were empowered by my stance to begin to assert themselves as well.

This was not, of course, an experience of complete victory. Al did not change his mind about very many things. The woman who worked with him on a collaborative paper seemed uncomfortable throughout the process and absolutely miserable at our conference at the end of the project, and she was never able to articulate her feelings in his presence. Equally important to me, however, was my failure to reach the one student who represented a clearly working-class background, a commuter who lived with her parents. While she remained in the class, she avoided any interaction with other students, including peer-group workshops and after-class conversations. Eventually, she stopped coming and never came back. Perhaps in an affluent residential university, the class differential may be the hardest thing to claim; it was one aspect of difference that I felt our class failed to validate. Still, we did experience some success. Al's presence did make it possible for issues to arise and be addressed that normally are subsumed in consensus; his presence made "difference" a concrete reality to students otherwise inclined to deny its existence. That denial is precisely what happened in the GA section, where the most outspoken male student was a large and affable football player. His genial acceptance of all I had to say served to deny its significance, I believe, in the same way that Al's presence highlighted it.

My conclusion, then, is that demonstrated practical differences contribute to an understanding of theoretical "difference." Clearly, we cannot import difficult students to each class simply as pedagogical tools; nevertheless, there are other ways to encourage students to claim their own ground. I have invited speakers who convincingly espouse political views or have lived experience vastly and obviously different from whatever the class consensus may be. One feminist poet, whose gentle personality seemed inappropriate to her radical poetry, created conflicts which students were forced to confront. Class readings setting forth radical views are also useful, but students often felt more free to devalue not only the writing but the writer, since that person is not known to them. Student papers highlighting examples of difference, when available, are more useful. One class read essays similar to the typical masculine and feminine papers in Elizabeth Flynn's "Composing as a Woman"; I asked students to vote first on which they preferred and then on which they thought were written by women. We discussed not only the differences marking each author's gender, but the significance of the fact that the class preferred the masculine narratives by wide margins.

There are no doubt other ways to foreground the many aspects of difference, but I feel most pleased that some of these worked well enough in my class to cause an earnest first-year woman to write in her class evaluation:

> The only thing I might change is the abundance of discussion on feminism. It divided the class, and from then on it seem to stay divided.

I agree with her. It did indeed stay divided, by articulated difference.

"What's in It for Me?" Two Students' Responses to a Feminist Pedagogy

Sara Farris

There were two important firsts in my teaching last fall. For the first time I was planning an overtly feminist teaching strategy in my composition class. In previous semesters my students have usually suspected me of being a feminist, they've accused me of it, and they've sometimes even identified with it; but until last fall I'd never made a point of announcing my feminism from the outset. The second first was that I was teaching on Miami's Hamilton campus, characterized by a mostly working-class student body and a wide range of ages; I had students who were recent high-school graduates testing the college waters while they lived at home and worked part-time, and I had students who were full-time workers returning to the classroom 20 years after high school. A third first was one I had not anticipated but that I appreciated nonetheless: for the first time I was not the only self-identified feminist in my classroom. This is not to say that I didn't run into the same kinds of hostility, mostly from male students, that I was used to getting from first-year students confronted with feminism in the classroom. And of course there were students who fit more or less comfortably in the middle, accommodating my feminism simply because I was the teacher and they were the students. But what I want to consider here are two students who represent the extremes—one, a woman, who came into my class as a feminist and who embraced my teaching strategies sometimes more enthusiastically than I did and the other, a man, who resisted everything about my class, including but not limited to my feminism.

Sheena is somewhere in her late forties or early fifties, with three children—one son in the armed forces, another in college, and a 12-year-old daughter. She's run her own business, she's a self-identified feminist, and since her husband's death a few years ago she's had sole responsibility for her family. Her writing experiences since high school and prior to the first-year college writing course were limited mostly to business. Sheena took one look at Natalie Goldberg's *Writing Down the Bones* and fell in love with Natalie's feminist/zen approach to writing. The first writing assignment was to browse through the book and write a one-page informal response paper. Sheena told us all how she sat out under a tree and filled three notebook pages, which she proudly read to the class. If, as Peter Elbow says, "the best test of a writing course is whether it makes students more likely to use writing in their lives" (136), then Sheena was a success for me.

In many ways, Sheena and Valerie, another woman about Sheena's age, took on a very traditional role in our class, playing the mother, not only with other students, but on occasion, with me. When I returned to the classroom after being sick for a few weeks, it was Sheena and Valerie who stayed after class to make sure I was taking care of myself, and, once that was settled, to swap surgery stories. Younger students often turned to Sheena and Valerie as the voices of experience, and they usually complied with good humor. Yet

Sheena was unwilling to be limited by the mother role and often challenged what she saw as unenlightened perceptions in her classmates of what it means to be a mother, a returning student, and a feminist. For one thing, she was very outspoken, something which at first surprised and daunted the younger men in the class. In a class discussion about the possibility of women going into combat, a young male student said that, as a country, we just weren't ready to see "our daughters" coming home in body bags. Sheena, whose oldest child would be sent to the Persian Gulf in a few weeks, angrily set him straight: "I am *no* more willing to see my son come home in a body bag than my daughter!" Sheena's comment about sons and daughters and body bags effectively silenced the sexist argument that women have no place in combat. bell hooks says that often "the very act of speech, wherein a woman talks to a man, carries embedded in that gesture a challenge, a threat to male domination" ("Feminist" 128). In the feminist classroom, then, this threat is at least doubled: not only is the teacher/authority figure a woman, but as the feminist pedagogy alters the traditional classroom dynamic, the other voices heard are likely to be women's.

Sheena's writing also challenged dominant ideology, or, as Toni Morrison terms it, the master narrative. Sheena wrote an astute class analysis of Connorsville, Indiana, a town she'd lived in as a newcomer, an upwardly mobile wife, and a socially awkward widow. She wrote about the impossibility of coping with a dying husband, three children, and her own grief. She wrote a letter-to-the-editor essay explaining that the strip-tease bars in Covington, Kentucky, did not merit the same protection under the law as the Robert Mapplethorpe photo exhibit across the river in Cincinnati. Once, in a class discussion about Miami's diversity statement, Sheena commented that the socioeconomic class differences between the students at Miami's main campus in Oxford and Hamilton's two-year campus were not the result of differing abilities as much as they were the result of the university administration's design. When I grinned and told her that was a dangerous idea, she took it as a compliment, repeating it later in the class to describe herself: "Well, you know me, I tend to be dangerous!"

My other example is James. I can't offer as detailed a description of James, which is part of my point—he brought nothing to the class, and as far as I can tell, took nothing away with him. James fit comfortably into a group I labeled privately as "the judges": a half-dozen white, male 18-year-olds who were determined that this feminist teacher was not going to con them into speaking or writing, let alone workshopping an essay. Clearly my position as a relatively young woman indicated to the judges that my authority in the classroom was questionable at best. Though they never said as much, I can safely assume that my feminism only reinforced their dismissal of me as an authority. It was a power struggle from day one. The judges were my failures; no matter what I tried—indulging them, ignoring them, making their nonparticipation the subject of class discussion—they were resolute.

James's workshop group demonstrates the problem: it routinely workshopped four essays in less than fifteen minutes and then looked expectantly at me, waiting for their next task to be assigned. When I talked to them about what I considered to be a dysfunctional group, they insisted that they got out of their workshop exactly what they wanted: nothing. Writing and revising were activities best pursued alone. Unlike Sheena's group and the other more successful workshops, where I observed productive collaboration, the members of James's group constituted a paradox: they were a collective of individuals, completely invested in the modernist and masculinist image of the writer struggling in solitude (see Brodkey, "Picturing"). Finally, I just let them be.

Curiously, I can't dismiss James's behavior as simple and willful opposition, as I did with the other judges. James occasionally made accommodating gestures toward participating in the community of writers. On one occasion in particular, James was genuinely if only briefly interested in a writing project. I'd brought in a sample student essay from my other class, David's narrative about his girlfriend being attacked and severely beaten. The essay was not an attempt to speak for Kristy; it was about David—his anger, his fear, and his struggle to cope with Kristy's anger and fear. The essay was powerful in part because it was immediate; David had gotten the call from the hospital the night before drafts were due for the first in-class workshop. When he got home from the hospital hours later, he threw out the essay he'd started and wrote about that night. A few days after reading David's essay, James decided he wanted to write an essay about his girlfriend's history of sexual abuse. But unlike David, who wrote about his own experience in relation to Kristy, James wanted to write about his girlfriend's experience. I suspected that this was pure accommodation: in addition to having read David's essay, we'd talked, in conjunction with the Take Back the Night March, about sexual assault and violence against women. So James had reason to believe that I'd go for this topic. To put the best face on it, however, I had to consider that James simply felt free to write about something that he previously wouldn't have thought was appropriate for composition class. But that's where the story ends. With James unwilling to workshop the paper with his classmates or to conference it with me and unable, apparently, to complete the project on his own, the essay never materialized. The masculinist concept of the writer struggling in solitude had failed James, and the feminist classroom had failed to convince him or he had failed to be receptive to the idea that there was another way to be a writer.

While I recognize the danger of focusing feminist scholarship on the needs of male students—reinscribing the male as the center of women's attention—as a teacher of women and men I have an obligation to question what feminism offers to all of my students. In her essay, "Feminist Focus on Men," hooks suggests that "there is not enough said about men, about the social construction of masculinity, about the possibilities for transformation" (127). It's fairly simple to see the immediate liberatory possibilities of feminism for women students. It's not so simple to recognize the liberatory possibilities of feminist pedagogy for male students. In part, this is because male students are unwilling to look to feminism for their own needs. hooks explains that "in the early stages of contemporary feminist movement, labeling men 'the enemy' . . . was . . . an effective way for women to begin making the critical separation that would enable rebellion to begin" (127).

For the feminist teacher, this "in the beginning" feeling recurs at the beginning of every semester of a first-year writing course, not because of the teacher, but because of her students. First-year students are nearly always either new to feminism, completely unfamiliar with it, or, more likely, fear and reject feminism based on shadowy misconceptions fed by erroneous mainstream media images. Women students are often only beginning the process of recognizing and rebelling against male domination. And, not surprisingly, male students nearly always react defensively to feminism, immediately moving to protect their male authority and privilege. We may lose patience with male students who reject feminism because they don't see its value in their lives, yet the truth is that women come to feminism for that very reason: there is something very real and immediate in feminism for us! At the same time, there is, or ought to be, something very real in feminism for male students.

"What's in it for me?" is the question asked by every student of every class, and rightly so. For Sheena, the answer to that question in my class was clear. For James it was not. Whether this was his failure or mine, I'm not sure. I have decided that for feminism to be truly transformative, feminist teachers, in collaboration with our students, must interrogate, dismantle, and create alternatives to oppressive patriarchal definitions of both masculine and feminine.

WOMEN'S BODIES IN THE COLLEGE WRITING CLASSROOM: THE THREAT OF FEELING EXPOSED

Jill Eichhorn

"Your self is separate from your body" (77). According to Emily Martin, this image is central in women's descriptions of their relationships with their bodies. In *The Woman in the Body,* Martin analyzes how 165 women of differing class and race backgrounds describe their bodily experiences. Relying on transcripts of taped interviews with these women, Martin dissects the metaphors they use to chart their perceptions of their bodies in relation to the dominant cultural ideology—how they reflect the dominant ideology and how they resist it. Martin's study focuses on women's perceptions of their experiences with menstruation, pregnancy, childbirth, and menopause; however, her study doesn't address the specific conditions of women college instructors in the classroom. How do the bodies of women composition instructors figure into the negotiations of power and authority in the classroom?

In "The Feminization of Composition," Susan Miller describes the cultural position of composition studies in the academy and the position of the instructors—primarily women—in that field. "Composition studies," Miller explains, "remains largely the distaff partner in a socially important 'masculine' enterprise, the cultural maintenance of linguistic dispositions of power and enfranchisement" (40). Composition instructors introduce students to the language of the academy, serving, then, as initiators who train their students to support and conform to the existing power structure. In other words, composition instructors are part of the equation that maintains the status quo. However, Miller also sees the potential of composition studies as a "culturally designated space for political action" (51), a space that can offer a counter-hegemonic critique of the academy because of its "low status" within its own superstructure. While I have consciously designed my composition class as a space for political action by focusing on connections between students' personal experiences and social issues, my own experience of pregnancy has led me to understand the political force of a female body in a traditionally male position of authority.

As a woman, not necessarily because I am a feminist, I become a symbol of maternal authority to my students. They expect me to be nice, loving, nurturing—and feel betrayed when I am not. Their cultural education as well as my own influences this dynamic. Miller traces the history of symbolic functions that constructs the composition teacher as nurse/mother/disciplinarian:

> [The composition instructor] is a nurse who cares for and tempts her young charge toward "adult" uses of language that will not "count" because they are, for now, engaged only with hired help; she is, no matter what her gender, the "mother"' (tongue) that is an ideal/idol and can humiliate, regulate, and suppress the child's desires. But she is also the disciplinarian, not a father figure but a sadomasochistic Barbarella version of either mother or maid. (48)

One way of disrupting my students' easy association of me as a maternal figure was, paradoxically, to draw attention to my pregnancy. While I have often had the opportunity to bring issues of women's bodies into discussion in my classroom, I haven't thought of my own body as a concrete example of difference in relation to the dominant male ideology—the cultural expectation that people in authority are male. In fact, because of that male ideology, I have tried in the past to physically disguise my difference. At the least, I have tried to wear clothing that minimizes my female shape. Notice here the self separate from the body: a feminist voice disassociating herself from a female body.

My pregnancy, however, made it impossible for me to deny my female body. As I moved into my sixth month of pregnancy, the changes and feelings of my body became my daily meditation. Less and less disguisable, I embodied difference from the dominant ideology. My responses to pregnancy are deeply connected to what our culture taught me about my body, responses grounded in the ideology I internalized as a teenager.

I was an early bloomer in those awkward years of adolescence, a surprising physical blooming for an otherwise ordinary looking child. In the summers, I loped up and down the beaches with a pack of girls. Learning to worship our bodies for the male attention they brought us, we focused on what our bodies looked like, not on what our bodies could do. We internalized the objectification of our own bodies, and the lessons were reinforced everywhere. Older boys wrote in my yearbook, "Keep that body and you'll go far." My father cracked jokes about the expense of a swimsuit that revealed more than it covered, and even a friend's mother, eyeballing me up and down one day on the beach, quipped, "You've got a million-dollar figure."

I was embarrassed by the messages in my yearbook and my father's jokes, as I was embarrassed by the comment of my friend's mother. What did all this attention mean? And yet, I knew that my body was drawing attention in ways I had never experienced before. My body was some kind of ticket—I just didn't know the destination. In a society ambivalent about the economic value of the work women do, there is never any ambivalence about the economic value of women's bodies. Like many women, I felt alienated in a culture that divorced my body from my sense of self.

The shape of a woman's body marks her difference in the culture, an external sign of the different processes she experiences bodily—menstruation, pregnancy, and menopause. Where in all the attention to my body was there recognition of these processes? The injunction to me at 14 was to keep that 14-year-old body. How could the part of me denying a female body celebrate the baby growing daily inside me?

During my first trimester, when I suffered from morning sickness from the time I got up until I went to bed, the classroom space was full of conflict for me in new ways. My energy sapped, I found it difficult to do little else than sit on the couch with my dog. While my body demanded that I stop my 16–17 hour days (the work day of most graduate students and faculty I know), the rest of my conscious feelings focused on guilt. I wasn't doing everything I should be doing in my classroom, I thought. I should be doing X, Y, and, of course, Z. Constructed in a split of body and self, my brain desperately tried to coach my body to ignore the biological forces in a flurry of activity inside me.

I considered discussing my physical discomfort with my students, but the fear of the unknown stopped me. I risked validating the notion that women physically are incapable of performing certain kinds of traditionally male jobs. Although I knew how to make the argument against this assumption, I didn't have the emotional energy for the confrontation. I feared, God forbid, breaking down in tears.

Emily Martin helps me re-evaluate my first trimester experience. Now, I can re-interpret my feelings of inadequacy as a form of political resistance. She describes women's bodies as countering the dominant forms in which time is socially organized. Analyzing the PMS literature and women's descriptions of their symptoms of PMS, she demonstrates women's valiant attempts to accommodate the organization of time that doesn't account for their bodies. She cites women's experiential statements, describing a cycle during which they function differently on certain days, in ways that make it harder for them to tolerate the discipline required by work in our society. Martin suggests that rather than perceiving this conflict as a flaw inside women, we can see the conflict as an insight into flaws in society.

Sharing with my composition students my conflicts as a woman in this male-dominated system is one way to fight the power structure that would use my skills against me. I wrote my students a letter, where I explained what it meant to me to be a feminist teacher and what it meant to me to be pregnant. Modeling the use of writing as a social practice through this letter, I opened my composition classroom as a space for counterhegemonic critique of the academy and the outside world it represents. Surprised by some of the fears I expressed, one female student replied, "Why were you so nervous to share your pregnancy with us?" Her question made me realize I was struggling with my own desires to keep my experience private. While I could use my pregnancy as a form of political resistance in the classroom, doing so made me vulnerable to the attention my students gave to my body. Later, in a discussion of the importance of integrating personal experiences in writing as well as in the classroom, I invited a discussion of my pregnant body. Before I knew it, I was fielding a barrage of questions about my pregnancy, my marriage, my life. Accustomed to sharing stories about my personal life with my students, I wasn't as willing to direct attention to my body. Yet, women's bodies in public space, space that has been organized and defined as male, can work symbolically and concretely as signs of resistance. Emily Martin explains:

> Women interpenetrate what were never really separate realms. They literally embody the opposition, or contradiction, between the two worlds. Sometimes the embodiment is private, as women menstruate through a day of work with no one else knowing or manage to conceal hot flashes, but of course the women themselves are acutely aware of what they conceal from others. Pregnancy, of course, cannot be concealed for long, and anyone who has looked for a job or continued one while pregnant cannot help but see the clash with which the two worlds, meant to be kept ideologically separate, collide. (197)

As my face turned crimson at the sudden turn of focus to my body and the baby growing inside me, I fought the urge to run, to silence my students' questions, to protect my body in ways our culture has taught me I must. Internally, I listened to the voice that said calmly to me, "They're just curious. You must share some of the life of your body with them if you want your female students to value their own bodily experiences and your male students to respect those experiences." To risk this vulnerability is to offer myself and perhaps some of my female students the chance to heal the split that separates our bodies and ourselves, the chance as well to critique the political structures which have created the split.

WATCHING OURSELVES: FEMINIST TEACHERS AND AUTHORITY

Karen Powers-Stubbs

> A little too much emphasis was placed on feminism in this class; this instructor should watch herself on this subject.

> I think the persuasion papers focused too much on feminism. Although it may be a good topic to write about, other, better subjects would also work. Not enough emphasis was put on social issues.

> There are slightly more impressionable minds than mine and it is not fair for them to be lambasted with a lot of feminist jargon, while the realist voice is represented by practically only me.
>
> This is English class, not feminism.

I hear my students' voices as I glean my first-semester evaluations and journal responses for suggestions to improve my teaching. I'm not surprised to read objections to the feminist values embedded in my pedagogy. What does surprise me is how willingly and vehemently my students dismissed my ideas and perspective—essentially, my authority—concerning a social issue such as feminism. Seemingly, this is a topic I should know something about since I'm a woman who happened to reach adulthood in the midst of the social turbulence of the late sixties and early seventies.

On second thought, I also question my authority in the classroom, even when the contested issue is one in which I have both a personal and professional interest. As a new teacher, my authority in the classroom was one among the myriad of issues on my mind as I prepared to teach for the first time last fall. But as a new feminist, my questions and anxieties about teacherly authority differed from those generally articulated by my fellow graduate students. In part because of the Feminist Sophistics seminar I took during the previous summer, I was all too aware that women in patriarchal social institutions are customarily relegated to powerless positions. As Margo Culley and others have convincingly argued, the authority commensurate with the role of teacher is diminished, if not entirely invalidated, by granting that authority to a woman. Not surprisingly, then, as a novice teacher only recently introduced to the transformative power of feminist pedagogy, I entered the classroom with conflicting ideas about my authority. For the most part, I vacillated between capitulating to internalized images of feminine decorum and forging new ideas antithetical to those traditional images. Yoking two seemingly incompatible personas—nurturer and authority—left me floundering in uncertainty.

From the beginning of the first-year composition course which provoked the student responses mentioned above, I defined my pedagogy as committed to challenging my students' and my own assumptions about how language use is related to classism, racism, and sexism. In our early discussions concerning the various definitions of writing and writers, I offered my reasons, based on my background in cultural anthropology, for viewing writing through a sociocultural lens. For me, it's not only obvious that we are shaped by the language we speak, it's equally clear that we have the power to reshape that language and, subsequently, restructure the social order. I was looking forward to exploring that idea with my students. But most of my primarily white, upper-middle-class, conservative students have been socialized to understand themselves as entirely free and autonomous individuals. They resisted.

In retrospect, I suspect that these elements typical of feminist pedagogy suggested to my students who embrace the male model of teacher as quintessential authority that the woman teacher is less intelligent and less professional than her male counterpart. Bennett and other researchers have argued that structured, current-traditional teachers are likely to be regarded by students as more organized and professional. On the other hand, feminist teachers who reject the banking model of education and often use collaborative methods are seen as less competent. Along similar lines, Sandler concludes that "students, whose teacher is trying to actively engage them in the learning process, may feel instead that she is not well-organized or does not have a good grasp of the subject" (9). As I reflect on my classroom experience, this conclusion probably applies—especially when I introduced the topic which threatened to complicate certain zero-order beliefs my students held about their worlds. But perhaps because I was a new teacher, as well as being new to feminism, I was relatively oblivious to just how highly charged the feminist classroom can be when the silent hierarchies of society are disrupted.

The contradictory nature of feminine authority was starkly highlighted for me last year during the course of a classroom project I proposed. The project itself was straightforward enough. Following two personal narrative assignments and one persuasive assignment dealing with campus issues, my fourth writing assignment asked students to write an argument dealing with a minority concern. We read articles about the minority status of women in American and other cultures and discussed the relationship between language and oppression (sexist language, in particular), the economic status of women, the media's perception of women, and violence against women. Although our discussion focused on women, issues surrounding any minority, such as ethnic, racial, or religious minorities, the disabled, or the elderly, were posited as fruitful subjects to examine.

This particular assignment did not play out as I had anticipated. Magda Lewis and Roger Simon summarize the troubling epiphany I experienced that week in my classroom: "The overwhelming experience of women in a society dominated by men is that of being silenced" (459). Although I was ostensibly the authority in the classroom, I too was a silenced woman. Given my students' attitudes about feminism, it seemed that any argument I could offer from the feminist perspective was predestined to be dismissed as disqualified knowledge. Ironically, although my position as teacher granted me the authority to present my view through readings and discussion, my students' nearly unanimous rejection of both my experiential knowledge and my scholarly knowledge worked, in effect, to silence me. The class as a whole (with the exception of one minority female student) systematically denied that social inequity shapes our culture despite my argument to the contrary. My dilemma is exemplified in our discussion of Miami's song, the lyrics of which were modified only recently to embrace the daughters of the school as well as the sons. Most of the students scoffed at the outcry over the original sexist lyrics, declaring the protest as "petty" and "trivial." Racism, classism, and sexism were seen as problems that had been successfully adjudicated in the past, and, if they hadn't been, they weren't worth arguing about anyway.

In an effort to repudiate the oft-heard and pervasive contention that feminists are "whining" over imagined slights, I provided what I thought was solid evidence that women and their accomplishments are devalued in contemporary society. Claiming that women are disproportionately victims of violence, I cited the disturbing statistics: every hour 16 women confront rapists, a woman is raped every six minutes, 3 to 4 million women are battered each year, every 18 seconds a woman is beaten, 3 out of 4 women will be victims of at least one violent crime during their lifetime (Salholz et al. 23–24). Yet these statistics were met with suspicion, if not outright hostility. Two particularly skeptical male students interrogated me about the source of these numbers. Even my distributing the text from *Newsweek,* which acknowledged the Senate Judiciary Committee as the impeccable source, failed to convince at least one male, who emphatically denied the implications of the statistics and claimed they were more than likely "inflated." The glares and body language of most of the other students in the class signified tacit, if not vocal, agreement.

Since we had productively addressed many other volatile issues, I hadn't anticipated my students' steadfast unwillingness to debate this one. I remember feeling vulnerable and unprepared as my tenuous grasp on authority dissolved. It seemed that I was the authority in the classroom only as long as I remained within prescribed boundaries.

My point is not that I'm disturbed by dissension in the classroom. On the contrary, I see furrowed brows and impassioned speech as markers of actively engaged students. I'm most satisfied with my teaching when my students argue as they leave the classroom or linger to have the last word after class is officially over. Class discussion up to this point in the semester had been interactive and dialogic. Unfortunately, this was not the case when the subject was women's issues. For those three class sessions, the class collectively and mutely stalked out when I indicated that our time was up. Even more importantly, in marked contrast to our typical discussions, these class sessions on women's issues were marked by binary oppositions—the one minority student and I stood as adversaries to the 16 primarily vocal men and the remaining six primarily silent women. Lewis and Simon reasoned that men "are united in their shared relationship of dominance over their women: they are dependent on each other to maintain that domination" (458). Disturbingly, not only were the men unified in their resistance, most of the women supported the men in their silent rejection of my ideas about the social implications of language.

Fortunately, conversations with my students, specifically about women's issues, continued for the remainder of the semester, occasionally in class, but primarily in dialogue journals. For the most part, the anger and denial exhibited by my students eventually moderated into productive questioning. One male student and I carried on a conversation in his journal about my hyphenated name for weeks. And we were accomplishing one of the goals I have for my writing class: discovering new ideas and modifying old ones through writing. When the teacher/course evaluations were returned to me after the conclusion of the course, I was somewhat surprised to find that all except one of my students deemed the course a resounding success. Apparently, even those students who most stringently objected to my feminist stance considered the course valuable.

As I approach the beginning of a new semester, I realize that the contradiction inherent in "woman teacher" is even more complex than I had surmised. My experience convinces me that the gender-related expectations that students hold are tenacious and difficult to disrupt. Yet, paradoxically, I'm encouraged by the students who protested that feminism is misplaced in the composition classroom. Despite their heartfelt objections, those students were, nonetheless, persuaded to weigh, measure, and consider the social environment and the place of writing and language within that environment. Significantly, women's issues were obviously still on their minds at the end of the course. As yet another new semester approaches, I am, as usual, rethinking my composition syllabus with the help of my students' responses. Ever mindful of my student's admonishment to "watch myself' on the subject of feminism, I plan to incorporate discussions of gender and language. Perhaps my "realist" voice can find a place within the heteroglossia to maintain that this is English class *and* feminism.

TEACHING ACROSS AND WITHIN DIFFERENCES

Susan C. Jarratt

After trying for several years to finesse my feminist position in the writing class, I finally decided last fall to conduct an "overtly" feminist composition class. By that I meant most of all that I would use the word "feminism" from the very beginning to describe my pedagogy—in my syllabus, in daily discussion of pedagogical decisions with students, and in a final letter to the students describing and evaluating our work together. Both national and local factors worked against a discourse of feminism at Miami University. The popular media have been gloating for some time over the decline of feminism, along with other progressive social movements, during the conservative eighties. Susan Faludi's *Backlash* documents this phenomenon in painstaking detail. In tune with the national chilling of feminist fervor, some students at our Oxford campus reserve a special distaste for the "feminism" that disrupted the normal social life of their university within recent memory. Five years ago an undergraduate women's group staged a courageous sit-in at the administration building to protest the forced hiring of a man in the all-woman escort service. That year, protests of a sorority date auction and of a beauty contest held by the men's glee club further alienated, even disgusted, many students who have no experience of social protest as a legitimate form of participation in public affairs.

For newer students several years away from those local events, "feminism" still comes from an alien language. Like "Marxism" and "socialism," it names an alternative worldview often demonized by schools, churches, and the media in the attenuated public discourse in our society. Even after I've convinced my students to complicate their assumption that anyone calling herself (or even himself) a feminist seeks the end of love, intimate heterosexual relations, marriage, family, and the male of the species, there remains the genuinely threatening critique feminism offers of those gendered social conventions they've worked so hard to master and that serve as their very survival skills in the frightening new world of the university outside the classroom.

Despite these impediments, my 17 first-year students, my undergraduate teaching fellow, and I had a fine semester that fall. Class discussions were lively but respectful, the writing was engaging, student evaluations were high. It seems that we experienced this success through a paradoxical opening and closing of multiple differences. Though the gesture of naming myself and my class "feminist" opened a chasm between me and my students, various kinds of solidarity were forged behind and within our work together.

I think my own self-assurance was an important personal difference from past teaching experiences. Though I engaged in activism in the sixties, it was more counterculturally than politically motivated. Without a history in the feminist movement, I've often felt like a late-comer without the necessary credentials. In the past, I most often introduced social issues within a rhetorically based pedagogy and sometimes expressed my own views on issues students chose to take up, but I did not name myself with a particular ideological position. They labeled me with their own terms—former hippie, liberal—but I kept an ironic distance from those labels. To announce myself as something was a completely different strategy, a different rhetoric of the classroom, one I now felt comfortable with. In closing with the name "feminist," I modeled for students a committed but provisional social identity, good only until the withering away of sexism (not to be confused with the withering away of men)! The problem for both conservative students and also, paradoxically, for some radical teachers is that "feminism" names only one site of social difference: gender. But defining feminism for myself and my students as a theoretical vehicle for naming multiple social identities and for analyzing the play of language and power at those various sites moves it beyond a narrow identity: politics. More simply put, I convinced them that there was more to "feminism" for us than my own gender.

Having just completed the Feminist Sophistics seminar and conference made a more communal difference. It marked a moment of connection for the participants between composition/rhetoric as a field and feminism. Certainly feminism is far from the first political intervention in the writing classroom. From long before the beginning of the recent creation of composition as an academic field, teachers and scholars have engaged politics in and of the classroom. Greg Myers, James Berlin, Richard Ohmann, and many others have chronicled the junctures of radical politics and the teaching of writing during this century. The connection with feminism has been later and perhaps more tentative (see Flynn, "Composing"), but seeing the growth of a group of feminist fellow travelers specifically in the teaching of writing was significant for me as a teacher. As I stepped into the classroom, I felt supported by a group. The inevitably agonistic experience of counterhegemonic cultural work was ameliorated.

In another more material way I wasn't alone in the classroom last fall. I was assisted throughout the term by an undergraduate Teaching Fellow. Miami offers to English majors interested in education the opportunity to assist a faculty member in teaching a lower-division class. Theresa Squires had been in a class I taught the previous spring on women and writing. As a sophomore, Theresa was beginning to discover a feminist consciousness and was passionately interested in social issues in the classroom. Her presence as an older student, a self-described "brown girl" (with parents of different racial backgrounds), and a social being in process had a powerful influence on the class. She attended all the classes, read all the students' papers and wrote comments on them, contributed to decisions about writing and reading, and joined in class discussion. Though the two of us shared some general sympathies, we sometimes had different opinions on issues discussed in class. So Theresa never functioned simply as a "yes" person, just reinforcing a party line. Rather, she served a significant role for the students in mediating my authority as an older, tenured faculty member offering a counterhegemonic pedagogy. For me, she was a source of support, a sounding board, and a reality check on student concerns and lives. Her presence bridged the student/teacher difference.

"How many feminists does it take to change a light bulb?"
"One—and it's *not* funny!"

Another element of our experience last fall was my serious decision to use humor in my feminist classroom. I may be more sensitive than others to the bad rap feminists get about being humorless because I am generally a pretty serious person. Because students both male and female feel that their most deeply valued personal interests are threatened by feminism, I made an effort to lighten the burden of relentless critique (see Shor). By using humor, I communicated that I could laugh at myself and other feminists and that I cared enough about my students to share the pleasure of laughter with them. But I didn't suggest that feminism wasn't something I took seriously. Laughing together made us co-conspiring cultural critics, bound us together as a group, cutting across the social boundaries we were simultaneously working to demarcate through our writing and reading about difference. After I started the semester with the joke above, we fell into a pattern of sharing jokes at the beginning of class each day. We noticed that lots of jokes were funny at someone else's expense, so we tried to find ones that weren't or figure out why people's laughter hurts others. Too often, though, I found myself analyzing for my students why the jokes others brought in were sexist, racist, classist, etc. That role gave me too much power and, of course, killed the humor of the joke. Power shifts when the students themselves have control of language tools—a principle at the heart of the composition revolution.

I think the most powerful fusion across difference came from sharing with my students tools of sociolinguistic analysis—tools the students both applied and critiqued. By naming my pedagogy and myself feminist, I wasn't communicating that the writing class should be a platform for my views about specific issues. It meant that becoming a responsible language user demands an understanding of the ways language inscribes difference. My students had only to agree to use the analytic tools I provided (see Bizzell). In this way, my pedagogy may resemble a more instrumentalist composition theory. For example, instead of taking my word that adding concrete details would improve a personal narrative, I asked my students to take my word that naming their own social locations would ground their stories in socially specific, and thus more socially responsible, accounts of personal history. Instead of persuading my students that "information" is socially constructed, I made them graph the data from a national news source along two axes of social difference—race and gender. When we looked at TV and film, I set them the task of focusing not only on the medium as text but on its production and reception as well, questions generated by work in cultural studies. I didn't tell them what the outcome of these processes would be because I didn't know myself, nor did I tell them what to make of the outcomes. But it was clear to all of us that the politics are in the techniques of analysis. Requiring students to perform the practices above is different both from demanding that they share my views and from teaching them to write unified, coherent five-paragraph themes—all political acts.

Again, the difference for me in this moment of feminist teaching was a reduction of difference between me and my students. We were collectively engaged in a process of cultural critique and production, an engagement reflected in their evaluations: "I'm addicted to this analysis stuff!" Very few, if any, of my 17 students were ready to sign up as feminists at the end of the semester, but that was not my goal. Most of them were ready to describe themselves as language users engaged in a socially located and responsible practice of analysis and production. The point of my account is not that differences should disappear, it is that socially oriented and personally satisfying composition teaching can happen across and within different kinds of difference.

Feminist Pedagogy: Experience and Difference in a Politics of Transformation

Adriana Hernández

As a woman and a Latin American studying in an American university, I was a particular embodiment of difference bringing a very particular personal experience to the Feminist Sophistics Group. Since I belonged to a different department—Educational Leadership—and I was not teaching a composition class, my role was to participate in the collective process of reflecting and questioning our assumptions and conclusions and to advance the creative task of legitimizing a transformative practice while departing from standard procedures. At the core of the project were two main concerns in feminist theorizing: experience and difference. My particular question for our project concerned the relation between specific classroom experiences and the generalization demanded by theory. In reviewing the five accounts of classroom experience above, I see that they can be grouped into three clusters around issues of the female teacher's authority and the supportive versus oppositional voices of students.

The Controversial Legitimation of Personal Experience.   In one cluster we can place Jill Eichhorn's sharing of her experience of being married and pregnant, accepted and even welcomed by the class, alongside Karen Powers-Stubbs experience as a mother coming back to college and coming out as a feminist, which her students resisted in spite of her openness to inquiry and her willingness to share. The initial resistance the students had toward the introduction of feminist issues to Jill's classroom and their sense of betrayal because of her refusal to enact a mothering role as a teacher turned into a "barrage of questions." Were they relieved that she finally fit into the dominant role for women? Did the students understand the personal in the classroom in terms of its social construction and political value? Jill literally embodied an authority that was a violation of a masculinized public space, but one which did not radically challenge the world views (and future plans) of her students. For her the composition classroom worked as a space wherein she could enact an alternative example of teacher authority while healing "the split that separated her body from herself." This is a concrete case in which feminist pedagogy worked in a process of self and social transformation.

Karen also found herself challenged in her authority as a woman teacher and in her expertise on a social issue such as feminism. While the focus of Jill's work in the process of enacting a feminist pedagogy was on bodily experiences, the force of Karen's attention was on language, its connection to racism, sexism, and classism. Karen felt empowered to address women's issues by the fact that she returned to school after a 10-year hiatus to stay home with her children. While she saw this as a strength, her students seemed to resent the radicalization of her mothering experience into an outspoken concern for minority issues. It seems to me that Karen's willingness to challenge and interrogate not only her own assumptions but her students' with respect to language and power relations was very menacing to them. Here students felt threatened by the private intermeshed with the public: the figure of mother stepping into political issues within the setting of the college classroom. Students denied all legitimacy not only to Karen's experience but also to the information provided: i.e., the statistics on violence against women published by *Newsweek* (Salholz et al.) and presented according to the dominant model of "fact knowledge." These two cases suggest that women's experience seems to be recognized more easily as a source of knowledge when coming from traditional social roles defined according to the dominant ideology (mother/wife) but not when linked to counterpractices or resistance. Another aspect to take into account is that when experience is recognized, it seems to be conceptualized not as socially constructed but as personal in the sense of private, and, therefore, depoliticized.

Embodying Difference.   In another two groupings of these teaching accounts, the question becomes: How did the members of the group work "difference" according to the various positions taken up by their students? In the cases of Susan Jarratt and Sara Farris, the counterhegemonic analysis of language and power, the problematic of women's oppression, and female authority in the classroom were mediated by others besides themselves in the class. Susan had a non-white undergraduate teaching fellow who was openly engaged in feminist issues and other social concerns. Sara could count on the support of two middle-aged women who were very enthusiastic about her position and took strong stands in different situations. The presence of other people in the classroom articulating resistance to the norm provides the possibility to work in a dialogical process. In this way, different voices can be heard, the material is not presented in linear mode as "fact," and knowledge gets produced as a process. This process is not so easy to accomplish when the teacher is the only one embodying difference and the risk of being caught in a binary opposition is greater. It is very difficult to provide provisional social stances with which the students may identify in order to articulate difference and give room for transformation and emancipation when the teacher is positioned to defend herself constantly and the students do not have alternate possibilities besides the one offered by her.

This was the case in a third grouping of accounts. Sara Farris, Karen Powers-Stubbs, and Karen Hayes all faced strongly resistant students in their classes, with various results. Sara had success despite her "judges"; Karen Powers-Stubbs worked with her resistant students in conferences and through journals; Karen Hayes valued her single outrageous voice of difference. The presence of these classroom voices is in some measure a matter of chance; we can offer no general rules to be followed in these or any of the multitude of other possible combinations of voices or "selves" in the composition classroom. It seems to me that a recognition of the classroom as a space where tensions about race, gender, class, and other differences are articulated is the first step away from a monological conception of pedagogy that reduces all consideration of formative processes to a language of methods and techniques. What these different combinations of voices, shifting alignments among students and teachers, and various assessments of success and failure by the teachers themselves have in common is the process of struggle.

An Ongoing Process of Transformation.   Magda Lewis and Roger Simon, a student and a teacher writing collaboratively, speak eloquently on the issue of struggle:

> It is the experience of the reality of lived differences that critical pedagogic practice must claim as the agenda for discussion. This means that both students and teacher must find space within which the experience of their daily lives can be articulated in its multiplicity. In practice this always implies a struggle—a struggle over discourse as the expression of both form and content, a struggle over interpretation of experience, and a struggle over "self." . . . It is a struggle that makes possible new knowledge that expands beyond individual experience and hence redefines our identities and the real possibilities we see in the daily conditions of our lives. The struggle is itself a condition basic to the realization of a

process of pedagogy: it is a struggle that can never be won—or pedagogy stops. (469)

Feminist pedagogy is a practice that addresses the complexity of educational phenomena, both within the school setting and outside it in wider cultural spheres. It is discourse that, while framed within larger concerns of social theory, engages immediate concerns of everyday life. Through these accounts we have been concerned with the immediate classroom context, although not in terms of technique or recipe. We cannot say, for example, that Powers-Stubbs's presentation of information according to the dominant model of "fact knowledge" was a mistake. She reasoned that, given the conservative bent of her students, they would be responsive to information about violence against women and she would be able to open a space of discussion. That this was not the case does not lead us to discourage the use of information in the classroom: i.e., we would not draw here a conclusion about the strategy or a recommendation for specific practice. Rather, we read this experience as an example of the strongly ingrained negation of unsettling social problematics on the part of some students. This example, like the others, speaks for an ongoing pedagogical practice that redefines itself constantly in terms of personal and social investments.

Feminist pedagogy is a flexible practice that does not tie itself to dogmatic rules which prescribe teaching in a certain way to everyone in all circumstances. Instead, the feminist classroom legitimizes struggle as positive and productive; it provides the arena to analyze contradiction, identification, and resistance. As feminist teachers we struggle to persuade students to acknowledge our authority in the classroom: to make a place for women's knowledge and experience. At the same time we struggle to discover, respect, and work within the differences our students bring with them to class. In our title we ask, What's the difference? Through these accounts and reflections we seek neither to overcome struggle nor to erase difference but to promote collective participation in a rhetorical process of engagement with transformative possibilities for us all.

WORKS CITED

Bauer, Dale M. "The Other 'F' Word: The Feminist in the Classroom." *College English* 52 (April 1990): 385–96.

Bauer, Dale M., and Susan C. Jarratt. "Feminist Sophistics: Teaching with an Attitude." *Changing Classroom Practices: Resources for Literary and Cultural Studies*. Ed. David B. Downing. Urbana: National Council of Teachers of English, 1994. 149–65.

Bennett, S. K. "Student Perceptions and Expectations for Male and Female Instructors: Evidence Relating to the Question of Gender Bias in Teaching Evaluation." *Journal of Educational Psychology* 74 (April 1982): 170–79.

Berlin, James A. *Rhetoric and Reality: Writing Instruction in American Colleges, 1900–1985*. Carbondale: Southern Illinois UP, 1987.

Bizzell, Patricia. "Power, Authority, and Critical Pedagogy." *Journal of Basic Writing* 10.2 (Fall 1991): 54–70.

Brodkey, Linda. "Picturing Writing: Writers in the Modern World." *Academic Writing as Social Practice*. Philadelphia: Temple UP, 1987. 54–86.

———. "Transvaluing Difference." *College English* 51 (October 1989): 597–601.

Culley, Margo, et al. "The Politics of Nurturance." *Gendered Subjects: The Dynamics of Feminist Teaching*. Ed. Margo Culley and Catherine Portuges. Boston: Routledge, 1985.

Elbow, Peter. "Reflections on Academic Discourse: How It Relates to Freshmen and Colleagues." *College English* 53 (February 1991): 135–55.

Faludi, Susan. *Backlash: The Undeclared War against American Women.* New York: Crown, 1991.

Flynn, Elizabeth A. "Composing as a Woman." *College Composition and Communication* 39 (December 1988): 423–35.

———. "Composing 'Composing as a Woman': A Perspective on Research." *College Composition and Communication* 41 (February 1990): 83–89.

Friedman, Susan Stanford. "Authority in the Feminist Classroom: A Contradiction in Terms?" *Gendered Subjects: The Dynamics of Feminist Teaching.* Ed. Margo Culley and Catherine Portuges. Boston: Routledge, 1985. 203—07.

Giroux, Henry A. *Schooling and the Struggle for Public Life.* Minneapolis: U Minnesota P, 1988.

Goldberg, Natalie. *Writing Down the Bones: Freeing the Writer Within.* Boston: Shambhala, 1986.

Holbrook, Sue Ellen. "Women's Work: The Feminizing of Composition." *Rhetoric Review* 9 (Spring 1991): 201–29.

hooks, bell. "Feminist Focus on Men: A Comment." *Talking Back: Thinking Feminist, Thinking Black.* Boston: South End, 1989. 127–33.

———. *Yearning: Race, Gender, and Cultural Politics.* Boston: South End, 1990.

Hunter, Susan. "A Woman's Place *Is* in the Composition Classroom: Pedagogy, Gender, and Difference." *Rhetoric Review* 9 (Spring 1991): 230–45.

Jarratt, Susan C. "Feminism and Composition: The Case for Conflict." *Contending with Words: Composition in a Postmodern Era.* Ed. Patricia Harkin and John Schilb. New York: MLA, 1991. 105–25.

Lather, Patti. *Getting Smart: Feminist Research and Pedagogy with/in the Postmodern.* New York: Routledge, 1991.

Lewis, Magda, and Roger I. Simon. "A Discourse Not Intended for Her: Learning and Teaching Within Patriarchy." *Harvard Educational Review* 56 (October 1986): 457–72.

Martin, Emily. *The Woman in the Body: A Cultural Analysis of Reproduction.* Boston: Beacon, 1987.

Miller, Susan. "The Feminization of Composition." *The Politics of Writing Instruction: Postsecondary.* Ed. Richard Bullock and John Trimbur. Portsmouth: Boynton/Cook, 1991. 39–53.

Morrison, Toni. *A World of Ideas.* With Bill Moyers. Public Television. New York Public Library. n.d.

Myers, Greg. "Reality, Consensus, and Reform in the Rhetoric of Composition Teaching." *College English* 48 (February 1986): 154–74.

Ohmann, Richard. *Politics of Letters.* Middletown: Wesleyan UP, 1987.

Rich, Adrienne. "Taking Women Students Seriously." *On Lies, Secrets, Silences.* New York: Norton, 1979. 237–45.

Runciman, Lex. "Fun?" *College English* 53 (February 1991): 156–62.

Salholz, Eloise, et al. "Women Under Assault." *Newsweek* 16 July 1990: 23–24.

Sandler, Bernice Resnick. "Women Faculty at Work in the Classroom, or, Why It Still Hurts to Be a Woman in Labor." *Communication Education* 40 (January 1991): 6–15.

Shor, Ira. *Critical Teaching and Everyday Life.* Boston: South End, 1980.

Trimbur, John. "Consensus and Difference in Collaborative Learning." *College English* 51 (October 1989): 602–16.

Weiler, Kathleen. *Women Teaching for Change: Gender, Class, and Power.* South Hadley: Bergin, 1988.

23 Participatory Rhetoric and the Teacher as Racial/Gendered Subject

CHERYL L. JOHNSON

Nowhere are the related issues of essence, identity, and experience so highly charged and so deeply politicized as they are in the classroom. Personal consciousness, individual oppressions, lived experience—in short, identity politics—operate in the classroom both to authorize and to de-authorize speech. "Experience" emerges as the essential truth of the individual subject and personal "identity" metamorphoses into knowledge. Who we are becomes what we know; ontology shades into epistemology.

—Diana Fuss, *Essentially Speaking*

If anything I do, in the way of writing novels (or whatever I write) isn't about the village or the community or about you, then it is not about anything. I am not interested in indulging myself in some private, closed exercise of my imagination that fulfills only the obligation of my personal dreams—which is to say yes, the work must be political.

—Toni Morrison, "Rootedness"

"Floating signifiers," I whispered.

—Patricia Williams, *The Alchemy of Race and Rights*

According to Toni Morrison in "Rootedness: The Ancestor as Foundation," a text may evoke a participatory relationship between itself and the reader (341). The text is not the sole repository or source of meaning for the reader; it merely provides the opportunity for, or titillates the reader into, a textual marriage. In her discussion of the intimate relationship between the reader and the text, however, Morrison does not consider the possibility that some readers are not alone with the literary work; a third party—a teacher—may join the reader and the text, thus providing another voice and text to be deciphered. This role becomes interestingly complicated when the author and

From *College English* 56 (1994): 409–19.

major characters of a text share with the teacher the marked identity of black-ness or femaleness, or both. As a black woman who teaches courses on the lit-erature of black women writers and criticism and who incorporates some of these texts in other courses not specific to black women writers, I have won-dered how much my students' reading of my racial/gendered body informs their reading of the literary texts. Specifically, as Diana Fuss suggests in the above epigraph (113), do students empower me as an absolute authority on black womanhood (and, therefore, the literature of black women) because my *experience* of this gives me an infallible handle on the "true meaning" of the text? Am I "read" as a representation of essentialized black womanhood, and, if so, what is that "reading," and how much do I participate in or contribute to students' ideas about the nature of black women? My thoughts about these questions resemble less a way-made tapestry than an unevenly stitched crazy quilt, with pieces, sometimes torn and stained, from my forty-three-year-old race-gender-class-academic wardrobe. I have come to realize that if RuPaul is right—we are all crossdressers—then my identity as an African-American woman professor is both confused and confusing; these racial/gendered/academic signifiers float in restless waters. Race and gender conspire in the construction of my role as teacher and my students' interpretation of an African-American literary text. This conspiracy results not only from the social, cultural, and political contexts in which I continue to come of age, but also from the students' gaze, which is informed by their own socially con-structed readings of race and gender and the relationship of these to literature.

The questions I continue to ask myself about the social construction of the student's gaze, the body as text, the spoken/written text(s) as text, and the perils of participatory rhetoric occasion my attempts to continue my interior/exterior dialogue with myself and others about these issues. The primary informing agent is my own shifting and subjective understanding of how, in the tradition of W. E. B. DuBois's representation of double consciousness, I simultaneously position myself and have been positioned in the academy. This Janus-faced positioning situates and displaces my pedagogical methods, style, and content.

In "Rootedness," Toni Morrison describes the "participatory relationship between the artist or the speaker and the audience" in the creation of meaning (341). For her, what is left out of the text is supplied by the reader; thus, both the text and the reader are involved in an intimate dialogue. This dialogue, according to Morrison, "should try deliberately to make you stand up and make you feel something profoundly in the same way that a Black preacher requires his congregation to speak, to join him in the sermon, to behave in a certain way, to stand up and to weep and to cry and to accede or to change and to modify—to expand on the sermon that is being delivered" (341). This par-ticipatory relationship is, then, analogous to "call and response"—the use of language to draw both speaker and audience into a conversation marked by strong emotions and intimacy. Call and response is a significant part of tradi-tional black religion; the calls are familiar and the responses are anticipated by each party. Both the call and the response are part of the participants' cultural knowledge; the speaker and the audience supply cultural understandings that facilitate the creation of meaning in the spoken text.

Morrison's desire for a reader's participation in the literary text is not necessarily shared by other writers; nevertheless, her ideas help me as I think about the ways in which students, especially white students, read African-American literature and the ways in which I as a racial/gendered subject might affect students' experience of reading. Clearly, by comparing reading to a black form of worship, Morrison collapses the oral/written dichotomy and represents reading as not only an intimate, shared experience but also a spiritual one, capable of evoking profound feelings. Such responses, however, depend upon the participant's "immersion" into the literary text—a baptism by words, if you will—in which a cleansing or at least transforming experience is anticipated, even desired, by the reader. This joyous intimacy, characterized by a willingness on the part of the reader to be submerged into culture-specific signs and signifiers within black women's literature, certainly strengthens the political impact of Morrison's writings. Her argument that writers "should be able to make it unquestionably political and irrevocably beautiful at the same time" (345) counters formalist attempts to dichotomize black literature into either a didactic or an aesthetic mode and chastises those who would argue that any work of literature which attacks racism or any other evil in our society is "tainted." Rather, Morrison's "feeling is just the opposite; if it has none, it is tainted" (345).

Morrison's analogy between reading and religious worship, or maybe the sense in which I have extended it, is problematic in at least three ways. First, it assumes that readers will approach a literary text with a willingness to be vulnerable to this "immersion." This is not necessarily true, especially as more and more universities incorporate required multicultural curricula. Some students may read such requirements as intrusions on their academic study and actually resent texts which explore racial, ethnic, gender, or religious differences. Even courses which incorporate minority texts alongside always/already canonized texts may contain students who argue that such inclusions displace "classic" literary texts. Attitudes such as these may inhibit these students' ability to immerse themselves into a literary text in the participatory way Morrison describes.

Second, Morrison's analogy assumes that her readers have access to the culturally specific references which would allow them to participate in the creation of meaning. Without such access, readers will impose their own understandings, which may be informed or misinformed, depending upon the reader's cultural experience or knowledge. This is not to argue that meaning is fixed, rigid, and unbending within the text. Despite the attempts of some purists, language refuses to stand still—preferring to be-bop or hip-hop within its own semantic possibilities. Nevertheless, just as sociolinguists such as Labov and Smitherman have alerted us to the ways in which attitudes about language can determine our perception of racial difference, readers who encounter a racially, culturally, or linguistically different text may read their perceptions of these differences into the text, manipulating the language to conform to their culturally learned assumptions. Third, as mentioned earlier, Morrison's analogy assumes that only the reader and the text will be involved in the creation of meaning; she does not envisage another party—a teacher, for instance—contributing to the creation of meaning, forming a readerly "ménage à trois," so to speak. When students encounter a professor enclosed in a racial/gendered body, her very presence in the classroom inaugurates the creation of another decipherable text. For example, her role as teacher/professor signifies a power and an authority which Eurocentric history and contemporary media representations have denied her. Instead, the figurations of the black woman as mammy, maid, and welfare queen are prominent in Western cultural memory. How, then, can students refigure the black woman in their consciousness? And how are they to read the African-American text in the presence of this African-American female body?

Interactions with non-black students responding to African-American texts have informed my questions and concerns on this issue. One such student visited me in my office at the University of Wisconsin–Milwaukee and explained why he could not finish reading James Baldwin's *Go Tell It on the Mountain*. The violence in it, he said, was intolerable because it reminded him of an incident in which his father and a co-worker were robbed by some black men, and the co-worker was killed. The realization that his father could also have been killed was still so powerfully a part of his consciousness that reading Baldwin's novel evoked again his pain and, I think, his association of violence with black men. I remember being stunned at the connection he made between the novel and what had happened to his father. Nothing in the novel resembles the real occurrence; if anything, the violence in the novel is domestic, inflicted by the father on his wife and children. The narrator is a young man who struggles to understand the actions of his father, who uses religion to justify his violence and to imprison his family. The focus of the novel is on deliverance, on saving oneself from the tyranny of another's personal history and demons. Yet I remember thinking that this young man, my student, would not be able to hear my objections to his interpretation of the book. His impressions of black men were informed by what had happened to his father as well as the racial tension in Milwaukee and racist representations of black men. As I think back on that meeting, I re-experience my feelings of helplessness—how can I combat a society which has a long history of racial distortions and stereotyping and, within the last few years, has offered contemporary updates: pictures of Willie Horton, the beating of Rodney King, and the Thomas-Hill proceedings? My contradictory roles raised their clenched fists at each other: should I use this opportunity to explain the horrors of racism and how it participates in the creation of violence against us all? Or should I show empathy and compassion for my student, which he might read as compliance with his interpretation of the novel? Are these two narratives—Baldwin's novel and my student's story—so far apart that they cannot intersect at any point? Do their specific discursive properties or logic resist or downright forbid synthesis? It was clear to me that my student separated and privileged one narrative over the other. He did not want to understand why the incident happened; he wanted a look of horror to refigure my facial features, signifying a shared sense of fear, disgust, and vulnerability. Black men would become the "Other"; I would be the black person who is an exception to the rule.

Maybe, for me, writing on this subject is my act of contrition; what did my student's "telling" of his story do for him? Did I become his confessor—granted the power and authority by the academy to forgive him for his sin of responding with such horror to Baldwin's novel? Did I absolve him from his appropriation of Baldwin's story about his father, even as this student juggled the details so that they accommodated his own father's story? As a racial/gendered authority figure, I had the power not only to release him from his obligation to complete the assignment, but also to forgive his misreading of the novel.

Further complicating my struggle over the professional/humane/right response was my puzzlement over why this student had "crossed the line" and become personal with me. How had he "read" me? In "Black Women Intellectuals," in *Breaking Bread: Insurgent Black Intellectual Life*, bell hooks discusses how perceptions of black women as "inherently" nurturing and caring, even obsequious, disrupt any appreciation of their intellectual prowess. Many black women, she argues, are constructed into the mammy role, "nurturing and sustaining the life of others" (154). She states further that "Black women in all walks of life . . . complain that colleagues, co-workers, supervisors, etc. ask them to assume multipurpose caretaker roles, to be their guidance counselors, nannies, therapists, priests" (154). Certainly, I did not want to be a mean, stern disciplinarian who lacked compassion for this student or the capacity for empathy, but I resented his crossing the line and entering my professional space because, in so doing, he redefined my professionalism by imposing considerations outside of both my professional domain and Baldwin's novel. Those considerations complicated our interaction by producing various yet symbiotic discourses about race relations, violence within the black community, representations of black men, and the supposedly mimetic nature of black literature. Being an African-American literary critic is not enough; I must also address any other issues related to race. As an article in *The Chronicle of Higher Education* on blacks who work at predominantly white colleges states, "there are expectations that you are a minority encyclopedia, capable of explaining the black perspective on any given campus issue or development" (Palmer 19). Perhaps my strongest reaction to my student's story was sadness that he could not read and appreciate Baldwin's exquisite book, at least not at that time, because extraliterary voices blurred or completely obliterated Baldwin's own voice and those of his characters. Ultimately, my desire to understand my student's pain and his reconstructing gaze produced a third person who was professor/confessor; his reading of my racial/gendered body convinced him that I would not intrude on his reading of *Go Tell It on the Mountain*, even though his personal history misinformed his experience of the novel.

Another student could not finish reading Gayl Jones's *Corregidora*. This novel tells a complicated, painful story of the sexual degradation and psychological abuse of two black slave women and of how their stories inform the consciousness and sexuality of their female descendants, Ursa Corregidora (the narrator) and her mother. This white female student reacted strongly to the explicit references to the female body and to the vivid descriptions of the sexual abuse and rape of the black women slaves. She did not tell me why reading the book was so painful to her, but she implied that she had been the victim of sexual abuse and that the memories of that experience still devastated her. As this young woman sat before me, in tears, I found it impossible to require her to read Jones's novel. Separated by race and age, both of us still shared an understanding of the vulnerability of our bodies. Although I have never experienced what the women in the novel did, the fictionalized account of their humiliation gives me some sense of what my great-grandmother may have endured because her race and gender denied her ownership of her own body. The empathy I felt for my student's feelings arose not only from my historical perspectives on race, gender, and the body but also from the fear that my body could be violated and the recognition that many young girls and women have lived or are living that horrible reality. Nevertheless, I felt that the student had appropriated the slave women's story and made it a testament to her own pain, while not allowing it to inform her of the pain of black slave women. Furthermore, by not completing the novel, my student did not witness Ursa's attempts to find the language, through blues songs and other women's narratives, that would liberate her from the burden of her ancestors' history of forced concubinage. Slowly, Ursa comes to understand the construction of women's sexuality outside of procreation and her own need to reconstruct herself in her own terms according to her desires and needs. My student's participation in Ursa's story allowed her, like the male student who could not finish *Go Tell It on the Mountain*, to appropriate the text according to her own experiences. She erased the historical references, the race of the female characters, and the voice of the narrator, and her own story became the dominant text. My inability or unwillingness to force her to suspend her own subjectivity compromised my professionalism and my commitment to the integrity of African-American literature.

These episodes obliged me to examine not only how the students in question read these African-American novels, but also how they read me and the effect of their readings on my own subjectivity: I am trying to understand how my race and gender construct my role as a professor, my pedagogical style, and my ideology about African-American literature. If identity politics would seem to authorize my speech about African-American literature—if " 'experience' emerges as the essential truth of the individual subject and personal 'identity' metamorphoses into knowledge," in Diana Fuss's terms (113)—this is not the only dynamic at work: because of their readings of my identity, these white students felt authorized to invoke their own experience in ways that not only "de-authorized" me but effectively silenced Baldwin and Jones.

I will admit to the extraordinariness and specificity of the examples I have given thus far. Clearly, many students live lives of quiet or noisy desperation, but most of them will not tell us their stories, nor will they necessarily react to African-American literature as did the students presented above. A more common occurrence would be the situation I encountered last semester in my Composition and Literature course. The texts we used included a literature anthology and a novel, Ralph Ellison's *Invisible Man*. This book, so brilliant in its complexity and artistic sophistication, has baffled literary critics, so I expected to encounter some student anxiety and confusion. The greatest problem was trying to engage students in a discussion about the novel; they refused to ask questions or to respond to mine. One student finally said that she simply did not like the novel, and since we had only read about a hundred pages, I wondered what could have allowed her to form her opinion so soon.

As I thought back on my attempts to discuss certain scenes, I realized that some of them might pose problems for the students, especially as they wrestled with them in the presence of a black teacher. For example, in the prologue, the narrator, upon encountering a white man who uses a racist term, begins to beat the man and almost kills him (4). Most of the students were quiet during this discussion, and I now wonder if the image of a black man beating a white man, despite the reasons, made them uncomfortable; how could they feel sympathy for the narrator if he was engaging in behavior which they had been taught to view as evidence of his "essential" violent nature? I remember trying to engage them in a discussion of why the narrator reacted so violently to the white man by asking what racist name the man called the narrator. No one said a word. Finally, I uttered the infamous n-word—nigger—and I remember not their discomfort but their relief that I, and not one of them, had said the word. Were they concerned about the specific act of uttering that word in my presence? What, they may have asked themselves, would be my response to them? Would I be offended as that nasty word hung suspended in the very air that separated us? Did they want to admit to knowing that word? If they did reveal their awareness of the word, would I assume that they had used it? My saying the word relieved them of directing that word in my direction, of seeming to name me, even though I created the context in which the word would be placed.

Another scene which occurs early in the novel is the Battle Royal. That our narrator was set up to fight other black men for the entertainment of white men clearly presents another instance of racism to the students, and I am learning that many white students believe that scenes such as these are meant to produce feelings of guilt on their part. They argue that although those racist incidents may have occurred, they should not be held responsible since they, of course, are not racist. But just as they found ways to negotiate their feeling about that part of the Battle Royal, the students then confronted the part with the naked, dancing blonde woman who has a small American flag tattooed on her belly (19). How, then, to discuss the obvious desire of the black men for the woman without confronting again the stereotype of black men as savage, sexual animals who lust after white women? How to talk about the white woman as the object of desire in front of a black woman whose brown body is the antithesis of the white woman's? And how to synthesize the American flag and a white woman's body with race and desire without confronting their own values, which may be in conflict with those of the racial/gendered body standing in front of them? Silence gives them some protection from the issues and from me, the authority figure who knows all the righteous answers about race and gender.

These examples all refer to the displacements and tensions I have experienced as a black female professor teaching African-American literature to white students. The differences between us are clearly demarcated in our experiences of race and/or gender, and these differences manipulate our readings of both literature and each other. What may be erroneously suggested here is that the relationship between a black professor and black students would be harmonious because both, supposedly, locate themselves culturally, socially, politically, historically, and intellectually at an all-encompassing black/African-American site. If such a location exists, it is a tentative and unsteady one, affected by time and place of encounter. In other words, there is no fixed African-American ideology; black students may inscribe one or more various, sometimes conflicting, codes onto the body of the black professor, such as Afrocentricism, black nationalism, womanism, feminism, assimilation, or other perspectives arising from each student's subjectivity. Black professors are often expected to interpret or fashion these codes into academic masks or costumes which would signify their commitment to a particular ideology about race and gender.

What is clear, however, is that despite a desire on the part of some blacks for a racial ideology—constructed as a defense against racism—which would unite African-Americans around common goals and ideals, various and sometimes dissonant perspectives frustrate attempts for intraracial unity. There is no monolithic black essence, and the very desire for such an essence can be dangerous. Critics such as Henry Louis Gates and Hazel Carby, for example, warn us about the dangers of essentializing "blackness" because this only facilitates racist notions about racial and gendered differences. Ironically, these notions, when positioned as the cultural and intellectual property of African-Americans, may actually empower black students who use their experiences of difference as sources of knowledge about black culture and literature. In the classroom, such experiences grant voice, authority, and authenticity to those who previously have been dismissed as irrelevant to American history and culture; on the other hand, these oral testaments to "the black experience" may simultaneously silence those who do not share the same cultural background.

As a black woman professor, I have often found myself in the difficult situation of negotiating between two internal, warring voices. One insists that I allow my black students, who have never had such an opportunity before in their collegiate experience, to "own" a course on black literature. For example, more than a few black women students have pointed at passages in Toni Morrison's *The Bluest Eye* and said, "Yes, I know that," exhibiting a poignant familiarity with Pecola's tragic story as well as a startling exhilaration that what they may have whispered to themselves, what they may have accepted as an Absolute Truth—that dark skin is a signifier of all that is evil and ugly in the world—can be the subject of discussion in a classroom whose walls had only before heard what Shakespeare or Chaucer or Eliot had to say. The other voice argues that such a gesture on my part constitutes a "feel good" type of pedagogy that empowers black students but may, even though unwittingly, silence the other students. It is my professional responsibility, this voice continues, to assure each student access to the text and the class discussions.

It is, however, the black students' intimacy with black literature that most strongly approaches Morrison's concept of participatory reading. As these students recognize within the literary work their African-American communities, their neighbors, the jazz/blues/gospel/rhythm-'n-blues–like quality of the language, and the daily glories, tensions, and mundanities growing out of (or despite) racism and sexism, the "call and response" creation of meaning Morrison speaks of occurs. My racial/gendered presence may either promote this textual "chorus" by allowing its continuation or disrupt it by inviting "other" voices into the discourse. Wherever I locate myself, on either side or in some hazy middle-space, my body becomes an inscribed text, affecting the students' reading and participation in the literature.

I suspect that my experiences are not unique to me. Maybe there was some safety in teaching the "old" curriculum because we could place some distance between us and the text; our participation was not personal, and our delight in the text was lofty, even sublime, or objective and scientific. It is clear, however, that as we continue to find and include other, previously marginalized voices in the curriculum, we will encounter some students who will resist what we require them to read, and some who will challenge our ability to teach certain texts, arguing that our very presence and voice displace the cultural integrity of the text. Perhaps the most troublesome situation we may face would be some students' insistence that we articulate a particular stance or ideology about race, gender, class, ethnicity, or sexual preference. Amid conflicting discourses in the classroom, we will struggle with the desire to allow all students' voices to inform the discussion, while understanding that some of these voices may alienate the African, Asian, Hispanic, Native-American, or gay students; rightfully, they may refuse to be "minority representative for the day" and ask us to speak for them with compassion and knowledge.

Certainly, this array of responses and expectations, even as they challenge our authority in the classroom, will force us to examine our own personal and professional ideals and to participate in the reading and discussion of multicultural literature in ways which may be disturbingly revealing. We must, of course, continue to study the history, literature, and criticism of the groups our students represent. But knowledge will not be enough. Students will come to our classes with troubling questions, fears, and illusions about gender, race, and difference. Many will read literature seeking understanding that their experience does not provide, but often their responses to texts will be shaped in complex ways by their readings of our own racial/gendered bodies. These readings, as they reveal cultural, social, and historical definitions of race, gender, and class in this culture, will problematize our position in relation to the literature. As painful as this may be, I believe that we have no other choice but to allow space in the classroom for such encounters with our students and to confront, finally, the persistent distortions, lies, and mythologies surrounding race, gender, and other kinds of difference.

NOTE

I am indebted to John Heyda, Valerie Ross, Charles Spinosa, and Edgar Tidwell for their contributions to this essay.

WORKS CITED

Baldwin, James. *Go Tell It on the Mountain*. 1953. New York: Dell, 1985.

Ellison, Ralph. *Invisible Man*. 1952. New York: Vintage, 1990.

Fuss, Diana. *Essentially Speaking: Feminism, Nature, and Difference*. New York: Routledge, 1989.

hooks, bell. "Black Women Intellectuals." *Breaking Bread: Insurgent Black Intellectual Life*. bell hooks and Cornel West. Boston: South End P, 1991. 147–64.

Jones, Gayl. *Corregidora*. 1975. Boston: Beacon P, 1986.

Morrison, Toni. "Rootedness: The Ancestor as Foundation." *Black Women Writers: A Critical Evaluation*. Ed. Mari Evans. New York: Anchor P, 1984. 339–45.

Palmer, Stacy E. "In the Fishbowl: When Blacks Work at Predominantly White Colleges." *The Chronicle of Higher Education* 14 (Sept. 1983): 19–21.

Williams, Patricia. *The Alchemy of Race and Rights*. Cambridge: Harvard UP, 1991.

24

Rend(er)ing Women's Authority in the Writing Classroom

MICHELLE PAYNE

Michelle, is it okay if I don't come to conference tonight?"

The rest of Kyle's peers were making their way out of the classroom, talking about the fate of our team-taught writing course. As a class, we had just tried to "democratically" plan the rest of the course by negotiating four different proposals the students had spent the last few weeks creating in small groups. The process of negotiation this period had been quite chaotic, as most democratic processes are, especially when they are experiments. Amid this chaos, Kyle, an eighteen-year-old journalism student who had begun the course by asking whether other sections were taught more "traditionally" than it seemed mine would be, had spent his time in class this day trying to read a novel despite my presence next to him. When I suggested he put the book away, he grunted and remained silent the rest of the period, hanging his head. As he had made clear to me before, he had no interest in planning a writing course he didn't believe he could learn from anyway. Now he was asking my permission to skip a conference, a group conference, no less.

"Why do you want to skip conference?" I asked. My back was to the blackboard. Only a few inches taller than mine, Kyle's stocky, broad frame was poised to go out the door.

"I have too much other stuff to do."

"I think you need to decide whether you want to stay in this class or not." Motionless, he stared at me.

"What?"

"It seems to me you don't agree with what we're doing and don't believe you can learn from this situation, and there are plenty of other courses to choose from. I think it would be in your own best interest to take another section. I created this course to be designed by students so that everyone could find a space to get what they wanted out of it. You don't have to be here if it isn't meeting your needs." I took a deep breath, noticing from the corner of

From *Taking Stock: The Writing Process Movement in the 90s*. Eds. Lad Tobin and Thomas Newkirk. Portsmouth, NH: Boynton/Cook, 1994. 97–111.

my eye the three male students who were waiting for our conference. I knew, based on my previous conferences with Kyle, what was coming next—he would challenge me, try to intimidate me, get defensive, and try to deflect from my point.

"When did I say I didn't want to be in this class? I don't remember saying that. I don't understand what you're talking about." He faced me squarely now, fixing his unblinking, dark brown eyes as firmly on me as he had positioned his feet firmly on the ground.

"It's the sixth week of classes and you haven't done the dialogue journal, you haven't even begun your learning log, and your last paper, which didn't even fulfill the assignment, makes it loud and clear you don't intend to learn anything in this class. Your body language in class announces your apathy and resistance. Technically, I could fail you not only for failing to do the work but for being mentally absent in class a number of times and then not coming to conference tonight." Remember, I said to myself, stay focused on the point.

"What do you call being mentally absent? If you just mean not talking, then half the people in this course should fail. I worked in my group—just ask them. I put time in and they'll tell you I contributed a lot. How can you say I was mentally absent?"

"I'd say reading a book in class is being mentally absent."

"I thought what we were doing in class today was stupid."

Was it stupid? Did anyone else feel that way? Had we accomplished anything? Should I have said something when Karen said she didn't see why we should read in a writing course? When Amy said we should only write for ourselves?

"Why was it stupid?" I asked.

"Because it was like high school." In the writing he *had* turned in he had repeatedly criticized his "liberal" high school, particularly his English teachers who made students write about their "feelings."

"Well, there are twenty-seven other students in this class who think this is college. If you don't think so, then you need to find another section. You don't have to be here. And I don't have to teach apathetic students. I'm tired of teaching students who don't want to be here. The whole premise of this course is that students need to participate in their own learning. If that isn't what you want, then you need to find another section." After several weeks of Kyle's passive-aggressive behavior, I was beyond frustration.

"I was going to ask you if I could audit it."

"You need to talk to the director about that. But I suggest you change sections."

"I can't drop this class. I need it. And about that last assignment—I thought you told us that if we didn't like an assignment, we could write about whatever we wanted. . . ."

"I find that hard to believe. Why would I create a specific assignment and then say that?" Had I said that?

"I don't understand why you think I'm apathetic. I never said that. Plenty of other students seem apathetic to me. Why are you focusing on me?"

"Not turning your work in and reading a book in class seem like convincing evidence to me. And you just said you thought the class today was stupid." Was I only focusing on him? Was this only one incident that I was blowing out of proportion?

"But I haven't been like that all semester. . . ."

"Kyle, what do you think you need to do to pass this class?"

"Turn in my portfolio. Show up for class."

"No, Kyle, you need to learn something. You need to put some effort into learning something about your writing, and you need to not only do all the work, but participate in class."

"You can't fail me if I turn a portfolio in. If I show up for class and do all the work, you can't fail me. What about all those other people who are apathetic and not doing their work?" He folded his arms across his chest and stood with his feet wide apart.

I wanted to say, "Watch me." I hesitated. He was asking important questions, even if they were deflecting from our discussion of his own behavior. Did he know of other resistant students trying to deceive me? Could I really fail him for all these reasons? Would the director support me? Would he think I was out of line?

"The portfolio is only part of your grade. You haven't done all your work, and your attitude in class has given you two absences. If you have a problem with this, you can talk to the director of freshman English. For the moment, you have to decide whether you're going to stay for this conference."

"I guess I don't have any choice."

I re-create this incident in such detail because it represents for me not only one of the most difficult situations in being a writing teacher, but one of the most significant issues of being a female academic. Despite James Berlin's criticism of the belief that "[my] privately determined truths will correspond to the privately determined truths of all others" (1988, 486), I want to argue that what I have experienced as a female graduate teaching assistant in a Composition and Literature doctoral program may speak to more female academics and writing teachers than I (we) realize. But, maybe not. It may be, as I once heard a professor say of Richard Rodriguez, that I'm speaking out of my own neuroses. Or, as Kyle once said of Rodriguez and Nancy Sommers, I may be writing one of those "confessional narratives" that seems to have no particular audience except the self. Regardless, what I hope to do here is explore the ways in which my personal history, my gender, and my education in composition and critical theory have created for me a rather interesting, sometimes frustrating, always conflicting internal dialogue about my own authority (and authority in the abstract) that often renders me hesitant and distrustful, vulnerable and decentered. In doing so, I will harken back to those "prior texts" in composition and post-structuralist theory that seem most useful to my task, and I will also share a good deal of my personal history.

And that makes me nervous.

As much as I value the marriage of public and private discourse, academic and personal writing, I find it increasingly difficult to "allow" myself to "indulge" in such a marriage in my own writing. It's hard enough to write a piece where my voice "appropriates" the discourse of others and uses that discourse to further my own argument. To invite my own experience into the dialogue seems particularly . . . threatening. I've always feared that one of these days, someone would come along like Toto and inadvertently slide the curtain away to reveal that the Wizard of Oz wasn't quite who he made himself out to be. By sharing my personal experience, and certainly my feelings, I may be inviting someone to come along and determine I am unfit, unstable, too emotional to be in a position of power—that my presentation of efficiency and capability is exactly that, a presentation. A pretty common feeling for many of us, I know, but one that has become increasingly difficult for me to shake. The more frequently I'm in positions where I need to "authorize" myself, the more threatened I feel. I think this is what Peter Elbow means when he says "there is what I would call a certain rubber-gloved quality to the voice and register typical of most academic discourses—not just author-evacuated but showing a kind of reluctance to touch one's meanings with one's naked fingers" (145). Well, I'm about to touch my meanings with my naked fingers.

I rarely read about students like Kyle who reject process teaching, or about teachers like me who feel riddled with self-doubt. In our continuing reevaluation of the teaching of writing, we have created a pedagogy (at least one) that we believe, on some level, will reach every student and bring out his or her latent powers of language. In blaming current-traditional writing instruction for the hatred students felt toward writing and for their poor writing skills, we have almost defined ourselves as the "saviors" of students—and of learning in general. In bringing students to the center of our classrooms, we have taken them more seriously, granted them more respect and intelligence than had been acknowledged before, and this is good, this is important. But in my experience it has left little room for the growing anger I feel at apathetic students (anger that is created, in part, I think, by the belief that my success as a teacher depends on reaching everyone). It has left little room for exploring my experience as a writing teacher, specifically those moments when I'm not quite sure I'm making the best choices. In romanticizing our students, we may have inadvertently silenced a very important part of the teaching of writing—our experiences as complex individuals who don't always have everything figured out and who interact with, affect, and are affected by complex students. This is not to say we haven't written about "not having things figured out" or that all the various pedagogical theories in our field have an evangelistic tenor to them. It is to say we need to pay closer attention to our beliefs about our students and about ourselves as teachers. And we need to write about them. Although the situation with Kyle is not the worst case I've dealt with, it strikes me as painfully emblematic of the "heteroglossic" (in all its connotations) nature of my teaching experience.

I was angry, had been angry for a number of days, that Kyle could sit so calmly in class and make comments pointing out the absurdity in what I was saying or trying to get the class to do and that he could sit in conference with me, late at night with no one else around, and refuse to answer questions like

"What are you trying to do in this paper? What ideas do you have for revision?" only to get defensive when I would, at his request for more directive comments, share my various responses and ideas for his paper. I was simply tired of having at least one male student—but usually more—who had no problem telling me, often in writing that I didn't know what I was doing, that he didn't like the course or what I was asking him to do, and that he didn't feel like he was learning anything. "I'm paying for this course. I came here to learn from *your* knowledge—how can I possibly create a course to teach me something I don't know yet?"

Although his behavior was unacceptable to me and the philosophy of the course, I could see his point. I had sat in on the various groups of students as they talked about the goals of a college writing course, their past experiences, what they thought the roles of teachers and students should be in creating an "exceptional" learning experience. Prior to this group work, they had individually been writing in response to a sequence of assignments, reading (Paulo Freire and Richard Rodriguez), and researching about learning and education under my own guidance. I had developed the questions I thought they needed to consider—I wanted their plans to be informed decisions to the extent they could be. I had anticipated an outbreak of creativity and excitement. What I saw was excitement that gradually gave way under the pressure of time, the struggles of negotiating and accommodating so many personalities and ideas, and what I sensed was an increasing fear that they wouldn't really learn much in this course. What I realized as I sat in on their planning sessions was that I had a lot more to offer these students than I realized—ways of creating the experiences they wanted and helping them to learn something about writing from those experiences. I also realized that in planning this course, they were coming in with so many beliefs about writing that I didn't agree with (but that didn't surprise me), that I didn't think were productive, that I didn't want them to walk away with. This grand experiment was beginning to look too risky. I was experiencing the same self-doubts I always do when I teach: Was this the right thing to do? Am I wasting their time? Have I created a too-difficult task? A too-easy one? Will they give up, decide they can't learn from this class, and turn into passive, "good students" who humor the teacher just to get through the course? Should I, as Bartholomae, Bizzell, Delpit, and others say, be teaching them what they would need to know about writing in the university instead of asking them to participate in determining what they might need or want to know and do?

I would call this an identity crisis. In asking my students to design their own course, I was opening myself up as a teacher for criticism and doubt, inviting them into a relationship with me that was more co-equal than many of them had experienced with teachers before, and also inviting them into my own personal and professional struggle with who I am as a writing teacher. Together, we were asking: What is a teacher? What does she or he do? Why? What is her or his relationship to students and their relationship to her or him? From the perspective of many "libertarian pedagogies," as well as many process, student-centered pedagogies, this situation is ideal—students and teachers are learning from each other, both learning within a community of people reflecting on their world and their place in that world. I have certainly embraced these values or I wouldn't have created such a class. But from the perspective of a woman who was socialized to have what post-structuralists call a "split subjectivity," who already commands from most students less authority and power than a man, yet who has embraced pedagogies and post-structuralist theories that decenter authority and who also sees the value of "apprenticing" students into the academy, asking students to question my authority was overwhelming at best, debilitating at worst.

In exploring this "identity crisis" and how I see my conversation with Kyle as emblematic of it, it would be nice if I could create a palimpsest, a multi-voiced text whose columns speak back and forth to each other as they seem to in my head. Unfortunately, that would be too difficult to read and to produce on paper, so I'll have to settle for a linear text that tries as best it can to weave these multiple voices in and out in a productive tension.

Personal History as Text

As many social constructionist and post-structuralist theorists have argued, an individual is more than a unitary, coherent self—she or he is "constructed" of all the prior texts and prior discourses she or he has engaged with. I have very little difficulty agreeing with this; my sense of self has always seemed fragmented, fluid, and dialogic. Because of my personal history, I have been "constructed" around a certain view of myself that many post-structuralists might find . . . inviting. In many ways I am a series of texts that all seem to "deconstruct" themselves regularly. In spite of all my efforts to the contrary, my attempts at authorship—in all the connotations of that word—usually end up dismantling themselves. In other words, post-structuralist theory has merely given me language with which to discuss processes I have been experiencing for years now. Ironically, this makes critical theory both comforting—I have a language for my experience—and threatening. It just intensifies the internal conflict and self-doubt that seem crippling in situations with students like Kyle.

One of the most powerful discourses that has influenced my identity as a writing teacher—and that is often ignored in theoretical and pedagogical discussions—has been my experience as a woman from an emotionally abusive childhood home. In sharing this I am quite conscious of the myriad reactions I might receive. Not only am I making myself vulnerable, but I'm "telling on" my family and breaking the cardinal rule of most academic work—keep your distance, be objective and theoretical. Many, though not all, of us seem to value students writing about their family life and care about our students not just as writers but as people, yet we seem reluctant to share publicly the various ways our own private lives have influenced us as scholars and teachers. We are quite willing to turn a psychoanalytic eye on "literature" and use psychotherapeutic methods in the writing classroom, but do we ever think about ourselves in these terms? Do we ever consider the impact our theoretical and pedagogical ideas might have on those of us who didn't have "normative" childhoods? We are only beginning to understand how our students' family experiences may influence their learning and behavior in our classes, and it seems equally important that we begin to understand what may be influencing us. Maybe these are issues that can only be worked out in a therapist's office. Then again, maybe these are issues that can't wait for the therapist's office.

We have certainly learned a great deal about what it means to be female in this culture, particularly when it comes to women's social and intellectual experiences. My own experiences might sound familiar to many. Very early in life I was convinced that I was as gullible, naive, irrational, and emotional as my father and younger brother said. Whenever I had an opinion about something, they would argue with me, sometimes through intimidation, always to the point of me getting "emotional." In their bastardized version of logic, my personal experience was always skewed and my responses were emotional over-reactions to their simple, clear, rational points of view. Even as an undergraduate, when I came home one weekend and shared with my father, a dentist, what I had learned male doctors had done to marginalize and criminalize midwives and to radically change the experience and function of childbirth for women, he became increasingly angry. He couldn't believe, he said, that I could be so gullible and uncritical, believing everything I read or heard from a teacher. How could I expect to function in this world believing everything I read? I tried to explain what I had read, recapitulating the argument as best I could given that I was quickly losing confidence in my ability to remember anything. My father pointed out everything I didn't know about this issue, including the incredible benefits of modern medicine, reinforcing my belief that I was, as he had always said, merely a bookworm who knew nothing more than what I read and couldn't function outside the limits of the university.

My father once told me that my brother, on the other hand, had natural talent and "understood" things, even though his grades didn't reflect it. I had gotten through school and done well, from my father's perspective, by the sheer force of my desire to please, not by any intellectual prowess on my part. This reinforced my already pervasive belief that I was "faking it" and would one day be discovered as a fraud. This inability to trust myself was reinforced by my father's reaction to our sibling fights. My brother would try to humiliate me verbally and, no matter what we were arguing about, I was always stupid and wrong, and certainly too emotional. Even though I felt my brother was being a jerk, my father often told me it was my fault, and this compounded my sense that I was easily deluded. Although my father and brother now realize the debilitating impact all this had on me, it has seemed from the time I was in second grade, when my father attributed the sexual abuse I had suffered from his cousin to my over-active imagination, that my sense of self has been constructed around a belief that I am usually and easily deluded.

At least three of the arguments that have historically been used to dismiss women's experiences are (1) she's deluded, irrational, "mad"; (2) she's just angry and emotional—it will pass; and (3) she created the situation herself.

Interestingly, Kyle, the student I began this piece with, used all of these arguments, besides physical intimidation, to undermine my authority at various points in the semester. The conversation with Kyle I have re-created evoked memories of my father and brother, and I struggled not to fall back into my role of "victim" and allow him to convince me that I was at fault, that I was simply angry and picking on him, or that I was under an "illusion" about his behavior and feelings and couldn't see what was going on around me with the other students. A week after our first conversation, Kyle brought the subject up again after class, saying he didn't understand why I was so "down" on him. "You're just upset that I don't agree with your teaching philosophy, that's all," he said. Through a series of verbal attacks, reminiscent of my brother's, he essentially told me I was making this all up, I was creating a double standard because I didn't like him, my anger was not justified, I didn't know how to teach, I had no power over him. Later, when Kyle and I were discussing this with the director, I said, "Kyle, one of the central issues here is that you don't respect me. You don't believe that I have anything to offer you." He nodded his head.

COMPOSITION THEORY AS TEXT

When a female teacher walks into a first-year writing class, she inevitably evokes responses from students a male teacher most likely does not. Students come in with so many assumptions about teachers, authority figures, and women as teachers and authority figures that how a teacher interacts with students becomes incredibly important. Most process, student-centered pedagogies define the teacher's primary role as facilitator, the one who creates an "enabling environment" where students can experience the process of discovery, the "motivating force of revision." The teacher is a questioner who sits back and lets the student tell her where the draft is leading him, modeling for him the questions he needs to ask himself in order for the teacher to be needed no longer. A writer herself, the teacher is patient and listening, responding to where each student is coming from.

In this model, the teacher is nurturing, non-directive, non-content oriented. Her authority derives from her experience as a writer, but more importantly from her partnership with the students. In order for the best learning to take place, the hierarchy of power must be broken down so teachers and students learn from each other and share authority (though sometimes we speak of "transferring" the authority and power to students). For theorists like Paulo Freire, the classroom becomes democratic and communal; for someone like Donald Murray, the institutionally endowed power of the teacher is evident primarily in the pressure to write daily, participate in workshops, and come to conferences. For many teachers—particularly, I imagine, for women—decentering the teacher's authority feels comfortable, manageable. If, as Carol Gilligan (1982) says, women are attuned to relationships and try to avoid threats to those relationships, a co-equal, non-authoritarian, non-confrontational writing classroom seems ideal.

That was certainly my response when I began studying composition my senior year in college. I was preparing to teach the following year as a master's student and I was terrified I wouldn't know what I was doing. "What right do I have to be in front of the classroom?" I asked my professor, Mary Fuller. "I'm only four years older than my students. I know so little about writing. . . ." Mary assured me, as did the writings of Murray, Elbow, Emig, and Knoblauch and Brannon, that my experience as a writer was all I needed to qualify me as a writing teacher. I didn't have to lecture, I didn't have to demonstrate my knowledge to my students in careful commenting on their texts. I was comforted. After all, I did the non-directive thing well. Having been my brothers' caretaker from the time I was ten, I was nurturing, responsible, and adept at creating non-threatening environments. I had been responsible for everyone's feelings and fearful of their anger and displeasure, so I became a chameleon, trying to prevent "unpleasant" situations by understanding everyone's point of view and reading everyone's mind. The last thing I wanted to do was put myself into a position of responsibility that carried overt power and authority—power and authority meant humiliation and silencing for me. I felt I would either stand before my students to be revealed as a fraud, or I would silence them and create hostility.

It soon became evident, however, that decentering my authority was not creating the situations I read about in the journals. My students were not motivated by their writing—they took advantage of my openness and unwillingness to create friction by doing as little work as possible. I had been following my interpretation of the Murray-method of response, and when a student said, "Nowhere—I like this draft just fine," to my question, "Where is this draft leading you?" I didn't know what to say. I knew the draft wasn't "good enough," but then again, the students were the ones determining what was good, what felt right, not me. I was there primarily to facilitate their natural impulse to write and give them the freedom to write about whatever they wanted so they could shake off the shackles of high school writing teachers. (In effect, it seems, I was exchanging my power and authority for their comfort and affection.) They were supposed to be learning to enjoy writing and learning again. My class was supposed to be the one they would never forget. Instead, they seemed to sit back and write with the same attitude they did in high school—I'm not learning anything, but I have to do this anyway.

Gradually, I changed my style. I was starting to read people like David Bartholomae and Joseph Harris, and their arguments about empowering students with academic discourse made sense. As a graduate student I was certainly aware that I had to learn academic conventions and personas—I was an apprentice who knew that personal-experience papers wouldn't get past the professor's desk. Plus, I was discovering through a rhetoric class that if I had known anything about logic and argumentation, I would have known how to defend myself against my brother and father's mal-adaptations of it. I'd always known language was empowering, and now I was learning *how* it was empowering. Why not share that with students?

I worked my way into creating sequences of assignments around a single topic that asked students to "theorize" from their experiences what it meant to, say, conform in our society, or to play roles, or to be a female. I structured the class with assignments that still asked them to write personal-experience papers and that eventually led to open topics, and I maintained the same nurturing, flexible, non-authoritarian stance I had assumed in my less-structured classes. I still talked about the writing process and writing to discover. The only thing different was that I was handing out general assignments. The students by and large, after the first four weeks, reacted with open frustration. Instead of male students trying to flirt with me and get out of doing any work, some of them began to respond hostilely in their writing. ("This is bullshit." "I can't believe you picked this story. It's stupid." "I don't care about this.") They began to act out in class—falling asleep, not working in their groups, and goofing off. Whether their behavior can be attributed to the way I asserted my "control" over their writing or to what I now see as a general trend in this kind of behavior, I'm not sure. Whatever the case, their behavior complicated my already conflicted internal dialogue about my role in the writing classroom and the extent and nature of my "control" and "authority."

After a series of unusually passive and quiet students (with noticeable exceptions) who I feared had not learned much from my course, I was about ready to give up on teaching. I realize now that how my classes responded to my teaching—their resistance and apathy—translated for me into failure. The students could see that I had no real power, just as my brothers had seen it. Plus, no matter what I taught, I seemed condemned to fail: the dialogue in the field about what and how we should be teaching corresponded well with my personal conflicts and experiences with the emotional and the "rational," what had been marginalized for me and that which marginalized it.

In other words, I knew firsthand that Western male (academic) discourse was empowering: I had come to believe such discourse was what I needed. But I also knew it was threatening, used to disempower, and I wanted to value my feelings and personal experiences, not continue to marginalize them as my father and brother (and education) had done. So what should I teach? Should I ask the women to learn a new discourse that for many is threatening? Should I encourage them to write from their strengths in personal, self-reflective pieces? Should I encourage the men to learn new ways of thinking about themselves and relationships or reinforce the discourse that seems based on a devaluation of such personal discourse?

The way academic discourse has been structured seems to demand that this is an either/or choice. Bartholomae's metaphors of mastery and appropriation for acquiring academic discourse seem anathema to what has traditionally been associated with women's values and experiences. At the same time, as Lisa Delpit (1988) has argued, we can't empower disempowered students by refusing to teach them the power language. Ironically, this "public" discussion of these issues is incredibly personal for me. I cannot separate them, especially now that I have language to talk about their differences. In this sense, such a dialectic is productive, stimulating. But as I said before, when I walk into the writing classroom so well versed in this debate, knowing that some students value non-directive teaching and others value explicit teaching, I feel like double-exposed film.

I want to add one more element to this discussion before I move on to the post-structuralist critique of these dichotomies. I would argue that the choices set up by the process-model/academic discourse debate create a no-win situation for a female teacher. If she chooses the non-directive approach and works to share authority, it might reinforce the men's devaluation of her as an authority figure (and invite them to turn that power differential in their favor, as Kyle tried to) inappropriate for women (even though the women might feel comfortable with a co-equal teaching situation). If the teacher decides to teach academic discourse (which seems to demand more direction), she might create resistance in the men at a "woman" holding power over them and resentment in the women for disturbing the relationships with them and with the men (especially in a period like now when women reject anything that will label them—or any other woman—"feminist" or "bitch").[1]

A female teacher's authority, though endowed by a degree and the university, is tenuous no matter which pedagogy she embraces. And if teaching is a matter of persuasion in the classical rhetorical sense, then women may have a more difficult time being taken seriously by their students when the very fact of their gender undermines their ethos. As much as I wish this weren't the case, my power and authority—my effectiveness as a teacher—is dependent on how much power and authority my students grant me (in addition to the support the administration grants me). When they can't even agree on what constitutes "legitimate" authority, and I'm still torn myself, what do I do on Monday morning?

POST-STRUCTURALIST THEORY AS TEXT

Deconstructive critics, as I understand their method, would consider the previous paragraphs a deconstructive moment. I tried to demonstrate that our traditional definitions of "authority"—a teacher's authority—can be "decentered" when we begin to take into consideration what happens when the marginalized term (women have not traditionally been considered authority figures) is brought into the system. Authority is not transcendent or transmissible. It is arbitrary and contingent, definable only in relation to its opposite.

For a number of people, post-structuralist theory seems jargony, elitist, unnecessarily abstract, and sometimes nihilistic. I have certainly experienced it as all these things. But as I said earlier, I have also experienced post-structuralism as something that describes my experience of myself and my world. Very few things have remained stable for me, and structure and power have always seemed arbitrary and conflictual. What people said was not necessarily what they meant, so signifiers and signifieds only rarely seemed to line up. To this day, with the help of post-structuralist theory, I can still argue myself into and out of any situation or feeling, as well as into utter hopelessness. I have welcomed difference and criticized power relations, arguing for multiplicity and tolerance.

But when I am in charge of a classroom of students, when I carry some form of indoctrination, how does multiplicity and tolerance work? I have relatively specific goals (which are constantly in flux) and I try to direct the classroom so that students can learn something, but what if my goals are in conflict with a student's (like Kyle's)? What happens when I ask students to critically consider the role of teacher and student and redesign their course to meet what they determine their needs are? Where do my needs and what I think is important fit in? Does the class have to be either the students' or the teacher's? Do I have to "give up" power for them to become empowered? What if they decide I don't know what I'm doing as a result of the questioning I have asked them to do?

If we are arguing in literary theory that we need to redefine the canon to reflect multiple views, and that this means we must consider the literary piece within its own culture and its culture's values, does this also mean we must consider each student (and his or her paper) within his or her own culture, regardless of how it conflicts with our own? I'm not arguing here for a return to a universal standard or the dominance of one discourse community over another. I'm primarily wondering how I can possibly *not* marginalize someone in the classroom, especially in a situation where we are required to evaluate students' work. Should I, for example, sit down with Kyle and try to "talk this through" by sharing what I sense is going on, as one of my colleagues suggested? When it seems that Kyle operates within a community where authority figures are direct about their requests and their information, would that work for me, trying to do what Delpit says is a white, middle-class method of making my power inexplicit through a series of questions that imply commands (289)? As a feminist, should I be disturbed or enraged (which I am at times) that I have to put up with more from male students like Kyle than my male colleagues do? In my efforts to be tolerant and egalitarian, do I have to value male values that I see as ultimately hurtful?

I realize that critical theorists don't see their value system leading inevitably to relativism and "anything goes"—they value the dialectic, the discussion that occurs when conflicting paradigms engage each other. Ideas and people are ultimately changed in the bargain. But for someone like me, whose sense of personal power was eroded from childhood on, and who knows that power does exist and is held by certain people, being a deconstructive text is becoming more and more debilitating. Theoretically, we are not unitary individuals with one "self" we need to find in order to be whole. We are multiple selves that have been constructed over time from the various "texts" we have encountered. I have organized this chapter based on that premise. But right now, I would really like to have a unitary self, a set of values that I can live by, even though I know they are not absolute and probably not common. I would like to be comfortable walking into class with a plan I will stick by no matter how many students grumble. I'd like to know my students *are* learning something from my class. I would like to be able to comfortably tell someone like Kyle that he cannot stay in my class and to know that I won't get sued by his parents for discrimination or fired for not being able to "handle" discipline problems—and that I won't get tossed out of the profession for having the "wrong"' attitude toward students.

NOTES

   I want to thank two people who have been significant to the development of this article: Tom Newkirk, who urged me to get this out of my computer and into the hands of other readers, and my husband and colleague, Steve Barrett, whose support, ideas, and many conversations helped me to see my way through the web of conflicting feelings and ideas that had begun to undermine my teaching and my sense of self. He encouraged me to write my way through a difficult situation, and I did. Thank you.
   1. See especially Susan Jarrett's "Feminism and Composition: A Case for Conflict" in Harkin and Schilb's *Contending with Words*, 105–23.

WORKS CITED

Bartholomae, David. "Inventing the University." *Journal of Basic Writing* 5 (Spring 1988): 109–28.

Berlin, James. "Rhetoric and Ideology in the Writing Class." *College English* 50 (September 1988): 477–94.

Bizzell, Patricia. "Cognition, Convention, and Certainty: What We Need to Know About Writing." *Pre/Text* 3 (1982): 213–44.

Delpit, Lisa D. "The Silenced Dialogue: Power and Pedagogy in Educating Other People's Children." *Harvard Educational Review* 58 (August 1988): 280–98.

Donahue, Patricia, and Ellen Quandahl. *Reclaiming Pedagogy: The Rhetoric of the Classroom.* Carbondale: Southern Illinois University Press, 1989.

Elbow, Peter. "Reflections on Academic Discourse: How It Relates to Freshmen and Colleagues." *College English* 53 (February 1991): 135–55.

Emig, Janet. *The Composing Processes of Twelfth Graders.* NCTE Research Report No. 13. Urbana, IL: NCTE, 1971.

Friere, Paulo. 1970. *The Pedagogy of the Oppressed.* New York: Herder and Herder.

Gilligan, Carol. *In a Different Voice: Psychological Theory and Women's Development.* Cambridge: Harvard University Press, 1982.

Harkin, Patricia, and John Schilb. *Contending with Words: Composition and Rhetoric in a Postmodern Age.* New York: MLA, 1991.

Harris, Joseph. "The Idea of Community in the Study of Writing." *College Composition and Communication* 40 (1989): 111–22.

Knoblauch, C. H., and Lil Brannon. *Rhetorical Traditions and the Teaching of Writing.* Upper Montclair, NJ: Boynton/Cook, 1984.

Murray, Donald. *Learning by Teaching.* Portsmouth, NH: Boynton/Cook, 1992.

Rodriguez, Richard. "The Achievement of Desire." *Hunger of Memory.* New York: Bantam, 1982.

Summers, Nancy. "Revision Strategies of Student Writers and Experienced Adult Writers." *College Composition and Communication* 31 (December 1980): 378–88.

25 Coming Out in the Classroom: A Return to the Hard Place

MARY ELLIOTT

The secret contains a tension that is dissolved in the moment of its revelation. . . . It is surrounded by the possibility and temptation of betrayal; and the external danger of being discovered is interwoven with the internal danger, which is like the fascination of an abyss, of giving oneself away.

—GEORG SIMMEL

The fascination with the "secret" of lesbian and gay identity and with the abyss a gay or lesbian teacher crosses to come out in the classroom should have spent itself by now. More than a quarter-century after Stonewall, what was once transgressive should have lost its pedagogical shock value and assumed its place alongside other milestones of America's troubled social history. Indeed, testimonials to the positive purposes and effects of coming out appear more and more often in journals such as *Radical Teacher* and *Feminist Teacher*, at conferences, in collections of essays on feminist pedagogy, and in the avalanche of recent work on gay and lesbian studies. Most recent work on coming out assumes a political position that privileges disclosure over non-disclosure and self-naming over a pretense to "neutrality," seeing these as strategies that resist conservative institutional pressures to preserve the silence and invisibility enshrouding gay and lesbian identities.

No doubt, a pedagogy of disclosure and visibility can challenge tautological claims that historical social absence justifies and explains further social absence. One of my straight colleagues informed me last year, for example, that "gay issues" should not be taught in undergraduate composition classrooms because these issues have not yet received the decades of media attention (and thus, I inferred, the historical legitimacy) that issues of racism and sexism have received. This determination somehow to "miss" the media coverage of gays in the military (dating at least from the mid-1970s *Time* cover story on Leonard Matlovich), the massive coverage of AIDS history for over a decade, and recent feature articles in a range of mainstream periodicals on the

From *College English* 58 (1996): 693–708.

cultures and civil rights issues of gays and lesbians, as well as regular inclusion of gay and lesbian issues and characters on television talk shows, sitcoms, and dramas over the past five years, displays an intractability that, however resolute, is not uncommon. What concern me, though, are not the resistances of political and cultural conservatives—these are old and familiar obstacles—but our own resistances as gays and lesbians to acknowledging the emotional and physical tolls of public self-disclosure that most coming-out narratives reveal, whether they appear in mass media or in anthologies of essays concerned with gay, lesbian, or feminist pedagogy.

What the narratives elide, or mention only briefly and then recoil from (as an issue and experience), is the act of giving away the secret, that terrifying crossing of the abyss. One after another, these narratives present a minute glimpse of the dread, panic, confusion, and uncertainty of the actual moment of disclosure and then, as if mimetically reproducing the performance of the coming-out act itself as an uncomfortable (always) or even shameful (sometimes) but necessary ordeal, move on as quickly as possible and without comment to lengthy pedagogical, ethical, and sociological defenses of the coming-out process. Often, the defenses are buttressed with charts, graphs, interpretations, and assessments of positive student response surveys.

Such work is absolutely necessary to the eventual professional legitimizing of gay and lesbian issues, literature, students, and teachers. But the labor of the body and the emotions—which always begins the real content of theory, analysis, and persuasion in these narratives—is abandoned at a price. Perhaps we feel that our political or personal development should have delivered us beyond "the hard place"—the pounding hearts, shaking voices, sleepless nights, and hours of strategizing with friends. "If it's this hard to come out," we chastise ourselves, "maybe I'm not ready." Often, we compare our experiences with those of our friends or colleagues, for whom coming out seems to have been wholly unproblematic. Indeed, there may be many who have come to regard coming out as a simple act of personal, political, or pedagogical housekeeping, one that produces little or no physiological stress. Others, beneficiaries of feminist, postmodern, and queer theories in and out of university classrooms of the 1980s and '90s, may regard the issue itself with non-comprehension or even with contempt that it remains an issue at all.

But the issue persists *as* an issue within particular contexts. My primary point of reference throughout this essay, the context within which coming out seemed most dangerous, is an undergraduate composition course in critical writing that is required of most students at my Midwest university to satisfy the English proficiency requirement for graduation. The course itself has been scrutinized by the university in response to accusations of a "liberal agenda" by a conservative local press and community. Would it be easier if the course were taught in Berkeley or San Francisco or New York City? Emphatically, it would, although censorship of gay and lesbian materials in libraries and schools occurs in these areas as well, and the recent dismantling of affirmative action policies by the Regents of the University of California should temper glib assumptions about "tolerant" regions and administrations. Does it matter whether the course is required or elective? Yes, perhaps even more emphatically, since the charges of political "indoctrination" leveled at an out lesbian or gay instructor could be more damaging when the course is a high-stakes graduation hurdle than when it is an elective course in lesbian literature, gay and lesbian studies, American novels, or literary representations of aging. I have taught all of these courses during my doctoral work in cultural studies at my university, but the "hard place" I refer to in this essay is the composition classroom, a pedagogical arena where I—and, by extension, my very supportive department—am most vulnerable to attack.

As early as the 1974 "Homosexual Imagination" issue of *College English,* the politics of visibility was interpreted as a mandate for coming out. Guest editors Louie Crew and Rictor Norton stated then that "Coming out is not strictly a matter of conscience: it is an academic responsibility" (288). The 1984 "Gay and Lesbian Studies" issue of *Radical Teacher* reflected a continuing concern with the problems and politics of coming out. Ten years later, however, editors Henry Abelove, Richard Ohmann, and Claire Potter can write in the introduction of the 1994 "Lesbian/Gay/Queer Studies" issue of *Radical Teacher* that coming out is no longer a pressing subject for their contributors. The 1994 editors speculate that, while "apparently the politics of such decisions are less on the agenda for public discussion now than ten years ago," it is also true that "whether or when to be out is still, of course, a decision loaded with consequences for lesbian and gay teachers" (2). This nicely embodies the ambivalence of the discourse on coming out, a discourse that would like to move beyond the issue but continues to acknowledge its recurrent trauma.

Very few writers provide practical suggestions for methods of coming out (exceptions are Mittler and Blumenthal; Adams and Emery). Yet at a recent CCCC all-day workshop for lesbian and gay teachers, I observed that such suggestions seemed to engage most of the participants, even those who had taught for many years. Richard Mohr's 1992 touchstone discussion in *Gay Ideas: Outing and Other Controversies* has inspired a vigorous and complex debate both in support of his claim that outing and being out may not violate individual privacy (Chekola) and in opposition to it (Mayo and Gunderson; Barbone and Rice).

Often as these discussions appear in academic anthologies and as editorials in lesbian and gay publications, however, the political consequences they analyze generally remain abstract, and I suspect that for many coming out remains an unfashionable but very real dilemma. When, for example, I return to friends or colleagues who initially presented themselves as fearlessly out in their own classrooms, they often present instead another, less cavalier, more angst-filled version of the story—one whose emotional terrors more closely resemble my own. For many, if not most of us, it seems that although we are amply supplied with assumptions about what the coming-out experience should be like, we do not have a vocabulary for the emotional and corporeal experience itself. We risk humiliation if we come out awkwardly or fearfully and risk feelings of personal failure if we cannot quite push ourselves over the abyss. We berate ourselves further with the conviction that if we truly had our political and personal houses in order, this trauma would not be happening to us.

But any student of phobias understands that it is the undifferentiated character of the unknown that produces the kind of shaking, trembling, irrational response suffered by many gays or lesbians in the coming-out moment: if we cannot see the source of our fear or measure the effects our actions will have, then the power of these unknown causes and consequences can assume unlimited proportions. As Sandra Bartky has suggested of women's shame, for example, the power of shame's "corrosive character" and the "peculiar helplessness" it produces inheres "in the very failure of these feelings to attain to the status of belief" (95). Although such fear responses are classically and intractably phobic and therefore beyond the reach of reasoned control, it would be facile to suggest that they may be dismissed as "internalized homophobia." What internalized homophobia supplies us with is the kind of "double consciousness" articulated by W. E. B. DuBois as the internalization of white racism in black consciousness: "It is a peculiar sensation, this double consciousness, this sense of always looking at one's self through the eyes of others, of measuring one's soul by the tape of a world that looks on in amused contempt and pity" (3). Many of us cannot avoid seeing ourselves as we have been taught to imagine that others see us. Often, this consciousness, because it was learned prior to or contemporaneously with our own sexual formations, accompanies us as an internalized counter-voice to our self-constructed voices of positive identity and subjectivity. But analyses of double consciousness are ultimately not very helpful. First, the accusation of internalized homophobia is self-blaming; second, internalized homophobia is so undifferentiated as a symptom that it provides no clarification of our own feelings and no guidelines that could assist us in overcoming its alleged effects.

Other vocabularies for the subjective experience of coming out might well be more clarifying and insightful. The discourses of fear, shame, secrecy, lying, and self-disclosure, well established within the conversations of ethics, psychology, and popular culture, can be applied to the experiences of abject terror, self-doubt, and self-recrimination that these narratives disclose (and then foreclose). I suspect that resistance to the possibilities inherent in these vocabularies resides, again, in the sense that we have advanced beyond such "negative" terms as "fear," "shame," and "secrecy." I also suspect that what motivates us to avoid such loaded and negative terms is our conviction that we are too advanced personally, socially, or politically to return to language that might re-pathologize us. But a closer look might very well help us to differentiate the nameless presences in the abyss we wish to cross and, if not eliminate them altogether, at least re-frame them so that responses that first appear phobic or shameful can be more openly understood and managed.

> People are ashamed of being ashamed. . . . So we don't talk about it, we don't express it, and we don't acknowledge it. We say we're uncomfortable, or "It was an awkward moment" — these are code words for shame. (Karen 49)

Shame, it might finally be said, transformational shame, is *performance*. I mean theatrical performance. (Sedgwick, "Queer Performativity" 5)

Most coming-out narratives begin with moments in which, regardless of the content or context of the coming-out moment, the physiological difficulty of crossing the abyss typically leaves the narrator shaken, if not overwhelmed altogether. Such moments, each registering the corporeal effects of coming out, have been recorded in a number of anthologies of pedagogical theory (Jennings; Kissen; Parmeter; Segrest; Stein; Wright). Judith McDaniel writes in 1979:

> I announced that *Rubyfruit Jungle* was due on Monday. I told them about the picaresque novel and Fielding and socially unacceptable or shocking behavior. And then I stopped. I couldn't say the word "lesbian" in my own classroom. I spent that weekend in a panic. How the hell was I going to teach this book? What could I say about it? Was my own sexual preference relevant to teaching this novel? (131)

A later narrative, published in 1988, registers the costs of brazening out an encounter with a confrontational student:

> "Hey Ms. Stein, what do you call a girl homosexual?" The room is suddenly silent. Taking a deep breath, I try to respond naturally. "The word is lesbian." She persists, asking how to spell it. "Lesbian is spelled LESBIAN," I say evenly, attempting not to blush or avoid eye contact. (Stein 4)

Recently, Bob, the sole male student in a small class of nine students, asked me at the final meeting of my American Novels class what I would be teaching next semester, adding that he would be interested in taking another class with me. "Lesbian Literature," I replied. Although I had anticipated the question for some time, it produced a very long moment in which I felt absolutely alone. Bob and I and some of the others were able to smile at each other. It was, after all, a recognizably humorous moment. But my warmest, most open, and articulate student looked shattered and was unable to resume any sort of eye contact for many minutes. When she did speak again, it was to mention for the first time the boyfriend that she was "thinking of hooking up with."

But focusing on the negative effects of coming out is problematic within any forum, and some gay and lesbian educators focus less on the experience and its affective consequences than on the importance that coming out has for establishing an openly gay faculty presence and forwarding gay curricular issues (Malinowitz, *Textual Orientations;* Harbeck; Khayatt). In order to solicit a range of responses on these issues, my colleague Thomas Piontek and I led a roundtable discussion entitled "Out of the Closet and into the Classroom— NOT!" at a conference on politics and ethics held on our campus. We rehearsed, in the form of a mock debate, some arguments in favor of coming out: (a) passing and secrecy are destructive to self-acceptance and political change; (b) any secret, if intuited by the students as a secret, becomes a "dirty" secret, encouraging sub rosa speculation and derision; (c) coming out challenges dominant thinking and institutional heterosexism; (d) coming out provides a model and personal contact for gay, lesbian, and heterosexual students alike, facilitating the unlearning of prejudice.

We also listed reasons for not coming out. First, the positional authority of an out teacher may inhibit or silence student candor, driving hostility underground. Some writers, though they seem to be in the minority, caution against coming out to entire classes (though not to individual students) because of the silencing effect it might have on heterosexual students (Luboff). David Bergman states, "I prefer to think I'm in the classroom to teach a course, not to involve the students in my psychodramas." Bergman postpones disclosure of the sexuality of the gay authors his class studies to avoid "pigeonholing" and "dismissal" or the danger that his students will read the work exclusively "through the lens of the author's sexuality" (5). As Sissela Bok suggests, "institutional practices of self-revelation may bring solace, alleviation of guilt, group acceptance, personal growth, even self-transcendence, but they are also unequaled means for imposing orthodoxy of every kind" (*Secrets* 88). In the forum, however, we found it difficult to see the silencing of prejudice as harmful; we questioned whether the airing in the classroom of homophobic or sexist or racist views could ever be construed as positive and concluded that it could not.

Second, the neutral space of the classroom would be compromised by coming out. We challenged this assertion, as well, by contending that the classroom is never a "neutral" space. Neutrality, we agreed, is a universal cultural default setting which is almost always presumed to be heterosexual and white; it is not available to those who cannot "pass" as either or both.

Third, the progressive curriculum of any composition program could be threatened by community objections to a teacher, especially an out lesbian or gay teacher, using materials that focus on lesbian and gay culture and issues. As Evelyn Beck has expressed it, a teacher must mediate between the tension of "caring for the self (by being out) and protecting the program (by remaining somewhat closeted)" ("Out" 233). Thus, lesbians and gays may find themselves in the position of protecting the very institutions that exclude them, and their students, from full participation (although institutional invisibility cannot benefit or "protect" anyone). Undergirding this tension, obviously, is what Harriet Malinowitz describes as a fear that students will "reread us within the cultural fiction of demonization that Simon Watney has described" ("Transforming" 2). In "School's Out," Watney describes the way in which the identity of the homosexual in Britain and America between the 1960s and 1990s has been figured as less than human, a force of corruption that "promotes" homosexuality to youths by representing it as equivalent to heterosexuality. Thus, homosexuals pose a threat that can be countered only by the imposition of more restrictive laws and legislation.

We addressed other concerns as well over the course of the forum: our fears of being disliked, rejected, physically harmed, or even killed by our students; losing our authority; being accused of playing partisan politics with students' lives; losing our guise of impartiality; not being protected as a "diverse" or "cultural" class within our university (and therefore vulnerable to the ignorance or malice of any institutional authorities who might wish to harm or eliminate us); and our shame over our own vulnerability.

The performance of indeterminacy in the classroom as an alternative to coming out, and the problems such an alternative raises, became the focus of discussion here. Strategies for undermining and destabilizing the various "regulatory systems" targeted by the audience can be useful, though also deeply problematic, as I will discuss later. Clothing can provide playful ways of deconstructing gender stereotypes by converting coming out into a performance act (by straight, gay, lesbian, bisexual teachers alike), layered *on* the body instead of a speech act originating *from* the body; a male teacher wearing a T-shirt stating, "I'm not a lesbian" or a female teacher wearing one that reads, "I'm not gay but my boyfriend is" (and obviously, an exchange of shim would further deconstruct the categories) could produce discussions that would not threaten either the teacher or the students. Pronouns can be destabilized ("He loves him"; "She married her best friend's wife"). If "coming out" as "lesbian" or "gay" seems mired in identity politics, as many in the audience suggested, and "being out" reproduces a kind of gay and lesbian or butch/femme essentialism (we all know how various versions of "out" are supposed to look, act, talk, move), perhaps "acting out" could best accomplish various indeterminate and inherently performative gender role identities.

The collapse of gender and personal identities into the performance of indeterminacy presents problems, however. First, performative roles are constructed along extant models: flirting on the edges of the "outness" continuum, along the chasm between personal and political, private and public, truth and lie, comfort and terror is only possible because others have crossed those lines to create the categories that we may now elect to perform. Performances of indeterminacy by women teachers, in particular, should not preclude historical consciousness of waves of feminism that challenged various manifestations of women's visibility and invisibility from the 1848 convention of American women in Seneca Falls, New York, to the 1995 Fourth World Conference on Women in Beijing. These legacies profoundly affect the ways in which women continue to occupy public space and claim public political identities such as "pro-choice" or "lesbian," for example, regardless of how they may also elect to distinguish themselves from such legacies. It matters, in other words, whether performance of identity constitutes subversive play or just more self-effacement.

Second, and this derives from the first point, if indeterminacy becomes a means and an end in itself, does it not perpetuate the invisibility of gay and lesbian teachers and students who are already threatened socially, physically, and emotionally precisely because their presence is not sufficiently visible, legible, audible in their families, classrooms, and communities? Can the gender play of postmodern pedagogy and mainstream fashion do the political work necessary to counter the anti-gay movement's weekly gain in power and numbers or even the status quo assumptions of average undergraduates, many of whom, because their own sexual identities are at stake, sympathize with the goals and methods of that movement? Such performances constitute a sort of passing that, as Claudia Card observes, is "analogous to (perhaps an instance of) at least a pretense of servility. Like servility (real or pretended), it impedes one's ability to protest" (200).

Third, what shall we do with the fact that some of our bodies cannot disembody identity, no matter how articulated or performed, that we can no longer pass (if we ever could) because we are too butch or too femme, and that our differences may be as legible and essentialized as those of color or age or health or mobility? Coming from such bodies, can discussions or performances of gender possibilities convince anyone of their fluidity? Regardless of (and because of) how we think, speak, act, and move, we will *be* out and read as straight, gay, lesbian, transsexual, asexual in varying degrees of purity and synthesis.

As long as this is true, that the body projects a subtext, imitative though it may be, that itself undermines attempts to claim or disclaim it verbally, performances that attempt to dismantle that subtext or to deny its primacy run the risk of appearing fraudulent or grotesque. I wish to distinguish here between fraud and drag. Both performances derive their charge from the play of incongruities between the body's text and the clothing, speech, and gestures that layer it. Both strategies appropriate, flaunt, and deconstruct power dynamics; yet fraud is failed drag, emptied not of the possibilities of multiple referentialities but of the possibilities of achieving and reflecting subjectivity and integrity within these referentialities.

Indeterminacy raises more questions than I have addressed here: Do such strategies subvert or deepen the silence and invisibility of gay and lesbian student and teacher presences in the classroom? Do they ignore the public importance of gender representations in and out of the classroom, as I suggested earlier? Do they subvert or challenge the operations of shame, taboo, and fear already surrounding issues of sexual difference and delay the time in the perhaps utopian future when coming out will no longer be necessary? What I do know is that indeterminacy elides the problem of terror. The preference to sublimate the destabilizing tremors of fear into the exhilarating theater of indeterminacy is understandable, but it does not resolve the root ambivalences. Fear, then, begins the story, and, with no apparent bridge across the abyss, the story for many of us ends abruptly there—at the hard place.

––––––––––

Often, we feel politically compelled to come out yet privately ambivalent about the ethical purposes that coming out would serve in some pedagogical contexts. Susan Parr writes of the pedagogical implications of raising ethical issues within classrooms or disciplinary contexts where ethics is not the subject, as is arguably the case in the required undergraduate composition classroom. She suggests, in support of her own opinion that ethics should become a part of even unrelated undergraduate curricula, that because students are demonstrably ignorant of events such as the Holocaust, Vietnam, and Watergate:

> they really do lack a sense of the connection of events and of causality . . .
> it becomes understandable why they deny individual responsibility. By
> the same token, it also becomes clear why they seem so indifferent to
> learning the skills of careful and critical reading and of clear and logical
> writing. If individual action is of no significance in the world, then there
> is no real reason to try to understand others or to communicate one's own
> ideas. (194–95)

Perhaps this chilling summary explains some of the lethargy we see in students
(for example, their almost hostile reaction, often, at being asked in undergraduate composition classes to find topics that interest them). At the same time, and
despite this often disconcerting realization, students are unfailingly receptive
to stories, to writing them, reading them, and hearing them. If non-ethics
classes can or, as Parr would claim, should raise ethical issues, can those issues
be raised, in part, through readings of gay and lesbian stories?

Making clear one's own stake in discussing a gay or lesbian text, far from
silencing students, could, if carefully handled, legitimize their own very different stake in the same or another text and help them to become part of or
even to rewrite the "story" on their own terms, as Harriet Malinowitz's recent
book *Textual Orientations: Lesbian and Gay Students and the Making of Discourse
Communities* so convincingly argues. Students could learn then, for perhaps
the first time, to make a direct connection between their own "individual
actions" or positions and those of others, particularly when those "others" are
physically and not just textually present in the room.

Larry Ehrlich's observation in 1981 that the university, like the church and
the family, has failed to provide opportunities for "the free, unfettered discussion of alternative lifestyles" (139) seems still to be true. Heterosexual identities are the foundation of most discussions, and Malinowitz makes a
persuasive case for challenging this:

> Divisiveness within the composition community about the appropriate-
> ness of this inclusion [of gay and lesbian texts] has largely emerged from
> divergent notions of the place of ideology itself in composition classes.
> The argument at its surface level has been about whether or not ideology
> belongs in a writing class; at a deeper level, it is about *which* ideology
> belongs in a writing class, since new historicists, deconstructionists, and
> social constructivists have shown that culture is never neutral, unmedi-
> ated, or value free. ("Extending Our Concept" 133)

Parr's and Malinowitz's arguments should provide motivation for the instructor debating the ethical consequences of coming out. Since dominant ideologies are already present in the classroom, the debate over coming out need
no longer hinge on whether the gay or lesbian instructor is "contaminating"
the classroom with ideology itself; rather, he or she is simply setting one ideology alongside another and helping the students to make critical distinctions
between them and also to make connections between those ideologies and
their consequences or, in Parr's terms, between "events" and "causality"

(194). For example, the issue of coming out within different historical and cultural contexts (as gay, as Jewish, as feminist . . .) could be raised and the following questions asked: What are the ways in which heterosexuality or Christianity are assumed? What would it mean to discover that the "gay" teacher was actually straight or the "straight" teacher gay? (Berg et al. 32).

If being perceived as an ideologue who imposes radical ideologies on students is one of the fears preventing us from coming out, what are some of the others? Besides the fears of losing the students' respect and affection, of undermining our own authority, of appearing partisan, of being accused of "promoting" gay or lesbian sexuality, more basic losses threaten us. To return for a moment to the undifferentiated abyss, Ehrlich describes in the following passage the bland, faceless anonymity of most audiences:

> In some respects it might be easier for gay persons to disclose themselves to a fellow advocate or an avowed homophobe than to the less polarized personalities, the somewhat non-descript individuals representing most of the encounters encompassed in a lifetime . . . the non-public, apparently uncommitted encounters represent a substantial threat. (133)

It is difficult for me not to imagine the affiliation with dominant institutional power behind each of these friendly, young, predominantly white male faces in my Midwest undergraduate composition and literature classrooms. What is perhaps most terrifying about them is the probability that they are ignorant of the power they embody. Eve Sedgwick suggests, however, that the real enemy of institutional heterosexism is not gay sexuality specifically but the "excessive" character of sexuality in general:

> Our culture still sees to [sexual passion's] being dangerous enough that women and men who find or fear they are homosexual, or are perceived by others to be so, are physically and mentally terrorized through the institutions of law, religion, psychotherapy, mass culture, medicine, the military, commerce and bureaucracy, and brute violence.
>
> . . . teachers are subject to being fired, not only for being visibly gay, but, whatever their sexuality, for providing any intimation that homosexual desires, identities, cultures, adults, children, or adolescents have a right to expression or existence. ("Pedagogy" 152)

As Malinowitz observes, gay-hating is justified "by overlaying the real discussion with a hyperbolized one" ("Extending Our Concept" 130–31) so that gay and lesbian representations are distorted into images of impossibly promiscuous, bestial child-abusers, as attested in *The Gay Agenda*, a nineteen-minute anti-gay video produced by an Oregon church to support removal of antidiscrimination protections. This hyperbolization of sexuality is obvious when one recalls that at other specific historical moments the targets of white male accusations of hypersexuality have included Jews, blacks, and women, as Sander L. Gilman has argued. Perhaps, then, awareness or renewed awareness of the fact that we are not alone in this succession of scapegoating, ridicule, and erasure can help us to make the crossing. We are in excellent historical company.

> The notion of the secret as a form of poison or infection has long antecedents. Ellenberger traces the concept of what he calls the "pathogenic secret" back to primitive healers, and to magnetists and hypnotists who worked at drawing painful and intolerable secrets into the open.
>
> (BOK, SECRETS 8)

> The confession became one of the West's most highly valued techniques for producing the truth . . . one confesses one's crimes, one's sins, one's thoughts and desires, one's illnesses and troubles; one goes about telling, with the greatest precision, whatever is most difficult to tell.
>
> (FOUCAULT 59)

Boundaries between self and other, personal and political, private and public are constantly being renegotiated in the classroom. What is self-disclosure and how much is too much? Evelyn Beck's 1983 essay "Self-Disclosure and the Commitment to Social Change" describes self-disclosure as follows:

> In any given situation we may tell a great deal about ourselves without ever thinking of it as self-disclosure. We only begin to call it self-disclosure when we talk about ourselves in situations where one would not expect certain kinds of information to be announced. According to patriarchal concepts, anything personal in the classroom would have to be considered self-disclosure. Socially unacceptable or difficult facts are almost always considered self-disclosure, too. Moreover, I think our own comfort level with information we give also determines whether we perceive ourselves to be self-disclosing or "just talking." (286)

Self-disclosure implies the personal, the unacceptable or difficult, and the uncomfortable; self-disclosure of sexual orientation surely packages all three. Perhaps just this much clarity—that coming out will necessarily entail self-disclosure (as opposed to a more comfortable fantasy of oneself as disclosing a vague "societal Other")—can stabilize the moment of crossing. Beck suggests that the "state of being ready to self-disclose" when the disclosure is "most congruent with, and most organic to the teaching act" is more important than idealizations of acts of self-disclosure ("Self-Disclosure" 291). Self-disclosure in the congruent or "golden" moment rather than the incongruent moment can mitigate fear by removing much of the artificiality and sense of "wrongness" from the disclosing moment, a sense that can be confused with the value of the disclosed content itself.

In crossing the abyss, do we expose a secret that should no longer be a secret, thereby draining it of its destructive power—or do we appear to confess, thereby imputing criminality to our practices and feelings? And what distinguishes privacy from secrecy? Janet Wright, writing in 1993, claims that "coming out is not a discussion of intimate sexual details" but "a discussion of identity" (25); others have made the same point (Card 205; Mohr 17). Yet that public "identity," because it is predicated upon private taboo sexual practices, can never achieve full status *as* an identity in the heterosexist mind. Coming out will almost always, therefore, feel more like the confession of a secret than we who live within the consciousness of a complex gay and lesbian culture would wish.

Sometimes the "secret" leaks out and confesses itself. Even when I do not choose to disclose myself as a lesbian to my composition classes, for example, I am consistently read that way by my students. At some point in the semester, when they begin to feel comfortable with each other, they begin to speculate about me. I observe this, I overhear it, and it is sometimes reported to me by the students themselves. To maintain a pretense of "neutrality" in the face of this patent failure to "pass" feels like a pathological choice. To do nothing is intentionally to deceive, through what Bok calls "messages meant to mislead . . . to make [others] believe what we ourselves do not believe. We can do so through gesture, through disguise, by means of action or inaction, even through silence" (*Lying* 13).

Yet simply to announce my sexual orientation as I hand out the class syllabus unproductively fragments my identity and polarizes the students in relation to that fragmentary self-representation in a way that seems no less deceptive. I prefer to come out spontaneously to students at the "golden moment." Such moments occur during class discussions and thus provide a relevant context for self-disclosure. Though brief (and thus all too easy to defer until their enabling contexts have passed), such moments can produce the same effects as more deliberate and premeditated coming-out acts. For me, the effects include a crashing heart and a sense of having stepped into a vacuum that provides no easy way back into my own body, let alone the classroom.

To return to the issue of sub rosa student speculation, the content of the course does not, in itself, insulate the teacher from scrutiny. In a gay and lesbian studies course, where I am vocally and unproblematically out as a lesbian, the students then need to read what *kind* of a lesbian I am, even as they read what kind of a person, woman, teacher I am. But in this situation I become contextualized not within a heterosexual paradigm, where I can only be a lesbian, but within the lesbian paradigm, where I can occupy and speak from and to a multiplicity of sexualities and identities.

> Pathological shame is an irrational sense of defectiveness, a feeling not of having crossed to the wrong side of the boundary but of having been born there.
> (Karen 47)

For the gay or lesbian teacher or student, the "wrong side" often seems to be the only side, because the "right side" is inaccessible. This very inaccessibility contributes to the paralyzing sense of ambivalence that inheres in the coming-out act, rendering it as potentially self-shaming as it is self-liberatory. Quite simply, the coming-out gesture asks something of its putatively straight audience: "Accept me" — "Don't accept me" — "See what we have in common" — "See what we don't have in common." It opens up a fundamentally monologic, not dialogic, relationship because the direction of the act is always from the gay or lesbian speaker to the straight listener. Straight people seldom come out as straight to gay people and even less often to other straight people, unless the presence of a gay interlocutor or the discussion of a gay issue seems to require that remarks be prefaced with a defensive disclaimer ("I'm not gay myself, but . . .").

A gay or lesbian teacher, then, faces a double terror and a double crossing: he or she must not only cross a one-way bridge, but in doing so must toss away his or her sack of institutional power and protection en route. Paradoxically, at the very moment when the teacher breaks away from the safety of heterosexual privilege and institutionally sanctioned professional identity, students may be most likely to see her or him as part of a generic "them" which they identify with the university: "this *class*," they complain, "is trying to shove a lifestyle down my throat." In this case, a teacher's survival will depend on the institutional response to student accusations of a "gay agenda." Unfortunately, many administrators would rather withdraw tacit and overt institutional protection than risk the political and economic costs of defending their faculty against such charges.

Only if the students can see the teacher as an individual rather than an "agenda" is there hope of that teacher forging the kinds of new and productive ways of thinking, writing, and working with the students that most of the coming-out testimonials describe. Malinowitz describes this transformational potential: "By coming out to my students and inserting a lesbian and gay discourse into the class, I am divesting those students of their ignorance and their entitlement to prejudice, and am investing them with responsibility to negotiate meanings" ("Transforming" 3).

The experience of coming out can rarely be reduced to an intellectual exercise that follows from a series of political decisions; reductive assumptions such as these, under which we all labor for a while, only perpetuate unreasonable expectations that the crossing will be emotionally neutral because we have determined that it should be so. In fact, though, the task demands of us the same "responsibility to negotiate meaning" that we require of our students, and that negotiation cannot take place in an emotional vacuum. To understand this from the outset will be our most powerful strategy.

WORKS CITED

Abelove, Henry, Richard Ohmann, and Claire B. Potter. Introduction. *Radical Teacher* 45 (Winter 1994): 2–3.

Adams, Kate, and Kim Emery. "Classroom Coming Out Stories: Practical Strategies for Productive Self-Disclosure." Garber 25–34.

Barbone, Steven, and Lee Rice. "Coming Out, Being Out, and Acts of Virtue." Murphy 91–110.

Bartky, Sandra Lee. "Shame and Gender." *Femininity and Domination: Studies in the Phenomenology of Oppression.* New York: Routledge, 1990. 83–98.

Beck, Evelyn Torek. "Out as a Lesbian, Out as a Jew: And Nothing Untoward Happened?" Garber 227–34.

———. "Self-Disclosure and the Commitment to Social Change." *Learning Our Way: Essays in Feminist Education.* Ed. Charlotte Bunch and Sandra Pollack. Trumansbury, NY: Crossing P, 1983. 285–91.

Berg, Allison, Jean Kowaleski, Caroline Le Guin, Ellen Weinauer, and Eric A. Wolfe. "Breaking the Silence: Sexual Preference in the Composition Classroom." *Feminist Teacher* 4.2–3 (1989). 29–32.

Bergman, David. "The Gay and Lesbian Presence in American Literature." *Heath Anthology Newsletter.* Lexington, MA: D. C. Heath, 1993. 5–7.

Bok, Sissela. *Lying: Moral Choice in Public and Private Life.* New York: Pantheon, 1978.

———. *Secrets: On the Ethics of Concealment and Revelation.* New York: Pantheon, 1982.

Card, Claudia. *Lesbian Choices.* New York: Columbia UP, 1995.

Chekola, Mark. "Outing, Truth-Telling, and the Shame of the Closet." Murphy 67–90.

Crew, Louie, and Rictor Norton. "The Homophobic Imagination: An Editorial." *College English* 36.3 (November 1974): 272–90.

DuBois, W. E. B. *The Souls of Black Folk.* Millwood, NY: Kraus-Thomson Organization, 1973.

Ehrlich, Larry G. "The Pathogenic Secret." *Gayspeak: Gay Male & Lesbian Communication.* Ed. James W. Chesebro. New York: Pilgrim P, 1981. 130–41.

Foucault, Michel. *The History of Sexuality, Volume I: An Introduction.* (Paris: Editions Gallimard, 1976.) New York: Vintage, 1990.

Garber, Linda, ed. *Tilting the Tower: Lesbians Teaching Queer Subjects.* New York: Routledge, 1994.

Gilman, Sander L. *Difference and Pathology: Stereotypes of Sexuality, Race, and Madness.* Ithaca: Cornell UP, 1985.

Harbeck, Karen M., ed. *Coming Out of the Classroom Closet: Gay and Lesbian Students, Teachers, and Curricula.* New York: Harrington Park P, 1992.

Jennings, Kevin, ed. *One Teacher in 10: Gay and Lesbian Educators Tell Their Stories.* Boston: Alyson, 1994.

Karen, Robert. "Shame." *Atlantic Monthly,* Feb. 1992: 40–70.

Khayatt, Madiha Didi. *Lesbian Teachers: An Invisible Presence.* Albany: State U of New York P, 1992.

Kissen, Rita M. "Gay Culture and Straight Jackets: Teaching and Action at a Midwestern University." *Radical Teacher* 43 (Fall 1993): 40–43.

Luboff, Gerald F. "Making Choices: Determining the Need to Be Out." Abstract of paper presented at the panel "Coming Out in the Classroom: Teacher Identity and Student Experience," Annual Meeting of the Conference on College Composition and Communication, Cincinnati, OH (March 19–21, 1992). *Variant* 4 (July 1992): 7–8.

Malinowitz, Harriet. "Extending Our Concept of Multiculturalism: Lesbian and Gay Reality and the Writing Class." *Vital Signs 3: Restructuring the English Classroom.* Ed. James Collins. Portsmouth, NH: Boynton/Cook-Heinemann, 1992. 128–50.

———. *Textual Orientations: Lesbian and Gay Students and the Making of Discourse Communities.* Portsmouth, NH: Boynton/Cook, 1995.

———. "Transforming Teacher and Student: The Benefits of Being 'Out.'" Paper presented at the panel "Coming Out in the Classroom: Teacher Identity and Student Experience," Annual Meeting of the Conference on College Composition and Communication, Cincinnati, OH (March 19–21, 1992).

Mayo, David J., and Martin Gunderson. "Privacy and the Ethics of Outing." Murphy 47–65.

McDaniel, Judith. "Is There Room for Me in the Closet?" *Gendered Subjects: The Dynamics of Feminist Teaching.* Ed. Margo Culley and Catherine Portuges. New York: Routledge and Kegan Paul, 1985.

Mittler, Mary L., and Amy Blumenthal. "On Being a Change Agent: Teacher as Text, Homophobia as Context." Garber 3–10.

Mohr, Richard D. *Gay Ideas: Outing and Other Controversies.* Boston: Beacon P, 1992.

Murphy, Timothy F., ed. *Gay Ethics: Controversies in Outing, Civil Rights, and Sexual Science.* New York: Harrington Park P, 1994.

Parmeter, Sarah-Hope. "Four Good Reasons Why Every Lesbian Teacher Should Be Free to Come Out in the Classroom." Parmeter and Reti 44–58.

Parmeter, Sarah-Hope, and Irene Reti, eds. *The Lesbian in Front of the Classroom: Writings by Lesbian Teachers.* Santa Cruz, CA: HerBooks, 1988.

Parr, Susan Resneck. "The Teaching of Ethics in Undergraduate Nonethics Courses." *Ethics Teaching in Higher Education.* Ed. Daniel Callahan and Sissela Bok. New York: Plenum P, 1980. 191–203.

Sedgwick, Eve Kosofsky. "Pedagogy in the Context of an Antihomophobic Project." *South Atlantic Quarterly* 89.1 (Winter 1990): 139–56.

———. "Queer Performativity: Henry James's *The Art of the Novel.*" *GLQ* 1.1 (1993): 1–16.

Segrest, Mab. "Confessions of a Closet Baptist." *Reading for Difference: Texts on Gender, Race, and Class.* Orlando, FL: Harcourt Brace Jovanovich, 1993. 369–72.

Stein, Anza. "What's a Lesbian Teacher to Do?" Parmeter and Reti 4–16.

Watney, Simon. "School's Out." *Inside/Out: Lesbian Theories, Gay Theories.* New York: Routledge, 1991. 387–401.

Wright, Janet. "Lesbian Instructor Comes Out: The Personal Is Pedagogy." *Feminist Teacher* 7.2 (1993). 26–33.

26   *"When and Where I Enter": Race, Gender, and Composition Studies*

SHIRLEY WILSON LOGAN

Only the BLACK WOMAN can say "when and where I enter, in the quiet, undisputed dignity of my womanhood, without violence and without suing or special patronage, then and there the whole Negro race enters with me."

—ANNA JULIA COOPER

Black women have a long history as communication specialists, teaching facility with language to those who needed it most—free and enslaved Africans in America—throughout the nineteenth century. When the educator Anna Julia Cooper addressed the Washington, DC, Convocation of Colored Clergy of the Protestant Episcopal Church in 1886, she was continuing a tradition among black women of public speaking and teaching begun many years before. In her speech "Womanhood a Vital Element in the Regeneration and Progress of a Race," from which the title of this essay is taken, Cooper suggests that if the neglected black woman enters, then a fortiori the more highly regarded members of her race accompany her. But the speech also mentions the unique significance that black women and all women possess when they enter new situations, by virtue of what Cooper calls, in another essay, the "feminine . . . side to truth" ("Education" 60). By claiming for women this special influence, Cooper applies the nineteenth-century suffragist argument from expediency, based on the claim that women were indeed fundamentally different from men and that this different, "feminine side" entitled them to a place in the public sphere (Kraditor 43–74). She gives the Episcopalian leaders a thorough tongue-lashing for the church's failure to attract more than the black educated elite. More significant, she condemns the leaders' neglect of southern black women, "at once both the lever and the fulcrum for uplifting the race" (73). Her post-Reconstruction black women stepped tentatively into the public space occupied by those who had denied them room throughout the century. Black women entering writing classrooms at the end of the twentieth century

From *Feminism and Composition Studies: In Other Words.* Ed. Susan C. Jarratt and Lynn Worsham. New York: Modern Language Association, 1998. 45–57.

share common experiences with their nineteenth-century foresisters. And, of course, much has changed.

In this essay, I review briefly the teaching activities of a few nineteenth-century black women. I believe such a review is an important first step toward understanding some of the racial and gender issues facing higher education today. Contemporary discussions about black women educators should be set against the historical backdrop of this deeply rooted tradition, because that backdrop corrects the short-sightedness inherent in the current perception of diversity that sees all difference as ahistorical. This perception too often assumes that people of color are just now beginning to take part in developing and shaping American culture, however defined. I then address some of the issues facing black women professors generally and those teaching writing in particular, using two of my own experiences as examples. I close by suggesting some ways in which the tensions surrounding black women who teach in predominantly white institutions might be converted into catalysts for change.

I am keenly aware that although I was asked to write this essay for a collection on feminism and composition, many of the writing concerns addressed here do not arise strictly from the professor's gender or from the gender of the students. They arise from a conflation of gender and race and subject matter and setting, a conflation that for me is difficult if not impossible to sort out. Marsha Houston reminds us that "women of color do not experience sexism *in addition to* racism, but sexism *in the context of* racism; thus, they cannot be said to bear an *additional* burden that white women do not bear;" instead, they "bear an altogether *different* burden from that borne by white women." Houston characterizes burdens as "multiple, interlocking oppressions" (49). Frances Harper, the nineteenth-century author, lecturer, and women's rights activist, was faced with this kind of burden when she announced to suffrage leaders that she supported the Fifteenth Amendment, which gave black men the vote but not women. She considered sex the lesser question (Stanton, Anthony, and Gage 391). In other words, sex became an issue for her only in the larger context of race. While less certain than she of the ranking of oppressions, I do want to acknowledge confliction. But I still hope that what Jerome Karabel, describing some of bell hooks's insights, calls "a shock of recognition" (27) will be evoked in others who read the following descriptions of classroom encounters, wherever they find themselves, and that it will stimulate future conversations and ultimately effect changes in classrooms and curricula.

NECESSARY WORK

A legion of black women went into teaching before and after emancipation, responding to the need for literacy education in the North and South. In 1836, Mary Ann Shadd Cary, as staunch a feminist as she was an antislavery woman, opened a school for black children in Wilmington, Delaware, then settled in Canada West to teach black emigrants for the American Missionary

Association; there she became the first black newspaperwoman, editing the *Provincial Freeman*. Susan Paul, daughter of a prominent minister, ran her own school for blacks in Boston in the 1830s. By 1837, Sarah Mapps Douglass had established a school in Philadelphia, which for a while provided the only opportunity for black women to receive a high school education. Frances Harper taught briefly before launching her career as an antislavery lecturer in 1854. In 1856, Charlotte Forten became the first black teacher of white children in Salem, Massachusetts; she later volunteered to teach free black men and women on the Sea Islands of South Carolina. Cooper, Cary, Paul, Douglass, Harper, and Forten are typical of the many nineteenth-century black women who not only chose a career in teaching but also helped establish schools. Teaching was considered a proper and highly respected profession for black women. According to Dorothy Sterling, most of these women were "northern born, middle class, single, and childless. Almost all were in their twenties, with an above-average education acquired at Oberlin, the Institutes for Colored Youth, or at normal schools near their homes; almost all had taught locally before going South" (263).

The wish that African American teachers in particular be hired for the work of literacy education is already apparent in the 1872 observations of one northern missionary, Charles Stearns. He argued, during Reconstruction, that black teachers were preferable because they would have faith in their students' ability to learn, the students would be more receptive to them, black teachers would understand the students' needs better, and black teachers would serve as role models (qtd. in Alexander 168–69). These advantages resonate today in requests to hire additional African American faculty members at predominantly white institutions, where too many students of color begin, but do not complete, their higher education. According to the *Journal of Blacks in Higher Education,* "less than three quarters of black college freshman [enrolled in NCAA Division II and III schools] return to college for their sophomore year" ("Retention Rates").

Evidence of the response to this nineteenth-century call to racial uplift and self-help is clear in Fannie Barrier Williams's 1893 speech to the World's Congress of Representative Women:

> In twenty-five years, and under conditions discouraging in the extreme, thousands of our women have been educated as teachers. They have adapted themselves to the work of mentally lifting a whole race of people so eagerly and readily that they afford an apt illustration of the power of self-help. Not only have these women become good teachers in less than twenty-five years, but many of them are the prize teachers in the mixed schools of nearly every Northern city. (109)

Such phrases as "prize teachers in the mixed schools" remind us that Williams spoke at a time when evidence of intellectual competence was required and offered explicitly. Similar evidence is perhaps no less necessary today, when phrases such as "bright black woman" are too frequently interjected oxymoronically into academic conversations.

Those pioneer teachers of literacy performed the same role that many writing teachers do today, who, Susan Miller reminds us, are hired to teach composition not to the "already entitled" but to the unentitled and those "only tentatively entitled to belong in higher education" ("Feminization" 45). While the early teachers were not necessarily preparing their students for higher education as it is now understood, they were preparing them for survival in a strange culture. The teaching of the unentitled and the tentatively entitled has been described as foundational, preparatory, preliterate, and, in the view of many today, is "distasteful but necessary cultural work" (46). In the euphoria of nineteenth-century post-Civil War America, blacks optimistically viewed this necessary cultural work as a means of preparing black people to take their place in American society.

A NECESSARY PRESENCE

The early educators were teaching in settings quite different from those in which black women find themselves today. Most taught a range of courses; they taught not only reading and writing but also geography, Latin, Greek, and mathematics. Today's highly specialized classes satisfy the careerist students' demand for an immediate superficial relevance in every course. Semester offerings now include a proliferation of upper-level writing courses, such as business, technical, medical, and legal writing. Nineteenth-century black women largely taught students with little prior education, of all ages, hungry for knowledge. Black women today typically teach college students with a family tradition of education, in classes where women, too, are perceived as other. Unlike what we now call multicultural classrooms, where the teacher usually belongs to the majority culture, in the classroom under consideration here the students are predominantly white and the teacher is a woman of color.

Another difference between then and now is that today black women are not present in legions. According to the October 1994 survey report of the National Center for Education Statistics, as of fall 1992 only 2.8% of full-time faculty members in English and literature at accredited United States postsecondary institutions were identified as black non-Hispanic female. White males made up 45.2%, white females 45%, and black males 2.1% of the total (United States 14). Of part-time faculty members in English and literature, 2.6% were black female, 0.5% black male, 61% white female, and 29.5% white male. (The racial-ethnic categories of American Indian, Asian, and Hispanic completed the percentage distributions [16].) Unfortunately, the category of English and literature does not indicate how many primarily teach composition. We do know that roughly two-thirds of all composition teachers are female (Miller, "Feminization" 41). These percentages are not surprising. They are evidence of the "hegemonic compromise," about which Miller writes, "As statistics about who writes composition theory and who administers composition programs tell us, neither describing composition as a discipline nor asserting its equality has 'worked' on the actually gender-coded professional circumstances of those who teach writing" (49).

What is also clear is that few English faculty members are black and female, and few of those, if they are tenured or on a tenure track, are likely to teach composition, especially at predominantly white institutions where black women are seen as commodities too precious to use in this manner. (Departmental assumptions about what subject areas are valuable do not support such use.) But since writing takes place—or should take place—outside the traditional composition classroom, we can imagine this scenario: a black female teacher, white students, and students of color having conversations about writing.

In *Teaching to Transgress,* bell hooks recalls her experience as the black female teacher in such a setting. She points out that "the majority of students who enter our classrooms [in predominantly white institutions] have never been taught by black women professors. My pedagogy is informed by this knowledge, because I know from experience that this unfamiliarity can overdetermine what takes place in the classroom" (86). In another section of her book, she contrasts her estranged situation at a white institution with the normative classroom presence of a white male professor, whose casual dress and manner said that he was there "to be a mind and not a body," and she observes that only those in power have "the privilege of denying their body" (137). Describing her own efforts to apply the tenets of Paulo Freire's liberatory education to create an environment where all voices are respected, hooks learns that the professor cannot make a classroom exciting by her enthusiasm alone, especially when faced with this unfamiliarity. Discussions of the need to empower students in a multicultural classroom usually invoke images of the self-isolated students of color sitting in the corner eyeing their white teacher suspiciously or tentatively. But what of classes where most if not all students are white? To what extent might their views be suppressed because the class is taught by a woman of color? Cheryl Johnson calls this situation "the teacher as racial/gendered subject," in which the professor is perceived as a "representation of essentialized black womanhood" (410). The presence at the front of the room is read as a signal that now oral and written expressions of ideas may need to be suppressed lest they offend the person who will evaluate them. All too often my students submit stifled prose that sticks to stock responses to racial issues, issues that beg for critical consideration. The students perceive this kind of writing as safe for them because it is non-threatening to me. The challenge for the teacher in such a class is to create an environment that encourages the free expression of ideas even when they may be unpopular. This situation is more than merely the opposite of white teacher versus student of color because the reversal of classroom roles by color no longer mirrors conventional societal hierarchies. Elizabeth Flynn reminds us that efforts to encourage women students in particular to write with power and authority can have only limited success because "individual classroom instructors are not sufficient to bring about powerful writing." She argues that "changes in the social and economic order must be made as well" ("Studies" 149). Societal constraints, along with the racial presence of the black female professor, surely limit that professor's attempts to empower her students as writers.

WRITING AND OUTSIDE INTERFERENCE

The following descriptions of two classroom episodes are based on my experience as a black woman teaching courses in composition and rhetoric at a predominantly white university. They certainly do not represent the whole situation, or even the whole of my experience. And they should not be read exclusively as tales of what Houston refers to as the "triple jeopardy" of race, gender, and class (48)—and, in this instance, for class we should read academic discipline. Indeed, some may consider my affiliation with rhetoric and composition the greatest jeopardy, the second-class status of writing teachers having been well documented. But as the Anna Cooper epigraph to this essay implies, these jeopardies should perhaps be labeled differences instead, differences that can act as a force for change. Further, I hope that for my telling of my episodes I will not be given the essentialist label of the anthropological "native informant" who is presumed to speak for an entire group (hooks, *Teaching* 43).

In a course in advanced academic writing, some of my students had difficulty critiquing a section of "Letter from Birmingham Jail," by Martin Luther King, Jr., which I had assigned for rhetorical analysis. Enrolled in the class were students who had fulfilled the upper-level writing requirement and were seeking further writing instruction; English majors concentrating in language, writing, and rhetoric; and a few graduate students writing theses—all experienced writers. Thus I was especially disappointed to find their responses filled with glowing praise for King and his accomplishments. The students seemed reluctant to suggest that there was any flaw in the writing of a revered leader, reluctant even to support their praise with specific examples. Glowing but generalized praise often masks the condescension that denies a text serious critique. But I suspect that something more than condescension was operating here. Although we had studied various tactics of rhetorical analysis, I think that with King's letter there was too much external societal interference for these students. The difficulty they had with the assignment may have had nothing to do with the racial identity of the instructor, but generalized prose is common when race is involved. Perhaps they feared that any critical comments would be interpreted as racist.

Describing a similar silence in a communication class during a discussion of "ethnic cultural differences among women," Houston concedes that her students' fear of saying the wrong thing was valid and adds that "in a society where racism, like sexism, remains pervasive, speaking in nonracist ways is difficult, especially when the topic is racial differences" (46). My students may well have been reacting to an instance of what hooks characterizes as unfamiliarity overdetermining the classroom environment. No doubt I could have better explained and modeled rhetorical analysis, a genre that challenges most students. I could have chosen a text by someone or about something less racial, less controversial. But surely, rather than keep silent, we need to engage in democratic conversations about divisive topics like race and gender, and in a variety of public spaces, especially in classes designed to enhance effective communication.

In another course on rhetorical theory, we listened to Fred Morsell's compelling recording of Frederick Douglass's well-known 1852 speech "What to the Slave Is the Fourth of July?" I then distributed copies of the speech and asked the class to identify some of its stylistic features as a way of applying an earlier reading of book 4 of the *Rhetorica ad Herennium*. In response, one female student wrote two dense pages in defense of America, stating that she didn't see why Douglass was complaining about the treatment of slaves. After all, she argued, the Irish immigrants had as many difficulties as the slaves, yet they overcame them. In conclusion she said that if people didn't like this country, they should not have come here. Her response indicated that she had not heard Douglass's speech at all but instead was reacting to contemporary reverberations emanating from the racial nature of the subject. This student had contributed little to class discussions, and her prior papers had not been particularly enthusiastic. Because of my nurturing pedagogical impulse, mixed generously with a lifetime of covert and overt suppression of my opinions, I made no negative comments, afraid that they would discourage the student's future participation.

Susan Jarratt addresses this problem in an essay on feminist pedagogy in the composition class. Stressing the need for a "more carefully theorized understanding of the multiple forms of power reproduced in the classroom," she points out that "differences of gender, race, and class among students and teachers provide situations in which conflict does arise, and we need more than the ideal of the harmonious, nurturing composition class in our repertory of teaching practices to deal with these problems" ("Feminism" 13). It would have been easy enough for me to point out to my student that she had not fulfilled the requirement of the assignment, that is, to identify selected tropes and their uses to persuade. The challenge I faced was to respond constructively to the paper she did write. In my written comments, I suggested that the arrival histories of the two groups—Irish Americans and African Americans—might account for the differences in the two groups' experiences. We met briefly after class to discuss her need to address the assignment. Trying to tap into and rechannel her interest in the speech, I suggested that she reexamine the speech to determine what specific language choices of Douglass might have elicited such a strong response in her. I invited her to make an appointment with me to talk further about how to do this as well as to talk about some of the objections she had raised to Douglass's arguments. She declined the opportunity to revise and chose instead to submit a stylistic analysis of another text, one that in her mind was less controversial.

Cheryl Johnson notes that as more multicultural texts are incorporated into the curriculum, some students may view them "as intrusions on their academic study and actually resent texts which explore racial, ethnic, gender, or religious differences" (411). Although to some extent texts have always explored difference, certainly the differences are embodied to a greater extent today in those who teach the texts. Should I have chased my student down the hallway or called her dorm to demand that she make an appointment? I had given the class a brief introduction to Douglass—most knew little about him—and reminded them that the event of his speech took place before the Civil War and emancipation; but perhaps I should have devoted a portion of a class session to a discussion of African American history. I chose to let my student decide how she wanted to respond to my evaluation of her essay. Her subsequent class participation increased considerably, even though the two of us never had our follow-up discussion of Douglass. True, the remaining course texts were not by or about African Americans. I was not entirely satisfied with the outcome but accepted my student's analysis of a substitute text. I saw in all this a small pedagogical victory, feeling that our encounter helped her realize that I was open to discussion about the *r* word. She was just not ready to have such a discussion with me. I was reminded that teaching, like learning, can never be a neutral act. As Sharon Crowley writes:

> We can look at our students as people who bring the discourses of their communities into the classroom with them. Their discourses are not always pleasant to hear and read, riddled as they may be with racism, sexism, and elitism. But we acknowledge students' languages as their own these days, more profoundly than we used to. And we don't deny the ugliness and alienation of the world outside the classroom anymore, and we don't kid ourselves that our classrooms are, or can be, warm huggy refuges from that world. ("Letter" 324–25)

ACKNOWLEDGING DIFFERENCE

In both the courses described above, an assignment asked white students and a sprinkling of students of color to give a critique of a text by an African American, a critique to be read and evaluated by their African American teacher. But black students face this situation in reverse—white author, white teacher—all the time, as they make their way through white institutions. It is interesting that many of my black students struggled with the same two assignments—perhaps for related racial reasons. After describing several black teacher–white student encounters in her literature class, Johnson cautions:

> What may be erroneously suggested here is that the relationship between a black professor and black students would be harmonious because both, supposedly, locate themselves culturally, socially, politically, historically, and intellectually at an all-encompassing black/African-American site. If such a location exists, it is a tentative and unsteady one, affected by time and place of encounter. In other words, there is no fixed African-American ideology; black students may inscribe one or more various, sometimes conflicting, codes onto the body of the black professor, such as Afrocentrism, black nationalism, womanism, feminism, assimilation, or other perspectives arising from each student's subjectivity. (416)

The periodicals *College English, College Composition and Communication, Teaching English in the Two-Year College,* and the *Journal of Advanced Composition* have all featured articles on white students and students of color developing voice in the college classroom.[1] Indeed, the role of race and gender in the teaching of writing needs to be studied from a variety of perspectives. I have been focusing here on just one perspective: black professors, especially black women professors, trying to create in multicultural contexts an environment where students, especially women students, can comfortably express opinions. If we do not consider strategies for constructive critique of the opinions put forth in this triply complex convergence of gender, race, and class, then, as hooks writes, we will "engage in a form of social amnesia in which we forget that all knowledge is forged in conflict" (*Teaching* 31). If we desire peace and harmony in the classroom instead of welcoming dissent, we will be dancing around or smoothing over important issues. In a composition class, where a writer's well-argued opinions often constitute the content, students and teachers may avoid topics that are controversial. It becomes safe to discuss only the "them" not represented in the classroom. We need to devise ways to speak the unspeakable, to talk about and have students write about issues surrounding race and gender, in composition classrooms and in all classrooms.

Joyce Middleton describes a series of "introductory class rituals." To establish a framework for discussion, she "asks students to question unchallenged assumptions about race, literacy, and teaching" (104) and helps them develop a vocabulary for talking about those assumptions. At the beginning of one semester, Middleton had her students read two contrasting texts and discuss some of the issues they raised. One text was an editorial from a local newspaper, filled with "unchallenged racial stereotypes" and "ridiculous analogies" (104). She chose a blatantly racist text to unify the class against material that they would all agree was biased. The second text was an essay by bell hooks in which it is argued that love of blackness is a form of resistance against racism. During the discussion of this piece, tensions emerged as the class struggled with the notion of loving blackness without rejecting whiteness. As a final opening strategy, Middleton had the class work its way through a list of concrete but invisible white privileges. This exercise shed light on hooks's essay. Middleton's framework establishing helped students understand what is involved in unlearning racism. A black woman teaching at a predominantly white university, Middleton employed an up-front approach to the unspeakable, which seemed especially appropriate for that course's subsequent readings. Such an approach can reduce the anxiety produced by unfamiliarity.

Concern for helping students develop voice and authority in the writing classroom should not lead teachers to abdicate their positions as writing experts. But there is a great difference between a teacher who is an authority in the subject matter and one who squelches ideas. I believe that all students have strong opinions about most things and that they will not be afraid to express them in an encouraging environment. Yet many lack the argumentative skills needed to support their opinions and the adaptive skills needed to address different audiences. The students who wrote extended

King encomiums instead of the assigned rhetorical critiques may have considered themselves skillful accommodationists, carefully adapting text to audience. The student in the second classroom episode clearly had strong opinions but needed more practice in connecting argument to evidence—and in retrieving accurate evidence. Critiquing the open-classroom movement of the eighties, Lisa Delpit speaks of the continuing need to teach skills "within the context of critical and creative thinking" (384). I am not opposed to teaching skills along with helping students express ideas and find voice. It may be that our students need skills more than ideas. We won't always change their opinions—and perhaps we should not—but we certainly have a responsibility to teach them how to express those opinions and to challenge the assumptions that support them. A facility with language may be the most liberating pedagogy we can offer.

Black women are especially challenged to teach communication skills in settings where they must often first overcome resistance to their very presence. But hooks suggests that rather than attempt to deny identity, we take a closer look at "the presence of teacher as body in the classroom, the presence of the teacher as someone who has a total effect on the development of the student, not just an intellectual effect but an effect on how that student perceives reality beyond the classroom" (*Teaching* 136). A step is surely taken toward achieving our goal of helping students become more effective written communicators when in designing our courses and assignments we pay attention to the interaction among teacher, student, and subject matter in a variety of multicultural contexts. Fine-tuned "introductory class rituals" like those described by Middleton, establishing the appropriate framework for teaching and learning, would also discourage the sort of evasive writing that my students produced. Jarratt sees these "collisions of gender, race, and class" as opportunities for improving pedagogy: "Recognizing the inevitability of conflict is not ground for despair but the starting point for creating a consciousness in students and teachers through which the inequalities generating those conflicts can be acknowledged and transformed" ("Feminism" 119).

Difference can be a force for change. Yet it would be naive to think that the simple presence of a black female teacher guarantees change. Taking exception to hooks's characterization of the movement toward multicultural pedagogy as "tantamount to a revolution," Tom Fox reminds us:

> There's a danger in thinking of multiculturalism as a revolution that has already occurred. The small changes toward more inclusiveness and diversity in our curriculum and pedagogy don't seem anything like a revolution. And even those small changes are in danger of backsliding into monoculturalism. Actually there's been minuscule success in hiring people of color in universities across the country, baby steps toward a more inclusive, more constructive curriculum, pedagogical changes only by a tiny few, and only a slight increase in the representation of students of color in higher education. (567)

Still, it is certainly worth exploring and exploiting Anna Cooper's claim that black women enter uncharted territory with the unique and valuable perspective of their race and gender, especially in a time when achieving gender, racial, and communicative equality is critical.

NOTE

1. See, for example, Gary Olson's interview with hooks; Terry Dean's "Multicultural Classrooms, Monocultural Teachers"; and *Teaching English in the Two-Year College* 21. 2 (1994), a special issue on multiculturalism in the writing classroom, edited by Frederic Gale.

WORKS CITED

Alexander, Adele Logan. *Ambiguous Lives: Free Women of Color in Rural Georgia, 1789–1879.* Fayetteville: U of Arkansas P, 1991.

Bullock, Richard, and John Trimbur, eds. *The Politics of Writing Instruction: Postsecondary.* Portsmouth, NH: Boynton/Cook-Heinemann, 1991.

Clifford, John, and John Schilb, eds. *Writing Theory and Critical Theory.* New York: MLA, 1994.

Cooper, Anna Julia. "The Higher Education of Women." *A Voice from the South.* 1892. New York: Oxford, 1988. 48–79.

———. "Womanhood a Vital Element in the Regeneration and Progress of a Race." Logan 53–74.

Crowley, Sharon. "A Letter to the Editors." Clifford and Schilb 319–26.

Dean, Terry. "Multicultural Classrooms, Monocultural Teachers." *College Composition and Communication* 40 (1989): 223–37.

Delpit, Lisa D. "Skills and Other Dilemmas of a Progressive Black Educator." *Harvard Educational Review* 56 (1986): 379–85.

Flynn, Elizabeth A. "Composition Studies from a Feminist Perspective." Bullock and Trimbur 137–54.

Fox, Tom. "Literacy and Activism: A Response to bell hooks." *Journal of Advanced Composition* 14 (1994): 564–70.

Gale, Frederic G., ed. *Multiculturalism in the Writing Classroom.* Spec. issue of *Teaching English in the Two-Year College* 21 (1994): 91–160.

hooks, bell. *Talking Back: Thinking Feminist, Thinking Black.* Boston: South End, 1989.

———. *Teaching to Transgress: Education as the Practice of Freedom.* New York: Routledge, 1994.

Houston, Marsha. "The Politics of Difference: Race, Class, and Women's Communication." *Women Making Meaning: New Feminist Directions in Communication.* Ed. Lana F. Rakow. New York: Routledge, 1992. 45–59.

Jarratt, Susan C. "Feminism and Composition: The Case for Conflict." *Contending with Words.* Ed. Patricia Harkin and John Schilb. New York: MLA, 1991. 105–23.

Johnson, Cheryl. "Participatory Rhetoric and the Teacher as Racial/Gendered Subject." *College English* 56 (1994): 409–19.

Karabel, Jerome. "Fighting Words." Rev. of *Teaching to Transgress* and *Outlaw Culture,* by bell hooks. *New York Times* 18 Dec. 1994, sec. 7: 27.

Kraditor, Aileen. *The Ideas of the Woman Suffrage Movement, 1899–1929.* Garden City: Doubleday, 1971.

Logan, Shirley Wilson, ed. *With Pen and Voice: A Critical Anthology of Nineteenth-Century African-American Women.* Carbondale: Southern Illinois UP, 1995.

Middleton, Joyce Irene. "Back to Basics; or, The Three R's: Race, Rhythm, and Rhetoric." *Teaching English in the Two-Year College* 21 (1994): 104–13.

Miller, Susan. "The Feminization of Composition." Bullock and Trimbur 39–53.

Olson, Gary A. "bell hooks and the Politics of Literacy: A Conversation." *Journal of Advanced Composition* 14 (1994): 1–19.

"Retention Rates of African-American College Students." *Journal of Blacks in Higher Education* 6 (1994–95): 56.

Stanton, Elizabeth Cady, Susan B. Anthony, and Matilda Josyln Gage. *History of Woman Suffrage.* Vol. 2. 1881. New York: Sourcebook, 1970.

Sterling, Dorothy. *We Are Your Sisters: Black Women in the Nineteenth Century.* New York: Norton, 1984.

United States. Dept. of Education. *Faculty and Instructional Staff: Who Are They and What Do They Do?* Washington: Natl. Center for Educ. Statistics, 1994.

Williams, Fannie Barrier. "The Intellectual Progress of the Colored Women of the United States since the Emancipation Proclamation." Logan 106–19.

27 Reading and Writing Differences: The Problematic of Experience

MIN-ZHAN LU

This essay explores a feminist writing pedagogy that asks teachers and students to examine the political uses and abuses of personal experience when reading and writing differences. As feminist critics have forcefully cautioned us from the perspective of current debate on issues of identity, difference, and representation in literary, cultural, and marginality studies, the right of one class to speak is always based on the oppression and silencing of another (hooks, *Yearning* and *Teaching;* Minh-ha; Probyn; Spivak, "Can"). These critics argue that in validating the authority of the personal, academic feminist readers need to reflect on their privileged social location and be vigilant toward the tendency to invoke experience as an inherent right that erases differences along lines of race, class, gender, or sexual identity. We need to imagine ways of using experience critically: experience should motivate us to care about another's differences and should disrupt the material conditions that have given rise to it.

Using my attempt to teach Sandra Cisneros's short story "Little Miracles, Kept Promises" in a writing-intensive literature class cross-listed with the women's studies program at Drake, a private university in the Midwest, I describe a tendency among us to put our gendered experience forward as a critical criterion for subsuming differences and to separate issues of gender from those of race, class, or sexual identity. I propose teaching practices aimed at combatting this tendency through experimentation with ways of making critical use of our gender experience. I argue that composition pedagogies based on revision through sequenced reading and writing assignments— revision defined as a means for exploring different ways of seeing—can be used to advance the feminist project of making experience work both experientially and analytically. Such pedagogies are put forward in David Bartholomae and Anthony Petrosky's *Facts, Artifacts, and Counterfacts* and *Ways of Reading*.

From *Feminism and Composition Studies: In Other Words.* Ed. Susan C. Jarratt and Lynn Worsham. New York: Modern Language Association, 1998. 239–51.

Cisneros's story portrays life near the Texas-Mexico border through a series of short letters left before the statues of saints. When asked to interpret the story, most of my students write about those letters in which issues of gender play a prominent role. My students' papers suggest a shared interest in contesting gender inequality. They also suggest that this interest is enabling, that it helps them connect with lives portrayed in the story that would otherwise appear foreign and strange to them. But their interest in confronting sexism is accompanied by a general indifference to the interlocking of sexism with other forms of oppression. That indifference results in simplistic readings of the letters. To illustrate, I use my students' responses to two letters in the Cisneros story, one signed by Adelfa Vásquez and the other by Barbara Ybañez.

Students often read Adelfa's letter as an example of the older generation's adherence to traditional female roles and Barbara's letter as evidence of the younger generation's struggle against such gender construction. Two sentences toward the end of Adelfa's letter stand out for my students: "Zulema would like to finish school but I says she can just forget about it now. She is our oldest and her place is at home helping us out I told her" (222). One student reads the sentences as pointing to "a culture that intended for the women to stay home and not get an education." Another asks, "If she [Zulema] were male, would an education be granted? . . . The household chores would completely fall into the hands of Adelfa, if Zulema goes to school. Adelfa is confining Zulema to the traditional Mexican role of women." Students do discuss other parts of the letter, such as Adelfa's plea for "clothes, furniture, shoes, dishes, . . . anything that don't eat" (222) and the inadequate disability check the family receives. But such discussion tends to appear in a different section of the students' papers, in the context of the poverty experienced by members of the community. Students approach the Vásquez family's financial plight as separate from rather than intertwined with Adelfa's attempt to convince Zulema that her place is at home. The possibility that Zulema, being the oldest, is needed at home to help relieve the family's economic stress seems overruled by students' conviction that Zulema is needed to help out with house chores, even though there is no reference to that concern in Adelfa's letter. Students' initial interpretation of Adelfa's letter suggests that students are making two assumptions: first, that issues of gender are not interrelated to issues of economic class and, second, that gender divisions are solely a matter of who does the chores around the house.

The same conceptual framework is evident in student approaches to the letter signed by Barbara Ybañez. One student writes, "Ms. Ybañez doesn't want to be subservient to a man. She wants to find someone who will 'cook or clean and look after himself.' Her letter also reveals that she thinks men can become a 'pain in the nelgas.' As another woman, Teresa, says in her letter, men can become 'a heavy cross' that restricts the freedom of the female."

Two other aspects of Barbara's letter stand out for my students: Barbara identifies herself as "Ms. Ybañez," and she is college educated. As one student puts it, "Ms. Ybañez represents the younger generation who are no longer willing to play the traditional gender roles because they have had the benefit of education." But few students refer to the third paragraph of Barbara's letter: "I would appreciate it very much if you sent me a man who speaks Spanish, who at least can pronounce his name the way it's supposed to be pronounced. Someone please who never calls himself 'Hispanic' unless he is applying for a grant from Washington, DC." (222).

Their lack of interest in this section again indicates a tendency to separate issues of gender from those of ethnicity. It is also telling that the few students who do refer to this section focus on Barbara's wish to find "a man who speaks Spanish." In their papers they place this fact in a discussion of the younger generation's concern to retain ethnic ties or cultural heritage. My students all ignore the last sentence of the paragraph, where Barbara articulates an interest in a man who shares her contempt for the official label "Hispanic" that Washington, DC, assigns to people like her. Furthermore, while many students notice her description of herself, "Ms.," no one refers to her description of the "educated" man she seeks: Chicano. My students' silence on these aspects of Barbara's letter suggests their identification with the hegemonic indifference to racial and ethnic differences.

In many ways, my students' initial interpretations of Cisneros's story exemplify the kind of essentialism that operates in unreflecting use of the personal in some versions of feminism and that has been powerfully critiqued by feminists on the margin. The feminist dictum that the personal is political has taught us to recognize the centrality of the gendered experience in the production of knowledge. But as feminists on the margin have repeatedly pointed out, recognition of the primacy of experience, in its most limiting forms, can be an essentializing force and erase differences; such "feminism becomes a password misleading us into a false notion of 'oneness' with all women purely on the grounds of gender" (McRobbie, "Politics" 52). Too often, the gendered experience of the academic researcher or reader (white, straight, middle class) functions as a universalizing term to overwrite the experiences of others under study. I don't think it is a coincidence that most students enrolled in my course say they are white, of European descent, from middle-class or upper-middle-class families, and committed to feminist issues and that their papers on Cisneros's story demonstrate a yearning for universality. Some of my students later point out, when writing about their self-location as readers, that they are drawn to certain experiences in the story because they have to some degree lived them. As one student puts it, "As much as I try to focus on point of view other than the one I am used to, it may sometimes be that I read a little bit of myself in the text." Many have been told, or know female friends who have been told, to stay home and finish the dishes, and many know parents who don't think education is important for "girls." They have or know of fathers and boyfriends who wouldn't share household chores. And they have been told to take German to keep up their ethnic ties. These experiences have not only figured in and fed into the questions the students bring to Cisneros's text but also have kept the students from attending to the differences between the familiar story of oneself and the story of an other. The task facing a teacher is to help students rethink ways of using personal experience so that readings through the personal will not be at the expense of other stories and selves.

Wrestling with this problem, I have been influenced by the work of feminist critics on the margin who approach the issue from the perspective of the debate in feminism and cultural studies over issues of identity, difference, and representation. Elspeth Probyn argues for the need to theorize the self as a "double entity," as something that is not "simply put forward" but, rather, "reworked in its enunciation" (1–2). She argues that it is useful to think of experience as working on two levels. Experience can testify to "an immediate experiential self" (16), one revealing the gendered, sexed, classed, and racial facticity of being in the social. But experience can also be used to recognize an epistemological self, a self that politicizes itself by analyzing the material conditions that gave rise to it and that posits ways of changing those conditions while transforming itself in the process. Using Raymond Williams's concept of the structure of feeling and Michel Foucault's notion of the care of the self, Probyn explores how feminists might make experience work on both the experiential and analytic levels. Probyn posits three analytic possibilities for experience. First, experience can be used to analyze the facticity of our material being—the composition of the social formation that creates us (21). Second, it can be used to reveal connections that, in its weakest form, it conceals—conceals, because experience can mask the construction of its own ground. Third, experience can impel an analysis of one's differentiated relations to levels of the social formation (21). The first two kinds of analysis can help us consider not only what our experience allows us to reach toward but also what it might prevent us from reaching. It can prevent us, for example, from reifying itself into the sole criterion for critical analysis, as most of my students seem to have done when interpreting the Cisneros story. Analyzing our experience along these two lines can move us toward the third possibility, where the self is used not as an end in and of itself but as the opening of a perspective that allows us to conceive of transforming ourselves with the aid of others. In this way the self becomes not a mirror of us but, as Stuart Hall puts it, a "representation which is able to constitute us as new kinds of subjects and thereby enable us to discover spaces from which to speak" ("Cultural Identity" 237).

Exploring the analytic possibilities of experience in the three directions mapped by Probyn offers alternative uses of the personal for readers who, like my students, are committed to contesting gender inequality in the United States today. It can help such readers learn ways of reading that use their gendered experience but do not efface difference through omission. This exploring makes them reflect on the connections between various systems of oppression masked by their experience and imagine ways of disrupting their potential implication in other forms of discrimination. A teacher should initiate a series of readings and writings that help students revise their habitual approaches to difference by encouraging them to experiment with alternative ways of using their experiential selves. We need assignments that ask students to explore the analytic possibilities of experience by locating the experience that grounds their habitual approach to differences; by sketching the complex discursive terrain out of and in which the self habitually speaks; by investigating how that terrain delimits our understanding of differences along lines of race, class, sex, and gender; and by exploring personal and social motivations for transforming one's existing self-location in the process of rereading and rewriting.

One composition pedagogy that helps students use their experience critically is to have a sequence of reading and writing that prompts them to investigate and test different ways of seeing and to use that inquiry for revising their familiar ways of seeing (Bartholomae and Petrosky, *Facts* and *Ways*). I look for texts that call attention to the interlocking of all systems of domination (race, class, sexual identity, religion, ethnicity, age, education, physical norm, gender), that validate the primacy of experience while using it critically, and that offer a vocabulary for theorizing the politics of the personal in feminist projects. Through the years, I have used texts by such feminist critics on the margin as Gloria Anzaldúa, bell hooks, Kobena Mercer, Audre Lorde, Adrienne Rich, Gayatri Spivak, and Trinh T. Minh-ha.

The works of hooks and Minh-ha help my students explore the potential uses and abuses of our gendered experiences when we read and write differences. hooks's essay "Reflections on Race and Sex" speaks to my students with particular power because it is aimed at feminists and liberation workers who, like them, yearn to eradicate oppression (*Yearning* 13) but tend to take an either-or approach to discrimination along lines of sexual identity, gender, class, and race. Furthermore, the essay appeals to them because hooks's argument for focusing on the interlocking of all systems of oppression is grounded on incidents that are close to home—a crime in the news, a personal account of an attack on a woman by a black man. The students are eager to apply hooks's approach to their daily life—and to their initial readings of Cisneros's story. Another essay that my students feel applies to their situation is Minh-ha's "Difference: A Special Third World Women Issue." They are particularly struck by her argument that the "'wo-' appended to 'man' in sexist contexts is not unlike 'Third World,' 'third,' 'minority,' or 'color' affixed to woman in pseudo-feminist contexts." Minh-ha convinces them of the need to examine their yearning for universality, that is, the tendency to efface difference through the notion of a generic woman reified from the experiences of white, middle-class heterosexuals (97). The essay also gives them some concrete ideas on how to combat that yearning.

Reading these essays along the line of the potential use and abuse of one's gendered experience in the process of reading-writing differences helps my students and me posit alternative perspectives and thus locate rationales for rereading Cisneros's "Little Miracles" to revise their initial papers. The following is an example of the kind of revision assignment that can come out of such a reading:

Assignment A

"Progressive folks must insist, wherever we engage in discussions of . . .
issues of race and gender, on the complexity of our experience in a racist, sexist society."

— BELL HOOKS

"The understanding of difference is a shared responsibility, which requires a
minimum of willingness to reach out to the unknown."

—TRINH T. MINH-HA

For this paper, use our class discussions of the essays by hooks and
Minh-ha to reread Cisneros's story and critique your initial interpretation
of this story in your last paper.

When rereading the Cisneros story, try to approach it from the perspective of the interlocking of issues of race, class, sexual identity, religion,
and gender. When critiquing your paper, consider the extent to which
you were able to fully acknowledge the complex experiences portrayed
in the letters. Locate moments in your paper where you might be said to
have taken an either-or approach to the complex interlocking of various
systems of domination.

As you can see, the purpose of Assignment A is to ask students to reread
Cisneros's story and their initial interpretation from an alternative perspective, one they have formulated from discussing two essays by two feminist
critics. This alternative perspective directly challenges the tendency in those
who wish to end sexism to subsume differences, a tendency that surfaces
in most of my students' papers but supports those who structure their approaches on the wish to end other forms of domination as well. Rather, it asks
students to become more self-conscious about the ways in which their interest
in combating one particular form of oppression might delimit—enable as
well as prevent them from reading-writing differences. Such a revision assignment is best accompanied by one that helps students use their lived experiences of social domination to locate personal and social reasons for trying out
this alternative perspective. My class reads Anzaldúa's essay "La consciencia
de la mestiza: Toward a New Consciousness" to explore ways of using the figure of the mestiza to examine the structural underpinning of experience and
to talk about its analytic possibilities. Anzaldúa depicts the mestiza as that
juncture where beliefs and forces cutting across lines of race, class, gender, sex,
ethnicity, and religion collide (387). The image of collision grounds the personal in a complex discursive terrain. Anzaldúa argues that the first step of the
mestiza is to take inventory of the baggage inherited from her ancestors—
beliefs, values, and viewpoints—so that she "puts history through a sieve,
winnows out the lies, looks at the forces that we as a race, as women, have
been a part of" (390). My students and I find the image of putting history
through a sieve helpful for projecting ways of using our experiential selves to

examine the extent to which our viewpoints illuminate as well as tell lies about our inscription in interlocking systems of oppression. We interpret the sieve as the mestiza's determination to end all forms of oppression. It can help her decide which notions of the familiar to surrender and to which foreign ways of seeing and thinking she should make herself vulnerable. The act of taking inventory and putting history through a sieve offers us a vocabulary for talking about how we as readers can use experience to rework our habitual approaches to differences.

Our reading of the mestiza provides us with another revision assignment:

Assignment B

"As I looked for common passions, sentiments shared by folks across race, class, gender, and sexual practice, I was struck by the depths of longing in many of us. . . . [T]here are many individuals with race, gender, and class privilege who are longing to see the kind of revolutionary change that will end domination and oppression even though their lives would be completely and utterly transformed. The shared space and feeling of 'yearning' opens up the possibility of common ground where all these differences might meet and engage one another."

— BELL HOOKS

"Her [the new mestiza's] first step is . . . a conscious rupture with all oppressive traditions of all cultures and religions. . . . Deconstruct, construct. She becomes a *nahual,* able to transform herself into a tree, a coyote, into another person."

– GLORIA ANZALDÚA

For this assignment, use the image of the mestiza to locate personal-social motives for revising your initial paper on Cisneros's "Little Miracle" from the perspective put forward by critics such as hooks and Minh-ha.

The following are some questions to get you started:

Take inventory of your personal experiences of oppression along lines of race, gender, class, sex, ethnicity, age, education, physical norm, geographic region, or religion. Which type(s) of discrimination are you most familiar with? In what particular forms? Which have you had least experience with? Why?

Consider the extent to which your personal history might affect how you enact your yearning to eradicate oppression. What particular viewpoints and forces of which you have been a part can be used to advance your interest to combat which type(s) of oppression? Why? What particular "familiar" viewpoints and privileges must be surrendered for you to end which type(s) of oppression? Why? Which foreign ways of seeing and thinking might you need to make yourself vulnerable to? Why?

Examine the ways in which your personal history might have affected your ability to attend to the interlocking of all forms of oppression when you approached differences, such as reading Cisneros's "Little Miracle" in your original paper. For example, how have your experiences in certain forms of oppression enabled you to relate to certain aspects of the text? How has your (lack of) experience in other forms of oppression kept you from engaging with other aspects of the text?

As someone yearning to end discrimination and transform yourself, how might you revise your reading of Cisneros's "Little Miracle" so that your immediate interest in ending particular form(s) of oppression could enhance your interest in rather than keep you from deconstructing other form(s) of oppression operating in society and portrayed in Cisneros's text?

Together, Assignments A and B can motivate students to revise their initial approach to Cisneros's story. Although in our class discussion we focused on the applicability of the image of the mestiza to our approaches to Cisneros's story, we also learned to use the image to analyze the thoughts and actions of several characters portrayed in the story and analyze as well the author's position. Taking inventory, quite a few students observed that their Protestant or nonreligious background made it initially difficult for them not to see as foreign, primitive, or silly the practice of writing letters and leaving charms to "idols." That and their wish to respect cultural differences led them either to avoid discussing the text's references to religion or to approach those references strictly as a unique cultural heritage. Such self-reflection led one student to complicate her gender reading of Barbara's letter by taking into consideration the intersection of gender, race, and religion:

> She doesn't want to be subservient to all "masters": a man, a government, or a god which is keeping her from what she believes she deserves. She is not afraid to say what she wants, even if it is not what the *masters* have chosen for her. She asks for someone "who's not ashamed to be seen cooking or cleaning or looking after himself." She wants someone who never calls himself "Hispanic," when knowing this is the identification expected by those handing out grants in Washington DC. And she tells the Saint that if the Saint doesn't send her the "man" she asks, she will "throw him back" and "turn [the] statue upside down." Ms. Barbara Ybañez understands that she has "put up with *too much* too long." She believes she is too intelligent, powerful, and beautiful to put up with *any* of the *masters* running her life.

Attention to her habitual indifference to issues of religion, race, and class led another student to revise her reading of another letter in Cisneros's story signed in code, by a "B2nj1m3n T." In her original paper, this student pointed out that Benjamin probably does not feel safe to write about his "love sadness" for another man in either Spanish or English because homosexual feelings are not acceptable to either community. In her revision, she added, "It is also significant that Benjamin writes to not just Christ but the 'Miraculous Black Christ of Esquipulas.' A black Christ would probably better understand and be able to intercede in Benjamin's behalf because he would understand the prejudice Benjamin faces."

Another student, taking inventory, felt authorized to use her experience as a practicing Catholic and an "older generation" woman, which originally marked her as the other in this classroom, to explore the function of saints for the least powerful of the congregation: women and the poor. She revised her reading of Adelfa's letter by pointing out that "since the male of the house was on disability, the burden of supporting the family falls on other members of the family, including Adelfa and Zulema—the oldest child. St. Martin de Porres was Adelfa's choice of saint because as founder of an orphanage, he knew the problems of feeding hungry children. So he would understand Adelfa and help her make Zulema 'see some sense.'" Writing about her personal history also motivated this student to complicate the notion of ethnic ties that surfaced in the class's interpretation of why characters who think like feminists, such as Ms. Barbara Ybañez and Rosario (Chayo) De Leon, would leave letters and charms to the saints:

> Rosario decides that "all that self-sacrifice, all that silent suffering" of her mother and grandmother is "not me." But she also realizes, because of the taunts she suffered from her relatives when she declared her intention of remaining single and becoming an artist, that "those who suffer have a special power"—"the power of understanding someone else's pain." This taught her to be proud to be "her mother's daughter and her ancestor's child."

At the same time, reviewing the particularity of her Catholic experience, this student becomes more attentive to the particularity of the Catholic experience portrayed in Rosario's letter:

> To Rosario, the Virgin Mary is not "Mary the mild." For in the Catholicism of her people, [Mary's] name is also the Coalaxopeuh and "our mother Tonantzin," someone with the "power to rally a people when a country was born" and with "Dominion over Serpents." In pleading to the Virgencita, Rosario is saying that she has discovered from her ancestors a powerful weapon for fighting oppressions. And she means to use it to fend off the hurt she feels from the derision she gets from her mother and relatives because she wants to stay single and become an artist.

These revisions, prompted by a sequence of reading and writing assignments that ask students to consider alternative approaches put forward by critics, show that exploring the structural underpinnings of one's experience can motivate students to revise their habitual approaches to differences. That is, writing the personal can motivate students both to use unfamiliar approaches and to use the familiar critically. Writing the personal also authorizes students whose backgrounds are other than those of a majority of the class to use the specificity of their lived experience to open up alternative approaches to the text. For example, writing about his experience as a short person, one of the four male students located a lived reason not only for confirming his intellectual alignment with feminism but also for becoming more aware of his lack of interest in issues of class.

Revision assignments should be followed by an assignment that asks students to theorize the critical use of experience they have enacted so that they can more self-consciously employ this method in the future and outside the classroom:

Assignment C

For this assignment, use the thoughts you have generated doing the last two assignments to write a revision of your original paper on Cisneros's "Little Miracle." When you have finished your revision, comment on a separate sheet of paper about your experience in doing this sequence of assignments. How would you characterize the use of personal experience in this process? How many directions did you take? Which of these directions do you find necessary but difficult? Why? How did you go about overcoming such difficulties?

By such a sequence of reading and writing assignments, composition studies can contribute to students' rethinking the use of self and experience in feminist enunciation. With radical thinkers like Paulo Freire and with the debate on issues of identity, difference, and representation in literary, cultural, and feminist studies, composition has a long tradition of developing critical pedagogies aimed at helping one reflect on one's self-location as a reader-writer and explore ways of changing how one reads, thinks, and lives. The sequencing of reading and writing assignments is not the only method available to compositionists interested in rethinking the use of self and experience in feminist approaches to differences.

The need to explore other ways of utilizing our expertise in critical pedagogy to make experience work both experientially and analytically is urgent for those of us resisting the hegemony of neoconservatism in the United States of the 1990s. As hooks points out in *Teaching to Transgress,* "family values" has become a fix-all magic phrase in discussions of current social problems. Especially alarming is that the family evoked in such discussions is one in which sexist roles are upheld as a stabilizing tradition. Not surprisingly, this vision of family is coupled with "a notion of security that suggests we are most safe with people of our same group, race, class, religion, and so on" (28). The neoconservative rhetoric of "family values" encourages us to subscribe to a social amnesia about the real cause of our problems: the intertwining of racial, sexual, economic, and gender oppressions and the consequent social segregation. The move toward social isolation and amnesia is also prominent in both liberal and conservative models of multiculturalism in college and university classrooms, where cultural diversity is often studied without rigorous reflection on the privileged location that authorizes our right to study and speak about differences. Given such a pervasive conservatism, we should more actively mobilize our expertise in critical pedagogy and feminist thinking to call attention to the interlocking of all systems of oppression in our everyday lives, whether we are debating a solution to social problems like violence and poverty or trying to reach a multicultural interpretation of a text like "Little Miracles."

The feminist project of making experience work on both the experiential and analytic levels is particularly valuable in combating the hegemony of neo-conservative rhetoric, because of feminism's continual emphasis on the primacy of firsthand knowledge. My students' papers on Cisneros's "Little Miracles" show that my students not only have this knowledge but also know how to make it a criterion for critical analysis. I find it heartening that, despite the privileged class and racial background of most students in the private, midwestern campus where I teach, the work of colleagues in the university to establish a women's studies program has produced a sizable number of students versed in the use of the experiential for critical analysis. If we can move them to recognize that gender is not the only determinant of our identity and that to end sexism we need to use our gendered experiences analytically to fight all forms of oppression, we can broaden our alliances in the struggle against neoconservatism. Furthermore, learning to make experience work both experientially and analytically in our day-to-day teaching and learning can unite teachers and students across the lines of race, class, gender, and sexual identity. We can mobilize our lived experiences of one form of discrimination to end social amnesia about other forms of discrimination. In that critical space differences can and must engage one another. For it reminds us that in spite of our best intentions, social isolation and amnesia can result from unreflective use of the experiential and that no one system of discrimination—gender, race, or class—can be eradicated if we do not use our lived experiences analytically to stop other forms of domination.

NOTE

An earlier version of this article was given as a keynote address at the University of Maine Conference on Multiculturalism. My thanks to members of the audience and to Bruce Horner for their comments.

WORKS CITED

Anzaldúa, Gloria. "La consciencia de la mestiza: Toward a New Consciousness." Colombo, Cullen, and Lisle 386–95.
Bartholomae, David, and Anthony Petrosky. *Facts, Artifacts, and Counterfacts: Theory and Method for a Reading and Writing Course.* Upper Montclair: Boynton, 1986.
———, eds. *Ways of Reading: An Anthology for Writers.* 2nd ed. Boston: Bedford, 1990.
Cisneros, Sandra. "Little Miracles, Kept Promises." Colombo, Cullen, and Lisle 221–32.
Colombo, Gary, Robert Cullen, and Bonnie Lisle, eds. *Rereading America: Cultural Contexts for Critical Thinking and Writing.* 2nd ed. Boston: Bedford, 1992.
Hall, Stuart. "Cultural Identity and Diaspora." *Identity, Community, Culture, Difference.* Ed. Jonathan Rutherford. London: Lawrence, 1990. 222–37.
hooks, bell. *Teaching to Transgress: Education as the Practice of Freedom.* New York: Routledge, 1994.
———. *Yearning: Race, Gender, and Cultural Politics.* Boston: South End, 1990.
McRobbie, Angela. "The Politics of Feminist Research: Between Talk, Text, and Action." *Feminist Review* 12 (1982): 46–57.
Minh-ha, Trinh T. "Difference: A Special Third World Women Issue." *Women, Native, Other: Writing Postcoloniality and Feminism.* Bloomington: Indiana UP, 1989. 79–116.
Probyn, Elspeth. *Sexing the Self: Gendered Positions in Cultural Studies.* London: Routledge, 1993.
Spivak, Gayatri Chakravorty. "Can the Subaltern Speak?" *Marxism and the Interpretation of Culture.* Ed. Cary Nelson and Lawrence Grossberg. Urbana: U of Illinois P, 1988. 271–311.

28 On Becoming a Woman: Pedagogies of the Self

SUSAN ROMANO

Future historians examining the particulars of late twentieth-century writing instruction doubtless will conclude that college-level literacy entailed significant practice in the assumption of alternate identities. Evidence of pseudonymous and anonymous electronic conferencing, of MOO sessions where fictive personae are required or encouraged, and of personal Web-page selves composed from multiple media will persuade these historians that writing teachers using electronic forms considered the idea of invented, multiple selves integral to literacy formation.

This essay takes you back to the early years of teaching with computer technologies—1986, 1987, and 1988—when teachers in networked classrooms using realtime conferencing software first began experimenting with what I call pedagogies of the self, teaching practices that undermine unitary concepts of self and induce students to take on alternate identities. For evidence, I turn to transcripts of online teaching archived at the University of Texas at Austin Computer Research Lab (CRL). In effect, I re-run in slow motion the magnetic tapes that have recorded the making of selves during realtime electronic conferencing, freezing frames to examine closely the range of subject positions made available to students—women students in particular—through their interactions with teachers and classmates. Electronic technologies not only alter our language practices, they provide both mechanism and impetus for reconsidering topics of long-standing interest to teachers and theorists of language, and the relationship of language to self is just such a topic. Across the centuries, theories of rhetoric have offered specialized vocabulary for figuring this relationship. Aristotelian ethos refers to the tailoring of self for persuasive purposes. Renaissance rhetoricians coined sprezzatura to signify an oscillating, contradictory self, whose artful instability constituted decorum (Lanham). Eighteenth- and nineteenth-century Scottish rhetorical theorists understood self as mind; hence the study of psychology directed the teaching of rhetoric

From *Passions, Pedagogies, and 21st Century Technologies.* Ed. Gail E. Hawisher and Cynthia L. Selfe. Logan: Utah State University Press, 1999. 249–67.

(Horner). Kenneth Burke proposed identification—self location in relation to others—as the central mechanism of persuasive rhetoric. Poststructuralists, argues Linda Brodkey, "articulate relations between a possible self and a possible reality (which includes possible others)" (238). Postmodernism conceives the subject as multiple, competed for, and constituted in discourse. Finally, information age rhetoricians newly theorize subjectivity as a process of morphing or, to use a different metaphor, as the recombination of social identities (Balsamo; Haynes; Heath).

Whereas rhetorical theory addresses the relationship of self to language and provides a vocabulary for articulating this relationship, histories of rhetorical education (or writing instruction) examine the pedagogical procedures by which ideologies (including ideologies of the self) are transmitted to consciousness, or, alternatively, how pedagogies at the level of everyday practice constitute ideologies. In either philosophy of education, teachers are not absent from scenes of writing instruction because pedagogies, whether objectivist or epistemic, transmissive or social constructionist, are designed and implemented by teachers. I make this point because teachers using electronic conferencing technologies have frequently represented their influence on classroom discourse as negligible, celebrating their diminished presences and ceding classroom management to software applications. Eager, perhaps, that their institutionally conferred authority not undermine a student-centered model of education, they neglect conceptualizing a rhetorical authority designed neither to control knowledge nor win arguments with students, but rather to assist the development and maintenance of equitable discursive environments. I find, however, that teachers' reluctance to imbricate themselves in student discourse does not preclude their enactment of rhetorical authority.

"Rhetorical authority" implies both the use of persuasive language and an understanding of how discourse is working in a particular environment at a particular time. "Rhetoric" is a richly nuanced term, situated variously within different systems of knowledge, and historically, a "rhetorical" practice has been complex and specialized, something other than mere verbal presence among others. Indeed, Aristotle begins the *Art of Rhetoric* by making this very distinction:

> [F]or all [persons] up to a certain point, endeavor to criticize or uphold an argument, to defend themselves or to accuse. Now, the majority of people do this either at random or with a familiarity arising from habit. But since both these ways are possible, it is clear that matters can be reduced to a system, for it is possible to examine the reason why some attain their end by familiarity and others by chance and such an examination all would at once admit to be the function of an art. (I, i)

Granting that success in argument is well within the reach of those who practice speaking among others regularly, and certainly not out of reach of those who rely upon fortune alone if such persons are willing to take bad fortune along with good, Aristotle argues for an analysis of the differences. Presumably, the habitually successful disputant has tacit knowledge that well might be systematized so that interactive, public reasoning (or argumentation) becomes a discipline, that is, an art made accessible both theoretically and practically. Although Aristotle conceives success in terms of winners and losers of particular arguments, a teacher inserting herself into the electronic conference is perhaps more interested in exercising an authority that fosters equitable discussion.[1]

By its innovative character, much of our teaching in interactive electronic environments continues to fall into the category that Aristotle might refer to as "chance" teaching, and which Plato disparagingly would call "cookery," for teachers in computer-mediated environments necessarily test the uses of electronic technologies for writing instruction on the spot, by trial and by error, risking chance outcomes. To examine the differences between electronic conferences left to chance and electronic conferences whose teachers practice a rhetorical authority, I examine conference transcripts logged early in the history of computers and writing, when all software features were innovative. Not only do these transcripts make available for analysis many examples of classroom discourse, they also provide access to numerous electronic discussions during which teachers analyze their own innovative practices. Hence a researcher has access not only to student discourse, alongside evidence of teachers' discursive presences, but also to the conversations whereby teachers begin to newly theorize writing instruction from practice itself, to the process of transforming risky pedagogy to disciplinary art. Researching online teaching is an interpretive practice, for I have had to read over the shoulders of teachers and students, so to speak, tracing out patterns perhaps invisible to these participants, despite their active presences at the very discursive events under scrutiny. As lurker historian, I read primarily from a teacher's perspective, with interest in outcomes but without responsibility for them, and I read at a more leisurely pace.

The scene of my investigation, then, is the online classroom; the object of inquiry, pedagogy; the human beings in question, students and teachers; the focus, women students. Focusing on women is appropriate for investigating the relationship of self to language in online environments on two counts. First, women not infrequently report that finding a satisfactory location from which to speak as women is not as simple as we would like it to be.[2] It follows that people who experience participation in online conferences as liberatory might wish to stop and listen closely to opposing accounts. Second, at the site whose documents comprise my research materials, gender issues pervaded classroom discourse. Gender became topical, for instance, when students read Deborah Tannen on conversation analysis, when they studied representations of women's speech in cartoons of the 1970s, when they debated implementing non-sexist language in the classroom, and when they read Helena Viramontes in tandem with Ernest Hemingway.[3] Gender became topical even when teachers did not so intend, for students frequently invited each other to a gendered social identity from which to read both print texts and the texts they were engaged in building online.

SEIZING THE DAY

Revolutions provide opportunities for the marginalized to participate in the rearrangement of the social, political, and economic hierarchies that affect their lives, and a media revolution is no exception. Our current media revolution offers opportunities to propose new social arrangements with an array of writing tools. It provides especially rich opportunities for women's activism because a gap between old and new literacy conventions has been forced, and the already legitimized concepts of "innovative" and "alternative" may be used to advantage by those who wish to wedge innovative and alternative selves into the new discourses. The proliferation of representational venues encourages women to fragment unitary conceptions of the female by representing selves in graphic and textual shapes not easily categorizable.

We need not be naive, however, in assuming unilateral correspondences between new media representations and the various civil, economic, and political arrangements that govern material lives,[4] nor even in assuming automatic correspondences between women's new self-representations online and equity in virtual space. Faced with building opportunities galore and few guarantees of outcome, we may wish to retain issues of equity in the form of open-ended questions: How do textual or graphical representations affect social arrangements both on and off line and what accounts for the variable effects?

Discussions of equity and computers often turn to the technicalities and politics of providing access, for this is an area over which we can plot remedial action. It is more difficult to imagine how change is effected rhetorically, once physical access to virtual spaces is provided. Indeed, it seems that our metaphors mark the very limitations of our imaginations. The metaphors of space and frontier frequently employed to describe online life contribute to the mystification of social arrangements in virtual environments just as they did during westward expansion. Such metaphors propose that once provided the vehicles by which to access virtual space, women are unstoppable in their quest for self-empowerment: they need only get there and fill the space. We might begin inquiry into the space metaphor by asking women pioneers whether they would confine "ease" in occupying the spaces to matters of technical access.

Indeed this was one of the questions Gail Hawisher and Patricia Sullivan addressed when researching professional women's uses of electronic media. For twenty-eight days, thirty women conversed about their occupancy of e-spaces, a term used by the researchers to designate human cultures constructed by way of networked, online activities. Some women reported that difficult physical access did indeed prevent satisfactory online presence, but others located difficulty or ease in the discursive environment itself. Of these latter, some reported complete satisfaction with their online cultures; others, some satisfaction for the chance to speak without interruption; and still others, dissatisfactions sufficient to induce them to abandon certain e-spaces in frustration and anger. Although the researchers were anxious not to allow accounts foregrounding discontent to override those of satisfaction, they were interested in the narratives documenting perceived inequities, and so am I, not because I wish to affirm women's victimization, but, on the contrary, because I believe that close examination of the discursive mechanisms causing dis-ease may promote the discipline and art of producing equitable discourse. My investigation borrows from Joan Wallach Scott's understanding of historiographical practice:

> Perhaps the most dramatic shift in my own thinking came through asking questions about *how* hierarchies such as those of gender are constructed or legitimized. The emphasis on "how" suggests a study of processes, not of origins, of multiple rather than single causes, of *rhetoric or discourse rather than ideology or consciousness.* (4; second emphasis mine)

I am less interested in dramatic episodes of flagrant, misogynist conduct, such as the infamous rape on LambdaMOO (Dibbell) than in the quotidian discursive events that de-neutralize the spaces available, enhancing or eroding their desirability as suitable locations from which to speak.

UNDER PSEUDONYM

The 1987, 1988, and 1989 records of online teaching at the University of Texas at Austin Computer Research Lab do not indicate whether teachers spoke directly to students about subjectivity. Teachers did, however, report a particular fascination with pseudonymous conferencing, a practice certainly instrumental in altering subjectivity. During a 1988 graduate seminar, for example, graduate student and faculty instructors discussed the possible effects of pseudonymity on their students' sense of the relationship of self to language as experienced during online discussion. "FORUM" (now "InterChange") refers to the realtime conferencing module of the Daedalus system. The following excerpt is taken from the middle of the conference:

> LESTER FAIGLEY: Nonetheless, it is fascinating how you feel compelled to jump into the discussions in FORUM when it is so easy to sit back and listen in an oral discussion without participating. I'm going to pass out the last transcript from my E309 class. The students all took pseudonyms. I also invited JoAnn Campbell. The text we discussed is an ethnography called THE COCKTAIL WAITRESS. It's interesting that not only did everybody participate, but that everybody participated almost immediately, even though I had no idea who was doing what. I want to use this transcript as a text to analyze, particularly the week after next.
>
> GRADUATE STUDENT: Lester, let's use pseudonyms for one of our sessions. Imagine the possibilities.
>
> GRADUATE STUDENT/CRL TEACHER: I have had similar success in my E309 class with pseudonymous FORUMS. I'm wondering why students jump in so easily, playfully. I talked to one girl in my class who said she assumed a persona exactly opposite of the way she felt she was, and said absurd statements that

contradicted her own beliefs, just to see how people reacted and to see what it felt like to say those things.

LESTER FAIGLEY: Are you suggesting that we go with pseudonyms next time?

GRADUATE STUDENT/CRL TEACHER: Lester: In a word, yes. Pseudonyms (and no-names) make for very different FORUMS. In such a confident and outspoken bunch as this, we might not notice it, but in my English 309 class, where there are people who are afraid of their ideas sounding stupid, the pseudonymous FORUM was a smashing success.

GRADUATE STUDENT: I think the pseudonym idea is great. I think of all shy freshman writers so reluctant to express an opinion.

These off-the-cuff messages begin the process of building theory from practice, and although not explicitly articulated as such, two distinct theories of self and language are set forth during the sequence. One theory proposes that a student writing under pseudonym "outs" a formerly hidden or inhibited self through language ("shy freshman writers . . . reluctant to express an opinion"), and the other, that pseudonymity enables the construction of selves in language ("[a student] assume[s] a persona exactly opposite of the way she felt she was").[5] The first theory accommodates a writer's sense of self set free from social/discursive constraints, able to take advantage of the virtual spaces at her disposal, whereas the latter envisions pseudo-selves positioned within a social/discursive environment, regardless of space. Indeed, testing alternate personae in the company of others entails careful observation of the effects of one's speech within a particular environment.

During the above conversation, the instructors introduce several kinds of evidence supporting continued use of pseudonymity: near universality of student participation (formerly fearful students speak out), degree of student enjoyment (students jump in playfully), and increase in students' repertoires of possible discursive positionings (a student tries on different personae to see how the class reacts). Although the first two arguments are not specific to writing instruction, the third argument certainly is. If teachers of interactive argumentation begin with the premise, then, that pseudonymous conferencing is advantageous because it expands the range of subject positions available to students, then they would necessarily conclude that the practice of pseudonymous conferencing at Texas in the early days taught this lesson only erratically. Records indicate that some students taking on prefabricated literary personae created discursively impoverished characters. "Betsy Ross," to use an example from a pseudonymous conference featuring women in history, was unable to imagine herself speaking outside the confines of her needle. Her remarks consisted entirely of offers to sew for others, and she devised no alternative discursive action. Not infrequently, students in pseudonymous conferences withdrew into prefabricated literary or historical worlds, articulating new selves that were hard pressed to converse productively across spans of time and genre, as when Moby Dick and George Washington struggled to find common ground. Still others were encouraged by pseudonymity to set out information about their personal lives that would be withheld under "real" (or regularly appearing) identities. Yet apparently pseudonymity was considered by most CRL instructors a universally excellent classroom activity, and no evaluative distinctions among pseudonymous sessions were forthcoming during these years.[6]

Although large claims about the pedagogical value of pseudonymity cannot be based on fragmentary evidence, such evidence indeed can serve to frame the issues it raises. If the purpose of pseudonymous and other pedagogies of the self is to teach that identity is a construct, that subjectivities may be altered at will or by circumstance, or that language is not transparent, then the particularities do not much matter. So long as a student practices constructing, reconstructing, altering, and fictionalizing the self, the lesson is learned. If, however, teachers are invested in the shape of the discourse they wish students to produce online, in expanding the range of students' discursive options, and in producing equitable discursive environments, they will need to examine more carefully the means that best serve these purposes. The question becomes, then, not "What are the technical means by which we can problematize student identities?" but rather, "To what ends do we do so?"

INTERROGATING THE FEMALE SUBJECT

Under certain circumstances, pseudonymous discussion may dramatize for students the argument that gender is a cultural and linguistic construct, and this lesson is known in culture studies jargon as "the interrogation of subjectivity," an educational procedure enabling people to apprehend the social forces at work in the formation of self-consciousness (Johnson). Implementing pseudonymity at Texas, however, may have served a more immediate purpose: establishing an equitable environment. For when gender became topical in sessions conducted under "real" social identities, the subjects placed under severe interrogation usually were women. Male students frequently antagonized female students by essentializing their behaviors, and it would become incumbent upon women to accept, refuse, or ignore the category "women," or to challenge the undesirable characteristics assigned to the category before speaking from within it, before allowing their experiences as women to openly inform their arguments.[7] Each option—to accept, refuse, ignore, or challenge—carries an array of immediate discursive consequences for the women students undergoing this form of interrogation. Indeed, the onus placed on women is striking. And to say so is by no means to fault the instructors who chose readings about women and by women in order to build women into the daily work of the language classroom. Nor should we necessarily fault male students who engaged, in many cases, not in the locker room dialectics described by Christine Boese in "A Virtual Locker Room," but rather in the familiar cultural practice of light, cross-gender teasing. Still, by being targeted, women students are more apt to experience the effects of a pedagogy of chance whose results are unpredictable, a matter of fortune. That is, by becoming the subjects under interrogation when gender is introduced into discussion, some women may indeed take advantage of the opportunity to become more savvy and "empowered" by practicing self-location within discourse when the going is tough. Others, however, may become silent or otherwise discursively disempowered, unable to find satisfactory locations from which to argue well.

Unpredictability of outcomes (or chance teaching) thus may be partially responsible for the election of pseudonymity as the medium of choice for interrogating gender, subjectivity, and language, at the CRL and elsewhere. Indeed, Donna LeCourt and Cynthia Haynes, in separate articles, have begun theorizing feminist subjectivity in networked environments from the practices they observe and participate in. Both researchers ground some of their observations in data produced during pseudonymous conferences, and both assume the exclusionary nature of discourse, its impermeability, its easily invoked hostility to women's presences, and the inadequacy of traditional rhetorics for theorizing procedures or providing satisfactory strategies for rhetorical action. Both invoke French feminist theory and reject expressivist rhetoric (one of the theories under consideration in the University of Texas CRL), finding expressivism an ineffective means for challenging patriarchal discourses. Whereas the tactics Haynes and LeCourt advocate may resemble various expressivisms by the inclusion of emotion as part of discursive repertoire and by the relaxation of politeness and decorum, these tactics are better understood as calculative discursive moves and their authors as among Lanham's "cynical connoisseurs of language" (146).

Haynes argues specifically for abandoning a cherished feminist practice—a politics of location that relies heavily upon space metaphors—believing this metaphor ineffective when translated to virtual environments. Advocating instead a feminist seizing of what is decidedly new in realtime virtual environments—speed and motion—and following Cixous, Haynes envisions feminist activists "flying through" but not occupying the spaces provided by programmers and/or wizards, whose likely masculinist persuasions and ideologies are merely constraining. Developed from images of motion, speed, and shape, a feminist "position," according to Haynes, is "amphibious," less a location than a process of making disorder.

Similarly (but following Irigaray), LeCourt advocates using virtual spaces to "jam" discourse in order to create self-representations not contingent upon the dominant. Citing from pseudonymous course transcripts, Le Court provides examples of discursive episodes where both women and men purposely disappoint the expectations associated with the provision of writing spaces. Feminist action is achieved when writers accede to expectations by occupying space and speaking within conventional roles, then subvert these very roles by taking on multiple subject positions from within a single identity. Repetitious acquiescence to a traditional role achieves, in the end, an effect of mockery. Haynes demonstrates this very technique in part three of her essay (@gender). In preparation for the development of LinguaMOO, Haynes interviews a wizard from PMC (*Post Modern Culture*) MOO, ostensibly to inform herself more fully about pre-programming verbs (or emotes) for MOO participants. During the course of a short interview, Haynes writes "Cynthia smiles" and "Cynthia nods" seven times and otherwise signals support by murmuring "I thought so," "hmmm," "yes," and "I see" in a hilarious qua sobering parody of the friendly, supportive, space-ceding, female interviewer.[8]

Both Haynes and LeCourt provide necessary visions, theories, and vocabularies—the beginnings of a new rhetoric of the self—for feminist performances in online environments. The classroom example I provide in the last section of this essay supports their work by illustrating the discursive mechanisms by which "free" space becomes baggaged with properties preventing women students from successful discursive occupation of that space. I hope to justify Haynes's and LeCourt's critiques of the commonplace among computer compositionists that providing physical access to virtual space suffices and that empowered self-representation is easily accomplished. However, the assumptions underpinning my argument differ somewhat from those of both Haynes and LeCourt. Rather than cast all discourse in the role of patriarchal villain and principal opponent, I conceive discourse as more pliable and responsive to manipulation, less in need of violent disruption, although by no means innocent. Such a theory of discourse enables me to assign to teachers and other participant rhetorician/rhetors some responsibility for partial and temporary remedies for exclusionary events, an assignment that requires careful readings of discursive environments and careful writing—in short, a rhetorical authority. My alliance with Haynes and LeCourt may weaken at the link where their revolutionary tactics brush up against my reformist ones. But a weak link, I believe (and hope they will agree), does not preclude the alliance.

I do not, for example, privilege pseudonymity at the expense of simulating possible selves under "real" names. Because we may reasonably assume that a good portion of women's professional and personal online work will be performed under their stable, off-line identities, certainly women will benefit from understanding and practicing self-representations under these identities. Gender erasure, argues Teresa De Lauretis, must be considered in light of its consequences:

> Do[ing] away with sexual difference altogether . . . closes the door in the face of the emergent social subject, . . . a subject constituted across a multiplicity of differences in discursive and material heterogeneity. Again, then, I rewrite: If the deconstruction of gender inevitably effects its (re)construction, the question is, in which terms and in whose interest is the de-re-construction being effected? (25)

Indeed, even without pseudonyms, electronic conferencing tends to destabilize a writer's sense of self. In realtime discourse, a range of available subject positions becomes visible to writers, and the idea of a possible or temporary self existing among possible alternatives becomes more apparent, if the writer/reader attends closely. The apparent separation of self from body that electronic conferencing enforces, or, put another way, the appearance before one's eyes of a simulated self who then scrolls right by and must be made by its author to reappear repeatedly in ever-changing rhetorical contexts, announces to students something about the constructive power of language and something about the limitations of linguistic constructs as well. Illusions of control are swiftly undermined by the diminished likelihood of long-term gain or fixed returns on a writer's choices. Successes online are fleeting, and rewards for careful construction of ethos are strikingly ephemeral.

Constructing or assuming alternate identities, however, is not synonymous with conceptualizing the relationship between language and self. Indeed, rhetorics or textbooks designed for undergraduate writing instruction in or outside of computer classrooms seldom provide discussions of self. Barry Brummett's 1994 textbook *Rhetoric in Popular Culture* is an exception. Although not designed for online environments, it does include an explanation of how reader subjectivities form in response to a text:

> The Marxist scholar Louis Althusser (1971) and others (for example, Hall 1985) have argued that texts ask those who read them to be certain kinds of subjects. To be a certain kind of subject is to take on a sort of role or character; these theorists argue that rather than having any single, stable, easily located identity, we do nothing but move from one subject position to another. In a sense, then, the power that a text has over you has a lot to do with what kinds of subject positions it encourages (or forces) you to inhabit. (98)

Unfortunately, Brummett's treatment suffers a partial loss of explanatory power when applied to online environments because it grants mobility to the reader only, who is said to take up subject positions ranging from "preferred" to "subversive," with respect to an inert text. Indeed, Brummett cautions students that "a subject position is not a character in the text itself" (98) and so marks the significant limitation of his approach for teaching in online environments, where participants indeed are characters in the texts they produce. Brummett positions readers as rhetorical analysts only, whereas in online environments, they are writers as well, required simultaneously to analyze and produce discourse, to be rhetoricians, rhetors, and subjects under construction by others as well.

Although the classical term *ethos* currently governs the idea of self and language in networked writing classrooms at Texas, and although students use the term with some success for both analysis and production of discourse, its presence derives not from the practice-based theories of teachers in the CRL, but rather from an off-line syllabus introduced in computer classrooms in 1991. Working from a substantial knowledge of digital text, Richard Lanham has suggested that the Renaissance term sprezzatura might prove useful for theorizing digital hermeneutics, but to my knowledge this term is not in use, either as vocabulary for theorists or as a tool placed at the disposal of students. Although the teacher featured in the extended example below does not provide students with conceptual tools for considering their discursive options, his rhetorical pedagogy—his discursive art—attends carefully to the reluctance that women students exhibit when asked to take up subject positions as women, and he works to provide a broader range of possibilities from which they might construct their arguments.

ATTENDING TO WOMEN'S SPACES: A PEDAGOGY OF THE SELF

Prior to the Hopwood decision, the University of Texas at Austin sponsored a summer program for minority scholarship students residing in Texas, and enrollees were mostly Latina/os and African-Americans. According to archival records for summer 1988, a first-year writing course for students in this program was designed around texts documenting the communication practices at a variety of work environments. I have selected passages from three different electronic conferences performed during this course, tracking the specific discursive events that invite women students to speak as women even as the strength of such a discursive positioning is eroded. I track women's decisions to take up the position or sidestep it and the instructor's efforts to expand the range of available subject positions to all students.

Readings assigned in preparation for the first conference were taken from Studs Terkel's *Working,* a collection of workers' narratives transcribed from oral interviews. Just prior to the following excerpt, the instructor has suggested several times to students engaged in lively discussion of some of the men's narratives that they turn to the women's texts. Finally they respond to his urging, and one student observes that possibly the most difficult aspect of one woman's job is the lying she is required to do. Anxious, perhaps, to thicken this thread of discussion on women, the instructor responds as follows:

INSTRUCTOR: It's interesting that both Sharon Atkins and Enid Du Bois talk about lying on the job.

And perhaps because the phrasing of this message invites the response that women lie because they are women, the instructor reframes the observation, suggesting instead that workers might lie because of working conditions:

INSTRUCTOR: Can you think of other jobs that require people to lie regularly?

Together these questions lay out an analytical terrain accommodating both essentialist readings of women and cultural readings of working conditions. They extend an offer to women to occupy the category "woman" and respond from this subject position, to occupy the category "worker" and respond from that position, or to occupy both or neither. Rhetorical decisions for women are immediately complicated, however, by a message that begins the ongoing process of larding the category "woman" with additional "information":

DAVID: I wasn't surprised by Jill Torrance [one of the narrators in *Working*] in the least. Most women, excluding UT women, aren't as materially minded as others may think. . . .

David draws the following response:

ANGELICA: David, did you only exclude UT women because there are women in this room with you?[9]

Previously, Angelica had hedged when the instructor offered the subject position "women," responding with a story about a female friend who regularly lied on the job. Her message to David constitutes another evasion, yet marks her interest in issues of gender and rhetoric. Rather than contest, which possibly would entail speaking as a woman, Angelica queries the rhetoric of the discussion at hand, reading for author intention, reading for the effects of writing on other writers.

When the question of women's "natural" or habitual shyness becomes topical during a subsequent discussion about computer-networked writing, once again women students must decide whether to respond as women, that is, to take up subject positions as women, or to devise other places to stand. In the ensuing discussion associating computers with freedom to speak, several participants propose that the networked machines free the women to say whatever they want, invoking the expressivist theory of networked writing ("shy freshman writers so reluctant to express an opinion"). This time, women do respond as women, yet gratuitous information about the nature of women shapes their responses. The following sequence omits messages not directly relevant to my argument:

ALEJANDRO: David, if it were not for computers, how many of us would be expressing our opinions as openly as we are now? I feel that the personal atmosphere is much better.

INSTRUCTOR: David, I think computers separate people if we were all just talking to computers. But since we are all hooked up together, we can come up with a lot more ideas as a group because we can all "talk" at once.

GORDON: It's true what Alejandro said about computers. If we didn't have these things most of us (especially the girls) would be very shy and, therefore, wouldn't express their feelings like they do here. I'm not saying anything to get the girls mad, but most girls are quiet when discussion are taken about and they are called upon. What do you think, females?

KATY: I have to disagree with you, Gordon.

GORDON: Why, Katy?

ANGELICA: Gordon, I personally feel exactly the same way you do. I know that if we were sitting in a classroom I would not talk as much. It is a lot easier for me to talk to the class using the computer.

MARA: I agree with Gordon that this interaction with the computer and the class is a lot more beneficial than an oral discussion, but I do feel that girls can be just as vocal as boys if the guys just give them a chance.

GABRIELA: Well, Gordon, most of us are not shy. At least, I don't think I am. It is sort of hard to go up and talk to someone, especially a guy, without them thinking you want something or that you are interested.

KATY: If we (females) have a comment to make on a particular subject, then we usually state [it] unless you (males) are monopolizing the whole discussion.

GORDON: Normally we do, but we'll be nice and hear your opinions.

ANGELICA: Gordon, are you trying to say that the males have the option to let the females voice their opinions?

MIGUEL: Katy, sorry, but it would be impossible for us (males) to monopolize the whole discussion, considering the computer will print responses as fast as you can type them in. And we are not saying anything out loud, so we can't drown you out.

DAVID: Katy, what you did is very typical and transparent. Why play it off on the guys when it is the girls that usually don't enter discussions? Also, the people that always talk the most are girls and they stop when they are asked to do so. Women are just contrary.

JOHN: Katy, you know that guys want to make their points across. So, if someone says something wrong, a guy is less hesitant to disagree. Girls may want to get something across, but they feel if they interrupt someone, they better make sure they have their facts or evidence straight.

ANGELICA: Miguel, I understand what you are saying and that is true, but David is really getting on my nerves. There are so many things I want to say to him. I just wish I had the guts to tell him.

The argument as to whether women are free to choose when and how to speak, both off- and online, and/or whether they are constrained by male monopolies is about how discourse works when gender becomes a factor in its production and analysis. Here women students demonstrate their attentiveness to the constraints of discourse even as they speak. While refusing to locate gender difference in shyness or reasoning power, they argue and demonstrate that they experience discourse differently from men, in both offline and online environments. For example, before Gabriela can reason about computer-based communication, she must clarify that what may look to men like shyness might better be understood as self-protection. Katy asserts that men typically monopolize conversations, thereby calling men to male subjectivity, a position Gordon readily accepts, as does Miguel, who asserts a corollary to the "women are now free" proposal: that technology actually prevents men from monopolizing conversations. Although the women who become involved in the discussion eventually affirm the advantages of networked conversation, they resist the essentializing of all experience in networked environments. Angelica's final ironic remark about not having guts to speak assures us that for her, even in computer-mediated environments, there are strong stakes that impinge upon her discursive choices. Evidently it is less a question of spaces available, than of the quality of those spaces.

When students read John Train's "For the Adventurous Few: How to Get Rich," an essay on global free enterprise, and Ehrenreich and Fuentes's "Life on the Global Assembly Line," an essay about working conditions for third-world women, the instructor carefully positions himself outside student discussion by asking students what Ehrenreich and Fuentes would say to Train and introducing his question via a student comment. Simultaneously, he avoids direct invocation of "women" and thus eases the pressure on women to respond as women to questions about women. Angelica takes up the topic proposal and produces an argument referring to women as "they":

INSTRUCTOR: Mara says that Ehrenreich and Fuentes would likely despise Train's attitude. What would Train have to say about them?

ANGELICA: The authors of "Life on the Global Assembly Line" would feel very different. They felt that the women are exploited in the Third World and as far as they are concerned there are no business ethics for the women. They are practically treated like slaves in the Third World.

Several messages later, Steve names women as the primary audience for the article, thus calling women students to a possible subjectivity from which to respond:

STEVE: The way Ehrenreich and Fuentes keep mentioning how the women are working for such low wages, it seems to me that this essay is addressed more to women.

The instructor follows Steve with a message on women (not reproduced here) whose length strongly supports a Third-World-women discussion thread without directly calling women students to gendered subjectivity. He adroitly directs Ehrenreich and Fuentes's arguments to the Latina/o members of the class but frames his question as a question about culture, not about women:

INSTRUCTOR: Ehrenreich and Fuentes make some specific claims about the culture of Mexico—that it makes it easier to exploit women. At the end they say that because a woman's reputation is so important in Hispanic culture, women will "bend over backward to be respectable" and thus cause no trouble for the employer. Do you think this claim is accurate concerning Hispanic culture?

Two men address the question first, Alejandro pointing out strengths of Latin culture (being able to take care of yourself and speaking out for what is right) and John evidently rearticulating the claims that working-class women in Latin America must either work or get married. Angelica, on the other hand, undertakes the task of guarding against broad assertions about women and their actions. She challenges essentialized representations of Latinas and confronts the growing number of restrictions becoming operative in this locally constructed environment. I cannot speak for Angelica's intentions but can assert that her words serve within this discursive environment to clear once more a space for women of Latin descent to speak without encumbrances:

ALEJANDRO: Hispanic culture does stress the reputation of women, but they do not necessarily stay out of trouble. Another characteristic that is stressed is being able to take care of yourself, which means speaking out for what is right.

JOHN: I feel the claim is accurate because those Hispanic women have a choice of either getting married to someone or stay on the job. The thing is if you don't have a husband, then crying is the only thing that these women can do. The authors said that the men will not stay on the job after working a couple of times, so women will do it.

ANGELICA: In certain parts of Mexico where the women do not know any better, I think that this is true about them bending over backward to be respectable, but it is not like this in all of Hispanic culture. I think that once these women come to a country like America, they lose that claim.

The instructor interposes two more long messages, one on the politics of foreign investment in Mexico and the other on working conditions and entrepreneurship in South Africa, ending by offering all students subject positions as business executives. The geographic areas he names called students to ethnicity as well, albeit obliquely:

INSTRUCTOR: . . . So what would you do if you were the executive of a company that had a factory in a country with no laws protecting its workers?

MARCOS [still on the woman question and likely not having seen the instructor's new post]: Angelica, I think that Hispanic women should revert to that type of thinking. Don't you agree?

ANGELICA: Marcos, I do not feel that they should revert to that type of thinking. Why are you trying to make me mad?

JOHN: I'm not going to say anything about Marcos's comment because I don't want any lady in here mad at me.

GABRIELA: In my opinion most Hispanic women are very conscientious about their reputation. It is very evident in the United States. I have been to Mexico several times and it is very common to see several women that are prostitutes, and they are all mostly young.

STEVE: If I had a company in South Africa I would try to change the working conditions for the blacks, but if it got to the point that it was costing the company too much, then I would have to do whatever is best for the company.

ANGELICA: It would be real easy to say that I would try to improve the working conditions, but in reality I would probably, to some extent, take advantage of these poor people. It all depends on what your heart and mind allow you to do. If you can live with yourself after you run over these people, then you will get your profit; otherwise, it is better just to stay out of it.

GABRIELA: A lot of difference in a person's response will depend on if that person is dealing with people of his own race. If I had a company in Mexico, I don't think I would exploit my own people. It is very likely that my ancestors were probably treated like this and I do not think I could go in there and do the same.

In this first-year course composed primarily of African-American and Mexican-American students, the instructor introduces the ethnicity question with careful subtlety, via articles on the effects of Third-World capitalism.

The ethnic subject position is not thrust full force upon them, but is offered, nevertheless, and taken up in the above excerpts—by Latina/os and likely (although I can't be sure) by African-American men. Gendered subjectivities for women have been offered by the instructor previously and often, but most recently during this session in combination with the discussion of Third-World, working-class women, and when complicated by the introduction of questions of reputation and morality, the Latinas are put on the spot, for the woman position has become quite vulnerable and disempowered. Once the instructor offers "executive" as subject position, however, he has many takers.

Donna Haraway writes that women's experiences are "structured within multiple and often inharmonious agendas" (243), and this conference provides a sense of what this powerful insight might mean. When women are asked to encode their experiences within a specific classroom-produced discourse, even one designed and executed with great care for equitable practice and populated by polite, intelligent discussants, they comply, if they choose to do so, under local constructions of the category "woman." When Gabriela is offered "executive" in addition to "worker" as a subject position alongside a heavily baggaged "Latina," she finds an adequate position from which to relocate morality in places other than women's psycho/sexual behaviors, which had been introduced and sustained as characteristics typical of being Latin and female. As entrepreneur and "person," she writes using a male-gendered pronoun; she is able to resituate morality within business ethics. In addition, she proposes ethnicity or roots (ancestors) as causal forces for her ethical decisions: "If I had a company in Mexico I don't think I would exploit my own people."

Perhaps even more crucial to the production of equitable discourse is the possibility that when many women are present and differ in their self-representations, then "women" as a category—represented variously—can be taken back from its reductive forms and rebuilt as a multiple. Both constrained and enabled by the shape of local conversation, the women students in this virtual classroom demonstrate some success in figuring "Latina" as a multiple construct, situated variously within different geographical, socio-economic, and psycho-sexual arenas, but the question remains as to whether their proposal for women's diversity was influential among the discussants.[10] Noteworthy as well is Mara's role. Although Mara did not participate directly in the more confrontational episodes, she did provide useful metacommentary (indeed one wishes she might have said more), naming what for Angelica and Gabriela was not easily namable if they wanted to retain their positions as public reasoners rather than fractious antagonists speaking from disempowered discursive locations.

THE IMPOSSIBLE DREAM

I have not discerned in the archival records examples of students either male or female creating new emotions (Haynes). I am unable to say comfortably that Gabriela or Angelica or Katy or Mara spoke their contradictory selves within a single voice (LeCourt) or whether they shifted shape in ways that might be considered amphibious (Haynes). I am more comfortable saying that Gabriela, for example, was finally able to combine satisfactorily a number of the subjectivities made available to her in order to speak about a possible ethical self and possible ethnic self placed in a possible position of power. Indeed, the metaphors of recombination found occasionally in the work of Ann Balsamo and Shirley Brice Heath might be usefully aligned with those of Haynes and LeCourt, for still we have no adequate terminology to account for the exclusionary tendencies of discourse while attending to the making of online selves.

Gabriela, who may well have finished her coursework and graduated in 1993, is not available for commentary on my interpretation of her writing. I cannot provide her reading of the particular excerpt of online discussion I have magnified for inspection; likely she would not remember it. If by chance she were to have become a Marxist feminist in the interim and were to offer her own retrospective reading, quite possibly she would object more strongly to the economic binary—exploited and disempowered worker versus entrepreneur—than to the tainted, gendered subject positions that I am more concerned with. She might read the segment not as a provision of multiple subject positions for a woman's recombination but rather as entrapment within the false ideologies of capitalism. Still, I offer my non-definitive reading of this excerpt as an example of teaching with some (partial) comprehension of the disadvantages for women who would speak from gendered spaces and their reluctance to do so. I offer it as example of a teacher's attempt to put rhetorical authority to good use, as an example of online teaching that leaves marginalization and inclusion neither to the spaces provided by the software nor to chance.

Teachers allotting class time to electronic conferences and committed to sponsoring equitable discursive environments find themselves awkwardly positioned with regard to their own assignments. Certainly, we should consider each session a new and untainted episode of interactive writing, but also, I argue, we should suspend naiveté about the benevolence of online discourse and acknowledge its exclusionary as well as inclusionary history. Positioned institutionally as constructivists, as instigators of student writing, and as the parties responsible for assuring its value, teachers may wish to distinguish between virtual space and discursive space, taking action to assure an ample range of discursive positions for all students. The above excerpts demonstrate the delicacy of so doing—the small turns of phrase by which the instructor carefully, gingerly makes offers to students of possible selves. Even so, he is not able to extricate himself from his connections to these selves and from his own responsibility for their being. He may be faulted, perhaps, for not providing an "elsewhere," that place to stand outside oppressive discourses, or for providing sets of binaries—male-female, worker-entrepreneur—as materials for students' self-construction. Nevertheless, there is art and sound method to his cookery.

NOTES

1. One of the early Daedalus instructor manuals addressed the issue of conferences gone awry by proposing that most difficulties arise from students' psychological immaturity.

2. Early in the history of online writing instruction, for example, two titles appeared in the 1990 special edition of *Computers and Composition:* "Sharing Authority on a Synchronous Network: The Case for Riding the Beast" (Marshall Kremers) and "Taking Women Professors Seriously: Female Authority in the Computerized Classroom" (E. Laurie George). Although both articles placed under careful scrutiny budding notions of virtual utopias, the grammatical discontinuity between sharing (authority) and female (authority) signals important conceptual differences. Whereas Kremers conceives authority as distributive, however difficult the process of distribution, George understands authority as a situated, cultural construct and finds practicing authority in her environment irrevocably linked to gender.

3. These examples are taken from transcripts of Daedalus InterChange sessions logged from Fall 1987 through Spring 1989.

4. Joan Landes documents the unfortunate results of revolutionary opportunity in the aftermath of the French Revolution, when subordinate positions for women were reconfigured through their idealization as keepers of virtue and the attendant excision from public life.

5. Surveying both undergraduate and graduate students in 1987 and 1988, Jerome Bump reported this very distinction in students' perceptions of self in online environments. Although most students in his survey were pleased with the increased freedom of expression and with the reprieve from a politeness enforced by peer opinion, others conceived their activities as a roleplaying, an understanding that defused accusations of insincerity ("Radical Changes" 57).

6. See Minock and Shor, "Crisscrossing Grand Canyon: Bridging the Gaps with Computer Conferencing," for a report on uses of pseudonymity that expand discursive options for students.

7. In his ethnography of a single University of Texas course, Wayne Butler documents one woman's inability or unwillingness to sustain a feminist perspective and concludes that her feminism was not strong enough to sustain the pressures of the discursive environment.

8. Haynes supplements her theorizing with education. She writes: ". . . I have constructed (in collaboration with Jan Rune Holmevik of Oslo, Norway) a text-based virtual reality environment called LinguaMOO where I train our teachers and students to pursue alternate writing activities and alternate classroom dynamics" (@gender par. 37).

9. I have provided pseudonyms for the students represented here, and their messages are lightly edited (spaces inserted, for example) for the sake of reader comprehension.

10. Gabriela has previously sent a confusing and perhaps defensive message, but one that insists upon differences within the Hispanic woman category: "In my opinion, most Hispanic women are very conscientious about their reputation. It is very evident in the United States. I have been to Mexico several times, and it is very common to see several women that are prostitutes, and they are all mostly young." Angelica writes, "but it is not like this in all of Hispanic culture."

WORKS CITED

Aristotle. 1982. *"Art" of Rhetoric.* Trans. J. H. Freese. Cambridge: Harvard UP–Loeb.

Balsamo, Anne. 1995. *Technologies of the Gendered Body: Reading Cyborg Women.* Durham: Duke UP.

Boese, Christine. 1999. "A Virtual Locker Room in Classroom Chat Spaces: The Politics of Men as 'Other.'" In *Feminist Cyberscapes: Mapping Gendered Academic Spaces,* ed. Kristine Blair and Pamela Takayoshi. Stamford, CT: Ablex. 195–226.

Brodkey, Linda. 1994. Making a Federal Case Out of Difference: The Politics of Pedagogy, Publicity, and Postponement. *Writing Theory and Critical Theory,* ed. John Clifford and John Schilb. New York: MLA. 236–61.

Brummett, Barry. 1994. *Rhetoric in Popular Culture.* New York: St. Martin's P.

Bump, Jerome. 1990. Radical Changes in Class Discussion Using Networked Computers. *Computers and the Humanities* 24: 49–65.

Burke, Kenneth. 1950. *A Rhetoric of Motives.* New York: Prentice-Hall.

Butler, Wayne Michael. "The Social Construction of Knowledge in an Electronic Discourse Community." Diss. U of Texas, Austin, 1992.

De Lauretis, Teresa. 1992. *Technologies of Gender: Essays on Theory, Film, and Fiction.* Bloomington: U of Indiana P.

Dibbell, Julian. 1996. A Rape in Cyberspace; or How an Evil Clown, a Haitian Trickster Spirit, Two Wizards, and a Cast of Dozens Turned a Database into a Society. In *High Noon on the Electronic Frontier: Conceptual Issues in Cyberspace,* ed. Peter Ludlow. Cambridge: MIT P. 375–95.

George, E. Laurie. 1990. Taking Women Professors Seriously: Female Authority in the Computerized Classroom. *Computers and Composition* 7: 45–52.

Haraway, Donna J. 1997. *Modest witness@second millennium. FemaleMan meets OncoMouse.* New York: Routledge.

———. 1991. *Simians, Cyborgs, and Women: The Reinvention of Nature.* New York: Routledge.

Hawisher, Gail, and Patricia Sullivan. 1997. "Women on the Networks: Searching for e-Spaces of Their Own." In *Other Words: Feminism and Composition,* ed. Susan Jarrett and Lynn Worsham. New York: MLA.

Haynes, Cynthia. 1997. *Practicing Safe Rhetoric: The Passion and Paradox of Ethics in Educational MOOs.* Haynes and Holmevik.

——— and Jan Rune Holmevik, ed. 1998. *High Wired: On the Design, Use, and Theory of Educational MOOs.* Ann Arbor: U of MI P.

——— and Jan Rune Holmevik, Beth Kolko, and Victor J. Vitanza. 1997. "MOOs, Anarchitexture, Toward a New Threshold." *The Emerging CyberCulture: Literacy, Paradigm, and Paradox,* ed. Stephanie Gibson and Ollie Oviedo. Cresskill, NJ: Hampton P, 2000.

Heath, Shirley Brice, and Milbrey W. McLaughlin. 1993. *Identity and Inner-City Youth: Beyond Ethnicity and Gender.* NY: Teachers College P.

Horner, Winifred Bryan. 1996. *Nineteenth-Century Scottish Rhetoric: The American Connection.* Carbondale: Southern IL UP. 1993.

Johnson, Richard. 1986–1987. "What Is Cultural Studies Anyway?" *Social Text: Theory/Culture/Ideology* 16: 38–80.

Kremers, Marshall. 1990. "Sharing Authority on a Synchronous Network: The Case for Riding the Beast." *Computers and Composition* 7: 33–44.

Landes, Joan B. 1988. *Women and the Public Sphere in the Age of the French Revolution.* Ithaca, Cornell UP.

Lanham, Richard A. *The Electronic Word: Democracy, Technology, and the Arts.* Chicago: U of Chicago P, 1993.

———. "The Implications of Electronic Information for the Sociology of Knowledge." *Leonardo* 27, 1994: 155–163.

LeCourt, Donna. 1999. "Writing (Without) the Body: Gender and Power in Networked Discussion Groups." *Feminist Cyberscapes: Mapping Gendered Academic Spaes.* Ed. Kristine Blair and Pamela Takayoshi. Stamford, CT: Ablex. 153–75.

Minock, Mary, and Francis Shor. 1995. Crisscrossing Grand Canyon: Bridging the Gaps with Computer Conferencing. *Computers and Composition* 12: 355–65.

Scott, Joan Wallach. *Gender and the Politics of History.* New York: Columbia UP, 1988.

29

Bi, Butch, and Bar Dyke: Pedagogical Performances of Class, Gender, and Sexuality

MICHELLE GIBSON, MARTHA MARINARA, AND DEBORAH MEEM

Current theories of radical pedagogy stress the constant undermining, on the part of both professors and students, of fixed essential identities. Trinh Minh-Ha, for example, describes an "Inappropriate/d Other who moves about with always at least two/four gestures: that of affirming 'I am like you' while pointing insistently to the difference; and that of reminding 'I am different' while unsettling every definition of otherness arrived at" (8). Elizabeth Ellsworth applies Minh-Ha's idea to "classroom practices that facilitate such moving about" and the nature of identity that obtains in such classrooms:

> Identity in this sense becomes a vehicle for multiplying and making more complex the subject positions possible, visible, and legitimate at any given historical moment, requiring disruptive changes in the way social technologies of gender, race, ability, and so on define Otherness and use it as a vehicle for subordination. (113)

In the stories that make up this article, we hope to show our own strategies, partial and varied though they are, for disrupting several assumptions that animate the dynamics of the academy: the assumption that the university represents a set of attributes that can be acquired by various Others that will enable them to realize a stereotyped dream of success, the assumption that the process of acquiring such attributes involves jettisoning undesirable traits and associations that the Other has brought with her, the assumption that power in the academy is consistently associated with a predictable and unchanging set of personal characteristics, and the assumption that professor self-presentation must reflect only those "power" characteristics and no other.

Presented as a set of theorized narratives in three voices, this article examines the way three feminist, queer teachers of writing experience and perform their gender, class, and sexual identities. We hope to critique both the academy's tendency to neutralize the political aspects of identity performance and the essentialist identity politics that still inform many academic discussions of

From *College Composition and Communication* 52 (2000): 69–95.

gender, class, and sexuality. Through our "stories," we hope to complicate the notion that identities can be performed in clean, organized, distinct ways by examining and theorizing our own experiences of class, gender, and sexual identity performance. We want to acknowledge the conscious ways we perform our multiple subjectivities and to examine our political/economic/ pedagogical uses of those performances. In short, we want to move beyond the essentialist act of situating ourselves as scholars authorized to speak about specific issues; we want instead to argue for a kind of universal authorization of discourse. We present these three "papers" as one multivoiced article because the narratives seem to us to be alive both with continuity and with conflict, and we believe that maintaining the integrity of each voice helps highlight its relationship to (and against) the others.

BI: PLAYING WITH FIXED IDENTITIES

Late last Friday afternoon, as I do every Friday after work, I stopped at Kroger to pick up groceries for the weekend. I don't like the complication of grocery shopping when I'm hungry and tired and thinking about the paper I'm writing or the assignments I need to put together. On this particular Friday, the juice aisle was blocked by a young woman shopping with her daughter. The little girl, who couldn't have been much more than three, sat in the grocery cart while her mother asked her what kind of juice she wanted. Not an unusual scene, except that there were no limits placed on the child's choices. No "I have a coupon for Ocean Spray Cranapple 64 ounces, the Welch's White Grape Juice is on sale, and the 28-ounce Kroger Apple Juice is two for one, so you can have one of those." It's not that I don't believe in giving children choices, but there are always financial limits to the choices my children can make. And time limits as well. This little girl was reveling in the power of her choices and had already changed her mind three times, each time just as her mother reached for the juice she had asked for. Because I was in a hurry and becoming annoyed, I said, "After you change your mind three times, all the juice disappears." The little girl sat up in the grocery cart seat, looked straight at me for a few long seconds, flexed her little slippered feet, shook out her golden locks, touched her rosy cheek, and said, "Oh, you're one of those people that makes up stories." "Yes," I answered her, "but all my stories come true." I knew she meant the *magic dream princess secret identity riddle treasure* kind of story, not the kind of stories I tell in writing classes. But I had to wonder as I finished my shopping and drove home if the stories I tell don't at least try to serve the same purpose as the mismatched, mistaken identity fairy tale where all the characters figure out who they *really* are by the end, where knowing who they *really* are means they get to live happily ever after. Despite the inability of the storytellers of personal narratives to easily manipulate a happy ending or any ending at all, storytelling is the way we compose our lives; all identity, all social construction, begins with narratives. Although my stories and many fairy tales represent a struggle for identity, the difference between fairy tales and personal narratives comes from autobiography's necessary interplay of fiction and reality, the constant dialogue between an emerging identity and social institutions. My stories are different from fairy tales because they represent people and culture in process; there is no fixed identity, no happily ever after. I have to wonder why if I can feel that pea under my mattress, I'm still eating cold porridge.

The nexus created by the juxtaposition of that uncomfortable pea and the cold porridge illustrates an important connection between autobiography and social critique; the writing of individual lives actively constructs culture and politics by establishing the narrative codes, the parameters of subject and community. Both our cultural context (the cold porridge) and social identity (feeling that hard pea) depend on their reciprocal relationship for structure and definition. The narratives told about social institutions are embedded in or with the narratives of individuals whose lives, whose joys and pains, and whose struggles for survival have been involved with building, manipulating, and rebuilding the cultural context(s) in which they form their social identities. And these identities give us a critical apparatus, one that enables us to reflect on how and why we tell stories and how we use our stories to produce culture.

The stories told by both lesbians and working-class academics help form class consciousness and serve a strategic political purpose. In marking stories "lesbian" or "working class," the lives contained therein are less invisible and give the narrators—students and faculty—a political site from which to speak and act. Playing with the notion of an "essential voice" allows the storytellers to claim a recognizable, politically engaged identity from a narrative that is already academically codified; however "speakable," this politicized voice emerges from a self-empowerment that hinges on an appeal to universalities of class and sexuality, a self-empowerment that depends on binary oppositions. We think we tell stories to illustrate the particular, to demarcate culture as marked and shaped by difference. Claims of universalism have given way to the demands of the particular, but the particulars have their own universalisms. Most lesbian and working-class autobiographies, rather than defying the fixity of identity, merely redraw the boundaries and serve to categorize individual subjects as different from those defined as "straight" and "professional." These stories create a common experience, and the personal narratives suggest that there is something coherently the same about all lesbians, about all working-class persons, and, consequently, something coherently the same about the "straight" or "middle-class" experience that is being resisted. But there are stories that conform to neither category of identification.

Using lesbian and working-class experiences to strive for a political identity is both significant and necessary; I have no wish to deny those voices their political direction. But the communal voice that is created tends to erase the differences within those communities and ignore the complex, intertwined relationship between public and personal narratives. Consequently, writing students—working class or middle class, gay or straight—either embrace or resist the collective voice and often find themselves defending a "real me" that is a mix of essentialist beliefs about good and bad thinking, right and wrong behaviors, and inclusion and exclusion. "Their own" interpretations of social texts tend to be ahistorically driven and grounded in universals. Writing students define "real me" voices as safe, static, inherent, and inviolate; public voices, though, are required to listen to other public voices, and listening can cause uncomfortable changes. The tension, the uncertain space writing teachers and students find between the familiar, "real me" voice and an emerging public voice should not necessarily be resolved with already codified positions; rather, the tension should be a space to work from and with because the language of any personal narrative contests static identities. Defining the personal, the "real me" as the product of an individual (but universally human) psyche would construct rhetorical studies as insular and drained of political content, ideological analysis, and intellectual rigor (the tools necessary to understand and change social hierarchies and cultural institutions). In parallel fashion, recognizing identity as grounded or fixed in particular political locations negates the possibility for inter-reference between any two narrative landscapes. Because the formation of any story is not fixed within some individual identity or within an established public position—but rather is formed among competing public and private voices—identity, the writer's story and voice, includes the writer's shifting relationships with the peculiarities of our culture.

Despite the complexities of self-construction, the dependence of cultural identity on a dualistic system of thought makes it impossible for me to come out of the closet; when one can be "straight" and "lesbian" simultaneously, one doesn't get an already codified, easily recognizable closet narrative. In this case, difference is more than a presence; it is a pressure that acts constantly, if unevenly, along the boundaries constructed by "straight" and "lesbian" narratives. This pressure promises heterosexual protection with its already disclosed rules of social recognition while still shifting the contours of sexuality and desire. Bisexuality, defined as an incomplete dominance of either sexual trait, defies easy social categorization; it is an identity without visible rules, almost without referent.

Because a politically productive identity demands a culturally recognizable political self (or at least someone who can make up her mind), the closet story I live in is without a collective identity. Entangled in the dynamics of difference, my public identity as both lesbian and straight is as conflicted as my private identity. In a similar fashion, no one can be both professional and working class; so one's "new" identity is perceived as a positive step up, a successful crossing of class barriers. The resulting narrative reflects the American Dream, the "rags to riches" story, and *The Little Engine That Could.* In these narratives, "working class" has a transient quality, and a successful performance makes the previous identity go away. Those are the fairy tales; the reality is an identity that never quite fits, is never quite comfortable, authentic, or believable. The politics of the professional narrative promises the dream of the street, but cannot carry with it the drama of labor, cannot live back in the neighborhood.

Recently, back for a short visit to the neighborhood where I lived most of my adult life, I found myself sitting in my sister's kitchen at 6:30 on a Saturday morning wishing someone else—anyone else who could figure out her new coffeemaker—would wake up. I decided finally to walk the seven blocks up Putnam Avenue to the market where I worked for the eight years it took me to finish my undergraduate degree. I knew the Faricellis would have hot coffee. When I walked in the back door, Mace (the produce manager) looked at me and said, "So Marta, what are ya' dreamin'? Bring in the newspapers and the hard rolls." The hard rolls weren't on the back porch and that resulted in an argument I had listened to every morning as Patrice and Johnny the butcher yelled back and forth in a mixture of English and Italian. This particular argument started with the missing hard rolls and escalated to the conflicts between genders. I found the whole scene amusing and comfortable.

The comfortable feeling I recognized even before I finished making the coffee—I knew what to expect here, what I could safely say, and what would get me in trouble. (And I knew how to work the coffeemaker.) The amusement came from a different space. I could now observe them from a distance, an educated distance that kept me from being a part of or really caring about their argument, a distance that in fact made it possible for me to analyze the argument and realize why Patrice always won. Before I left the market for one final time, more final than the last time I left, I collected hugs and kisses, heard "we're so proud of you" and "don't be a stranger." I promised I wouldn't, but I knew I already was, because if I had made the kind of success the Faricellis could understand an autographed photo of me shaking Johnny's hand would be hung up on the wall behind the deli counter and I'd be able to order filet, large shrimp, casaba melons, and asparagus like their successful customers. So, there's that uncomfortable pea, planted under my mattress the minute I went back to college. I can talk or write about my working-class past, but I no longer live in it. I have no *real* identity there, and I have no *real* identity in the professional class; I only have the dream.

The dream state makes one unable to belong to a particular social identity because the lack of authenticity, however problematic the concept, makes one's class, as well as one's sexual orientation, invisible. I once had a student who, when angered by the text we were discussing, loudly proclaimed, "I don't believe in lesbians." There I stood, feeling like Tinker Bell as her life breath slipped away and her little twinkling light faded from sight, hoping that some child somewhere would proclaim, "I do. I do believe in fairies" and clap his or her hands so I could continue to live. I asked my students to clap for me, but most of them just appeared confused or thought I was joking and with good reason: I'm not lesbian by every definition and certainly not by the definitions of students who cling to the sexual stereotypes that construct their worlds. I don't look like a dyke and I have two children. Caught in the tension between individual desires and communal cohesion, the flux of my identity resists the established parameters of subjectivity and community. This rebellious identity really is a matter of both believing and resisting, but it can't be shaped by the clapping of hands.

What it can be shaped by is exploring the differences within difference and welcoming the friction that an animated identity represents. This difference undermines the very idea of identity and becomes a conflicted, but productive, space in which signifiers and codes of cultural representation are questioned. The space created by opening up identity allows for a more open-ended model of collective identity and poses hard questions about the nature and definitions of political subject positions as one is both enlarged and oppressed by constantly shifting alliances. In the classroom, this space lies in the often tense relationship between students' experiences and what they are learning in class. In the same class where I felt like Tinker Bell, the students who hadn't dropped the class were reading and discussing a poem by David Budbill, "Roy McInnes." At one point the narrator of the poem states, "When you shake his hand his grip is warm and gentle / and you can feel the calm he carries in his person / flow into your arm" (14–16). Questioning what Budbill might have meant by writing these lines resulted in a discussion about whether or not the narrator was "male" or "female." Most of the class finally decided the character was female because "men," real or fictive, "don't shake hands with each other like that." For most students who lack different cultural experiences, the question of physicality is always a question of sexuality, especially female sexuality. I thought at first that I would merely offer the definitions of the difference between *affection* and *sexual desire,* but the three pairs of eyes from the three lesbians in the class challenged me: "You're one of us, Dr. Marinara. Don't cop out on us." So, instead, knowing those differences are not as acute as social mores would like us to believe, I asked the students to blur the emotional differences between affection and sex, sexuality and physicality. We began the discussion by making a list on the board of those people in our lives whom we "touch warmly," for whom we feel a deep emotional, almost electric bond. We put the "same sex" experiences, the hugging of friends and relatives, in a separate column. I mentioned not being able to keep my hands off my children, how burying my face in my younger daughter's hair and smelling her sun-warmed scalp is a sensual experience, an affection that cannot be divorced from the physical experience of touching. Others shared their experiences of enjoying the touch of warm fingers, the smell of soft skin. Somewhere along the way, most of the class agreed that it is physically satisfying, not just emotionally satisfying, to hug our friends. The class left that day with no clear definitions, with a narrator whose gender and sexuality couldn't be determined, whose physical affection could not be wholly separated from sexuality or sensuality, a narrator who had to speak from difference.

The "About the Author" page inserted at the end of my dissertation reflects my difference from the academy, as does the epigraph I chose for the beginning. My dissertation opens with a few bars of Bruce Springsteen's "Thunder Road" and ends with my life up until that point. My story of singing with a rock band; hitching cross-country with my best friend Rachel; working for Dunkin' Donuts, Baskin-Robbins, and the Whitneyville Market; giving birth to one daughter and adopting another overwhelms the last line about receiving graduate degrees. I think I "got away" with this because I was expected to put those experiences in the past and behave like a professional from then on.

My students also feel the pressure to give up something about their lives in order to take on the new, professional roles or careers they are trying so hard to achieve. What makes this giving up so difficult is the fact that most of our cultural texts have been shaped by persistent binaries: working class/ professional class, heterosexual/homosexual, college preparation/vocational. Choosing a subject position seems to entail resisting a previous position or identity. Like many writing faculty who want their classrooms to be a "contact zone" where students can reflect on and negotiate identities within different cultural perspectives, I find telling stories of living with an identity that moves in and out of centers of power and combines often conflicting identities to be a useful pedagogical tool.

I tell stories to explain my feminist position, a position that was shaped by my working-class life: When I was in my late twenties, I worked the grave-yard shift at Dunkin' Donuts. One night a customer leaned over the counter and bit my cheek because, as he explained, my earrings looked like fishing lures. The other customers, all male including two police officers who were drinking their "free" coffee at the end of the counter, laughed as if this were the funniest thing they'd ever heard (and sadly enough, it probably was). There was nothing I could do at that point, no possible resistance except for serving him regular coffee instead of decaffeinated and the stalest donut I could find. I've told my students about the boss I had when I was a waitress (and I'm purposefully saying waitress rather than waitstaff because I think there is a difference) who every day offered me $100 not to wear a bra to work. I needed that job, so every day I said, "For $300, I might consider it." Some of my students will tell me that this was sexual harassment; they can't believe someone who changes every "mankind" in their papers to "humankind" would have put up with it. We talk about the sexual harassment lawsuits that make it to *Court TV*. They are all high-profile cases, and the women involved are most always professionals, women with some power, women who are not working class. For many working-class women, sexual harassment is just another unfortunate part of the workday.

Sexual harassment, under the guise of the inability to work with difference, is still a part of my everyday life. Last quarter I taught an advanced composition class in which most of the students were planning careers in education, most of the students were non-traditional, and all of the students were female. Toward the end of the quarter, the classroom had become a comfortable working environment, and the students had developed an open, tolerant way of speaking about and sharing their differences from one another as they worked out problems in their essays. I was unprepared for what happened the day we were to discuss Adrienne Rich's "When We Dead Awaken: Writing as Re-Vision." A large percentage of the students couldn't or wouldn't work with Rich's theories, life, or poetry because she is lesbian. I never thought that a class whose inside joke was "you don't need a penis to do that" would be so threatened by a woman who theoretically in language and materially in her life and politics resisted and then rejected penises altogether. Threatened by Rich's collective "we," the women in the class felt compelled to take a position that resisted Rich's inclusive definition of "lesbian." But the term "lesbian" for Rich referred to "nothing so simple and dismissible as the fact that two women might go to bed together." I had made the mistake of becoming too comfortable with this class; by enjoying what made us all the same, I had forgotten how different I am from many women. When one of the students said, "Maybe we shouldn't talk about this. There aren't any of *them* in here, are there?" fear almost kept me silent. But instead I did what I've always done when I've felt harassed or threatened. I used sarcasm: "Let's check and see who has 'lesbian' tattooed on their butt." I told them that I did and talked about how my life causes me to read Rich's essay in ways that were different from their readings, in ways that found her language intellectually stimulating rather than threatening. We moved into a discussion about how our lives shape our theoretical positions and how theoretical positions shape our lives and politics. But for the most part the class was silent. The journal entries I received, however, were plenty loud:

> Rich tried to justify her actions by blaming culture and men, rather than acknowledging her own problems with sex.
>
> Rich's unhappiness is innate and she shouldn't point a finger at outside forces or the cultural environment.
>
> Rich's "awakened" way of life was degrading in the 70s and is now as well.

And, of course, I had to read an awful lot of quasi-biblical, Christian with a capital C rhetoric as well. Most of the class completely missed out on Rich's insistence on feminine language, a language that begins with "the act of looking back, of seeing with fresh eyes, of entering an old text from a new critical direction" (467), and moves on to "renaming." No longer willing to share my life, I answered their journal entries with academic, theoretical arguments, something useful I had learned in graduate school.

The last piece we discussed in this class was Joyce Carol Oates's short story "Theft." The class was still, for the most part, and silent. But one student brought up the question of Marya's denial of her lesbian sexuality as contributing to the stresses that made her steal, an interpretation that had in previous classes remained invisible. A few students were even willing to discuss Marya's love for Imogene and found a place for this love within other cultural stories of attraction and betrayal. Several passages where Marya describes Imogene or watches Imogene walk across campus were used to highlight this interpretation. I brought up the question of difference between the heterosexual relationships in the story and Marya's and Imogene's relationship, and some of the class discussed how the best friendships can survive sometimes blurred sexual boundaries and changing roles. A very small triumph to be sure, but the stories of teaching writing are fed by such successes, by the little workings with difference.

Differences between identities that are comprehended as absolute stifle the multiplicity of difference. The controlled dramatic or dynamic quality of a teacher's flexible identity as a bisexual and working-class academic can accommodate both an understanding of the necessity for an essential, collective consciousness to engage political issues and the equally compelling need to continually question this political identity. Keeping identity from becoming "fixed" leaves room to construct other useful political positions, still more "Other" places from which to speak. Increasing our understanding of those who tell stories from the social margins means exploring contradictions — the changing shapes of difference — so we can locate ourselves within/as the process of negotiating class and sexuality.

BUTCH: PERSONAL PEDAGOGY AND THE BUTCH BODY

In the late 1980s, I participated in a seminar series designed to help faculty members trained in traditional disciplines "retool" (a decidedly non-feminist word choice) with a view toward teaching interdisciplinary women's studies courses. There for the first time I encountered a chart (which I now know to be commonly used in introductory women's studies classes and elsewhere) outlining two areas: (1) some of an individual's multiple identities and (2) the relative experience of privilege associated with each. Through positioning myself on this chart, I was able to articulate to myself for the first time some of the ways I partake of unearned privilege: through my whiteness, through my family's adequate middle-class income, through access to education and other entranceways into a lifetime of status and financial security. At the same time, I was able to see how two specific aspects of my identity operated to deny me privilege: my femaleness and my lesbianism. (For the moment I'll ignore the butch aspect of my lesbian identity.) I began to understand how I occupy both the center and the margins of American society.

I focus on the implications of my identity presentation for my personal pedagogy and my collegial experience in the academy. I argue that many issues of diversity are so fully embodied that they cannot be meaningfully discussed, but rather exist primarily in the realm of performance. I believe that in my writing classrooms, the kind of multicultural consciousness I hope to encourage can arise at least as much from my own performance of (multiple) personal identities as from *Life Studies, Living in America, Writing About Diversity* or any other anthology. And I believe that in my interactions with colleagues, strange and (sometimes) wonderful transformations frequently take place at a visceral, not an intellectual, level. Don't get me wrong: I don't preach, and I don't act. But I have observed, for instance, that my femaleness, complicated both by a butch self-presentation and by the fact that I have children my students' ages, leads students and colleagues to react to me in ways that indicate their (not fully conscious) awareness of multiple, incongruent identities.

I suppose I should begin by pinning down what I mean by the word "butch." In lesbian parlance, the terms butch and femme refer to "qualities that exert a mutual attraction" related to stereotypical notions of masculinity and femininity (Laporte 210); the butch is "a lesbian whose self-identity takes on aspects of the traditionally 'masculine'" (Tracey and Pokorny 12). In the early twentieth century, the butch was seen as a "mannish lesbian," an invert, containing the soul of a man in a woman's body. By mid-century, butch and femme "roles" organized working-class lesbian bar culture, even to the extent that, as Elizabeth Kennedy and Madeline Davis have written, "For many women, their identity was in fact butch or fem, rather than gay or lesbian" (5). The lesbian-feminists of the 1970s rejected the butch/femme binary because they felt that rigid same-sex gender roles replicated the oppressive sexism of the larger society. What they forgot was that the very rigidity of butch/femme roles had given lesbians much-needed visibility in the years after World War II. After a decade underground, butch/femme reemerged as a form of "lesbian erotic identity" (Nestle 14) during the "lesbian sex wars" of the 1980s. As Arlene Stein puts it, "Eighties butch-femme—if it can accurately be termed such—is a self-conscious aesthetic that plays with style and power, rather than an embracing of one's 'true' nature against the constraints of straight society" (434–35). Today, in the era of lesbian chic, butch is a woman's performance of the stereotypically masculine.

In connecting my own butch gender performance with my experience as an academic, I want to tell three stories. The first took place in the late 1980s, when I coordinated an ongoing study of computers and basic writers. In gathering data, we ended up with some intriguing results that didn't fit anywhere in our stated purpose. Seven faculty took part in the study, three men and four women; over a period of four and a half years, the seven of us taught developmental writing to over 1,000 student participants. Every student completed a standard course evaluation at the end of the quarter. On a whim, we looked at the evaluation results by professor's sex and found that, taken together as a group, the three men averaged higher ratings in *instrumental* categories (knowledge, fairness) while the four women as a group averaged higher ratings in *affective* categories (helpfulness, availability). This result was, of course, the expected trend based on the research. But when we compared the four women with one another, we found another trend: Two of the women received much higher affective than instrumental scores while the other two (myself and another woman) had instrumental scores as high as the men's and affective scores just slightly lower than those of the other two women's. We theorized at the time that this result was obtained because the two of us women who scored high in instrumental categories are more butch than the other two women, who are more traditionally feminine. We considered having all seven faculty participants take the Bem Sex-Role Inventory test and actually measure the degree of (stereotypical) masculinity and femininity that each of us projects. We didn't do it, because we had enough on our hands just analyzing the data that pertained to the computer study, but now I wish we had. I suspect that the two butches would have scored high in masculine traits, which might very well have explained the difference in how our students reacted to us.

The second story is a coming-out story. In October 1994 I received a phone call from Jay Schatz, a TV reporter for Cincinnati's Channel 12 news, asking me to be a "sample dyke at work" for a feature timed to coincide with National Coming-Out Day. We arranged that he would film me in my writing class the next morning; I requested that he not arrive until half past the hour because I had not yet come out to the students in that class and needed some time to get past that sometimes thorny moment. When class began the next day, I launched into my coming-out speech: "Channel 12 is doing a feature on lesbians and gay men at work, and since I'm a lesbian and this is my work, they are coming to film us. If any of you prefer not to be shown on TV, let me know, because they'll be here any minute." There was a beat of silence, that moment of dysphoria every queer experiences every time we come out. Then a young man sitting near me pulled off his baseball cap, ran his fingers through his hair, and said, "How do I look?" Everyone laughed and the filming went off without incident. The point is that my coming out surprised no one, because, as Kristin Esterburg writes, in all areas "the coding of lesbians as not feminine *and therefore in some way masculine* predominate[s]" (276). As a butch or masculine woman, I project a "lesbian" persona without formally coming out.

The third story tells of my relationship to a (certain type of) male colleague. I should explain that I have been at the University of Cincinnati for sixteen years and am now a full professor. As such I have been involved in college and departmental policy planning, especially in the area of reappointment, promotion, and tenure (RPT). Since 1990 I have chaired two major college committees, one on the evaluation of teaching and the other on the revision of the college RPT guidelines. In the fall of 1997, I served for one quarter as acting academic dean of the college, a position I did not seek and agreed to fill only until a full-time person could be hired. That said, my story begins with the RPT guidelines committee during 1996–97. As chair, I was already struggling with a number of difficult personalities on the committee (you know them, I'm sure: the prima donna, the whiner, the obstructionist) and trying to keep the group on task and at least a little bit focused. On this committee was a man I'll call Professor Bluster, who at the time was recently tenured and also serving as chair of the committee that reviews promotion and tenure dossiers at the college level. In the few months that he had chaired that committee, he had done such a lousy job that faculty members throughout the college were calling for the elimination of the entire committee. Nevertheless, Professor Bluster thought he knew everything about how academic units should govern themselves, and he made it abundantly clear to the guidelines committee that he intended to tell us what we needed to know, while of course never volunteering for any of the real grunt work. My strategy for dealing with him was simply to allow him to say his piece, do a quick read of how the rest of the committee felt about it, then either bring his idea up for a quick decision or thank him for sharing and move on. He never protested openly, and the committee concluded its work in timely fashion. Later that year, however, I heard from another colleague that Professor Bluster had cornered her in her office and complained, "That Deb Meem—she's so bossy!" Here again I suspect it's my butchness that troubled Professor Bluster. Had I been a man, he would not have hesitated to bring all committee work to a halt in order to engage in a pissing contest with me. As a butch woman, however, I had a certain power over him; he clearly perceived me as being immune to male feather-ruffling and intimidation. In other words, his usual strategies for getting attention were useless, and all he could do was call me bossy later on.

These three stories illustrate how my butch performance (and I use that word hoping you will attend to the difference between, say, *dramatic* performance and *embodied* performance) impacts my various interactions in the academy. Because I am butch, I am visible as a lesbian; I am often asked, for instance, to be the "token dyke" on campus. Students come out to me, or ask me for advice; colleagues want to discuss queer issues with me, or include me on a panel. These responses, plus those from my three stories, indicate that students and faculty see my butchness as powerful, especially as contrasted with femme experience, which is mostly invisible. The power of butch performance seems to me to derive from what I described earlier as "multiple, incongruent identities." I do not see butch as an "identity" per se (although in some ways I could be said always to have been butch, from earliest childhood through marriage to a man to now), but rather as a chosen gender performance. I agree with Patti Smith, who said, "As far as I can tell, being any gender is a drag" (Stein 378, epigram). Judith Butler picks up on this idea: "If gender is drag . . . then gender is a performance that *produces* the illusion of an inner sex or essence or psychic gender core; it *produces* on the skin, through the gesture, the move, the gait (that array of corporeal theatrics understood as gender presentation), the illusion of an inner depth" ("Imitation" 28). What she is saying here is that butch drag looks like, and may even be experienced as, a "psychic gender core." But this essence is far more complex than "what you see is what you get," that is, a woman dressing like a man and appropriating not only the outward signs, but also some of the power and influence, of masculinity. Butler is helpful here again: "the 'identification' with masculinity that appears as butch identity is not a simple assimilation of lesbianism back into the terms of heterosexuality" because "in both butch and femme identities, the very notion of an original or natural identity is put into question" (*Gender Trouble* 156, 157).

This idea of multiple, or confusing, simultaneous identities brings me back to the chart I mentioned (Figure 1).[1] Those of you who are familiar with this chart as it appears in women's studies texts will recognize that I have added butch and femme in the "privileged" (top line) and "oppressed" (second line) positions, respectively. As I circle my various identity categories, I notice that I am "privileged" 5 to 4. Right away this complicates the assumption that as a woman and a lesbian, I am uniformly oppressed in the academy. Further, when the identity category "butch" is figured as powerful (as my three stories have shown it can be), even lesbianism can be reconceptualized. In short, these categories must be seen as fluid. Butch was an oppressed identity in the 1950s specifically because butch lesbians were visible and, therefore,

FIGURE 1 Multiple, Simultaneous Identities

Male	Middle Class	Heterosexual	White	Young, Middle-Aged	Able-Bodied	Thin	Christian	Butch
Female	Working Class	Lesbian, Gay	Of Color	Old	Disabled	Fat	Non-Christian	Femme
	Impoverished	Bisexual, Trans-Gendered						

targets for harassment, discrimination, and violence. Femme lesbians, precisely because they were *invisible*, had greater access to jobs and relative immunity from harassment (at least, from harassment based on their lesbianism; as women they were just as vulnerable as their straight sisters). Today, however, butch visibility in the academy can provide access to a certain kind of power; the relative invisibility of femmes makes it difficult for them to connect with sources of lesbian community in or out of the academy. Experiences of relative privilege and oppression thus resist consistency.

Continuing this line of reasoning, I am also led to observe that the very existence of the chart and the commonness of its usage in the academy tend to privilege its "oppressed" categories. Let me tell one final story. I am a member of a listserv for lesbian academics, and recently I "lurked" the list during a discussion of the possible connection between childhood sexual abuse and adult lesbian identity that turned into a flame-throwing exchange about elitism and privilege. The principal flamer is a woman in her final year of graduate school who claims that her identities as working class, Latina, and butch lesbian operate together to deny her privilege in the academy. While I would not venture to claim that she has never been denied privilege on account of her multiple "second row" identities, I would propose that those identities also privilege her, since, as Diana Fuss writes, "in the classroom [and, I would add, in the academy in general] identities are nothing if not commodities" (115). The flamer's chief error is assuming that identity categories are fixed, both in themselves and in the experience of privilege or oppression attached to them. The concept of strategic essentialism holds that an oppressed group may claim its identity as an essence for the purpose of gaining political power— that, for instance, lesbian and gay activists may plead, "We were born this way; we've always been this way; it's not our fault; don't discriminate against us." I see the flamer as adopting a strategic essentialist stance in order to stake out a space for herself as oppressed, and therefore deserving of at least recognition and at most reparations. Fuss acknowledges the utility of this practice, but insists that we in the academy need to interrogate identity and its uses; "we need," she writes, "both to theorize essentialist spaces from which to speak and, simultaneously, to deconstruct these spaces to keep them from solidifying" (118). If it is true, as Judith Butler says, that fixed "identity categories tend to be instruments of regulatory regimes" ("Imitation" 13), then complicating our own multiple identities is a revolutionary act. The stories I have told here have been intended to problematize the simplistic identity schematic represented by the chart. In my classes, in my college, and in the world, I will insist on owning, and performing, all of my incongruent identities; I'll continue being the butch with kids.

BAR DYKE: A COCKTAIL WAITRESS TEACHES WRITING

In *Poisoned Ivy: Lesbian and Gay Academics Confronting Homophobia,* Toni McNaron argues that "remembering one's past . . . constitutes a radical political action. For those of us who have been told, overtly or subtly, that our existence is not quite valid, insisting on having and shaping memories into coherent form constitutes disobedience on a personal level and destabilization on a cultural level" (8). To my mind, McNaron's argument can be taken even a step further. In an academic climate where postmodern theories that focus on the performative nature of identity prevail, political action necessitates not only giving voice to but also performing memory, especially as it relates to the construction of identity. Many academics have memories that can challenge traditional beliefs about who is willing and able to function effectively in the academy, as well as about what it *means* to function effectively in the academy. Those memories help construct nontraditional academic identities that, if performed fully and openly, can deconstruct notions about who university students and faculty are and force the academy to respond more fully to the needs of diverse populations.

One way I make my identities overt is to think like a constructivist but act like an essentialist. Whenever a circumstance allows for it, I perform my identities as a femme lesbian, a survivor of family violence, and a recovering mental patient. One such circumstance arises every couple of years. At the University of Cincinnati, faculty who wish to be reappointed, promoted, or tenured are required to submit dossiers of their work. These dossiers contain evidence of achievement in three areas—professional activity, service, and teaching—as well as self-evaluation statements for each area. The dossier goes through several levels of evaluation, one of which is performed by a college-wide committee. A few years ago, when I was being evaluated for reappointment, that committee returned my dossier to me, saying that while they felt that my work in each of the areas clearly exceeded expectations, they were "disquieted" by my self-evaluation statements. Specifically, the committee believed that I identify too strongly with students and that I should not admit in a professional document that I did not follow a traditional academic path. They suggested that I remove references to my work as a cocktail waitress, refrain from discussing my connections to students who are unfamiliar with academic expectations, and "write tweed" (their phrase).

The return of my dossier with these suggestions reminded me that, though many academics talk about diversity, the academy itself persists in seeing the university as tweed: white, middle class, and heterosexual. This mentality is exactly the mentality that many of my peers in composition studies and I try to subvert when we insist upon speaking our memories and performing our diverse and multifaceted identities. Our colleagues, though, don't always share our enthusiasm for experiential data. For instance, in *Sexing the Self,* sociologist Elspeth Probyn says that when she revealed in an article about anorexia that she was anorexic, a reviewer responded with criticism, arguing that the problem with "postmodern America [is that] the natives are now writing their own ethnography" (12). So when my colleagues on the college committee read my dossier they were responding not only to their individual discomfort with what I had written but also to the disjuncture between my values and the values they have learned as participants in their own academic disciplines.

Here is one of the passages the committee found problematic:

I do not have a traditional academic background, and I believe that is one of my greatest strengths as a University College faculty member. I just barely graduated from high school, then I muddled around working as a cocktail waitress, selling cars, peddling insurance door-to-door, and living what could be called an aimless existence before I met someone who suggested that I attend college. Only because the "college life" seemed more inviting than the life I had been leading, I began attending a two-year college in my hometown. Then, only because I actually graduated from Hutchinson Community College and someone else suggested that I go on to get my bachelor's degree, I went to a four-year college in Maryland. Then, only because I didn't know what kind of a job I could get with a bachelor's degree in English and someone else suggested that I go to graduate school. I went to Ohio University to get my graduate degrees.

What probably stands out most about this statement is how benign and understated it is. When I wrote this passage I really didn't think much of it. In fact, I was a bit concerned that I had said too little in my general self-evaluation. What seemed as clear to me as what I had said was what I had not said. For instance, even though I was extremely tempted, I didn't write about the fact that the work I did as a cocktail waitress was done at a lesbian bar known for its girl drag shows and for its drag team, which was named for the Village People's song, "Macho Man." I didn't talk about the fact that I believe I got quite a bit of training for being a teacher and running a classroom from my experiences as the emcee for those drag shows, from "working a room." I didn't say that, as emcee, I put my rhetorical skills to great use when I wrote lewd, rhyming introductions for the drag "kings," as we called them. In short, while I knew when I wrote that passage that I was confronting some traditional beliefs about who becomes an academic, my awareness of what I left out of it led me to believe that it was pretty mundane.

And, when a representative of the College Reappointment, Promotion, and Tenure Committee (let's call her Dr. Gatekeeper) called me to set up a meeting to discuss my dossier, I had no idea that she might want to discuss this passage. However, what she told me was that this passage was particularly troubling to the committee, whose members believed it "dangerous" to my professional well-being. She explained that a candidate for reappointment must appear to be "as much like upper-level administrators as possible." The committee, she informed me, was interested in and engaged by my self-evaluation statements, but they believed them "artless" in the sense that passages such as the one above make me sound as if I misunderstand the nature of the university. She said that references to work experience such as cocktail waitressing and admissions that both my existence before I started college and my college career were "aimless" would make me seem to the provost and his peers as if I were not worthy of membership in the academic community.

Had I been more prepared for this kind of reading of my dossier, I might have told Dr. Gatekeeper that Diana Fuss says, "Personal consciousness, individual oppressions, lived experience . . . operate . . . both to authorize and to de-authorize speech" (113). I might have explained that my experience of the academy, both as a student and as a faculty member, had led me to believe that many of my identities—particularly those like the ones I discuss in my self-evaluation statement—are just what Dr. Gatekeeper's comments indicated they are: unauthorized. I might have said that in the four years I spent as an undergraduate I had almost never read any piece of literature that was at all related to my experiences as a lesbian or as a survivor of family violence and institutionalization. I remember no more than two instances in which my teachers discussed issues related to lesbians or represented family life in a way that I recognized. Even in my Psychology of Women course there was no mention of lesbianism, and I was the only person who broached the subject of family violence. In short, my experience was de-authorized not by denial but by silence.

As a faculty member working from a position of relative power, then, I feel a great need to authorize those experiences by giving them voice and by performing them. However, Dr. Gatekeeper's goals (and those of the committee she represented) are clearly different from mine. It's too easy to say that she hoped to protect the status quo; I think her motivations were more complex than that. After all, she honestly believed that she was protecting my interests by instructing me in the ways of the academy. Her relaying of the committee's accusation that my writing was "artless" was her way of sending me the message that she believed I wrote what I did out of naiveté. During our conversation she told me several times that administrators are not creative, that unlike faculty who are also scholars, they reject intellectual complexity in favor of familiarity. Dr. Gatekeeper wanted me to see her as my ally, as one who shares my political consciousness but knows better than I do how to gain power and use it effectively. I, on the other hand, felt at least vaguely confident that I had shown sufficient progress in the three areas under review and wanted to mobilize my confidence into political action.

In performing her function as gatekeeper, my advisor was even more troubled by the following section of my dossier than she had been by the previous one:

> It's 8:10 a.m. on a Wednesday morning and I have just announced that . . . we will . . . sign on to the computers and use them for a classroom activity. Tom, who . . . informs me every day that he probably knows more about computers than I do, is particularly excited. . . . [H]e raises his voice above mine and bellows out instructions that are confusing to everyone in the room. Suddenly, about ten students raise their hands and wave frantically. I hear things like, "What have I done?" "My computer doesn't work; the screen is blank," and "It's all screwed up!" Tom keeps yelling, I ask everyone to calm down, Tom keeps yelling. Finally, I snap, "Not another word, Tom." While I get everyone else to the same screen, Tom writes an e-mail to me in which he says that I humiliated him. When I am able to return to my computer, I respond that he is absolutely right, that a teacher should never make her students feel humiliated. In his next e-mail to me, he says that he has never been apologized to by a teacher before and says, "You are a great English teacher, my greatest ever."

Mary, a student in my 8:00 a.m. English for Effective Communication class, is making her third attempt to pass the course. She is shy; most of the time she looks down at her lap or holds her book in front of her face. During a conference, she tells me she has been hospitalized for depression but that now she is ready to "get back into life and get through college." One day she comes running into class twenty minutes late. Her hands are shaking and she is breathing hard as she takes her seat. After class, she approaches me and explains that she has been in an automobile accident and that it was her fault. She tells me that she was praying and not paying attention to where she was going when she hit a car that was turning in front of her. In a moment of insight, I put my hand on her shoulder and ask, "Were you praying with your eyes closed?" She turns, waves her finger in my direction, and says, "Professor Gibson, *that* was my mistake."

Brian writes an angry journal entry about the paper he has just completed. He says that English teachers are awful people who don't care about their students or about writing. He seems to be challenging me to make negative comments about his paper so that he can characterize me as "just like the rest of them." During a conference, I ask Brian to explain his journal entry, to help me understand its motivation, and to work with me to find a way for us to have productive discussions about his writing. In what turns out to be a fifteen minute soliloquy, he tells me that he grew up in a small town, that his father is in prison for armed robbery, and that his English teacher in high school seemed to blame him for his father's tendency to be a "violent asshole."

Though it is difficult to admit, I strongly identify with Tom, Mary, and Brian. Like Tom, I know what it is like to be insecure, to try to alleviate that insecurity by acting in ways that seem inappropriate and odd to those around me, and to feel humiliated when I am confronted about my behavior. Like Mary, I started college only a short while after being released from a hospital where I was treated for depression; I was frightened and shy, and most of the time I felt like I was driving and praying with my eyes closed. And like Brian, I grew up in a small town where it seemed as though everyone knew about my violent family, considered us "white trash," and treated me accordingly. Tom, Mary, Brian, and I started college believing ourselves uniquely inadequate and fearing that our inadequacies were visible not only to our peers, but also to our teachers.

When I submitted my dossier, I knew that this part of my teaching self-evaluation statement was different from what I had seen in other dossiers. I also knew from listening to hallway chat that the committee was particularly concerned that our self-evaluation statements not make our students look different from, by which they meant inferior to, students in the rest of the university. Many of my colleagues believe that our college, which is the only open admissions unit on the University of Cincinnati's main campus, gets a bad rap because it focuses too much on its underprepared students. I disagree. I believe that our college has a unique opportunity to force the university to rethink its definitions of words like *student, success,* and *access.* Therefore, I was trying to engage in what Fuss calls "trading on" identity and experience. As a constructivist who believes strongly in the multiplicity and liquidity of identity and acknowledges the necessity of problematizing it, I know that identity can be used to "purchase" power. Using the "truth" of my experience, I constructed an identity as a formerly impoverished, scared, and shy student who had no idea how to perform in the academy until I was transformed by education into a rather outspoken middle-class professor of English. By construct, I do not mean that I lied; everything I said about myself in that introduction is true to my experience. What I do mean is that I chose in this instance to use my experience as currency, to use the familiar transformation metaphor to buy from the administrators I knew would read the dossier some understanding of my students' unique situations and potential.

I wanted to perform for those administrators an identity they usually associate with students they characterize as "not college material" and then complicate it with an identity they usually associate with professionals they characterize as "successful." I believed that if I was "out" about some of my experiences, I could mainstream (intellectually speaking) the experiences of students who face similar circumstances. And, because I did not want my students to be further disenfranchised by my attempts to buy them some power, I was extremely careful and thoughtful about the process I used to do that work. In short, I was trying to walk a thin line between using personal experience, or performing memory, to authorize a new kind of discourse and overwhelming my readers with information so unfamiliar that it seemed inappropriate.

In my conversation with Dr. Gatekeeper, and in the notes she gave to me to "guide revision," I was told that the college committee was extremely troubled by my admission that I feel such intense connection to my students. I was informed that, as a faculty member submitting a dossier for reappointment, my task is to identify with administrators, not students. Sitting beside me on the sofa in her office, sipping a cup of tea that she warmed with hot water from the silver pot on her desk, Dr. Gatekeeper explained that I needed to develop a better sense of my place in the academy if I wanted to advance at an appropriate rate. Astonished and perplexed, I finally asked Dr. Gatekeeper what would happen if I did not revise my self-evaluation statements or if I only made small, editorial changes. Her answer was that nothing would happen because my vitae showed sufficient achievement in teaching, service, and scholarship to merit reappointment.

In the end, I made only cosmetic changes to my dossier, and I received a positive letter from the college committee. I was able to follow the old feminist adage "the personal is political" and to disobey in the way McNaron suggests we should by "having and shaping [my] memories into coherent form" (8). And, throughout my discussion of my experiences with Dr. Gatekeeper, I have followed McNaron's lead. After all, I have given the representative from the college committee a rather obvious pseudonym; I have disclosed all kinds of personal information in what Probyn would call an intellectual "striptease";

and I have presented a text that pretty much insists that identity is constructed of memory and experience.

What would happen, though, if I assumed for a moment that Dr. Gatekeeper would be more accurately named Dr. Radical Constructivist and that her motive was to launch a rather leftist interrogation of the essentialist assumptions behind my adoption of identities? Suppose we assume that Dr. Radical Constructivist was asking questions similar to those asked of Probyn's work by feminist critic Laura Marcus:

> How can autobiography's emphasis on the individual, the development of the self and the confluence between author and textual "I," be reconciled with political and theoretical perspectives skeptical of traditional concepts of subjectivity, individualism, and textual authority? (Probyn 13)

Could it be that my attempts to authorize an intellectual discourse for students and faculty whose identities are constructed of memories like mine actually de-authorize that discourse? I know that stories like mine can be used to create silence. Let me give you an example.

I belong to a listserv of colleagues from composition studies. One of the most common strands on the list has to do with issues related to personal power in the academy. Recently, one of the white male members of the list was trying to discuss his feelings of relative powerlessness when compared to other white males. Female members of the list responded angrily, arguing that even when white men are not aware of it or try not to use it, the culture automatically endows them with unearned privilege. The man who had argued his powerlessness responded to those criticisms by explaining that in his dysfunctional family he was expected to take on much of the work and responsibility that would traditionally have been given to his mother. Then he described his family's circumstances in some detail. His disclosures were met with utter silence; no one on the list pursued the power issues originally under discussion; no one responded at all. To my mind, what happened there was that the man whose disclosures stopped the conversation attempted to complicate the issues at hand, but his attempts were so personal that no one knew how to critique his argument or the highly personal disclosures that informed it. The man's disclosure, then, de-authorized critical discourse that might have brought us all to a more complex understanding of the way gender functions to empower and disempower in the academy.

If the committee representative is Dr. Radical Constructivist rather than Dr. Gatekeeper, she might have been asking me to reconsider the effectiveness of my approach. She might have been correct when she characterized my self-evaluation statements "artless," if artlessness has to do with not accomplishing my goals. If my intellectual/emotional striptease did nothing to help me create a space in the academy for students and faculty who perform identities such as femme lesbian, survivor of family violence, or recovering mental patient, then all that it did accomplish was to leave me standing buck naked in front of an audience. As is probably obvious, I believe that constructing and performing our nontraditional identities through personal experience is an inherently political act designed to transform the public spaces we inhabit from oppressive realms into inclusive realms. However, I also believe that, without consistent interrogation, over time acts that originate as political resistance can become familiar and institutionalized, thereby losing their power to create change.

CONCLUSION

Compositionists committed to creating classrooms in which traditional academic power structures are problematized and critiqued must also commit themselves to interrogating their own positions in those classrooms. We must think seriously about the identities we bring with us into the classroom, remain conscious of the way those identities interact with the identities our students bring, and insert ourselves fully into the shifting relationships between ourselves and our students at the same time that we resist the impulse to control those relationships. It is not enough for teachers merely to include in their curricula readings about race, class, gender, and sexuality, for the traditional inclusion model fails to challenge the academic mindset that assumes the centrality of white, middle-class, male, heterosexual values and desires. We must instead make ourselves acutely aware of and constantly responsive to the interplay of identities—both our own and those of our students. The stories we have told here emphasize the shifting nature of our own personal and academic identities. "Bi" presents herself as between comfortably recognizable identities: neither wholly at home among her working-class former neighbors nor thoroughly assimilated into the academic middle class, neither safely straight nor stereotypically lesbian. "Butch" stresses the paradoxical nature of power in the academy, according to which "dyke" becomes less a liability than a "drag" choice that can be traded on. "Bar Dyke" illustrates the disjuncture among her own need to express herself in an authentic voice, the "tweed" rejection of that voice, and her sense that even what seemed most risky in her self-presentation in fact understated the lived reality. We offer them not as models for teachers, but rather as possibilities for complicating the experience of Otherness in the academy.

NOTE

1. Note that in the second and third columns I add a third "least privileged" category. Of course, on one level, this third category complicates the relentless binary oppositions that lent the original chart its shape. More than this, however, the sexuality column asserts that even in the context of heterosexual privilege, lesbians and gay men rank higher than bisexual or transgendered people. This ranking is because in our culture "lesbian" and "gay" are assumed to be coherent identities, while bisexuality and transgender are so fluid—and contested—as to resist the consistency of definition and the relative safety of coherence.

WORKS CITED

Budbill, David. "Roy McInnes." *Working Classics: Poems on Industrial Life.* Ed. Peter Oresick and Nicholas Coles. Chicago: U of Illinois P, 1990. 30.

Butler, Judith. *Gender Trouble: Feminism and the Subversion of Identity.* New York: Routledge, 1990.

——. "Imitation and Gender Insubordination." *Inside/Out: Lesbian Theories, Gay Theories.* Ed. Diana Fuss. New York: Routledge, 1991. 13–31.

Ellsworth, Elizabeth. "Why Doesn't This Feel Empowering? Working Through the Repressive Myths of Critical Pedagogy." *Feminisms and Critical Pedagogy.* Ed. Carmen Luke and Jennifer Gore. New York: Routledge, 1992. 90–119.

Esterburg, Kristin G. "'A Certain Swagger When I Walk': Performing Lesbian Identity." *Queer Theory/Sociology.* Ed. Steven Seidman. Malden, MA: Blackwell, 1996. 259–79.

Fuss, Diana. *Essentially Speaking: Feminism, Nature, and Difference.* New York: Routledge, 1989.

Kennedy, Elizabeth Lapovsky, and Madeline D. Davis. *Boots of Leather, Slippers of Gold: The History of a Lesbian Community.* New York: Penguin, 1994.

Laporte, Rita. "The Butch-Femme Question." *The Persistent Desire: A Femme-Butch Reader.* Ed. Joan Nestle. Boston: Alyson, 1992. 208–19.

McNaron, Toni A. H. *Poisoned Ivy: Lesbian and Gay Academics Confronting Homophobia.* Philadelphia: Temple UP, 1997.

Minh-Ha, Trinh. "Introduction: She, the Inappropriate(d) Other." *Discourse* 8 (1986/1987): 3–9.

Nestle, Joan. "Flamboyance and Fortitude: An Introduction." *The Persistent Desire: A Femme-Butch Reader.* Ed. Joan Nestle. Boston: Alyson, 1992. 13–20.

Oates, Joyce Carol. "Theft." *Ways of Reading.* Ed. David Bartholomae and Anthony Petrosky. 4th ed. Boston: Bedford Books, 1996. 471–507.

Probyn, Elspeth. *Sexing the Self: Gendered Positions in Cultural Studies.* London: Routledge, 1993.

Rich, Adrienne. "When We Dead Awaken: Writing As Re-Vision." *Ways of Reading.* Ed. David Bartholomae and Anthony Peterosky. 4th ed. Boston: Bedford Books, 1996. 549–62.

Stein, Arlene. "All Dressed Up, But No Place to Go? Style Wars and the New Lesbianism." *The Persistent Desire: A Femme-Butch Reader.* Ed. Joan Nestle. Boston: Alyson, 1992, 431–39.

Tracey, Liz, and Sydney Pokorny. *So You Want to Be a Lesbian?* New York: St. Martin's/Griffin, 1996.

Masks and Other Drapings: A Reconsideration (or Reconciliation?) of "Participatory Rhetoric and the Teacher as Racial/Gendered Subject"

CHERYL L. JOHNSON

ll life is rhythm.

–Ustad Alla Rakha, Master of Hindustani Classical Music

A few months ago, I visited the Art Institute of Chicago and saw a special exhibit on art from Somalia. Although I have seen many African art exhibits, and I have various African masks and statues in my home as part of my private collection, in those two or three museum rooms I experienced an epiphany of sorts. I have always known, at least intellectually, that these masks and ceremonial dress were worn during ceremonies and rituals, whether to pay homage to ancestors, appeal to a deity for special favor, or express an ontological understanding or reconciliation. But as I gazed upon these masks and head dress, featuring intricate cultural carvings with lines and shapes, some framed by abrupt, elongated representations of parts of the human or animal body, whether phallic or female, I realized that these stunningly beautiful wood objects were once situated on someone's head or pressed against the flesh of someone's face, that sweat drenched the interior and exterior of the mask as the wearer performed the historical, social, and/or spiritual symbols inscribed onto the contours of the mask. One of the exhibited costumes was layered with yards and yards of brightly colored material, so that as the dancer whirled, the layers fanned into an array of colors, dazzling in their rhythms, their syncopation. But I wondered, how does the dancer negotiate the contours and demands of the costume with his own body? At what point do the performer and dress become one, congruent in their movements, with sweat so intense that the dyes created a tattoo of sorts on the skin of the performer?

When I wrote "Participatory Rhetoric," I understood that I was a performer of sorts, but I did not consider how heavy and cumbersome—psychologically, intellectually, and emotionally—the masks and costuming were. Realizing that students were reading my body along with the African American texts, I performed rituals, with language styled by its own ceremonial dress and masks, that were designed to signify both my personal and professional locations. Teaching, then, has never been for me simply the transmission of information; instead, it has facilitated my desire to have students interrogate difference, step outside the margins of their own discourses and discursive practices, and reconsider their ideologies, whether shaky or scared. I imagined that the language of texts and I performed a fascinating rhythm—fashioning meaning: "signifyin." But, just as any visitor to a museum who gazes upon an object taken out of its cultural context imposes meaning on that object based on her own culturally framed references, my students read my performances and the African American texts from their own readings of race and gender as eighteen- to twenty-one-year-olds. Clearly, my rituals and costuming were not merely fastidious: Many students approached my performances with an anthropological perspective, ready to reread the symbols, resituate their cultural references. But for other students, the burden of their cultural understandings would not allow intervention, or these were significantly diffused, muted. Just as African art was and still is seen as primitive by those who do not know its cultural markings, students who are not part of African American culture or communities misread my performances.

So, nearly a decade after publishing "Participatory Rhetoric," I am still concerned about the ways in which students participate in the construction of meaning of African American texts. And I still worry about my responsibility to respect the integrity of their readings while enticing them to enter another interpretive space, framed by gender, race, class, and sexuality issues. My performances, however, are now less dazzling. My masks are lighter, my costuming less intricate. These drapings are simply too heavy, and I am more interested in investigating the small spaces between the masks and drapings and my own skin and mind—juxtaposing/conflating the inner-outer: the performance, the rhythm.

Feminism and the Politics of the Profession

Part Five: Introduction

LEE NICKOSON-MASSEY

Professional issues have been and continue to be a concern of feminist compositionists, as the academy has not been immune to sexism in the workplace. The articles that follow present varied approaches to confronting working conditions in composition. Included are examinations of how working conditions for women have improved over the last several years but also of how much needs to be done, sentiments that echo the field of feminism and composition. Scholars have noted, for example, that college-level teaching positions have traditionally been reserved for men and that the only positions regularly available to women were in composition. This "feminization" of composition has contributed to the devaluation of composition as an academic field. Moreover, even as composition remains one of the most receptive fields for women, many still face problems common to women in other professions—lower pay, lower levels of job security, and fewer opportunities for advancement.

Wendy Bishop, in her 1990 article, "Learning Our Own Ways to Situate Composition and Feminist Studies in the English Department," argues against academics labeling themselves as "feminist" or "compositionist" in a climate that devalues some areas of English studies. Attaching these labels to ourselves, she argues, works to reinforce the dominant approach to the field as hierarchical—the literature scholar and critic once again becomes elevated, while the teacher of composition or women's studies finds herself marginalized once again. In a narrative composed for this collection, Bishop subsequently reflects on the reception of her essay; she addresses the schism between literature and composition and the values associated with each and suggests we work with and mentor graduate students to create change in the academy.

In "Composing 'Composing as a Woman,'" Elizabeth Flynn reflects on the factors that influenced her work, including her often-cited essay "Composing as a Woman," and on the resistance she faced to publish the essay because it drew upon multiple disciplines, genres, and research methods. She introduces the essay as an effort to address specific comments the original essay received from its *College Composition and Communication* reviewers; to

illustrate that feminist work can successfully draw from humanism, empiricism, and feminist theory; and to increase awareness among "composition
specialists who are unaware of or unconvinced of the relevance of work in
feminist studies to their investigation of student writing."

Susan Miller addresses the negative connotations associated with feminist approaches to composition and suggests that we must challenge the belief
that composition is itself a marginalized field; she asks why, how, and by
whom has it been marginalized. Hers is a self-reflective, rigorous feminist
argument, one that aptly represents the debates often heard throughout the
field at the time. Miller calls for political action to change the negative conno-
tation of the "feminization" of composition and for intellectual and practical
movements toward gender balance in composition studies. She explores the
status of females as occupying lower positions in the hierarchy of the academy
and gives an informative history of the marginalized positions of English,
composition studies, and women teachers. Miller promotes composition studies as a "culturally designated space for political action." She concludes with
suggestions for catalysts of change, presenting composition as containing the
discourse of the majority and thus an effective place for "counterhegemonic
intellectual politics."

Janice Lauer and Lynn Bloom each write of women's status in the field,
based on their own experiences. Lynn Bloom's approachable narrative details
her personal history as a woman in the field. She relates horror stories of
teaching part-time at one university: Though she had earned a doctorate, she
found that she did not warrant an office with a telephone of her own. She tells
about additional struggles to find a voice as she found herself moving from
institution to institution, all the while fighting to legitimate herself, her position within the field, and the field itself. Those looking to get a glimpse into
the life of an esteemed compositionist, as well as those seeking a personal
account from an established scholar, will enjoy reading of the many challenges, frustrations, and successes she encountered during the course of
her career. Then Lauer highlights the marginalized status of women in the
field by addressing the negative connotations often associated with feminist
approaches to composition. This essay supplies a concise and helpful history
of English studies that explores the character of the field throughout the years.
She discusses what historical events and pedagogical movements may have
influenced the feminization of the field.

Finally, Eileen Schell argues that feminist work needs to challenge the
metaphors and narratives that reinscribe women in restrictive or oppressive
roles. Referencing prevalent stereotypes that represent teachers as mothers
and female professionals as engaged in housework, she notes that the fact that
more and more women are entering the field does not mean that feminist pedagogy has also experienced an increased presence in composition. To her,
composition is seen as a "service" course that teaches "skills" and that it is
thus often considered to be "drudge or apprentice work." Consequently,
Schell notes, little institutional status is attributed to those part-time and/or
graduate students (most of whom are women) who teach composition. She

adds that, when we do hear women's voices, it is from the few who have "made it": There are few women in leadership positions, just as few of the field's published articles are authored by women. Ultimately, then, she argues that feminization becomes exploitation and questions what "women's work" means to the profession.

Although unique in approach and perspective, the essays in this section present a history of composition as affected by imbalance or inequity as a call for reflection and change. These authors challenge readers to consider a current tension in the field: Women have come to share a strong voice in composition teaching, research, and scholarship, but is it (has it been) enough to "have a voice"? What does it mean to have a voice? What might we have given up for our successes in a field still heavily influenced by traditionally male modes of rhetoric and institutional hierarchy? And last, these essays serve as reminders for us to engage other imbalances based on class and ethnicity and investigate the ways the issues addressed by feminists in composition cross boundaries of difference.

30 *Learning Our Own Ways to Situate Composition and Feminist Studies in the English Department*

WENDY BISHOP

We all know that it is possible to hold conflicting intellectual and emotional positions simultaneously; many personalities inhabit us in our lives as teachers, scholars, mothers, fathers, community members, speed offenders, friends, lovers. It is primarily when we move into that rarefied air of our professional lives—say, when we open the door to an English department meeting—that we give ourselves over wholeheartedly to what Mary Savage describes as "academentia." At that moment, our carefully negotiated and necessarily composite personality shivers, cracks, faults, and folds under, and we resay ourselves, becoming decontextualized as a "Shakespearean," a "Melville specialist," or, in the lesser ranks, a "feminist," "compositionist," "fiction writer," or "poet." When we label ourselves in this way, we agree to the dominant method of distinguishing areas in English studies, what Gerald Graff calls the field-coverage model, a model that isolates and elevates the literature scholar and critic and isolates but devalues the generalist.

Too often, in entering these singular terrains, women travel nervously, alone, with few maps or guidebooks, while the current-traditional "body" of English studies is very able to absorb our nervousness and discontent. By creating separate women's studies programs, designating fields like "composition" and "feminist studies" or allowing only minimal authority for writing program administrators, the establishment is free to conduct department business as usual.[1] Meanwhile, marginalized cultures within or beside the department's dominant culture, alienated, co-opted, or about to be co-opted, sit silently around that meritocratic table, feeling concerned.

NEGOTIATING RULES AND CROSSING BOUNDARIES

When I was a "good" girl in high school, I completed my classwork scrupulously and found a part-time job in order to save money for future college expenses. The first morning at Woolworth's, I didn't forge right out to the mixed joys of working the candy counter, but was kept in the drafty upper

From *Journal of Advanced Composition* 10 (1990): 339–55.

regions of the store to read the rules-and-regulations manual, after which I signed a paper saying I understood and agreed. Most jobs I held after that—generally part-time, poorly paid, and sure to encourage my pursuit of the examined life—included a quick run-through of parameters. There was always a rules-and-regulations manual. Always, that is, until I entered the more discreet and elite work force of the English department. During my years as a TA, part-time lecturer, full-time renewable instructor, and, finally, tenure-line professor, there were rules but they were not written; there were communities but they were usually not friendly or open.

In my earliest days in academia, I wanted and needed more guidance in many ways. I was a woman. I was naive. And I was traumatized by much of what I experienced. I had "converted" suddenly and enthusiastically from studio art to creative writing and literature, and professors had welcomed me to their undergraduate classes. But in the transition to graduate-level work, something happened: my place as a class member in good standing was usurped. I entered a world where the prevailing hierarchy was visible if not explicit, as Adrienne Rich describes it:

> Look at a classroom. . . . Listen to the voices of the women and the voices of the men; observe the space men allow themselves, physically and verbally, the male assumption that people will listen, even when the majority of the group is female. Look at the faces of the silent, and of those who speak. Listen to a woman groping for language in which to express what is on her mind, sensing that the terms of academic discourse are not her language, trying to cut down her thought to the dimensions of a discourse not intended for her . . . or reading her paper aloud at breakneck speed, throwing her words away. ("Taking" 244–45)

As a female initiate into graduate English studies, I was no longer expected to have a voice.[2]

Equally, reading the traditional canon under paternal guidance was going to change me. Patrocinio Schweickart illuminates the problem: "For a woman . . . books do not necessarily spell salvation. In fact, a literary education may very well cause her grave psychic damage: schizophrenia 'is the bizarre but logical conclusion of our education'" (41). For instance, although I had become an English graduate student because I loved reading and writing, the texts I loved to read were no longer sites of enjoyment. Rather, they were sites of struggle where my (generally) male professors were enmeshed in a critical game of vast proportions. These professors were Titans struggling in the bleak "publish or perish" universe, while I, uninitiated, was naively expecting to savor great works with their guidance. But the critical wars were not considered suitable for seminar discussion, the primacy of particular great works was not questioned, and the woman student progressed through literature studies as usual, reading against herself. Schweickart also reminds us of the disturbing end-result of such reading: we create a personality untrue to itself, for this is "the consequence of the invocation to identify as male while being reminded that to be male . . . to be universal . . . is to be *not female*" (42).

After completing master's-level work in creative writing, I continued on through a quick, unhappy stint in literature to composition and ESL. I was "guided" into community college teaching by a literature advisor when I failed to pass one of three days of qualifying exams for a Ph.D. in English (literature) and, no longer a good girl, refused to take the exams again. At that time, teaching composition and ESL was considered a respectable "trade."

Years later, finally, happily, I chose deeper work in rhetoric and composition. Yet I've never given up my allegiances to those first areas of study, and I constantly work to reintegrate them into my life. Not to do so would be to lose my culture, my pedagogical and writing life experiences. For me, to be only a poet, or a feminist, or a compositionist is not enough. Nevertheless, traditional scholars warn me not to try to cross field boundaries. Says Martin Mueller:

> A great deal of interdisciplinary work in English departments is deficient precisely in the virtue it claims for itself because scholars approach interdisciplinary work too casually. Stick to your knitting is sometimes good advice. We would all benefit from a healthy respect for our own expertise and an equally healthy apprehension of the difficulties involved in venturing on other territory. (9)

Mueller tries to find a middle ground in the critical-theory/literature-studies wars, never once mentioning feminist or composition issues. Sticking to my knitting in a traditional English department would include, I expect, not allowing learning from my low-status pasts to inform my present professional status. That is, if I intend to "do" criticism or direct graduate students' theses, I should not dilute boundaries by admitting to having taught ESL or liking to write poems. Cross-disciplinary work, it must be remembered, challenges the existing field-coverage model.

As a participant in English studies, I do not want to stick to my knitting, for, like many others, I do not want to undergo the deracination that Patricia Bizzell suggests may occur to minority-culture students, who must forget where they have come from in order to survive their journey through the academy. Students try to resolve a dialect problem as they accede to the preferred school dialect, a dialect that they need to learn in order to successfully master the discourse conventions of their chosen fields or the academic community at large. Or they may need to learn a new way of thinking entirely, mandating a change in their world view. Bizzell holds that students who are asked to change their world view risk deracination, and she argues for closer study of the ways that academically enforced acculturation affects them (Bizzell, "What Happens"). And, I would add, how academically enforced acculturation affects women, often all composition teachers.

RESISTING DERACINATION IN ENGLISH STUDIES

Women risk deracination as they attempt to enter the tacit and dominant culture of English studies, literature, and critical theory. Often adrift without mentors, "good" girls are offered few choices and denied voice: they may learn to read and act like a man or be stopped short by the gatekeepers, as Dale Spender reminds us:

> For gatekeepers are in a position to perpetuate their own schemata by exercising sponsorship and patronage toward those who classify the world in ways similar to their own. Women are by no means the only "outsiders" but they are a significant group and there is considerable evidence which suggests that women's schemata does not at times "match" with men's. (191)

When these gatekeepers hold the rules and regulations in their heads and don't share them, marginalized individuals won't succeed very well or quickly.

Sometimes gatekeepers respond with counterarguments to critiques of the patronage system, invoking the relative-oppression and the quality-work arguments. In the former argument, gatekeepers may compare "(white) women's status with that of black and poor men (not black or poor women), as a means to label women's concerns trivial" (Aiken et al. 267). In the latter argument, individuals, often men and always insiders, claim that access is open for women or marginalized constituencies like part-time teachers or graduate students. If they aren't succeeding, it's probably because they haven't completed the requisite degree or don't do "quality work" — not because they don't know the rules or because they are denied access. Here is a version of this argument:

> You will only be outsiders as long as you define yourselves that way. Any time you want to get on the bus, you can. All you have to do to get on the bus is some quality work. Yes, it is a meritocracy. But that's all it is. Nothing else — not race, professional status, gender, religion, clothes style, sexual orientation, or brand of underwear — decides whether or not you succeed in getting recognized. Graduate students can do it if they choose to, although usually it takes longer than graduate school lasts. You can certainly begin in grad school. I'm a reader for six different journals, and I can tell you from my experience that good work gets published. ("CCCC Voices" 213)

This quality-work view is held in literature studies but also in composition studies, despite claims that the professional meetings and community of composition studies are friendlier, more open, and more accessible than those of the Modern Language Association or Associated Writing Programs. This belief does not keep novices in composition — women and men alike — from sometimes feeling they've entered new and discouraging terrain without maps or guidebooks. Here is part of a graduate student's anonymous critique of CCCC, the critique that prompted the "quality-work" response above: "If I am ever an Insider, standing at podiums reading my papers, extolling the virtues of teaching writing, what will I have really gained? A more comfortable room, a more self-assured voice, and a sense of uneasiness as I remember what I left behind" ("CCCC Voices" 199). Clearly, this is the voice of a person worried about the effects of gatekeeping and deracination.

Both the relative-oppression and quality-work arguments ignore issues of marginality and feminism in composition studies where, as Elizabeth Flynn reminds us, gatekeepers still flourish. She refers to her recent (and eventually successful) attempt to publish "Composing as a Woman," a theoretical essay informed by feminism. As she relates, the essay "is thoroughly feminist in perspective and method. . . . The reviewers of the piece seemed to be offended by my criticisms of the field, though, so I decided to shift the emphasis of my discussion, focusing on the positive rather than the negative" (88). Flynn's view is at variance with the quality-work argument offered by the male composition scholar above.[3] These voices of dissent should remind us that the rules-and-regulations manual is not always available for everyone.

In the same vein, Maxine Hairston reminds us:

> But our experience [in composition studies] is much like that of the women's movement. One can look at how far we have come and rejoice at our progress, or one can look at the barriers that still exist and become discouraged. I believe, however—and once more the situation is analogous to that of many women—the major reason we get discouraged is that our worst problems originate close to home: in our own departments and within the discipline of English studies itself. (273)

As compositionists, we interact daily with what Hairston calls the "intimate enemy," members of the traditional English department. Her argument here is possibly for secession—that writing find a new home. Terry Eagleton argues even more persuasively that this new home might be a new and unified department called rhetoric. Clearly, secession has been the solution for some feminists who have built separate women's studies programs within existing university structures. In some cases, separation has resulted in strength, allowing marginalized cultures to circumvent the tendency of the English department's field-coverage model to absorb their interests in isolated intra-departmental pigeonholes. In other cases, secession has resulted in further alienation and erasure of any campus profile, problems that seem similar to those experienced by some writing-across-the-curriculum programs.

In composition studies, those of us involved with feminist issues who intend to exist within English departments and to encourage such existences might further learn from Rich:

> Today women are talking to each other, recovering an oral culture, telling our life stories, reading aloud to one another the books that have moved and healed us, analyzing the language that has lied about us, reading our own words aloud to each other. . . . To do this kind of work takes a capacity for constant active presence, a naturalist's attention to minute phenomena, for reading between the lines, watching closely for symbolic arrangements, decoding difficult and complex messages left for us by women of the past. It is work, in short, that is opposed by, and stands in opposition to, the entire twentieth-century white male capitalist culture. (*On Lies* 13–14)

We need to become active for ourselves while observing these issues with "a naturalist's attention to minute phenomena." We need to remain active while realizing that we are a formidable challenge to the status quo. We need also to learn from Susan Aiken and her colleagues, who address the resistance that comes in response to attempts to change: "Curriculum integration is . . . an exceedingly complex undertaking. . . . Those who direct it should anticipate resistances that will shift—in both kind and intensity—according to the changing chemistry of the groups involved. Because resistance assumes such protean forms, there is no single right way to proceed" (273).

Nevertheless, we may accomplish much by learning from ourselves. To start, we can recognize that what we have learned from studying multicultural students in writing classrooms can illuminate our own positions. There is a connection between what we do to enable those students to negotiate academic lives and what we may do to resolve our own lives within the culture of the English department. Certainly, we need to explore new attitudes and practices for learning and knowing: neighborliness, *praxis,* feminist mentoring, and encouragement of "believing" behaviors. Arguments for these positions come from composition and feminist theory and pedagogy. We need to examine our world to see where we might go in light of such explorations, questioning whether through active intervention we may not be able to do for ourselves what Bizzell suggests we do for our students: "offer them an understanding of their school difficulties as the problems of a traveler to an unfamiliar country—yet a country in which it is possible to learn the language and the manners and even 'go native' while still remembering the land from which one has come" ("Cognition" 238). We and our graduate students are much like the students that Bizzell considers, and we are traveling inward, into forbidden territory.

LEARNING FROM OURSELVES

Discussing multicultural writing students, Terry Dean suggests that "teachers need to structure learning experiences that both help students write their way into the university and help teachers learn their way into student cultures" (23). Kevin Davis voices a parallel understanding, finding that basic writers are "neither deficient and in need of remediation nor developmentally unadvanced; they are, instead, quite adept users of different languages, capable of explaining who they are, where they are headed, and why they want to get there" ("What I Learned" 35). Joy Ritchie adds to and extends these ideas: "Learning to write and teaching writing involve us and our students in a process of socialization and of individual becoming" (153). All three writers pinpoint the transactional nature of such learning.

Additionally, Davis claims a need for "translation" so that students' "language can be understood by members of other cultures" (35). Both Dean and Davis point out, too, that those from the dominant culture need to interact with and enter into the minority cultures' concerns. But can we, as feminists and compositionists, engage the dominant culture of literature faculty members in our lives even as we engage in theirs?

Other theorists working with students from marginalized cultures offer concerns equally as insistent. Lucille Schultz, Chester Laine, and Mary Savage suggest that college writing teachers need to resolve their own class biases before trying to resolve intra-departmental biases. College writing teachers can accomplish this by realigning themselves with elementary and secondary writing teachers through collaboration and, thus, breaking down the hierarchical and elite system of thinking that insists "knowledge should be created at advanced levels of the educational system and applied or carried out at lower levels; and . . . that the language and discursive practices of each educational level should be separate and distinct" (147). It is easy to see that such hierarchical thinking works against composition and feminist studies within the English studies department but less easy to see our own faults—that we also work against precollege writing teachers (who are often female) simply by ignoring connections between our practices. In this sense, the enemy is even more intimate than Hairston suggests. Even as we complain about our own impoverished positions, we may be the oppressors of writing teachers in the precollege writing world.

What, then, do those working with culturally marginalized individuals suggest? Dean says that he has found success building bridges and translating across cultures by including cultural and language topics in class, using peer response groups, publishing class newsletters, bringing campus events into classroom discussions, and encouraging the use of anecdotes ("What I Learned" 28–36). Patrick Hartwell suggests that we need to access "underlying postures toward language" by "banishing teacher talk," "investigating literacy events," and looking at our metaphors and narratives. Echoing Rich's call for a naturalist's attention to detail, Hartwell further suggests that we use classroom ethnographic observation, that we watch and explicate ourselves, teachers and students alike (12–16).

The anthropological model of teachers who learn as they teach is supported by the research of Mary Belenky and her colleagues in *Women's Ways of Knowing*. They argue for "connected teaching," in which the teacher views herself or himself as a participant-observer in the classroom: "A connected teacher is not just another student, the role carries special responsibilities . . . an authority based not on subordination but on cooperation." They further claim that "connected teachers are believers. They trust their students' thinking and encourage them to expand it" (227).

Hairston offers several suggestions as well. She urges us to realize that literature professors are not listening to us, to stop being angry and wasting energy, and to pay attention to the inner voice—to stop trying to be "good." To accomplish this, she suggests that we become productive and publish and network with fields outside our own and with the professional (nonacademic) world (278–82).

Finally, Savage offers instant relief in "neighborliness," claiming that "neighborliness is an antidote; it is not a new direction, paradigm, consensus. Rather it is an instant, homeopathic remedy that allows the body to come back to its senses" (16). For Savage, neighborliness is "praxis, practical activity, like teaching people to read, or helping women provide better nutrition for infants, or accompanying a grieving family at a wake" (16). This type of *praxis* is founded on Freirean pedagogy and Christian ecumenical work in which neighborliness "establishes both closeness and distance in the critical interrogation of life" (16). As she points out, such a critical interrogation of life is being undertaken by "pastoral workers in Latin America [who] are curing their own clericism by asking a central question: whose cry do I hear, toward whom do I move, whose interests do I serve?" (17). Savage's suggestion is strongly rooted in a feminist perspective, and she suggests that "writing teachers capitalize on their womanliness, their 'limnality' (their living at the limits, on the margins of the system), and that they approach one another as neighbors" (18).

TURNING TOWARD NEW GRADUATE STUDENTS

Whose cry do I hear? At times I hear many, but I want to attend here to the novitiate, the official new member of the English department community. We need to pay close attention to our "young," those temporarily (and sometimes permanently) marginalized male and female TAs, the next generation in the changing department of English, the people that we may come into contact with in exciting and valuable ways. These are the individuals that I move toward, for it just may be that the entrenched literature-studies professional is too obdurate to change. Remember Hairston's "intimate enemy," and look at her war imagery. Remember that Dean, Davis, and Ritchie tell us that those who develop critical consciousness, enter into dialogue with minorities, and cross cultural boundaries are both agents of change and themselves changed.

Simply put, those individuals with strongly developed classification systems may find it impossible to change; they have more at stake, more to lose.[4] Additionally, for those in power, intentional change can be seen as giving in, becoming the enemy, and, in the case of men, becoming female. Aiken and her colleagues found this occurring in an institutionally sanctioned project, a curriculum integration seminar designed to aid university faculty in incorporating feminist concerns into courses: "Unfortunately, participants who transcended masculinist preoccupations and attempted to voice feminist positions frequently found their contributions ignored or discounted by others in the groups or found themselves subtly classed as 'female' by their [male] colleagues" (269).

Rather than go to war, to insist on change in those for whom change entails great risks and who may even react with punitive or repressive measures against department subcultures, I look toward the new graduate student, who is not yet such a fixed product, who is still in the process of becoming.[5] No adult comes to a graduate program as a blank slate, but new graduate students are voluntarily enrolling in a process that can have profound effects on who they are and who they become. For example, Carol Berkenkotter, Thomas Huckin, and John Ackerman trace the writing development of a new student in rhetoric and linguistics who learns to write like a rhetorician. John Schilb critiques this case study because the researchers, he feels, do not illuminate the ideological biases of the culture this student was asking and being asked to enter, nor, Schilb feels, do the researchers come to terms with the political and ethical issues of academic acculturation. Since graduate students represent great potential for English departments, we should explore public and private channels for teaching critical consciousness to these soon-to-be peers. As the next wave of composition and feminist workers, and as newly aware literature faculty, these students have the potential to make changes that we have sometimes despaired of making.

Forums for graduate students can and should include an introductory course in "English Studies" that goes far beyond the required bibliography, research, and criticism courses currently offered.[6] Such a course would be concerned with knowledge-making, with philosopher Gilbert Ryles's often quoted distinction between "knowing that" and "knowing how," a distinction summarized by David Foster:

> "Knowing that" and "knowing how" are two different kinds of knowledge, not antecedent and consequence. "Learning *that*" is "acquiring information," becoming "apprised of a truth"; "learning *how*" is "improving in ability," or "getting trained in a procedure." These two capacities are both exercises of intelligence, but are not associated in a simple cause-and-effect fashion." (117)

In most graduate programs, the bibliography, research, and criticism course focuses on knowing *how,* while knowing *that* about the professions is incidental information, program lore, academic rules and regulations transmitted by word of mouth from mentor to mentee or puzzled over by graduate students in midnight lounges. To exercise both knowing capacities, the introductory graduate seminar should also focus on knowing *that.*

In such a course, we might question our own history by examining texts like James Berlin's *Rhetoric and Reality,* Graff's *Professing Literature,* Toril Moi's *Sexual/Textual Politics,* and Joseph Moxley's *Creative Writing in America.* These books can help us begin to know *that* because their authors share a determination to examine the historical and ideological conditions that influence our lives within the English department. By including works related to all areas of English, a redesigned, historically aware, multicultural seminar in English studies can begin to offer graduate students important contexts and a forum for question-making. In such a seminar, questions could be asked about how our intertwined but varied subdisciplines have come into being and, often, into serious conflict. Such a seminar would work against the traditional assumption that "students should be exposed only to the results of the controversies of their teachers and educators and should be protected from the controversies themselves" (Graff 261).

Within this participatory seminar, we can also use activities similar to those in multicultural classrooms, including anecdote and storytelling, for telling stories is a neighborly act that can illuminate the academy's ways. Our narratives can also be considered "change-active." Linda Brodkey argues for critical ethnographies in which the writer's voice "is made most audible by interrupting the flow of the story and calling attention to the fact of the narration" in order to be "theoretically sound and honest to draw attention to one's ideological position as a narrator" (73). Critically conscious historical discussion will bring up the political and ethical issues of academic acculturation.

And questions will be raised. What does it mean to study literature, writing, critical theory, and rhetoric in the English department? Whose cry do we hear? Toward whom do we move? Whose interests do we serve? Questions promulgate dialogue. As we do with our multicultural students, we may interact in diaries, journals, and peer groups, telling anecdotes and stories, examining processes, developing critical consciousness on a range of department- and profession-specific concerns. Using Elisabeth Daumer and Sandra Runzo's suggestions, we could "focus on experiences of being unable, or denied the right, to speak for oneself and on incidents of racial, sexual, and linguistic oppression and assertion" or describe "a time when someone changed or distorted their language," or consider "telling a story of personal significance to another who then retells it to the class," or encourage a student to "write about herself in a context that she thinks social conventions have generally denied her" (55–56) — as I did when I began this essay. We can discuss whether quality work does count, how it counts and who says so, and how it should be done. We can discuss gatekeepers and conventions. Through such discussion, we can illuminate the ideological bases of all groups involved: gatekeepers and gatecrashers, dominant and minority cultures, males and females.

VALUING MENTORING AND BELIEVING

Neighborliness can extend beyond the graduate seminar to those departments too small or too conservative to transform the curriculum. Women in composition (and men who value such alternatives) can provide new and positive mentoring models to female and male students new to the profession. Mentors can develop for and articulate to graduate students their sense of the operative rules and regulations governing the department and field; such articulation may well serve mentors to better understand their position, too. Reminding us that "mentoring is not only an intellectual relationship but also an emotional one," Kathleen Schatzberg-Smith explains its benefits:

> Productivity is enhanced by affiliation with a mentor. This in turn stimulates the novice's career advancement. The protégé also gains access to a professional network that would not be so readily available without the assistance of the mentor. . . . The mentoring relationship provides in a sense a safe haven in which the protégé can take risks and develop personal and professional values and style. (48)

Certainly, mentoring provides a wonderful opportunity for those new to the field, yet mentoring opportunities are often restricted for women.[7]

We need new ways to view mentoring. Belenky and her colleagues offer one in the "midwife teacher," an individual who utilizes connected teaching and believes in and cooperates with students: "Midwife-teachers focus not on their own knowledge (as the lecturer does) but on the students' knowledge. They contribute when needed, but it is always clear that the baby is not theirs but the student's" (218). Janet Emig describes an analogous mentoring model: "Teaching writing is more like what is classically the maternal role than the paternal role and that is to make certain that something grows. And you do it any way you can"(132). As Dixie Goswami suggests, this mentoring model is based on a progression, a mentor serving "first, as collaborator with a student, next as reformulator for a student, and finally as audience, as a very particular kind of audience" (qtd. in Emig 132). A nonhierarchical mentoring model makes sense, for by becoming a first collaborator, first reformulator, and first audience for young academics, we might just reduce our collective "academentia."

The benefits of such mentoring are explained from a Jungian perspective by Daniel Lindley. Lindley claims that successful teachers tap the "student" in themselves and the "teacher" in their students, transferring authority from teacher to student, who ultimately finds that "her inner teacher is all she needs. She can do the work on her own" (164). In essence, successful teachers enable a student to become a successful self-learner, just as successful feminist mentors could enable a graduate student—in literature, composition, or creative writing, female or male—to become a successful academic: one who has critical consciousness and expects to perform in a neighborly fashion, one who has achieved a measure of holism and is able to use both male and female behaviors, one who explores ideologies and explicates and critiques his or her beliefs.

Being a positive mentor to many students is not impossible if we redefine our concept of mentoring, as Nel Noddings does: "I do not need to establish a lasting, time-consuming personal relationship with every student. What I must do is to be totally and nonselectively present to the student—to each student—as he addresses me. The time interval may be brief but the encounter is total" (qtd. in Belenky et al. 225).

Encouraging believing behavior can also promote neighborliness within our departments, helping us to make sure that something grows. Peter Elbow encourages us to develop both doubting and believing capabilities, viewing both methodological doubting and believing as essential learning activities. He claims that we more often doubt than believe, needing only one disconfirmation to abandon an assertion; however, proof of the nonexistence of a disconfirming instance is very difficult if not impossible to provide. He claims that doubt too often caters to "our natural impulse to protect and retain the views we already hold" (263). Elbow calls for balance and integration: doubting and believing are both necessary for broadening our intellectual repertoire.

Valuing believing behavior and realizing its connection to *praxis* may foster such integration. Drawing on Richard Berenstein's work, Schultz, Laine, and Savage discuss *praxis:* "Praxis, or critical practice, therefore, is neither the highly theoretical knowledge of the advanced scholar nor the technician-like knowledge of those asked only to carry out ideas, but practical activity which continuously involves judgment and reflection" (150). We practice judgment and reflection in our classrooms and seminar rooms as we develop what Stephen North has called (not always flatteringly) teachers' "lore." We can share this lore that is based on judgment and reflection by using anecdotes and narratives, if we gather our understandings carefully in diaries and teachers' journals and begin to see ourselves as teachers/researchers/ethnographers/naturalists. We can reap the productive results of metacognition and become aligned with feminists who advocate *praxis* as well. Schweickart claims that "feminist criticism . . . is a mode of praxis. The point is not merely to interpret literature in various ways; the point is to change the world" (39).

LISTENING TO OUR VOICES

In this essay, whose interests do I hope to serve? Again, Rich offers insight: "What interests me in teaching is less the emergence of the occasional genius than the overall finding of language by those who did not have it and by those who have been used and abused to the extent that they lacked it" ("Teaching" 67–68). What interests me in teaching graduate students is not finding the original genius but helping to give voice to those who want and need voices, for silencing still occurs. Two simple examples passed into my critical consciousness lately. Reading the *Chronicle of Higher Education,* for example, I learned with little surprise that some academics intend never to change. Here is what I read, a news item on the new MLA-sanctioned guidelines for avoiding gendered language:

> Edward A. Cowan, an assistant professor of German at the University of Texas at Arlington, tells *The Chronicle* that using "he" is grammatically and stylistically correct because the masculine pronoun is by definition without gender when used as a generic pronoun. He writes that he plans to continue using "normal English," adding, "if that is 'sexist,' then so be it." ("In Box")

And, while reading the *AWP Chronicle,* a newsletter that represents creative writing programs around the country, I listened to poet Maxine Kumin and learned:

> Every six months or so another critic of the contemporary culture parachutes among us with the bad news that poetry is dead. Joseph Epstein's "Who Killed Cock Robin?" essay employs so much ammunition in the service of cramping us poets even deeper "into the dark corner poetry now inhabits" that I can only throw up my hands and agree with him.
>
> Things are indeed bleak, but we women poets can hardly be held accountable. In this didactic and learned essay peppered with the names of the dead great poets . . . we don't amount to much. Although, to quote Carolyn Kizer (not cited by Epstein), "we are the custodians of the world's best-kept secret: / Merely the private lives of one-half of humanity," only the sacred deceased triumvirate of Dickinson, Bishop, and Moore are mentioned. . . . It would seem that we have blundered into an all-male profession by mistake and may therefore ask to be excused. (15)

Whose interests do I serve? My own, of course, but I also try to listen to graduate students. I listened recently to MFA students enrolled in a graduate-level seminar in creative writing in which I tried to practice what I preach here—critical consciousness, feminist mentoring, neighborliness, and believing. Certainly, I did not practice all these behaviors successfully, but in response to semester-end questions designed to gauge their learning in the seminar, they said such things as these:

> I hadn't considered the issue of sexism in the field of teaching creative writing. I had thought about it in terms of literature and the male-dominated canon but not in terms of the workshop. And I think when I sensed sexist behavior, such as male teachers flirting with female students, I told myself I was misreading the situation. Now I think I am more sensitive to it in the academic community—and more resentful when I see it going on. Across the board, male teachers are still setting the norms without being sensitive to female students. I guess I have changed in that with what I have learned, I'm a little more critical of how workshops are conducted and how teachers treat students.

> Maybe what it all boils down to for me is that students get the respect they deserve in classrooms. I don't think it matters what we're teaching—literature, composition, or creative writing—what we're helping students to achieve is the ability to empower themselves through language. When we understand this, the tools—literature, essays, poems, stories, or criticism—take on an equal weight. One is no more primal than the other. What is most important is that students experience language, discover it, and clarify their relationship to it.

Engaging in "change-oriented" teaching means that we must proceed with care, both for our students' and our own sakes. If we provide new models, our students will consider them.

Maintaining a questioning stance means, too, that we question ourselves. Listen to writer and teacher Katharine Haake as she doubts and believes herself:

> For me it is much easier to say what I do wrong: I talk too much, I am not nurturing enough, I don't make effective enough use of collaboration. As for what I think I may do right, what I want is not to be the focus of the classroom, and what I do to allow for this shift is . . . provide a theoretical context by addressing such issues as how discourse operates to constitute ourselves and the world, and what happens to writing in the absence of an author. I also make explicit my own ideological assumptions, including my various stances as a feminist that extend to embrace those who are marginalized in other ways as well, by race, by class, by belief, by status: blacks, for instance, or students themselves. I work to establish a common critical practice that can empower students by giving them control over their own work. And there is one other thing: I listen very, very closely, for we are all working this language together, clumsily, eagerly. (Haake, Alcosser, and Bishop 2)

And listen to writer and teacher Kevin Davis as he considers his own writing classrooms and makes suggestions for good teaching:

> What I'm suggesting is asking questions you don't know the answer to, letting students establish meaning, accepting whatever answer they produce as their answer, perhaps seeking a little clarification. . . . You don't have to know any answers to teach; you only have to know the right questions. And you'll know the right questions when you see them. (Letter)

The questions we each need to ask may be simple: whose cry do I hear, toward whom do I move, whose interests do I serve? Asking these questions helps us to cure our own "clericism." And the mentoring model may be simple: first collaborator, first reformulator, first audience. Yet the results of our activities will be productive and dangerous. Neighborliness is not passive but active *praxis*. Feminist mentoring is not ideologically free but self-analytical and self-critical, based on belief and premised on engaging ourselves to ask the right questions. The rules-and-regulations manual does and should change. Our constant endeavor is to help translate it into the language of graduate students and then to be, in turn, translated by them into the best academics we can be.[8]

NOTES

1. On the authority of writing program administrators, see Olson and Moxley.

2. See also Bolker; Sperling and Freedman.

3. I contrast Flynn's assertions that gatekeeping does exist—she felt she had to modify her essay to pass the scrutiny of gatekeepers who did not value feminist claims—to Robert Connor's assertions that composition publishing is not based on "race, professional status, gender, religion, clothes style, sexual orientation, or brand of underwear"—not to beatify or vilify either writer but simply to show that gender has influenced the perceptions of these equally prominent members of the composition community. In fact, as did other readers, I appreciate Connor's openness in identifying himself to the graduate students who wrote "CCCC Voices." Nevertheless, when James Raymond, *College English* editor, reviewed submission and publication patterns during 1985–86 and compared them with earlier figures, his data showed that gender and professional status do influence editorial reality, at least in that prominent composition forum (556).

4. I discuss this issue further in *Something Old, Something New: College Writing Teachers and Classroom Change.*

5. See Stewart for a story of curriculum change and resistance in which a department chair dismantles a threateningly successful rhetoric program within his English department.

6. Also see Stewart for a suggestion that the same type of rethinking is needed in the undergraduate English major.

7. On the restriction of mentoring opportunities for women students, see Hall and Sandler.

8. My thanks to Kevin Davis and Katharine Haake, peers whose thinking always helps me to think, and more recently to Bonnie Braendlin for careful and supportive reading and to Don McAndrew—a mentor in all the best ways.

WORKS CITED

Aiken, Susan Hardy, et al. "Trying Transformations: Curriculum Integration and the Problem of Resistance." *Signs: Journal of Women in Culture and Society* 12 (1987): 255–75.

Belenky, Mary Field, Blythe McVicker Clinchy, Nancy Rule Goldberger, and Jill Mattuck Tarule. *Women's Ways of Knowing: The Development of Self, Voice, and Mind.* New York: Basic, 1986.

Berkenkotter, Carol, Thomas Huckin, and John Ackerman. "Conventions, Conversations, and the Writer: Case Study of a Student in a Rhetoric Ph.D. Program." *Research in the Teaching of English* 22 (1988): 9–44.

Berlin, James A. *Rhetoric and Reality: Writing Instruction in American Colleges, 1900–1985.* Carbondale: Southern Illinois UP, 1987.

Bishop, Wendy. *Something Old, Something New: College Writing Teachers and Classroom Change.* Carbondale: Southern Illinois UP, 1990.

Bizzell, Patricia. "Cognition, Convention, and Certainty: What We Need to Know about Writing." *Pre/Text* 3 (1982): 213–43.

———. "What Happens When Basic Writers Come to College?" Conference on College Composition and Communication. New York, March 1986.

Bolker, Joan. "Teaching Griselda to Write." *College English* (1979): 906–8.

Brodkey, Linda. "Writing Critical Ethnographic Narratives." *Anthropology and Education Quarterly* 18 (1987): 67–76.

"CCCC: Voices in the Parlor." *Rhetoric Review* 7 (1988): 194–213.

Daumer, Elisabeth, and Sandra Runzo. "Transforming the Composition Classroom." *Teaching Writing: Pedagogy, Gender, and Equity.* Ed. Cynthia L. Caywood and Gillian Overing. Albany: SUNY P, 1987. 45–64.

Davis, Kevin. Letter to the Author. 2 May 1989.

———. "What I Learned in Basic Writing: Negotiating Commitment." *Research in Teaching Developmental Education* 5 (1988): 35–42.

Dean, Terry. "Multicultural Classrooms, Monocultural Teachers." *College Composition and Communication* 40 (1989): 23–37.

Eagleton, Terry. *Literary Theory: An Introduction.* Minneapolis: U of Minnesota P, 1983.

Elbow, Peter. "Methodological Doubting and Believing: Contraries in Inquiry." *Embracing Contraries.* New York: Oxford UP, 1986. 253–300.

Emig, Janet. Interview. *The Web of Meaning.* Ed. Dixie Goswami and Maureen Butler. Upper Montclair, NJ: Boynton, 1983. 132–34.

Flynn, Elizabeth. "Composing 'Composing as a Woman': A Perspective on Research." *College Composition and Communication* 41 (1990): 83–89.

Foster, David. *A Primer for Writing Teachers: Theories, Theorists, Issues, Problems.* Upper Montclair, NJ: Boynton, 1983.

Graff, Gerald. *Professing Literature: An Institutional History.* Chicago: U of Chicago P, 1987.

Haake, Katharine, Sandra Alcosser, and Wendy Bishop. "Teaching Creative Writing: A Feminist Critique." *AWP Chronicle* 22.2 (1989): 1–6.

Hairston, Maxine. "Breaking Our Bonds and Reaffirming Our Connections." *College Composition and Communication* 36 (1985): 272–82.

Hall, Roberta, and Bernice B. Sandler. "Academic Mentoring for Women Students and Faculty: A New Look at an Old Way to Get Ahead." Washington, DC: Association of American Colleges Project on the Status and Education of Women, 1983. ERIC ED 240891.

Hartwell, Patrick. "Creating a Literate Environment in Freshman English: Why and How." *Rhetoric Review* 6 (1987): 4–20.

"In Box." *Chronicle of Higher Education* 26 April 1989: A13.

Kumin, Maxine. "The World's Best Kept Secret." *AWP Chronicle* May 1989: 15.

Lindley, Daniel A., Jr. "The Source of Good Teaching." *English Education* 19 (1987): 159–70.

Moi, Toril. *Sexual/Textual Politics: Feminist Literary Theory.* London: Routledge, 1985.

Moxley, Joseph, ed. *Creative Writing in America: Theory and Pedagogy.* Urbana: NCTE, 1989.

Mueller, Martin. "Yellow Stripes and Dead Armadillos: Some Thoughts on the Current State of English Studies." *ADE Bulletin* 92 (1989): 5–12. Rpt. in *Profession 89.* New York: MLA, 1989. 23–31.

North, Stephen M. *The Making of Knowledge in Composition: Portrait of an Emerging Field.* Upper Montclair, NJ: Boynton, 1987.

Olson, Gary A., and Joseph Moxley. "Directing Freshman Composition: The Limits of Authority." *College Composition and Communication* 40 (1989): 41–50.

Raymond, James C. "College English: Whence and Whither." *College English* 49 (1987): 553–57.

Rich, Adrienne. *On Lies, Secrets, and Silence: Selected Prose 1966–1978.* New York: Norton, 1979.

———. "Taking Women Students Seriously." *On Lies* 237–46.

———. "Teaching Writing in Open Admissions." *On Lies* 51–68.

Ritchie, Joy S. "Beginning Writers: Diverse Voices and Individual Identity." *College Composition and Communication* 40 (1989) 152–74.

Savage, Mary C. "Writing as a Neighborly Act: An Antidote for Academentia." *ADE Bulletin* 92 (1989): 13–19.

Schatzberg-Smith, Kathleen. "Passing the Torch: Mentoring and Developmental Education." *Research in Teaching Developmental Education* 5 (1988): 47–51.

Schilb, John. "Ideology and Composition Scholarship." *Journal of Advanced Composition* 8 (1988): 22–29.

Schultz, Lucille M., Chester H. Laine, and Mary C. Savage. "Interaction among School and College Writing Teachers: Toward Recognizing and Remaking Old Patterns." *College Composition and Communication* 39 (1988): 139–53.

Schweickart, Patrocinio. "Reading Ourselves: Toward a Feminist Theory of Reading." *Gender and Reading.* Ed. Elizabeth Flynn and Patrocinio Schweickart. Baltimore: Johns Hopkins UP, 1986. 31–62.

Spender, Dale. "The Gatekeepers: A Feminist Critique of Academic Publishing." *Doing Feminist Research.* Ed. Helen Roberts. London: Routledge, 1981. 186–202.

Sperling, Melanie, and Sarah Warshauer Freedman. "A Good Girl Writes Like a Good Girl: Written Response to Student Writing." *Written Communication* 9 (1987): 343–69.

Stewart, Donald C. "What Is an English Major, and What Should It Be?" *College Composition and Communication* 40 (1989): 188–202.

31 Composing "Composing as a Woman": A Perspective on Research

ELIZABETH A. FLYNN

"Composing as a Woman" was published in *CCC* in December of 1988 (423–35). It argues that the newly emergent field of composition studies feminizes previous conceptions of the nature of the composing process but that, unfortunately, the field has not engaged feminist research and theory in any sustained and systematic way. It argues, further, that feminist work on gender differences in social and psychological development—especially Nancy Chodorow's *The Reproduction of Mothering* (U of California P, 1978); Carol Gilligan's *In a Different Voice* (Harvard UP, 1982); and Mary Belenky, Blythe Clinchy, Nancy Goldberger, and Jill Tarule's *Women's Ways of Knowing* (Basic Books, 1986)—is useful in examining student writing and in suggesting directions that a feminist investigation of composition might take.

In writing "Composing as a Woman," then, I had rather broad professional and research interests. But one of *CCC's* anonymous reviewers of the manuscript identified the audience as "composition generalists" and observed that "this is just the kind of essay I would like to have most of my teaching colleagues read." This same reviewer also observed, though, that "there is no extensive empirical research presented here. The examples drawn from student writing serve only as illustrations of the points, not as a basis for inductive argument." The message was clear—the essay would probably not be of interest to researchers because it was *not* research.

"Composing as a Woman" may appear to be aimed primarily at classroom teachers because it contains a section entitled "Pedagogical Strategies." This section, though, was a later addition to the essay included at the suggestion of editor Gebhardt and several reviewers. I certainly consider the piece to be research, and I definitely intended an audience of researchers and theorists. The audience I had in mind was composition specialists who are unaware of or unconvinced of the relevance of work in feminist studies to their investigations of student writing. I make this clear in my statement of purpose: "I will show how . . . [feminist] research and theory may be used in examining

From *College Composition and Communication* 41 (1990): 83–89.

student writing, thus suggesting directions that a feminist investigation of composition might take" (425). I also suggest some research questions that others might pursue: "Do males and females compose differently?" "Do research methods and research samples in composition studies reflect a male bias?" (425)

Quite possibly the essay does not appear to be research because it is not clear which research tradition I am working within. The essay does not obviously conform to the procedures and methods of research in the sciences or social sciences, for instance. It is not an experiment or a case study or an ethnography. Work that hovers on the blurred edges of several traditions is not legitimate, is not research, it would seem.

"Composing as a Woman" is the result of an extended and complicated process of discovery, a merging of a number of different research traditions — humanistic, empirical, and feminist being the most prominent. The essay reflects the diverse influences that have affected my reading and writing over the course of my career — literary scholarship, theory, and criticism; feminist literary criticism and theory; reading research and theory; composition research and theory. The result is an essay whose genre is difficult to identify. A brief description of my varied intellectual pursuits and of the process involved in composing the essay should help illuminate the assumptions that underlie the study and the reasons for the choices I made as I undertook my research.

BACKGROUND

I was trained as a graduate student to be a literary scholar, to do historical research that would help explain the meaning of literary texts, but also to be a literary critic, to interpret literary texts. Toward the latter part of my career as a graduate student I became interested in literary theory and in feminist theory and feminist literary criticism, and these interests resulted in a dissertation that attempted to define feminist literary criticism by linking it to other critical approaches, especially Marxist, archetypal, and neo-Aristotelian. I was hired at Michigan Tech, though, as a composition and reading specialist who would contribute to the development of Tech's writing-across-the-curriculum program. I was able to reconcile my interest in literary theory and my new responsibilities as a reading specialist by developing an interest in reader-response theory and criticism. I pursued my commitment to feminist inquiry by focusing on the relationship between gender and reading, especially the reading of literary texts.

Reconciliation of my commitment to feminist inquiry and composition studies was much harder, though. Connections between composition theory and feminist literary theory were more difficult to make, and there was no community of feminist composition specialists to nurture my inquiry. I somehow felt I had to suspend my feminism when I put on the hat of the composition specialist. Sometimes it was suspended for me. When I was introduced at talks I gave on writing across the curriculum, for instance, the introducer often ignored the work I have done in feminist studies, sometimes apologizing later for having done so and clearly embarrassed that it was there at all.

"Composing as a Woman" was my attempt to bring about this reconciliation. But reconciliation did not come easily—the essay took years to write. At the 1983 CCC convention I delivered a paper entitled "Writing Strategies of Male and Female Students." The paper was a somewhat humorous discussion of essays submitted in a first-year composition class. It made for a good paper but was hardly publishable. One problem was that I was unable to make strong connections between the writing of my first-year students and the feminist literary theory with which I was familiar. There seemed to be an enormous gap between the descriptions, explanations, and arguments I was receiving from my first-year students and the discussions of the poetry and novels of women writers. Research and theory that attempted to account for the connections among women writers, Elaine Showalter's *A Literature of Their Own* (Princeton UP, 1977), for instance, or for the relationship between the male canon and the female writer, Sandra Gilbert and Susan Gubar's *The Madwoman in the Attic* (Yale UP 1979), for instance, did not seem to illuminate the work of the student writers I was examining. What I needed was research and theory that better explained the mindsets of my highly unself-conscious and unliterary students. So I put the paper aside, determining that I would come back to it when I had more compelling explanations for what I was finding in the student essays.

I discovered Chodorow, Gilligan, and Belenky et al. through my investigation of the relationship between gender and reading. Their work seemed especially well-suited to an examination of student interactional patterns and provided me a new way of interpreting my data. Not surprisingly, my new interpretive framework produced an entirely different essay. The student papers I had previously analyzed were transformed, yielding entirely new meanings. In the original paper I had looked at the narrative, expository, and argumentative essays of ten students in a first-year English class, focusing on differences in setting (the women students tended to set their essays in interior spaces while the men set theirs outdoors), conception of self (the women students had difficulty describing female role models whereas the men had no difficulty describing male role models but never described female ones), and attitude toward authority (the women students described submission to authority or contained rebellion whereas the men more often described direct and open conflict). In revising the essay, I decided to look only at the narrative essays because the narratives were descriptions of interaction and seemed especially well-suited to theories of psychological and social development. I also felt that the essays written in the different modes were too diffuse to work with. I needed a more focused sample. My first attempt at revision of the original paper was a talk I delivered at the University of Calgary the summer of 1987. The original essay I submitted to *CCC* was a revision of the talk. In the talk and the revision of the talk, I was not yet able to demonstrate convincingly to my reviewers or to myself that there was a connection between the theory I presented and the student examples I discussed. I revised the *CCC* essay by narrowing the sample once again, this time by limiting the discussion to the four narratives that appear in the final essay. Only the lead of the Calgary talk remained intact. Faint traces of the discussion of the student narratives I omitted in the revision remain in the form of a brief summary of the other student papers I could have used to make my argument (431).

"Composing as a Woman," then, is the result of a complex process of inquiry that parallels my own development as a scholar, critic, and researcher. I would not have undertaken the project had I not had a strong commitment to and background in feminist criticism and theory and had I not felt the need to try to figure out what it might mean to be a feminist composition specialist. On the other hand, I had also participated in the composition community almost from its beginnings and was therefore quite familiar with research traditions quite different from humanistic ones. It will be useful to try to sort through these diverse influences, focusing especially on three—humanism, empiricism, and feminism.

HUMANISM

Unlike scientific inquiry, in which the central project is often the testing of theory, humanist inquiry emphasizes the application of theory for the purpose of providing a meaningful interpretation. Frequently, the theoretical position informing an interpretation is unstated, unacknowledged. The aim of humanistic inquiry, like scientific inquiry, is to persuade. In humanistic inquiry, though, the illustrative example is often sufficient evidence to support a claim. The example may be an informative one or a representative one, to use Kenneth Burke's terms (*A Grammar of Motives,* U of California P, 1969, 59–61), but the researcher need not defend the selection of an example with quantitative data. The example persuades if it is appropriate and sufficiently elaborate.

I do not mean to suggest that all humanistic inquiry is monolithic in its assumptions and methods. In literary studies, for instance, the New Critics believed in the objectivity of the literary text and argued for a scientific approach to the analysis of literature that would remove from consideration the intention of the author, the subjectivity of the reader, and the historical tradition out of which a text arose. A literary text was an object to be deciphered, a well-wrought urn, to use Cleanth Brooks' term. The tradition within which I am firmly rooted, reader-response criticism and theory, is a reaction against the New Criticism and against a positivistic belief in the objectivity of literary texts. The subjective criticism of David Bleich represents an extreme version of the reader-response position, emphasizing the reader's participation in the making of meaning in the process of interpreting a literary text. In *Subjective Criticism* (Johns Hopkins UP, 1978), Bleich describes the interpretive process as an intersubjective process, a process motivated by the purposes and goals of the interpretive communities to which we belong. We interpret for a reason, and our interpretation becomes a symbolic act, a "resymbolization" that can be negotiated with others. A less extreme position is that of Louise Rosenblatt in *The Reader, the Text, the Poem* (Southern Illinois UP, 1978). She also emphasizes the importance of the reader in the reading transaction but sees that the text plays an important role as well. According to Rosenblatt, reading is not a subjective process but a transactional one. Reader and text are transformed as they transact with one another.

"Composing as a Woman" is humanistic in that it is centrally concerned with the interpretation of texts, in this case student texts. Like the literary critic, I have used theory to illuminate written documents, to explain them. In "Composing as a Woman" I have used the work of Chodorow, Gilligan, and Belenky et al. to interpret student papers. I am not attempting to prove that their positions are sound. I am not testing theory. Nor am I attempting to arrive at predictive conclusions. Instead, I am using their discussions of social and psychological development to explain the narratives I received in a first-year composition course and, more generally, to demonstrate that it and other feminist research and theory are useful in the analysis of student writing. The essay is aimed at composition specialists who are not familiar with feminist studies, and it attempts to persuade them that feminist theory has a bearing on composition studies. It supports the claim through use of examples, discussions of student essays that are illuminated by the theory.

Empiricism

It would be difficult to be a composition specialist these days without being influenced by empirical approaches to the study of student writing. The influence of scientific and social scientific methods has been widespread and, often, salutary. Empiricism is not synonymous with positivism, though. In a positivistic tradition, research methods are considered to be value neutral, and the aim of research is to arrive at universal laws, to test theory. The process of testing involves comparing what the theory says should occur under certain circumstances with what actually does occur. "Facts" that are presumably theory neutral are collected and tested by theory-neutral methods.

Research can be empirical without being positivistic. The "interpretive anthropology" of Clifford Geertz is a good example. Geertz, in his essay "Thick Description: Toward an Interpretive Theory of Culture," explains that in interpretive anthropology, "the essential task of theory . . . building is not to codify abstract regularities but to make thick description possible, not to generalize across cases but to generalize within them" (*The Interpretation of Cultures*, Basic Books, 1973, 26). What he calls "cultural theory," therefore, is not predictive. Its aim is to yield defensible interpretations as new phenomena arise that need to be interpreted. Theory continues to be meaningful as long as it can be fruitfully applied to new interpretive problems. It enables comprehension of the particular subject in society and in social life. Further, interpretive anthropology is a science whose progress is marked "less by a perfection of consensus than by a refinement of debate" (29). Interpretations are presented and defended, negotiated, argued for.

The research and theory introduced in "Composing as a Woman" enabled me to read the student papers I received in fruitful ways, allowed me to describe them. I applied theory that has been used in one context to a different context, attempting to produce defensible interpretations of new phenomena that needed to be interpreted. The examples I presented were not mere illustrations of the theory presented, though, as I make clear in the essay (431). Rather, they illuminate the theory, demonstrate its significance in a new way. The juxtaposition of evidence or data and the theory leads to a new synthesis, a new way of thinking about the theory and about student writing.

FEMINISM

Feminist inquiry is hardly univocal. Some of the richest feminist research has been solidly humanistic in approach, the considerable body of feminist literary theory and scholarship, for instance. As I suggested earlier, though, I found it difficult to make connections between this body of scholarship and my task at hand, the interpretation of student essays. Much more useful was the "feminist empiricism" of Chodorow, Gilligan, and Belenky et al.

Sandra Harding, in the conclusion to her *Feminism and Methodology* (Indiana UP, 1987), describes feminist empiricism as an approach that challenges the incomplete ways empiricism has been practiced, not the norms of empiricism themselves (183). Traditional empiricism, according to Harding, insists that the social identity of the observer is irrelevant to the adequacy of the results of research (183). Feminist empiricists, in contrast, claim that feminists (male or female) as a group are more likely than non-feminists to produce claims unbiased by androcentrism. They are more likely, in other words, to produce persuasive results. Further, feminist empiricists argue that traditional empirical research tests hypotheses generated by what men find problematic in the world around them and does not direct researchers to locate themselves in the same critical plane as their subject matters (184).

Feminist empiricism is hardly the equivalent of feminist positivism, though, according to Harding. Indeed, a feminist positivism is a contradiction in terms. A feminist approach is necessarily an interested one and is necessarily skeptical of claims of the value-neutrality of research methods, theories, and facts. Such claims all too often mask androcentrism. Research which is presumably value neutral usually reflects the concerns of one group, white males, to the exclusion of others, often women and people of color.

The work of Carol Gilligan and of Belenky et al., which I discuss in "Composing as a Woman," can be seen as a form of feminist empiricism. These researchers, trained in traditional disciplines, take as a starting point their dissatisfaction with the androcentric bias of much traditional empirical research. They place themselves within their studies, explaining their personal motivations and describing their affiliations with other feminists and with the feminist communities to which they belong. Both *In a Different Voice* and *Women's Ways of Knowing* describe empirical studies that make use of interviewing as a method of data collection. In both books, though, the discussion of research methods is very sketchy. The central arguments of both are advanced through elaborate analyses of the interviews themselves, hence both books might be seen as "interpretive psychology," the equivalent of Geertz's interpretive anthropology. And both books create as well as test theory. Gilligan demonstrates the limitations of Lawrence Kohlberg's stages of moral development but in the process elaborates her own, using as her central metaphor the powerful images of the ladder and the web. Belenky et al. demonstrate the limitations of William Perry's stages of intellectual development and in the process create an elaborate taxonomy, a new way of describing intellectual development.

"Composing as a Woman" is thoroughly feminist in perspective and method. I begin by identifying those aspects of composition studies that might be seen as liberatory from a feminist standpoint—its feminization of our notion of the composing process, for instance. I then demonstrate that despite its perpetuation of enlightened ways of thinking about writing, the field of composition studies has strangely resisted feminism. I do not dwell on the price the field has paid for ignoring women's issues, relegating my observations (complaints) to footnote #3 (434). The original draft of the essay sent to *CCC* was considerably more critical of the field, emphasizing that although many prominent composition specialists are women, much of the theoretical work upon which composition theory has been built was done by men—Britton, Vygotsky, Piaget, to name a few. And too often that work has been appropriated by women composition specialists without a critique of its androcentrism.

The reviewers of the piece seemed to be offended by my criticisms of the field, though, so I decided to shift the emphasis of my discussion, focusing on the positive rather than the negative. But I did not acquiesce when one reviewer found the term "feminist" to be problematic, because it "carries several different meanings for different communities," and suggested that I used the term "gender related" instead, especially since Gilligan and Belenky et al. might not be considered "orthodox" feminists by some readers. My essay would have been an entirely different one had I substituted "gender related" for "feminist" and had I avoided designating Gilligan and Belenky et al. feminists.

Feminism is integral to the argument of "Composing as a Woman" and could not have been edited out of the essay. It provided an interpretive framework. But it also provided me research questions that had not previously been asked: What does it mean to compose as a woman? Do women and men compose differently? These questions, admittedly, have a political agenda. If we can establish difference, then we have taken a first step toward establishing dominance. I would like to think that my readings of the student examples are persuasive because I have been true to them and have not simply imposed a framework on them. The extended process of revision that my reviewers encouraged me to undertake insured that I would deal with the examples in their complexity, recognizing the contradictions inherent in them. I found myself limiting the sample at each stage of the revision process because I felt that in prior iterations I was oversimplifying, providing thin rather than thick description.

———

The word *research* derives from the French *recherche* and suggests a quest, an investigation. Research procedures and methods evolve and develop as fields of inquiry evolve and develop. Such procedures and methods are meant to enable discovery, not to impede it. New research questions necessitate new methods. If we introduce feminist inquiry into the field of composition studies, we inevitably alter it, call into question its assumptions and procedures. I welcome such an introduction and urge that the resulting studies be legitimated by being recognized as research.

32   *The Feminization of Composition*

SUSAN MILLER

I realize that my title may unintentionally fail to frame my purpose, for it easily leads in two directions. "Feminization" calls to mind both positive new moves in composition to gender-balance research and teaching and negative associations with the actual "feminization" of a field that collects, like bugs in a web, women whose persistently marginalized status demands political action. But I have chosen this potentially slippery term precisely, to point a new reading of composition studies that places both the political action that we obviously need, and many new intellectual and practical movements toward gender balance in composition studies, against a prevailing negative cultural identity that "the feminization of composition" implies. Paradoxically, positive internal desires to gender-balance our field are contained by a negative, insistent external feminization in the phallocentric community where it was born. Much of the field's past, its continuing actual experience, and its usually overlooked but important symbolic associations result from a defining, specifically from a gendered, cultural call to identity.

By using the phrase "call to identity," I mean to bring to mind a group of related leftist political and feminist theories that explain identity formation as a result from a cultural context. Identities do not, in these views, result from the preexisting or essential qualities of a person, or of an area of social action, itself. Instead, they come into being through a cultural context of which we are already a part. This context is partially made up of a framework of assumptions and approaches, a superstructure, that places both individuals and certain kinds of social action in fairly well-enclosed cultural spaces, where they have names and identifiable discursive practices. These identifying spaces are hierarchically disposed, but cultural invitations to inhabit them are not simple edicts from on high. We tacitly accept these identities to maintain the superstructure that we live in, in a process of hegemonic consensus. The "low" is contained by its implied participation in a total system.

From *The Politics of Writing Instruction: Postsecondary.* Ed. Richard Bullock and John Trimbur. Portsmouth, NH: Boynton/Cook, 1991. 39–53.

In regard to gender and the "low" situation of females, this reasoning emphasizes that categories of identity, or "subjectivities," map both individuals and groups (see Eagleton, "Subject" 95). For instance, a female may be constituted as "a mother" and therefore as a person who will sacrifice her personal separateness to attend to the frequent and private bodily needs of young children—elimination, cleanliness, and nurturance. But the culture also produces "motherhood," a symbolic domain that places a particular woman's self-sacrifice in an acceptable image of *the* Mother, a figure who occupies an idealized space of veneration. For many feminist theorists, it is well understood that no matter what range of individual biological, intellectual, social, economic, class, or other qualities people of the female sex may exhibit, this and other female identities (e.g., "wife," "whore," "girl") participate in similar cultural calls to "womanhood." This "hood" effectively cloaks differences to assure that females (and males) are socially identified by imaginary relations to their actual situations.

Many feminists also point out that, within this process, the identity of the female person was specifically differentiated as "woman" to supplement, complement, oppose, and extend male identity. This separation of genders first organized cultures for their biological, economic, and social survival. A female's particularity or her ignorance of such category formation could not at first excuse her and has not later excused her from the cultural identity devised to ensure the continuity of traditions that regulate property, power, and status within and among communities.

I outline these theories and some of their corollaries because I want to argue that this view of lower-status female identity—including both its critique of dominance and submission and its view of historical requirements imposed for the sake of survival and tradition—is embodied by composition studies. A similar cultural call acting on composition has, that is, created the field's unentitled "place" in its surroundings and has limited both its old and its new self-definitions. This call and responses to it maintain the regular range of results that follow from the field's most common, as well as its most innovative, practices. Recent reactions to this call often attempt to overcome the field's feminization, but composition remains largely the distaff partner in a socially important "masculine" enterprise, the cultural maintenance of linguistic dispositions of power and enfranchisement.

To support this claim, I want to review "facts," a history, and relevant symbolic associations that negatively feminize composition, despite (and in concert with) some of our best efforts to overcome this identity. Making my case depends, I realize, on persuasively joining information we already know and accept about the status of composition to both a historical context and a larger symbolic domain that is usually preserved to explain purposes, practices, and status in more entitled cultural sites. We habitually, at least among ourselves, quote statistics and tell personal tales about the professional situation of the field and its members, but we rarely account for and evaluate these (quite accurate) perceptions from a theoretical perspective, to show how they arise from, and contribute to, the superstructure they maintain.

We can, then, begin uncovering the feminization of composition by reviewing some concrete bad news we already know. In fact, in the actual life-world of anyone who teaches English, the field is largely the province of women. As Sue Ellen Holbrook has so carefully shown in her essay "Women's Work," the sexual division of labor that characterizes all jobs has equally characterized composition. Holbrook points out that in decades when women have "risen" in the academy, at least in numbers, they have concurrently assumed lower ranks in subject areas associated with feminine pursuits — home economics, physical education, humanities, social sciences, and education. They have, on average, been paid 18 percent less than men; as late as 1986, they earned but 85 percent of what men in the humanities earned. In addition, women hold the part-time appointments in academic institutions. In 1976, women occupied 25 percent of full-time positions, but 38 percent of the part-time positions.

As we know, a large proportion of this part-time work force is housed in departments of English, where composition is usually taught. These paraprofessionals, to use Holbrook's term, occupy the lowest hierarchical status by virtue of their association with composition teaching itself, typically characterized as *elementary* teaching that is a *service* tied to *pedagogy* rather than theory (9). Holbrook estimates that two-thirds of all who teach composition are female. Two-thirds of the NCTE College section membership are women. In 1986, 65 percent of the program participants at the Conference on College Composition and Communication were female; in 1987, 58 percent were female. (In 1986, 45 percent of the participants at the MLA convention were female.)

Holbrook also points out that the gendered hierarchy these figures represent is repeated within composition as a sub-field of English Studies. In composition research, for instance, the hierarchy that subordinates women is maintained: Men appear to publish a greater percentage of articles submitted to *College English* (65 percent); books by men dominate in selective bibliographies (approximately 70 percent); male authors overwhelmingly dominate in "theoretical" (as against nurturant, pedagogical) publication categories (12–13). Holbrook's analyses of these demonstrable proportions and of the historical position of women as faculty in universities give her good grounds for inferring that "men develop knowledge and have higher status; women teach, applying knowledge and serving the needs of others, and have lower status" (7–8). Her inference is further supported by other concrete facts: according to her 1981 count of unambiguous first names, 71 percent of the members of the Association of Writing Program Administrators are men (13), and 73 percent of the programs Carol Hartzog described in her *Composition in the Academy* are administered by men who outrank the female majority of teachers they supervise (23).

These and other ways that the field of composition mirrors traditional "women's roles" are such normalized parts of our daily experience that we may overlook the seemingly contradictory self-images they force us to accept. That is, we are on the one hand so well persuaded that composition is, as Holbrook says, nonintellectual, pedagogical, service-oriented work that we hardly wonder that it is given over to women. We can, no matter how quickly we would deny our nobility in doing so, easily accept that composition is a field for "women and children," teachers and students whom we expect to be tentative about their commitments to "real" education, that which we (again, easily) assume will chronologically follow writing courses. But we also retain equally deep cultural images that thoroughly convince us that composition teaching is the "important" mission that English studies as a whole was constituted to perform. We see it as the locus for the best sense of the cultural literacy that is the imagined important mission of a university as a whole. Learning to read and write, we easily acknowledge, assures the continuation of our civilization. Our most "civilized" and powerful citizens—college graduates—must be confident, fluent producers and equally skilled analysts of discourse. But we are also accustomed to confessions that composition teaching, and composition research, are not something that "regular" (meaning powerful, entitled, male-coded, theoretical) faculty do. This apparent contradiction in the social text around composition studies deserves a great deal of attention, for it is here that the female identity of composition, clear in the facts I have just cited, becomes a larger "feminized" identity that is situated in a specific history that has its own cultural implications.

To get at this history, we can notice that the low status of composition (which is curiously seen as both the cause and the effect of the statistics Holbrook compiled) has always tied composition to "work" in a specific pairing with literary study, the "play" of English. As Richard Ohmann has pointed out, "Writing and Reading: Work and Leisure" describes the totality of English Studies (*Politics* 26–41). That is, the judgmental manual labor of composition opposes entitlements that females in the academy only rarely claim: relaxed mental contemplation, reflection, and most recently a more powerful "theory" of literary study. Consequently, to understand the well-established contradiction between the low-status and inverted female majorities in composition and its importance as "civilizing work," we need to look at the field's original and still most prevalent institutional position. It is the counterpart, the handmaiden, and low-order basement attached to vernacular literary study.

We can reasonably infer that this relationship is a product of the first disposition of composition instruction in new departments of English established in the late nineteenth century, both in England and in America. We have a great deal of historical evidence that the entirety of English, because it was comprised of vernacular language and literature, not the mystified classics, was at first associated with dilettantish, womanish images of belles lettres. It was, that is, letters for belles, identified as a "pink sunsets" tradition of teacups and limp wrists. But this symbolically gender-coded vernacular subject was also, in fact, taught by women in the mechanics and industrial institutes where its advanced courses first appeared, pointedly to address the imagined greater need for "civilizing" students in these institutions. Women taught English even in more elitist schools after its spread (Doyle 23). But notwithstanding an elitist implimatur, "English" was perceived as a "soft," not rigorous or difficult subject, an extension of the popular extracurriculum of polite learning into privileged educational institutions.

Nonetheless, English quite quickly assumed academic centrality, arguably because it was seen as a way to establish national unity among those who were not already entitled to a classical education, but who were being newly admitted to postprimary education. Terry Eagleton's *Literary Theory: An Introduction* argues forcefully that vernacular literature and language study became both the content and the idiom of the modern "parent" country because it included precisely the "poor man's classics," a nationalist substitute for religion. He cites George Gordon, an early professor of English at Oxford: "England is sick," Gordon said in his inaugural address, "and English literature must save it. The Churches (as I understand) having failed, and social remedies being slow, English literature has now a triple function, still, I suppose, to delight and instruct us, but also, and above all, to save our souls and heal the State" (quoted in Eagleton, *Literary Theory* 23). Lest we think this agenda supported only new British English studies, we must remember that similar ideas flourished even more readily in America. There they had been prepared for by an early Puritan morality that had led the *New England Primer* to rhyme "Thy life to mend/This book attend" (Tchudi 4–5). Lindley Murray's infamous *English Grammar, Adapted to the Different Classes of Learners* (1795) taught parsing to "discipline the mind" and to help students write "with propriety" (Tchudi 6). Arthur Applebee, in *Tradition and Reform in the Teaching of English,* quotes one mid-nineteenth-century teacher/reformer who demonstrates American continuities of this tone in an equally moralistic and chauvinistic justification for vernacular literary study: "The first great aim in the literature course is a training for citizenship by a study of *national* ideals embodied in the writings of American authors, our *race* ideals as set forth by the great writers of Anglo-Saxon origin, our *universal* ideals as we find them in any great work of literary art" (my emphasis; Applebee 69).

Consequently, the entire complex of activities associated with "English" began its competition for a place among established academic subjects with a gendered, but blurred, spiritual identity. And this identity applied equally to the grammatical instruction that for Hegel was "the alphabet of the Spirit itself" (Graff 29). English originally had *actual* associations with a distaff, "soft" study of vernacular language and literature, which had formerly trained children of both sexes in the preliminaries to the rigorous classical education pursued further only by boys. But in establishing English Studies as a university-level discipline competing against the classics and against an equally plausible scientific center for the curriculum, promoters of English Studies asserted its *imagined,* or symbolic, manly associations with religious and nationalistic ideals.

Charles Eliot, the president of Harvard most often identified as the inspiration for the "new university" in which this blurred identity of English studies was to flourish in America, clarified how these contradictory associations were to become systematic practice in his 1869 inaugural address. There he announced that "English" would be the center of the new curriculum. This subject would ensure something like the unity that men educated in the earlier classical colleges had necessarily shared, despite the newly practical and more fragmented curriculum that characterized more "relevant" effort. But, Eliot qualified, this new Harvard education would be bestowed on two sorts of potential recipients—those already entitled, from "refined" homes, and the "new" student, the person whose hold on good character and correct values was only tentative and who needed to receive both principles and a test (Douglas 129).

The principles—national, race, and universal—were to be learned in vernacular literary study. But the moral test, which would necessarily precede exposure to these principles, was the "test" of English composition. It became embodied only four years later, in both the well-documented Harvard Entrance Exam and "the" course in composition. This course was supervised by Adams Sherman Hill, the journalist and former classmate of Eliot's who was recruited to supervise it. It was thereby defined as a device for winnowing and sifting within the newly elevated, central, field of English. Composition was, then, established to be a place where Harvard could assure the worthiness, moral probity, and fitness of those who might otherwise slip through the newly woven net that would now take in additional, *but only tentatively entitled,* students. In this form, as Ohmann has said of its speedy national adoption, "it spread like kudzu" (33).

The actual establishment of university-level departments of English required a further professional implementation of this educational agenda, a "base" cooperating with this new superstructure. To inculcate literary principles, it was necessary to overcome the "nonserious," gender-coded, image of English by emphasizing its new departments' attachments to philology and to traditional methods of teaching classical language and literature, in order that the subject's work, and its professionals, would be perceived as "hard" (Graff 38). To compete against science and other subjects like traditional rhetoric, which had always been learned and taught in combative, exclusively male contexts, these departments had to overcome traditional, feminine, negative images of vernacular literary study. But they also had to implement Eliot's "test." To organize the discriminations and reassurances about social entitlement that Eliot's new vision of postsecondary curricula meant to maintain, the course in composition had to be a place to house those who studied and taught subjects that were now preliminary in a new sense. Divorced from the old college curriculum in classics, "composition" was defined for the first time as preliterary (or preprincipled), not as a part of rhetorical education for those already entitled eventually to "speak."

Even discounting the economic or survival needs that are often cited to explain composition's importance in the origins of English departments, composition conveniently, and precisely, contained within English the negative, nonserious connotations that the entire field might otherwise have had to combat. In mutuality with literary study, it enclosed those who might not "belong," even as it subsumed the soft, nonserious connotations of vernacular study. It became a place that the "best men" escape from, as we learn both from elaborate placement testing systems and from the frequency with which histories of English and of rhetoric describe Francis Child's release from teaching rhetoric courses at Harvard. But composition was nonetheless the symbolically essential way to verify the social and moral credentials of those admitted to the new university. Given an original societal demand in this cultural call to an identity for composition, we can explain the seeming contradiction between its status as women's work and its ceremonial cultural importance as the essence of an elegantly cooperative pair. Actual "woman's work" filled a necessary symbolic (and often actual) "basement" of literary studies in an easily understood process of identity formation.

The objects of this cooperation, composition students, of course have another subjectivity, or category of identity, that follows from the feminization I am describing. They took an entrance examination whose results were often made public to humiliate them, attended classes that enrolled one hundred or more students in their earliest, introductory exposure to "English," and were taught by ancillary help who were "supervised" rather than admitted to collegial academic freedom. The new pecking order in English departments connected these students to concrete manifestations of the "work" of composition described by Ohmann. For them and their teachers, composition was in fact, as it was in the newly established sustaining mythology of "English," work of a menial, backbreaking sort. "Daily themes" required daily writing and marking (Kitzhaber 169). But since the purpose of assigning these themes was to reveal the fitness of a new student "body"—the unentitled new student's spirit manifest in the physical surface of his language—this heavy, corrective workload was perfectly arranged to accomplish the introductory course's goals. This backbreaking (or more accurately, mind-boggling) work was fit, that is, for tentatively entitled employees of the academy, like women, just as the work of producing correct essays on inconsequential subjects was and remains with few exceptions a task for students whose verbal propriety is in question. It is work required of "new" students in any era, imposed on the majority who are taken to be only tentatively entitled to belong in higher education (Miller, Chapter 3).

But this new educational culture also supplied an acceptable covering mythology that accommodates both the work of composition teaching and its corrective treatment of students' linguistic bodies. Composition teaching, that is, took place in a historically well-established symbolic domain that invited cooperation with distasteful but necessary cultural work. The call to "work" was overlaid on already accepted religious images of grammatical correctness, Hegel's "alphabet of the Spirit." Just as the taxing demands of motherhood give mothers an imaginary relation to a venerable image of *the* Mother, the corrective task of dealing with writing by students who were now identified as only tentatively suitable for the social rewards of university enrollment provided its workers with a covering myth of the "English teacher." This particular cover story endows the composition teacher of whatever disposition, experience, or relation to status with qualities much like those of the mythologized mother: self-sacrifice, "dedication," "caring," and enormous capacities for untheorized attention to detail. But this figure is ambivalent. It also symbolizes authority, precision, and eternally validated, impeccable linguistic taste, qualities that prompt those who meet composition teachers to expect censure and disapproval.

As this duality suggests, composition teaching is not simply "motherhood," a service to father texts. The social identity of the composition teacher is intricately blurred, in a matrix of functions that we can understand through the instructive example of Freud's description of the "feminine," which was formed at about the same time that composition courses and their teaching first achieved presence in the new university. Despite the problematics feminists point out in his work, Freud's description of associations that contain ambivalently situated women can be seen as a reliable historical account of nineteenth-century sexual mythologies. His description of the Mother/Maid, a blurred dream figure whom he revised over time, suggests why our resistance to changes in the cultural image of composition teaching is so deep.

Freud first dreamed of his family nurse, a common member of the nineteenth-century bourgeois household, whom he later transformed into "mother." The nurse in his dream "initiated the young Freud in sexual matters" (Stallybrass and White 157). But later, in Freud's writing about "femininity," "the nurse has been displaced by the mother" (157). In various writings, Freud by turns associated seduction and bodily hygiene with motherhood and with the maid, at one time calling the maid the most intimate participant in his initiations and fantasies, and at another thinking of these matters in relation to perfect motherhood. In *The Politics and Poetics of Transgression*, Peter Stallybrass and Allon White infer that because the nineteenth-century bourgeois family relegated child care to nurses, the maid both performed intimate educational functions and had power over the child. "Because of his size, his dependency, his fumbling attempts at language, his inability to control his bodily functions" (158), the child could be shamed and humiliated by the maid. But paradoxically, it is more developmentally "natural" to desire the mother than the maid, who is "hired help," so actual interactions with a nurse/maid might be fantasized as having occurred with the mother for whom the maid stood in.

It is fair to suggest that analogous symbolic blurrings still encode teachers of composition, even if we set aside comparisons between the "low" work of composition teaching and this representation of intimate work that at once corrects, educates, and seduces the young initiate. This analogy explains some otherwise troubling contradictions in the ways we habitually conceive of composition teachers, if nothing else. The bourgeois mother and maid, that is, each represent comfort and power, the contradictory endowments required of the service-oriented teacher of students who are, despite their actual maturity, sentimentalized as preeconomic, presexual, prepolitical children (Ohmann, *English* 149). The mother (a "pure" Victorian symbol) was the source Freud turned to for explanatory information about the maid. The mother was also, with the father, an authority. He displaced these associations of comfort and power onto the maid, but she was also given actual "dirty" work. Thus the maid was an ambivalently perceived site for dealing with low, unruly, even anarchic desires and as yet uncontrolled personal development, the qualities of freshman writing highlighted in much composition pedagogy.

The Wolfman in Freud's writings developed great anxiety about his formal lessons in Latin, the public, formal, consequential language about which his comforting yet ambivalently perceived nursery maid knew nothing. The requirement, that is, to "'forget' the baby-talk of the body" (Stallybrass and White 166) created great ambivalence about his own body's functions, just as the process of forgoing "home" vernacular language for formal, publicly criticized English compositions displaces the vernacular linguistic confidence of most students. But the composition student is learning a "home," vernacular language *again,* as a formal system that now has public consequences, and is taught in that situation by the maid who is also a designated mother/power figure, not the new schoolmaster whom Wolfman encountered. Again, the cultural "importance" of composition is overlaid on its demeaned place in the family romance of English Studies.

Consequently, the potential identification between the low-status composition teacher and tentatively entitled "young" students creates yet another blurring. Students in their "practice" composition courses expect both infantile freedom from the embarrassment that the mother/power figure in the "real" family causes *and* those same embarrassments, in the form of corrections and information about propriety and "appropriateness" in a formerly familiar language. This at once comforting and powerful, but public and displaced, figure becomes a blurred point of transference for the student's anxieties over the maturation that inevitably accompanies developmental moves toward public language.

Consequently, the figure of a composition teacher is overloaded with symbolic as well as actual functions. These functions include the dual (or even triple) roles that are washed together in these teachers: the teacher is a nurse who cares for and tempts her young charge toward "adult" uses of language that will not "count" because they are, for now, engaged only with hired help; she is, no matter what her gender, the "mother" (tongue) that is an ideal/idol and can humiliate, regulate, and suppress the child's desires. But she is also the disciplinarian, not a father figure but a sadomasochistic Barbarella version of either mother or maid.

These are deeply held images, whose power is evident in their appearance as humorous stereotypes even among the people whose characteristics and practices contradict them. These images from nineteenth-century bourgeois culture had their own historical precedents, which ironically clarify the readily accepted view that the individual composition teacher is a culturally designated "initiator," similar to a temple priest or priestess who functions to pass along secret knowledge, but not to participate freely in a culture that depends on that knowledge. Strict regulations, similar to those devised to keep "hired help" in its place, prevent those who introduce the young to the culture's religious values and rites from leaving their particular and special status. These mediators between natural and regulated impulses are tied to vows, enclosed living spaces, and/or certain kinds of dress, the categories we might compare with composition teachers' self-sacrificing acceptance of work without time for contemplating its implications, their traditionally window-less offices, and the prissiness expected, at least in the past, in their personal presentations (Lerner 123–141).

This blurred initiating role, whether it is described as a religious/sexual initiation or as the groundwork now symbolically placed "under" an edu-cated public's discursive practices, has been unstable in any context. Cultures never codified it even in ancient times, when socially separated *grammaticus* and *rhetor* competed, as Quintilian noted, over who should initiate students into rhetorical composition (*Institutes,* II.1). Consequently, the teacher of com-position is assigned not only these roles, which might involve the initiating care, pedagogic seduction, and practice for adulthood provided by nurses in bourgeois homes. In addition, this teacher must withhold unquestioned acceptance, represent established means of discriminating among and evalu-ating students, and embody primary ideals/idols of language. This initiator, who traditionally has a great deal at stake in the model-correctness of his and her own language, must also *be* the goddess, *the* mother tongue, the discursive culture to which the student is introduced.

It might be countered that this complex call to identity contains any teacher of any introductory course claiming to initiate students into "essen-tial" cultural knowledge. But the composition teacher consciously and un-consciously introduces students to the culture's discourse on *language,* which is always at one with action, emotion, and regulatory establishments. This teacher is always engaged in initiations into the textual fabric of society and thus will always be in a particular and difficult relation to the superstructural regulation of that society. We see this difficulty daily, in the experience of those who are both demeaned by their continuing *ad hoc* relation to status, security, and financial rewards yet are given overwhelming authority by students, institutions, and the public, who expect even the most inexperienced "English teacher" to criticize and correct them, even in settings entirely removed from the academy. In these and many other ways, the complexly feminized cultural call to identity imposed on teachers of composition is maintained, even after they themselves censure early mechanistic teaching and its obviously regula-tory practices.

This censure signifies positive moves to redefine composition as a disci-pline, i.e., "composition studies" (see North 9–17), and to establish it as an academically equal partner in English departments. Such obvious, normal reactions from members of a marginalized culture unquestionably bode well for the fully theorized approach to writing and its instruction that could change the cultural expectation that its teachers be only initiating, service-oriented, self-sacrificing, practical people. But in view of the feminized iden-tity I have established, the motives behind actions to "change" composition need cautious critiques. As statistics about who writes composition theory and who administers composition programs tell us, neither describing com-position as a discipline nor asserting its equality has "worked" on the actually gender-coded professional circumstances of those who teach writing. These motives have not resulted in acknowledging the gender-coded call to identity that marks the field's cultural history or in offering alternatives to the deep but blurred structures of identity I have described. Our continuing tacit cooperation with hegemonic superstructural values cannot be underestimated, nor can the hegemonic compromise that continues to constrain the field be "overcome," or "combated," with male-coded fortitude.

We have examples of such fortitude in attempts to follow the formative counterpart of composition, literary study, into an entrenched, privileged, "equal" academic position. The problem with such attempts at equality is that they contribute, no matter how inadvertently, to an improved status that continues the patriarchal hierarchy in which they begin. Despite their perfectly understandable motivations and the positive results for both the theory and practice they have created, "equalizing" privileges between composition and literature, or between composition and any other established field, signifies acceptance of values that ignore the beginnings and contradict the purposes of current composition teaching and research.

For instance, neoclassical histories of composition that insist on its intellectual continuity with ancient rhetoric create both a content and a form for composition history that should give us pause. These histories do not normally focus on composition as a discrete product of American discourse education, whose connection to rhetorical instruction was ruptured, not merely interrupted, by Francis Child's 1875 negotiated defection from Harvard's Boylston Chair of Rhetoric to concentrated literary research. Nor do they consider other historical events, some of which I have described, in which the test-hungry National Committee of Ten, Eliot at Harvard, and his henchman Adams Sherman Hill began a mechanistic, corrective course without even honorific connections to rhetorical education. Neoclassical histories do not, that is, point out the hegemonic significance of establishing a *freshman* writing course to winnow and sift students in place of—not as a version of—traditionally later, upper-class instruction for postgraduate public discourse.

In an otherwise admirable attempt to give composition a history and thus allow it (as many have said of needed women's history) to participate as an agent rather than an overlooked object in its own system of significance, neoclassical histories inadvertently approve of traditional academic privileges embedded in the fabric of hegemonic "traditions" and their overbearing "common sense." Focusing on a limited "intellectual" history of composition to the exclusion of its material circumstances implicitly places composition in academic "Big" history, where it will accrue entitlements from "authority and the ancients." But this tactic also sustains the hierarchies and privileging mechanisms that those in the field complain of so often.

Similarly, inevitable desires to demonstrate that composition is a research field have in some forms assumed that "research" must be empirical and scientific. This attitude, by no means universal among composition researchers, values "hard" data, "rigorous" methods, and what are taken to be generative "results" that will spawn further study. The intellectual contributions of this form of research are not at issue, but it is politically important to notice that claims for its powerful, masculine academic position imitate quite closely the "scientific" spirit that motivated and legitimized literary New Criticism earlier in this century. The "purified" (ahistorical, intransitive, theorized) "processes" of writers and newly "objective," disinterested methods of studying them allow composition to claim, as literary studies did under New Criticism, that it has an object of study and that it can discover self-contained "meaning" in the act of writing apart from its contexts — in the "act itself."

This particular way to code composition as academically male, like neoclassical historicism, indicates a felt need to overcome its feminized cultural identity. But displacing either the symbolically "soft" or the actually marginalized status of the field and its female majority will not be accomplished by "combating" that identity, to achieve a success designed to imitate the totalizing effects of New Criticism's reign. And neither research that creates a male identity for composition studies nor historiography that links it to a Big picture actually fulfills this disguised desire. Both, that is, potentially alienate composition from consequential status among those who have historically had all the "principles" endowed to English. One adopts methods and vocabularies that ring false among many who already resent "science" as a field with which they have always competed, and the other focuses on a rhetorical educational history from which literary studies purposefully sets about to estrange itself.

My reasoning implies, I know, that no movement from within composition studies could ever do more than reform the basic structure of its identity and that we should all at this point perform the intellectual/sexual submission we were culturally called to, to "lie back and think of England." As Althusser (following Marx) wrote about the cooperation of seemingly "new" and "traditional" ideologies (before he acted out his personally held ideological privileges by murdering his wife), "every child knows that a social formation which did not reproduce the conditions of production at the same time as it [was] produced would not last a year" (quoted in Macdonnel 28). But going beyond Marx, he also argued that attempts to overcome what we take to be hierarchical dominance often sustain the hierarchy, the "means of production," in which ideologies install us. Althusser's argument clearly applies to specific "new" moves in composition like those with which I have taken issue. These and many other intellectual and "practical" moves toward equality for composition reproduce the hegemonic superstructure by implying that bourgeois social climbing and successful competition for intellectual "clout" are legitimate signs of improvement. Although they take many seemingly unrelated forms, they are *politically* unified attempts to become equal in, and to sustain, a hierarchy that their supporters often claim to be overturning.

Nonetheless, the negative feminization of composition need not last forever.

The field might, that is, enjoy a different, if not a "new," identity, precisely as a culturally designated space for political action. Composition studies has always had the process available to it that active feminists and African-Americans have employed to transform their marginalized cultures into sites where cultural superstructures and their privileging results are visibly put into question. Composition professionals can also uncover and describe what is at stake for larger cultural maintenance in the marginalized status of their field. By raising a different voice in an active conversation about the feminized actual, historical, and symbolic status of composition professionals and their students, we can, that is, begin to reveal existing counterhegemonic structures in the field's existing practices and intellectual positions. An *actually* improved status depends on openly consolidating the field's resistances to the cultural superstructure that first defined it.

My primary purpose has been to accomplish part of the first, conversational goal, but the second process of intellectual redefinition would re-represent the negatively "feminine" field as irrefutably counterhegemonic, not as a victim stuck in webs of compromise. For instance, composition might be redefined as a site culturally designated to teach *all* students, not an elite group. It therefore already is an encompassing site for empowering, not for repressing or "correcting," the discursive power of the majority. In addition, the field might highlight (as many have recently done) the status of its female majorities and the constructed marginal identity of its always "new" students. By drawing concrete attention to the ways in which political issues are played out in a contemporary academic situation that was first constructed on anti-feminist principles, it would ask neocolonial administrators to recognize, and to be accountable for, the political implications of their enduring definitions of "composition" as the central institutional site for colonizing and regulating otherwise questionable, nontraditional entrants to the academy.

Other frequently noted characteristics of composition equally define it as an already designated place for counterhegemonic intellectual politics. The field addresses writing-in-progress (and writing as process), not writing as an immutable textual product. It thereby overtly claims that categories of "high" and "low" texts are social, not essential, categories. "Good" writing, as composition must define it, is the result of established cultural privileging mechanisms, not of pure "taste." The field thus vividly demonstrates, in practice and in theory, that a mixture of ideas, timing, entitlements, and luck have designated some rather than others as "important" writer/thinkers. The field's most productive methods of evaluation also judge writing by situational rather than by universal standards and thus insist on the arbitrariness of evaluations and their relativity to particular power structures. Additionally, the field's research opens rather than closes borders among established fields, thereby arguing that making new knowledge is a shared rather than isolated process, a matter of cooperation rather than of disciplined competition.

Each of these often stated but persistently unpoliticized practices and insights in the field have positioned it to transform its negatively feminized identity by engaging intellectual as well as practical political actions. As the institutional site designated as a passive enclosure for "unauthorized" discourse, composition has simultaneously been designated as a marginalizing power. But this enormous power to contain the discourse of the majority can be, if its professionals wish to claim it, the strength that re-represents the field's negative feminization. Composition is *also*, that is, an active existing site for dismantling particularly troublesome versions of hegemonic discursive "common sense" — particularly the exclusivity, humiliation, repression, and injustice hidden in nineteenth-century bourgeois moralities.

We have frequently translated these counterhegemonic implications of the field's practices and intellectual positions into signs of an undifferentiated "vitality" or "energy." But this abstract "energy" can be plugged into interventions that would undo concrete political structures that have a great deal at stake in negative images of composition teaching and the writing of students. Composition is not, that is, a modern place to celebrate a liberal "healthy pluralism" that reforms systems around it. It contains active resistance to the exhausted social situations that produced both its negative feminization and "traditions" that should have become cultural embarrassments long ago. As Kristeva has said in resisting traditional definitions of females, we can transform our own negative identity by understanding the implications of composition as "that which is marginalized by the patriarchal symbolic order" (quoted in Moi 166).

WORKS CITED

Applebee, Arthur. *Tradition and Reform in the Teaching of English: A History.* Urbana, IL: NCTE, 1974.

Douglas, Wallace. "Rhetoric for the Meritocracy." In Richard Ohmann, *English in America.* New York: Oxford UP, 1976, 97–132.

Doyle, Brian. "The Hidden History of English Studies." In *Rereading English.* Ed. Peter Widdowson. New York: Methuen, 1982, 17–31.

Eagleton, Terry. *Literary Theory: An Introduction.* Minneapolis: U of Minnesota P, 1983.

———. "The Subject of Literature." *Cultural Critique,* No. 2 (Winter 1985–86): 95–104.

Graff, Gerald. *Professing Literature: An Instructional History.* Chicago: U of Chicago P, 1987.

Hartzog, Carol. *Composition in the Academy: A Study of Writing Program Administration,* New York: MLA, 1987.

Holbrook, Sue Ellen. "Women's Work: The Feminizing of Composition." Unpublished ms. of 1988 presentation at CCCC, St. Louis, MO.

Kitzhaber, Albert. "Rhetoric in American Colleges: 1850–1900." Unpublished diss. University of Washington, 1953.

Lerner, Gerda. "Veiling the Woman." In *The Creation of Patriarchy.* New York: Oxford UP, 1986.

Macdonnel, Diane. *Theories of Discourse: An Introduction.* Oxford: Basil Blackwell, 1986.

Miller, Susan. *Textual Carnivals: The Politics of Composition.* Carbondale, IL: Southern Illinois UP, 1991.

Moi, Toril. *Sexual/Textual Politics.* New York and London: Methuen, 1985.

North, Stephen. *The Making of Knowledge in Composition: Portrait of an Emerging Field.* Portsmouth, NH: Boynton/Cook, 1987.

Ohmann, Richard. *English in America.* New York: Oxford University Press, 1976.

———. "Writing and Reading: Work and Leisure." In *The Politics of Letters.* Middletown, CT: Wesleyan UP, 1987. (Chapter 3).

Stallybrass, Peter, and Allon White. *The Politics and Poetics of Transgression.* Ithaca: Cornell UP, 1986.

Tchudi, Stephen N. *Explorations in the Teaching of Secondary English: A Sourcebook for Experimental Teaching.* New York: Dodd, Mead, 1975.

33   *Teaching College English as a Woman*

LYNN Z. BLOOM

During my first year of doctoral work I spent all my savings on a lifetime membership in NCTE. Already, in my first year as a TA, I knew I loved to teach. Nothing less than a lifetime commitment to the profession I was preparing to join could express that love.

It has taken thirty years to find the voice, the place in the profession, to tell the stories that follow. When the events occurred, I would never discuss them, silenced by guilt, shame, anger, and embarrassment. Like discussing childbirth (which for the same reasons I never did either until a recent reunion with college roommates), it would not have been ladylike. But two years ago at a summer conference, a one-hour session on "gender and teaching," attended by women and men alike, metamorphosed into two nights of telling life-saving stories.[1] And so I tell you what it has been like to teach college English as a woman, to become a member of the profession I now and ever embrace anew. Call me Lynn.

I. MY JOB AS VENTRILOQUIST'S DUMMY

Once upon a time, as a newly minted PhD with a newly minted baby, I got the best part-time job I've ever had, a half-time assistant professorship at a distinguished midwestern university. Unusual for the early 60s, and unique to that institution, my job was created in response to the dean's estimate of an impending shortage of faculty. "It's going to be hell on wheels facultywise around here for the next five years," he said. So I was hired for exactly half of a full-time job: half the teaching load, half the advising and committee work, half the regular benefits. Our second child was born, conveniently, during my second summer vacation. Though not on a tenure track, I did have a parking space; it seemed a fair exchange. I taught freshman composition, of course, and sometimes sophomore lit surveys. I even taught in a room that overlooked the playground of our children's nursery school.

From *College English* 54 (1992): 818–25.

During the whole five years I taught there, I never expressed an original opinion about literature, either in class or out. In the course of my very fine education at one of our nation's very finest universities, taught entirely by men except for women's phys. ed. where they allowed a woman to teach us how to develop graceful "posture, figure, and carriage," I learned, among other things, that only real professors had the right to say what they thought. Anyway, in the 50s there were no concepts, no language, to say what I, as a nascent feminist critic, wanted to say. I tried, in a fifteen-page junior year honors paper, "Milton's Eve did too have some redeeming virtues." The paper was returned, next day, in virgin condition, save a small mark in the margin on page two where the professor had apparently stopped reading, and a tiny scarlet C discreetly tattooed at the end. In shame and horror at getting less than my usual A, I went to see the professor. "Why did I get a C?" I was near tears. "Because," he said in measured tones, drawing on his pipe, "you simply can't say that." End of discussion. I did not sin again.

I had majored in English because I loved to read and to write, and I continued to love reading and writing all the way through graduate school. But somewhere along the line, perhaps through the examples of my professors, measured, judicious, self-controlled, I had come to believe that my job as a teacher was to present the material in a neutral manner, even-handedly citing a range of Prominent Male Critics, and let the students make up their own minds. It would have been embarrassing, unprofessional, to express the passion I felt, so I taught every class in my ventriloquist's dummy voice. Indifferent student evaluations reflected the disengagement this approach provoked—"although she's a nice lady," some students added.

Editing textbooks didn't count. Only the other women who taught freshman composition part-time took this work seriously. (Collectively we were known to the male full-time faculty as the "Heights Housewives," as we learned from the captions on the witchlike cartoons that would occasionally appear on the bulletin board in the English Department office.) I had collaboratively edited a collection of critical essays on Faulkner intended for freshman writing courses, signing the book contract in the hospital the day after the birth of my first child. I was working on two other collaborative texts. The English department invited my Faulkner collaborator, a gracious scholar of international reknown, to come to campus to lecture on the subject of our book, but they did not invite me to either the lecture or the dinner for him. The university's public relations spokesman nevertheless called and asked if I'd be willing to give a cocktail party for him, at my expense. That may have been the only time I ever said "no" during the whole five years I taught there.

Freshman composition didn't count. I was so apprehensive about publishing original writing in my own name that when my husband Martin, a social psychologist, and I collaborated on an article about a student's writing process, I insisted that we submit it in Martin's name only. Only real professors with full-time jobs could publish academic articles, and I knew I wasn't one. *College English* accepted it by return mail. "Now do you want your name on it?" Martin asked. "You should be first author." "Yes," I said. "Yes."

My work in nonfiction didn't count. I proudly told the department chair that I was beginning research on a biography of Dr. Benjamin Spock, soon to retire from his faculty position at the same university. I had access to all the primary sources I needed, including Spock himself. "Why don't you write a series of biographical articles on major literary figures?" asked our leader, whose customary advice to faculty requests for raises was "Diversify your portfolio." "Once you've established your reputation you can afford to throw it away by writing about a popular figure." I thanked him politely and continued my research, a logical extension of my dissertation study of biographical method. I could learn a lot about how people wrote biographies, I reasoned, if I wrote one myself. And because I couldn't say to the children, "Go away, don't bother me, I'm writing about Doctor Spock," I learned to write with them in the room.

Ultimately, I didn't count either. A new department chairman arrived soon after I began the biography. His first official act, prior to making a concerted but unsuccessful effort to abolish freshman English, was to fire all the part-time faculty, everyone (except TAs) who taught the lowly subject. All women but one. He told me privately, in person; a doctorate, after all, has some privileges, though my office mate learned of her status when the chairman showed a job candidate the office, announcing, "This will be vacant next year." He was kind enough to write me a letter of recommendation, a single sentence that said, "Mrs. Bloom would be a good teacher of freshman composition." I actually submitted that letter along with a job application. Once.

II. On the Floor with the Kitty Litter

One of the textbooks so scorned during my first part-time job actually got me my first full-time job, two years later. The department had adopted it for the freshman honors course, and the chair had written an enthusiastic review. Then, dear reader, he hired me! This welcoming work enabled me to find my voice. After ten years of part-time teaching, as bland as vanilla pudding, I felt free to spice up the menu. Being a full-time faculty member gave me the freedom to express my opinions about what we read and wrote and to argue and joke with my students. My classes became noisy, personal, and fun. Two years later, I received tenure, promotion, and an award for good teaching. But after four years in Indiana, my husband was offered a job in St. Louis too good to turn down. I resigned to move.

My voice was reduced to a whisper. I could find no full-time job in St. Louis in that inhospitable year of 1974 when there were several hundred applicants for every job. In hopes of ingratiating myself with one or another of the local universities, I taught part-time at three, marginal combinations of writing and women's studies. I taught early in the morning, in mid-afternoon, at night, coming and going under cover of lightness and darkness. It didn't matter, for no one except my students knew I was there anyway. Department chairmen wouldn't see me; with insulated indifference faculty—even some I'd known in graduate school—walked past my invisible self in the halls. For administrative convenience, I was paid once a semester, after Thanksgiving, $400. Fringe benefits, retirement, the possibility of raises or continuity of employment were nonexistent. At none of the three schools did I have any stationery, mailing privileges, secretarial help, telephone, or other amenities—not even an ID or a library card. I was treated as an illegal alien. Nowhere did I have an office, until I finally begged for one at the plushest school, frustrated and embarrassed at having to confer with my students in the halls on the run. After several weeks, the word trickled down that I could share space with a TA—and, as it turned out, her cat, which she kept confined there. This office symbolized my status on all three jobs. It was in a building across campus from the English Department, where no one could see us. It was under a stairwell, so we couldn't stand up. It had no windows, so we couldn't see out, but it did have a Satanic poster on the wall—shades of the underworld. The TA had the desk, so I got to sit on the floor next to the kitty litter. I stayed there, in the redolent dark, for a full thirty seconds.

Then my voice returned, inside my head this time. Its message was powerful and clear, "If I ever do this again, I deserve what I get." I did finish the semester. But I never went back to that office. And I never again took another job that supported such an exploitative system, even though that meant commuting two thousand miles a week to my next job, a real job, in New Mexico. "Go for it," said Martin, and took care of the children while I was away.

III. POISON IN THE PUBLIC IVY

Four years later we moved again to eliminate my cross-country commute. Through research support, graduate teaching, directing a writing program, and supervising some sixty TAs and part-time faculty, my New Mexico job had given me a grownup voice. I was beginning to talk to colleagues throughout the country, at meetings, through my own publications and those of my students, and I was looking forward to continuing the dialogue on the new job as Associate Professor and Writing Director at a southern, and therefore by definition gracious, Public Ivy.

As I entered the mellowed, red-brick building on the first day of class, a colleague blocked the door. "We expected to get a beginning assistant professor and wash *him* out after three years," he sneered. "Instead, we got *you*, and *you'll* probably get tenure." I took a deep breath and replied in a firm voice, "You bet."

"We" contains multitudes; one never knows at the outset how many. Although the delegated greeter never spoke to me again, it soon became clear that *we* meant a gang of four equal opportunity harassers, all men, all tenured faculty of long standing, all eager to stifle my voice. Their voices, loud and long, dominated all department and committee meetings and, word had it, the weekly poker games where the decisions were really made. I could do no right. I was too nice to my students; everybody knows that undergraduates can't write. I was merely flattering the students by encouraging them to publish; that they did indeed publish showed they were pandering to the public.

My writing project work with schoolteachers was—aha!—proof that I was more interested in teaching than in literary criticism; misplaced priorities. My own publications, ever increasing, were evidence of blatant careerism. I received a number of grants and fellowships; just a way to get out of teaching. The attendant newspaper publicity, though good for the school, reflected badly on my femininity.

Although I was heard in class and, increasingly, in the profession at large, I had no voice in the departmental power structure. The gang of four and, by extrapolation, the rest of the faculty, already knew everything they needed to know about teaching writing; they'd learned it long ago as TAs. Faculty development workshops were a waste of time. The college didn't need a writing director anyway; the students all wrote well, the faculty all taught well, and Southern Public Ivy had gotten along for two hundred years without a writing director. Why start now? As a way to forestall my imminent tenure review, this hospitable group initiated a review of the position of writing director. If they could demonstrate that there was no need for the job, despite the thousand students enrolled every semester in required freshman English, not to mention the upper-division writing courses, oversubscribed and with waiting lists, and the initiative in other departments for a writing-across-the-curriculum program, I would not have the opportunity to come up for tenure. Because the review was, of course, of the job and not of the person in it, I, of course, could not be consulted; that would compromise the impartially of the process. Nor could I discuss the ongoing review with colleagues; ditto. Or the department chair; ditto. Or the dean; ditto, ditto.

The review began in September of my second year. Nobody identified its criteria; nobody told me what it covered; I could not ask. Occasionally a friendly colleague would sneak into my office during that very long fall semester and tell me that he was so anguished by the proceedings he wanted to resign from the review committee; *sotto voce* I urged him to stay on it. A borrowed voice was better than none. Rumor had it, I heard, that I was talking to a lawyer. How unprofessional. Oh was I? I whispered. The campus AAUP president heard about the review; write me a letter, he said, outlining what's going on, and I'll send it to the national office. So I did. And he did.

Then, on a clear crisp evening in January, tenure became irrelevant. Our family dinner was interrupted by the phone call that every parent dreads. Come right away.

We saw the car first, on a curve in the highway near the high school, crushed into a concrete telephone pole. Next was the rescue squad ambulance, lights revolving red and white, halted amidst shattered glass. Then the figure on the stretcher, only a familiar chin emerging from the bandages that swathed the head. "He was thrown out of the back seat. The hatchback door smashed his face as if he'd been hit with an axe," said the medic. "I'm fine," said our son, and we responded with terror's invariable lie, "You're going to be all right."

After six hours of ambiguous X-rays, clear pictures finally emerged long after midnight, explaining why Laird's eyes were no longer parallel—one socket had simply been pulverized. The line of jagged-lightning stitches, sixty in all, that bolted across his face would be re-opened the next day for reconstructive surgery. "Don't go out in a full moon," sick-joked the doctor, howling like a banshee. "People will mistake you for a zombie."

Laird had to remain upright for a month so his head would drain, and our family spent every February evening on the couch in front of the wood stove, propping each other up. Every day the writing directorship review committee asked by memo for more information; every day I replied, automatically. I do not know, now, what they asked; I do not know, now, what I answered; or what I wrote on student papers; or what we ate, or read, or wrote checks for during that long month.

But I do know that in early March the AAUP's lawyer called me and his message was simple: "A university has every right to eliminate a position, or a program, if there is no academic need, if there are no students in it, for example. But it cannot eliminate a position just to get rid of the person holding the job. If Southern Ivy does this, they'll be blacklisted." He repeated this to the department chair. When the department voted, in its new wisdom, in late April to table the review of the writing directorship until after I had been reviewed for tenure, a friend, safely tenured, whispered to me, "You just got tenure." The thick copies of the committee's review were never distributed; I was awarded tenure the next year—and left immediately to become department chair at Urban State University, tenured, promoted to professor, with authority to have an emphatic voice. The review was never reinstated, says a faculty friend still at Southern Ivy; for six years the writing directorship went unfilled.

IV. Escaping the Rapist

Fortunately, even as department chair I could continue to teach, and I often taught Women Writers. One day my class, not only writing intensive but discussion intensive, began arguing about Joyce Carol Oates's "Where Are You Going, Where Have You Been?" Some claimed that Arnold Friend, "thirty, maybe," who invades Connie's driveway in "an open jalopy, painted a bright gold," his eyes hidden behind mirrored, metallic sunglasses, is in love with the pubescent teenager about whom "everything has two sides to it, one for home and one for anywhere that was not home." Others asserted that from the moment they met, Arnold's "Gonna get you, baby," signalled the abduction with which the story concludes. Though he does not lay a finger on his victim, Friend does, they pointed out, threaten to burn down her house and kill her parents—scarcely acts of love. After screaming for help into a disconnected phone until she loses her breath, Connie has no more voice and walks sacrificially out into the sunlight and Friend's mockingly waiting arms. "What else is there for a girl like you but to be sweet and pretty and give in? . . . You don't want [your family] to get hurt. . . . You're better than them because not a one of them would have done this for you."

Such compelling evidence clinched the debate, and I decided to reaffirm the students' interpretation with a life-saving story of my own. "A decade earlier," I began, taking a deep breath. I had never thought I would tell this story to my students. "My husband, adolescent sons, and I were camping in Scandinavia. But it was a dark and stormy night in Stockholm, so we decided to spend the night in a university dorm converted to a youth hostel for the summer. At 10 P.M., the boys tucked in, Martin and I headed for the showers down the hall. He dropped me off in front of the door decorated with a large, hand-lettered sign—Damar. Women. Frauen. Dames.—and went to the men's shower at the other end of the long corridor. As I groped for a light switch in the pitch black room, it struck me as odd that the lights were off at night in a public building. The room was dead silent, not even a faucet dripping. I walked past a row of sinks to the curtained shower stall closest to the window, where I could leave my clothes and towel on the sill.

"As I turned, naked, to step into the shower, a man wearing a bright blue track suit and blue running shoes shoved aside the curtain of a shower stall across the aisle and headed toward me. I began to scream in impeccable English, 'Get out! You're in the women's shower.' He kept on coming. My voice had the wrong words, the wrong language. I screamed again, now into his face, looming over mine as he hit me on the mouth. I screamed again, 'Get out!' as he hit me on the cheek. My mouth was cut, I could taste the salty blood as he hit me again in the head. I began to lose my balance. 'If he knocks me down on the tile,' I thought, 'he'll kill me.' Then I thought, still screaming, 'I don't want my children to hear this.'

"Then time slowed down, inside my head, the way it does just before you think your car is going to crash when it goes into a skid, and the voices, all mine, took over. One voice could say nothing at all for terror. I had never been hit before in my life. How could I know what to do? The man in blue, silent, continued to pummel my head, his face suffused with hatred, his eyes vacant. Another voice reasoned, 'I need to get my clothes and get out.' 'But to get my clothes I'll have to go past him twice.' 'I should just get out.' Still I couldn't move, the whirling blue arms continued to pound me. I was off balance now and afraid of falling. Then the angry message came, etched in adrenaline, 'I didn't ask for this, I don't deserve it, and I'm not going to take it.' I ran naked into the corridor."

The bell rang. "You're right," I said. "Oates's story is about violence, not love." The students, whose effervescent conversation usually bubbled out into the corridor as they dispersed, filed out in silence.

That was on a Thursday. The following Tuesday, an hour before our next class meeting, a student, svelte and usually poised, came into my office, crying. "What's the matter?" I asked. "Saturday night," she said, "I was walking home alone—I live alone—and heard the phone ringing in my apartment. When I rushed in to answer it I must have left the door open. Because after I'd hung up, when I went into the kitchen a man stepped out from behind the curtain, grabbed me from behind, and shoved a gasoline-soaked rag over my face. As he began to wrestle with me, he ripped my shirt trying to throw me down. Suddenly I heard your voice in my head, repeating the words you'd said in class, 'I didn't ask for this, I don't deserve it, and I'm not going to take it.' I ran, screaming, into the street and flagged a passing policeman. You saved my life."

"No," I said, "you saved your own life."

CODA

The computerized NCTE membership card says that my lifetime membership expires in 1999. As the date draws closer, I write headquarters about this. Several times, and still no answer.

I will have to raise my voice. My commitment to teaching English is, after all, for life.

NOTE

1. See also my essay "Hearing Our Own Voices: Life-Saving Stories" in *Writing Ourselves into the Story: Unheard Voices from Composition Studies,* ed. Sheryl I. Fontaine and Susan Hunter (Carbondale: Southern Illinois UP, 1992), 89–102.

34 *The Feminization of Rhetoric and Composition Studies?*

JANICE M. LAUER

Last year, I was invited to speak at a conference whose theme was the feminization of composition.[1] This topic coincided with another discussion I had been following in our journals: the emergence of Rhetoric and Composition as a scholarly field. In preparing my talk, I began to raise several questions like: What is meant by feminization in these discussions? Can we assume that composition is feminized? Are the discourses on disciplinary formation and on feminization already woven together? If not, should they be? This essay explores these questions, making distinctions and telling stories that offer an alternative perspective.

Let me begin with the feminization of composition. My rereading of many of these discussions[2] leads me to conclude that their statements about feminization apply largely to composition *instruction,* not to Rhetoric and Composition as a *scholarly field.*[3] The two reasons generally advanced are the numerical predominance of women and the nature of composition pedagogy. Accounts agree that women do most of the teaching of writing from the university level to elementary school as either full- or part-time instructors. Many descriptions of recent pedagogies maintain that instructional practices, particularly of expressive and critical pedagogies, are marks of feminization because they are collaborative, student centered, and nurturing. A few, however, dissent. Susan Jarratt and Evelyn Ashton-Jones, for example, problematize collaboration as a desirable feminine pedagogy. Lil Brannon contends that the expressivists and people like Giroux, Shor, Freire, and Rose are reinscribing patriarchy by invoking masculine heroic narratives of conquest as traditional male Romantic heroes who, like the rugged individual in the Dead Poet's Society, work against all odds to make a difference.

Some historical accounts of nineteenth-century composition position it as feminized in contrast to rhetorical instruction and the emerging professionalization of English Studies. Robert Connors argues that the demise of agonistic rhetorical instruction in persuasive public discourse, which he contends had

From *Rhetoric Review* 13 (1995): 276–86.

largely characterized male education up through 1850, was related to the entrance of significant numbers of women into higher education in the nineteenth century. These women were excluded from taking oral rhetoric and assigned to a more "appropriate" course called composition. He goes on to illustrate that this course gradually introduced important changes: moving from challenging and judgmental student-teacher relationships to those that were nurturing and personalized, from oral rhetoric to writing, from argument to a multimodal focus that privileged explanation, and from abstract, distanced subjects to more personal assignments (6).

But this early feminization of composition instruction was not characteristic of the disciplinary formation of English Studies, which was occurring during this same period. As Holbrook has explained, English Studies became professionalized through a process of dissociating from feminine culture by making itself a body of scientific knowledge constructed by specialists, distancing itself from feminized composition instruction and the preponderance of women teaching at the secondary and elementary levels. She reports that starting in the 1880s through the next 80 years, English Studies emphasized the ascending power of the PhD and the primacy of scholar-training over teacher-training in English graduate programs. Men were recruited to college teaching, and efforts were made to change the image of English professors away from that of "unproductive" or unnatural men. During this period women experienced difficulty in finding places within the crystallizing English Studies. Holbrook documents that men receiving PhDs in English jumped from 68 in 1930 to a high of 1,476 in 1941, whereas the number of women rose from 28 in 1930 to only 44 in 1941 as English Studies strove to make itself a science ("Manful Enterprise" 26).

This masculine *ethos* of English Studies was matched by its graduate pedagogy. Don Stewart depicts George Kittridge, the Harvard English Department's emperor, as arrogant and bullying, with a pedagogy described later by Francis Child as "turning doctoral dissertations into a device for killing the last spark of sensibility in the future teacher of literature and for sending out clones to dominate English departments across the country" (64). Although Stewart points to exceptions like Fred Newton Scott, he doesn't refute the dominance of the Kittridge pedagogy. In my graduate literature courses in the sixties at the University of Michigan, the feminine wasn't palpable either. The smart tactic for breaking into publication was to ridicule or demolish the interpretations of others, a practice true also in linguistics, where the structuralists were in mortal combat with the transformationalists. This was the academic context in which Rhetoric and Composition began to form as a scholarly field. Did it resist this *ethos*?

To address this question, I will consider several accounts of our disciplinary formation, asking whether these narratives of our development have been tales of feminization. The first is North's important account, which describes early research in Rhetoric and Composition as a methodological landrush, in which group after group of investigators "scrambled to make their claim to a portion of what they have perceived to be essentially virgin territory" (23). Far from feminization, these metaphors reek of competition, territoriality, border disputes, and conquest. A second version of the field's origins can be found in citation histories. An example is a recent *CCC* essay titled "*College Composition and Communication:* Chronicling a Discipline's Genesis" by Phillips, Greenberg, and Gibson that, while offering a valuable construction of the field's intertextuality, nevertheless is limited to textual evidence and hence does not support feminization, as I will explain below. A third narrative, told by Nystrand, Greene, and Wiemelt, in "Where Did Composition Studies Come From? An Intellectual History," contends that a true academic community emerged only when empirical research on the composing process, especially by Flower and Hayes, married (their metaphor) theoretical conceptions. The authors present important insights into the relationship between the emerging Composition Studies and larger epistemological changes in criticism and linguistics, as these fields moved from formalism through the structuralist lens of social-construction to dialogism. But their interpretation of the field's beginning relies only on a study of texts, ignores gender, and even occasionally misrepresents some developments. For example, the authors state that Corbett's book, *Classical Rhetoric for the Modern Student*, published in 1965, "motivated a number of writing teachers to reassess the value of teaching rhetorical invention as a means of guiding students' thinking" (278). This imaginative reconstruction of the field's early research on invention makes a subtle move, characterizing interest in rhetorical invention as pedagogical and sweeping inventional theorists (including a few women) into an anonymous group of "writing teachers." My own experience differs. When I began my dissertation on invention in contemporary rhetoric at the University of Michigan in 1964, I was not motivated to do so by Corbett's book but rather by an intellectual curiosity about the state of rhetorical invention in composition and an interest in new studies of heuristics. Further, I was not part of a group of nameless writing instructors doing so.

In a fourth version of the field's development, *Textual Carnivals*, Susan Miller, when speaking of composition studies, interprets the field's choice of the phrase *process paradigm* to a sense of blurred identity instead of to an androgyny that would have given equal privilege to the two terms. As the field formed, she maintains, it used the term to associate itself with the scientific, the "harder disciplines," distancing the field from soft, unorganized theories of composition and thereby producing a new grotesque (140–41). In "The Feminization of Composition," Miller urges a cautious critique of efforts to define the field as an academically equal partner in English departments. She warns of tacit cooperation with hegemonic superstructural values that she believes lurk in efforts to maintain an intellectual continuity with ancient rhetoric.

The last representation of the field's development that I will mention here is Beth Flynn's two articles on "Composing as a Woman." In her first essay, Flynn starts by calling the field feminized because it "changed the conception of how writers write and how writing should be taught," a conception she attributes to both women and men (423). But she concludes: "For the most part, the fields of feminist study and composition studies have not engaged each other in serious ways" (425). In the second essay two years later, she contends that "much of the theoretical work upon which composition theory has been built was done by men . . . and too often that work has been appropriated by women composition specialists without a critique of its androcentrism" (88). While both essays argue for introducing feminist inquiry in all its rich complexity into composition research in the future, they also thereby express misgivings about the feminization of Composition Studies in the past and present.

Because all these versions of the development of the field of Rhetoric and Composition are based on considerations of the field's scholarship, they imply that at some mysterious moment a critical mass of publications rose up like talking heads and magically transformed into a scholarly field an enterprise that was viewed at the time as a service of dubious intellectual value. This focus only on publications makes the claim for feminization problematic because women haven't dominated publishing in composition. Theresa Enos's article, "Gender and Journals, Conservers or Innovators," surveys twelve of our journals, showing that men outnumber women as authors of articles except in two journals, *Basic Writing* and *The Writing Instructor*. Sue Ellen Holbrook, in "Women's Work: The Feminizing of Composition," reports that her 1986 analysis of Larson's bibliography showed that 66% of the authors were men and 34% were women, that in one year of *College English*, 65% of articles selected were by men while 33% were by women, and that in Weaver's *WPA* bibliography, 85% of the professional books were by men and 15% by women. She interprets these counts to mean that men have been the preeminent makers of knowledge in composition ("Women's Work" 210–11).

A counterargument might advance that even though men numerically dominate publishing, certain women's scholarship has been more theoretically fecund than that of men. But pursuing this line of reasoning risks promoting a kind of female tokenism or affirmative action which, as Barbara Bieseker notes, underhandedly affirms a cultural supremacy for a few women but devalues collective rhetorical practices (156–57). Another countertactic might be to demonstrate that doctoral programs in Rhetoric and Composition have enrolled more women than men. But we don't have that information. Neither the 1986 MLA report, Chapman and Tate's survey, nor the *Rhetoric Review*'s recent overview of doctoral programs considers gender.

So instead of turning to fecund influence or the number of doctoral students, I will offer here a supplement to the above accounts of the field's development by telling stories of my own experience with that formation. My stories will speak about the field's body—concrete events, individual efforts, and social interactions—that helped the field's professionalization. Like the body, these efforts have been taken for granted, unvoiced in our disciplinary accounts. As a genre, my stories might be dignified as synchronic history, which ethnographic historians argue can heighten awareness of informal or small-scale interactions that express important linkages and conclusions (Ervin 87), but because of space constraints, I can't provide the thick description that more rigorous ethnography requires. My anecdotes might also be called a kind of oral history that tells of activities largely occluded in the discursive histories of our field. Or one might end up calling these narrative renderings "unreconstructed essentialism," naive accounts, uncritically theorized and relying on personal authority. I'll let the reader position them.

Because in composition, the term *feminization* appears to mean the *dominance* or *predominance* of women, I will forgo this term and, at the risk of essentialism,[4] will foreground some "feminine" traits that have been "deliberately chosen and enacted critically by women and men, not essentialized features derived from marginalization or oppression" (Phelps 2). These traits have often been named as feminine:

- cooperative, relational, interdependent, and collaborative
- releasing in others their unexplored resources and transformative power
- viewing development as a web
- caring for another's development
- suffused with desire and joy

I will also speak of actions that bear three of Holbrook's features of women's work: service oriented, less well paid than men's work, and often devalued ("Women's Work" 202).

My first story revisions the emergence of the field as an act of conquering territory for ownership, replacing it with the metaphor of working together to clear space for sharing. The sense of an emerging field began for me as a growing social network, a web of friendship. In 1968 at the CCCC in Minneapolis, I attended an organizational meeting of the Rhetoric Society of America. At this meeting people from speech communication, philosophy, and English convened to form a society that would foster a resurgence of interest in rhetoric. At subsequent CCCC meetings, a few Rhetoric Society members met informally as a small special-interest group. One year in the early seventies (the date escapes me), a subgroup of us went out to dinner after our informal RSA meeting and continued to do so for several years. The regular members of this dinner group were Ed Corbett, Ross and Norma Winterowd, George and Mary Yoos, Richard Young, and me. While I don't remember our specific conversations over wine and salmon, I do recall that we discussed and dreamed about a serious field devoted to the study of written discourse. And we had fun; we became friends. I returned home each year with a sense of connection, a feeling of shared dedication to studying writing and to connecting rhetoric to composition. This group became a sustaining force, isolated as most of us were in English departments uninterested in rhetoric and disdainful of composition. Although the term *discourse community* would come much later, as I look back, one was forming. Was this a gendered experience? Of the Rhetoric Society members at these dinners, I was the only woman, but I felt no barriers.[5] I don't recall pieces of virgin land being auctioned or claims being staked. Nor were our conversations exercises in one-upmanship. Instead we traded stories about our adventures as local pariahs, and we shared ideas about writing.

And back at home in our institutions, we started to formalize the *study* of rhetoric and composition theory. Ed Corbett introduced rhetoric courses at Ohio State and directed a few composition dissertations (e.g., Andrea Lunsford's), while Richard Young began teaching courses in composition theory at the University of Michigan and directed some dissertations (e.g., Lee Odell's). Ross Winterowd started courses in rhetoric and literacy at the University of Southern California, while I developed courses in composition theory at Marygrove College and the University of Detroit and directed a rhetoric dissertation (James Porter's). From my perspective now, these predisciplinary acts seem pretty gutsy because they boldly positioned composition theory as appropriate subject matter for graduate study and, more importantly, they began to enlarge the web, introducing others into a community that was in its earliest phase of disciplinary formation.

Subsequently, some of that dinner group went on to construct doctoral programs: Ross Winterowd in 1975 at the University of Southern California, Richard Young in 1980 at Carnegie Mellon, and I in 1980 at Purdue.[6] Although the existence of these programs is now often taken for granted, I would argue that their formation helped construct Rhetoric and Composition as a scholarly field. And far from being acts of professional aggrandizement, the founding of these programs was fraught with political risks and challenges for the developers.

Other episodes in the formation of Rhetoric and Composition as a field were the summer and year-long NEH seminars, such as the one offered in 1978 by Richard Young, which introduced to Rhetoric and Composition a number of future theorists like James Berlin and Victor Vitanza. And in 1976 I started a summer two-week rhetoric seminar that was repeated for 13 years, first at the University of Detroit and then at Purdue. This educational context helped satisfy a growing desire and need for rhetoric and composition theory in the profession, drawing together some of the leading composition theorists and fifty to sixty interested English instructors each summer.[7] The experience of many of the participants who sought an understanding of this new field is voiced by one participant's evaluation of the seminar: "I came to see that rhetoric is a rich, varied, philosophical field that interests me as theory and as the basis for teaching composition. I never before was aware of its dimensions, its political, social, and cultural implications; nor its history."

The work of conducting these summer rhetoric seminars, the NEH seminars, and the doctoral programs strikes me as "feminine," helping to release in others unexplored resources and transformative power. And like casting stones into ponds, the initial efforts of these developers only multiplied into further responsibilities for them, like directing large numbers of dissertations, writing numerous letters of recommendation, and reviewing scores of people for promotion and tenure. Ed Corbett confided to me one time that he had written over 300 letters of recommendation that semester. Like women's work, these acts of program development, dissertation direction, and letters of recommendation are seldom highly rewarded by salary increases or lightened faculty loads. In my department, for example, no release time has been given for graduate program direction or for dissertation guidance, which on average entails our working with 35 dissertations in a given semester, a number several times higher than in literary studies.

Beyond these stories of program and seminar development, there are other disciplinary acts that continue the tale of the feminine. The first is bibliographic. While literary studies relies on the PMLA annual bibliography, in our field someone had to undertake that service. Women stepped forth to do it: in 1980 Win Horner published *Historical Rhetoric: An Annotated Bibliography of Selected Sources in English* and its two subsequent updating volumes, *The Present State of Scholarship in Historical and Contemporary Rhetoric.* In 1987 Erika Lindemann fought for the publication of the *Longman Bibliography of Composition and Rhetoric* and labored through five subsequent volumes as it changed to the *CCCC Bibliography of Composition and Rhetoric.* Now this important work is being done by two other women, Gail Hawisher and Cindy Selfe. Further, these bibliographic efforts have been collaborative, products of the whole field. Not to be ignored are the bibliographies in the *CCC* and *RTE,* done by Richard Larson over the years, and those in the *Rhetoric Society Quarterly* provided by George Yoos for over 20 years. These acts of service are crucial to disciplinary formation but engender little enthusiasm in departmental promotion and tenure committees.

In this same supportive category is journal and encyclopedia editing. Strong examples include Theresa Enos's founding of *Rhetoric Review,* George Yoos's long editorship of *Rhetoric Society Quarterly,* Victor Vitanza's efforts with *PRE/ TEXT,* and Stephen Witte and John Daly's initiation of *Written Communication.* The two encyclopedias—the *Encyclopedia of Rhetoric,* initiated and edited by Theresa Enos, and the Composition/Rhetoric portion of the *Encyclopedia of English Studies and Language Arts,* coordinated by me—provide outsiders and members of our field with collaboratively constructed accounts of the complex dimensions of teaching and studying rhetoric and composition. Yet such editorial work is rarely positioned high on the merit totem pole of the university.

All of these stories make a case, I would submit, that "feminine" acts by women and men have played a significant role in shaping the field, particularly from the sixties to the mid-eighties. But what about today? Has the field changed? In a earlier essay of mine, "Composition Studies: Dappled Discipline," I described the field as "permeated with a sense of community in which new work attempted to build on previous studies rather than to ridicule or demolish them" (27). I contended that "unlike the slaughter in some fields in which proponents of one persuasion struggled in mortal combat with those of another and unlike more covert warfare in which newcomers carved out niches for themselves by enlarging loopholes in previous work, composition scholars huddled together in the face of tidal waves of problems whose solutions demanded collaboration" (27–28). I called this a comedic tone in Lynch's terms, a "descent into the actual contours, the interstices, the smells of the beastie [wo]man" (28), into the dappledness of classrooms, literacy sites, workplaces, political forums. Today I might call this the world of the body, desire, pleasure, self-mockery, and care. Do these terms represent the tone today? Would I now speak of feminine traits? Not as readily.

There's a good bit of agon, ridicule, and displacement that bloodies our discourse. But the need for huddling together in the face of tidal waves of problems has not disappeared. While we throw more and more sand at each other, literacy research and composition instruction are in danger of drowning. Just two examples.[8] A few years ago, Phyllis Franklin told me that she had spent quite a bit of time interesting the Ford Foundation in funding literacy research. But when she drew some Ford representatives to a meeting with composition theorists and researchers, the composition people started bickering among themselves and the Ford group withdrew. More recently, Richard Larson's reports of the state of composition programs in the US paint a bleak picture in spite of decades of theory and research. Could it be that these programs stick to their safe current-traditional teaching in the face of baffling or off-putting conflicts?

Yet even as our internal quarrels escalate, through this agonistic fog, I glimpse some theorists, researchers, and editors still building networks and bridges instead of ideological fortresses. I see people continuing to construct educational contexts to empower others. These feminine traces strike me as converging into one of the new directions of postmodernism. Berry and Wernick note that some theologians and feminists like Irigaray are offering a new understanding of spirit, not as transcendent, not as the binary opposite of *body*, but as an insistence upon the bodily dimension of knowledge and the consequent "attainment of a new capacity for ethical action—whether this is described in terms of love, compassion, altruism or care" (4–5). Wyschogrod calls this new mode of existence "a postmodern expression of excessive desire, a desire on behalf of the Other" (5). Will this mode of existence prevail in rhetoric and composition studies? I hope so.

NOTES

For helpful responses to this essay, I wish to thank Janet Atwill and my two *RR* reviewers, Sharon Crowley and Lynn Bloom.

1. The annual conference sponsored by the University of Southern California's doctoral program in Rhetoric, Linguistics, and Literacy.

2. See, for example, Bauer; Flynn; Holbrook; Eichhorn et al.; Ervin; Hollis; Hunter; Miller; Osborn.

3. The distinction I make here in no way implies a hierarchical binary between composition as instruction and as scholarship. Nor do I think that these two senses of composition are unrelated: I have written elsewhere about the strong relationship between Composition Studies and writing instruction. But I do maintain that the two are not synonymous. Composition instruction had gone on for centuries before Rhetoric and Composition found an academic position as a scholarly discipline.

4. In her examination of the problem of essentialism, Diana Fuss keynotes her book with the following statement: "In and of itself essentialism is neither good nor bad, progressive nor reactionary, beneficial or dangerous. The question we should be asking is not 'is this text essentialist' (and therefore "bad")? but rather, 'if this text is essentialist, *what motivates its deployment?*'" (xi). She ends the book, saying that "'Essentially speaking,' we need both to theorize essentialist spaces

from which to speak and simultaneously to deconstruct these spaces to keep them from solidifying. Such a double gesture involves once again the responsibility to historicize, to examine each deployment of essence, each appeal to experience, each claim to identity in the complicated contextual frame in which it is made" (118).

5. Within the Rhetoric Society as a whole, however, women were a distinct minority. At the organizational meeting, I recall being the only woman. The first Board of Directors in 1968 had 17 men including Wayne Booth, William Irmscher, Henry Johnstone, Richard Larson, Ross Winterowd, Ed Corbett, and Donald Bryant (*Rhetoric Society Newsletter* 1). Only later did women take leadership roles, not from the ranks of speech communication or philosophy, but from the composition contingent of the RSA. In 1975 Dorothy Guinn, then a doctoral student in Rhetoric, Linguistics, and Literacy at the University of Southern California, was elected as a student member to the Board of Directors, and in 1976 I was elected. Dorothy and I continued on the Board as the only women until 1981, when I was reelected and joined by Win Homer and Honora Rocker from Carnegie Mellon; then in 1982 Lynn Worsham, a student member from the University of Texas at Arlington, was elected, followed in 1986 by Andrea Lunsford and Lisa Ede.

6. In telling this local story, I don't mean to imply that these were the only people developing doctoral programs or offering courses and seminars at this time. Certainly there were others like Joseph Comprone, Janet Emig, and James Kinneavy.

7. The faculty of the seminar were eight composition theorists each summer, including over the years Jim Berlin, Edward Corbett, Janet Emig, Linda Flower, James Kinneavy, Andrea Lunsford, Louis Milic, James Moffen, Gene Montague, Frank O'Hare, Walter Ong, Louise Phelps, Gordon Rohman, Ross Winterowd (who codirected the first seminar with me), and Richard Young. The participants were men and women from every state in the US and from Canada, with teaching experience ranging from thirty years to none: instructors, departmental chairs, deans, a vice-president; literary scholars, linguists, psychologists, and philosophers. They worked in large universities, regional colleges, community colleges, high schools, and elementary schools; in urban and rural schools, and on a reservation.

8. I am not hoping here for a mode of existence without any conflict, argument, or ideological differences—all are marks of a dynamic and growing field. I am talking about a tone of respect, a tolerant mode of professional interaction that does not demonize the "other."

WORKS CITED

Ashton-Jones, Evelyn. "Collaboration, Conversation, and the Politics of Gender." *Feminine Principles and Women's Experience in American Composition and Rhetoric.* Ed. Louise Wetherbee Phelps and Janet Emig. Pittsburgh: U of Pittsburgh P, 1995. 5–26.

Bauer, Dale. "The Other 'F' Word: The Feminist in the Classroom." *College English* 52 (1990): 385–86.

Berry, Phillipa, and Andrew Ernick, eds. *Shadow of Spirit: Postmodernism and Religion.* London: Routledge, 1992.

Bieseker, Barbara. "Coming to Terms with Recent Attempts to Write Women in the History of Rhetoric." *Rethinking the History of Rhetoric.* Ed. Takis Poulakos. Boulder, CO: Westview, 1993. 153–72.

Brannon, Lil. "M[Other]: Lives on the Outside." *Written Communication* 10 (1993): 457–65.

Chapman, David, and Gary Tate. "A Survey of Doctoral Programs in Rhetoric and Composition." *Rhetoric Review* 5 (1987): 1–3.

Connors, Robert J. "Women's Reclamation of Rhetoric in Nineteenth-Century America." *Feminine Principles and Women's Experience in American Composition and Rhetoric.* Ed. Louise Wetherbee Phelps and Janet Emig. Pittsburgh: U of Pittsburgh P, 1995. 67–90.

"Doctoral Programs in English." *Rhetoric Review* Special Issue 12 (1994).

Eichhorn, Jill, Sara Farris, Karen Hayes, Adriana Hernandez, Susan Jarratt, Karen Power-Stubbs, and Marian M. Sciachitano. "A Symposium on Feminist Experiences in the Classroom." *College Composition and Communication* 43 (1992): 297–322.

Encyclopedia of Rhetoric and Composition: Communication from Ancient Times to the Information Age. Ed. Theresa Enos. New York: Garland, 1996.

Encyclopedia of English Studies and Language Arts. General Ed. Alan Purves. Scholastic, 1994.

Enos, Theresa. "Gender and Journals, Conservers or Innovators." *PRE/TEXT* 9 (1990): 209–14.

Ervin, Elizabeth. "Interdisciplinarity or 'An Elaborate Edifice Built on Sand'?: Rethinking Rhetoric's Place." *Rhetoric Review* 12 (1993): 84–107.

Flynn, Elizabeth. "Composing as a Woman." *College Composition and Communication* 39 (1988): 423–35.

———. "Composing 'Composing as a Woman'": A Perspective on Research." *College Composition and Communication* 41 (1990): 83–89.

Fuss, Diana. *Essentially Speaking: Feminism, Nature, and Difference.* New York: Routledge, 1989.

Hawisher, Gail, and Cindy Selfe, eds. *CCCC Bibliography on Composition and Rhetoric.* 1991; 1992. Carbondale: Southern Illinois UP, 1993–1994.

Holbrook, Sue Ellen. "Manful Enterprise, Feminine Subject: Expressions of Gender in the History of Composition 1880–1950." Unpublished manuscript, 1990.

———. "Women's Work: The Feminizing of Composition." *Rhetoric Review* 9 (1991): 201–29.

Hollis, Karyn. "Feminism in Writing Workshops: A New Pedagogy." *College Composition and Communication* 43 (1992): 340–48.

Horner, Winifred, ed. *The Present State of Scholarship in Historical and Contemporary Rhetoric.* Columbia: U of Missouri P, 1983 and 1991.

———. *Historical Rhetoric: An Annotated Bibliography of Selected Sources in English.* Boston: Hall, 1980.

Huber, Bettina. "Appendix: A Report on the 1986 Survey of English Doctoral Programs in Writing and Literature." *The Future of Doctoral Studies in English.* Ed. Andrea Lunsford, Helene Moglin, and James Slevin. New York: MLA, 1989. 121–75.

Hunter, Susan. "A Woman's Place *Is* in the Classroom." *Rhetoric Review* 9 (1991): 230–45.

Jarratt, Susan. "Feminism and Composition: The Case for Conflict." *Contending with Words.* Ed. Patricia Harkin and John Schilb. New York: MLA, 1991. 105–23.

Larson, Richard. "Classes of Discourse, Acts of Discourse, Writers and Readers." *English Journal* 81 (1992): 32–36.

Lauer, Janice M. "Composition Studies: Dappled Discipline." *Rhetoric Review* 3 (1984): 20–29.

Lindemann, Erika, ed. *CCCC Bibliography on Composition and Rhetoric.* 1987; 1988; 1989; 1990. Carbondale: Southern Illinois UP, 1990–1992.

———. *Longman Bibliography of Composition and Rhetoric.* 1984–85; 1986. New York: Longman, 1987–88.

Miller, Susan. "The Feminization of Composition." *The Politics of Writing Instruction: Postsecondary.* Ed. Richard Bullock and John Trimbur. Portsmouth, NH: Boynton/Cook, 1991. 39–53.

———. *Textual Carnivals.* Carbondale: Southern Illinois UP, 1991.

North, Stephen. "Composition Becomes Composition." *The Making of Knowledge in Composition: Portrait of an Emerging Field.* Upper Montclair, NJ: Boynton/Cook, 1987. 9–17.

Nystrand, Martin, Stuart Greene, and Jeffrey Wiemelt. "Where Did Composition Studies Come From?" *Written Communication* 10 (1993): 267–333.

Osborn, Susan. "Revision/Re-Vision." *Rhetoric Review* 9 (1991): 258–73.

Phelps, Louise Wetherbee, with Janet Emig. "Editors' Reflections: Vision and Interpretation." *Feminine Principles and Women's Experience in American Composition and Rhetoric.* Pittsburgh: U of Pittsburgh P 1995. 407–25.

Phelps, Louise Wetherbee, and Janet Emig, eds. *Feminist Principles and Women's Experience in American Composition and Rhetoric.* Pittsburgh: U of Pittsburgh P, 1995.

Phillips, Donna, Ruth Greenberg, and Sharon Gibson. "*College Composition and Communication*: Chronicling a Discipline's Genesis." *College Composition and Communication* 44 (1993): 443–65.

The Rhetoric Society of America Newsletter 1 (December 1968): 1.

Stewart, Donald. "Collaborative Learning and Composition: Boon or Bane?" *Rhetoric Review* 7 (1988): 58–88.

Wyschogrod, Edith. *Saints and Postmodernism: Revisioning Moral Philosophy.* Chicago: U of Chicago P, 1990.

35 The Feminization of Composition: Questioning the Metaphors That Bind Women Teachers

EILEEN E. SCHELL

Over the past two decades, the field of composition has acquired the rather Janus-faced reputation of being "feminized," simultaneously welcoming the work of women while marginalizing them as part-time faculty, lecturers, and adjuncts. As Susan Miller notes, composition collects women "like bugs in a web," an apt simile for the current situation of female part-timers (39). Indeed, Sue Ellen Holbrook describes composition as a field "saturated by women practitioners, focused on pedagogy, allied with education departments and school teaching, conceived as having a 'service' and elementary place in the curriculum, and pervaded by paraprofessionalism" (211).

Hence, three important considerations keep the "feminization" metaphor alive for composition teachers. First, composition is regarded by many as a "service" course that teaches "skills." Second, composition has acquired the status of being "drudge" or apprentice work because it is labor intensive and low paying. Third, composition, with its reputation of being "service" oriented and unprofessional, has become the province of women part-timers, adjunct faculty, and graduate students with only a few tenured, full-time women faculty sprinkled in between.

Thus, the "feminization" metaphor has a double-edged meaning for women in composition, simultaneously signifying their presence as part-timers and adjuncts, while also signifying their absence in positions of power and influence. Yet "feminization" does not necessarily correspond with a move toward feminist positions. Instead, it defines the work of women composition teachers as both literally "female" and "feminized" in the pejorative sense. Donna Haraway's general definition of "feminized" provides a useful understanding of how "feminization" denotes marginalized status. To be "feminized" is to:

> be made extremely vulnerable; able to be disassembled, reassembled, exploited as a reserve labor force; seen less as workers than as servers;

From *Composition Studies/Freshman English News* 20 (1992): 55–61.

subjected to time arrangements on and off the paid job that make a mockery of a limited work day; leading an existence that always borders on being obscene, out of place, and reducible to sex. (Haraway 86)

For the past century, women have "feminized" the teaching profession (particularly in lower level and lower paid positions). As early as 1888, an investigator for the "Association for the Advancement of Women" declared that "67% of the teachers in the country were women"—a noticeable presence, yet along with that noticeable presence was a noticeable absence of women in positions of power—only 4% of those women occupied administrative positions" (Grumet 83). Women's entrance into the teaching profession corresponded with Horace Mann's emphasis on a pedagogy that fostered character training and moral development in pupils, the "proof of which must be the capacity for voluntary obedience to duty" (69). While Mann argued that female teachers were more suited to cultivating morality in their students, he also kept his eye on the fact that it was cheaper to hire women than men. For nineteenth-century women, teaching often meant taking low pay and accepting harsh working conditions under the guise of noble, maternal service. In *Mother/teacher,* a study of the feminization of American education, Redding Sugg writes: "The first profession opened to women consisted of the sale of sexual love and was called prostitution; the second, an initiative of nineteenth-century Americans, was a traffic in maternal love and was called pedagogy" (Preface).

While Sugg's analogy is extreme, he does point out the problems with exploitation endemic to the "feminized" field of teaching. Susan Miller describes the female composition teacher as having "qualities much like those of the mythologized mother: self-sacrifice, dedication, caring, and enormous capacities for untheorized attention to detail" (46). Women composition teachers continue to carry on the tradition of nurturing students, though not always unproblematically, as many have introduced feminist pedagogies as strategies of resistance and transformation. While feminist pedagogies resist patriarchal constructions of teachers, students, and the classroom, the metaphors commonly used to describe feminist teaching as "nurturing" and "mothering" risk being caught up in traditional inscriptions of the "feminine." The authors of "The Politics of Nurturance" state: "We are, inescapably, also [our students'] mothers—necessary for comfort, but reinforcing a feared and fearful dependency" (Culley et al. 14).

Unfortunately, constructing the female composition teacher as mother reinforces dominant culture's expectations for women as "natural" care-givers and nurturers. Furthermore, the image of the nurturing, sacrificing, mother/teacher is often held in opposition to the stereotype of the "arid, strident" feminist teacher. In the patriarchal economy of the university, feminist teaching is often regarded as the "locus of imbalance, fanaticism, [and] eccentricity" (Bauer 386). Overall, the stock images that depict women teachers as either nurturing mothers or fanatic feminists downplay the challenges that feminist teachers issue to their students. Adrienne Rich writes of these challenges as a refusal "to accept passive, obedient learning and insist upon critical thinking" (244). "We can become harder on our women students," she writes, "giving them the kinds of 'cultural prodding' that men receive, but on different terms and in a different style" (244). Feminist teachers can nurture their students, yet challenge them to think critically about their notions of gendered identity in the classroom and in the "world outside." Mediating the process between nurture and challenge, however, is a difficult task that leads to resistances and ambivalences among teachers and students. In "The Other 'F' Word: The Feminist in the Classroom," Dale Bauer argues that:

> each agent—whether teacher or student—is responsible as citizen for ethical choices, although those choices often involve contradictory positions. Because agency involves a complex intersection of historically conditioned practices, discourses, and customs or habits, choice is never unambivalent or easy or unmediated. (388)

In Bauer's description of the classroom, the feminist teacher is more aptly characterized as a mediator and facilitator instead of care-giving mother.

While feminist pedagogy provides a chance for composition teachers to challenge patriarchal ways of teaching writing, there is still the issue of inequity for women composition teachers. Like nineteenth-century schoolteachers, women composition teachers are still being paid less than their male counterparts and have fewer tenured positions. In 1980 two-thirds (approximately 64%) of the women in English departments (many of them composition teachers) were instructors, lecturers, or assistant professors (Holbrook 208). Furthermore, there is still a significant inequity in the number of articles published by women in the journals that shape composition studies, publication being the primary way institutions reward tenure, salary increases, release time, and travel money. Theresa Enos's 1988 mini-study on the number of females published as opposed to the number of males published in journals— such as *College English, CCC, Pre/Text,* and *Rhetoric Review*—demonstrates that men are more likely to be published despite the fact that they are a "minority" group in Rhetoric and Composition (213). These statistics should come as no surprise. The large number of unpublished, hence untenured, part-time women composition teachers corresponds to deeply ingrained social and economic traditions that have designated teaching as women's work.

Moreover, teaching composition is still regarded in many circles as a sort of English department "housework" in which women "tidy up" student essays with painstaking, careful commentary and hours devoted to students in one-on-one conferencing. Meryl Altman further unpacks the "composition as housework" metaphor with a series of specific associations. Composition, she writes, "carries low professional status; [and] in many places . . . doesn't really count as professional work at all (it is done by adjunct faculty and graduate students)" (501). In addition, teaching composition "is a task overwhelmingly performed by women; this is a national fact and problem, which no one in power talks about very much" (501). Hence, part-time composition teachers have much in common with the proverbial housewife who contributes greatly to the running of the household (or the university) but gets no actual recognition for it (e.g., tenure, salary increases, office space, resources).

As a "refugee" from the part-time, community college circuit, I am well acquainted with the feelings of disassociation and frustration that come from having an uncertain professional future. Part of what drove me from part-time composition teaching back to graduate school was not only the working conditions and low pay, but the fact that I felt too fragmented, alone, and cut off from conversations with my colleagues. All I had to do was look around me at the community college I worked at and I knew, by a quick head-count, that women were the shoestring part-timers and "freeway fliers" who traveled interstate I-5 daily, stopping to teach class after class at respective community colleges.

Now that I've returned to graduate school, I'm often told by my male counterparts that the fact that I am a woman and a feminist, combined with my Ph.D. in Rhetoric and Composition, will guarantee me a job and success. As one earnest male colleague bound for the MLA said, "I wish I was a woman this year. You women have it made—no one wants to hire white males." Behind that comment stands the misconception that being a "marketable" woman and being hired will lead to success, publications, promotion, recognition. The story remains only half-told. Admittance to a male-centered institutional hierarchy does not guarantee success. Once women are "in the door," the real difficulty begins. Sexual harassment, male professors who mentor then marry or have affairs with their female graduate students, inequity of pay and promotion are realities in institutions that are powered by men and staffed by women. As Adrienne Rich states:

> The university is above all a hierarchy. At the top is a small cluster of highly paid and prestigious persons, chiefly men, whose careers entail the services of a very large base of ill-paid or unpaid persons, chiefly women: wives, research assistants, secretaries, teaching assistants, cleaning women, waitresses in the faculty club, lower-echelon administrators, and women students who are used in various ways to gratify the ego. (136)

In this age of "post-feminist" thought, the social and economic issues at stake for women in composition are often ignored. Part of a challenge to feminist consciousness and feminist teaching seems to have been spurred by the postmodern emphasis on metaphors of the "feminine." French theorists such as Deleuze, Derrida, Lacan, and Lyotard have used the "feminine" to signify that which is outside the Cartesian subject. Thus, "woman" is used to signify a break or rupture with enlightenment values like Truth and Reason (the "feminine" becomes "untruth" and a turn away from reason). Elspeth Probyn further describes the postmodern use of "feminine" metaphors as an encoding process in which women, or impossible representations of them, serve as "images without referents, bits of the feminine manufactured in the media simulacrum. As such, they are essentially unconnected, not only to each other, but also to any political position" (35). One glaring example of this phenomenon occurs in critical discourse where it has become common for male theorists to adopt metaphors of the "feminine" as metaphors for reading, writing, and teaching. We have deconstructionist Jonathon Culler reading as a woman, Jacques Derrida writing as a woman, and male compositionists celebrating a "feminine" pedagogical style. This feminine metaphor "mania," in many cases, serves as a sort of linguistic version of the invasion of the "body snatchers." As Alice Jardine states: "To accept a metaphorization, a semiosis of woman . . . means risking once again the absence of women as subjects" (37).

Exploring how metaphors of the "feminine" operate is crucial to understanding how the symbolic functions in maintaining the oppression of women's material and social bodies. While it would seem that metaphors of the "feminine" put women into discourse, in actuality, these metaphors serve to reinforce traditionally inscribed feminine values within a patriarchal context. One obvious example is the time-worn maxim that women teachers are "naturally" more nurturing than male teachers and thus more willing to accept a "psychic income" as compensation for heavy teaching loads and stacks of freshman essays. In addition, this attitude leads to the widespread belief that the "feminization" of composition (the sheer number of women in the field) means that composition is a field heavily influenced by feminism, a field where feminists can flourish. Elizabeth Flynn counters that argument, stating that "the fields of feminist studies and composition studies have not engaged each other in a serious or systematic way" (425).

Since 1988, the feminist work of Flynn herself, Dale Bauer, Susan Jarratt, Susan Miller, Joy Ritchie, and others has provided a context in which feminists have posed questions. This work is the beginning of a dialogue about the "place" and "mission" of feminism in composition studies. This dialogue, however, is limited to those who have access to study groups, scholarly journals, and those who have time for reflection upon methodologies, goals, and directions. There are many women writing teachers who are part-time, scrambling to teach and grade papers as well as negotiating other obligations, chiefly home, family, and other employment. How can these women's voices and experiences be recognized?

One hopeful area for recognition of part-time women composition teachers is through the writing of feminist histories of the field that highlight the working conditions and experiences of part-time women faculty. Susan Miller's "The Feminization of Composition," Sue Ellen Holbrook's "Women's Work: The Feminizing of Composition," and Sharon Crowley's "Three Heroines: An Oral History" are valuable histories—or "herstories"—of the "feminization" of composition. Feminists in composition studies need to write more histories like these, histories that fill in the blanks that James Berlin, Stephen North, and other composition historians have left out in the parades of names, dates, and definitions of discourse communities. As Adrienne Rich writes: "Our history is the history of the majority of the species, yet the struggles of women for a 'human' status have been relegated to the footnotes, to the sidelines" (204). Many who are now graduate students and junior and senior faculty in composition studies have their professional beginnings in part-time composition teaching. Many will never forget the feeling of being fragmented, jumbled between multiple teaching jobs. Many are still in those very positions.

As composition studies continues to define itself as a profession, it is important that women's voices be heard—the voices of not only the full-time women faculty who have "made it," but women composition teachers who are struggling with difficult working conditions. Feminist compositionists need to question the metaphors that bind them as "mythologized mother/ teachers" and ask themselves to what extent they are being absenced by those metaphors. Through analyzing the way women composition teachers are constructed materially and metaphorically, and through writing the histories of women in our field, we can chip away at the grand master-narrative that has kept women in composition in a "feminized" position.

WORKS CITED

Altman, Meryl. "How Not To Do Things With Metaphors We Live By." *College English* 52 (1990): 495–506.

Bauer, Dale. "The Other 'F' Word: The Feminist in the Classroom." *College English* 52 (1990): 385–96.

Crowley, Sharon. "Three Heroines: An Oral History." *Pre/Text* (Fall/Winter 1988): 202–6.

Culley, Margo, et al. "The Politics of Nurturance." *Gendered Subjects: The Dynamics of Feminist Teaching.* Ed. Margo Culley and Catherine Portugues. Boston: Routledge, 1985. 11–20.

Enos, Theresa. "Gender and Journals, Conservers or Innovators." *Pre/Text* (Fall/Winter 1988): 209–17.

Flynn, Elizabeth. "Composing as a Woman." *College Composition and Communication* 39 (1988): 423–35.

Grumet, Madeleine. *Bittermilk: Women and Teaching.* Amherst: U of Massachusetts P, 1988.

Haraway, Donna. "A Manifesto for Cyborgs: Science, Technology, and Social Feminism in the 1980s." *Socialist Review* 14.2 (1985): 65–107.

Holbrook, Sue Ellen. "Women's Work: The Feminizing of Composition." *Rhetoric Review* 9.2 (1991): 201–29.

Jardine, Alice A. *Gynesis.* Ithaca: Cornell UP, 1985.

Miller, Susan. "The Feminization of Composition." *The Politics of Writing Instruction: Postsecondary.* Ed. Richard Bullock and John Trimbur. Gen. Ed. Charles Schuster. Portsmouth: Boynton/ Cook, 1991. 39–53.

Probyn, Elspeth. "Bodies and Anti-Bodies: Feminism and the Postmodern." *Cultural Studies* 1.3 (1987): 349–60.

Rich, Adrienne. *On Lies, Secrets, and Silence: Selected Prose.* New York: Norton, 1979.

Sugg, Redding S., Jr. *Mother/teacher: The Feminization of American Education.* Charlottesville: UP of Virginia, 1978.

36

Gender and Publishing Scholarship in Rhetoric and Composition

THERESA ENOS

Because women comprise the majority in rhetoric and composition, the field is often called a "feminized field." Disciplines where women excel—and are acknowledged—are devalued. A field where women are recognized as being highly competent and where they make up the majority generally has lower prestige, is taken less seriously, and is devalued because its work is seen as "women's work." Women's work is characterized by a disproportionate number of women workers (as in the academy's writing programs), it is service oriented (like the teaching of writing in the classrooms of institutions of higher education), it pays less than "men's work" (traditional forms of scholarship), and it is devalued (compared to males, females get fewer promotions and less pay). Thus, males as well as females in a feminized field suffer from salary compression and horizontal rather than upward "promotions."

Indeed, research shows that women are now the majority of tenure-track writing faculty in higher education. If we consider all college writing faculty (eighty percent of our part-time teachers and lecturers are female), we've had a majority of women for some time. And we know that 1987 was the watershed year for female rhetoric and composition hires in tenure-track positions. Of all job candidates holding degrees in rhetoric and composition that year, seventy percent were female. And information taken from the *MLA Job Information List* and a follow-up survey published in the *ADE Bulletin* show that of all candidates hired in rhetoric and composition that year, sixty-six percent were female; we know, therefore, that women are hired in proportion to their representation in the candidate pool. In doctoral programs housed in research universities, males comprise fifty-seven percent of the writing faculty, but, overall, women make up the majority of both faculty and students in rhetoric and composition. (For the survey data and their origin, see Enos, *Faculty*.) What's more, women in 1980 made up sixty-five percent of the participation

From *Publishing in Rhetoric and Composition*. Ed. Gary Olson and Todd Taylor. Albany: SUNY, 1997. 57–74.

in the NCTE College Section in contrast to forty-five percent in MLA. And in 1994, sixty-three percent of the CCCC program participants were women.

Like nursing, library science, and some areas of education, then, more women than men work in rhetoric and composition. Unlike these other disciplines, however, impressions from available data suggest that women who teach writing at the college level are under-compensated in terms of status and pay compared to their male counterparts. Some of these questions have been explored recently by Janice Lauer, who offers an alternative perspective to other discussions on the feminization of the field. Lauer's essay is an insightful critique of several "readings" of our history that make claims about the feminization of the field. In both her critique and her own story, she tends to separate teaching and scholarship in rhetoric and composition. In her view, *instruction* may be feminized because the majority of writing teachers are women; thus, the expressive, student-centered, and nurturing pedagogies can mark feminization. But Lauer argues that in scholarship the field has not been feminized because men publish more than women.

Lauer is correct that in rhetoric and composition men publish more than women; nevertheless, the perception is that teaching writing is women's work. But I believe, as Ernest Boyer argues, that the traditional mindset about higher education that tends to separate teaching from scholarship is what we should be reconsidering. My research over a number of years has shown that men publish more of their work in what we consider our "scholarly" journals, and women publish more of their work in our "pedagogical" journals. The research also points to a recent sharp increase in publication of women's scholarship. Nevertheless, there is still some distinction between how men and women define "intellectual work."

In this chapter, I want to (1) further explore perceptions between pedagogy and scholarship in rhetoric and composition, (2) discuss four studies on the ratio of male-to-female publishing, (3) present some problems that can prevent women from publishing as much as their male counterparts, and (4) offer some suggestions about publishing in rhetoric and composition journals.

Gender and Publishing

Boyer's research on publication shows that in all disciplines nationally males publish more than females. The fairly recent entry of females, in any numbers, into higher education, however, should be taken into account. In his survey of all categories of institutions in higher education, forty-two percent agree that it is difficult to achieve tenure without publications (the breakdown by type of institution: research, eighty-three percent; four-year, forty-three percent; liberal arts, twenty-four percent; two-year, two percent). Even in the four-year universities with their lack of doctoral programs (and sometimes limited resources for research) and in the liberal arts colleges where teaching is highly prized, tenure is still difficult without publication.

My own national survey in 1992 of over three thousand teachers of writing posed some forty-three questions about the professional lives of writing faculty, one section focusing on record of publication. Because I received smaller samples on this section of the questionnaire than the other sections, I can report only those percentages correlating to the number of publications for writing faculty in four-year and research universities (see Tables 1 and 2).

Statistics such as these indicate that the percentages of women in rhetoric and composition who have not published is significantly higher than the percentages Boyer found across all disciplines. Those tenure-track writing faculty in four-year universities who have published between one and ten articles are pretty equally divided by gender, but the writing faculty who have more than ten publications are predominantly male.

The data show a different picture in research universities. Although tenure-track, female writing faculty in research universities publish more than their counterparts in the four-year universities, women still comprise fifty-eight percent of the professors at this level who do not publish. And far more women in research universities have published only between one and five articles as compared to their male counterparts. Tenured or tenure-track women who have published between six and ten articles, however, make up fifty-five percent of this group. One of the more striking statistics in the survey shows that of those research-university, tenured or tenure-track writing faculty who have eleven or more publications, sixty-five percent are female. These percentages suggest a possible correlation between the majority of women hired since 1987, who would have been heavily involved in scholarship in preparation for the promotion and tenure process during the sixth year of employment, most likely the year 1993. Overall, males are still publishing more; the gap, however, is narrowing as increasingly more women are being

TABLE 1   Number of Published Articles by Tenure-Track Writing Faculty

Number of Articles Published	Four-Year		Research	
	Percent Male	Percent Female	Percent Male	Percent Female
None	31	69	43	58
1–5	50	50	5	95
6–10	48	53	45	55
11+	75	25	35	65

TABLE 2   Number of Published Articles by Non-Tenure-Track Writing Faculty

Number of Articles Published	Four-Year		Research	
	Percent Male	Percent Female	Percent Male	Percent Female
None	30	70	33	67
1–5	12	88	0	100
6–10	53	47	42	58
11+	48	52	56	44

tenured. Women are doing exciting and vigorous scholarship, yet, of all those in four-year and research universities who do not publish, sixty-six percent are women.

In addition to this national survey that was the basis for a book on faculty lives and gender roles, I have researched the percentage of female-authored articles in rhetoric and composition journals since 1982. I was drawn to the topic first because more than other fields rhetoric and composition, at least until fairly recently, has been defined more by journal articles than by books. (Until recently, there were few avenues for publishing books other than textbooks. Until the early 1980s, there were few writing journals, too, but opportunities for publishing still were better there, especially in NCTE's official journals.) I was also drawn to the topic when I conducted an informal survey of scholarly and professional books in rhetoric and composition that told me that seventy-seven percent of our field's scholarly books (not including textbooks) were male authored. This informal survey of books in our field led me to think about gender and publishing in our journals because I believe our journals more than books reflect the various voices and conversations going on in our discourse community.

The first survey's percentages, from 1982–1988, were stark and shocking. In the journals that we consider our most scholarly, far more men were published than women. Inversely, in the journals we consider pedagogical, women published much more than men. When I first reported the percentages in 1990, I think journal editors were the most shocked: the ratio of male-to female-authored articles published in our journals began to change. I don't know whether the percentages were so shocking that more women started doing more research and thus suddenly began to submit more articles (though I don't really think this is the case; I know that *Rhetoric Review* continued to receive more submissions from men), or that some of the more traditional editors saw their roles as more than gatekeepers, or that some peer review policies and procedures were changed. We didn't know much more in 1990 except that the sparse data we did have suggested a slight majority of women in the field. Also, the research in higher education showed that women considered themselves to be teachers first, spending less time on research than men, who considered research and writing to be their "real" work.

I updated the journal article study, adding publication by gender for 1988 and 1990 to show just how much the percentages had changed. My interest to update this research was spurred in part by James Kinneavy's statistics based on the index to Winifred Horner's second edition of *The Present State of Scholarship in Historical and Contemporary Rhetoric*. Of the 366 items in the index, 250 are male authored compared to the eighty-one female authored. (The other thirty-five entries are journals.) That about one-fourth of the authors are women seemed an encouraging ratio to Kinneavy: "Very few disciplines can make such a claim—except, of course, specialized disciplines like nursing" (qtd. in Enos, "Gender and Publishing" 314). The comparison between the two disciplines bothered me somewhat, because even though rhetoric and composition, like nursing, has more females than males, its knowledge-making through publications still comes from males more than females (with the one exception of writing faculty in research universities that I commented on earlier). In nursing it is the women who hold the positions of power and the males who are trying to break through the glass ceiling. In rhetoric and composition, women still do not have the power, pay, and real positions despite their numbers.

One change slowly taking place is a broadening of the definition of scholarship to better fit with what it is we do in rhetoric and composition. It is ironic that Boyer's definition of scholarship—discovery, integration, application, and teaching—has been the mosaic pattern of our working rhetoric for twenty-five hundred years. Boyer argues against the traditional German model of research and quantitative evaluation (which U.S. universities adopted and have maintained throughout this century) as only part of the four-patterned mosaic of scholarship that he envisions and that is so familiar to us in rhetoric and composition. One result of the traditional model, because it is at odds with the unique act of rhetoric and composition—to theorize practice and apply theory—is that many writing faculty, in order to earn tenure, have had to do research and publication in literature or creative writing instead of in rhetoric and composition—their area of scholarly interest and expertise and the area for which they were hired in the first place. Many faculty told me that only after tenure could they do the work in rhetoric that first attracted them to the field.

In updating the journal study, I found that the ratios of female-to-male publishing had changed significantly in three years; more women were getting published. In 1995 I again updated the survey, this time including 1991 through the available 1995 issues. The percentage of female-authored articles in our journals dramatically increased, the last column in Table 3 showing the increased percentage of women publishing.

Women are being published more in our journals. Whether the number of submissions to journals in rhetoric and composition has increased so that the percentage of increase correlates to the increased percentage of publication, I don't know, but I *can* speak for *Rhetoric Review*. Female-authored submissions

TABLE 3   Percentage of Male and Female Authors

Journal	1980–88	1988–90	1991–95	Increase (percent)
College English*	31	36	43	12
College Composition and Communication	37	41	55	18
Rhetoric Review	31	30	37	6
Journal of Advanced Composition	30	40	42	12
Pre/Text	24	36	47	23
Rhetoric Society Quarterly	19	27	30	11
Journal of Teaching	44	57	66	22
Journal of Basic Writing	58	51	69	11

*Since Louise Smith took over the editorship of *College English* in 1992, the percentage of female authors has increased to 46 percent.

to *Rhetoric Review* have remained about the same (though there's been a sharp increase in 1995); I still get more male-authored submissions. And the double-blind peer review process I began in 1983 has remained the same. As women have done more sustained work in the history and theory of rhetoric and composition, we do have, in some journals more than others, a chorus of female voices ringing out. And for the first time, we have a female editor of one of the two major NCTE journals: *College English.* Given the nature of our area of study and of the majority of women in rhetoric and composition, however, *College Composition and Communication* should have been the first.

In the next sections, I want to present some problems that particularly attach themselves to our professional history in rhetoric and composition, perceptions about our intellectual work, the realities of women's burdens in administering writing programs and mentoring students, the consequences of finding a voice, and questions about collaborative work.

DISTINCTIONS BETWEEN "RHETORIC" AND "COMPOSITION"

Although gendered perceptions of work are changing as more women enter the field, men and women overall in the academy but particularly in rhetoric and composition perceive their "intellectual work" differently. To men, *real* work in the field more often than not has meant writing books, doing research; work to women usually has meant teaching. According to my survey data, women writing faculty spend more time teaching than men. In the four-year university, women spend sixty-one percent of their time teaching compared to fifty-four percent for men. And in research universities, women spend forty-nine percent of their time teaching compared to forty percent for men.

The data show interesting correlations of time spent on research and both age and length of time tenured. Males spend more time on research than females overall (twenty percent to seventeen percent); by institution, however, there are significant differences. In two-year colleges, female writing faculty spend a little more time on research (eight percent) than do their male counterparts (six percent). In liberal arts colleges, the percentage is the same for both male and female writing faculty: thirteen percent. In the four-year universities, male faculty spend twenty-one percent of their time on research, while women spend only sixteen percent of their time doing research. In research universities, males spend twenty-nine percent of their time on research, while women's research takes up twenty-five percent of their time. According to the data, the older the faculty member and the longer tenured, the less research that person does. Those tenured in 1980 or before, for example, spend less time on research than those who were tenured later. And those age forty or less spend more time on research (twenty-two percent) than do faculty over forty (sixteen percent).

The pressure to publish in the early part of one's career in order to obtain tenure, and/or getting married and raising children (or not), surely affect an academic's scholarship. But the figures do suggest some correlation: if we know that those tenured in 1980 or after do the most research and if we know that more women than men have been hired in tenure-track positions since about 1987 so that women now are the majority in rhetoric and composition, then submissions by female writing faculty to journals would understandably increase. (Such data do not explain why female-authored publications rose to forty-six percent under Louise Smith's editorship of *College English*; editorial policy and politics also share a role in the increased publication of women.)

One problem with which we're increasingly having to deal is the very name of our area of study, most usually called "rhetoric and composition." The name calls up attitudes that can, and I think do, complicate our efforts to broaden the definition of what we do in rhetoric and composition. Although eighty percent of the survey respondents said their program or department made no distinction between "rhetoric" and "composition," twenty percent offered evidence that many English departments put the two terms into a dichotomous relationship. "Rhetoric" in some English departments means theory and history, rigorous scholarship, doctoral programs. "Composition" means service courses and association with only the undergraduate curriculum. The differing meanings of the two terms reflect an intellectual distinction, not a programmatic one. Rhetoric, a number of respondents said, is in their department more recognized as a discipline than composition, which is considered a service-oriented field.

Doing research on the theoretical and historical study of texts, style, structure, and persuasive use of language, and publishing in journals strongly associated with "rhetoric," have been the *sine qua non* for evaluating scholarship at most universities that have writing programs and especially doctoral programs in rhetoric and composition. No matter that "composition" already is part of "rhetoric"; no matter that rhetoric is not only the oldest of the humanities but also unique in that it is both a substantive art and a methodology. To do one's research in writing pedagogy is taking a career risk if the department does not have separate criteria for research in rhetoric and composition studies: it's harder to earn tenure if you're a specialist faculty in a research-oriented university, and it's harder to obtain a tenure-track position in either a four-year or research university if all your research focuses on pedagogy. Of those too few women who have made it to the "top" in the field, most if not all have done their work in the history and theory of rhetoric, not pedagogy. And they have published their work primarily in the journals considered the most scholarly. They are known for adding to our "body of knowledge"; their work is defined as knowledge constructing.

Mentoring/Nurturing/Administrating—Women's Burdens

In my survey the subject of administrative work elicited more angry, despairing, bitter narratives than almost any other topic, the majority of these voices belonging to women. Too often women are less protective of their time than men, but too often the faculty members with the greatest authority to make demands are male. (Department heads and writing program directors in our larger universities still are mostly male.) Within rhetoric and composition, male faculty tend to hold the real administrative positions with real titles while women faculty tend to handle the many details of day-to-day running of committees and the nitty gritty work with students that does not get recognized because it is less organized, less associated with a "position."

Administrative duties for writing faculty are both heavy and wide-ranging. Although faculty in research universities spend more time on administrative duties than their counterparts in other colleges and universities, all writing faculty spend a large percentage of their time on administration: research faculty, thirty-three percent; four-year, twenty-five percent; liberal arts, eighteen percent; two-year, eighteen percent. For seventy-one percent, their administrative work counts for tenure and promotion; however, that leaves twenty-nine percent whose administrative work does not count.

Women writing faculty take on a heavy burden of administrative work—too often a heavier burden than our male counterparts and without the same status derived from formal titles and commensurate compensation. And we know that such administrative work does not have the exchange value it should in promotion and tenure decisions. In her letter of "support" during my tenure review, my former dean, avowing herself a victim of gender discrimination and for years nurturing a reputation as an ostensibly strong supporter of women, wrote disparagingly of the administrative duties I'd taken on as an overload for five years (associate director of composition and coordinator for our TA teacher training, a year-long credit-bearing preceptorship and colloquia). This dean called these heavy administrative duties and responsibilities "quasi-administrative work."

The practice of burdening *untenured* faculty with directing a writing program falls mostly to women. Many times an untenured assistant professor who is a woman is given the job of director of first-year English so that change is kept to a minimum. Many times she is expected, or forced, to act as a caretaker rather than become an innovative administrator because to step out of the drawn lines means risking alienating tenured members of the department who most likely have had some hand in shaping the program.

For all of us, the unique mix and heavy burden of teaching and administrative work, along with the expectations for research and publication, is onerous. For women who have families, the pressure becomes greater. Women still bear most of the responsibility for family and home; women faculty often are torn between teaching and a "life." One of the stories I hear quite often is that a woman who is not married and/or who does not have young children can leave campus as late as five o'clock and still can have five to seven hours to grade papers, write from her research, or even relax during some evenings. A woman with family responsibilities might have only a couple of late-night or early-morning hours to prepare her classes. This difference is not recognized in any way that I can see—certainly not in publishing circles or in promotion and tenure reviews.

Along with the heavy administrative work that too often is not connected to a real position, women still are given much of the work of mentoring and nurturing students within the department. Seventy-one percent of the women who responded to the survey said their careers had been nontraditional because of changed or interrupted careers or because they had had no mentors in graduate school and most often not even one female professor in their field of study. Many of these women now spend inordinate amounts of time nurturing and mentoring because of their own experience of bias in the early part of their careers. And more of them are now realizing the dangers of mothering in the academy.

Mothering in the academy—whether it's through the nurturer in the writing program or the maternal teaching model—can carry with it a danger. Such a model can lead to our silencing in situations in which we might still be uncomfortable, or unable to deal, with conflicting parts of our identity. To be separate, individual, and autonomous may be emphasized too much when we speak about and live in the male-dominated arena of much of our professional lives. But we live in this world of faculty where, despite our numbers, we may not have worked out for ourselves how to maintain separate identities. If we make ourselves too available, too maternal, too caring, we risk not achieving a balance between our very natures and our careers. They should be the same; alas, they are not. A number of respondents to the survey commented on these problems that so many women who teach writing face, expressing that perhaps we should learn to stop mothering in the academy and to better balance nurturing with autonomy in order to guard our time.

So we women faculty can and often do find ourselves in a dilemma. We like to work with students; we don't guard our time carefully. We're already overburdened by administrative work, work that does not have exchange value with traditional scholarship. Mentoring was not explicitly included in any of the many department or university criteria that I saw while conducting the survey. And, no surprise here, nurturing was not mentioned. But here's the rub: if women scholars don't assume the additional responsibility of mentoring—especially for our female colleagues and students—then how can we change some of the destructive discriminatory practices still going on in our departments and programs?

KNOWLEDGE-CONSTRUCTING AND VOICE

As an editor who reads hundreds of manuscript submissions every year and as a teacher who works primarily with women graduate students, I know feminist theory well enough to see its siren-call to female graduate students who are working toward a career in rhetoric and composition in institutions of higher education and who already are trying to get published. Sometimes I think that "making knowledge" many times gets confused with "finding a voice." Let me tell a story to illustrate.

Several years ago I sent out for blind peer review a manuscript written by a woman who is known for her scholarship in the history of rhetoric. In the manuscript she had included a personal narrative about her mother trying to teach her to make cinnamon rolls when she was eight years old. I should say that this was a departure from the scholar's usual style, but part of her argument logically grew out of the narrative. It worked—I thought. When the reviews came back, one of the reviewers had objected to the narrative. This reviewer is male and is also well known for his work in the history of rhetoric. He is, furthermore—and I say this with conviction—extraordinarily supportive of women's work in the field. Although his review was overall supportive, he commented that the narrative should remain part of the "scholarly" manuscript on rhetorical history only if the author was one whose work was well known. That way, he said, the previous work would provide a context and make the personal part acceptable.

I suspect that a double-blind peer review system cannot eliminate bias— of course not, because the *words* are still there on the page. I'm not even sure that this would constitute gender bias anyway, though I know that the use of personal narrative can be viewed as "gender specific." Lately I have been rethinking the epistemological position that women's ways of composing are different from men's; women who have published the most might have a larger repertoire of "styles"—they've probably always had to be acutely aware of their audiences, given the economic, cultural, and social constrictions on them because of their sex. But it's not just women who use narration as a way of arguing, or personal narrative to create voice; the perception remains, however, that this is "female style," or that it is nonscholarly. I would have to agree with the peer reviewer who commented on the "cinnamon bun story" that indeed it's true, sadly enough, that the most highly recognized people in the field "get away" with having voice ride above content—and there are fewer women in the high-profile group of scholars in rhetoric and composition. James Corder, who is recognized for his style—his marvelous sense of voice—as well as his ideas, visited my campus in 1990 as part of our annual colloquia for writing faculty and TAs. Over coffee and pastries, graduate students were informally discussing with Jim his homespun, philosophical style. One student, who particularly admired Jim's writing style and who wished to be able to project as strong an ethos as Jim's, asked, "Could I write like you do and get published?" Jim answered, "probably not." We all laughed. We understood too. Jim talked about his problems years ago in getting published in *College Composition and Communication* and *College English* because the manuscripts he submitted weren't "scholarly" enough. He hasn't changed his style; his work is regularly published now, though. He has a name—and he has a voice.

Let me tell another story, this one about a manuscript submitted to *Rhetoric Review,* a feminist reading of Plato's *Gorgias.* The paper argued that "if a discursive practice exacts as its price for authorization the repression of feeling or of personal stakes in the practice, then that price is too high." The essay was based on an episode, told with much anger, about the female author's encounter with a "famous" male scholar at a conference who had, in his male way, dismissed her ways of thinking about authority and models of inquiry. The peer reviewers to whom I'd sent the manuscript all replied similarly: the piece set up binaries too neatly—and violently and angrily—without offering readers an alternative. One reviewer commented that the "conversational style and stream of ideas" was not the most effective way to present the point, this reviewer stressing that the author did have something important to share with readers. The reviewers thought voice got in the way, became more important than the argument.

The author subsequently revised and resubmitted the piece; she was not willing, however, to rethink the role voice and narrative played in the argument. I sent it to the same peer reviewers. The first reviewer to respond was "sorry not to be able to recommend publication," saying that the "personal narrative" was not appropriate for *Rhetoric Review,* that the essay "presents characterizations that are based on stereotypes. Those who disagree are giving in to the power structures, male professors are authoritarian, efforts by others who are not in agreement with the author are 'moves,' etc." This reviewer went on to express the hope that the "author will see these comments as my fairest and most sincere effort to comment on areas of need and not any sort of statement prompted by any other reasons than the scholarly criteria used to adjudicate an essay's merits." Another reviewer said:

> While you privilege "feelings" (the song came to mind more than once as I spent a great deal of time on the piece) and the "personal" (not really presented in away that I could understand, particularly considering the postmodern turn which you avoid even though it could help your case a lot), my reading saw a privileging of immediate sensation, not emotion or feeling. This privileging of sensation would ordinarily fascinate me, partly because I am in such great need of feminist responses. It does with, for example, the autobiographical work of Linda Brodkey and Marianna Torgovnick, whose autobiographical writing is so carefully, so thoughtfully, worked through. The series of sensations re-presented here are not really related to Plato. . . . They appear to be related to a desire to perform catharsis in front of the large audience of *Rhetoric Review* interpreters. . . .
>
> Jasper Neel in *Plato, Derrida, and Writing* presents his great anger toward both Derrida and Plato. He does so in a compelling, lucid, provocative way that I can and have used over and over in my writing and in my graduate and undergraduate classes. I hope that you will study how his book is made. He started out with lots and lots of hard study and difficult encounters with other writer/speakers. I also recommend that you immerse yourself in Derrida's "Plato's Pharmacy." Derrida, too, is mad at Plato. Many have been mad at Plato. Your piece assumes the stance that expressing this anger is a new kind of event. . . . I hope . . . that you will explore the difference between exposure of sensation to a supposedly public audience and exposure of insight to a group of readers.

Another reviewer who didn't "want to fall into traditional scholarly modes of critique" asked a graduate student to collaborate on the peer evaluation. But all of the reviewers had problems with the author's handling of, or confusion with, knowledge-construction and the expression of a particular view through voice. The author chose not to work with the four reviewers' suggestions; the manuscript, therefore, was rejected. Lest you are curious: two of the reviewers were female, two male.

We certainly need more research on how women's scholarship is evaluated. One of the few studies we have on this topic reports that women's scholarship in academia consistently is evaluated as being precise, thorough—and noncontroversial (Bernard). A few women who publish a lot and whose scholarship is perceived to be more in "composition," or the politics of composition, than "rhetoric"—women like Ann Berthoff, Maxine Hairston, Patricia Bizzell—have strong, political voices. They can be "controversial" in a way that traditional women scholars in the history of rhetoric, say Winifred Bryan Horner, are not. If a woman historiographer, however (Susan Jarratt, for example), "rereads" history, she can become well known, can become a controversial figure.

Women Scholars and Collaboration

Several years ago I reported on the amount of collaborative writing being published in rhetoric and composition journals. I was particularly interested in how many coauthored articles were by women working together. Belenky and her coauthors in *Women's Ways of Knowing* had described the collaborative process that produced their book as the wonderfully cooperative way in which women can work together. "It would seem," Elizabeth Flynn says in response to a published interview with Belenky, "that women are, in general, more cooperative than men, more connected to each other and hence more capable than men of collaborating successfully" (176). But women's emphasis on mutuality, concern, and support is difficult to implement in academia where conflict and competition are facts. Indeed, our educational structures have served to separate women from each other and from knowledge; new structures must be found that allow for connected knowing.

Also responding to this same interview, Marilyn Cooper comments, "It is a moot point whether competition is associated with men and collaboration with women because of innate differences or because of socially constructed ones; the current pattern is that women by and large prefer to work collaboratively and that because collaborative work is devalued and dismissed in institutions structured on the basis of competitive strategies, women's work is often devalued and dismissed" (180).

These comments by Flynn and Cooper generated my interest in examining the number of coauthored articles in several of our leading journals, especially since collaborative scholarship is perceived to be highly valorized in our field. What I found is that if women frequently collaborate in their scholarly work, much of it is not getting published. Although the number of female coauthored publications has increased slightly over the last two years, most of the collaboration that has resulted in publication since 1980 is with men—either two men working together or a woman with a man. So one obvious question that perhaps we should be asking, given Cooper's comment about women's work often being dismissed, is: Why then do women more often collaborate with men than with each other?

We know that in this country more males than females encounter difficulties with writing English in school, although more published authors are male. Research that has revealed ways in which males and females differ in their writing processes suggests that men delay writing while women plunge in. It would follow then that women would find it more difficult to coauthor with men than with other women. There's fertile ground here for integrated (and collaborative) studies of the gender politics involved in collaborative research as well as deeper research into writing processes themselves.

OVERCOMING OBSTACLES

Getting published means writing a lot, and disciplining our time. For women directing writing programs (and that's a great many of us) it's hard to give equal attention to teaching and research. Winifred Horner has been tireless in her efforts to help women learn from events in her own academic history; we should heed what she learned regarding the heavy administrative burdens placed especially on women when they should be doing research and writing. She scolds and cajoles: If you take on heavy administrative work—especially before tenure—make sure that it is with the agreement that one day a week—or two afternoons a week—you will not be in the office. This is your research time. Stick to it; whatever you do, do not even think you can work anywhere in the building where the composition office is. Do not even try to work at home. Go to the library. Hide, so no one can find you—and they will try. The "problem" will always be there in your office waiting for you the next morning; it can wait till then.

Another long-time administrator reminds me often that women must learn to "say no": "Jobs stick to an administrator as ticks to a dog; every job performed well leads to requests for two more." We need to learn how to discriminate better between essential duties and peripheral chores that can be delegated. As mentors, most composition studies faculty are overworked because they are popular with graduate students. This is important and delightful work though usually unrecognized and time-consuming. But too often more of the burden falls on female writing faculty for mentoring and role modeling because female graduate students now make up seventy percent of the typical program in rhetoric (Enos, *Faculty*). The burden is accepted female-to-female, often sacrificially, often preventing women faculty from pursuing their own research. In research universities, it takes women longer to get tenure than males: according to my survey, 6.9 years for women as compared to 5.7 years for men. As a result, for mentoring or (wo)mentoring—if it leads to delays in getting published—we are penalized *de facto* for our contribution to future scholars. One thing we can do is to define mentoring so that its activities are not split between nurturing (female) and "real work" (male). In addition, mentoring responsibilities must be both carefully delineated for and equally distributed among all faculty.

Even after having been a journal editor for fifteen years, I don't have any magic advice on how to get published; as teachers, however, I think we can do much to help demystify the publication process for our graduate students. Few of our seventy-two doctoral programs in rhetoric and composition offer their graduate students a seminar in writing for publication or a course in the rhetoric of scholarship (see Brown, Meyer, and Enos). Because courses like these focus on how knowledge gets disseminated in the field, they foreground the politics of publication: the discourse community of rhetoric and composition studies, knowledge-construction, editing and peer review roles, journal and article-type analyses, and the etiquette of submission. And, of course, such courses are a forum for ongoing invention, writing, peer response, revision. In our history and theory courses especially, if we're not already doing so, we need to start viewing the required graduate "research" papers as a succession of drafts. Despite our talk—and practice in the undergraduate writing classroom—of process and peer-group praxis, more of us can turn our graduate writing courses into discourse-discussion groups where research is seen as invention, where successive drafts of papers are brought in and discussed, rather than where the traditional semester-end research paper is produced (still our most usual practice, I suspect) and where the professor, seeing it for the first time, evaluates the paper to justify the seminar grade.

Creating an environment in which students are encouraged to shape their traditional research papers into publishable papers helps demystify the publication process and involves students in a conscious dialogue about distinctive journal "voices," thus dealing with real audience considerations. I would argue for this approach instead of faculty/student coauthoring. I do know that important publications have come out of collaboration between faculty and student, and I support collaborative work. To increase publishing opportunities, however, I think it better to create an environment where a "publishable" paper is the semester goal rather than the usual summative seminar paper, which by its very nature is a record of *what* the student knows instead of an essay showing *that* the student knows.

The essays in this volume offer much practical advice for professionals just entering the field. Although my primary purpose here has not been advising how one gets published, still I'd like to offer a few suggestions from experience. One of the steepest hurdles blocking knowledge-construction and publication is learning to gain a sense of situatedness. So, young scholars—more and more of you women—situate *yourself* in your research topic, and I can assure you that a voice will emerge that shows an active mind in the process of constructing. Always connect—learn to make connections that allow for exciting exploration so that all your written work in graduate school (or "before tenure" if you're in your first ranked faculty position) reflects a mosaic of discovery, integration, application, teaching. To make those connections, whatever your main interest (major period, figure, concept, application), *historicize.* Historicizing helps us to define and redefine rhetoric. Historical resonances help us to broaden our sense of ourselves as we challenge and then perhaps cross the limits of our frames of reference. Then theory and praxis more easily fit themselves into the expanded frame or new frames.

Suppose you most generally define rhetoric as, and identify yourself with, the teaching of writing. There's a whole range of issues there related to English studies at all educational levels and in all periods. A whole range of questions on how people actually read and wrote needs more research. Suppose you define rhetoric and composition as a theory of persuasion. Your research area is a universe populated by accepted theories—shaped by intellectual, social, economic, political, legal trends. Many commonly accepted institutionalized trends are waiting to be rewritten. Suppose you define rhetoric as socially constructed discourse. You have lots of ground to cover (and lots of company) and many choices about which discourse conventions to examine: who gets to speak, how they are allowed to speak, and what purposes discourse serves or, better yet, can serve. Treat each hurdle as a challenge rather than a barrier. I cannot promise you that the path toward publication smoothes out completely; I can promise you that you will find much reward along the way.

WORKS CITED

Belenky, Mary Field, Blythe McVicker Clinchy, Nancy Rule Goldberger, and Jill Mattuck Taruale. *Women's Ways of Knowing: The Development of Self, Voice, and Mind.* New York: Basic, 1986.

Bernard, Jessie. *Academic Women.* University Park: Pennsylvania State UP, 1964.

Boyer, Ernest L. *Scholarship Reconsidered: Priorities of the Professoriate.* Princeton, NJ: Carnegie Foundation for the Advancement of Teaching, 1990.

Brown, Stuart C., Paul R. Meyer, and Theresa Enos. "Doctoral Programs in Rhetoric and Composition." *Rhetoric Review* 12 (1994). Special Issue.

Cooper, Marilyn M. "Dueling with Dualism: A Response to Interviews with Mary Field Belenky and Gayatri Chakravorty Spivak." *Journal of Advanced Composition* 11 (1991): 179–85.

Enos, Theresa. "Gender and Journals, Conservers or Innovators." *Pre/Text* 9 (1988): 209–14.

———. "Gender and Publishing." *Pre/Text* 11 (1990): 311–16.

———. *Gender Roles and Faculty Lives in Rhetoric and Composition.* Carbondale: Southern Illinois UP, 1996.

Flynn, Elizabeth A. "Politicizing the Composing Process and Women's Ways of Interacting: A Response to 'A Conversation with Mary Belenky.'" *Journal of Advanced Composition* 11 (1991): 173–78.

Lauer, Janice M. "The Feminization of Rhetoric and Composition Studies?" *Rhetoric Review* 13 (1995): 276–86.

REFLECTIVE ESSAY

On "Learning Our Own Ways"

WENDY BISHOP

Becoming a tenure-line English department member and a writing program administrator led me into some bad clothes days. I remember escaping my office and ending up at a mall department store looking at racks of sale suits. This was some sort of halfway house or Dantean limbo where I could escape identity, feel neither fish nor fowl, WPA nor my own person, partner nor parent. I paused before I returned home to my family and briefcase full of unfinished day's business.

Becoming a department member is much like trying to dress right, to define oneself within and against one's community. For instance, I came to feminist theory and thinking late, but by 1990, when this essay was published in the *Journal of Advanced Composition,* I better understood women from my writing classrooms who would come in my office, close the door, and say, "I didn't say anything in class because I don't want to be labeled 'feminist' but. . . ." Time in the academy had sensitized me to the uses and abuses of gendered language, to the ways the men in my classes claimed and were comfortable with my attention, while the women—if I didn't work hard not to let it happen—would fall silent. And I was sensitized anew in my position as WPA to the "woman's work" I was asked to do as a supervisor-mentor to a program of sixty teaching assistants, as wife to the English Department.

In "Learning Our Own Ways to Situate Composition and Feminist Studies in the English Department"—written in late 1989—I use the voices of others to find my own voice. Like the student who closed the door, I had been silent until that point on these issues. The many citations in this essay are part of my intentional collage and call to (self) action. This essay resulted from mindless shopping *and* mindful reading, from going out of my way to find thinkers and theorists who felt right, who welcomed me, who helped me look under the surface of things, beyond appearance.

Returning to school in 1985 to study composition, I had discovered in myself the soul of a reference librarian: I learned to love indexes, to scout out citations, to hot-wire ideas and see where they would take me. In this essay, I see the shadows of much of the work I would do in the years that followed. Because I was writing to learn, I used as touchstone my own academic history, leavening research with confession and retrospection. Because I was writing to be heard, I pulled out the prose stops, called on metaphor and narrative, braided themes, and balanced sentences. I found that the tools of creative craft helped me care about revision. I aimed for an essay that would be more essay-like than the research reports I had just read in graduate school because I wanted to dress like the creative writer I had already trained to be *and* like the compositionist I was committed to becoming.

When the essay was published, the asterisks were removed and descriptive subheadings were inserted by journal editors to make it conform to house style, to add a linearity and inevitability I did not feel. Unusual for me, I called to complain about these changes. (I later called to apologize for complaining.) It was at this point in drafting composition essays that I decided style was an important part of my self-presentation. And of course, after this, I pursued issues of written style with a vengeance.

Rereading, I hear a first attempt to assert strongly but in a way I found palatable as a woman writing; my methods of argumentation were discovered somewhere in the badlands between critique and testimony. And though I aimed for collage, I also aimed for wholeness and connection. I wanted to be in dialogue with other scholars, with friends and students. This essay marks my first insistence that the creative and scholarly commingle.

A new-to-the-field essayist, certainly I was surprised I did not hear a great deal in response after publication, particularly because the scaredy-cat in me thought she had just yelled loudly and expected a howl or two in return. Knowing more now than I was able to speculate upon then about the ways of disciplinary worlds, I should have been even more gratified than I was at the conference moment when a colleague said he was teaching the essay in a graduate class, and another said she had actually read it.

The proof of process for me has been to observe that it is potentially more engaging for actor than audience, for writer than reader. While I can point to the genesis of several other of my essays in this one, see the fingerprint of the later compositionist I am now in the early compositionist I rediscover here, what I value most is the freshness, even boldness, of some of the writing moves I made. And as well, I am pleased to report that I believe in the voice, the points, and the pleas of this essay as much now as I did back then. I am glad to find more or less that I still look and dress much the same.

A SELECTED ANNOTATED BIBLIOGRAPHY IN FEMINISM AND COMPOSITION

Baliff, Michelle. "What Is It That the Audience Wants? Or, Notes toward a Listening with a Transgendered Ear for (Mis)Understanding" *Journal of Advanced Composition* 19 (1999): 51–70.

Baliff makes several arguments for (re)theorizing audience—the way we think about it and teach it. She analyzes classical theories of audience and rhetoric and critiques feminism for the ways its arguments have reified traditional binaries such as speaker-audience and male-female. She argues for a way of complicating listening and thinking about audience that is more in line with the image of the hermaphrodite.

Batson, Lorie Goodman. "Defining Ourselves as Women (in the Profession)." *Pre/Text: A Journal of Rhetorical Theory* (1988): 207–9.

According to Batson, women who pursue a career in the academy are faced with unique decisions: "We desire both to be in and of the profession, and radically to alter it as a profession. We must choose to openly attack from without, to infiltrate and effect change from within, to conform, or to make alternative arrangements" (207). Batson reflects on the status of women in the academy in the 1980s and speculates about a brighter future, looking to scholars like Irigaray for possibilities of change. Irigaray's call for the inclusion of ethics as an integral component of any field of study provides what Batson sees as a conception of composition studies that is inherently feminist in its approach.

Bauer, Dale M., and Susan C. Jarratt. "Feminist Sophistics: Teaching with an Attitude." *Changing Classroom Practices: Resources for Literary and Cultural Studies.* Ed. David Downing. Urbana, IL: NCTE, 1994. 149–65.

Bauer and Jarratt argue that the goals of feminism and rhetoric are change. They argue for a "feminist sophistics," which combines feminism and rhetoric. Their discussion offers a history of sophism, including feminist sophism, and outlines the possibilities such an approach contains for the writing classroom. The teacher is able to bring "anxiety about power" into focus, and the "naturalized operation of power" becomes the subject of the course (149).

Blair, Kristine, and Pamela Takayoshi, eds. *Feminist Cyberscapes: Mapping Gendered Academic Spaces.* Stamford, CT: Ablex, 1999.

This edited collection marks the moment when feminists using technology imagined multiple locations for feminists in cyberspace before the importance of the World Wide Web was evident. Nonetheless, the many issues raised about how technology, technological interphases, and discourses surrounding technology shape our pedagogy and our play are still relevant. In addition to offering interviews with leading figures in the field and the transcripts from a MOO with the collection's contributors, this book is broken into five "Maps of Location": The Body in Virtual Space; Constructions of Online Identities: Our Students, Our Selves; Discourse Communities Online and in Classrooms; Virtual Coalitions and Collaborations; and The Future: To Be Mapped Later.

Bleich, David. "Genders of Writing." *Journal of Advanced Composition* 9 (1989): 10–25.

Bleich attempts to recategorize writing as not just generic but gendered. "Genders of writing" highlight the political aspect of writing that genres of writing leave in the background. Drawing on discussions that problematize gender categories and extending them beyond the traditional two—male and female—Bleich says that genders/genres of writing exist yet are permeable and inevitably hybrid. Moreover, our tendency to make heterosexuality compulsory binds us to simplistic binaries that mask the complexities of genders and genres.

———. "Sexism in Academic Styles of Learning." *Journal of Advanced Composition* 10 (1990): 231–47.

Bleich highlights the feminist critique of contemporary science and intellectual life—that their discursive formations are exclusive of women's ways of knowing. He argues that such a critique essentializes women. Discursive formations that value essentialism, moreover, cannot distinguish between what is and what should be—a "covert principle" at work in intellectual thought that reproduces the social inequities bound up in contemporary social and intellectual institutions. Bleich proposes to counter this problem by replacing the "what has been and should be" reasoning with "announcement of values" or "political disclosure."

Brodkey, Linda. "On the Subjects of Class and Gender in 'The Literacy Letters.'" *College English* 51 (1989): 125–41.

Brodkey adopts the poststructural/social-constructionist argument that language constitutes subjectivity rather than passively reflects it. She applies the argument to composition pedagogy by positioning the classroom as an ideological space and the writer as inhabiting a subject position. Looking at letters exchanged between students and teachers in an experimental literacy class, she finds even well-meaning teachers trying to protect the discourse of the classroom from intrusion of class and gender issues (or, rather, she finds that discourse exerting its power over the correspondents), preserving the institutional power of the teachers and, in effect, withholding it from their students.

Carlton, Susan Brown. "Voice and the Naming of Woman." *Voices on Voice: Perspectives, Definitions, Inquiry.* Ed. Kathleen Blake Yancey. Urbana, IL: NCTE, 1994. 226–41.

Carlton takes up Linda Alcoff's theoretical exploration of essentialism in order to reframe Elizabeth Flynn's, Lynn Worsham's, and Susan Jarratt's work. Drawing on feminist philosophy, Carlton explores key terms, such as "voice," within "essentialist," "nominalist," and "positionalist" rhetorics to represent alternative readings of feminist scholarship and their relevance for compositionists. While these rereadings expose what Carlton considers "feminist philosophical impasses," they also offer feminist compositionists a range of possibilities to expand rhetorical options of feminist textual production and reception within and beyond the writing classroom.

Cayton, Mary Kupiec. "Writing as Outsiders: Academic Discourse and Marginalized Faculty." *College English* 53 (1991): 647–60.

Cayton addresses the marginalized position of adjunct and/or part-time teachers at the university level in the early 1990s. Though they may not realize it, such teachers, she writes, are members of the oppressed. Relying heavily on Freire, Cayton argues that the "paternal" positioning of the academy reinforces the perception of part-time faculty as disposable.

Collins, Vicki Tolar. "The Speaker Respoken: Material Rhetoric as Feminist Methodology." *College English* 61 (1999): 545–73.

Collins calls for developing a historiographic methodology based on a material rhetoric—what she defines as "the theoretical investigation of discourse by examining how the rhetorical aims and functions of the initial text are changed by the process of material production and distribution" (547). To do this, she examines the implications of materiality based on the 1837 *Account of the Experience of Hester Ann Rogers.* Analyzing the multiple ways this account is respoken and by whom, Collins shows how it matters very much who is speaking, as these revoiced texts can be made to tell new stories. Close attention to the material practices that make these accounts speak again, while avoiding the problems of appropriation, anachronism, and decontextualization, offers a methodology for approaching historical texts and the uses made of them.

Cooper, Marilyn M. "Women's Ways of Writing." *Writing as Social Action.* Ed. Marilyn Cooper and Michael Holzman. Portsmouth, NH: Boynton/Cook, 1989. 141–56.

Cooper suggests thinking about students' difficulties in writing as a combination of cognitive deficit and social difference models rather than one or another. Drawing on the work of Belenky et al. and Shirley Brice Heath, Cooper proposes a plan for developing a writing program for abused women.

De Beaugrande, Robert. "In Search of Feminist Discourse: The 'Difficult' Case of Luce Irigaray." *College English* 50 (1988): 253–72.

De Beaugrande outlines a feminist dilemma: If the (patriarchal) bias in language is so pervasive, how can we critique the bias without using and reinscribing it? He suggests we use experimental forms of discourse to think differently and get outside patriarchy. De Beaugrande describes the views of language as outlined by structuralism, poststructuralism, and feminism and then, in detail, explores Irigaray's project of "pursu[ing] experimental forms of discourse that might open up genuinely *new* alternatives, even in the face of history and power" (256).

Dickson, Marcia. "Directing without Power: Adventures in Constructing a Model of Feminist Writing Program Administration." *Writing Ourselves into the Story: Unheard Voices from Composition Studies.* Ed. Sheryl I. Fontaine and Susan Hunter. Carbondale: Southern Illinois UP, 1993. 140–53.

Dickson narrates her experience as a feminist writing program administrator in a position without power to make decisions or facilitate change. In part a response to Gary Olson and Joseph Moxley's "Directing Freshman Composition: The Limits of Authority" (*College Composition and Communication*, 1989), Dickson offers a critique of WPA responsibilities as outlined by Olson and Moxley. Dickson argues against any model of WPA that places authority in the hands of one person. She suggests a feminist approach to writing program administration, one that privileges collaboration as an alternative to traditional notions of the position, and concludes by presenting "seven characteristics that feminist administrative structures might hold in common" (152).

Dixon, Kathleen. "Gendering the 'Personal.'" *College Composition and Communication* 46 (1995): 255–75.

"Gendering the 'Personal'" is informed by a case study of two student writers—David and Elizabeth—and provides a discussion of how each person's self-expression represents acts that are socially constructed and bounded. Dixon argues for more self-reflexive research in writing studies (an area she asserts is currently overlooked and undervalued by the field). In addition, she describes the need for greater experimentation with alternate forms of discourse in an effort to get more voices "heard."

Ebert, Teresa L. "The 'Difference' of Postmodern Feminism." *College English* 53 (1991): 886–904.

To redress postmodern feminism's lack of political action, Ebert advocates what she calls a "postmodern materialist feminist theory" that repositions and resists postmodern feminist theory within systems, especially within social and political ones. Materialist feminism contains a political aspect in which meaning is determined by the sign, within a matrix of possible signs (ideology), and must be determined through social, not only textual, struggle.

————. "For a Red Pedagogy: Feminism, Desire, and Need." *College English* 58: (1996): 795–819.

Ebert writes against the ludic postmodern pedagogies of pleasure (citing Deleuze and Guttari, hooks, and Gallop's pedagogies of desire; Tompkins's pedagogy of nurturance; and Grosz's pedagogy of the body, which, according to Ebert, focus on economies of individual libidinal liberation and erase class consciousness). Ebert argues for a red feminist pedagogy of materialist critique that focuses on economics, politics, labor, and class to expose global patriarchal capitalism, declaring that this pedagogy will better enable students to see the connections between individual experiences and systematic relations of projection that produce these experiences.

Farrell, Thomas J. "The Female and Male Modes of Rhetoric." *College English* 40 (1979): 909–21.

This essay appears in the same issue as Joan Bolker's "Teaching Griselda to Write," making Thomas Farrell one of the earliest male voices in the area of feminism and composition. In this piece he explores differences in approaches to argumentation in terms of gender. Through a detailed discussion of these modes and various examples of their uses, Farrell concludes that the male mode is "probably better suited than the female mode for written discourse (920)." However, he does suggest that the best features of each mode could be blended to create an effective argument, but blending them well would require great skill on the part of the writer.

Finke, Laurie. "Knowledge as Bait: Feminism, Voice, and the Pedagogical Unconsciousness." *College English* 55 (1993): 7–27.

Finke provides the reader with a good example of a psychoanalytic approach to teaching writing by narrating her adaptation of psychoanalytic feminist pedagogy. Referencing Lacan and Freud, she looks at a particular case study and shows how a (teacher's) fragmented self plays itself out in the classroom. She argues that hers is only one of many feminist approaches to writing instruction and that all pedagogies (like theories) must be subjected to continual reflection and critique.

Fleckenstein, Kristie S. "Resistance, Writing, and Dismissing the 'I.'" *Rhetoric Review* 17 (1998): 107–25.

Fleckenstein critiques pedagogical approaches that construct an authorial "I" that simultaneously focuses on the rhetor while dismissing the material person. This dismissal, according to Fleckenstein, makes the rhetor seem to be a universal category open to all, when in fact this liberal subjectivity removes material markers of difference. Consequently, Fleckenstein sees the rhetorical

"I" as highly problematic, ignoring the material distinctions that different groups, such as men and women, face as this rhetorical "I" reinscribes the status quo. Fleckenstein argues for a composition pedagogy based on a third "I," "neither material nor rhetorical, but both simultaneously" (122).

Flynn, Elizabeth. "Composition Studies from a Feminist Perspective." *The Politics of Writing Instruction.* Ed. Richard Bullock and John Trimbur. Portsmouth, NH: Boynton/Cook, 1991. 137–54.

Flynn claims that feminism has had a strong impact on many disciplines (literary criticism, linguistics, speech communications) but only a limited impact on composition studies, in large part because of composition studies' fledgling institutional status at the beginning of the feminist movement. She suggests that there are established ways of thinking about language within composition studies that feminists can build upon and offers suggestions for future research, such as delineating a female rhetorical tradition, examining positivism's influence on composition studies, and recuperating ideas within composition studies that are compatible with feminism.

———. "Feminism and Scientism." *College Composition and Communication* 46 (1995): 353–68.

Flynn explores the limitations of attempting to "masculinize" composition studies, or gain institutional stature, through what she calls scientism, an identification with the social sciences and physical sciences. Such limitations include male bias in research methods, agendas that serve those in power, and reductive images of reading and writing. Flynn offers alternative ways for composition studies to gain authority without "masculinized" identification with institutional dominant fields, such as the sciences. These alternatives will foreground "democratic research practices and administrative pedagogical structures" (367) and can be seen in some of the self-reflexive practices and discourses of resistance in cultural studies and feminist studies.

———. "Gender and Reading." *College English* 45 (1983): 236–53.

Flynn presents the results of a study she conducted on the differences between the reading patterns and effectiveness of "mature" male and female readers. She suggests that when confronted with "disturbing stories," male readers either attempt to "dominate" the stories or discussions of the stories or they tend to "reject" stories. Women, on the other hand, are more able to interpret and interact with such stories. Reading, for women, insulates and frees them in ways not available in speech.

Frey, Olivia. "Beyond Literary Darwinism: Women's Voices and Critical Discourse." *College English* 52 (1990): 507–26.

Frey looks at thirteen years of *PMLA* articles, as well as selected articles from other journals, and finds that all articles but two rely on adversarial forms of argument. Building on models of female development that portray women as primarily concerned with relationships and contextual knowledge (in opposition to impersonal and abstract knowledge), Frey argues that, though many succeed in the adversarial form, women may be discriminated against by its universal acceptance as the standard in academic discourse.

Gerrard, Lisa, ed. *Computers, Composition, and Gender.* Spec. issue of *Computers and Composition: An International Journal for Teachers of Writing.* 16 (1999): 1–206.

This special issue of *Computer and Composition* attends to how gender influences people's relationship with technology. In addition to offering Gerrard's introduction, book and Web site reviews, and an ending commentary, the heart of the collection contains three sections: feminist theory in computers and composition, online opportunities for gender equity, and classroom research in computers, composition, and gender. Within the breadth of ideas, the focus remains on what Gerrard calls the "politics of computing." This politics looks at the nexus of genres (e.g., coming out stories, autobiographies, experimental hypertexts, conversation analysis) and advocacy (spanning age groups, genders, and sexualities). While fully aware of the difficulties faced by many, this collection imagines possibilities that technology may offer.

Gillam, Alice M. "Feminism and Composition Research: Researching as a Woman." *Composition Studies: Freshman English News* 20 (1992): 47–54.

Gillam uses Elizabeth Flynn's "Composing as a Woman" as a touchstone for narrating her experience as a woman in the academy and her ongoing struggle to "merge" her roles as a feminist and scholar. She critiques the term *feminization* as objectionable, a word she says "can be read as meaning either a female takeover of composition or a composition takeover of the feminine" (48), and addresses the effects various readings of *feminization* have had on the development of composition studies as a discipline. "Feminism and Composition Research" is a call to engage, continue, complicate, and critique the feminist conversation, whose goal, Gillam concludes, is to explore issues of scholarship, and whose interests such scholarship might serve.

Graves, Heather Brodie. "Regrinding the Lens of Gender: Problematizing 'Writing as a Woman.'" *Written Communication* 10 (1993): 139–63.

Graves suggests that theories of "composing as a woman" often draw on the essentialist assumption that women write in a particular ways because they are women. Pointing out ways that Kenneth Burke writes "like a woman" and ways Julia Kristeva writes "like a man," she argues that we need to think of gender in more nuanced ways—as a masculine-feminine split that is the result of "acculturation" rather than of an essential womanness.

Haswell, Janis, and Richard H. Haswell. "Gendership and the Miswriting of Students." *College Composition and Communication* 46 (1995): 223–54.

This article presents the findings of an empirical study of how gender affects responses to writing. Haswell and Haswell call for expansive response practices that foreground gender both as a lived experience and as a reading practice and that see genderedness as both intrinsic to writing and constructed through reading. Teachers should, therefore, teach "gendership" as a rhetorical inevitability rather than as a political issue in writing.

Holbrook, Sue Ellen. "Women's Work: The Feminization of Composition." *Rhetoric Review* 9 (1991): 201–29.

Holbrook provides a narrative of the feminization of the field of composition, defining feminization as "the process by which the field of composition has become associated with feminine attributes and populated by the female gender" (201). Holbrook uses a historical approach to chronicle what she perceives as the relationship between the status of women and the status of composition. She observes that women "disproportionately" occupy positions of lesser value in composition than their male counterparts. She concludes that composition will remain "women's work"—marginalized, practitioner based, "service" oriented—until teaching becomes more valued. Only when perceptions of teaching change will composition be more valued by our culture and society.

Hollis, Karyn, L. "Feminism in Writing Workshops: A New Pedagogy." *College Composition and Communication* 43 (1992): 340–48.

Hollis argues that workshops for teachers of writing, both in English departments and in writing across the curriculum programs, need to pay more attention to issues of gender in the teaching of writing. In particular, she suggests that workshop leaders should address gender in relation to classroom structures, the composing process, rhetorical situations and audiences, topics and genres of writing assignments, peer group dynamics, responses to written work, and the use of nonsexist language.

Hunter, Susan. "A Woman's Place *Is* in the Composition Classroom: Pedagogy, Gender, and Difference." *Rhetoric Review* 9 (1991): 230–45.

Hunter considers what she terms the "coincidences" between feminist and composition pedagogies. She calls for the need to question how successful each pedagogy is for different groups of students, paying special attention to those students studying business and technology. She argues that feminist teachers must ask themselves if a pedagogy that is "simultaneously subversive of such students' conventional beliefs [can make] self-authenticating possible" (231).

Jarratt, Susan C., and Nedra Reynolds. "The Splitting Image: Contemporary Feminisms and the Ethics of Ethos." *Ethos: New Essays in Rhetorical and Critical Theory*. Ed. James S. Baumlin and Tita French Baumlin. Dallas: Southern Methodist UP, 1992. 37–63.

This essay suggests a way out of the postmodern feminist dilemma of losing the self as a category by combining the sophistic definition of ethos and the postmodern feminist politics of location. Jarratt and Reynolds advocate making individuals aware of their constructed place in the social order. The authors evoke a "split self" from Haraway's "passionate detachment," which respects difference and works toward a web of connections among differently positioned subjects. For Jarratt and Reynolds, these split selves illustrate the multiple subject positions we all embody.

Juncker, Clara. "Writing (with) Cixous." *College English* 50 (1988): 424–36.

Juncker argues that "by opening ourselves to French [feminist] theories of writing, we teachers of composition, male and female, might actually engender new textual and pedagogical strategies within our field and beyond" (424). By fostering multiple types of writing that encourage both logic and play and by seeing students as writing from a feminine (marginal at the university) position, Junker asserts, composition teachers can dislocate the symbolic order of the university so that "we might enable student writers to (re)invent themselves and to inscribe *différance* in(side) academia" (434).

Knadler, Stephen. "E-racing Difference in e-Space: Black Female Subjectivity and the Web-Based Portfolio." *Computers and Composition: An International Journal for Teachers of Writing* 18 (2001): 235–55.

Knadler examines Web portfolios of his first-year students to argue that the postmodern feminist lauding of playful altering of identity is not persuasive to his middle-class African American female students. The transgressive cyborg possibilities of many (white) theorists do not resonate with these students, who want to re-embody and foreground the visibility and collectivity of African American women's bodies. In response to feeling continually "racially anonymous" (237) in their everyday lives—where, Knadler argues, the black female body seems to be e-raced—these students chose to self-fashion and re-embody the self via their Web pages. He argues that theorists need to see this self-representation within a different set of inflections than the prevalent theories offered by (white) postmodern feminist theorists.

Kraemer, Don J., Jr. "Gender and the Autobiographical Essay: A Critical Extension of the Research." *College Composition and Communication* 43 (1992): 323–39.

Kraemer critiques works by Flynn, Rose, and Sirc on gender and student narratives. He argues that the gender-related features scholars have identified in student narratives are simplistic and reinforce gender stereotypes. Kraemer suggests that gender is not a simple category into which men or women fit but is always a contradiction-filled location (as in the "virile male, dutiful husband" contradiction).

LaDuc, Linda. "Feminism and Power: The Pedagogical Implications of (Acknowledging) Plural Feminist Perspectives." *Pedagogy in the Age of Politics: Writing and Reading (in) the Academy*. Ed. Patricia A. Sullivan and Donna J. Qualley. Urbana: NCTE, 1994. 153–65.

LaDuc suggests that teachers must be willing to explore different points of view, including different versions of feminism. She says that we have to be "able to negotiate the terrain between complicity and coercion when students do put forth a position with which we are at serious odds" (158). She concludes by stating that as feminist teachers, we must engage in critical reflection in order to understand the ways in which our authority as teachers of writing affects our students and ourselves.

Lamb, Catherine. "Other Voices, Different Parties: Feminist Responses to Argument." *Perspectives on Written Argument*. Ed. Deborah Berrill. Cresskill, NJ: Hampton, 1996. 257–69.

Lamb revises her earlier position, in which she advocated mediation and negotiation as alternatives to the win-lose model of argument. In this essay, she recognizes conflict as a state of argument in which each party obtains a viable and legitimate subject position and thus as a valuing of difference. Nevertheless, even in situations of conflict, response should be sought over refutation and continuation of the conversation is vital, especially in situations where resolution seems impossible.

Looser, Devoney. "Composing as an 'Essentialist'? New Directions for Feminist Composition Theories." *Rhetoric Review* 12 (1993): 54–69.

Looser suggests that the feminist emphasis on the personal is problematic because it reifies the connection between women and the personal in an "essentialist" way. She argues that feminism does not need to have a perfectly unified front and that "the insistence on feminist unity at all costs is a theoretical and practical mistake" (66).

McCracken, Nancy, Lois Green, and Claudia Greenwood. "Gender in Composition Research: A Strange Silence." *Writing Ourselves into the Story: Unheard Voices from Composition Studies*. Ed. Sheryl I. Fontaine and Susan Hunter. Carbondale: Southern Illinois UP, 1993: 352–73.

The three authors reflect on their early research—individually and collectively—and find that each conducted research that revealed gender differences in student writing and/or teacher response to student writing. At the time of publication, however, each of the authors ignored gender differences and examined only other variables, reflecting the lack of attention to gender in professional discussions at the time.

Mullin, Joan A. "Feminist Theory, Feminist Pedagogy: The Gap Between What We Say and What We Do." *Composition Studies: Freshman English News* 22 (1994): 14–24.

Mullin writes of the need for feminist teachers of composition to promote student autonomy and "safety" in the writing classroom environment. Her argument is that building a sense of community in which student authors feel safe is crucial to establishing a "truly feminist" classroom. The key, as Mullin sees it, is to encourage students to see themselves as one community of writers with many members. Students should feel comfortable, then, defending themselves and the work of their peers in the classroom.

Osborn, Susan. "'Revision/Re-Vision': A Feminist Writing Class." *Rhetoric Review* 9 (1991): 170–83.

Osborn reports on her effort to construct a classroom situation in which two goals are realized. The first goal is to help students develop an understanding of the relationship between language and gender; the second is to help students see revision as an integral part of writing. "Revision," furthermore, is also "Re-Vision," a process of looking at texts in new ways not only to engender changes in the text but also to facilitate change in the ways the author views and represents her world.

Papoulis, Irene. "'Personal Narrative,' 'Academic Writing,' and Feminist Theory: Reflections of a Freshman Composition Teacher." *Composition Studies: Freshman English News* 18 (1990): 9–12.

Papoulis examines the binary opposition of narrative versus expository writing. She notes that expository writing is usually more highly valued, while narrative or personal writing is often described as a preliminary, easier kind of writing that leads students to expository writing. She argues that this binary is false, too simplistic, and that narrative can be as intellectually challenging as expository writing (if not more so). She further compares the binary narrative-expository writing with the nature-culture and female-male binaries, using the work of Ortner, Gilligan, and Chodorow.

Peterson, Linda H. "Gender and the Autobiographical Essay: Research Perspectives, Pedagogical Practices." *College Composition and Communication* 42 (1991): 170–83.

Peterson reports on a study of teacher response to autobiographical essays written by men and women. She found that women's essays, on average, were evaluated more favorably than those of men and asks whether the autobiographical genre inadvertently favors female writers. She argues that teachers need to examine why they assign autobiographical essays and how they respond to them. She concludes with three "pedagogical guidelines" (175), suggesting that (1) "personal writing assignments should not unwittingly privilege one mode of self-understanding over another" (174), (2) "reading suggested as models for assignments should include examples by and about masculine and feminine subjects" (175), and (3) "evaluation of personal essays should not privilege certain gender-specific modes of self-representations, nor penalize others" (175).

Qualley, Donna J. "Being Two Places at Once: Feminism and the Development of 'both/and' Perspectives." *Pedagogy in the Age of Politics.* Ed. Patricia A. Sullivan and Donna J. Qualley. Urbana: NCTE, 1994. 25–42.

Qualley recounts how feminist thought has shifted from an emphasis on essentialism to an emphasis on diversity. She argues that we need to understand and work with both perspectives, especially as students are learning about feminism. She concludes with a classroom scenario that shows how students' collaborative work forces them to take on new perspectives.

Regan, Alison. "Type Normal Like the Rest of Us: Writing, Power, and Homo-
    phobia in the Networked Composition Classroom." *Computers and Com-
    position* 10 (1993): 11–23.

Regan dismisses the euphoric notion that computers in the classroom are
going to "level the playing field" and allow traditionally disadvantaged
groups the possibility of unprecedented freedom in the classroom. Focusing
on homophobic responses in Interchange sessions, this article suggests that
traditional biases are often reproduced in computer-based classrooms.

Reichert, Pegeen. "A Contributing Listener and Other Composition Wives:
    Reading and Writing the Feminine Metaphors in Composition Studies."
    Journal of Advanced Composition 16 (1996): 141–57.

Reichert reflects on her relationship with her partner—living together without being married, having divergent interests in literature and composition—
as part of an examination of publications that discuss the state of the field. She
argues that the metaphor "feminization" creates another set of unhelpful
binary oppositions (such as feminine-masculine, in addition to literature-
theory).

Rhodes, Jacqueline. "'Substantive and Feminist Girlie Action': Women
    Online." *College Composition and Communication* 54 (2002): 116–42.

Rhodes argues for "an articulation of radical feminist textuality" in which
writers are seen as rhetorical agents who negotiate their goals within a network of discourses and identifications. Rhodes frames her argument by comparing radical feminism of the 1960s and 1970s with cyberculture today: both
movements produced a proliferation of "temporary texts," written with a
clear purpose, ambiguous authorship, and a public audience, and spread by
networks of personal contacts. Within these frameworks, the goal of radical
feminist textuality is to facilitate social transformation by interrupting dominant practices and conversations, what Rhodes calls narratives of textual capital and control. This model of feminist agency uses available technologies to
help participants build temporary networks within which they can negotiate
their identifications and their identities.

Rose, Shirley K. "Reading Representative Anecdotes of Literacy Practice; or
    'See Dick and Jane Read and Write!'" *Rhetoric Review* 8 (1990): 244–59.

Rose examines the relationship between gender roles and literacy narratives
by reading student narratives as representative anecdotes. Using a Burkean
methodology, she analyzes gender differences in students' autobiographical
accounts, noting that women often describe literacy as social engagement and
men as a quest for autonomy. She provides representative student narratives
and aligns her work with that of feminist scholars in psychology, women's
studies, and rhetoric.

Schell, Eileen, E. "Feminism." *Keywords in Composition Studies.* Ed. Paul
    Heilker and Peter Vandenberg. Portsmouth, NH: Boynton/Cook Heine-
    mann, 1996. 97–101.

Schell offers a concise definition of feminism or, more correctly, feminisms and traces its development and effect on composition studies. In the spirit of other *Keyword* articles, she briefly reviews key articles and key moments in feminism and composition and ends with a helpful bibliography. This short article offers a succinct definition of and introduction to feminism in the field.

Selfe, Cynthia L., and Paul Meyer. "Testing Claims for Online Conferences." *Written Communication* 8 (1991): 163–92.

Using both qualitative and quantitative analysis, this article examines the interactions of writing studies scholars on an asynchronous list to examine how gender and status affect online interactions. Selfe and Meyer find that gender and status play key roles even in the "egalitarian" forums that online conferences are expected to offer. If these interactions occur in this group, Selfe and Meyer find it likely that gender and status will affect classroom interactions as well.

Sirc, Geoffrey. "Gender and 'Writing Formations' in First-Year Narratives." *Composition Studies: Freshman English News* 18 (1989): 4–11.

Looking for gender-related differences, Sirc analyzes the essays of twenty-one male and twenty female white, middle-class, first-year writing students. He identifies seven categories of difference essential "to analyzing a writer's narrative in terms of gender" (5): authorial stance, nature of incident, tone, major frame, linguistic code, locus, and mention of the opposite sex. He concludes by arguing that we need to understand the "possibly debilitating ideological underpinnings" of writing formations such as narrative in order to "shore up hegemony" (10).

Sloane, Sarah. "Invisible Diversity: Gay and Lesbian Students Writing Our Way into the Academy." *Writing Ourselves into the Story: Unheard Voices from Composition Studies.* Ed. Sheryl I. Fontaine and Susan Hunter. Carbondale: Southern Illinois UP, 1993. 29–39.

Sloane examines "how gay and lesbian student writers compose themselves" (30). Drawing on personal experience and two case studies, Sloane highlights how academic texts, writing assignments, and classroom practices can alienate gay and lesbian students. Unlike many minorities, gay and lesbian students often have the choice of visibility, but this choice between self-revelation and self-concealment/silence and between authenticity and safety is set within the hostile context of homophobia and violence against gay and lesbians. Therefore, Sloane concludes, teachers should create classroom contexts where "difference is respected" and where "all minority writers find safe places to speak in their own voices" (38).

Spurlin, William J., ed. *Lesbian and Gay Studies/Queer Pedagogies.* Spec. issue of *College English* 65 (2002): 1–95.

The goal of this special issue is to examine how theories of difference—sexual difference in particular—have informed the English undergraduate curriculum. The contributors draw on scholarship including postcolonial, feminist, and critical race theory, as well as locate their inquiry in various sites, from diverse academic settings to diverse periods in literature (medieval to twentieth century). In these locations, contributors challenge the assumption that theory precedes practice. Instead, they highlight the ways queer theory and queer pedagogy are mutually informing. Recurrent themes in this special issue are questions of difference, of identity and performativity, and of contextual moments and situations.

Stygall, Gail, Laurel Black, Donald Daiker, and Jeffrey Sommers. "Gendered Textuality: Assigning Gender to Portfolios." *New Directions in Portfolio Assessment: Reflective Practice, Critical Theory, and Large-Scale Scoring.* Ed. Laurel Black, Don Daiker, Jeff Sommers, and Gail Stygall. Portsmouth, NH: Boynton/Cook, 1994. 248–62.

This essay recounts efforts to make writing assessment more equitable by offering portfolio assessment instead of a single exam to determine exemption credit for first-year composition at Miami University. They find that women fare better with the portfolio system, and they also find that conventional, binary constructions of gender affect raters' readings of essays that may "perform" gender in more complicated and ambiguous ways. Attention to the complexities of gender-related signification, including the possibility of rhetorical "cross dressing" or parody of traditional gender categories, in assessment calibration sessions can help make writing assessment more equitable.

Tedesco, Janis. "Women's Ways of Knowing/Women's Ways of Composing." *Rhetoric Review* 9 (1991): 246–56.

Responding to what she labels the Perry-Belenky, Clinche, Goldberger, and Tarule debate, Tedesco argues in favor of composition teachers using both of these positions as "valuable but distinct tools" (254). Tedesco critiques both Perry and Belenky et al. for not answering the questions they set out to address: Perry does not create a developmental model of college students but rather outlines how "Harvard University promotes and encourages relativistic thought and how male students respond" (246); Belenky et al. do not delineate women's ways of knowing but rather illustrate some women's ways of adapting to new situations. Nonetheless, taken together, the two models may complement each other and help composition scholars "unlock that mysterious process called 'composition'" (254).

Tompkins, Jane. "Pedagogy of the Distressed." *College English* 52 (1990): 653–60.

Tompkins notes that "our practice in the classroom doesn't often come very close to instantiating the values we preach" (653). Resisting this inconsistency, she reports finding success in trusting students, talking to the class about the class, remembering that less is more, offering what she has and not worrying about what she can't bring to class discussions, not being afraid of new things, and letting go (659).

Tuell, Cynthia. "Composition Teaching as 'Women's Work': Daughters, Hand-maids, Whores, and Mothers." *Writing Ourselves into the Story: Unheard Voices from Composition Studies.* Ed. Sheryl I. Fontaine and Susan Hunter. Carbondale: Southern Illinois UP, 1993. 123–39.

"Why do we do it?" Tuell writes a personal narrative detailing her experiences as a part-time instructor of composition, addressing what she argues is a systemic mistreatment of part-time faculty. Included in the essay is an argument on behalf of a new respect for quality teaching.

Wall, Susan V. "Rereading the Discourses of Gender in Composition: A Cautionary Tale." *Pedagogy in the Age of Politics.* Ed. Patricia A. Sullivan and Donna J. Qualley. Urbana, IL: NCTE, 1994. 166–82.

Wall reexamines a case study she conducted earlier in her career, rereading it through the feminist framework provided by Carol Gilligan and Belenky et al. She illustrates how the work by Gilligan and the Belenky collective provides her with a different understanding of her case, one that takes the gendered dimensions of the writer into account. She cautions that researchers need to be self-reflexive when they interpret students' work, realizing that their interpretations are always shaped—and limited—by current theoretical and ideological frameworks.

Whitaker, Elaine E., and Elaine N. Hill. "Virtual Voices in 'Letters across Cultures': Listening for Race, Class, and Gender." *Computers and Composition* 15 (1998): 331–46.

As the title indicates, this article explores how issues of race, class, and gender shape (mis)communication between two e-mail partners, one student from a high school and one student from a college. These private exchanges with a real audience highlight the need to teach students how to negotiate difference.

FURTHER READINGS
IN FEMINISM
AND COMPOSITION

Addison, Joanne, and Sharon James McGee, eds. *Feminist Empirical Research: Emerging Perspectives on Qualitative and Teacher Research.* Portsmouth, NH: Heinemann-Boynton/Cook, 1999.

Aisenberg, Nadya, and Mona Harrington. *Women of Academe: Outsiders in the Sacred Grove.* Amherst: U of Massachusetts P, 1988.

Alcoff, Linda. "The Problem of Speaking for Others." *Cultural Critique* 20 (1991-92): 5–32.

Anzaldua, Gloria. *Making Face, Making Soul: Haciendo Caras.* San Francisco: Aunt Lute Foundation, 1990.

Belenky, Mary Field, Blythe Clinche, Nancy Goldberger, and Jill Tarule. *Women's Ways of Knowing: The Development of Self, Voice, and Mind.* New York: Basic, 1986.

Berg, Allison, Jean W. Kowalski, Caroline L. Guin, Ellen Weinauer, and Eric A. Wolfe. "Breaking Silence: Sexual Preference in the Composition Classroom." *Feminist Teacher* 4 (1989): 29–32.

Butler, Judith. *Gender Trouble: Feminism and the Subversion of Identity.* New York: Routledge, 1990.

Caywood, Cynthia, and Gillian Overing, eds. *Teaching Writing: Pedagogy, Gender, and Equity.* Albany: State U of New York P, 1987.

Cixous, Helene. "The Laugh of the Medusa." *Signs* 1 (1976): 875–93.

Chodorow, Nancy. *The Reproduction of Mothering: Psychoanalysis and the Sociology of Gender.* Berkeley: U of California P, 1979.

Coates, Jennifer. *Women, Men, and Language: A Sociolinguistic Account of Sex Differences in Language.* New York: Longman, 1986.

Coates, Jennifer, and Deborah Cameron, eds. *Women in Their Speech Communities: New Perspectives on Language and Sex.* New York: Longman, 1988.

Culley, Margo, and Catherine Portuges, eds. *Gendered Subjects: The Dynamics of Feminist Teaching.* Boston: Routledge, 1985.

Daly, Mary. *Gyn/Ecology: The Metaethics of Radical Feminism.* Boston: Beacon, 1987.

DeBeauvoir, Simone. *The Second Sex*. New York: Random, 1952.

De Lauretis, Teresa, ed. *Feminist Studies, Critical Studies*. Bloomington: Indiana UP, 1986.

Delpit, Lisa. *Other People's Children: Cultural Conflict in the Classroom*. New York: New P, 1995.

Dooley, Deborah Anne, and Madeleine Grumet. *Plain and Ordinary Things: Reading Women in the Writing Classroom*. Albany: State U of New York, 1995.

DuBois, Ellen, Carolyn Korsmeyer, and Gail P. Kelly. *Feminist Scholarship: Kindling in the Groves of Academe*. Urbana: U of Illinois P, 1985.

Eldred, Janet Carey, and Peter Mortensen. *Imagining Rhetoric: Composing Women of the Early United States*. Pittsburgh: University of Pittsburgh: 2002.

Enos, Teresa. *Gender Roles and Faculty Lives in Rhetoric and Composition*. Carbondale: Southern Illinois UP, 1996.

Fishman, Pamela. "Conversational Insecurity." *The Feminist Critique of Language*. Ed. Deborah Cameron. New York: Routledge, 1990. 234–41.

Flax, Jane. *Thinking Fragments: Psychoanalysis, Feminism, and Postmodernism in the Contemporary West*. Berkeley: U of California P, 1990.

Flynn, Elizabeth, A. *Feminism beyond Modernism*. Carbondale: Southern Illinois UP, 2002.

Flynn, Elizabeth, A., and Patrocinio Schweickart, eds. *Gender and Reading: Essays on Readers, Texts, and Contexts*. Baltimore: Johns Hopkins UP, 1986.

Fonow, Mary Margaret, and Judith Cook. *Beyond Methodology: Feminist Scholarship as Lived Research*. Bloomington: Indiana UP, 1991.

Fontaine, Sheryl I., and Susan Hunter, eds. *Writing Ourselves into the Story: Unheard Voices from Composition Studies*. Carbondale: Southern Illinois UP, 1993.

Freire, Paulo. *Pedagogy of the Oppressed*. Trans. Myra Bergman Ramos. New York: Routledge, 1982.

Fuss, Diana. *Essentially Speaking: Feminism, Nature, and Difference*. New York: Routledge, 1989.

Gabriel, Susan L., and Isaiah Smithson, eds. *Gender in the Classroom: Power and Pedagogy*. Urbana: U of Illinois P, 1990.

Gallop, Jane. *Feminism and Psychoanalysis: The Daughter's Seduction*. London: Macmillan, 1982.

Gannett, Cinthia. *Gender and the Journal*. Albany: State U of New York P, 1992.

Garber, Linda, ed. *Tilting the Tower: Lesbians, Teaching, Queer Subjects*. New York: Routledge, 1994.

Gere, Anne Ruggles. *Intimate Practices: Literacy and Cultural Work in U.S. Women's Clubs, 1880–1920*. Urbana: U of Illinois P, 1997.

Gerlach, Jeanne, and Virginia Monseau. *Missing Chapters: Ten Pioneering Women in National Council of Teachers of English and English Education*. Urbana, IL: National Council of Teachers of English, 1991.

Gilligan, Carol. *In a Different Voice: Psychological Theory and Women's Development*. Cambridge, MA: Harvard UP, 1982.

Glenn, Cheryl. *Rhetoric Retold: Regendering the Tradition from Antiquity through the Renaissance*. Carbondale: Southern Illinois UP, 1997.

Gore, Jennifer. *The Struggle for Pedagogies: Critical and Feminist Discourses as Regimes of Truth*. New York: Routledge, 1993.

Grumet, Madeleine. *Bitter Milk: Women and Teaching*. Amherst: U of Massachusetts P, 1988.

Haraway, Donna. *Simians, Cyborgs, and Women: The Reinvention of Nature*. New York: Routledge, 1990.

Harding, Sandra, ed. *Feminism and Methodology: Social Science Issues*. Bloomington: Indiana UP, 1987.

———. *Whose Science, Whose Knowledge? Thinking from Women's Lives*. Ithaca, NY: Cornell UP, 1991.

Hennessey, Rosemary. *Materialist Feminism and the Politics of Discourse*. New York: Routledge, 1993.

hooks, bell. *Talking Back: Thinking Feminist, Thinking Black*. Boston: South End, 1989.

———. *Yearning: Race, Gender, and Cultural Politics*. Boston: South End, 1990.

———. *Teaching to Transgress: Education as the Practice of Freedom*. New York: Routledge, 1994.

hooks, bell, and Manning Marble, eds. *Feminist Theory: From Margin to Center*. second ed. Boston: South End P, 2000.

Hull, Gloria, T., Patricia Bell Scott, and Barbara Smith, eds. *All the Women Are White, All the Blacks Are Men, but Some of Us Are Brave*. New York: Feminist P, 1986.

Irigaray, Luce. *This Sex Which Is Not One*. Trans. Catherine Porter. Ithaca, NY: Cornell UP, 1985.

Jaggar, Alison. *Feminist Politics and Human Nature*. Totowa, NJ: Rowman & Littlefield, 1988.

Jarratt, Susan. *Rereading the Sophists: Classical Rhetoric Refigured*. Carbondale: Southern Illinois UP, 1991.

Jarratt, Susan C., and Lynn Worsham, eds. *Feminism and Composition Studies: In Other Words*. New York: Modern Language Association, 1998.

Kirsch, Gesa. *Ethical Dilemmas in Feminist Research: The Politics of Location, Interpretation, and Publication*. Albany: State U of New York P, 1999.

———. *Women Writing the Academy: Audience, Authority, and Transformation*. Carbondale: Southern Illinois UP, 1993.

Kristeva, Julia. "Women's Time." *Signs* 7 (1981): 13–35.

Lakoff, Robin. *Language and Women's Place*. New York: Harper and Row, 1975.

Lather, Patti. *Getting Smart: Feminist Research and Pedagogy with/in the Postmodern*. New York: Routledge, 1991.

Lewis, Magda. *Without a Word: Teaching beyond Women's Silence*. New York: Routledge, 1993.

Logan, Shirley Wilson. *We Are Coming: The Persuasive Discourse of Nineteenth-Century Black Women*. Carbondale: Southern Illinois UP, 1999.

———, ed. *With Pen and Voice: The Rhetoric of Nineteenth Century African-American Women*. Carbondale: Southern Illinois UP, 1995.

Luke, Carmen, and Jennifer Gore, eds. *Feminisms and Critical Pedagogy*. New York: Routledge, 1992.

Lunsford, Andrea A., Ed. *Reclaiming Rhetorica: Women in the Rhetorical Tradition*. Pittsburgh: U of Pittsburgh P, 1995.

Maher, Frances, and Mary Kay Tetreault. *The Feminist Classroom*. New York: Basic, 1994.

Malinowitz, Harriet. *Textual Orientations: Lesbian and Gay Students and the Making of Discourse Communities*. Portsmouth, NH: Boynton/Cook, 1995.

McCracken, Nancy, and Bruce Appleby, eds. *Gender Issues in the Teaching of English*. Portsmouth, NH: Heinemann, 1992.

Middleton, Sue. *Educating Feminists: Life Histories and Pedagogy*. New York: Teachers College P, 1993.

Miller, Susan. *Textual Carnivals: The Politics of Composition*. Carbondale: Southern Illinois UP, 1991.

Minh-ha, Trinh T. *Women, Native, Other: Writing Postcoloniality and Feminism*. Bloomington: Indiana UP, 1989.

Minnich, Elizabeth, Jean O'Barr, and Rachel Rosenfeld, eds. *Reconstructing the Academy: Women's Education and Women's Studies*. Chicago: U of Chicago P, 1988.

Moi, Toril. *Sexual/Textual Politics: Feminist Literary Theory*. London: Methuen, 1982.

Moraga, Cherrie, and Gloria Anzaldua, eds. *This Bridge Called My Back: Writings by Radical Women of Color*. Watertown, MA: Persephone P, 1981.

Nicholson, Linda J. ed. *Feminism/Postmodernism*. New York: Routledge, 1990.

Noddings, Nel. *Caring: A Feminine Approach to Ethics and Moral Education*. Berkeley: U of California P, 1984.

Payne, Michelle. *Bodily Discourses: When Students Write about Abuse and Eating Disorders*. Portsmouth, NH: Heinemann Boynton/Cook, 2000.

Phelps, Louise W., and Janet A. Emig, eds. *Feminine Principles and Women's Experience in American Composition and Rhetoric*. Pittsburgh: U of Pittsburgh P, 1995.

Rich, Adrienne. *On Lies, Secrets, and Silence*. New York: Norton, 1979.

Ritchie, Joy, and Kate Ronald, eds. *Available Means: An Anthology of Women's Rhetoric*. Pittsburgh: University of Pittsburgh, 2002.

Royster, Jacqueline Jones. *Traces of a Stream: Literacy and Social Change among African-American Women*. Pittsburgh: U of Pittsburgh P, 2000.

———. "When the First Voice You Hear Is Not Your Own." *College Composition and Communication* 47 (1996): 29–40.

Rubin, Donnalee. *Gender Influences: Reading Student Texts*. Carbondale: Southern Illinois UP, 1993.

Ruddick, Sara. *Maternal Thinking: Toward a Politics of Peace*. Boston: Beacon, 1989.

Russ, Joanna. *How to Suppress Women's Writing*. Austin: U of Texas P, 1983.

Schell, Eileen, E.. *Gypsy Academics and Mother-Teachers: Gender, Contingent Labor, and Writing Instruction*. Portsmouth, NH: Heinemann-Boynton/Cook, 1997.

Schell, Eileen E., and Patricia Lambert Stock. *Moving a Mountain: Transforming the Role of Contingent Faculty in Composition Studies and Higher Education.* Portsmouth, NH: Heinemann-Boynton/Cook, 2000.

Schmidt, Jan Zlotnik, ed. *Women/Writing/Teaching.* Albany, NY: State U of New York P, 1998.

Spelman, Elizabeth. *Inessential Woman: Problems of Exclusion in Feminist Thought.* Boston: Beacon, 1988.

Spender, Dale. *Man Made Language.* New York: Routledge, 1980.

Spender, Dale, and Elizabeth Sarah, eds. *Learning to Lose: Sexism and Education.* London: Women's Press, 1988.

Spivak, Gayatri Chakravorty. "Can the Subaltern Speak?" *Marxism and the Interpretation of Culture.* Eds. Cary Nelson and L. Grossberg Urbana, IL: U of Illinois P, 1988: 271–313.

———. *Outside in the Teaching Machine.* New York: Routledge, 1993.

Stone, Lynda, ed. *Education Feminism Reader: Developments in a Field of Study.* New York: Routledge, 1994.

Tannen, Deborah. *You Just Don't Understand: Women and Men in Conversation.* New York: Morrow, 1990.

Thorne, Barrie, Cheris Kramarae, and Nancy Henley, eds. *Language, Gender, and Society.* Rowley, MA: Newbury House P, 1983.

Tompkins, Jane. "Fighting Words: Unlearning to Write the Critical Essay." *Georgia Review* 42 (1988): 585–90.

———. "Me and My Shadow." *New Literary History* 19 (1987): 169–78.

Tronto, Joan. *Moral Boundaries: A Political Argument for an Ethic of Care.* New York: Routledge, 1993.

Weiler, Kathleen. *Women Teaching for Change: Gender, Class, and Power.* New York: Bergin and Garvey, 1988.

Williams, Patricia J. *The Alchemy of Race and Rights.* Cambridge, MA: Harvard UP, 1991.

Young, Iris Marion. *Justice and the Politics of Difference.* Princeton, NJ: Princeton UP, 1990.

NOTES ON THE AUTHORS

Pamela Annas is Professor of English at the University of Massachusetts/ Boston, where she teaches such courses as Contemporary Women Poets, Working-Class Literature, Personal Narrative, The Art of Poetry, and Writing as Women. Her books include *A Disturbance in Mirrors: The Poetry of Sylvia Plath* and, with Bob Rosen, *Literature and Society* and *Against the Current*. She has published articles on pedagogy, contemporary poetry, science fiction, and working-class literature. Other articles on feminist approaches to teaching writing have appeared in the anthologies *Argument Revisited; Argument Redefined* and *Teaching Writing: Pedagogy, Gender, and Equity*. She is on the editorial board of the journal *The Radical Teacher*.

Luann Barnes received her master's degree in communication development from Colorado State University, Fort Collins, and works as a full-time programmer and hypertext writer for the Colorado State University Online Writing Center.

Dale M. Bauer, Professor of English & Women's Studies at the University of Kentucky, is the author of *Feminist Dialogics* (1988) and *Edith Wharton's Brave New Politics* (1994) and the editor of collections on feminism and Bakhtin, a cultural sourcebook for "The Yellow Wallpaper," and *The Cambridge Companion to Nineteenth-Century American Women's Writing* (with Phil Gould, 2002). In addition to essays on feminist theory and nineteenth-century U.S. women's writing, she has been researching "sex expression" in American culture from 1860 to 1940.

Wendy Bishop, Kellogg W. Hunt Professor of English, teaches writing at Florida State University. She is the author or editor of a number of books, including *Ethnographic Writing Research, Teaching Lives, Thirteen Ways of Looking for a Poem, Metro, The Subject Is Research, The Subject Is Writing, In Praise of Pedagogy, Reading into Writing,* and several poetry chapbooks. She lives in Tallahassee and Alligator Point, Florida.

Patricia Bizzell is Professor and Chair, Department of English, College of the Holy Cross, Worcester, Massachusetts. At Holy Cross, she has directed the

Writers Workshop, the Writing-across-the-Curriculum Program, College Honors, and English Honors. She regularly teaches the Introduction to Women's Studies course, as well as courses in American women's literature and rhetoric and in first-year composition. Among her publications is *The Rhetorical Tradition: Readings from Classical Times to the Present,* co-authored with Bruce Herzberg (second edition 2001).

Lynn Z. Bloom is Board of Trustees Distinguished Professor and Aetna Chair of Writing at the University of Connecticut. She has received research awards from NCTE, NEH, and the U.S. Department of Agriculture. Her recent articles include "Freshman Composition as a Middle Class Enterprise" (1996), "The Essay Canon" (1999; forthcoming as a book in 2004), and "Living to Tell the Tale: The Complicated Ethics of Creative Nonfiction" (2003), all in *College English.* Her current books include *Composition Studies as a Creative Art: Teaching, Writing, Scholarship, Administration* (1998); *Composition in the New Millennium* (2003); *The Arlington Reader* (2003); and *The Essay Connection* (seventh edition 2004).

Kathy Boardman is Associate Professor of English and Director of the Core Writing Program at the University of Nevada, Reno. She teaches undergraduate and graduate courses in writing, autobiography and memoir, women's rhetoric, and the theory and practice of writing instruction. As co-director of the Northern Nevada Writing Project, she plans workshops and serves as co-instructor for summer institutes of K–12 teachers. She has recently completed essays on qualitative research seminars and on contingent instructorships in composition. With Gioia Woods, she is currently at work on an edited collection of critical articles about western American life-writing.

Joan L. Bolker, Ed.D., was an academician and is currently a clinical psychologist and writer who has consulted to thousands of blocked writers. She is the editor of *The Writer's Home Companion* (Owl Books, Holt, 1997) and the author of *Writing Your Dissertation in 15 Minutes a Day* (Owl, Holt, 1998), as well as the mother of two biology professors and the grandmother of a grandson known as "The Princeling."

Lillian Bridwell-Bowles is Professor of English, Director of the Center for Interdisciplinary Studies of Writing, and a member of the Center for Advanced Feminist Study at the University of Minnesota. She is a past Chair of the Conference on College Composition and Communication, the international organization for teachers of writing. Her first book, *New Directions in Composition Research,* outlined the emerging field of Composition Studies in the 1980s; her more recent work on feminist rhetoric and teaching includes a collection of essays entitled *Identity Matters: Rhetorics of Difference.*

Barbara DiBernard is Professor of English and Women's Studies and Graduate Chair at the University of Nebraska–Lincoln. She is a feminist teacher who does research on and teaches women's literature, lesbian literature, and literature and disability. Her other interests are gardening, birdwatching, walking, and swimming. Her most recent collaborations with Joy Ritchie have been bottlenose dolphin, coral reef, and crocodile research in Belize.

Lisa Ede is Professor of English and Director of the Center for Writing and Learning at Oregon State University. Her publications include *Work in Progress. A Guide to Academic Writing and Revising,* now in its fifth edition; *On Writing Research: The Braddock Essays 1975–1998; Essays on Classical Rhetoric and Modern Discourse* (with Robert Connors and Andrea Lunsford); and *Singular Texts/Plural Authors: Perspectives on Collaborative Writing* (with Andrea Lunsford).

Jill Eichhorn is Assistant Professor of English and Women's Studies at Austin Peay State University. As director of the Women's Studies Program, she coordinates the Clothesline Project and Take Back the Night and co-teaches an interdisciplinary course in conjunction with the student production of Eve Ensler's *Vagina Monologues.* She is working on the significance of public testimony through writing and the Clothesline Project in the healing of sexual trauma.

Mary Elliott received her Ph.D. in English from the University of Wisconsin–Milwaukee's Modern Studies Program in 1999. Her research and teaching interests include nineteenth- and twentieth-century American women's fiction, theories and histories of gender and sexuality, and cultural studies. She currently lives in the San Francisco Bay area.

Theresa Enos is Professor of English and Director of the Rhetoric, Composition, and Teaching of English Graduate Program at the University of Arizona. Founder and editor of *Rhetoric Review,* she teaches both graduate and undergraduate courses in writing and rhetoric. Her research interests include the history and theory of rhetoric and the intellectual work and politics of rhetoric and composition studies. She has edited or co-edited nine books and has numerous chapters and essays published on rhetorical theory and issues in writing. She is the author of *Gender Roles and Faculty Lives in Rhetoric and Composition.*

Sara Farris is Associate Professor of English at the University of Houston–Downtown, where she has taught for the past ten years. Her teaching and research interests include composition (especially developmental writing), American literature, poetry, young adult literature, and literature of the environment.

Elizabeth A. Flynn is Professor of Reading and Composition at Michigan Technological University, where she teaches courses in writing, reading, gender studies, and literature. She is author of *Feminism beyond Modernism* (Southern Illinois UP, 2002) and co-editor of *Reading Sites: Social Difference and Reader Response* (Modern Language Association of America, forthcoming), a sequel to her co-edited volume *Gender and Reading* (Johns Hopkins UP, 1986). She is founding editor of the journal *Reader.*

Sally Miller Gearhart grew up in Virginia and found her first love at a women's college. She received a B.A. in English at Sweet Briar College in 1952, her M.A. in Public Address at Bowling Green State University in 1953, and her Ph.D. in Theater at the University of Illinois in 1956. San Francisco State University hired her as an open lesbian and tenured her in 1974. She taught there for two decades, helping to found its radical Women's Studies Program and publishing three books. Scores of her articles and stories have been anthologized in feminist publications. Her groundbreaking feminist science fiction/fantasy novel *The Wanderground* was first published in 1978 and reprinted by Spinsters Ink in 2002. Her new Earthkeep Series of feminist science fiction/fantasy features three books: *The Kanshou, The Magister,* and *The Steward.* Gearhart is well known for her leadership, along with Supervisor Harvey Milk, in defeating the 1978 "Briggs Initiative" in California, which was designed to bar homosexuality and homosexuals from schools. She has also been an activist for animal rights and Earth First! and now lives on a mountain of contradictions with many cats and a blue-tick coon hound in a Mendocino County women's community.

Michelle Gibson is Associate Professor of English and Women's Studies at the University of Cincinnati, where she teaches first-year writing, basic writing, literature, and LGBT studies courses. Her work focuses on theorizing about gender and identity, particularly as they apply to the teaching of writing. Her articles have appeared in *Journal of Teaching Writing, Feminist Teacher, Writing on the Edge,* and *Studies in Popular Culture.* With Deborah Meem, she recently edited *Femme/Butch: New Considerations of the Way We Want to Go* for Harrington Press. She has served on the editorial board of *Journal of Teaching Writing* and on the executive board of the CCCC Caucus for Lesbian and Gay Professionals.

Gail E. Hawisher is Professor of English and founding Director of the Center for Writing Studies at the University of Illinois, Urbana-Champaign, where she teaches graduate and undergraduate courses in writing studies. She is co-editor of the journal *Computers and Composition* and has also published several books, including *Global Literacies and the World Wide Web* and *Passions, Pedagogies, and 21st Century Technologies,* which won the Distinguished Book Award at Computers and Writing 2000. With Cynthia Selfe, she is currently busy at work on a book-length study titled *Literate Lives in the Information Age: Stories from the United States.*

Karen Hayes, since earning the Master of Arts in 1991, has continued her interest in teaching writing, especially among those considered "different" in the traditional classroom. During her years at Clark State Community College, she especially empathized with older students returning to the classroom, because she began her own graduate work at age 35. Currently Hayes teaches at Wittenberg University in Springfield, Ohio, where she works with international students, Upward Bound students, and independent study adult learners, as well as the traditional population. She continues her own education by pursuing a second master's degree in teaching English as a second language at Wright State University, Fairborn, Ohio.

Adriana Hernández is on the faculty in the School of Education, University of Comahue (Patagonia, Argentina). She teaches undergraduate courses on Pedagogy within the tradition of critical pedagogy and on Gender and Education. She is currently directing a research project entitled "Discursive Practices about Sexuality in Primary Schools in Neuquén City." From 1998 to 2001 she held the position of Research Secretary at the School of Education, organizing two National Congresses on Educational Research (1999, 2001). She studied at Miami University, Ohio, where she received her M.A. in curriculum theory and her Ph.D. in education. An article from her doctoral dissertation, "Pedagogy, Democracy, Feminism, and the Rethinking of the Public Sphere," was published in 1997 by SUNY Press in the collection *Teacher Empowerment and School Reform,* edited by Henry Giroux and Peter McLaren. She can be reached via e-mail at adri54@data54.com or ahernan@uncoma.edu.ar.

Mary P. Hiatt is Professor Emerita of the Department of English at Baruch College of the City University of New York; she was teaching at Baruch when she wrote "The Feminine Style: Theory and Fact." Now retired from academe, Hiatt is currently writing nonfiction—in a terse, feminine style, of course.

Florence Howe is an author, editor, publisher, and teacher who has taught at the University of Wisconsin, Hofstra College, Queens College/CUNY, Goucher, the College at Old Westbury/SUNY, and the City University of New York. She was the first chairperson of the Commission on the Status and Education of Women at the Modern Language Association, where she served as president in 1973. Over the course of three decades, Florence Howe became the record keeper of Women's Studies Programs in the United States and abroad, as well as the historian of the movement. From 1972 to 1982 she served as editor of *Women's Studies Quarterly,* the first national journal to focus on feminist teaching. Ms. Howe is the author or editor of more than a dozen books and more than ninety published essays. Since 1970, when she helped to found Feminist Press, she has been its president. In 2000 Howe retired from the Feminist Press and her professorship at CUNY. Most recently, Florence Howe edited an unprecedented history of the women's studies movement, *The Politics of Women's Studies: Testimony from Thirty Founding Mothers.*

Susan C. Jarratt is Campus Writing Coordinator and Professor of English and Comparative Literature at the University of California, Irvine. Formerly Professor of English and Director of the Women's Studies Program and of College Composition at Miami University in Oxford, Ohio, she has published on ancient Greek rhetoric and issues of social difference in contemporary composition studies. She co-edited *Feminism and Composition Studies: In Other Words* (MLA, 1998) with Lynn Worsham and is currently working on a book about the rhetoric of the Second Sophistic, memory, and public space.

Cheryl L. Johnson is Associate Professor of English and a Women's Studies and Black World Studies affiliate at Miami University of Ohio. Her areas of research include African American women writers and criticism; African American literature, theory, and criticism; cultural studies; and sociolinguistics. She is currently working on a book that analyzes the representations of the language of servitude in black women's slave narratives and novels.

Catherine E. Lamb (Frerichs) is Director of the Pew Faculty Teaching and Learning Center and Professor of Writing at Grand Valley State University, Allendale, Michigan. Although she no longer publishes in feminist composition, she continues a strong interest in alternatives to traditional argument. Currently, she is working on a memoir of her parents, who were missionaries in Papua New Guinea for forty years.

Janice M. Lauer is Reece McGee Distinguished Professor of English at Purdue University. She received the 1998 CCCC Exemplar Award. For thirteen summers she directed a two-week international rhetoric seminar. Her publications include *Four Worlds of Writing: Inquiry and Action in Context, Composition Research: Empirical Designs, New Perspectives on Rhetorical Invention,* and *Rhetorical Invention in Rhetoric and Composition,* as well as essays on rhetorical invention, disciplinarity, writing as inquiry, composition pedagogy, and historical rhetoric.

Donna LeCourt is Associate Professor in the English department at the University of Massachusetts–Amherst, where she teaches courses in composition theory and cultural/critical approaches to composition. She has published essays in journals such as *Journal of Advanced Composition* and *Computers and Composition* and is currently completing a book tentatively titled *Identity Matters: Schooling the Student Body in Composition,* to be published by State University of New York Press.

Shirley Wilson Logan is Associate Professor of English at the University of Maryland, where, for seven years, she directed the department's Professional Writing Program. She teaches courses in composition, rhetoric, and African American discourse. Logan is past president of the Coalition of Women Scholars in the History of Rhetoric and Composition, serves on the executive committee of the MLA Division on the History of Rhetoric and Composition, and will serve as 2003 Chair of the Conference on College Composition and Communication. Logan co-edits the SIU Press series Studies in Rhetorics and Feminisms with Cheryl Glenn, is author of *We Are Coming: The Persuasive Discourse of Nineteenth-Century Black Women,* and editor of *With Pen and Voice: A Critical Anthology of Nineteenth-Century African-American Women.* She has essays in several collections, most recently, *Sister Circle: Black Women and Work.* She is currently working on a history of black sites of rhetorical education.

Min-Zhan Lu is Professor of English at the University of Wisconsin–Milwaukee, where she teaches courses in composition, cultural criticism, and life writing. Her books include *Shanghai Quartet: The Crossings of Four Women of China*

(Duquesne UP, 2001), *Comp Tales,* co-edited with Richard Haswell (Longman, 2000), and *Representing the "Other": Basic Writers and the Teaching of Basic Writing,* with Bruce Homer (NCTE, 1999). Her essays on the uses of cultural dissonance have appeared in such journals as *College Composition and Communication, College English, JAC: A Journal of Composition Theory,* and the *Journal of Basic Writing.*

Andrea Abernethy Lunsford, Professor of English and Director of the Program in Writing and Rhetoric at Stanford University, has designed and taught undergraduate and graduate courses in writing history and theory, rhetoric, literacy, and intellectual property. Before joining the Stanford faculty, she was Distinguished Professor of English and Director of the Center for the Study and Teaching of Writing at Ohio State University. Currently also a member of the Bread Loaf School of English faculty, she completed her Ph.D. in English at Ohio State University. Lunsford's interests include rhetorical theory, gender and rhetoric, collaboration, cultures of writing, style, and technologies of writing. She has written or coauthored thirteen books, including *The Everyday Writer, Essays on Classical Rhetoric and Modern Discourse, Singular Texts/Plural Authors: Perspectives on Collaborative Writing,* and *Reclaiming Rhetorica: Women in the History of Rhetoric,* as well as numerous chapters and articles. Recent essays include "Collaboration and Concepts of Authorship" (with Lisa Ede), *PMLA,* 116 (2001), 354–70.

Martha Marinara lives in Orlando, Florida, with her adopted daughter, Nikki. She earned an M.A. in Creative Writing from Southern Connecticut State University (1989) and a Ph.D. in Rhetoric and Composition from Lehigh University (1993). Marinara teaches writing and directs the Composition Program at the University of Central Florida. She writes poetry and fiction and has published most recently in *Southern Poetry Review, Xavier Review, FEMSPEC, Estuary,* and *Awakenings Review.* Currently, she is working on a collection of short stories. Marinara won the 1999 Central Florida United Arts Award for poetry.

Deborah Meem is Professor of English and Women's Studies at the University of Cincinnati and a longtime member of the CCCC Caucus for Lesbian and Gay Professionals. In addition to first-year composition and basic writing, she teaches women's literature and LGBT studies courses. She publishes in the areas of popular culture, composition studies, lesbian studies, and Victorian literature. Her edition of Eliza Lynn Linton's 1880 novel *The Rebel of the Family* was published by Broadview Press. With Michelle Gibson, she recently edited *Femme/Butch: New Considerations of the Way We Want to Go* for Harrington Press.

Susan Miller is Professor of English and Founding Director of the University Writing Program at the University of Utah. She teaches undergraduate and graduate courses in composition, rhetoric, literacy, and cultural studies. She has won two prizes for teaching and curriculum development. Each of her scholarly books—*Rescuing the Subject* (1989), *Textual Carnivals* (1991), and

Assuming the Positions (1998) — has won one or more national awards. She currently coordinates Utah's graduate degrees in rhetoric and composition and a cross-disciplinary Literacy Studies minor.

Michelle Payne is Associate Professor of English and Assistant Director of Writing at Boise State University. She administers the teaching assistant training program and teaches courses in nonfiction writing, composition and rhetoric, research methods, and feminist theory. She has published several articles, as well as two books, *Bodily Discourses: When Students Write about Abuse and Eating Disorders* and the textbook *The Curious Reader: Exploring Personal and Academic Inquiry* (coauthored with Bruce Ballenger).

M. Karen Powers-Stubbs is Assistant Professor of Writing and Linguistics at Georgia Southern University. Her current research projects include a feminist revisionary history of environmental rhetoric, a study of the classroom experiences of working-class students and teachers, and a collaborative investigation of the history of writing instruction at Georgia Southern University. She teaches graduate and undergraduate courses in sociolinguistics and contemporary rhetoric, an undergraduate course in the teaching of writing, and first-year composition.

Joy Ritchie is Professor of English and Director of Women's Studies at the University of Nebraska–Lincoln. She teaches composition and rhetorical theory, women's rhetoric, and composition and literacy courses for K–12 teachers. Her most recent book, co-edited with Kate Ronald, is *Available Means: An Anthology of Women's Rhetoric(s)*. Together they are now working on *Teaching Rhetorica,* an edited collection that examines the implications for teaching of recent scholarship on women's rhetorics.

Susan Romano is Assistant Professor of English at the University of New Mexico, Albuquerque, where she teaches in the professional writing concentration and is Associate Director of the Rhetoric and Writing Program. She has published articles on teaching writing by using electronic media, and her current work examines the teaching cultures and institutions of Mexico that have shaped rhetorical encounters and educational practices in the U.S. borderlands.

Jacqueline Jones Royster, Professor of English and Senior Associate Dean for Research and Faculty Affairs in the College of Humanities at The Ohio State University, has three complementary areas of interest: the rhetorical history of women of African descent, the development of literacy, and contexts and processes related to the teaching of writing. Among her numerous articles and books that illustrate this confluence of concerns in both literacy studies and women's studies is her most recent work, *Traces of a Stream: Literacy and Social Change among African American Women* (2000), which won the MLA's Mina P. Shaughnessy Prize. Other work includes being a member of the editorial collective and serving as senior associate editor of *Sage: A Scholarly Journal on Black Women* (1983–1996) when the collective published *Double Stitch: Black*

Women Write about Mothers and Daughters (1991 and 1993). In addition to editing *Southern Horrors and Other Writings: The Anti-Lynching Campaign of Ida B. Wells-Barnett* (1997), Professor Royster is currently compiling a co-edited collection (with Ann Marie Simpkins), *Calling Cards: Theory and Practice in the Study of Race, Gender, and Culture.* Professor Royster has served as chair of the Conference on College Composition and Communication and as chair of the executive committee of the Division on Teaching Writing of the Modern Language Association.

Eileen E. Schell is Director of the Composition and Cultural Rhetoric Doctoral Program and Associate Professor of Writing and Rhetoric at Syracuse University, where she teaches undergraduate and graduate courses in writing and rhetoric. She is the author of *Gypsy Academics and Mother-Teachers: Gender, Contingent Labor, and Writing Instruction* (Heinemann, 1998) and co-editor with Patricia Lambert Stock of *Moving a Mountain: Transforming the Role of Contingent Faculty in Composition Studies and Higher Education* (NCTE, 2000). Her work has also appeared in *College Composition and Communication, Composition Studies, Dialogue: A Journal for Writing Specialists, JAC,* and *WPA: The Journal of Writing Program Administration.*

Marian Sciachitano teaches courses on feminist theory, global feminisms, and "third world women" and film for the Department of Women's Studies at Washington State University. Her co-edited book project with Linda Trinh Võ, *Asian American Women: The Frontiers Reader,* is forthcoming from University of Nebraska Press.

Patricia A. Sullivan is Professor of English, Director of the Program for Writing and Rhetoric, and Ineva Baldwin Chair of Arts and Sciences at the University of Colorado, Boulder. Her research and teaching interests include feminism, class, and composition; cultural studies; and research methods and epistemology. She is co-editor, with Gesa E. Kirsch, of *Methods and Methodology in Composition Research* and, with Donna J. Qualley, of *Pedagogy in the Age of Politics,* and is currently working on a book titled *Narrative Knowledge and the Cultural Subconscious.*

Lynn Worsham is Professor of English at the University of South Florida, where she teaches undergraduate courses on women's literature, multiculturalism, and cultural studies and graduate courses on rhetoric and feminist theory. She is currently editor of *JAC,* a quarterly journal for the interdisciplinary study of rhetoric, culture, and politics.

Terry Myers Zawacki directs the WAC Program and the Writing Center at George Mason University, where she is on the English and Women's Studies faculty. Her most recent publications include "Telling Stories: The Subject Is Never Just Me," in *Questioning Authority: Stories Told in School,* and the coauthored articles "Is It Still WAC: Writing in Learning Communities" in *WAC for the New Millennium* and "Questioning Alternative Discourses: Reports from Across the Disciplines" in *ALT DIS: Alternative Discourses and the Academy.*

NOTES ON THE EDITORS

Gesa E. Kirsch is Professor of English and Research Fellow at the Center for Business Ethics at Bentley College in Waltham, Massachusetts. Her research and teaching interests include ethics, feminism, qualitative research methods, composition theory, and women's roles in higher education. She has written and edited a number of books, among them *Ethical Dilemmas in Feminist Research: The Politics of Location, Interpretation, and Publication; Women Writing the Academy: Audience, Authority, and Transformation; Ethics and Representation in Qualitative Studies of Literacy; Methods and Methodology in Composition Research;* and *A Sense of Audience in Written Communication.*

Faye Spencer Maor currently serves as Communications Coordinator for 1890 Programs at Lincoln University of Missouri. She has taught composition, news writing, photo journalism, and American and African American literature for more than fifteen years on the college level. Currently, she is completing her Ph.D. in Writing Studies from the University of Illinois, Urbana-Champaign. Her interests include the rhetoric of nineteenth-century African American women, the African American press, and issues of race and identity in the composition classroom.

Lance Massey is a Ph.D. candidate and instructor of academic and business writing at the University of Illinois at Urbana-Champaign. He is currently completing his dissertation on the disciplinary discourses of composition and has recently published an essay on ethnography in *Protean Ground: Ethnography and the Postmodern Turn.* His research interests include composition and rhetorical theories, feminism and composition, qualitative research methods, and disciplinarity.

Lee Nickoson-Massey teaches college writing, theories and applications of written communication, and business writing to international MBA students at the University of Illinois at Urbana-Champaign. She has recently published an essay in *Practice in Context: Situating the Work of Writing Teachers.* She also serves as an assistant editor of *College Composition and Communication.* Her interests include composition pedagogy and writing program administration.

She is currently completing her dissertation in Composition Studies at Illinois State University.

Mary P. Sheridan-Rabideau is Assistant Professor of English at Rutgers, the State University of New Jersey, where she teaches and researches on literacy, technology, and gender. She has published in *Written Communication, Computers and Composition,* and *Journal of Basic Writing.* She also served as an assistant editor of *Computers and Composition.* She is currently writing a book on gender and community literacy practices.

608

Pamela J. Annas. "Style as Politics: A Feminist Approach to the Teaching of Writing." From *College English* 47 (1985). Copyright © 1985 by the National Council of Teachers of English. Reprinted with permission.

Dale M. Bauer. "The Other 'F' Word: The Feminist in the Classroom." From *College English* 52 (1990). Copyright © 1990 by the National Council of Teachers of English. Reprinted with permission.

Wendy Bishop. "Learning Our Own Ways to Situate Composition and Feminist Studies in the English Department." *Journal of Advanced Composition* 10 (1990). Copyright © 1990 by the *Journal of Advanced Composition*. Reprinted with permission.

Patricia Bizzell. "Feminist Methods of Research in the History of Rhetoric: What Difference Do They Make?" From *Rhetoric Society Quarterly* 30 (2000). Copyright © 2000. Reprinted by permission of the Rhetoric Society of America.

Lynn Z. Bloom. "Teaching College English as a Woman." From *College English* 54 (1992). Copyright © 1992 by the National Council of Teachers of Writing. Reprinted with permission.

Joan Bolker. "Teaching Griselda to Write." From *College English* 40 (1979). Copyright © 1979 by the National Council of Teachers of English. Reprinted with permission.

Lillian Bridwell-Bowles. "Discourse and Diversity: Experimental Writing within the Academy." From *College Composition and Communication* 43 (1992). Copyright © 1992 by the National Council of Teachers of English. Reprinted with permission.

Jill Eichhorn, Sara Farris, Karen Hayes, Adriana Hernández, Susan C. Jarratt, Karen Powers-Stubbs, and Marian M. Sciachitano. "A Symposium on Feminist Experiences in the Composition Classroom." From *College Composition and Communication* 43 (1992). Copyright © 1992 by the National Council of Teachers of English. Reprinted with permission.

Mary Elliott. "Coming Out in the Classroom: A Return to the Hard Place." From *College English* 58 (1996). Copyright © 1996 by the National Council of Teachers of Writing. Reprinted with permission.

Theresa Enos. "Gender and Publishing Scholarship in Rhetoric and Composition." Reprinted by permission from *Publishing in Rhetoric and Composition* by Gary A. Olson and Todd W. Taylor, the State University of New York Press © 1997, State University of New York. All rights reserved.

Elizabeth A. Flynn. "Composing as a Woman." From *College Composition and Communication* 39 (1988). Copyright © 1998 by the National Council of Teachers of English. Reprinted with permission.

Elizabeth A. Flynn. "Composing 'Composing as a Woman': A Perspective on Research." *College Composition and Communication* 41 (1990). Copyright © 1990 by the National Council of Teachers of English. Reprinted with permission.

Sally Miller Gearhart. "The Womanization of Rhetoric." From *Women's Studies International Quarterly* 2 (1979). Copyright © 1979 by Elsevier Science. Reprinted with permission.

Michelle Gibson, Martha Marinara, and Deborah Meem. "Bi, Butch, and Bar Dyke: Pedagogical Performances of Class, Gender, and Sexuality." From *College Composition and Communication* 52 (2000). Copyright © 2000 by the National Council of Teachers of English. Reprinted with permission.

INDEX

Abelove, Henry, 413
"Academic Conventions and Teacher
    Expectations: A Feminist
    Perspective" (Sullivan), 318
academic discourse, 296–97
Acker, Joan Kate Barry, 155
Acker, Kathy, 190
Ackerman, John, 503
Addison, Joanne, 3, 591
Adler-Kassner, Linda, 185
afrafeminist, 77, 202, 203
    ideology, construction of, 222–26,
        229
    scholarship, 226–31
African-Americans, 144, 153, 154, 175,
        182, 190, 201–3, 274–77, 304, 348,
        488–89
    archival projects on, 209–17
    community, in, 223–24
    marginal status of, 207
    National Conference on Black
        Women's Health, 210
"After Words: A Choice of Words
    Remains" (Worsham), 22
Against Literature (Beverly), 171, 173
Ahmad, Aijaz, 163, 165
Aiken, Susan Hardy, 499, 501, 503
Aisenberg, Nadya, 591
Albrecht, Lisa, 295, 303
The Alchemy of Race and Rights
    (Williams), 154, 302, 388
Alcoff, Linda, 84, 85, 151, 175, 358, 577,
        591
Alcosser, Sandra, 508

Alexander, Adele Logan, 427
Alice (de Lauretis), 98, 100
al-Saadawi, Nawal, 172
alternative discourses, 295, 306
alternative writing, 323
Althusser, Louis, 266, 456, 531
Altman, Meryl, 554
AmazonCity, 190, 191
*Amazon City: Where She Is the
    Revolution*, 190
Anderson, Benedict, 160
Anderson, Worth, 155
Andreesen, Marc, 184
androcentrism, 127, 132, 134, 245
Anglo-American feminism, 83, 258
Annas, Pamela, xiv, 12, 30, 61–72, 597
Anthony, Susan B., 426
Anzaldúa, Gloria, 19, 67, 190–92, 195,
        304, 311, 440, 441, 442, 591, 594
Aphra, 41
Applebee, Arthur, 524
Appleby, Bruce, 594
Applied Grammatology (Ulmer), 118
"Archivists with an Attitude," 196
Arendt, Hannah, 285, 287, 290
argument
    feminist case against, 264–66
    writing without an, 308–9
"Argument as Emergence, Rhetoric as
    Love" (Corder), 287
Aristotle, 60, 271, 273, 284, 287, 448–29
articles published by tenure-track
    writing faculty, 560
Art of Rhetoric (Aristotle), 448

Asher, William, 135
Ashton-Jones, Evelyn, 542
Aspasia, 195, 197, 199
Astell, Mary, 195, 200
Atkins, Sharon, 457
Auerbach, Nina, 351, 355–56, 358
Austen, Jane, 267
author as construct, 257
authordoxy, 191
authority, rhetorical, 448
authorship, 180–92
  reinvention of, 261
The Author's Property (Logie), 190
autobiographical disabilities, 300
The Autobiography of Malcolm X, 275
Available Means: An Anthology of
  Women's Rhetoric(s) (Ritchie and
  Ronald), 3
The Awakening (Chopin), 36, 40

Backlash (Faludi), 380
Bakhtin, Mikhail, 285
Bal, Mieke, 168
Baldwin, James, 391, 392, 393
Baliff, Michelle, 575
Balsamo, Anne, 448
banking, education as, 283–84
Barbone, Steven, 413
Barker, Pat, 359
Barksdale, Jim, 187
Barlow, John Perry, 188
Barnes, Luann, 241, 321–37, 326, 327,
  330–32, 334–37, 597
Barthes, Roland, 105–6, 117, 118, 185
Bartholomae, David, 118, 402, 406, 436,
  440
Bartky, Sandra, 414
Bartz, Carol, 187
Basic Writing, 545
Bass, Ellen, 40
Bateson, Mary Catherine, 286
Batson, Lorie Goodman, 323, 575
Bauer, Dale, 6, 347, 351–61, 363, 553,
  554, 556, 575
Baym, Nina, 101
Beck, Evelyn, 416, 421
"Being an I-Witness: My Life as a
  Lesbian Teacher" (DiBernard),
  236

Belanoff, Pat, 323
Belenky, Mary Field, 5, 15, 245, 246,
  247, 260, 285, 315, 339, 505, 506,
  512, 514, 516, 517, 518, 569, 578,
  591
believing game, 268, 273, 274
Bellah, Robert, 260
Bell-Scott, Patricia, 211
Benedek, Emily, 187
Bennett, Robert A., 11
Bennett, S. K., 378
Berenstein, Richard, 506
Berg, Allison, 591
Bergman, David, 416
Berkenkotter, Carol, 503
Berlin, James A., 20, 21, 266, 267, 381,
  400, 504, 547, 556
Bernard, Jessie, 569
Berry, Phillipa, 549
Berthoff, Ann E., 9, 15, 16, 125, 244,
  269, 569
"Beside Ourselves: Rhetoric and
  Representation in Postcolonial
  Feminist Writing (Jarratt), 160–79
Best, Cynthia, 155
Beverly, John, 171, 172, 173, 174
"Beyond Anti-Foundationalism to
  Rhetorical Authority" (Bizzell),
  278
"Beyond Argument in Feminist
  Composition" (Lamb), 281–93
"Beyond Gender Difference to a
  Theory of Care" (Tronto), 152
"Beyond Literary Darwinism:
  Woman's Voices and Critical
  Discourse" (Frey), 317
"Beyond the Lonely Anthropologist:
  Collaboration in Research and
  Writing" (Gottlieb), 181
"Beyond the Personal: Theorizing a
  Politics of Location in
  Composition Research" (Kirsch
  and Ritchie), 140–59
"Bi, Butch, and Bar Dyke: Pedagogical
  Performances of Class, Gender,
  and Sexuality" (Gibson,
  Marinara, and Meem), 466–87
Bieseker, Barbara, 200, 545
bilingualism, 63

Bing, Rudolph, 45
Bird, Carolyn, 40
The Birth Project (Chicago), 302, 309
  "Beside Ourselves: Rhetoric and
  Representation in Postcolonial
  Feminist Writing (Jarratt), 160–79
Bishop, Wendy, xvii, 493, 496–509, 508,
  573, 597
Bitzer, Lloyd, 284
Bizzell, Patricia, 77, 142, 194–204, 278,
  295, 296, 355, 356, 359, 367, 383,
  402, 498, 501, 569, 597
Black, Alycia, 155
Black, Laurel, 588
Black Diaspora, 303
Black feminist thought, 206, 222
Blair, Kristine, 53, 576
Bleich, David, 323, 515, 576
Bloom, Lynn Z., xvi, 12, 17, 494,
  534–41, 598
Blow Your House Down (Barker), 359
Blumenthal, Amy, 413
The Bluest Eye (Morrison), 95, 96, 97,
  395
Boardman, Kathleen, xiv, xvii, 4, 7, 598
Boese, Christine, 453
Bok, Sissela, 416, 421, 422
Bolker, Joan, xiv, 13, 31, 49–52, 579, 598
Bolter, Jay David, 325, 326
Bonaparte, Louis, 161, 162, 175
Bono, Mary, 189
Bordo, Susan, 136
Born Female (Bird), 40
Boyer, Ernest, 559, 562
Bradstreet, Anne, 92, 93, 94
Brady, Laura, 9, 14, 163
Brannon, Lil, 406, 542
Braverman, Harry, 64, 65, 66
*Breaking Bread: Insurgent Black
  Intellectual Life* (hooks), 392
"Breaking Our Bonds and Reaffirming
  Our Connections" (Hairston), 245
Brewer, Rose M., 303
*Bridges of Power: Women's Multicultural
  Alliances* (Albrecht and Brewer),
  303, 304
"The Bridge Poem" (Rushin), 63
Bridwell-Bowles, Lillian, xv–xvii, 15,
  144, 240, 294–312, 598

Britton, James, 244, 518
Brodkey, Linda, 366, 367, 448, 504, 576
Brooks, Cleanth, 515
Brown, Stuart C., 571
Bruffee, Kenneth, 19, 269
Brummett, Barry, 199, 456
Budbill, David, 471
Bullock, Richard, 520*n*
Burgess, Anthony, 47
Burgos-Debray, Elizabeth, 171
Burke, Kenneth, 201, 221, 356–57, 361,
  448, 515
Butler, Judith, 19, 185, 477, 479, 591
Butler, Octavia, 227

Calderonello, Alice, 294
Cameron, Anne, 90, 99
Cameron, Deborah, 309, 591
Campbell, Karlyn Kohrs, 200
The Cancer Journals (Lorde), 96
Canterbury Tales (Chaucer), 49
"Can the Subaltern Speak?" (Spivak),
  161, 164
Carby, Hazel, 395
Card, Claudia, 418, 422
Carlson, Thomas J., 186
Carlton, Susan Brown, 577
Cartwright, Frederick, 45
Cary, Mary Ann Shadd, 426
"Castration or Decapitation" (Cixous),
  110, 111
Cayton, Mary Kupiec, 577
Caywood, Cynthia, 3, 14, 103, 283, 290,
  591
*CCC. See College Composition and
  Communication (CCC)*
CCCC. *See* Conference on College
  Composition and
  Communication (CCCC)
Cereta, Laura, 195
"Champing at the Bits: Computers,
  Copyright, and the Composition
  Classroom" (Logie), 184
Chapman, David, 545
Charney, Davida, 326
Chase, Geoffrey, 297
Chekola, Mark, 413
Cheney, Lynne, 100
Chicago, Judy, 302, 309

Child, Francis, 526, 530, 543
Chodorow, Nancy, 245, 246, 248, 250, 339–41, 512, 514, 516, 517, 591
Chomsky, Noam, 302
Choo-Meyer, BeeTin, 144, 145
"Choosing the Margin as a Space of Radical Openness" (hooks), 153
Chopin, Kate, 36, 40
"Chronicling a Discipline's Genesis" (Phillips, Greenberg, and Gibson), 544
Cisneros, Sandra, 436–23, 446
"Citing Cybersources: A Challenge to Disciplinary Values" (Leverenz), 184
Cixous, Hélène, 84–85, 103, 106, 107, 109–12, 114, 116, 118, 140, 166, 195, 264, 281, 299, 300, 302, 303, 309, 454, 591
Clark, Beverly, 155, 355
Clark, Gregory, 152, 283, 284
Clark, Suzanne, 11, 22, 352
Classical Rhetoric for the Modern Student (Corbett), 544
Classical Rhetoric (Kennedy), 307
class identity, 161–62. *See also* social class
classroom practice as site of activism, xiv–xv
Clément, Catherine, 166, 264
Clifton, Lucille, 51
Clinchy, Blythe McVicker, 15, 245, 246, 260, 339, 512
CMC. *See* computer-mediated communication (CMC)
Coates, Jennifer, 591
"Cognition, Convention and Certainty" (Bizzell), 501
Coles, William, Jr., 15
collaborative works, xvi, 146–47, 153, 180–91, 236, 239, 283, 305, 311
  antipathy towards, 259
  dialogic mode of collaboration. *See* dialogic mode of collaboration
  hierarchical mode, 257–58, 259
  modes of, 257
  overcoming obstacles, 570–72
  "Rhetoric in a New Key: Women and Collaboration" (Lunsford and Ede), 256–62

women scholars and collaboration, 569–70
College Composition and Communication (CCC), 7, 11, 13, 43n, 64, 140n, 185, 243n, 281n, 294n, 314n, 318, 363n, 433, 466n, 493, 512, 512n, 544, 548, 554, 563, 567
College English, 7, 11, 12, 13, 15, 17, 33n, 49n, 61n, 135, 180n, 196, 244, 351n, 388n, 411n, 433, 522, 534n, 535, 554, 563, 567
Collins, Patricia Hill. *See* Hill-Collins, Patricia
Collins, Vicki Tolar, 200, 577
Coming of Age in Mississippi (Moody), 40
"Coming Out in the Classroom: A Return to the Hard Place" (Elliott), 411–24
Common Woman (Grahn), 90, 91
communication, 30, 31
  intellectual ancestry, used in discovery of, 217
  as matrix, 58–59, 296
Composing a Life (Bateson), 286
"Composing as a Woman" (Flynn), xvii, 5, 133, 239, 243–55, 282, 315, 365, 369, 381, 500, 544
"Composing 'Composing as a Woman': A Perspective on Research" (Flynn), 5, 135, 282, 364, 493, 512–19
Composition in the Academy (Hartzog), 522
Composition in the University (Crowley), 21
Composition Studies/Freshman English News, 552n
compustura, 190
computer-mediated communication (CMC), 336
computer programs, authorship of, 183–89
Computers and Composition (Gurak and Johnson-Eilola), 184, 321n, 328
"Conclusion: Epistemological Questions" (Harding), 285
Conference on College Composition and Communication (CCCC),

xvii, 2, 125, 141, 154, 245, 282, 413, 499, 514, 522, 546
Bibliography of Composition and Rhetoric, 548
Intellectual Property Caucus website, 189
conferences, xvii
conflict, resistance to. *See* "Feminism and Composition: The Case for Conflict" (Jarratt)
conflict encounter, 56, 265
"Confronting the 'Essential' Problem: Reconnecting Feminist Theory and Pedagogy" (Ritchie), 79–102
Connors, Robert, 542
conquest/conversion model of interaction, 58–59
constructivism, 79, 85
Contending with Words: Composition and Rhetoric in a Postmodern Age, 103*n*, 263*n*
"Contextualizing 'Composing as a Woman' " (Flynn), 339–41
Cook, Judith, 592
Cooper, Anna Julia, 208, 209, 348, 425, 430, 434
Cooper, Marilyn M., 569, 577
copyright, 181–83, 188–90
Corbett, Ed, 544, 546, 547
Corder, Jim W., 287, 567
Corregidora, Ursa, 393
Corregidora (Jones), 393
Cosby, Bill, 95, 96
Cowan, Edward A., 507
Creative Writing in America (Moxley), 504
Crew, Louie, 413
Critical Teaching and Everyday Life (Shor), 276
Cross, Geoff, 258
Crowhurst, Marion, 244
Crowley, Sharon, 9, 14, 21, 431–32, 556
Crummell, Alexander, 208
Culler, Jonathan, 253, 556
Culley, Margo, 269, 553, 591
cultural differences, 144
cultural feminism, 83
"Cultural Identity and Diaspora" (Hall), 439

Daiker, Donald, 588
Daly, John, 548
Daly, Mary, 84, 302–3, 309, 591
Dantley, Michael, 355
Daughters of Copper Woman (Cameron), 90–91, 92, 93
Daughter's Seduction (Gallop), 107
Däumer, Elisabeth, 269, 276, 505
David, Deirdre, 217
Davis, Kevin, 501, 503, 509
Davis, Madeline, 475
Dawn (Butler), 227
Dean, Terry, 501, 502, 503
De Beaugrande, Robert, 114, 117, 118, 300, 578
de Beauvoir, Simone, 40, 80–81, 83, 90, 592
de Courtivron, Isabelle, 300
de la Cruz, Sor Juana Inès, 195
De Lauretis, Teresa, 85, 86, 98, 100, 267, 268, 455, 592
De Leon, Rosario (Chayo), 444
Deleuze, Gilles, 555, 579
Delpit, Lisa D., 4, 402, 407, 434, 592
de Pizan, Christine, 195
Derrida, Jacques, 555, 556
de Scudéry, Madeleine, 195
Deutsch, Morton, 288
Deveare, Anna, 190
dialogic mode of collaboration, 239–40, 256, 257–58, 259–60, 261
Dialogue, Dialectic, and Conversation (Clark), 283
Dibbell, Julian, 451
DiBernard, Barbara, 77, 80, 82, 83, 86, 88, 89, 93, 97, 234–36, 598
Dickinson, Emily, 258
Dickson, Marcia, 578
"Difference: A Special Third World Women Issue" (Minh-ha), 440
Digital Future Coalition Website, 189
digital material, authorship of, 183–89
Digital Millennium Copyright Act, 188
disadvantaged groups, 62–71, 81, 148, 149, 153
"Discourse and Diversity" (Bridwell-Bowles), 144, 295–313
discourse community, 546
disruptions, 9, 17–21

diverse discourses, xv–xvii, 23, 295, 300, 301
  professional samples of. *See* professional samples of diverse discourse
  student samples of. *See* student samples of diverse discourse
Dixon, Kathleen, 578
A Doll's House (Ibsen), 40
Don Quixote: Which Was a Dream (Acker), 190
Dooley, Deborah Anne, 592
Douglas, Wallace, 525
Douglass, Frederick, 431–32
Douglass, Sarah Mapps, 427
Doyle, Brian, 523
D'Souza, Dinesh, 174
DuBois, Ellen, 592
DuBois, Enid, 457
DuBois, W. E. B., 208, 220, 389, 414
DuMaurier, Daphne, 46
"Dyke Methods or Principles for the Discovery/Creation of the Withstanding" (Trebilcot), 271
Dyson, Esther, 185, 186
Dyson, Freeman, 185
Dyson, George, 185

Eagleton, Terry, 500, 521, 524
Ebert, Teresa L., 143, 578
écriture féminine, xvi, 76, 166, 103, 299
Ede, Lisa, xvi, 170, 180–82, 189, 196, 239–40, 241, 244, 256–61, 284, 290, 291, 305, 599
Ehrenreich, Barbara, 459–60
Ehrlich, Larry, 419, 420
Eichhorn, Jill, 155, 363, 373–76, 384, 599
Einstein, Albert, 54
Elbow, Peter, 15, 20, 266–71, 273–75, 308, 367, 370, 401, 406, 506
Eldred, Janet Carey, 592
Electronic Frontier Foundation, 188
electronic writing, xvi
Eliot, Charles, 524–25, 530
Elliott, Mary, 349, 411–23, 599
Ellis, Albert, 44
Ellison, Ralph, 39, 394
Ellsworth, Elizabeth, 264, 466
Emerson, Caryl, 356

Emig, Janet, 3, 8, 9, 11, 14, 15, 125, 244, 269, 406, 506, 594
emotion and experience, 194–205, 247
Empirical Designs (Lauer and Asher), 135
empirical research, 516–17
"Encouraging the Patriarchy" (Auerbach), 355
Encyclopedia of English Studies and Language Arts, 548
Encyclopedia of Rhetoric, 548
English in America (Ohmann), 527
English Journal, 7, 11
Enlightenment, 10, 135, 166, 174, 195
Enos, Richard, 194, 195–96, 197, 203
Enos, Theresa, 9, 11, 17, 545, 548, 554, 558–72, 561, 570, 571, 592, 599
Epstein, Joseph, 507
Equal Rights Amendment, xiv
Errors and Expectations (Shaughnessy), 125
Ervin, Elizabeth, 545
essential feminism, 85
essentialism, 79, 81, 84, 85, 298–99, 305
  risk of, 143–45
essentialist-constructivist debate, 82, 84
Esseveld, Johanna, 155
Esterburg, Kristin, 476
ethical dilemmas, 148–51
ethic of care, 152, 155, 156
ethics, 76–77, 96–98, 140, 152
  of research, 152–56
ethnobotany, 186
ethnography, 229–30
ethos, 322, 333, 456, 543
"Everyman's Guide to Critical Theory," 135
"Experience" (Scott), 10
experimental discourse, 300
experimental texts, 327, 330–31
expressivist pedagogy, 240, 267–68, 454
  feminist adaptation of expressivist composition, 269–71

The Fabric of Voices (Barnes), 331–34
Facts, Artifacts, and Counterfacts (Bartholomae and Petrosky), 436, 440

Faigley, Lester, 20, 21, 162
Faludi, Susan, 380
Fanon, Frantz, 160
Farrell, Thomas J., 19, 323, 579
Farris, Sara, 155, 363, 370–73, 385, 599
Fee, Elizabeth, 132, 136
Fell, Margaret, 195
"The Feminine Style: Theory and
    Fact" (Hiatt), 13, 29–30, 43–48, 64
feminine traits, 546
femininism, 19
femininist pedagogy, 16
"Feminism, Postmodernism, and
    Style" (Moi), 274, 276
"Feminism and Composition: The
    Case for Conflict" (Jarratt),
    263–80
*Feminism and Composition Studies: In
    Other Words* (Jarratt and
    Worsham), 3, 8, 425*n*, 436*n*
Feminism and Methodology (Harding),
    142, 517
"Feminism and Methodology in
    Composition Studies" (Sullivan),
    124–39
Feminism Beyond Modernism (Flynn),
    340
feminist collaborators, 291
feminist critique. *See* "Feminism and
    Methodology in Composition
    Studies" (Sullivan)
feminist discourse, 295, 298, 300, 303
Feminist Empirical Research (Addison
    and McGee), 3
feminist empiricists, 517–19
"Feminist Focus on Men" (hooks),
    372
feminist inquiry, 517–19
"Feminist Methods of Research in the
    History of Rhetoric: What
    Difference Do They Make?"
    (Bizzell), 194–205
"Feminist Politicization" (hooks), 144,
    371
*Feminist Principles and Women's
    Experience in American Composition
    and Rhetoric* (Phelps and Emig),
    3, 8
"Feminist Responses to Rogerian
    Argument" (Lassner), 287

Feminist Sophistics, 363–66, 377, 381,
    383
feminist studies and composition
    studies, 244–45
Feminist Theory: From Margin to Center
    (hooks), 220
feminization, 6, 19
"The Feminization of Composition:
    Questioning the Metaphors That
    Bind Women Teachers" (Schell),
    552–57
"The Feminization of Composition"
    (Miller), 373–74, 428, 520–33, 544,
    556
"The Feminization of Rhetoric and
    Composition Studies" (Lauer),
    542–51
Ferguson, Mary Anne, 251
Ferreira-Buckley, Linda, 196, 197, 203
*Fighting for Life: Contest, Sexuality, and
    Consciousness* (Ong), 264
Fine, Michelle, 145, 154, 155, 355
Finke, Laurie, 579
*Fires in the Mirror: Crown Heights,
    Brooklyn, and Other Identities*
    (Deveare), 190
Fish, Stanley, 142, 273
Fisher, Roger, 287, 288
Fishman, Pamela, 592
Fishman, Stephen, 155
Fitzgerald, Frances, 44
Flax, Jane, 143, 592
Fleckenstein, Kristie S., 579
Flores, Mary J., 321
Flower, Linda, 125, 244, 544
Flynn, Elizabeth A., xvii, 1, 5, 8, 12, 97,
    133, 135, 239, 243–53, 281, 282,
    285, 300, 315, 339–41, 364, 365,
    367, 369, 381, 429, 493, 500,
    512–19, 544, 556, 569, 577, 580,
    581, 592, 599
Fonow, May Margaret, 592
Fontaine, Sheryl I., 578, 584, 587, 589,
    592
foremothers, 15, 16, 244
"Form, Authority, and the Critical
    Essay" (Fort), 316
*Forms of Intellectual and Ethical
    Development in the College Years*
    (Perry), 247

Fort, Keith, 283, 316
Forten, Charlotte, 208, 427
"For the Adventurous Few: How to Get Rich" (Train), 459
Foster, David, 504
Foucault, Michel, 148, 266, 421
Fox, Tom, 434
Fragments of Rationality (Faigley), 21
Franklin, Phyllis, 549
Free Software Foundation, 187
Freire, Paulo, 101, 274, 276, 283, 297, 352, 353, 359, 402, 405, 429, 445, 542, 592
Freirean pedagogy, 503
French feminism, 83, 84, 104, 105, 166, 258, 281, 299, 300, 454, 555
Frerichs, Catherine E. (Lamb). *See* Lamb, Catherine
Freud, Sigmund, 108, 527, 528, 579
Frey, Olivia, 283, 317, 580
Friedman, Susan Stanford, 364
Frye, Marilyn, 62
functional texts, 327
Fuss, Diana, 388, 389, 393, 479, 481, 592

Gabriel, Susan L., 592
Gage, Matilda Joslyn, 426
Gale, Xin Liu, 196–97, 199–202
Gallop, Jane, 85, 86, 107, 274, 578, 592
Gannett, Cinthia, 132, 592
Garber, Linda, 592
Garvey, Amy Jacques, 208
Garvey, Marcus, 208
Gates, Bill, 183, 187
Gates, Henry Louis, 395
Gauthier, Xaviere, 298
Gearhart, Sally Miller, xiv, xvii, 30, 53–60, 264–66, 271, 272, 295, 299, 308, 600
Geertz, Clifford, 230, 516, 518
Geisler, Cheryl, 294
gender, 84, 132–38, 140, 143, 144, 234, 245–51, 270, 274, 275, 294, 305, 347–50, 364, 388, 436, 447, 466
    psychoanalysis and the study of gender, 246
"Gender and Journals, Conservers or Innovators" (Enos), 545

"Gender and Publishing Scholarship in Rhetoric and Composition" (Enos), 558–72
Gender and the Journal: Diaries and Academic Discourse (Gannett), 132
"Gender and 'Writing Formations' in First-Year Narratives" (Sirc), 132
gender-coding of profession, 520–33
gender differences in social and psychological development, 245–47
"Gender Influence: Reading Student Texts" (Rubin), 132
Gender Roles and Faculty Lives in Rhetoric and Composition (Enos), 11
gendership, 322
Gender Trouble (Butler), 477
genres, 327–28, 333
Gere, Anne Ruggels, xvi, 15, 190, 261, 592
Gerlach, Jeanne, 592
Gerrard, Lisa, 581
Getting Smart (Lather), 4
Getting to Yes (Fisher and Ury), 287, 288
Gibson, Michelle, 349, 466–86, 600
Gibson, Sharon, 544
Gilbert, Sandra, 291, 514
Gillam, Alice M., 581
Gilligan, Carol, 5, 132, 245, 246, 251, 252, 260, 270, 339–41, 405, 512, 514, 516, 517, 518, 592
Gilman, Sander L., 420
"The Girls in Their Summer Dresses" (Shaw), 252
Giroux, Henry, 274, 297, 355, 359, 365, 542
Glaspell, Susan, 97, 99
Glenn, Cheryl, 4, 8, 189, 196–200, 202, 203, 593
god trick, 142
Goldberg, Natalie, 370
Goldberger, Nancy Rule, 15, 245, 246, 260, 339, 512
The Golden Notebook (Lessing), 39
Gordon, George, 524
Gore, Jennifer, 593, 594
Gorelick, Sherry, 147
Gorgias (Plato), 567

Goswami, Dixie, 506
Go Tell It on the Mountain (Baldwin),
    391, 392, 393
Gottlieb, Alma, 181
Graff, Gerald, 496, 504, 524, 525
Grahn, Judy, 90, 91, 94, 97
A Grammar of Motives (Burke), 515
Graves, Heather Brodie, 581
Green, Lois, 18, 584
Greenberg, Ruth, 544
Greene, Stuart, 544
Greenwood, Claudia, 18, 584
Grego, Rhonda, 20
Grimaldi, William, 284
Grimké, Sarah, 195
Griselda. *See* "Teaching Griselda to
    Write" (Bolker)
The Group (McCarthy), 39
Grumet, Madeleine, 153, 553, 592,
    593
Gubar, Susan, 291, 514
Guin, Caroline L., 591
Guinier, Lani, 189, 191
Gulyas, Carol, 149–50
Gunderson, Martin, 413
Gurak, Laura, 184
Guy-Sheftall, Beverly, 211, 212, 218
Gyn/Ecology (Daly), 302
Gynesis (Jardine), 111
Gypsy Academics and Mother-Teachers
    (Schell), 20

Haake, Katharine, 508
Habits of the Heart (Bellah), 260
Haefner, Joel, 321
Hairston, Maxine, 125, 244, 245, 500,
    502, 503, 569
Hale, Sondra, 150
Hall, Stuart, 439
Handa, Carolyn, 321
Haraway, Donna, 19, 143, 323–25, 462,
    552–53, 583, 593
Harbeck, Karen M., 415
Harding, Sandra, 133–37, 142, 143,
    144, 154, 285, 517, 593
Hardy, Thomas, 40
Harlow, Barara, 171
Harper, Frances, 426, 427
Harrington, Mona, 591

Harris, Joseph, 21, 406
Hartwell, Patrick, 502
Hartzog, Carol, 522
Haswell, Janis, 322, 581
Haswell, Richard, 322, 581
Hawisher, Gail E., xiii, 4, 447*n*, 450,
    548, 600
Hayes, Karen, 155, 363, 366–69, 385,
    544, 600
Haynes, Cynthia, 448, 454, 455, 462,
    463
Heath, Shirley Brice, 146, 244, 260, 448,
    578
Hebdige, Dick, 105, 106, 113–14, 116,
    118
Heilbrun, Carolyn, 89, 98, 99, 256, 298,
    300–1
Hellman, Lillian, 105
Hemingway, Ernest, 449
Henley, Nancy, 595
Hennessy, Rosemary, 10, 23, 593
Henry, Madeleine, 196–98, 200, 201,
    203
Hernández, Adriana, 155, 363, 383–86,
    601
Herzberg, Bruce, 194
Hiatt, Mary P., xiv, 13, 29–30, 43–48,
    64, 72, 601
hierarchical mode of collaboration,
    257–58, 259
Hill, Adams Sherman, 525, 530
Hill, Carolyn Ericksen, 15–16
Hill, Elaine N., 589
Hill-Collins, Patricia, 153, 206, 211,
    222–23, 225
Hirsch, E. D., 111
Historical Rhetoric: An Annotated
    Bibliography of Selected Sources in
    English (Horner), 548
"Historical Studies and
    Postmodernism: Rereading
    Aspasia of Miletus" (Gale), 196
historicizing, 571
Hoagland, Sarah, 152, 153
Holbrook, Sue Ellen, 364, 522, 523, 543,
    545, 546, 552, 554, 556, 582
Hollis, Karyn L., 582
Holmes, Marjorie, 44
Holzman, Michael, 577

"Homosexual Imagination" (Crew and Norton), 413
hooks, bell, 4, 144, 153, 220, 274, 276–77, 303, 323, 324, 366, 367, 371, 392, 426, 429, 430, 434, 436, 440, 441, 442, 445, 578, 593
Horner, Winifred, 9, 244, 448, 548, 561, 569, 570
Horton, Willie, 391
Houston, Marsha, 426, 430
"How Cruel Is the Story of Eve" (Smith), 88
Howe, Florence, xiv, 12, 15, 17, 29, 30, 31, 33–42, 244, 601
Huckin, Thomas, 503
Hull, Gloria T., 593
humanistic inquiry, 515–16
Humanities in America (Cheney), 100
The Human Condition (Arendt), 285
Hunter, Susan, 365, 578, 582, 584, 587, 592
Hurst, John, 155
Hurston, Zora Neale, 99
Hutcheon, Linda, 182
hybrid form of academic discourse, 202
hypertext, 241, 321

Ibsen, Henrik Johan, 40
icons, 329–30
"Identification and Consubstantiality" (Burke), 357
"Identity and Expression: A Writing Course for Women" (Howe), 29, 244
I Dwell in Possibility (McNaron), 302
Images of Women in Literature (Feguson), 251
"Imitation" (Butler), 477, 479
immigrant academics as metonymic subjects, 163–71
In a Different Voice (Gilligan), 245, 246, 251, 260, 339, 512, 517
"In a Word: Interview," 165
inclusion, 9, 10–14
inferiority complex, 29, 31, 33, 35
In Other Worlds (Spivak), 353
"In Pursuit of Connections: Reflections on Collaborative Work" (Kennedy), 181

"In Search of Feminist Discourse" (de Beaugrande), 114
"In Search of Our Mothers' Gardens"(Walker), 90
"The Instability of the Analytical Categories of Feminist Theory" (Harding), 136, 285
intellectual ancestry, understanding, 217–19, 219
intellectual property, 182–91
interaction, conquest/conversion model of, 58–59
Internet, 183, 184
   safe spaces created for women on. See "On Becoming a Woman: Pedagogies of the Self" (Romano)
internship program, SAGE Writer/Scholars, 212–22
The Interpretation of Culture (Geertz), 516
interpretive community, 273
interrogating the context of academic discourse, 331–33
interrogation of subjectivity, 453
intervention, feminist, 321–37
Invention as a Social Act (LeFevre), 261
Invisible Man (Ellison), 39, 394
Irigaray, Luce, 84–85, 107–12, 117, 118, 163, 324, 334, 454, 575, 578, 593
"Is There a Feminist Method?" (Harding), 136
Is There a Text in this Class? (Fish), 273
It Ain't Me Babe, 41

Jaggar, Alison, 593
Jakobson, Roman, 163
Jardine, Alice, 111, 114, 556
Jarratt, Susan C., xv, xvi, xvii, 3, 8, 9, 14, 20, 75, 155, 160–75, 196–200, 202, 203, 240, 241, 263–78, 271, 278, 342–43, 363, 365, 380–83, 385, 425n, 431, 434, 436n, 542, 556, 569, 575, 577, 582, 593, 601
Jaszi, Peter, 182
Jay, Gregory S., 174, 355
Jennings, Kevin, 415
Jespersen, Otto, 300
Jessup, Emily, 321
Jewett, Sarah Orne, 99

Johnson, Cheryl L., xvi, 348, 388–97, 429, 431, 453, 488–89, 602
Johnson-Eilola, Johndan, 184, 325
Jones, Ann Rosalind, 300
Jones, Gayl, 393
Jordan, June, 63
Journal of Advanced Composition, 79n, 160n, 433, 496n, 573
Joyce, James, 251, 252
Juncker, Clara, 114–16, 281, 282, 285, 300, 583

Karabel, Jerome, 426
Karen, Robert, 414, 422
Kaufer, David, 294
Kaur, Manjit, 144, 145
Keller, Evelyn Fox, 146
Kelly, Gail P., 592
Kempe, Margery, 92, 93
Kennedy, Elizabeth Lapovsky, 181, 475
Kennedy, George, 307
Khayatt, Madiha Didi, 415
King, Martin Luther, Jr., 430
King, Rodney, 391
King, Stephen R., 186
Kinneavy, James, 561
Kirsch, Gesa E., xiii, xvii, 1, 2, 76, 77, 124n, 140–56, 147, 150–51, 593, 606
Kissen, Rita M., 415
Kitalong, Karla Saari, 184
Kittridge, George, 543
Kitzhaber, Albert, 526
Kizer, Carolyn, 507
Knadler, Stephen, 583
Knoblauch, C. H., 406
"knotty entanglement" of self and other, 145
knowers, 145–48
Kohlberg, Lawrence, 246, 518
Kolodny, Annette, 92
Korsmeyer, Carolyn, 592
Kowalski, Jean W., 591
Kraditor, Aileen, 425
Kraemer, Don, 143, 323, 583
Kramarae, Cheris, 595
Kristeva, Julia, 84, 85, 103, 104, 110–12, 116, 118, 195, 299, 533, 581, 593
Krochmal, Maurice M., 188

Kuhn, Thomas, 339
Kumin, Maxine, 507

Labor and Monopoly Capital: The Degredation of Work in the Twentieth Century (Braverman), 64
Lacan, Jacques, 555, 579
"La consciencia de la mestiza: Towards a New Consciousness" (Anzaldúa), 441
LaDuc, Linda, 583
Laine, Chester, 501, 506
Lakoff, Robin, 13, 63–65, 66, 71, 593
Lamb, Catherine, xv, xvii, 240, 241, 281–91, 323, 584, 602
Landow, George, 325, 326
Landry, Donna, 161
Langer, Suzanne, 261
language, 98
 ownership of, 180, 192
Language and Woman's Place (Lakoff), 13, 63–65, 71
Lanham, Richard, 325, 447, 456
Larson, Richard, 545, 548, 549
Lassner, Phyllis, 287
Lather, Patti, 4, 156, 325, 364, 365, 593
Lauer, Janice M., xv, 135, 494, 542–49, 559, 602
"The Laugh of the Medusa" (Cixous), 106, 109, 110, 111, 114, 116
Lawrence, D. H., 39
"Learning Our Own Ways to Situate Composition and Feminist Studies in the English Department" (Bishop), 493, 496–511
LeCourt, Donna, 241, 321–37, 454, 455, 463, 602
LeFevre, Karen Burke, 261, 290
Lenin and Philosophy and Other Essays (Althusser), 266
Lerner, Gerda, 219, 529
Lesbian and Gay Writing (Lilly), 305
"Lesbian Feminist Literary Criticism: A Summary of Research and Scholarship" (Olano), 305
lesbians, 96, 144, 234–36, 305, 411, 466
LeShan, Eda, 45
Lessing, Doris, 39
LeSueur, Meridel, 67, 71

Letter VII (Plato), 284
Leverenz, Carrie Shively, 184
Levertov, Denise, 40
Lewis, Magda, 4, 16, 264, 378, 379, 385, 593
liberal feminism, 83
libertarian pedagogies, 402
Liddell, H. G., 274
"Life on the Global Assembly Line" (Ehrenreich and Fuentes), 459, 460
Lifton, R. J., 40
Lilly, Mark, 305
Lindemann, Erika, 548
Lindley, Daniel, 506
Listening to Their Voices (Wertheimer), 201
"A Litany for Survival" (Lorde), 63
Literary Theory: An Introduction (Eagleton), 524
A Literature of Their Own (Showalter), 514
"Little Miracles, Kept Promises" (Cisneros), 436, 440, 442, 445, 446
Lives on the Boundary (Rose), 304
Logan, Shirley Wilson, 4, 19, 190, 348, 425–35, 593, 602
Logie, John, 184, 190
Longman Bibliography of Composition and Rhetoric (Lindemann), 548
Looser, Devoney, 584
Lorde, Audre, 63, 94, 96, 99, 298, 303, 304, 440
Lu, Min-Zhan, 19, 175, 296, 348, 436–46, 602
Luboff, Gerald F., 416
Luke, Carmen, 594
Lunsford, Andrea Abernethy, xv, xvi, 4, 8, 76, 125, 170, 180–92, 184, 196, 239–40, 241, 244, 256–61, 284, 290, 291, 305, 547, 594, 603
Lying: Moral Choice in Public and Private Life (Bok), 422
Lykes, M. Brinton, 260
Lyotard, Jean François, 110, 118, 555

Macdonnel, Diane, 531
MacDowell, Ruth, 46
MacLean, Gerald, 161
Macrorie, Ken, 15, 275

The Madwoman in the Attic (Gilbert and Gubar), 514
Maher, Frances, 594
Mailer, Norman, 45
The Making of Knowledge in Composition: Portrait of an Emerging Field (North), 128, 135
Malamud, Bernard, 44
male and female authors, percentage of, 562
male chauvinist, 265
male writing style, female writing style compared to, 43–48
Malinowitz, Harriet, 19, 415, 416, 419, 420, 423, 594
Malone, Lisa, 367
A Man and Two Women (Lessing), 39
Mani, Lata, 164
Mankiewicz, Frank, 45
Man Made Language (Spender), 260, 299
Mann, Horace, 553
Maor, Faye Spencer, xiii, xvii, 1, 2, 29–31, 347–50, 606
Mapplethorpe, Robert, 371
Marble, Manning, 593
marginality, 10, 142, 153, 154, 219, 220, 245
"The Margin at the Center" (Beverly), 172, 173
Marín, Lynda, 172
Marinara, Martha, 349, 466–86, 471, 603
Marks, Elaine, 300
Martha Quest (Lessing), 39
Martin, Emily, 373, 375, 376
Martin, Nancy, 244
Marx, Karl, 161, 162
Marxist perspective, 5, 85, 98, 174, 463
"Masks and Other Drapings: A Reconsideration (or Reconciliation?) of " 'Participatory Rhetoric and the Teacher as Racial/Gendered Subject' " (Johnson), 488–89
Massey, Lance, xiii, xvii, 1, 2, 239–42, 606
"The Master's Tools Will Never Dismantle the Master's House" (Lorde), 298

Maternal Thinking (Ruddick), 286
Matlovich, Leonard, 411
matrix, communication as, 58–59, 296
Maynard, Joyce, 45
Mayo, David J., 413
McCarthy, Lucille, 155
McCarthy, Mary, 39, 51
McClintock, Barbara, 146
McCracken, Nancy, 18, 584, 594
McDaniel, Judith, 415
McGee, Sharon James, 3, 591
McHenry, Elizabeth, 196
McIntosh, Peggy, 219
McLaren, Peter, 355, 359
McLaughlin, Milbray, 186
McNaron, Toni, 302, 479–80, 484
McRobbie, Angela, 438
mediation and negotiation as
    alternative to argument, 287–91
Meem, Deborah, 349, 466–86, 477,
    603
Meisenhelder, Susan, 296, 299
Menchú Tum, Rigoberta, 163, 170–75
mentors, 214, 226, 505–7, 509, 566–69
Mercer, Kobena, 440
Meridian (Walker), 251
Messer-Davidow, Ellen, 301
metalanguage of style, 43
metaphor, 160, 162
Methodism, 200–1
"Methodological Doubting and
    Believing: Contraries in Inquiry"
    (Elbow), 273
*Methods and Methodology in
    Composition Research* (Kirsch and
    Sullivan), 124*n*
metonymy, 9, 14–16, 160, 162, 163, 169,
    170
Meyer, Paul R., 571, 587
Microsoft, 187
Middleton, Joyce, 433
Middleton, Sue, 594
midwives, 15, 16
    teacher-midwife, 82–83, 505
Miles, Josephine, 9
Miller, Brandt, 155
Miller, Nancy, 182, 184, 185, 298
Miller, Susan, xvi, xvii, 20, 155, 373–74,
    428, 494, 520–33, 526, 544, 553,
    556, 594, 603

Minh-ha, Trinh T., 19, 145, 163, 167–70,
    172, 436, 440, 441, 466, 594
Minnich, Elizabeth, 594
*Mississippi Mind: A Personal Cultural
    History of an American State*
    (Yates), 302
Mittler, Mary L., 413
MLA Commission on the Status of
    Women, 11, 17
Modern Language Association, 258,
    259
Mohanty, Chandra Talpade, 160, 164
Mohr, Richard, 413, 422
Moi, Toril, 111, 166, 256, 274, 276, 299,
    300, 303, 504, 533, 594
monologic argument, xvi, 240, 283,
    285, 286–87
Monseau, Virginia, 592
Moody, Anne, 40
Moraga, Cherrie, 594
Moral Boundaries (Tronto), 153
Morrison, Toni, 94, 95, 97, 371, 388,
    389, 390, 391, 395, 396
Morsell, Fred, 431
Mortensen, Peter, 592
mother, image of, 526–28, 553
Moulthrop, Stuart, 326
Moxley, Joseph, 504, 578
Mueller, Martin, 498
Mullin, Joan A., 584
multiculturalism, effect of, 234
multiple texts, 328–30
multivocal texts, 241, 261, 323, 324,
    335–36
Murray, Donald M., 266, 267, 269, 275,
    296, 405, 406
Murray, Lindley, 524
Myers, Greg, 381

narratives of feminism, 7–23
National Conference on Black
    Women's Health, 210
National Council of Teachers of
    English (NCTE), xiii, 11
NCTE. *See* National Council of
    Teachers of English (NCTE)
Neel, Jasper, 568
negotiation as alternative to
    argument, 287–91
Negroponte, Nicholas, 185

Nestle, 475
Netscape, 184, 187
New Criticism, 515, 531
Newkirk, Thomas, 398*n*
Newman, Andrea, 44
Newton, Judith, 97
New York Times, 183
Nicholson, Linda J., 594
Nickoson-Massey, Lee, xiii, 1, 2, 493–95, 606
"Nineteenth-Century Craniology" (Fee), 132
Noddings, Nel, 152, 506, 594
nonformation, 161, 162
North, Stephen M., 128–32, 507, 529, 543, 556
Norton, Rictor, 413
Notes from the Second Year: Women's Liberation, 41
nurturing, 566–69
Nystrand, Martin, 544

Oakley, Ann, 146, 156
Oates, Joyce Carol, 44, 473, 539
O'Barr, Jean, 594
Odell, Lee, 547
Off Our Backs: A Woman's News-Journal, 41
O'Hara, John, 46
Ohmann, Richard, 381, 413, 523, 527
Olano, Pamela, 297–98, 305
Olsen, Tillie, 12, 317–18
Olson, Gary, 324, 558*n*, 578
"On Becoming a Woman: Pedagogies of the Self" (Romano), 447–65
"On Contradiction" (Tung), 56
On Destruction (Culler), 253
"On Distinctions Between Classical and Modern Discourse" (Lunsford and Ede), 284
"On Female Celibacy" (Kempe), 92
Ong, Rory, 196–200, 202, 203
Ong, Walter J., 110–11, 264
"On 'Learning Our Own Ways'" (Bishop), 573–74
On Lies, Secrets and Silence (Rich), 61, 68, 500
online discourse. *See* "On Becoming a Woman: Pedagogies of the Self" (Romano)

online writing, xvi
"On Second Thought" (Frye), 62
"Opaque Texts and Transparent Contexts" (Jardine), 114
Orality and Literacy (Ong), 111
"Orators and Philosophers in English Studies, or, The Rhetorical Turn Versus Schemes for Cultural Literacy" (Bizzell), 359
Osborn, Susan, 585
Othering, 155, 297, 325, 335
Other People's Children (Delpit), 4
"The Other 'F' Word: The Feminist in the Classroom" (Bauer), 351–62, 554
Outside in the Teaching Machine (Spivak), 165
Overing, Gillian, 3, 14, 103, 283, 290, 591
overvoice in emotions path, 329–30, 331
ownership
  of language, 180, 192
  of property, 181–82, 186

Paine, Charles, 100, 352, 353, 354, 355
Palmer, Phoebe, 195
Palmer, Stacy E., 392
Papoulis, Irene, 585
paradigms, 339
Parmeter, Sarah-Hope, 415
Parr, Susan, 418–19
"Participatory Rhetoric and the Teacher as Racial/Gendered Subject" (Johnson), 388–97
Passions, Pedagogies, and 21st Century Technologies (Hawisher and Selfe), 447*n*
Patai, Daphne, 148, 149, 151, 156
Paul, Susan, 427
Payne, Michelle, xvi, 349, 398–410, 594, 604
Peaden, Catherine Hobbs, 143
pedagogical imperative, 115–16
pedagogical strategies, 251–53
pedagogy
  expressivist, 240
  hypertext's implications on, 336–37

postcolonial feminism, 174–75
student-centered. *See* student-
centered courses
will to, 115
writing theory and, 79–102, 105
"Pedagogy of the Distressed"
(Tompkins), 317
Penelope, Julia, 298, 299, 303
pentimento, 105
Perelman, Chaim, 53
Perl, Sondra, 15, 244
Perry, William, 247, 518
personal essays, xvi, 314–20
persuasion, 264
as act of violence, 53–56, 264, 296
alternatives to, 56–60
rhetoric and, 53–60
Peterson, Linda H., 585
Petrosky, Anthony, 436, 440
Phaedrus (Socrates), 284, 307
phallocentrism, 107–9, 111, 256, 299,
324, 335
phallocrats, 106, 118
Phelps, Louise, 3, 8, 9, 14, 546, 594
Pheterson, Gail, 353
Phillips, Donna, 544
Philosphy in a New Key (Langer), 261
Piaget, Jean, 518
Piercy, Marge, 252
Piontek, Thomas, 415
Plato, 271, 274, 277, 284, 287, 449, 567
Plato, Derrida, and Writing (Neel),
568
Plaza, Monique, 105
*Poisoned Ivy: Lesbian and Gay Academics
Confronting Homophobia*
(McNaron), 479
political correctness, 234
political interpretations, 104–13
politics in writing, 30
feminist textual politics:
interrogating context and self,
322–25
The Politics and Poetics of Transgression
(Stallybrass and White), 527
"The Politics of Feminist Research"
(McRobbie), 438
The Politics of Letters (Ohmann), 523
"The Politics of Nurturance" (Culley),
353, 354, 553

*The Politics of Writing Instruction:
Postsecondary* (Bullock and
Trimbur), 520*n*
Porter, Nancy, 154
A Portrait of the Artist as a Young Man
(Joyce), 251
Portuges, Catherine, 591
postcolonial theory, 160–79
The Post-Colonial Critic, 165
poststructuralist feminism, 83, 85, 98,
448
postmodern discourse, 111, 448
postmodern feminist perspective, 142,
323, 324, 340
"Postmodernism and Gender
Relations in Feminist Theory"
(Kristeva), 111, 118
The Postmodern Condition (Lyotard), 118
Potter, Claire, 413
power, 285
Powers of Horror (Kristeva), 111
Powers-Stubbs, M. Karen, 155, 363,
376–80, 384, 385, 386, 604
Pratt, Minnie Bruce, 10, 154
praxis, 501, 502, 506, 509
*The Present State of Scholarship in
Historical and Contemporary
Rhetoric* (Horner), 548, 561
Problems of Dostoyevsky's Poetics
(Bakhtin), 285
Probyn, Elspeth, 436, 439, 480, 555
process paradigm, 544
process pedagogies, 14
productive conflict, xv
Professing Literature (Graff), 504
professional samples of diverse
discourse, 301–6
property
intellectual, 182–91
ownership of, 181–82, 186
proprietary knowledge, 186
Protagoras (Plato), 274, 277
"Pseudo-Theory" (Lyotard), 110
psychic wholeness, 219
"Psychoanalysis and the Polis"
(Kristeva), 104, 111
psychoanalysis and the study of
gender, 246
public discourse, admitting the
"personal" into, 140–59

Publishing in Rhetoric and Composition (Olson and Taylor), 558*n*

Qualley, Donna J., 583, 585, 589

Rabine, Leslie W., 105
race, 63, 95–96, 140, 144, 154, 234, 267, 270, 274, 275, 294, 303, 305, 388–97, 425–35
radical feminism, 83, 84, 100
Rakha, Ustad Alla, 488
Randall, Margaret, 172
The Reader, the Text, the Poem (Rosenblatt), 516
"Reading and Writing Differences: The Problematic of Experience" (Lu), 436–46
Reading Lacan (Gallop), 274
Reagan, Ronald, 355
Reclaiming Rhetorica, 4, 201
"Recomposing as a Woman—An Essay in Different Voices" (Zawacki), 314–20
"Recovering the Lost Art of Researching the History of Rhetoric" (Enos), 194
"Reflection on Race and Sex" (hooks), 440
"Reflections on 'Feminism and Composition: The Case for Conflict' " (Jarratt), 342–43
Regan, Alison, 586
regional alienation, 63
Reichert, Pegeen, 586
reinvention of authorship, 261
relational identification process, 248
Release 2.0 (Dyson), 185
"Rend(er)ing Women's Authority in the Writing Classroom" (Payne), 398–410
representation, 161
The Reproduction of Mothering (Chodorow), 245, 339, 512
Rereading the Sophists (Jarratt), 199, 271, 278
"Rescuing the Archives from Foucault" (Ferreira-Buckley), 196
Resistance Literature (Harlow), 171
The Resolution of Conflict (Deutsch), 288

"Rethinking Differences" (Kristeva), 110
"Revisiting 'Confronting the Essential Problem,' " 234–36
Reynolds, Nedra, xvi, 19–22, 582
"Rhetoric, Feminism, and the Politics of Textual Ownership" (Lunsford), 180–93
rhetoric, persuasion and, 53–60
Rhetorica, 4
rhetorical authority, 448
The Rhetorical Tradition (Bizzell and Herzberg), 194, 196, 204
"Rhetoric and Ideology" (Berlin), 266, 267
Rhetoric and Reality (Berlin), 266, 504
"Rhetoric in a New Key: Women and Collaboration" (Lunsford and Ede), 256–62
"Rhetoric in Dialectic: The Functional Context of Writing" (Clark), 284
Rhetoric in Popular Culture (Brummett), 456
Rhetoric of Motives (Burke), 356, 357, 361
Rhetoric Retold (Glenn), 4
Rhetoric Review, 4, 256, 256*n*, 542*n*, 548, 554, 561, 562–43, 567, 568
Rhetorics, Poetics, and Cultures (Berlin), 21
Rhetoric Society of America, 546
Rhetoric Society Quarterly, 4, 194*n*, 548
Rhodes, Jacqueline, 586
Rice, Lee, 413
Rich, Adrienne, 12, 15, 17, 61, 67, 68, 79, 87, 92, 94, 99, 128, 131, 140, 142, 195, 243, 244, 253, 294, 295, 299, 303, 365, 367, 440, 472–73, 497, 500, 502, 507, 553, 555, 556, 594
Richardson, Laurel, 260
Riddell, Sheila, 149
Ripoll, Tania, 298, 309, 310
Ritchie, Joy S., xiv, xv, xvii, 4, 7, 75–77, 79–101, 140–56, 143, 144–45, 147, 149–50, 234–36, 235, 298, 501, 503, 556, 594, 604
Rockwell, Norman, 366
Rodriguez, Richard, 400, 402
Rogerian argument, 287

Rogers, Hester, 200
Romano, Susan, 347, 447–63, 604
Ronald, Kate, 3, 594
Roof, Judith, 160
A Room of One's Own (Woolf), 51, 64, 65, 67
Rooney, Ellen, 165
"Rootedness: The Ancestor as Foundation" (Morrison), 388, 389
Rose, Mike, 304–5, 542
Rose, Shirley K., 586
Rosenblatt, Louise, 516
Rosenfeld, Rachel, 594
Rosenfelt, Deborah, 97
Ross, Betsy, 452
Royster, Jacqueline Jones, 3, 76, 189, 190, 196, 201–4, 206—31, 226, 261, 594, 604
Rubin, Donnalee, 132, 594
Ruddick, Sara, 285, 286, 594
Runciman, Lex, 366
Runyan, Marvin, 187
Runzo, Sandra, 269, 276, 505
RuPaul, 389
rupturing narratives, 155
Rushin, Kate, 63
Russ, Joanna, 301, 594
Ryles, Gilbert, 504

SAGE: A Scholarly Journal on Black Women, 201, 211, 215, 221, 226
SAGE Writer/Scholars Internship Program, 212–22
Salholz, Eloise, 379, 384
Samuelson, Pamela, 187–88, 191
Sandburg, Carl, 366
Sandler, Bernice Resnick, 365, 378
sapientia, 118
Sarah, Elizabeth, 595
Sarton, May, 301
Sartre, Jean Paul, 106
Savage, Mary, 496, 501, 506
Sayers, Dorothy, 51
Schatz, Jay, 476
Schatzberg-Smith, Kathleen, 505
Schell, Eileen E., xvii, 16, 20, 494, 552–57, 586, 594, 595, 605
Schilb, John, 503–4
Schlesinger, Arthur, 100

Schmidt, Jan Zlotnik, 3, 16, 595
Schniedewind, Nancy, 281
Schubert, Lisa, 306
Schultz, John, 15
Schultz, Lucille, 501, 506
Schweickart, Patrocinio, 91, 97, 152, 497, 507, 592
Sciachitano, Marian M., 155, 363–66, 605
The Science Question (Harding), 133
Scott, Fred Newton, 543
Scott, Joan Wallach, 10, 450
Scott, Patricia Bell, 593
Scott, Robert A., 274
The Second Sex (de Beauvoir), 40
Secrets: On the Ethics of Concealment and Revelation (Bok), 421
Sedgwick, Eve Kosofsky, 415, 420
SEEK Program, CCNY, 15
Segrest, Mab, 415
"Self-Disclosure and the Commitment to Social Change" (Beck), 421
Selfe, Cynthia L., 321, 447n, 548, 587
semiotic disposition, 111
Sexing the Self (Probyn), 480
sexual orientation, 294, 303, 305
lesbians. *See* lesbians
Sexual/Textual Politics (Moi), 111, 504
Shaman Pharmaceutical, Inc., 186
Shaughnessy, Mina, 15, 19, 125, 244
Shaw, Irwin, 252
Sheridan-Rabideau, Mary P., xiii, xvii, 1, 2, 75–77, 607
Shor, Ira, 276, 353, 359, 382, 542
Showalter, Elaine, 12, 514
"Silences" (Olsen), 317
Silko, Leslie, 94
Simmel, Georg, 411
Simmons, Charles, 44
Simon, Roger I., 264, 378, 379, 385
Sims-Wood, Janet, 211
Singular Texts/Plural Authors (Ede and Lunsford), 180, 290, 291, 305
Sirc, Geoffrey, 132, 587
Sisterhood is Powerful: An Anthology of Writings from the Women's Liberation Movement, 41
Slatin, John, 325
Sloane, Sarah, 587
Smith, Barbara Herrnstein, 100, 593

Smith, Catherine, 326
Smith, Patti, 477
Smith, Paul, 85, 98
Smith, Stevie, 88
Smithson, Isaiah, 592
social class, 63, 95, 140, 144, 234, 267, 270–71, 274, 275, 294, 303, 305, 466
social feminists, 323
socialist feminism, 83
"The Social Construction of Black Feminist Thought" (Hill-Collins), 222
Society for Technical Communication, 258
Socrates, 271, 274, 284
software, authorship of, 183–89
Sommer, Doris, 172–73
Sommers, Jeffrey, 588
Sommers, Nancy, 125, 244, 400
Sonny Bono Copyright Term Extension Act, 188
Sons and Lovers (Lawrence), 39
Sophists, 264, 271, 273, 274, 277–78
The Souls of Black Folk (DuBois), 220
Speaking Freely: Unlearning the Lies of the Fathers' Tongue (Penelope), 299
"Speaking in Tongues: A Letter to 3rd World Women Writers" (Anzaldua), 67
Speculum of the Other Woman (Irigaray), 107
Spelman, Elizabeth, 595
Spender, Dale, 135, 252, 260, 264, 295, 299, 303, 309, 499, 595
Spiderwoman, 187, 190, 191
Spigelman, Candace, 185
Spivak, Gayatri Chakravorty, 85, 92, 105, 161, 163–67, 169, 170, 172, 174, 277, 353, 436, 440, 595
Spock, Benjamin, Dr., 536
Springsteen, Bruce, 471
Spurlin, William J., 587
Stacey, Judith, 149
Stallman, Richard, 187
Stallybrass, Peter, 527, 528
Stanger, Carol A., 269, 270, 276
Stanton, Elizabeth Cady, 426
Stearns, Charles, 427

Stein, Anza, 415
Stein, Arlene, 475
Stein, Gertrude, 94
Steloff, Frances, 261
Sterling, Dorothy, 427
Stewart, Don, 543
Stewart, Maria, 195
Stock, Paricia Lambert, 595
Stone, Lynda, 595
strong objectivity, 154
The Structure of Scientific Revolutions (Kuhn), 339
student-centered courses, 264, 266, 275
student samples of diverse discourses, 306–11
Stygall, Gail, 588
"Style as Politics: A Feminist Approach to the Teaching of Writing" (Annas), 61–72
styles, analysis of writing, 44–48
Subculture: The Meaning of Style (Hebdige), 105
subcultures, 105–7, 111, 116
Subjective Criticism (Bleich), 515
"The Subject of Literature" (Eagleton), 521
"The Subject of Pedagogy: Lessons in Psychoanalysis and Politics" (Jay), 355
Sugg, Redding S., Jr., 553
Suleiman, Susan, 300
Sullivan, Patricia A., 76, 100, 124–38, 124*n*, 318, 450, 583, 585, 589, 605
Sutherland, Mason, 200
Syfer, Judy, 67
"A Symposium on Feminist Experiences in the Composition Classroom" (Eichhorn et. al), 363–87

Takayoshi, Pamela, 576
Taking Stock: The Writing Process Movement in the 90s (Tobin and Newkirk), 398*n*
"Taking Women Students Seriously" (Rich), 12, 61, 68, 243, 497
Talking Back (hooks), 4, 276
Tannen, Deborah, 449, 595
Tarule, Jill Mattuck, 15, 245, 246, 260, 339, 512

Tate, Gary, 545
Taylor, Sheila Ortiz, 13
Taylor, Telford, 44
Taylor, Todd, 558*n*
Tchudi, Stephen N., 524
teacher-midwife, 82–83
teacher-mother, 269–70
A Teaching Subject: Composition Since 1966 (Harris), 21
"Teaching College English as a Woman" (Bloom), 17, 534–41
Teaching English in the Two-Year College, 433
"Teaching Griselda to Write" (Bolker), 13, 31, 49–52
Teaching to Transgress (hooks), 429, 430, 434, 436, 445
Teaching Writing: Pedagogy, Gender, and Equity (Caywood and Overing), 3, 14, 283
Technologies of Gender (de Lauretis), 267, 268
technology, safe spaces created for women by. *See* "On Becoming a Woman: Pedagogies of the Self" (Romano)
Tedesco, Janis, 322, 323, 588
tenure-track positions, surveys of. *See* "Gender and Publishing Scholarship in Rhetoric and Composition" (Enos)
Terkel, Studs, 457
Tess of the D'Urbevilles (Hardy), 40
testimonio (Menchú Tum), 163, 171–73
Tetreault, Mary K., 594
Textual Carnivals (Miller), 544
Textual Orientations (Malinowitz), 415, 419
"Theft" (Oates), 473
theory hope of antifoundation, 142
thick cognition, 326
"Thick Description: Toward an Interpretive Theory of Culture" (Geertz), 516
Thinking Across the Curriculum, 214
Thinking Fragments (Flax), 143
Third World intellectuals, 163
third world women, 167, 169
This Sex Which Is Not One (Irigaray), 107, 108, 109

Thompson, Nancy, 20
Thorne, Barrie, 595
"Three Heroines: An Oral History" (Crowley), 556
Thurman, Howard, 216
Tobin, Lad, 398*n*
Tompkins, Jane, 301, 306, 317, 588, 595
Topics (Aristotle), 273
Torrance, Jill, 457
Toulmin, Stephen, 53
Towne, Laura, 208
Traces of a Stream (Royster), 3, 201
Tradition and Reform in the Teaching of English (Applebee), 524
Train, John, 459, 460
transformation, 161, 162
Trebilcot, Joyce, 271–74
Trifles (Glaspell), 97
Trimbur, John, 20, 365, 520*n*
Tronto, Joan, 152, 153, 595
Trump, Donald, 289
Trump, Ivana, 289
Truth, Sojourner, 94
Tuell, Cynthia, 589
Tung, Mao Tse, 56
Twilight Los Angeles 1992 (Deveare), 190

Ulmer, Gregory, 118
"The Undiscovered" (Bennett), 11
Up from Under, 41
Ury, William, 287, 288

Vásquez, Adelfa, 437, 444
"A View from a Bridge: Afrafeminist Ideologies and Rhetorical Studies" (Royster), 206–33
    the construction of an afrafeminist ideology, 222–26
    people who do intellectual work need to understand power and how they are affected by it, 219–22
    people who do intellectual work need to understand their intellectual ancestry, 209–17
    theory begins with a story too, 209–17
    "ways of doing" in afrafeminist scholarship, 226–31

Viramontes, Helena, 449
"A Virtual Locker Room" (Boese), 453
Vitanza, Victor, 547, 548
A Voice from the South (Cooper), 209
Vygotsky, L. S., 518

Walker, Alice, 90, 91, 251, 252
Wall, Susan V., 589
Warhol, Robyn R., 359–61
Washington, Booker T., 208
Washington, George, 452
Washington, Margaret Murray, 208
Washington Square (James), 36
Watney, Simon, 416
Ways of Reading (Bartholomae and
    Petrosky), 436, 440
Ways with Words (Heath), 146, 260
"A Web of Symbolic Violence"
    (Kitalong), 184
Webb, Patricia, 336
Weiler, Kathleen, 4, 274–75, 359, 365,
    595
Weinauer, Ellen, 591
Weis, Lois, 219
Wells, Ida B., 201
Welty, Eudora, 301
Wernick, Andrew, 549
Wertheimer, Molly Meijer, 201
West, Susan, 185, 191
"What Matters Who Writes?"
    (Lunsford et. al), 184
" 'When and Where I Enter': Race,
    Gender, and Composition
    Studies" (Logan), 425–35
"When the First Voice You Hear is Not
    Your Own" (Royster), 207
"When We Dead Awaken: Writing as
    Re-vision" (Rich), 12, 17, 87,
    88–90, 244, 472
"Where Did Composition Studies
    Come From? An Intellectual
    History" (Nystrand, Greene, and
    Wiemelt), 544
Whitaker, Elaine E., 589
White, Allon, 527, 528
"White English/Black English: The
    Politics of Transalation" (Jordan),
    63
white feminism, 166
"Who Claims Alterity?" (Spivak), 164

"Who Knows? Identities and
    Feminist Epistemology"
    (Harding), 153
*Whose Science? Whose Knowledge?
    Thinking from Women's Lives*
    (Harding), 142–44, 153, 154
"Why I Want a Wife" (Syfer), 67
Wicker, Tom, 46
Wiedenhaupt, Sonia, 155
Wiegman, Robyn, 160
Wiemelt, Jeffrey, 544
Willard, Frances, 195
William, Fannie Barrier, 427
Williams, Patricia J., 154, 302, 388, 595
Williams, Raymond, 439
Wilson, David, 149, 150
Winkelmann, Carol L., 326
Winterowd, Norma, 546
Winterowd, Ross, 546, 547
Without a Word (Lewis), 4
With Pen and Voice (Logan), 4
Witte, Stephen, 548
Wolfe, Eric A., 591
"A Woman Is Talking To Death"
    (Grahn), 97
"The Womanization of Rhetoric"
    (Gearhart), 30, 53–60, 264, 308
Woman on the Edge of Time (Piercy),
    252
The Woman in the Body (Martin), 373
Women: A Journal of Liberation, 40
*Women, Native, Other: Writing Post-
    coloniality and Feminism* (Minh-
    ha), 167
"Women and Fiction" (Woolf), 316
"Women and Honor: Some Notes on
    Lying" (Rich), 67
Women as Healers: A Noble Tradition,
    210
Women at Point Zero (al-Saadawi), 172
"Women in a Double-Bind: Hazards of
    the Argumentative Edge"
    (Taylor), 13
Women in America (Lifton), 40
"Women in the History of Rhetoric:
    The Past and the Future"
    (Sutherland), 200
"Women on the Breadlines"
    (LeSueur), 67
"Women's Exile" (Irigaray), 108

"Women's Nature and Scientific Objectivity" (Fee), 136

Women's Research and Resource Center, 209, 212

Women's Studies International Quarterly, 53n

"Women's Time" (Kristeva), 111

"Women's Voices" (Ripoll), 309

Women's Ways of Knowing (Belenky et. al), 245–47, 260, 285, 315, 339–41, 502, 512, 517, 569

"Women's Work" (Holbrook), 522, 545, 546, 556

Women Teaching for Change (Weiler), 4, 274

"Women Who Are Writers in Our Century: One Out of Twelve" (Olsen), 12

Women/Writing/Teaching (Schmidt), 3, 16

Women Writing the Academy (Kirsch), 147

Woodmansee, Martha, 181

Woolf, Virginia, 39, 40, 51, 64, 65–67, 92–94, 195, 299, 316–97

Working (Terkel), 457

Worsham, Lynn, xvi, 3, 8, 22, 76, 103–21, 425n, 436n, 577, 593, 605

Wright, Janet, 415, 421

Write to Learn (Murray), 266, 267

"Writing Against Writing: The Predicament of *Écriture Féminine* in Composition Studies" (Worsham), 103–23

"Writing and Reading: Work and Leisure" (Ohmann), 523

Writing a Woman's Life (Heilbrun), 256

Writing Down the Bones (Goldberg), 370

"Writing Multiplicity: Hypertext and Feminist Textual Politics" (LeCourt and Barnes), 321–38

writing samples
analysis of, 44–48, 64–67
computer analysis of, 44–48

The Writing Instructor, 545

The Writing or the Sex? (Spender), 135

"Writing (with) Cixous" (Juncker), 114, 282

Writing Without Teachers (Elbow), 266–68, 273

Written Communication (Witte and Daly), 548

written expression and identity, xiv

Wyschogrod, Edith, 549

Yates, Gayle Graham, 302

Ybañez, Barbara, 437, 444

Yearning: Race, Gender, and Cultural Politics (hooks), 366, 436, 440

Yoos, George, 546, 548

Yoos, Mary, 546

Young, Iris Marion, 152, 595

Young, Richard, 546, 547

Zawacki, Terry Myers, 5, 241, 314–19, 323, 605

Zlotnik, Jan. *See* Schmidt, Jan Zlotnik